Public display and public benefaction have seen to it that Royal patronage is rarely an entirely private matter. But even those who have seen the paintings, drawings, and furniture and other works of art shown in exhibitions in the Queen's Gallery or visited the Palaces and residences open to the public, may be surprised at the range of the collection.

Royal building – from the Tower of London, through the great medieval chapels, churches, and castles, the Banqueting house at Whitehall and on to the hospitals at Greenwich and Chelsea and the pavilion at Brighton – are a central theme in the history of British architecture. The royal collection itself is of an unparalleled magnificence and variety. This book shows how the collection reflects the taste and interests of successive royal builders and collectors. The ill[...]   [...]tings and drawings, buildings and furnitu[...]   [...]s and stamps, books and scientific instrume[...]

This is a portrait of one aspect of monarchy, a celebration of patronage and taste which, lik[...]   [...]'s Royal heritage be[...]

'A remarkable *tou[...]*
year' – *Observer*

'The gift book of [...]

'A most stimulat[...]
duced in a mann[...]
Antique Collector

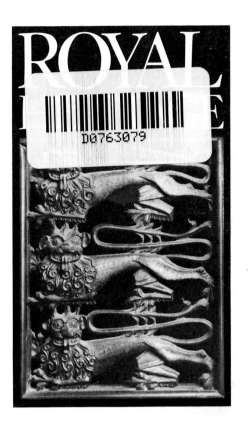

The detail on the front of the jacket is from *George IV when Prince of Wales*, painted by George Stubbs in 1791, the detail on the back from Aelbert Cuyp's *An Evening Landscape with Figures and Sheep*, c. 1650.

ROYAL HERITAGE

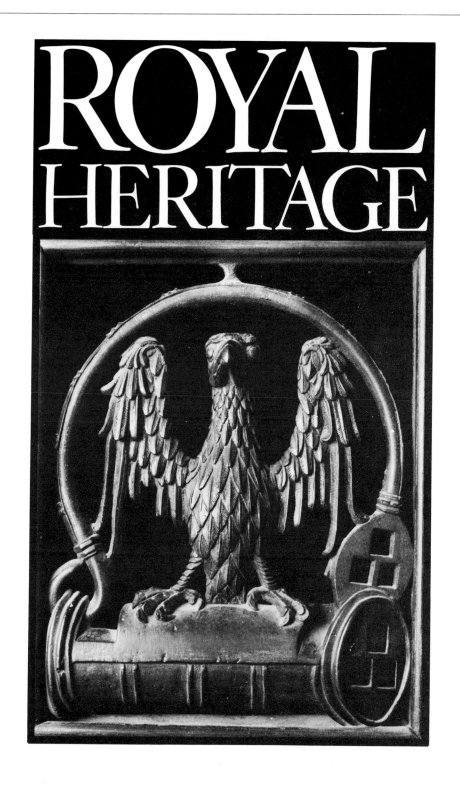

THE STORY OF BRITAIN'S ROYAL BUILDERS

AND COLLECTORS BY J. H. PLUMB

PUBLISHED IN ASSOCIATION WITH THE

TELEVISION SERIES WRITTEN BY HUW WHELDON AND J. H. PLUMB

BRITISH BROADCASTING CORPORATION

Published by the
British Broadcasting Corporation
35 Marylebone High Street
London W1M 4AA

Designed by Peter Campbell
Picture research by Diana Souhami

ISBN 0 563 17974 0

First published 1977
First paperback edition 1981
© Ferrymere Ltd 1977

Printed in England by
Jolly & Barber Ltd
Rugby, Warwickshire

CONTENTS

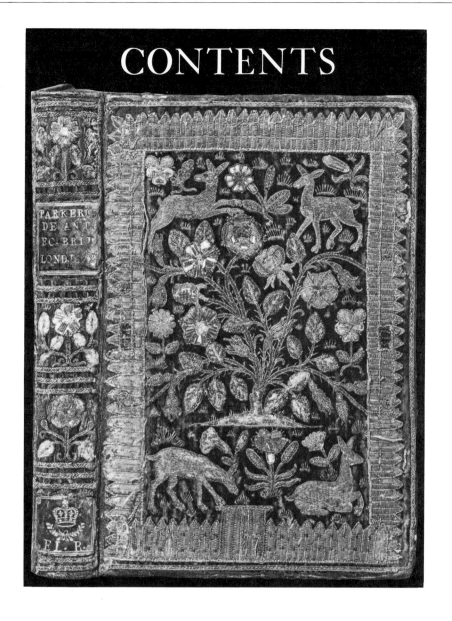

1 THE MEDIEVAL KINGS 11

2 THE TUDORS 43

3 THE STUARTS 93

4 THE HANOVERIANS 145

5 GEORGE IV 197

6 VICTORIA AND ALBERT 243

7 THE TWENTIETH CENTURY 287

MAKING THE FILMS 331

LIST OF ILLUSTRATIONS 343

Without the gracious permission of Her Majesty The Queen to view the extensive Royal Collections and buildings at Buckingham Palace, Windsor Castle, Kensington Palace, Hampton Court Palace, Balmoral Castle, Sandringham House, and elsewhere, this book could not possibly have been written. For such generous permission, we are deeply grateful.

We are also deeply grateful to Her Majesty Queen Elizabeth The Queen Mother for permission to view Clarence House and the Castle of Mey and Her Majesty's collections, and to Their Royal Highnesses The Duke of Edinburgh and The Prince of Wales for their close interest in both the book and the series, and for bringing so many important objects and works of art to our notice.

The custodians of the Royal Collections were unsparing in their time, energy and helpfulness and saved us from innumerable errors. We wish to express our gratitude in particular to Sir Oliver Millar, Surveyor of The Queen's Pictures; we came to appreciate not only his own impeccable scholarship but also the sensitivity of his understanding of the great works of art within his stewardship. He added to his generosity by saving the authors from many errors of detail. We are equally indebted to Mr Geoffrey de Bellaigue, Surveyor of The Queen's Works of Art, to Sir Robin Mackworth-Young, Librarian and Assistant Keeper of The Queen's Archives, and to Mr John Marriott, Keeper of the Royal Philatelic Collection.

We also wish to thank Mr John Charlton, former Principal Inspector of Ancient Monuments, Department of Environment, who gave up much of his time to show us round both Osborne House in the Isle of Wight and the Tower of London, and to his successor at the Department of the Environment, Mr Peter Curnow, who conducted us round Kew.

Our thanks are also due to the Lord Chamberlain, Lord Maclean, the Assistant Comptroller of the Lord Chamberlain's Office, Lieut. Col. J. Johnston, the Registrar, Mr Peter Hartley, and other members of the staff of the Lord Chamberlain's Office, who were tireless in their assistance in making arrangements to visit the collections and in providing illustrations for this book.

In the writing we depended on the assistance of many others, and particularly, of course, of all the members of the BBC production team. We all worked together for many months and book and series overlapped at many points. Our gratitude to the team as a whole knows no bounds. Their names are listed elsewhere as is proper. We would, however, like particularly to thank Mr Robert McNab, who was the chief research assistant for both the television scripts and this book, and Mr Joachim Whaley who undertook considerable research for us. J. H. Plumb was also particularly grateful to his secretary, Mrs Henrietta Napier, who struggled with innumerable drafts of ill-written chapters.

J. H. PLUMB
HUW WHELDON

The royal treasures of the British monarchy are of an unparalleled magnificence and variety. Works by almost every great master of painting are to be found in the royal collection – one of the finest of all Vermeers, magnificent Rembrandts, Rubens of spectacular quality. Portraits from Holbein to Winterhalter present a matchless panorama of our kings and queens, and those who served them. Hundreds of drawings by Leonardo da Vinci, exquisite examples of Michelangelo and Raphael; in paint or in pencil there is masterpiece after masterpiece. And the decorative arts are as splendidly represented as painting. The furniture from the seventeenth to the nineteenth century is outstanding, and the French furniture of the eighteenth century, collected by George IV, is the finest in the world. There are wonderful bronzes, exquisite china, magnificent suites of plate and glass; fine jewels, a multitude of miniatures. The armour would equip a regiment of princes. Indeed, the royal treasures are almost endless in their variety, but they would be even more impressive had our monarchs not given, time and time again, splendid gifts to our national institutions. Two enormous libraries, including illustrated manuscripts of the greatest rarity, were given to the British Museum, and now form one of the most important sections of the British Library. Queen Victoria gave Renaissance masterpieces to the National Gallery. The Maritime Museum at Greenwich, the Science Museum at Kensington, the Imperial War Museum, and many others, have been the recipients of royal gifts. Indeed, the royal collections were never intended as merely personal possessions. In the seventeenth century Samuel Pepys loved to stroll through the galleries at Whitehall Palace to look at the King's pictures which were open to gentlemen. Today the Queen's Gallery, established by Her Majesty, presents a continuous display of exhibitions, prepared with such imagination and scholarship that they have greatly enriched the cultural life of London. Furthermore there is rarely a major exhibition in any European capital or centre of art in which one will not find loans from the British royal collections.

As with artistic treasures, so with the royal buildings; they, too, have helped to create our heritage. The great central keep of the Tower of London, built by William the Conqueror, introduced Norman architecture into England, and nearly 1000 years later Osborne and Balmoral, partly designed by the Prince Consort, had a profound influence on the development of nineteenth-century domestic architecture. As with the royal treasures, the royal palaces have rarely become the private homes of the monarchy. In the Middle Ages, and for long after, most of the business of government was done there; as the king moved, so did his counsellors, and the armed retainers needed to protect them; hence the size of Windsor or the Tower of London which, for hundreds of years, were royal palaces. Main roads ran right through the palaces of Westminster and Whitehall; St James's Park was taken over by the citizens of London from the palace whose courtyards were always open to the world; the garden had provided its only privacy. These palaces were never, and have never become, dead museums or exclusive homes. Tens of thousands of men and women are invited to Buckingham Palace every year. For most of the year one can tramp over the magnificent deer forests and policies of Balmoral. The gardens of Sandringham have long been a mecca for tourists, but now the house itself may be visited. Indeed, privacy has usually proved elusive to our kings and queens.

The palaces and their contents are both the beneficiaries and the victims of time. The great collection of art formed by Charles I was dispersed by the commonwealth; the castles built by the Plantagenet kings fell into ruin. Nonsuch and Richmond, two great Renaissance palaces, have vanished. Greenwich was replaced by a hospital. And yet how much of the past persists. In Windsor and in the Tower there are nearly a thousand years of continuous royal history. And time and time again it has been the monarchs themselves who have preserved and restored these great buildings. Charles II, George III and George IV saved and embellished Windsor; George V and Queen Mary revived Holyrood-house and completed the plans initiated by Charles II in the seventeenth century. As with the royal treasures, preservation of the castles and palaces has been as important as addition — perhaps more so.

Both the palaces and their contents are redolent with Britain's history, and contain so many mementoes of our country's past. Along the ramparts of the Tower Sir Walter Raleigh walked, dreaming of El Dorado; five centuries earlier the young Norman princes had taken their knightly vows in the tiny but perfect chapel of St John. Through the window of the Banqueting Hall in Whitehall Palace Charles I stepped out on that bitter January day in 1649 to his execution. The Bible that he read and annotated for his son is still in the royal collection, so is the bullet that killed Nelson and the despatch brought posthaste by the blood-stained Major Percy to tell of the victory of Waterloo. Nearer our own time there is the ancient samurai sword with which the Japanese surrendered to Lord Mountbatten at the end of the second world war.

Moving as these historical objects and palaces are, peopled with the ghosts of so many famous men and women who have moulded our history, the royal collection has a deeper significance. Monarchy changes with changing time. Each society, from the Middle Ages to the present time, has created an image of monarchy which has given a sense of coherence and often of purpose to the nation at large. Each society has imposed its expectations on monarchy, requiring from it both a life-style and beliefs in conformity with the powerful social and political forces of the nation. The great virtue of the British monarchy has been, except on very rare occasions, its capacity to adapt to the needs and aspirations of the nation which it has ruled for so long. And the fascination and interest of the royal collection lies not only in the objects and buildings them-selves, but also in the way they reflect the changing role of monarchy. Seen in relation to their time, to the kings and queens who built or bought them, they deepen our understanding of the course of our history and the roots of our society today.

I

THE MEDIEVAL KINGS

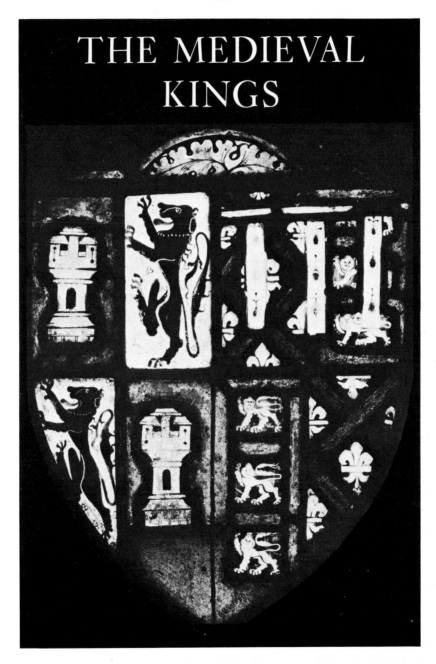

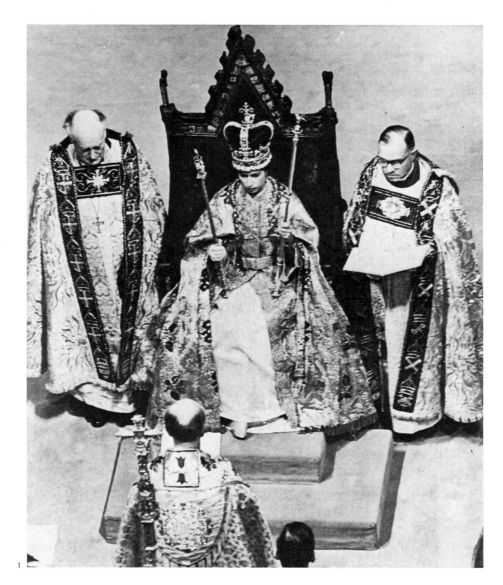

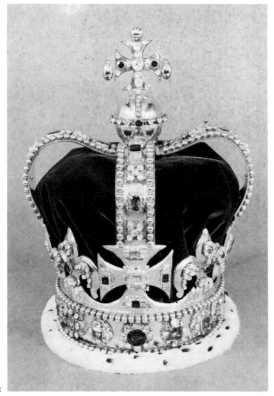

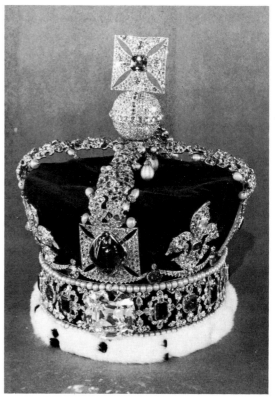

The ancestry of Queen Elizabeth II goes right back to the ancient Saxon kings of Wessex, the heartland of Anglo-Saxon England; perhaps even to Cerdic, first King of Wessex, about whose existence scholars still debate, who is said to have died in 534. Nothing is left of these early kings, although a hint of how they lived, and of the riches which they possessed, can be derived from the treasure trove of Sutton Hoo, with its great silver dish, made probably in Byzantium, and its magnificent ship used for the burial of a prince. All the objects are more splendid and more sophisticated than one might expect. From these Anglo-Saxon days there remain many charters, some well-preserved illuminated manuscripts, old collections of laws, coins in some abundance, a few jewels, here and there an ancient church; from time to time the spade reveals the foundation of a farm or, as at North Elmham in Norfolk, a Saxon cathedral. The great chronicles which dedicated monks kept for century after century, the epics which were passed from bard to bard, the prayers that priests wrote down, have enabled generations of dedicated scholars to reconstruct much of the story of that vast stretch of time over which the Anglo-Saxon monarchy ruled from the fifth to the eleventh century. Yet even the most famous, Alfred the Great and Edward the Confessor, remain shadowy figures.

It is from these distant Saxon days that some of the most precious symbols of monarchy date, and the most important of its rituals – the coronation ceremony. Despite slight changes over the centuries, the crowning of Queen Elizabeth II in 1953 bore a very close resemblance to the ceremony performed at Bath on Whit Sunday, 973, when St Dunstan crowned Edgar. Even then the ceremony was a very ancient one; parts of it are possibly Roman in origin, others derive from the way the primitive teutonic tribes chose their chieftains. When the Archbishop of Canterbury presented the Queen to the four corners of the congregation in Westminster Abbey, to the shouts of acclamation from the boys of Westminster School, he was following the custom of the Dark Ages, when kings had to be elected or accepted by their chieftains before the religious parts of the ceremony took place.

In these early Saxon and Plantagenet coronations the holiest part of the ceremony, as now, was the anointing with Holy Oil, which ultimately derives its authority from the Old Testament, when Solomon was anointed by Zadok the priest and Nathan the prophet. The royal regalia used in this part of the service are the oldest of the crown jewels: a gold ampulla, or chrism, which holds the oil that is poured through an eagle's beak into a gold spoon. The ampulla dates back to the fourteenth century, and the spoon, though repaired, is most probably that used in the coronation of King John in 1200. The anointing with oil confers on the monarch a sacred priestly function, setting him apart from other men. It is this priestly aspect of kingship which gives the monarch healing powers – the sacred touch by which scrofula and other diseases were cured. Throughout the Middle Ages, and long after, right down to the reign of Queen Anne in the eighteenth century, kings and queens touched their kneeling subjects at special ceremonies in the hope of healing them. This 'touch' added a special sanctity to monarchy.

Temporal rule is symbolised in the rest of the ceremony. The monarch is presented with a magnificent jewelled sword of state, representing earthly power. The medieval sword vanished long ago, although we

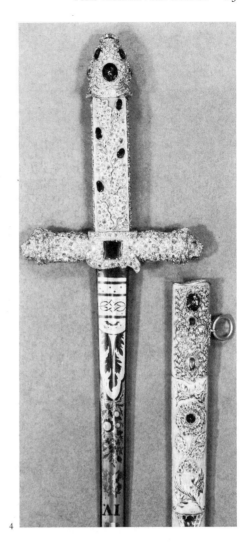

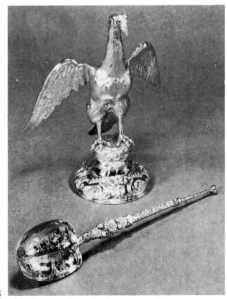

1 The Coronation of Her Majesty Queen Elizabeth II, Westminster Abbey, 2 June 1953. 2 St Edward's Crown. 3 The Imperial State Crown. 4 Hilt and Scabbard of the Jewelled Sword made for the Coronation of King George IV. 5 The Ampulla and Spoon

know that it was regularly used at the coronations. The present sword was made for the coronation of George IV, and has been used ever since. It is made of a dull gold which sets off to perfection the diamonds, sapphires, rubies and emeralds that form the national emblems of the rose (England), the thistle (Scotland) and the shamrock (Ireland) with which it is embellished. On the cross piece are the golden heads of lions or leopards which were adopted by Richard I, Coeur de Lion, as his badge, and have been used by all subsequent kings and queens.

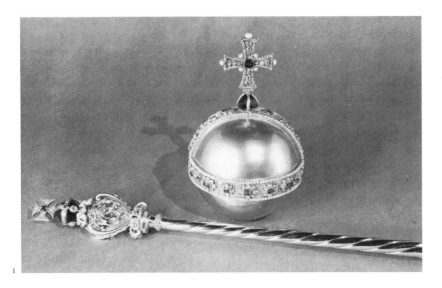

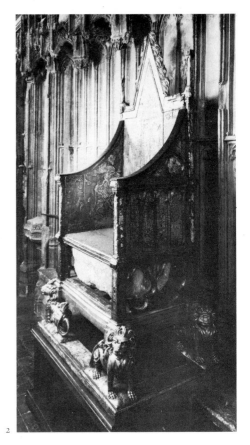

Then the monarch is robed in majesty, crowned, holding the orb in his right hand, perhaps the most sacred of all the coronation regalia, which symbolised the dominion of the Christian religion over the world, and in his left the sceptre, symbolising regal authority and justice. The sceptre which is now used has an outstanding diamond, the Star of Africa, below the cross, which enfolds an exceptionally fine amethyst. The moment of crowning is almost as important as the anointing. The crown itself was made for Charles II in 1660, although it is called St Edward's Crown, after St Edward the Confessor, the last but one of the Saxon Kings – a man venerated for his piety. The old medieval crown, which very probably went back to St Edward's time, was broken up, along with the rest of the regalia, after the execution of Charles I. Its fate is not entirely certain – there is a possibility that the priests of Westminster Abbey preserved parts of it, or that Cromwell did, and the present crown may contain elements that stretch back a thousand years. The crown is very heavy – nearly five pounds – and it is studded with over four hundred precious stones. Apart from St Edward's Crown, there are other crowns used for separate occasions, or during the different parts of the coronation ceremony. The most important is the Imperial State Crown, made for the coronation of Queen Victoria, which contains the oldest of the royal jewels – a sapphire that belonged to St Edward the Confessor, or may have done; a huge ruby that certainly belonged to Edward the Black Prince, son of Edward III; vast pearls that Elizabeth I used for earrings; and another huge sapphire that was owned by the Stuart kings. Crowns were the most important symbols of royalty regularly worn by medieval kings. In public only an archbishop could place the crown on the king's head; not even the monarch could do it himself. In private he could, but he alone – no one else. And on any occasion of importance that

1 The King's Orb and the Sceptre with the Cross
2 King Edward I's Coronation Chair, Westminster Abbey
3 The south face of the White Tower of the Tower of London
4 Detail from the Bayeux Tapestry of Harold crowned King

took place in the privy chambers of a king, he would place a crown on his own head – even to dine, if he had an important guest!

Since Edgar's day, the coronation service has become more elaborate and with more varied symbols – jewelled swords and golden spurs and vivid canopies of state. In contrast with the dazzling colours of the crown jewels and the brilliant heraldry of the canopies is the coronation chair itself, worn by time, chipped and cut by vandals. This ancient throne was made in 1301 to house the Stone of Scone, upon which the kings of Scotland had always been crowned. It was taken from them by Edward I. This stone may reach right back to neolithic times, the seat of the Bronze Age chieftains whose counterparts in England were responsible for Stonehenge.

The crown jewels are the great symbols of monarchy. For centuries they have been kept in the Tower of London, whose great stone keep was raised by William the Conqueror to awe Londoners as well as guard them. And it was also a royal palace, lived in century after century, growing in size and complexity right down to Tudor times, but always dominated by the White Tower which the Conqueror had built on the mound thrown up by the Romans.

William I was a tough, hard-headed warrior who took a vast risk in invading England. He only just won the Battle of Hastings, a victory which is celebrated in one of the most remarkable pieces of embroidery in existence, the Bayeux Tapestry, which tells the story of the Conquest, showing us how William shipped his horses and how he feigned defeat in order to gain ultimate victory. A tough warrior, but a pious man, he raised Battle Abbey as thanks to God for his victory over Harold on the field of the battle itself. The Battle of Hastings changed the course of English history as no other battle has done. It even changed our language, drawing it away from German, bringing it much closer to French and Latin. William was Duke of Normandy, and for the next 400 years our medieval kings were greatly concerned with their French possessions. William I was also a hard-headed administrator, as well as a brilliant and tough warrior. He ordered his clerks to compile what is now called the Domesday Book. This was, for its time, an extraordinary enterprise; no less than an attempt to describe the land ownership of his new kingdom: what was forest, what was tilled, the value of everything.

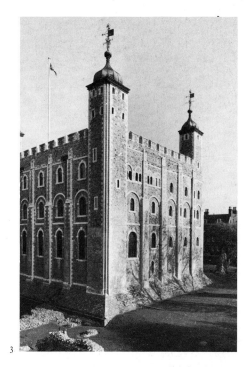

3

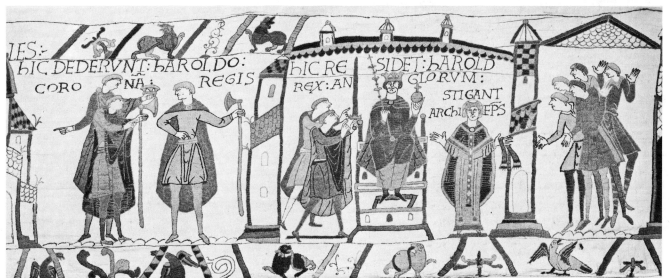

4

The King took possession of all the land, and then parcelled most of it out amongst his followers, but on very strict terms. They had to produce fighting men for his use, fully armed and mounted. And to do this their tenants and their serfs had to provide money and services.

The Anglo-Saxons had been scattered thinly across the land and even the Danes, who had seeped into England in the ninth century, came only in small groups of fighting men with their wives and families, not, indeed, in vast numbers. Much of England, in 1066, was forest – some famous, like Sherwood, others obscure and forgotten, like Leicester. The greatest was the New Forest, which William I partly created, extending it from Windsor to the Solent. These great forests had special laws to preserve the game. They were needed not merely for entertainment; hunting kept the bowmen in practice, and the warrior exercised his horses as well as himself. They were as carefully created and preserved as the royal palaces themselves. The fallow deer which kings loved to hunt may have been a curse to the peasantry living on the edge of the forest, but the maintenance of the forests, which was a matter of deep concern to kings and their ministers down to the eighteenth century, helped to preserve wild and beautiful land in the twentieth century for all to enjoy.

The rich farming lands of England had been a prey to invasion for a thousand years – Romans, Jutes, Angles, Saxons, Danes – but these Normans were the last. They hammered down the native population with great castles. From Richmond in the north to Dover in the south, from Norwich in the east to Chester in the west, and all the land between. The halls of the Saxons gave way to the bleak stone keeps of the Normans. They mobilised the military strength of England, making it the greatest power in western Europe.

These early kings were first and foremost warriors, for war was endemic in this feudal world. It brought profit in the shape of ransom, booty and plunder, and to the victorious, valuable rights in land. Yet they were far more than warriors. In the heart of William the Conqueror's White Tower is St John's Chapel, built in 1080. Here young squires, having bathed, were enjoined to spend a night in prayer before the day of their knighthood. Like kings, they dedicated themselves to the Church. At his coronation William swore to protect the Church and to maintain its privileges, and this was no idle gesture. The medieval kings and the Church were closely bound together, and much of their building and patronage was in the service of the Church which itself helped to civilise a tough, quarrelsome, warrior-dominated world. As well as being warriors and priests, kings were also lawgivers, a function every whit as important as war and religion. They appointed judges, and at the last appeal they were the judge. Their function, however, was to declare what the law was – not make new laws – and enforce it. These duties of medieval monarchy are enshrined in great royal buildings; the king, the lawgiver, at Westminster Hall; the king, the priest, in many cathedrals and churches, but above all in Westminster Abbey; and the king, the warrior, not only in the Tower, but also in stupendous castles, from Caernarvon in Wales to Chinon in France.

The Dukes of Normandy acquired England by conquest, but marriage and inheritance brought them an empire which stretched from Scotland to the Pyrenees. They were more powerful, richer too, than their overlord, the King of France, to whom they owed homage for their lands

The Norman chapel of St John the Evangelist in the White Tower, Tower of London

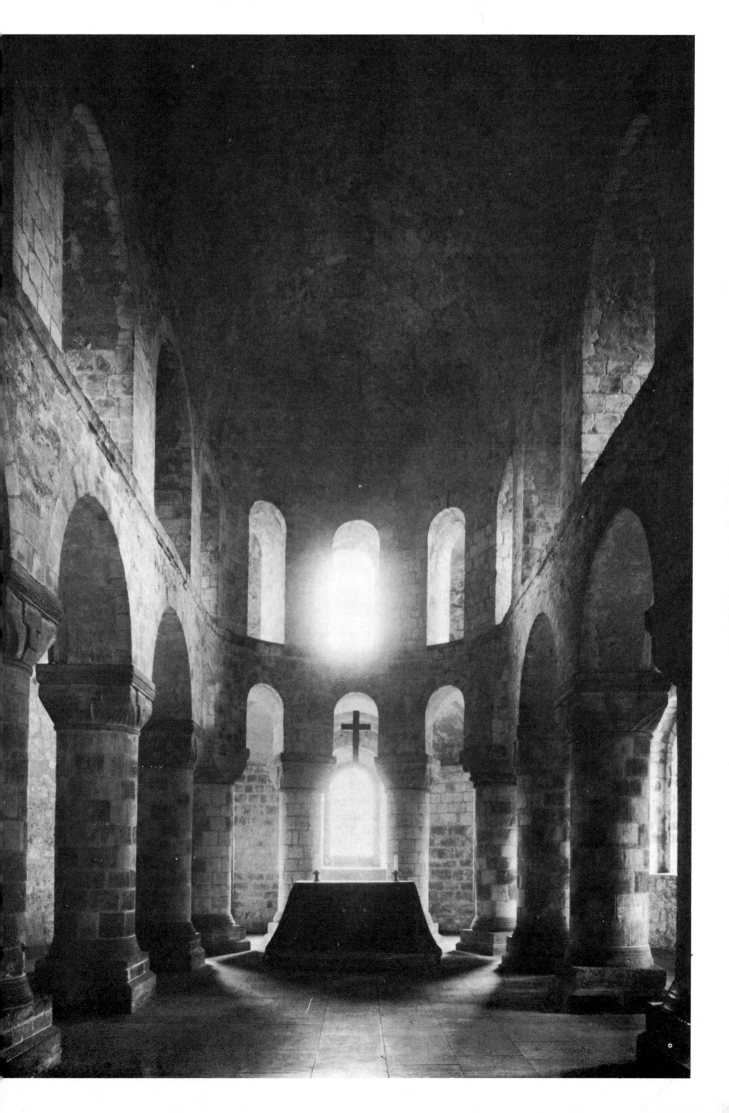

in France; and so they were constantly locked in disputes with the French King, disputes which began with intrigue and flared constantly into war. These conflicts forced our earliest medieval kings to be constantly on the move, crossing the Channel, holding their high courts at Winchester, Westminster and Gloucester, hunting a while in their forests, and then back to their lands in France. For a century and a half, after 1066, no King of England was born in England, and King John, who died in 1216, was the first of the Plantagenets to be buried here, in Worcester Cathedral. And so for the first royal tombs it is necessary to go to France, to Chinon in the rich farming land of the Loire, whose crossing it protects. This was the favourite castle of Henry II, the greatest of all the Plantagenets – restless, quick-tempered (he bore the responsibility for the murder of St Thomas à Becket in Canterbury Cathedral), a fierce and competent general, an even better administrator and governor, a tireless, small, barrel-chested man, quick in decision, adroit in diplomacy. Worn out with ceaseless activity, he came to Chinon to die, and to be buried in his favourite Abbey, the Abbey of Fontevrault, which he and his wife, Eleanor of Aquitaine, had founded and embellished. Their great warrior son, Richard Coeur de Lion, the crusader king, who fought so brilliantly in the Holy Land, was also a great castle-builder, raising one of the most majestic of all France at Gaillard to protect his crossing of the Seine, as Chinon protected the crossing of the Loire. He too was buried at Fontevrault. Their effigies are great works of art, some of the finest of these early centuries: Henry II, Richard I, and near to Richard I that of his mother, the formidable Eleanor of Aquitaine – formidable in riches, in power and in learning, one of the most cultured women of these early centuries. She brought up Richard to be far more than a tough warrior. Both his mother and his father were great patrons of learning, his father liking law and history and theology, his mother preferring poetry and music. Indeed, Richard wrote verse well, and when held for ransom by the German Emperor on the way back from the crusades, wrote a haunting song, one of many that he composed, but his *King Richard's Chanson* has echoed down the centuries.

Although the crusades brought Richard enduring fame, they wrecked the great Empire which he had inherited from Henry II. During his long

1 and 2 The tombs, in painted stone, of King Henry II, and of King Richard I and Eleanor of Aquitaine, at Fontevrault Abbey

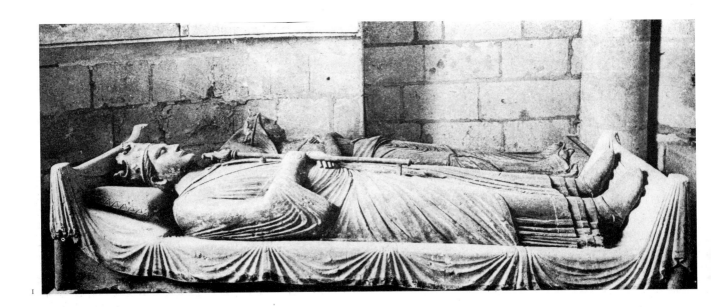

absence there were rebellions, plots, a general weakening, and his early death brought further disaster. His brother John, who succeeded him, lost Normandy. John's failure, and the endless difficulties with his rebellious nobles about taxation, brought him, in 1215, to Runnymede, to the greatest humiliation of any of his line, but one of the great milestones in English history. Here he signed *Magna Carta*, which for centuries was regarded as the foundation of an Englishman's liberties; indeed, it became that, but at the time it was largely John's rebellious barons who got the liberty. Within a year the barons were once again in rebellion. Even worse, they offered the English crown to the King of France. John fought magnificently, but he took ill, lost his baggage, caught fever, and died at Newark Castle. He was not a great builder of castles like his father and brother (although he did build a splendid small castle at Corfe) but he was a highly cultivated, intelligent king, not wise always in his judgments, but far from being the wicked, incompetent king of legend. He may, too, have been a great patron of gold and silversmiths if, as is quite possible, King John's Cup, now in the possession of King's Lynn Corporation, was really his. John lost his baggage in the fens, and this cup was dredged up there. It is so sumptuous that it must be royal. The workmanship is the very best that the early thirteenth century could produce. If it was John's, then he was a most discerning patron.

Both the sumptuous workmanship of the cup and the rebellions of the barons speak of the strains and the changes that medieval society and, indeed, kingship itself was undergoing. The baronage was steadily becoming rooted in the counties of England, building castles, great and small, that every decade increased in luxury. Often they were more willing than not to pay a tax (so long as it was light) than go to war or send their armed retainers. They therefore regarded King John quite differently from the way their ancestors had viewed William the Conqueror, a successful warrior king who brought victory, bounty and comradeship in arms. Now they were more concerned with money and the good things which money could buy – gold and silver plate, tapestries, brilliant clothes, and the silks and spices which the crusaders had brought back from the East – rather than war. Their wealth was

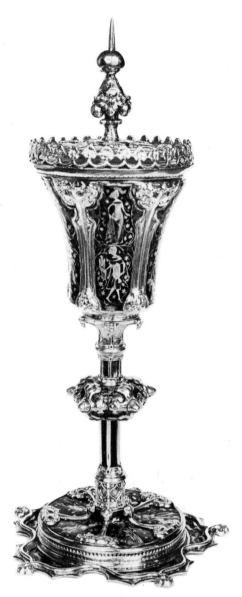

King John's Cup, King's Lynn

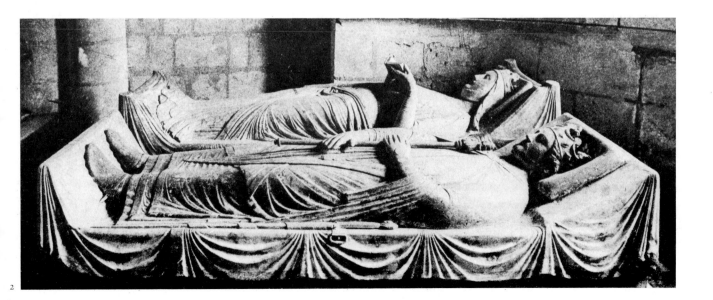

2

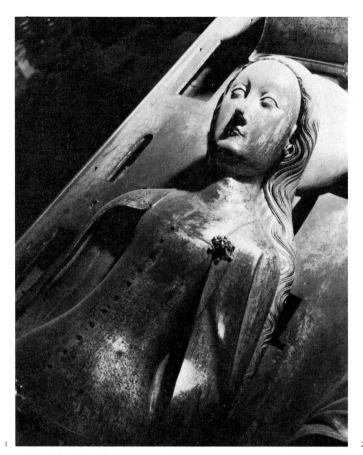

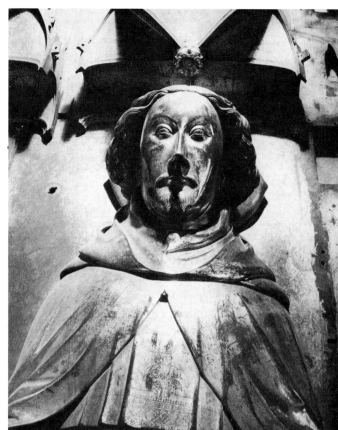

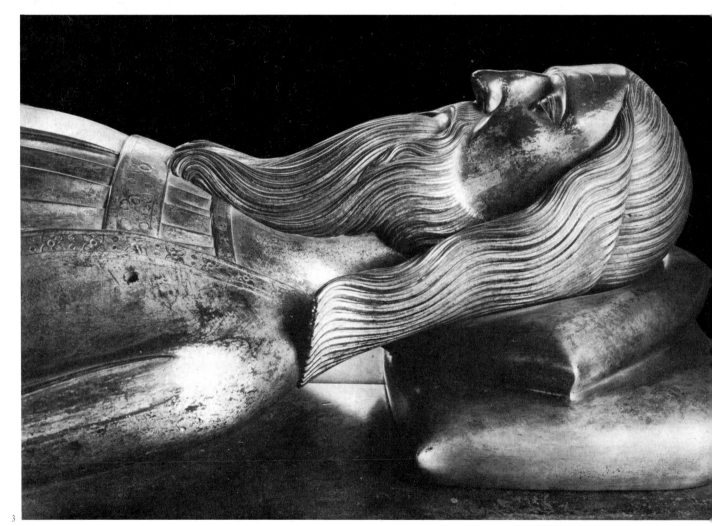

Bronze effigies of 1 Anne of Bohemia (1366–94) and 2 King Richard II (1367–1400) by Nicholas Broker and Godfrey Prest, Westminster Abbey.
3 Gilt copper effigy of King Edward III (1312–77), Westminster Abbey

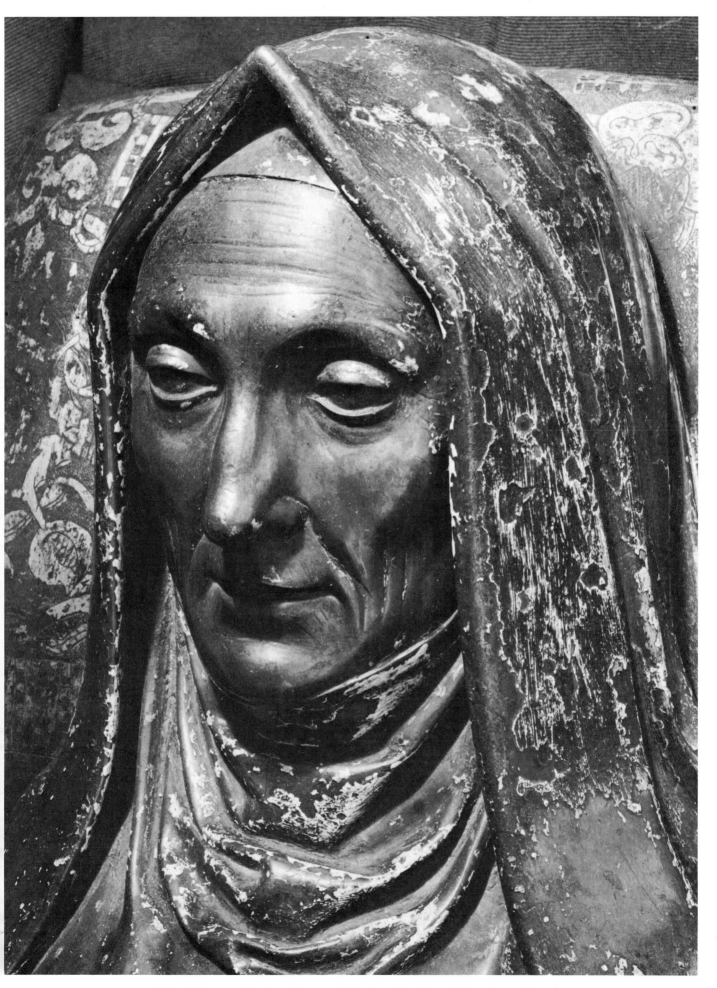

Effigy of Margaret Beaufort (1443–1509), by Pietro Torrigiano, Westminster Abbey

derived from privilege, from liberties (quite different, this, to liberty), liberties were usually rights to evade taxes or impose local ones. These often conflicted with the king's right, and his power clipped their wings, whilst his wars, win or lose, cost them money. If they went to war with him, many of them felt the time would have been better spent on their estates. Just as the baron's life was becoming more sophisticated, more stable, and far more expensive, so was the king's, and his need for money was as great as theirs. Royal armies were becoming more professional, so from time to time kings also preferred to tax their barons rather than summon them to war. But the king's idea of a just tax was a large one. Hence there was plenty of room for conflict between the king and his barons. There had been long before John came to the throne. It is not surprising that the thirteenth century witnessed one of the great developments of English law. As litigation grew, the definition of rights became essential, and new institutions were needed to deal with ever-increasing legal business.

In early Plantagenet days the king's judges went about with him, and the medieval court was always on the move because the king had to travel in order to rule. Because of growing complexity of government, and also because the king was so very frequently in France, the judges and the exchequer began to stay in London from Henry II's reign. The judges went on assizes, that is journeys round the kingdom – they still do – but their roots were in London. Westminster Hall became the home of law and justice. Begun by William Rufus as a great Banqueting Hall, it is almost the only part of the great medieval Palace of Westminster that is left. Nearly three centuries later, Richard II renovated it and gave it a new roof – perhaps the greatest hammer-beam roof to survive from the High Middle Ages. But from Henry II's day it had become the heart of the courts of justice. In time, each court acquired its own place. On one side of the door sat the Court of Chancery, on the other the Court of King's Bench; in the middle of the west wall, the Court of Common Pleas. In a room nearby was the Court of the Exchequer, which dealt with taxes and finance; so, until the nineteenth century, the hall teemed with lawyers, with men and women come to obtain justice. And, if this was not enough, it was also full of shops. A crowded, bustling place, for over 600 years it remained the heart of the life of the palace. It was always open to the public, for it was most important that justice could be seen to be done, and that, too, strengthened monarchy, for judges were the king's judges, justice was royal justice. Even today judges are men apart, neither legislators nor civil servants, a separate part of government. Then they were separate, but not independent. Under a strong king, the king's writ ran, but there were unsuccessful kings, such as John, as well as weak ones like his pious son, Henry III, and then the law might favour the baronage. So law, in the Middle Ages, like so much else, was a battleground; neither written nor closely defined, it was a matter of custom and interpretation; the barons and the great towns wanted more liberties, kings wanted them to have less. The Church, too, was always trying to escape from the king's legal grip and cling to the more constant authority of Rome.

So strife there was in plenty, particularly during the thirteenth century. Yet out of it came the great balance of power between the king and parliament, which consisted not only of nobles summoned by the

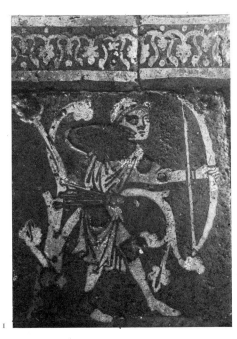

1 and 2 Details of tiles from the floor of the Chapter House, Westminster Abbey

king, but also representatives from the shires and boroughs. Parliament met when the king called it, and it assembled wherever he was – Northampton, Leicester, Gloucester, York, Winchester, but very often in the Palace of Westminster, where it still remains. Then the House of Commons sat in the Chapter House of Westminster Abbey, the great Church of the Palace. The Chapter House is one of the great triumphs of medieval architecture and one of the greatest pieces of royal patronage. The weight of the vast roof is born by one slender column of marble! For its time, a miracle of technology. Originally the chapel was a blaze of colour, of azure, red and gold; and Simon de Montfort, the champion of the commons, denounced it as a wanton royal extravagance when they met there for the first time in 1256 (just three years after it was completed). But one generation's extravagance is often the artistic glory of the next. The encaustic tiled floor remains in all its beauty, for it was covered for three centuries by a wooden floor. The different coloured tiles tell the stories and legends of the Abbey as the great wall paintings (some, alas, lost) tell of Christ's life. It was a daring building for its day, but triumphantly beautiful, and gave immense satisfaction to Henry III, whatever his baronial opponents might say.

At the age of nine, in 1216, Henry had inherited the crown and a land so torn by war that he was the one king not to be crowned at Westminster, but at Gloucester. Nevertheless, England enjoyed a surging prosperity, a rich Renaissance, particularly in architecture and sculpture. Henry was extremely pious and, unlike his Plantagenet ancestors, very English, although he appreciated French art. He began to cultivate English sentiment, and lay claim to its historic past. The founder of Westminster Abbey had been the saintly Edward the Confessor, whom Henry III venerated. So Henry tore down the old Norman Abbey and raised the Westminster Abbey that we know as a memorial to St Edward. With great pomp and ceremony, Henry himself acting as a pall-bearer, the coffin of Edward was moved and placed in the new, splendid, jewel-bedecked tomb behind the high altar. The jewels have gone, with the gold that encrusted it, ripped out at the Reformation as idolatrous, but the tomb itself remains, and so do the carvings which commemorate the events of the Confessor's life.

What attracted Henry III to Edward the Confessor was not only that he was wholly English, but also because he enshrined the ideal of holy, priestly monarchy – the king as a part of the Church, not merely its defender. As Peter of Blois wrote about the King's grandfather, Henry II, 'I would have you know that to attend upon the King is something sacred, for the King himself is holy; he is the anointed of the Lord.' All the Plantagenets prided themselves that they could work cures by touching the sick; they were most successful with 'plague affecting the groin and the healing of scrofula'. Henry III's son, Edward I, held the record for miraculous healing, curing some 1736 people in the year 1300. To underline their humility and their closeness to Christ, these kings washed feet and distributed alms to the poor on the Thursday before Good Friday, Maundy Thursday. The feet washing is over, although the Queen's attendants still wear aprons as symbols of it; the money – Maundy money – is specially minted for the occasion, the ceremony has persisted since the Plantagenets, King after King, century after century, and still performed by our own Queen.

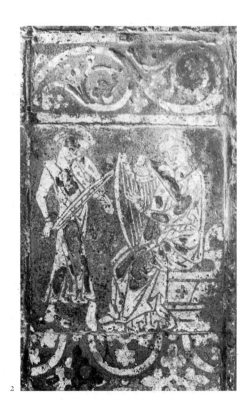

2

Henry III built as no other monarch had built before him. The great soaring chancel of Westminster Abbey was far higher than any cathedral in Britain. He took his ideas from France, the rounded apse is unusual for England, but patronised English architects. The scale, however, was so vast that he died before the abbey was half-finished. His son, Edward I, named piously after the Confessor, could not afford the sums his father had poured out, and the work went slowly on for 150 years, but the style never changed. So what we see at Westminster Abbey – soaring buttresses, flying columns, magnificent perspective – is Henry III's dream realised.

Henry, however, intended Westminster Abbey to be not merely a memorial to Edward the Confessor, but a sepulchre for kings, a magnificent royal burial ground near to the saint who had once ruled their land. Henry himself was the first to be buried there. As with his ancestors at Fontevrault, a magnificent effigy was placed over his tomb, sculpted by a great medieval artist, William Torel. In a sedilia nearby are the life-size paintings of Henry III and his son, Edward I. No saint he, but a great warrior who subdued the Welsh and hammered the Scots. And all about Henry's tomb are those of his descendants, some of the finest medieval royal tombs in the western world. Curiously enough, Edward I's tomb never received an effigy and remains plain. His grandson, Edward III, another warrior king, who trounced the French at Crécy and Poitiers, is shown in an effigy which is regarded by many as the most outstanding of them all. It is in brass, and although the beard is stylised, the features were said to be a true likeness of the King – perhaps the first realistic portrait of any English king. The sides of the tomb are covered with the figures of his numerous children, led by the eldest, the Black Prince, an even greater warrior. His own tomb, resplendent with his armour, is at Canterbury Cathedral, but that of his son, Richard II, is in Westminster Abbey, near to Edward III's, and alongside that of his wife, Anne of Bohemia, to whom he was utterly devoted. The portrait in the abbey of Richard as a young king, much restored as it is, is one of the finest of the Middle Ages, moving in its lifelike depiction of a vulnerable boy.

Perhaps the greatest monument of these medieval kings, however, is that raised for Henry V, in whose reign the English soldiers achieved their greatest victory against the French, at Agincourt, so great a victory that Henry V was able to marry the Daughter of France, Katherine, which led to his own son, Henry VI, being crowned King of France as well as of England. But Henry V, much to his country's grief, died young, 'too famous', as Shakespeare wrote, 'to live long'. He died in France in 1422. His body was embalmed and brought back to England in a vast solemn procession, a hundred monks in white robes singing their dirges as it wound its way slowly to Westminster Abbey. In this grove of royal graves a magnificent chapel was raised to his memory. Detailed sculptures show events in his life, his coronation, and on horseback among the tents of his soldiers.

For centuries afterwards, most Kings and Queens came to rest in the abbey, the strong and the weak, the young and the old, the successes and the failures. Although it is now cluttered with the tombs of the famous – admirals, generals, statesmen, poets, writers, musicians and actors, it remains essentially the church of the British monarchy, where the

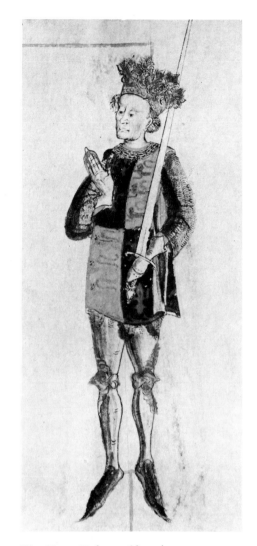

King Henry V, from a fifteenth-century manuscript collection of histories of Kings in the British Library, London

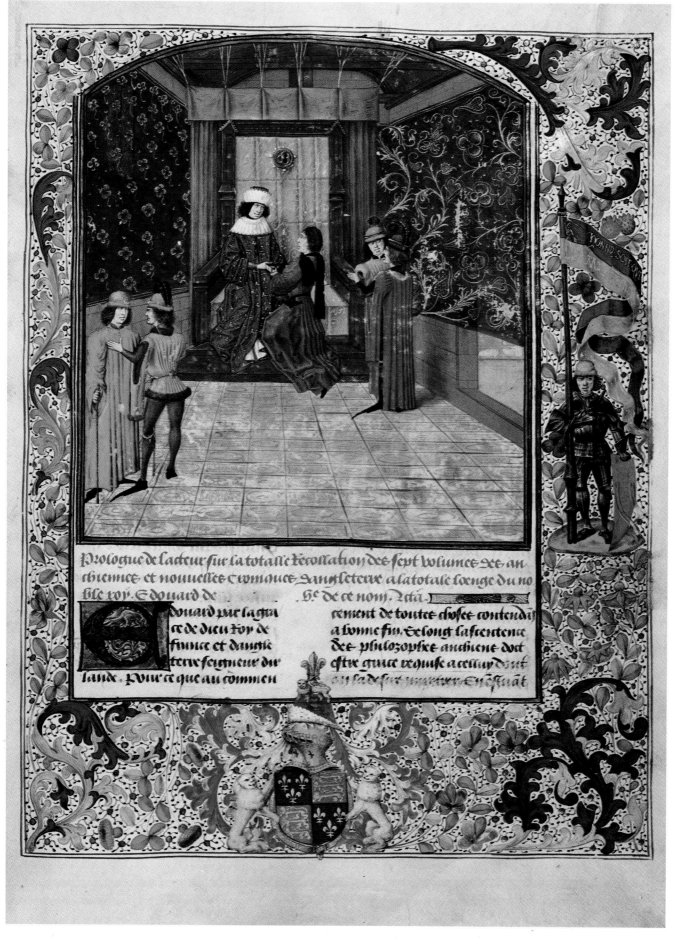

Wavrin presents his Chronicles to King Edward IV. *Les Anchiennes Et Nouvelles Chroniques d'Angleterre*

The history of the middle ages was recorded in illustrated manuscripts. Those in the British Library, from the old Royal Library, were for the most part presented to the Museum by King George II in 1757

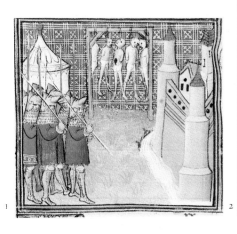

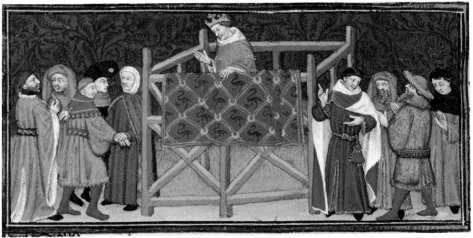

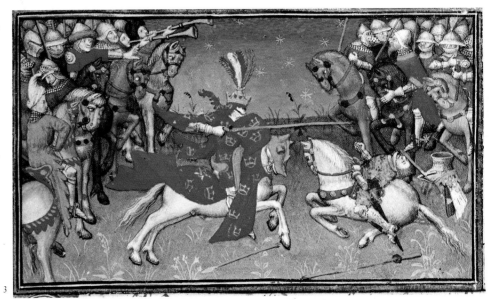

1 Warriors encamped at the walls of a town; five victims hang from the gallows. From *Les Chroniques de Saint Denis*. 2 From a scaffolding rostrum, the King addresses his subjects. From *L'Histoire d'Alexandre le Grand*. 3 In a joust at full gallop, one knight flies from his horse. From *L'Histoire d'Alexandre le Grand*. 4 The coronation of King Richard II. From *Les Anchiennes Et Nouvelles Chroniques d'Angleterre*. 5 King William I, enthroned, head of Church and State. From *The Chronica Majora*, by Matthew Paris

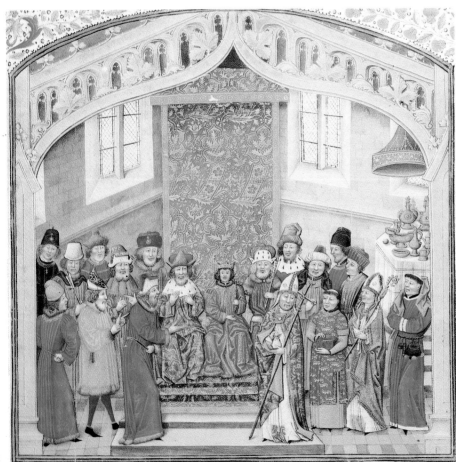

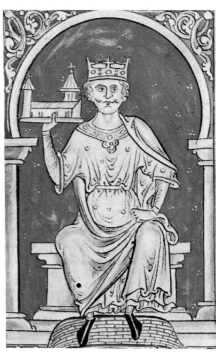

Opposite: The building of the Tower of Babel. From the French version of 'The Book of Hours' of John, Duke of Bedford, Regent of France (brother of King Henry V)

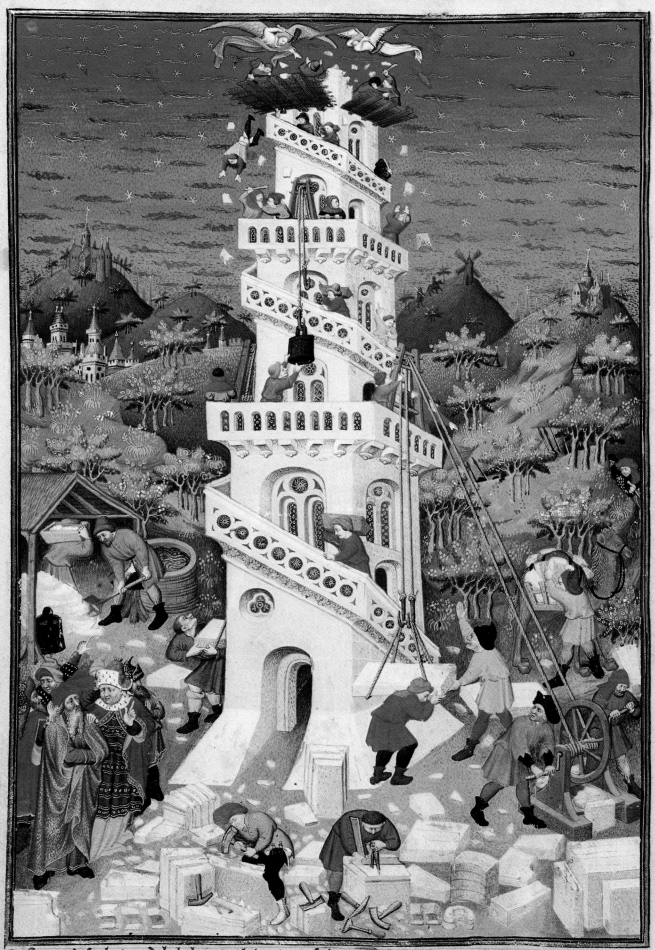

Comment on edifia la tour de babiloine. et le languege fute mue en .lxxij. languegues. et les anges la despecerent

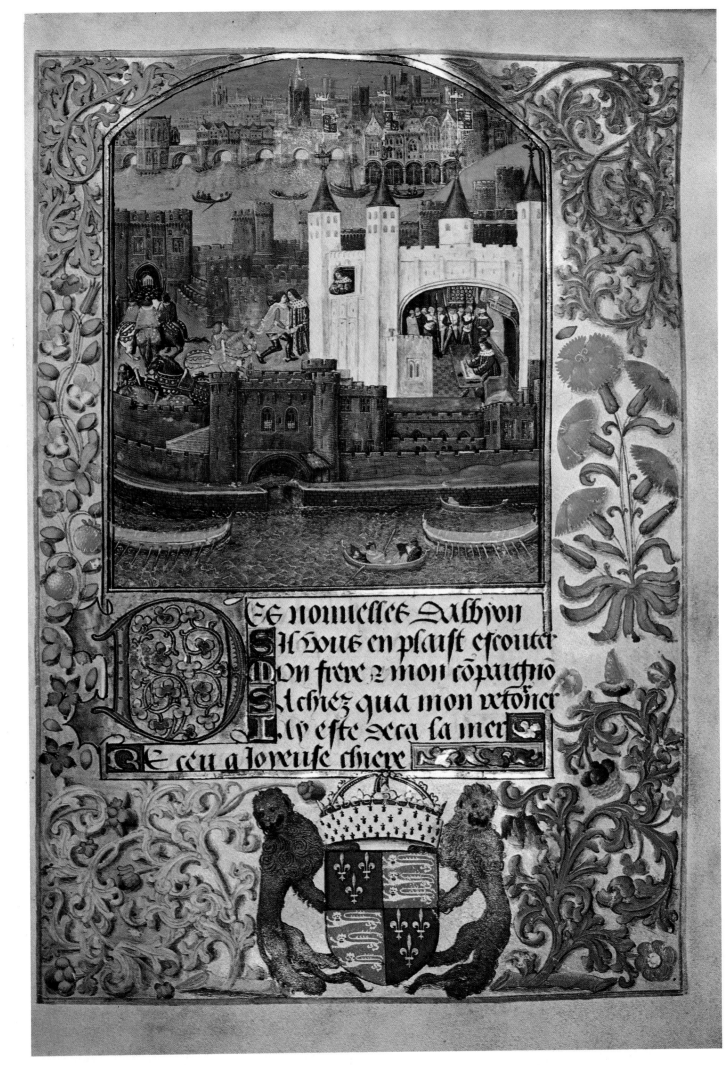

dramatic moments of each reign were staged – coronation, marriage, burial. But in the Middle Ages the abbey also had another function. Often abbeys and even cathedrals were used in ways which, to us, seem extremely secular – there were shops, for example, in St Paul's, and towards the end of the Middle Ages Caxton set up his printing press in a room of Westminster Abbey. Edward I, however, used a room there for the examination of his coinage.

Kings were responsible for all coinage. The king's head and name stamped on coins was a guarantee of their authenticity and value. Throughout the thirteenth century coinage began to be increasingly used, even in remote market towns, and with this increase came an increase in forgers, and even more of clippers who clipped off a little silver here and a little silver there. So it became important to declare officially the standard of any year's coinage, the amount of silver it contained and its weight. In 1279 Edward I instituted the Trial of the Pyx in one of the most secure vaults of the abbey – now known as the Chamber of the Pyx. At the trial the newly minted coins were carefully weighed, at the same time an equally careful check of the impression on the coin being made against the plate that made it. In 1281 these trials became public – not very public, but a few witnesses were present to authenticate what was done. Similar trials have continued ever since. Only in modern times, however, were they moved to the Mint. In the Chamber of the Pyx there were chests of new coins waiting for their testing, and because it was so carefully guarded the crown jewels and the coronation regalia were also kept there. Robbers have attempted to break in, and one who was caught was flayed alive and his skin hammered to the door of the chamber – traces of it are still visible.

Money Edward I needed, and money Edward I had – if not in the abundance he required. And certainly not enough to finish his father's great abbey at Westminster, which was low on the list of priorities. A long, lean man of six feet two inches, nicknamed 'Longshanks', Edward I welded the crown and the baronage together after long decades of mutual distrust and conflict. Medieval kings were never truly successful without victory in war; and Edward provided victory in plenty. His greatest success came in Wales. The Welsh princes had revolted and harried the coastal roads and borders from their great refuge in Snowdonia with its complex, easily defendable valleys. These marauding bands – they were little more – provoked Edward, indeed, incensed him, and on 17 November 1276 he decided to settle the Welsh question once and for all. He marched into Wales, taking with him masons and carpenters, and as soon as he reached Flint, he planned and started to build a formidable castle. Then, having caught and killed the princes, he went on to build castles on a scale that was almost megalomanic. The huge castles of Conway and Caernarvon, the lesser bastions of Harlech and Beaumaris, were the ring of fortresses which were intended to dominate Snowdonia for ever, and to become the heart of Edward's Welsh government. The walls of Caernarvon were modelled on those of Byzantium, the greatest medieval bastion in Europe. The castle is immense, masons and carpenters were brought in from Kent, Norfolk, Devon, Northumberland, and all the shires between. And it must be remembered that they came on foot, carrying their tools and possessions on their backs, walking day after day in small groups from every corner of Britain. They came in their

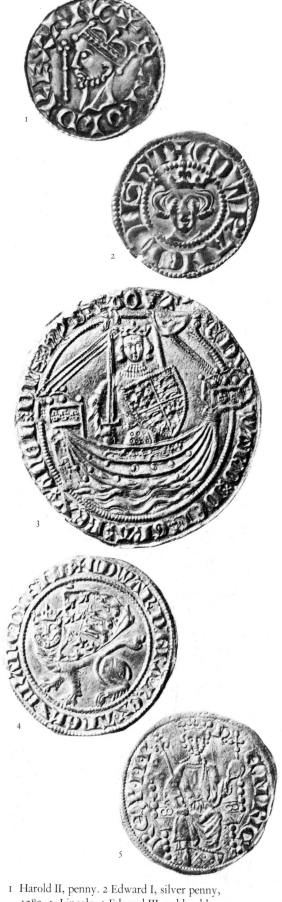

1 Harold II, penny. 2 Edward I, silver penny, 1280–1, Lincoln. 3 Edward III, gold noble, 1360–9, Calais. 4 Edward III, gold half-florin, 1344, London. 5 Henry III, gold penny, c. 1257, London. British Museum, London

Opposite: A late-fifteenth century view of London, from *The Poems of Charles of Orléans.* Charles is shown writing in the White Tower

hundreds, for they were bidden to build fast. The equivalent of at least £10 million in modern money was poured into this gigantic building, which is a walled city as well as a castle. Edward's policy of sweeping away all mementoes of the old Roman town was quite deliberate. There was a belief still current that Caernarvon had been the home of the father of the Emperor Constantine, who built Byzantium – hence the way Caernarvon was built – but not only that, Edward I intended Caernarvon to be his royal capital in Wales. Before the castle was half built, in 1284, he was there with his pregnant Queen. The child proved to be a son, and Edward subsequently made him Prince of Wales – a title normally held by the eldest son of the reigning monarch ever since. Yet no further heir has ever been born in Wales, and the ceremony of investiture was only revived in 1911 (on the suggestion of Lloyd George), when the future Edward VIII was invested. The only other investiture was that of the present Prince in 1969.

Caernarvon Castle

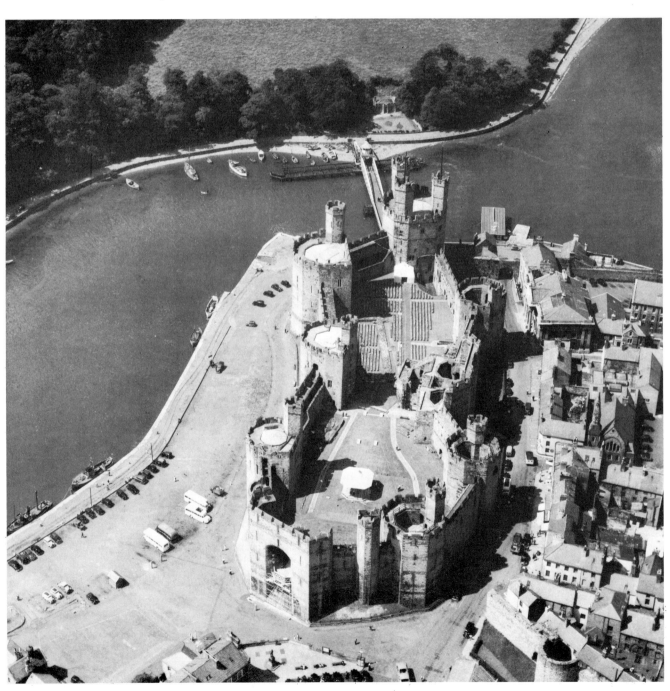

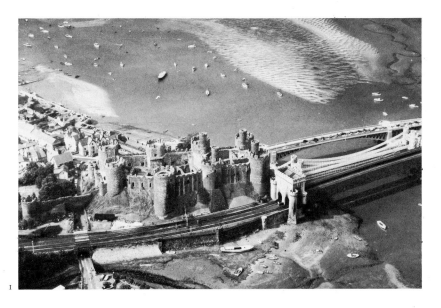

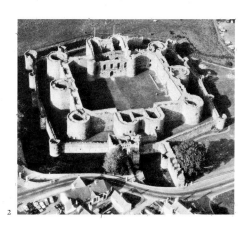

1 Conway Castle. 2 Beaumaris Castle

Once the Prince was born, the restless King moved back into England to hammer the Scots – a greater threat than the Welsh – but the castle building never ceased in Wales. Indeed, Caernarvon was never finished; it was too vast, and there were too many other castles to be built worthy of monarchs. Conway Castle, another walled city, built on a superb site guarding one of the main routes into Snowdonia, was almost as expensive and as elaborate as Caernarvon. It contained magnificent towers and halls, designed for a royalty that was never to live there. Caernarvon and Conway were to be the seats of government, and so Caernarvon remained for centuries. But there were also other castles, a little simpler, and built for purely military purposes, like Harlech and Beaumaris. Nevertheless even these bastions by the sea were huge and costly, and employed hundreds of workmen for decades. Nor did they prove highly defensible, because they were never fully manned. Caernarvon was sacked in a rebellion ten years after it was begun. Harlech succumbed to Welsh insurgents between 1403 and 1409; Criccieth, another large castle built across the bay from Harlech, was captured by Owen Glendower in 1404 and partly destroyed. Beaumaris fared somewhat better, but even Beaumaris was never completed.

Nevertheless, ten new castles built by Edward I are, in their way, the most impressive architectural achievement of the kings of the Middle Ages, and a remarkable feat of complex organisation. The resources of the whole country, from the borders of Scotland to the Channel, had to be mobilised; money to pay the workers had to be strapped to the backs of pack horses at the mints of Nottingham, Westminster and the Tower of London, and conveyed to Wales. Furthermore, the workers had to be housed and fed, not only themselves, but their wives and children, who often came with them and worked with them. The methods were primitive and arduous, but the organisation was a tribute to England's chancery or civil service, acknowledged from the days of Henry II to be the most efficient in the western world.

One of the great problems of the Middle Ages was the question of authenticity. Where so many privileges and rights of property depended on a written statement or charter for proof, forgers abounded. The papacy, which was particularly vulnerable (few monasteries jibbed at forging a papal bull), developed a complex system which involved subtle

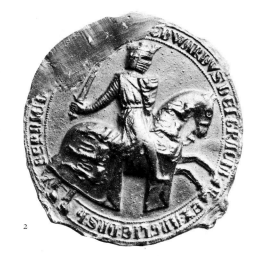

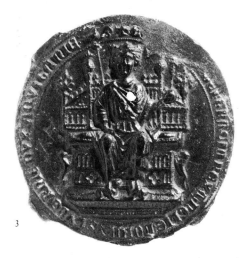

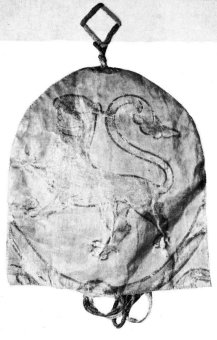

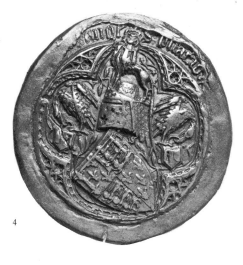

uses of language that changed from year to year, as well as elaborate seals. In England, the chancery largely depended on seals as defence against the forgers. These varied from the Great Seal of England, fixed to important documents of state, to smaller privy seals; the chamberlains and justiciaries and great officers of state possessed their own official seals. Such seals needed to be both intricate and solemn, and the royal seal developed its own artistry and beauty. Edward I's seal was a noble seal, but not comparable to that of his grandson, Edward III, whose seal is one of the most beautiful to have survived.

These seals bring beauty to the charters, but the arduous clerical work is best displayed by the rolls, on which all the immense details of wages and materials were meticulously kept. Few realise that the civil service, with its records going back to the twelfth century, is as royal in its origins and early development as Westminster Abbey or the Tower. And wherever the king and his court went, a small army of clerks (usually priests) followed him. It was not an easy life, serving a restless warrior such as Edward I, who was as passionately interested in law as he was in war.

Indeed, Edward I proved himself to be as great a lawgiver as a warrior. He called parliament after parliament in order to give greater solemnity and power to the laws that he promulgated by statute. He brought

1 A charter of King Edward I, 1280–1, granting land in Boreham and Little Waltham to Waltham Holy Cross Abbey. The Public Record Office, London.
2 and 3 The Great Seal of King Edward I.
4 The Privy Seal of John of Gaunt. All from the British Library, London

system and order to the complex patterns and contradictions of the feudal law which had grown up over generations. He defined the role of the Church in relation not only to Rome, but also to the holding of land. He greatly strengthened the structure of royal government, and it is not surprising that he acquired the sobriquet of 'the English Justinian' after the great codifier of Roman laws. And yet we know very little of the inner life of this powerful, effective king. One glimpse only: his wife, Eleanor of Castile, suddenly died at Lincoln in 1290 and his grief was so great that he raised a beautiful Gothic cross with a statue of the Queen at every place where her coffin rested on its slow journey to Westminster Abbey. The Eleanor cross at Hardingstone, near Northampton, has survived with least damage and alteration (the final cross, at Charing Cross, is a substitute). When her body reached Westminster, the Queen was buried with great pomp and her effigy in gilt brass was made by William Torel, who had made Henry III's effigy. No king has raised such superb or so numerous memorials to his wife – surely an indication of personal loss and grief, as well as regal splendour.

When Edward I died in 1309 he left a powerful and stable kingdom. England possessed the most centralised government in the western world. Wales had been totally defeated, Scotland crushed, his own baronage subdued. His laws had been declared and imposed. Few English kings had been such masters in their own realms. Yet kingship in the High Middle Ages depended greatly on the personality of the king, on his capacity to impose his will on his mighty subjects who could easily, if they banded together against him, raise armies as large and as powerful as his own. His son, Edward II, and his grandson, Edward III, illustrate this truth to perfection.

Edward II made mistakes. He chose the wrong type of favourites – sharp, witty, greedy. His barons rebelled, defeated him, and imposed heavy terms that wrecked the power of the monarchy and strengthened theirs. He struggled once more against them, but was deposed and put to a hideous death in Berkeley Castle – a victim not only of his barons, but of his wife and her lover. This was the terrible inheritance of his son,

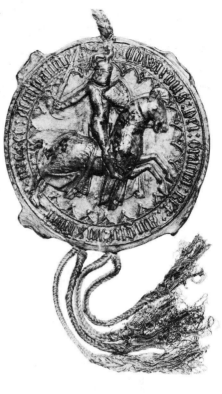

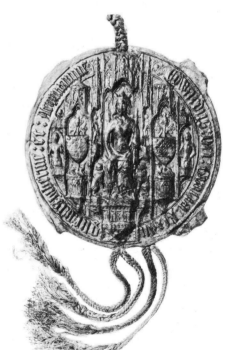

The Great Seal of King Edward III

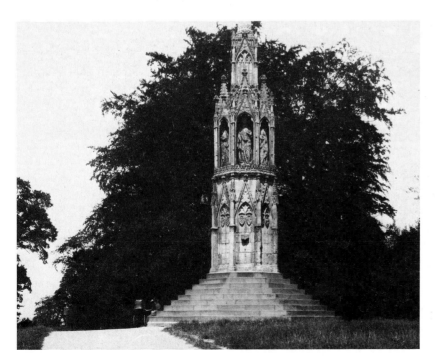

The Eleanor Cross at Hardingstone, near Northampton

Edward III. Yet within a few years he had established his royal authority, imposed his will on the unruly baronage, and stimulated great prosperity by judicious foreign alliances that gave advantages to English wool merchants. The power of the monarchy rose to new heights. A natural warrior like his grandfather, Edward invaded France, both to extend his own lands and to protect English trade. He won victory after victory, and so began the Hundred Years War, which was to bleed France almost to death, to bring the English spectacular successes in battle and, briefly, even the kingdom of France itself.

Once again the English kings were moving from the borderlands of Scotland to those of Spain, but no matter how far the medieval kings might roam, they were drawn back to London, the heart of their kingdom, prosperous and alive with trade, if plague-ridden. Too un-healthy to live in, the kings made their palaces close by. Situated, as it was, on the edge of the great forest in which the Plantagenet kings loved to hunt, Windsor was remarkably suitable. There was also the Tower, closer to London and, like Windsor, a great palace as well as a great fortress. It is hard to imagine the life of the court in these vast castles during the High Middle Ages, the Age of Chivalry. They are hard, cold, grey buildings, made, one might think, merely for war. The great towers – the Bell Tower, the Bloody Tower, the Wakefield, the Lantern Tower, and so round the walls, tower after tower back to Beauchamp and Bell, were raised by those great builders, Henry III, Edward I, Edward III, and his grandson, Richard II. The great towers of Windsor make the same impression – might and main; war and the mailed fist. Yet, within, these great grim fortresses were the abodes of kings, ablaze with colour, and thus echoed with music and songs and the sound of the dance or of a poet such as Chaucer reading his poetry.

Amongst the great collection of medieval books given by George II to the British Library, there is an illustrated manuscript which tells us a great deal about the High Middle Ages in a single illustration (see page 28). At first sight it looks rather childish, with its lack of perspective and the rather gauche way the artist has removed a wall of the Tower to show us what is happening inside; but his aim was not only to delight the eye with his sumptuous blues, reds, greens and golds, but to tell a story. He shows us London, with its bridge, and he deliberately creates a sense of riches by filling the Pool with shipping. Inside William the Conqueror's great White Keep is a French nobleman, Charles, Duke of Orléans, richly dressed in warm clothing, attended by French servants, and guarded by

The Treaty of Calais Chest, *c.* 1360. The inscription refers to peace made at Calais between the Kings of England and France

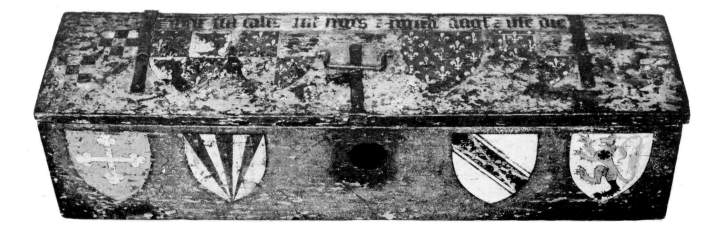

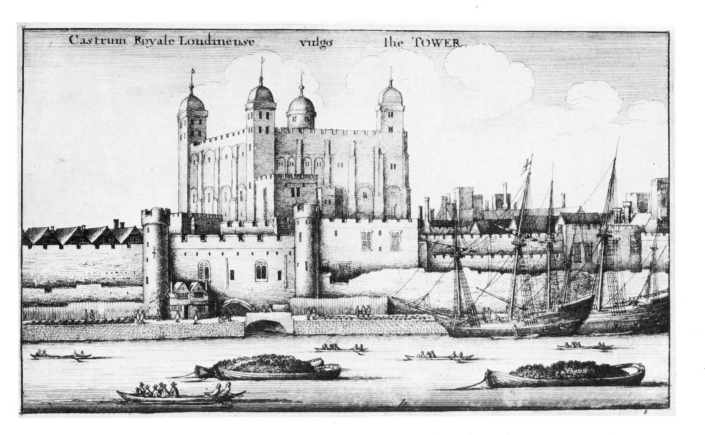

English soldiers, sitting comfortably at his huge desk, writing his poetry. He lived there in great comfort, leading a civilised life of music, poetry, reading, and, of course, dalliance, for girls were not denied him for the twenty-five years until he could raise his huge ransom. He had been captured in 1415 at Agincourt. Had he been a humble foot-soldier, death would almost certainly have come very quickly, the body stripped of its clothes, and left for someone else to bury. But a knight, a squire – anyone, indeed, who was mounted or armoured – was valuable. The higher his lineage, the greater his value, and a part of the art of medieval war lay in capturing such valuable prizes alive.

Of course, the knights also proclaimed boldly who they were. Indeed, heraldry developed in order to proclaim their names. This colourful art began as a simple shield painted in bold colours with a device that proclaimed Mowbray, Vere, Beauchamp, Grosvenor, or Cholmondeley. As time passed the painted devices on these shields became more complex and elaborate. Shields were often hung in the hall, partly as a decoration and partly to proclaim the honour and dignity of the owner, for they would indicate his descent, the families he was related to, or, if a king, the countries over which he claimed sovereignty. The crests of the helmet or the pennants that fluttered from his lance might also indicate the value of the prize sought in battle, and also the badges worn by the armed retainers around him. This flamboyance of shield, crest and badge, boasting 'come and get me', was matched by great daring. Heroic exploits were greatly prized, particularly if associated with the crusades against the heathen, or with unrequited love. Richard I died through an act of almost wanton courage, and was revered for it. Hence there developed a kind of poetry of war which we call 'chivalry'. And chivalry was elaborated by the warlike ritual games which developed into jousting tournaments when fully armed and mounted knights would charge

Wenceslas Hollar's engraving of the Tower of London, mid-seventeenth century. In the foreground is the Traitor's Gate

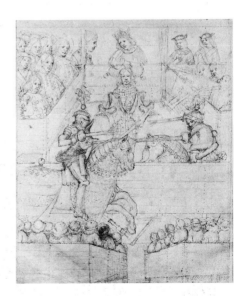

A joust, from *The Life and Acts of Richard Beauchamp, Earl of Warwick*, by John Rous, *c.* 1485. British Library, London

each other at full tilt in the hope of dismounting the other and gain, maybe, a favour from the ladies who watched.

Naturally such a world where individual prowess, acts of bravery and selfless devotion were venerated soon produced its heroes and its cults. Henry III, as we have seen, had made a cult of Edward the Confessor, the ideal king, but Edward was a real, an undeniable historic figure, but far back in time lurked a shadowy figure, King Arthur, about whom legends had already accumulated. Stories of King Arthur, his knights, the ladies they loved, the deeds they performed, were woven into epic tales, and so powerful did this cult of King Arthur become at Henry III's court that his brother Richard, Duke of Cornwall, even built a vast castle at Tintagel on Cornwall's wild northern coast because it was supposed to be the site of the legendary Camelot, Arthur's home. The cult of chivalry, with its chansons and gestes, meant that minstrels, bards and storytellers were welcome at the courts of the princes.

As often happens, the development of a more sophisticated and luxurious way of life had been aided by a simple technological advance. In the Dark Ages kings and their retainers had lived together in great halls – these are a feature of the great Norse sagas and of the Anglo-Saxon epic poems such as *Beowulf* – huddled about the central fire, whose smoke curled up through an open hole in the roof. Towards the end of the eleventh century the chimney was invented, and gradually improved, so that fires could give out heat, but suck up the smoke in quite small rooms. Not only did privacy become more possible, but small rooms encouraged greater intimacy and heightened individualism which can

The Wilton Diptych, c. 1394–9. King Richard II is presented by his patron saints, King Edmund, Edward the Confessor and John the Baptist, to the Virgin and Child. The reverse side, opposite, shows arms attributed to Edward the Confessor, with the quartered royal arms of France and England and Richard's personal emblem of the white hart (also embroidered on the dresses of the eleven angels and on the gown of the king). National Gallery, London

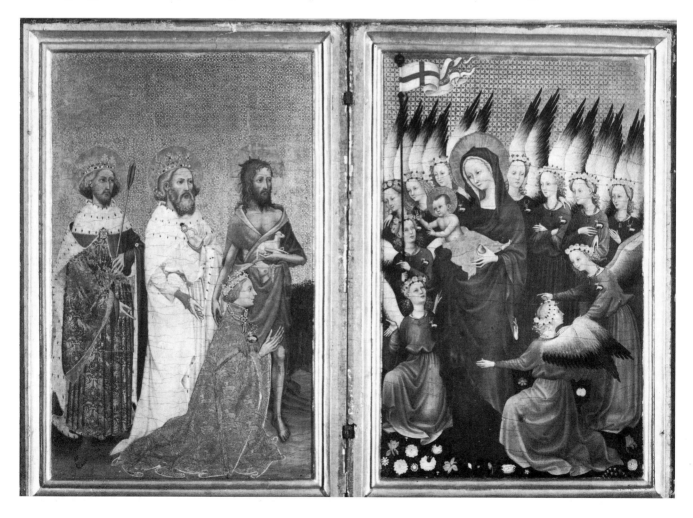

express itself in decoration, in all the embellishments that medieval art could bring. In Jean de Wavrin's *Chroniques d'Angleterre*, which the author presented to Edward IV, we see pictures, brilliantly painted, of such rooms. These rooms, hung with tapestries, sometimes tiled in marble, were as sumptuous as the clothing noblemen wore when they were out of their armour. They loved to listen to the great romances of chivalry – the stories of King Arthur and his knights, or the *Song of Roland*. And they enjoyed, too, the gentle satire of Chaucer, the father of English poetry, who is shown in another manuscript, reading to the court. In his great *Canterbury Tales*, Chaucer praised the chivalrous knight, but knew how to mock the self-seeking cleric and the over-refined nun, or laugh at the rollicking Wife of Bath.

Chaucer was a great favourite at the court of Richard II, whose reign marked a new height in English culture – in architecture, in sculpture, in literature and in painting. Richard's portrait in Westminster Abbey is far removed from the stylised representations of earlier kings. The same quality infuses the greatest masterpiece of this age – the Wilton Diptych. The powerful features of Richard's patron saints, St Edmund, the English Martyr, St Edward the Confessor, and St John the Baptist, contrast strongly with the delicate young prince, with his flock of attending angels. Equally beautiful is the painting on the reverse of the White Hart, the personal badge of Richard. Few, alas, of these great paintings, and there must have been many, have come down to us.

The pictures which we do possess are almost all to be found in the illuminated manuscripts. Although chronicles, particularly famous

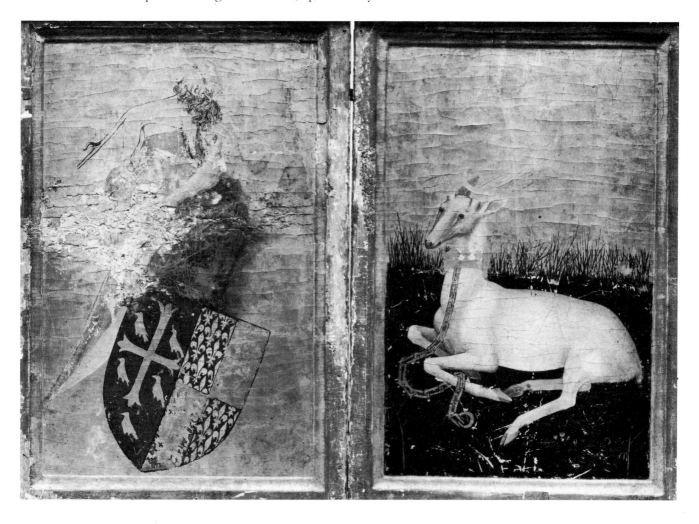

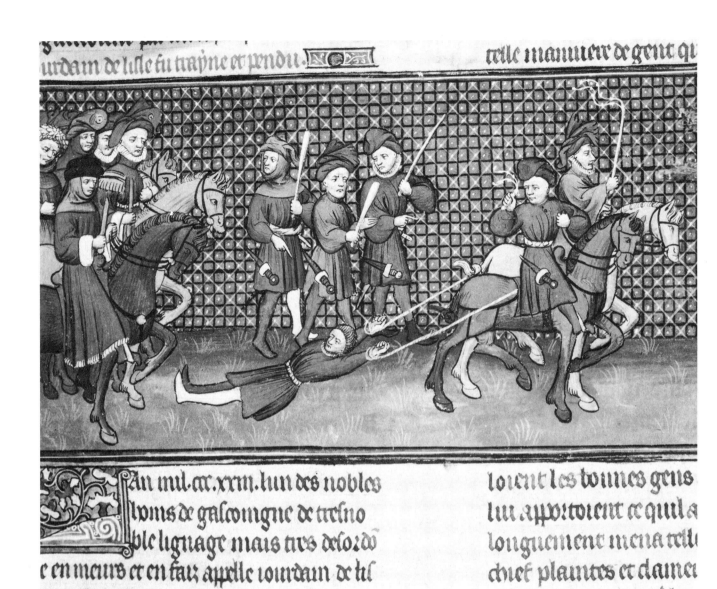

Manuscript illustration from *Les Chroniques de Saint Denis*. The British Library, London

chronicles like those of Froissart, who wrote about the wars between England and France, or of Villehardouin, who wrote about the Crusades, are not uncommon, the vast majority of these books are of an ecclesiastical nature – missals and books of hours that were used in the performance of the daily rituals of the church. A formal attendance at mass was expected daily of the king, the queen, and the great officers of state. The ceremony was elaborate and brilliantly colourful; even when the king was on campaign priests, and usually a bishop or two, would accompany him. So quite early the monks who were largely responsible for the beautiful calligraphy and illumination of the Middle Ages began to produce illuminated missals and books of hours of quite exquisite beauty. Many remained in the royal collection for centuries; others were acquired for Henry VIII by his antiquary, John Leland, when the monasteries were dissolved in the 1530s. The whole collection of medieval books was given by George II to the British Museum in 1757 – a foundation present, along with a vast library, but these manuscripts represent one of the most generous of all royal gifts to the nation.

Particularly evocative is a missal which records the order of the coronation, which was given by Richard II to Anne of Bohemia, who was crowned after their marriage in 1382. He was fifteen, she sixteen. Richard fell deeply in love with his bride, a very intelligent girl who became the major support of a king whose judgment was often clouded with doubt and weakened by indecision, and who was far more gifted in the adornment of life than the practice of politics, and whose end, like that of all weak medieval kings, was tragic and bitter; deposed and destroyed by his own subjects.

These sumptuous books, more decoration than text, took years to complete, and by the standards of the day were extremely expensive. The bill survives for a book somewhat comparable to Anne of Bohemia's missal. It is a little more ornate, but was written about the same time, 1384, for the Abbot of Westminster, and it cost £34 13s 7d (about £700 in modern money – not cheap for a prayer book). The next century saw even more costly books. Some, like *Les Très Riches Heures du Duc de Berry*, established themselves as masterpieces of European art, comparable to the finest of old masters. The equivalent in England is *The Book of Hours*, written for John, Duke of Bedford, the warrior brother of the warrior king, Henry V, who was regent for his son, Henry VI. This is thick with gold leaf, sumptuous in colour, with exquisitely painted miniatures – one of the most famous being that of the Duke kneeling before England's patron, St George. Even more splendid is the Sobieski *Book of Hours*, a

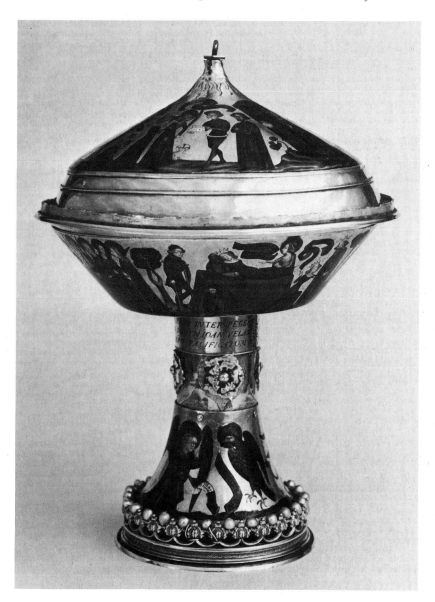

The Royal Gold Cup of the Kings, made in 1380/81 by order of the Duc de Berry for Charles V of France and given to King Henry VI by the Duke of Bedford. The stem was lengthened during the reign of King Henry VIII and included Tudor roses. British Museum, London

jewel of a book, still remaining in the royal collection, held back by George IV who loved great works of art, when he gave his father's library to the nation.

The High Middle Ages were ablaze with colour, their clothes, their books, their cathedrals, their castles – strong, bold colours, the colours of warriors. For war was at the heart of it all; for the last 200 years of the Middle Ages England was either at war with France or convulsed with civil war: the Hundred Years War and the Wars of the Roses, when two branches of the royal family, Lancaster and York, fought for the crown. These wars possessed two faces, one bitter, cruel, as wars always are – nor do the illuminated manuscripts hide death, destruction, burnings, pillage, rape – and the other of chivalry, of the courtly knight, devoted to his lord, the obedient and loving servant of his lady, a master of the arts of war, full of courage, courteous to his enemies, but always resplendent in the crests and badges that proclaimed his rank and name.

Knighthood, like chivalry, became a cult, and Edward III created the Knights of the Garter at Windsor – their motto, *Honi Soit Qui Mal Y Pense*, Shame to Him who Thinks Evil of It, was supposedly said when Edward III picked up a lady's garter. The order soon became very exclusive, conferred on kings and princes and the greatest men of the realm – a rival, indeed, to the famous *Order of the Golden Fleece* of Burgundy. And so it has continued, a tribute to a romanticised past, when each year the twenty-four garter knights – men of outstanding distinction in our country's life – go in procession at Windsor for a service of dedication. Such an Order needed a worthy, regal setting. At first a small chapel at Windsor was used, but then Edward IV raised St George's Chapel to house the order. St George's Chapel, Windsor, is one of the greatest royal ecclesiastical buildings, a splendid example of perpendicular Gothic, comparable to Eton Chapel just across the Thames, or King's College Chapel at Cambridge, both founded by Henry VI. As splendid as the vaulting are the stalls of the garter knights. Each knight is given a stall, and above hang their banners; on death these are removed, but their heraldic plates remain (one of the oldest is Lord Bassett's, a knight who fought with the Black Prince at Poitiers – tough, resourceful, chivalrous). These plates antedate the building but are a remarkable roll-call of the garter knights. A team of gifted carvers, led by William Berkley, took seven years to make the stalls. Some of the panels show successes of the time – one depicts Edward IV meeting the King of France, Louis XI, at the Bridge of Pecquiney, where for once they made not war, but peace, and completed a treaty of friendship.

The pageantry of chivalry stimulated all the decorative arts, and left us objects of enduring beauty, but we must not forget the darker side. Henry V was succeeded by his son, Henry VI, when a mere infant. Henry V's great conquests in France fell apart; factions struggled for power, and soon England was lashed by civil war. In some parts of the countryside there was an almost total breakdown of law and order; in others, like London which had a strong local government, life and trade flourished, almost indifferent to the clatter of feudal armour.

The flower of chivalry destroyed itself, nobleman after nobleman dying on the battlefield or the block. Henry VI, like Henry III, was a man of natural piety, a great builder but an incompetent king, and victory finally came to Edward IV. Edward built a great palace at Eltham in

St George's Chapel, Windsor, showing the vaulted ceiling and the stalls of the Garter Knights

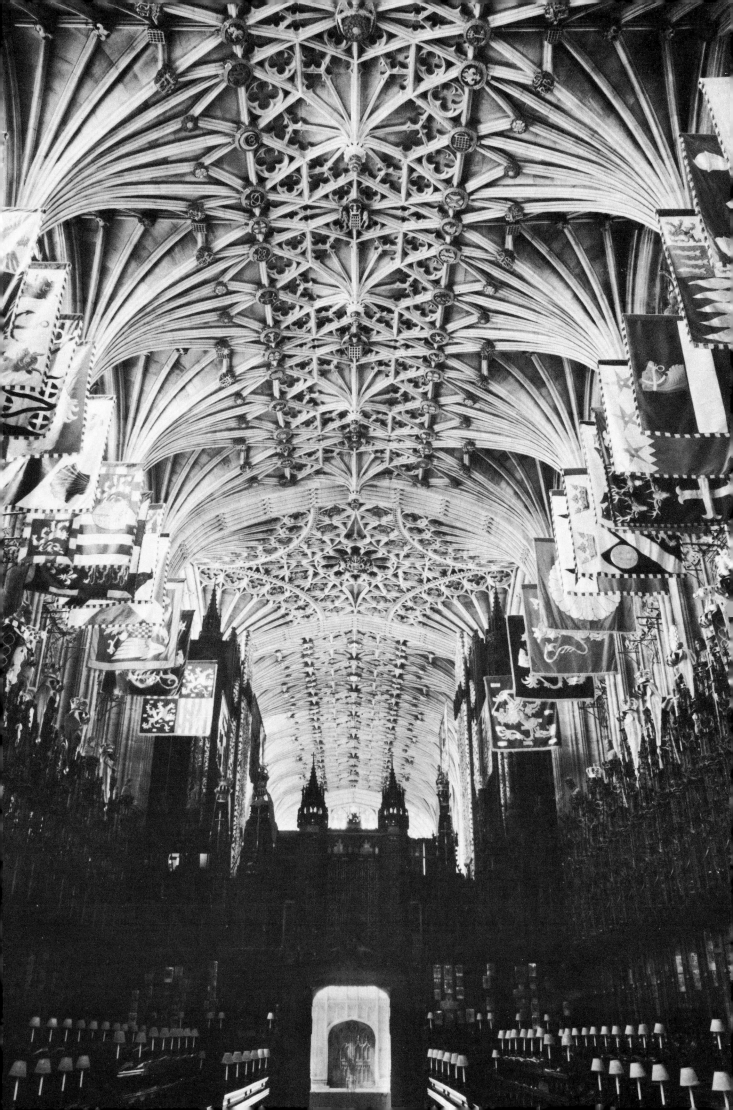

Kent, whose Hall is more symbolic of the age than the wild exploits of Henry V at Agincourt. With its great hammer-beam roof and large windows it looks forward to a new age. Even to us Eltham is modern; it looks forward to the Tudors, to our own world. And so does Edward IV. True, he led his armies, jousted in tournaments, loved histories and illuminated books, but he was also concerned with trade relations, with good and just government, as close to the merchants of London as to the great feudal magnates, perhaps closer. And close, too, to the new humanism that had rooted itself in London and the burgeoning Universities of Oxford and Cambridge. The feudal magnates, like the feudal monarchy, were going the way of the dinosaurs, their day was over. As Chief Justice Crewe wrote, 'Time hath his revolution; there must be a period and an end to all temporal things, *finio rerum*, an end of names and dignities. For where is Bohun? Where's Mowbray? Where's Mortimer? Nay, which is more and most of all, where is Plantagenet? They are intombed in the urns and sepulchres of mortality.'

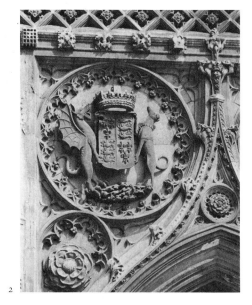

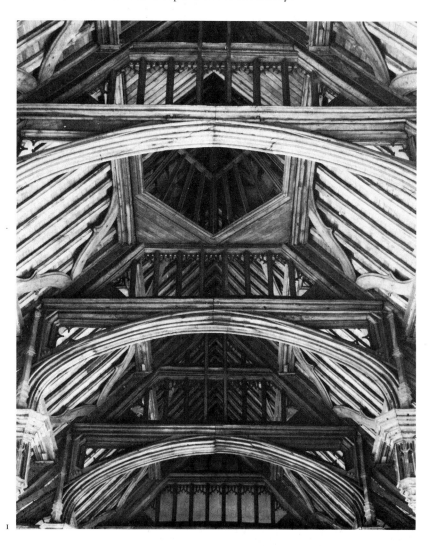

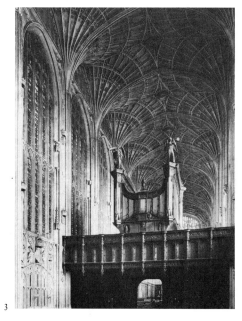

1 The hammer-beam roof in the great hall of Eltham Palace, Kent.
2 Detail of the Royal Arms from the south porch of King's College Chapel, Cambridge
3 The nave of King's College Chapel, Cambridge

THE TUDORS

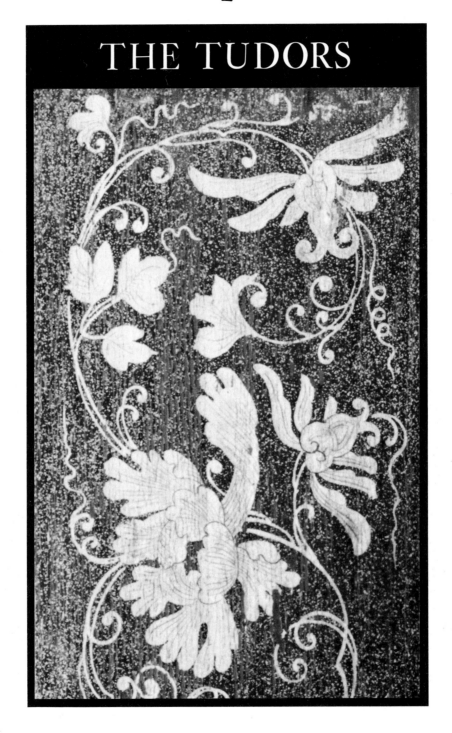

England hath long been mad, and scarr'd herself . . .
O now let Richmond and Elizabeth,
The true succeeders of each royal house,
By God's fair ordinance conjoin together!
And let their heirs, God, if thy will be so,
Enrich the time to come with smooth'd-fac'd peace.

So Shakespeare wrote of the Battle of Bosworth Field that destroyed Richard III and brought the Tudor dynasty to the throne. For decades civil war had intermittently raged as two royal houses – Lancaster and York – had fought each other for the crown. Edward IV had established a firm grip on the country, but died too soon. His heirs were young princes who disappeared in the Tower, and civil war had flared up again. But Bosworth, in 1485, was a decisive battle, a great turning point, that marked the beginning of the modern age for generations of historians. Ages, however, do not change so instantly, not even in revolution, and this was no revolution. Old forms of government were not changed, but slowly modified and often, as with parliament, given a new vitality. Nor was feudalism destroyed in a few years, and the great nobles still continued to live in fortresses with their armed retainers. Even the style and colour of life did not change overmuch or quickly; some of the finest of all Gothic architecture – King's College Chapel, Cambridge, for example – was being built in the early sixteenth century. And heraldry, that peculiarly medieval art, received a new lease of life with the Tudors; chimney-pieces, tombs, the ceilings of libraries were emblazoned with fantastic achievements and quarterings. Yet turning point it was. When the Tudor dynasty came to an end in 1603 a new Britain had come into being, and between 1485 and 1603 England was ruled by some of England's greatest kings and queens.

Henry Tudor, Duke of Richmond, the founder of the dynasty, became Henry VII in 1485. He was an administrator of outstanding ability. He devoted his life to eliminating treason, to consolidating his power, to reconciling the great factions, and securing the acceptance of his family in Britain and Europe, which he did by a series of judicious marriages – marrying one daughter to the King of Scotland and his son to a princess of Spain. In consequence he had little time for building, and not much for patronage. He had a shrewd sense of the value of history, however, as a buttress to authority. His claim to the throne rested on might, on the decision of battle, for his genealogical claims were at best shaky. So he took over the past, called his eldest son Arthur, after the mythical King Arthur of the Round Table, whose chivalrous exploits had recently been told by Sir Thomas Malory and printed by Caxton in the first year of Henry's reign. Henry also made a cult of the national saint, St George. One of the few pictures of his reign show him and his family in an attitude of religious devotion whilst above them St George, beautifully fitted out in Tudor armour, slays the dragon. He was early to realise the new power of the press and of the written word, and in 1488 he invited Polydore Vergil, the Italian humanist historian, to write the history of England in return for a considerable amount of clerical patronage. Vergil took so many years over his work that the King was dead before it appeared. History was to be used to denigrate all enemies of the Tudors and to demonstrate how their own coming to power was the unfolding of God's

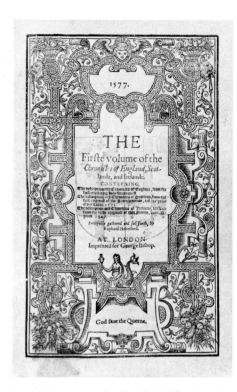

Frontispiece to Raphael Holinshed's *Chronicles of England, Scotlande and Irelande*, 1577. British Library, London

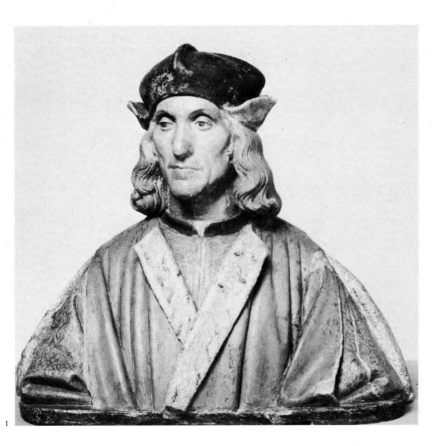

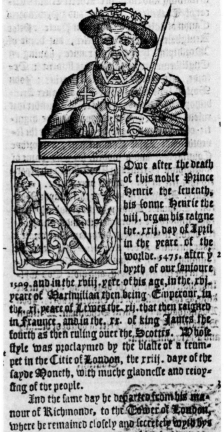

will and England's destiny. This determination to control the past in their own interests remained a preoccupation of the Tudor monarchy generation after generation. Sir Thomas More, the great writer and statesman of Henry VIII's reign, began the blackening of Richard III's reputation which culminated in Shakespeare's play; the great chronicles of history written in the middle decades of the century by Holinshed, Baker and others were paeans of praise to England's historic destiny and, as might be expected, immensely flattering to the Tudors.

Henry VII brought peace to his country, in spite of an occasional rebellion and tumult. By judicious treaties he helped to stimulate the prosperity which had begun to burgeon in the cloth trade during the fifteenth century. He loved money and kept it, frequently checking his own detailed accounts; he loved it well enough to leave a full treasury for his son. In spite of his careful financial ways he added three great courtyards to Greenwich Palace which became one of the favourite homes of his granddaughter, Elizabeth I. He also pulled down the old palace of Sheen, replacing it by a more modern Renaissance building which he called after his ducal title of Richmond in Yorkshire. Only fragments of it survive – a gateway, some walls and timber work embodied in later buildings. As it was so convenient for London he went there for hunting. His own park no longer exists – Charles II created the present Richmond Park – but in one or the other dynasties of British kings have hunted their deer along the banks of the Thames.

Henry realised the value of grandeur as well as money, and he left a very large sum to his son for the purpose of building a splendid tomb in the chapel at Westminster Abbey which he had created for the purpose. He chose the site quite deliberately to emphasise the claim to the past which he had asserted in naming his eldest son Arthur. He wanted to lie near to the chapel of St Edward the Confessor, the ideal of British

1 Pietro Torrigiano, bust of King Henry VII. Victoria and Albert Museum, London. A similar bust, of King Henry VIII, is in the Metropolitan Museum of Art, New York (see page 49).

2 The first column from the chapter on King Henry VIII from Holinshed's *Chronicles*. British Library, London

kingship, and so link himself with the most revered of Saxon kings.

The chapel, which was finished in 1519 some ten years after Henry's death, is a spectacular piece of perpendicular Gothic architecture. The fan-tracery of the roof is outstanding, as was the stained glass (alas, mostly destroyed) by the great Flemish glazier, Barnard Flower. The carving of the stalls, the statuary, the emblems in bronze and stone, all proclaim Henry VII's claim to the heritage of England – red and white roses of Lancaster and York, the portcullis of the Beauforts (his mother's family who were descended from Edward III), the greyhound of Richmond, the leopards of England, the dragon of Wales, and the badge of Edward IV, whose daughter Elizabeth he had married. What to us are pleasing patterns – nowhere, perhaps, more pleasing than in the bronze gates of Henry's chapel – declared their genealogical and historical message to a contemporary as clearly as traffic signs. No wonder that Francis Bacon, viewing this chapel generations later, should write that 'King Henry VII dwelleth more richly dead than he did alive in any of his palaces'.

The great glory of Henry VII's chapel, transcending even the majestic architecture and the rich and emblematic decoration, are the tombs. The effigies were the work of a great Italian sculptor, Pietro Torrigiano, a quick-tempered artist who broke Michelangelo's nose in a brawl. Torrigiano's work breathes with the spirit of the Italian Renaissance, with its deep sense of human individuality and its preoccupation with the beauty of natural things – the texture of a dress, the fragility of a rose

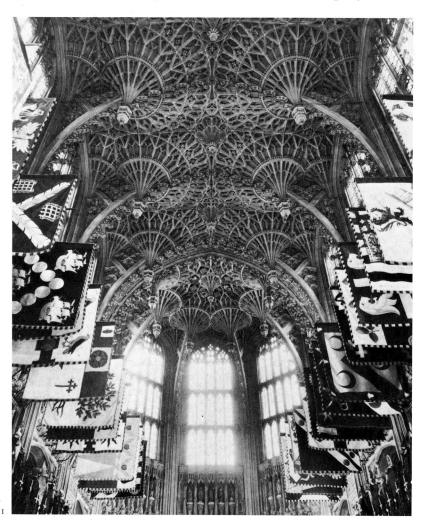

1 King Henry VII's Chapel, Westminster Abbey. Designed probably by Robert Vertue, it was built for the King at the beginning of the sixteenth century.

2 Within the Chapel, the tomb and effigies of King Henry VII and Elizabeth of York, designed by Pietro Torrigiano. Commissioned in 1512 and completed *c.* 1516

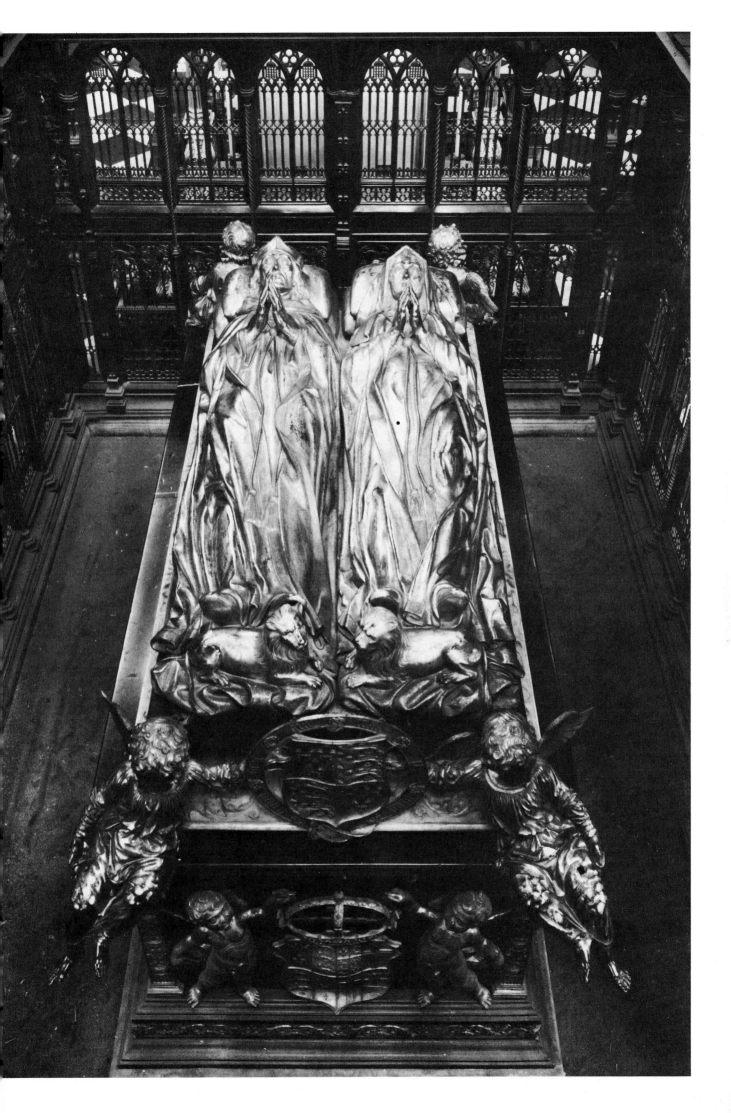

(for there is a rose on one of the tombs, quite beautiful and natural). In his work the break with the Gothic past is clear and sharp and the tombs that he designed, so appropriate for a Florentine church, make a vivid contrast to the fine perpendicular Gothic of Henry VII's Chapel, that in essence is purely medieval. The effigies of Henry VII and his wife are exceptionally expressive, but even they are surpassed by that of Lady Margaret Beaufort, the King's mother (see page 21). The finely modelled hands of an ageing woman and the delicately carved, lined face make this Torrigiano's masterpiece. It is particularly fitting that the epitaph, which states but does not inflate her virtues, should be by the humanist scholar, Erasmus, for she was the generous patron of the new learning of which he was the most distinguished practitioner. Lady Margaret's close adviser was Cardinal Fisher, and through him she was linked with the men who were introducing the great achievements of European learning into England. She was interested in printing, and gave support to Caxton and Wynkyn de Worde, the first English printers, whose presses were set up in the precincts of the Abbey. She used her great wealth to endow Christ's College with large estates. She also founded St John's College at

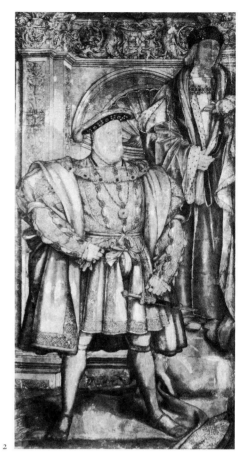

2

1 Hans Holbein *King Henry VIII. c.* 1536. Thyssen Gallery, Lugano
2 *Henry VII and Henry VIII.* The Chatsworth Cartoon, 1536–7, for part of the fresco at Whitehall, which was destroyed by fire in 1698. National Portrait Gallery, London
3 Painted terracotta bust of King Henry VIII by Pietro Torrigiano, now in the Metropolitan Museum of Art, New York. The bust is similar to that of Henry VII on page 45 and Henry VIII kept them in his study at Whitehall

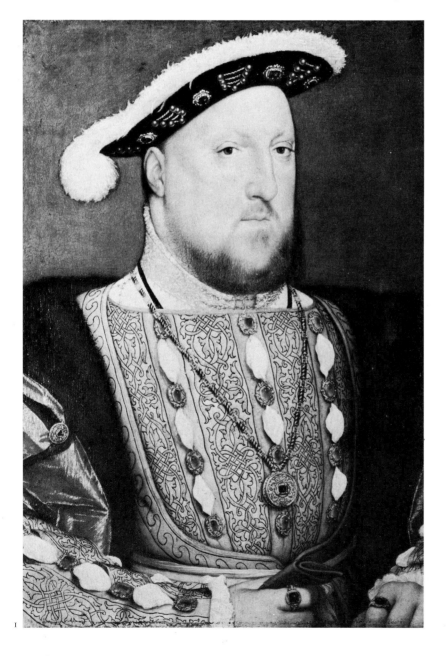

1

Cambridge, and set up professorships of divinity at both Oxford and Cambridge; and to Christ's, where she spent a great deal of time, she bequeathed magnificent plate – a silver-gilt cup and cover of exquisite workmanship, which had belonged to her uncle, Humphrey, Duke of Gloucester, and many items that she had commissioned from the finest silversmiths of her time. She was very close to her grandson, Henry VIII, and the powerful almost academic intelligence which is such a marked characteristic of the Tudor dynasty may have stemmed from her.

And so the stage was set for Henry VIII. The dynasty firmly rooted; the crown rich; an ambitious king; a king everyone knows. His name has resonated down the centuries. Huge, dominating, despotic, a consumer of wives. The image we instinctively call to mind is that of Hans Holbein. The king towers up in this picture, powerful legs, huge chest, vast shoulders, heavy brutal face with narrow, watchful, distrustful eyes – an overbearing image of ferocious yet regal power, an image that, once seen, implants itself indelibly on the memory. Thus the young Henry VIII, who charmed everyone he met, is obscured by this great but over-used portrait that is so untypical of the first twenty years of his reign.

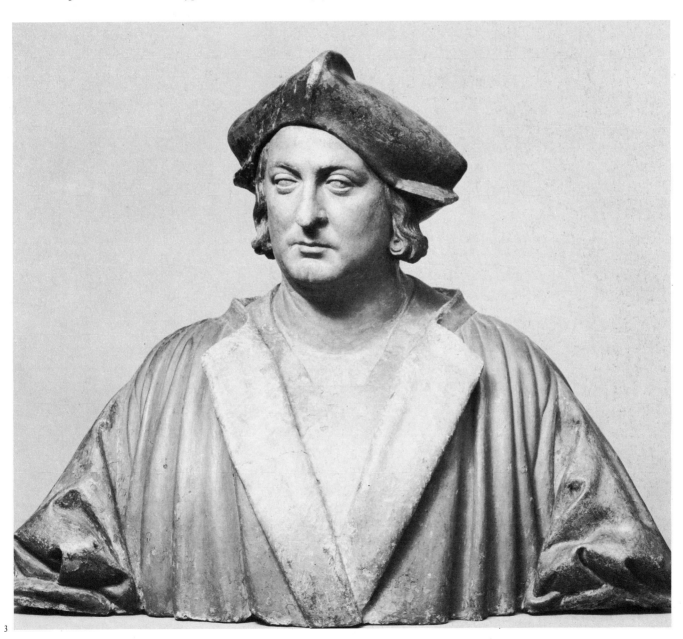

3

Henry VIII was a brilliant, gifted young man, devout, scholarly, musical, athletic. Very tall – six feet or more – with blond hair, verging to red, and a smooth skin; his face, according to the Venetian Ambassador, 'so very beautiful that it would become a pretty woman'. He was happily, very contentedly married to Catherine of Aragon, herself a witty, learned, charming girl some six years older than Henry. They had a daughter, and confidently expected, in the fullness of time, a son. Henry lusted for life – for magnificence, for the grandeur that was so much a part of the age of the Renaissance into which he had been born; but he had a sharp eye for beauty and a keen ear for music, and his love of grandeur was combined with artistic delight. As Sir Thomas More wrote, 'What may we not expect from a king who has been nourished on philosophy and the nine muses'.

Henry wanted to outshine the princes of Europe. He had the means and the innate taste to do so. He set about the task with gusto. He was aided and abetted by Cardinal Wolsey, a butcher's son of extraordinary administrative gifts, a priest with vaunting ambition. Wolsey had acquired preferment early, accumulated power with the dexterity of a skilled politician, and exploited the riches of the Church with the unslakable thirst of a robber baron. He loved princely magnificence as much as the young King, and in the hope of becoming pope encouraged him to make his presence felt on the European stage – a theatre of activity which drew Wolsey like a magnet, but in which he acted with far less skill and certainty than he did at home. Even so, Wolsey rapidly became a prince of the church and Papal Nuncio, the Pope's representative in England, as well as Archbishop of York and Chancellor of England. It is not surprising that he lived and moved in regal state, and, to gratify his love of splendour, built the first great palace at Hampton, far bigger than the King's at Richmond. Not a great deal of it remains, but one room, called his closet, does. It gives a good idea of Wolsey's taste, and his passion for the Italian High Renaissance is reflected in the elaborate Italianate ceiling. He may have been responsible for Torrigiano's visit to England, but certainly was for the presence of Maiano, another Italian artist, who sculpted the terracottas of Roman Emperors that adorned his palace.

So the steady tide of Renaissance influence (learning from his grandmother and the arts from Wolsey) which was to bear Henry VIII along to princely magnificence and extravagance had already taken hold in England. War, however, had always been the duty and the pastime of princes. Kings were first and foremost warriors. They not only fought wars, but also they practised the arts of war for fun. In arms, kings must excel. Henry VIII did. He shot the bow and the cross-bow to perfection, and the new weapons of musket and pistol and great cannon fascinated him. Inventive of mind, ingenuity intrigued him, and he experimented trying to combine old weapons with new. In the Tower armoury there is what seems to be a spiked club and doubtless could be used as a spiked club, but in fact it disguises three pistol barrels – an idea, after all, that was to develop centuries later as the bayonet and rifle.

More impressive than the weapons are the accoutrements of war. Naturally, the majesty of kings demanded the finest armour (and powerful horses as fully armoured as their riders). Royal armour, in Henry VIII's day, had become elaborate (yet efficient), costly, and

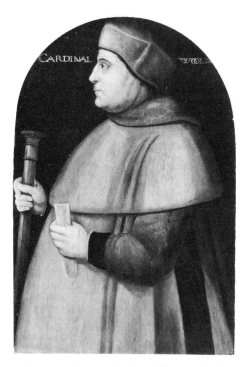

Thomas Wolsey, Lord Chancellor, Cardinal and Archbishop of York. National Portrait Gallery, London

exquisitely decorated. Much to Henry VIII's dismay, he was forced to buy the very best armour abroad. Emperors, kings and princes could, however, give *him* armour. The Emperor Maximilian I presented him with what is, perhaps, the most fantastic helmet made in the sixteenth century. It is utterly grotesque, with great curling ram's horns, and hideous face with staring eyes which, quaintly enough, turns out to be a joky caricature of the Emperor himself! Made by Europe's finest armourer, Conrad Sensenhofer of Innsbruck, it was part of an extremely lavish suit of tilt armour. But Henry could give nothing of such quality in exchange. So, with his usual energy, he imported German and Flemish armourers, and set them up in a workshop on his manor at Greenwich. Soon they were producing magnificent work – both for use and for show – and in a style as distinctive as the Austrian or the Milanese. In the Tower there is a very fine suit of armour for foot combat beautifully made by the Greenwich armourers for Henry VIII when he was middle-aged which betrays how vast he had become – the belly is enormous.

The Greenwich armourers went on producing splendid suits for England's kings and princes over the next hundred years. Nevertheless, Henry VIII's finest armour, indeed, one of the finest suits still in existence – the famous silvered armour – was made in Flanders. It is so beautifully articulated that it behaves almost like a skin. The joints move with superb ease, and in its pristine state, all silvered over and chased in gold, it must have made Henry, sitting on a horse clothed to match, into a demigod, awesome, overwhelming, dazzling. Not surprisingly the chasing tells the story of the martyrdom of St George.

Such splendid suits were not for battle. They were a part of the pageantry of monarchy, used only at the great ceremonial tournaments that adorned the public occasions of a monarch's life. It was a sport that Henry loved; and his jousting lances were specially hollowed to reduce the risk of injury. Even so he took a very bad fall and permanently injured his thigh, which gave him bouts of intense pain. This injury may have been partly responsible for the ferocity and uncertainty of his temper in middle age.

The most spectacular tournaments that the western world has ever seen took place in June 1520 at the Field of the Cloth of Gold, when Henry VIII and François I of France entertained each other. Henry embarked at Dover on his great ship, the *Grace de Dieu*, alive with colour and heraldry, blazoned with Tudor emblems, sails and streamers painted in gold leaf; a king's ship, if ever there was one! By 1520 Henry was regarded as one of the most magnificent princes of Europe, because of the splendour of previous royal meetings. He had fought at the Battle of the Spurs, met the Emperor Maximilian I, entertained his successor, Charles V, at Dover, but there was nothing to compare with the Field of the Cloth of Gold. In many ways it was a boasting match which would have delighted one of those chiefs of the Kwakiutl Indians of British Columbia, who pour gifts on each other to show their own greatness. François I lusted for magnificence in art and show as much as Henry VIII. He had persuaded the aged Leonardo da Vinci to leave Italy for his court at Amboise. For him Benvenuto Cellini, the great craftsman of the High Renaissance, had modelled and cast in gold what generations of discerning cognoscenti have regarded as the finest salt-cellar of all time. Painters, poets, decorators, artists of all kinds flocked to his palace at

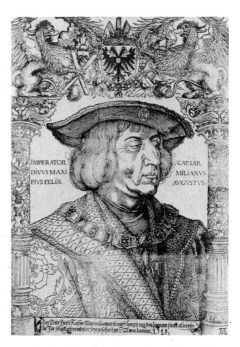

Albrecht Dürer, Woodcut portrait of Emperor Maximilian I. 1518

Fontainebleau. To take on such a king in wanton and extravagant display was no light matter.

The meeting took place at the Val d'Or, near Calais. Special temporary palaces were run up; a fabulous tent, painted to look like brick, housed a gilded banqueting hall. Henry took with him 2865 horses and 3997 people, including almost the entire nobility of the realm. François I brought 22 superb, specially woven tapestries of the History of Scipio, designed by Giulio Romano. Henry possessed 2000 fine tapestries, and Wolsey 436, so they no doubt met the challenge.

The Field of the Cloth of Gold was the greatest of all Renaissance spectacles. Nothing practical in terms of diplomacy was achieved, but in the way that the King, and his court, and above all Cardinal Wolsey, wanted most, it was a resounding success. It proclaimed the strength, the riches, the majesty of England, no longer a barbaric isle, but a brilliant, rich, sophisticated monarchy. One Italian was so swept away that he said Leonardo da Vinci could not have done better. During the feasting and jousting extravagant presents were exchanged. A silver-gilt salt-cellar, given later by François to Henry, and now in the possession of the Goldsmith's Company, illustrates the costly nature of these gifts. The memory of this meeting remained vivid, and Shakespeare described it to perfection. 'Today the French all clinquant, all in gold, like heathen gods shone down the English; and tomorrow they made Britain India; every man show'd like a mine.' Naturally the King wished to have a record of this splendiferous event, and two pictures – or copies – still exist in the Royal Collection, one of his setting out, the other of the scene at Val d'Or itself as he went to meet the French king. In both the symbols of the kingdom, as well as Henry's personal badges, are stridently obvious – a great Welsh Dragon and, of course, St George who was the ever-enduring symbol of English chivalry.

Orders of chivalry had long been a part of the mystique of monarchy, and Henry VII had given great importance to the establishment of St George as England's patron saint, a concept supported and stimulated by his son, who was just as concerned as his father to identify himself with his country's historic and mythical past. Membership of the orders of chivalry possessed a further value – as a part of the never-ending exchange of gifts between monarchs to cement alliances, arrange marriages, or just to cultivate good will. With the membership of the Garter, for instance, went a splendid collar or necklace and a fine jewelled representation of St George slaying the dragon. The Duke of Urbino was so delighted to be made a member of the order that he sent over the famous Italian Baldassare Castiglione, whose book, *The Courtier*, was regarded as the bible of chivalrous behaviour. He brought with him as a gift a magnificent picture of St George killing the dragon by Raphael. Lost to the Royal Collection in the seventeenth century, it is now in the National Gallery in Washington. The cult of chivalry, of St George and the Garter, was not just fun or play-acting, but a vital part of the magnificence of monarchy, emphasising the religious, semi-divine nature of the prince and his courtiers.

When the Reformation came later in Henry VIII's reign, advanced protestants saw the Order of the Garter as heathen, or popish, or both, and the advisers of Henry's son, Edward VI, half-heartedly tried to eradicate St George. But they failed, and Elizabeth I was quick to reunite

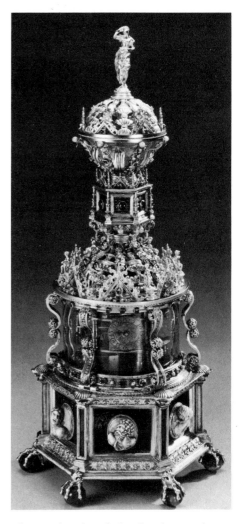

The Royal Tudor Clock Salt. The French silver-gilt salt-cellar probably given by François I to King Henry VIII. Worshipful Company of Goldsmiths, London

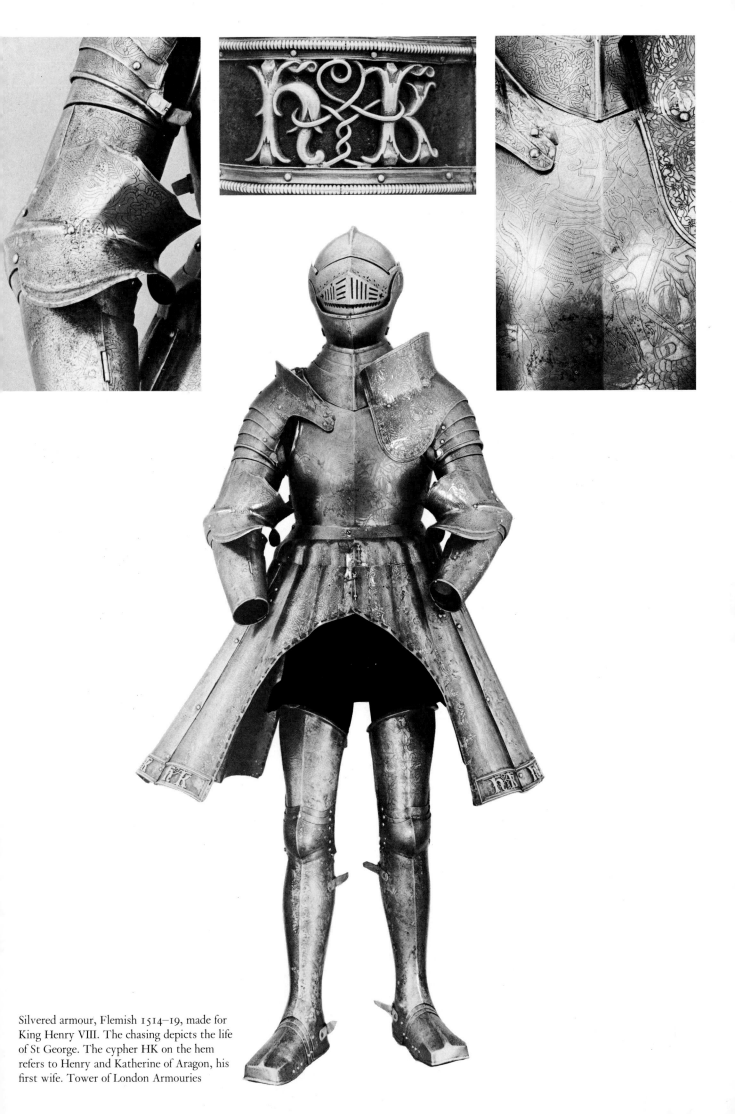

Silvered armour, Flemish 1514–19, made for
King Henry VIII. The chasing depicts the life
of St George. The cypher HK on the hem
refers to Henry and Katherine of Aragon, his
first wife. Tower of London Armouries

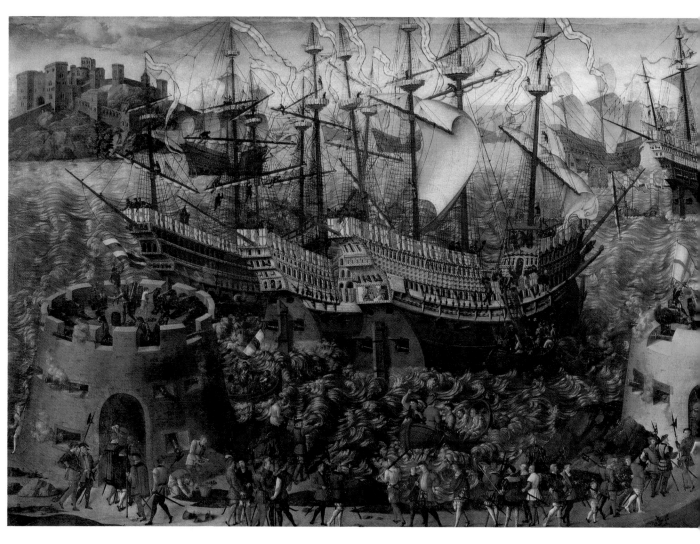

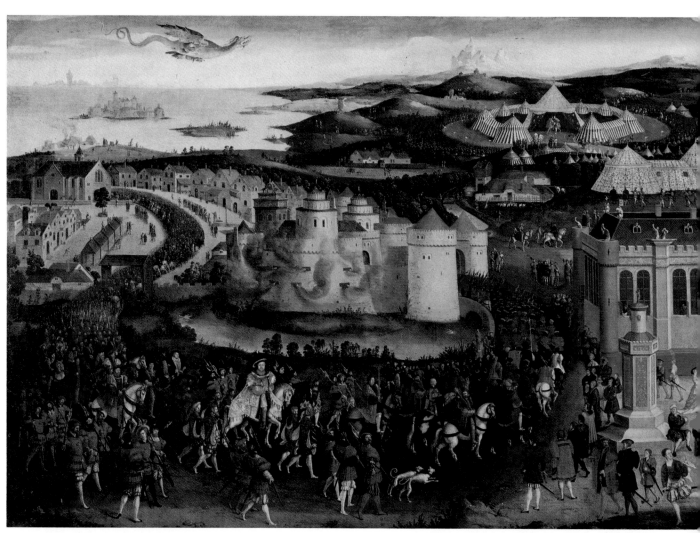

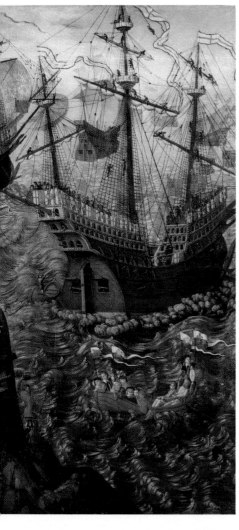

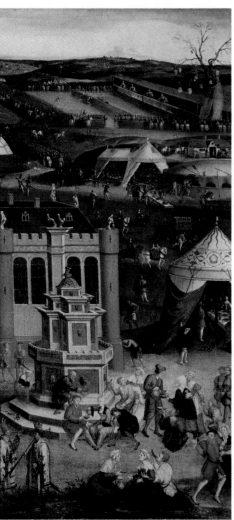

The Field of the Cloth of Gold. The meeting between King Henry VIII and François I in 1520, painted in the mid-sixteenth century. Top, *The Embarkation of Henry VIII*. The scene at Dover as Henry set sail. On the left is Dover Castle. The King's ship, centre right, with gold sails is probably the *Henry Grace de Dieu*, one of the largest English ships afloat at the time. Below, *The Field of the Cloth of Gold*. Many separate incidents are shown. In the left foreground, King Henry and Wolsey ride, in procession, into Guisnes. In the centre background Henry VIII and François I meet in front of a large golden tent. In the foreground is a special palace, built for the reception of Henry and his Queen, Catherine of Aragon. The fountain is running with wine, and some of the spectators are the worse for drink

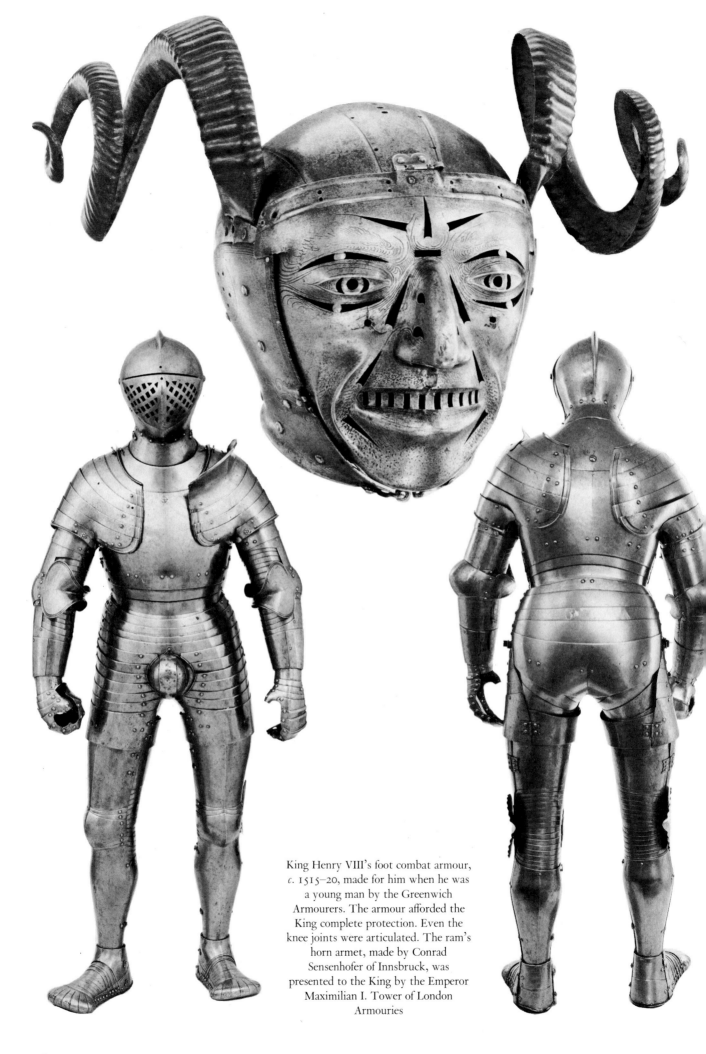

King Henry VIII's foot combat armour, *c.* 1515–20, made for him when he was a young man by the Greenwich Armourers. The armour afforded the King complete protection. Even the knee joints were articulated. The ram's horn armet, made by Conrad Sensenhofer of Innsbruck, was presented to the King by the Emperor Maximilian I. Tower of London Armouries

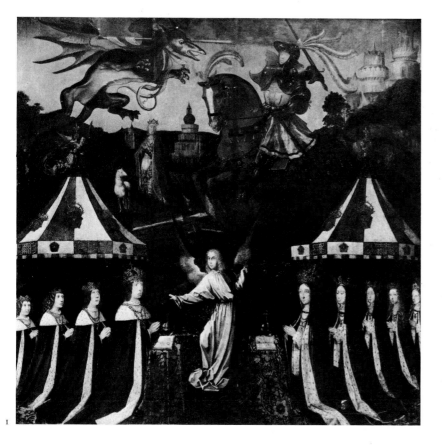

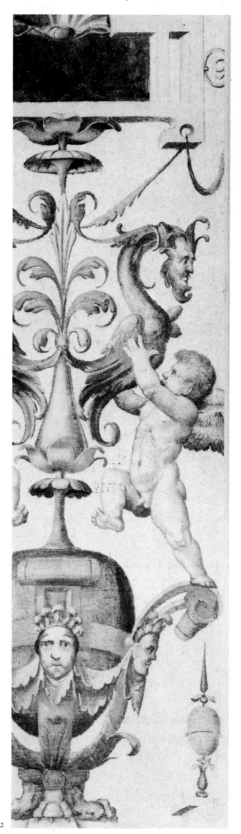

1 Artist unknown, *The Family of Henry VII with St George and the Dragon.* Henry kneels with three sons and Elizabeth of York kneels with four daughters. Before the King are an open book, sceptre and orb. Henry contributed to the development of the cult of St George.

2 Detail of the original panelling from Nonsuch, now at Loseley Park, Guildford

England and St George. Indeed, one certain portrait of her in the year she came to the throne is in the Blue Book of the Garter. Like her father, Elizabeth cultivated chivalry intensely, and Sir Henry Lee, her Master of Ceremonies, staged spectacular jousts and pageants with such remote classical and literary allusions that only a woman of Elizabeth's high intelligence and knowledge could grasp them. But their main message was clear enough then, as it had been in Henry VII's picture: kings and queens were demigods, and St George their nation's patron saint. But that is to run on, for Henry VIII did far more than just engage in boasting matches with other kings and encourage chivalry.

In the sixteenth century the majesty of monarchy increasingly expressed itself through buildings – grander, greater, more formidable than any belonging to a subject. Henry VIII's palace of Westminster was, however, devastated by a fire in 1512; hardly a building was left standing, except Westminster Hall and the small Jewel Tower. The King was forced to occupy the Tower of London, building there new rooms and fine state apartments for his queen. Then he built a palace at the Bridewell, in which the great painter Hans Holbein was responsible for some of the interior decoration. Like the Tower, this proved too small and cramped, and so he went on to build St James's, perhaps, after Buckingham Palace, the royal palace which still spells monarchy to most tourists. His most astounding palace, however, has vanished, Nonsuch, rightly so named, for it was an architectural fantasy, but we can get an excellent idea of its quality from paintings and drawings made during the century after it was built, when it became a favourite home of Henry VIII's daughter, Queen Elizabeth I. And there are a few relics. Some of the panelling with grotesques was moved to Loseley Park when Nonsuch was pulled down in the reign of Charles II.

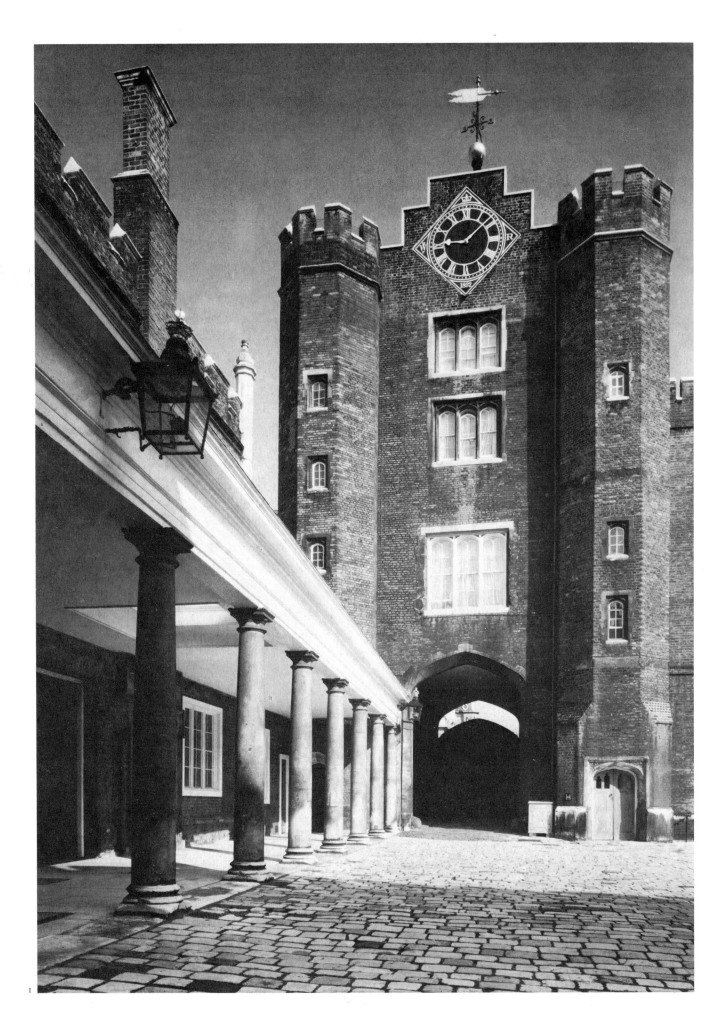

By 1538, when Henry VIII began Nonsuch, he had acquired another palace of great magnificence. In the late twenties the King was becoming disenchanted with Wolsey – not openly, but the Cardinal sensed it, and realised that his great palace at Hampton, richer, costlier, larger than the King's close by at Richmond, caused Henry VIII considerable irritation. So he made a present of it all – buildings, furniture, tapestry, plate – to the King – the greatest gift to a monarch a subject ever made. The King accepted with alacrity. Hampton Court became his favourite palace outside London, at least until he started Nonsuch, and he began at once to embellish it. Much of what we see of Hampton Court today is the work of Henry VIII, although it also contains much, particularly in what were the servants' quarters and the kitchens, that dates from the time of the Cardinal. The two major surviving additions Henry made are the chapel and the Great Hall. He replaced the roof of the chapel, the elaborate ceiling below is almost riotously rich in effect, with its painted and gilded fan vaulting and plump putti playing on their pipes.

The Great Hall is entirely Henry VIII's work. It has, again, an elaborate and finely carved roof, and there is a splendid musicians' gallery. It took five years to build, even though, during the winter months, the masons and carpenters worked by candlelight. Some decorators, carvers and glaziers of great skill were brought from Flanders, although the chief designers were English. One great convenience of the hall was that Henry's superb astronomical clock was visible from the oriel window. This elaborate clock possesses three dials which give the time of the day, the position of the moon and the relation of the stars, as then understood, with the earth. The earth, of course, is placed firmly in the centre of the universe, a position from which Copernicus was to displace it a few years later. However, his discoveries took decades to be accepted, and the great clock of Hampton Court remained a wonder of the age. It was probably designed by Nicolas Kratzer, a mathematician and astronomer from Germany, who had tutored Sir Thomas More's children. His knowledge fascinated the King, who appointed him to his household. Clocks and watches were at this time in a very rapid state of development and Henry VIII patronised many clockmakers, including

1 St James's Palace. The Clock Tower, built for King Henry VIII in 1533.
2 Nonsuch Palace in 1582, an engraving by Georg Hoefnagel

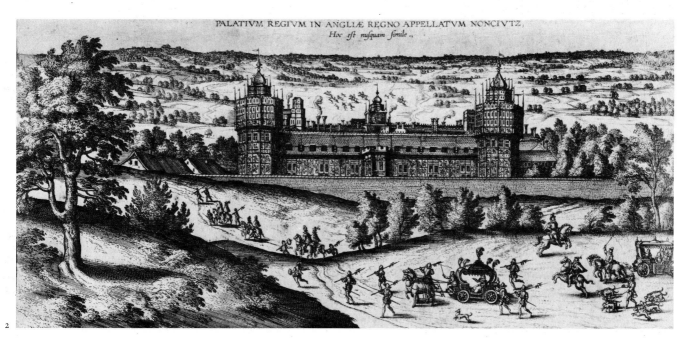

PALATIVM REGIVM IN ANGLIÆ REGNO APPELLATVM NONCIVTZ,
Hoc est nusquam simile.,

2

the Frenchman, Nicolas Oursian, who we know built this clock for the King.

Young and athletic, the King also needed sporting facilities when he was at Hampton Court. He built the tennis court – the enclosed court for royal or real tennis, which still exists and is still in use – and a tiltyard which has now disappeared – partly under the gardens, partly under the restaurant – only a turret remains. There spectacular jousts took place before covered stands – filled not only with the court, but also with the richer citizens of London. It was the one Tudor sport organised on somewhat of a modern scale.

However, it is wrong to think of Henry VIII merely as a handsome athlete addicted to games, pageantry and chivalry. He was highly intellectual, with a natural bent for abstruse theological argument, and a very tough statesman; and he cultivated men of learning as much as administrators. Like the jousts and the pageants, these intellectuals were expected to enhance that image of the monarchy which the Tudors so carefully cultivated. Great painters, great musicians, great writers were a necessary adornment to a Renaissance Court. Fortunately one, a marvellously accomplished artist from Basle, Hans Holbein the younger, drew and painted Henry's court, and so we possess a brilliant gallery of portraits of Henry's courtiers. Holbein was the greatest sixteenth-century artist to work in England. Although he painted religious pictures, of which there is a fine example which entered the royal collection later, his portraits are outstanding. He had a profound perception of character, and his portraits, although at first glance they seem blunt and direct, are full of nuance: a quality which, perhaps, is even more apparent in his drawings. The face of Sir Thomas More radiates intelligence, sensitivity, and that obstinate integrity which took him to the block on Tower Hill; indeed, the painting of Sir Thomas More and his family must have been one of Holbein's greatest pictures. The original, alas, was destroyed by fire, although copies remain; the original drawing still exists at Basle. More, Henry's chancellor, the great humanist and gifted author of *Utopia*, as well as books on theology, morals and history, contrasted vividly with Wolsey. He was pious, ascetic, learned, and Henry loved to argue with him about theology, as he had done with Wolsey, who had introduced the King to the great medieval philosophers, Duns Scotus and Thomas Aquinas. More brought another sort of learning to the court. He was a friend of the great European scholar, Erasmus of Rotterdam, and invited him to England, which he visited twice. Erasmus was deeply impressed by Henry VIII. 'You would say that Henry was a universal genius,' he wrote. 'He has never neglected his studies; and whenever he has leisure from his political occupations, he reads or disputes – of which he is very fond – with remarkable courtesy and unruffled temper.' And later he said that the King had so many learned men around him that his court was rather a 'Temple of the Muses'. These interests were shared by Queen Catherine, 'a miracle of learning', she was called. Indeed, Henry VIII created a scintillating, scholarly court in the 1520s. This, as we have seen, was fashionable amongst sixteenth-century princes, but Henry VIII did not simply listen; he took part in the arguments, which he deeply relished as an equal. The King's own reputation for piety and learning was derived from a famous pamphlet which he had been encouraged to write by

Hans Holbein. Design for a dagger handle. British Museum, London

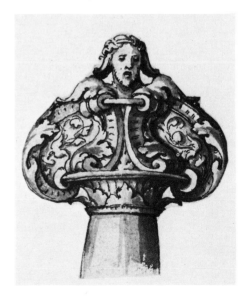

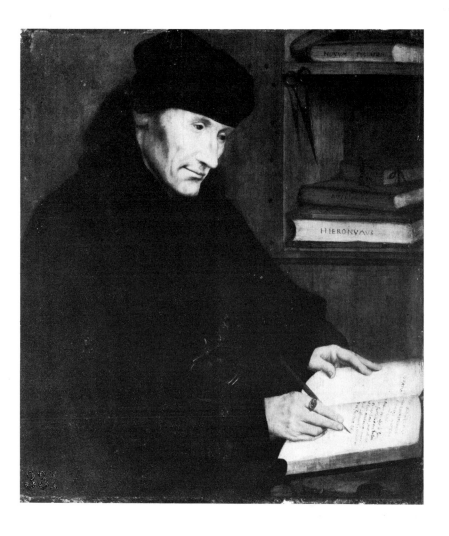

After Quentin Matsys, *Erasmus*

Wolsey. A ferocious attack on Martin Luther, the protestant reformer, *The Defence of the Seven Sacraments*, earned Henry the title of *Fidei Defensor*, the Defender of the Faith, granted to him by the pope in the golden bull of 1524, a title British monarchs have used ever since.

It was Erasmus who had been responsible for Hans Holbein's journey to England, a piece of remarkable good fortune for the development of English art. Holbein's pictures, including his miniatures, captivated the young Nicholas Hilliard who studied them and copied them carefully, learning from Holbein and using his techniques. Hilliard went on to become the greatest miniaturist of the second half of the sixteenth century, making popular a genre which stimulated other painters of great distinction. Holbein was at first befriended by Sir Thomas More, in whose household he lived for a time. Other early patrons were Warham, the Archbishop of Canterbury, and Sir Henry Guilford, a boon companion of the King and the Comptroller of his household. However, Holbein was soon monopolised by the King and, like any other Renaissance artist of genius or mere talent, was expected to turn his hand to any design his master might desire. He designed a ceiling at Whitehall, fireplaces at Bridewell, a temporary banqueting hall, title pages of books, and jewels, as well as painting the portraits, especially to create an awesome image of Henry himself, which was to become the official and most enduring portrait of the King.

Holbein's great fresco in Henry's Privy Chamber at Whitehall was destroyed by fire in 1698, but Charles II had had a copy made; and the

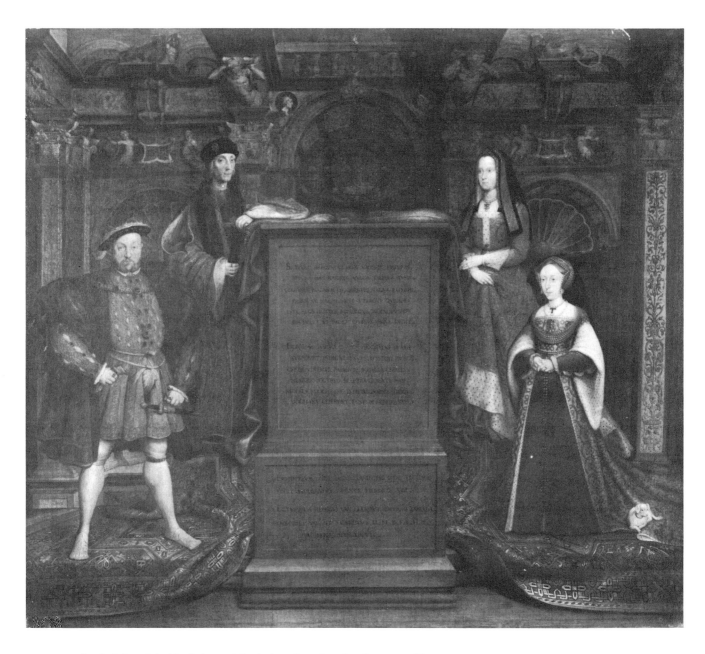

cartoon, the left-hand half of the original drawing for the fresco, still exists in the National Portrait Gallery. Henry VIII dominates the picture; although his father, Henry VII, is just behind him, the King is larger than life, awesome and majestic, almost superhuman, as kings were thought to be – a perfect image of Tudor kingship. In 1537, when Holbein painted the fresco, Henry's life had already taken on some of the quality of an epic saga. By then the power of the pope in England had been abolished, and the drift towards protestantism was well under way. Although Henry had acquired power and authority almost unmatched in our history, he ruled over a divided and troubled land.

The catastrophic events of the 1530s were triggered by the intensity of his faith, or, in our terms, superstitions. Like most men of his age, he believed in signs and portents. He maintained an astrologer at court to read the messages of the stars, and he himself kept a sharp weather eye open for the signs of God's approval or lack of it. Catherine of Aragon's inability to produce another child after the birth of her daughter, Mary, worried the King for years. She had been his brother's wife, and therefore, strictly speaking, forbidden to him by the laws of the Church.

Remigius van Leemput, *Henry VII, Elizabeth of York, Henry VIII and Jane Seymour*. Copied for Charles II from the life-size fresco painted by Hans Holbein for King Henry VIII in 1537 on the wall of the Privy Chamber in Whitehall, which was destroyed by fire in 1698. The remaining fragment of the cartoon for the fresco is reproduced on page 48

The marriage, strictly defined, was incestuous. Of course, all the necessary papal dispensations had been obtained, but Henry became a prey to worry about the validity of his marriage, although for years he was unable to come to any decision. Oddly enough, throughout his life the King hated decisions. His worries, however, came to a head when he fell in love with Anne Boleyn, the daughter of Sir Thomas Boleyn, one of Henry's courtiers. She was a strange, wild woman with plain features but wonderful hair, and oddly, and to some most sinisterly, she had six fingers on one hand.

Reluctant to become a mistress, eager to become a queen, Anne drove Henry frantic – he wrote her love poems, good ones, and passionate love letters, 'written with the hand of that secretary (ie himself) who in heart, body and will is your loyal and most ensured servant, H.' And that was true. The more she resisted, the more he wanted her, and the more important divorce from Queen Catherine became. However, Henry went to incredible lengths to try first to get the pope's sanction to divorce, and when that failed, the approval of all the learned theologians of Europe's universities. But divorce, in the end, could only come one way, by the breaking with Rome, the casting out of the pope's power, which led finally to the dissolution of the monasteries and the slow beginnings of the protestant reformation in England. Henry married

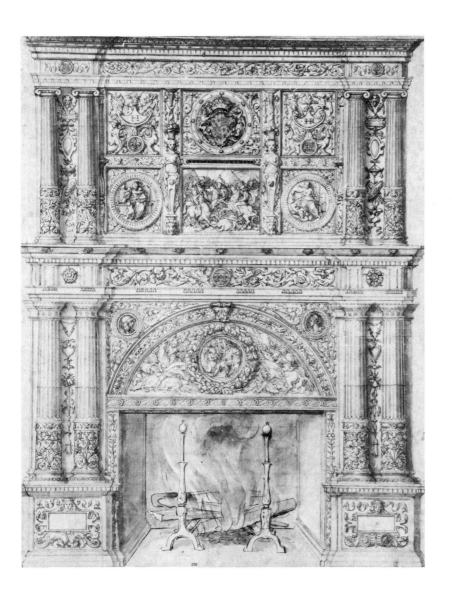

Hans Holbein. Design for a fireplace at Bridewell Palace. British Museum, London

Anne, and anticipated with joy the prospect of a male heir. With new wealth from the monasteries and a new bride, he plunged into a riot of building, feasting, and regal splendour. The great additions to Hampton Court were built for Anne, particularly the Great Hall. Henry was besotted with love as all could see. And, as if one palace were not enough for her, he built St James's too. Of his building there, the beautiful Tudor Friary Court and that great landmark of London, the Clock Tower, which had Henry's and Anne's initials placed boldly on it, remain.

He did not build only for himself. A great patron of education, like his grandmother, he had taken over Wolsey's College at Oxford, now Christ Church. At Cambridge he richly endowed Trinity College, whose great gate he still adorns (with a chair leg in his hand as a sceptre!), and poured money into King's Chapel, paying for the splendid stained-glass windows – the finest in Britain – by the Flemish artists Galyon Hone and Barnard Flower, who were the King's own glaziers. Perhaps his most magnificent gift, and once again one sees the intertwined H and A, is the organ loft and screen in this chapel. It is perhaps the greatest Renaissance carving in England, again done by the Italians whom the King greatly favoured.

Henry's interest in the organ was deeply personal. He was a fine musician who reached very competent professional standards. He was fascinated by the skill needed for difficult keyboard music. He was an excellent performer on the virginals and mastered the organ, which in the sixteenth century was a very complex instrument. He was equally adroit with wind or string instruments, and played the recorder as well as the lute. As he possessed a fine singing voice, he liked to accompany himself on the lute while he sang songs of his own composition. In 1509, the year he came to the throne, he wrote both words and music for the charming song 'Pastime with Good Company'. The next year he is said to have written two five-part masses, as well as songs and ballads, while he was

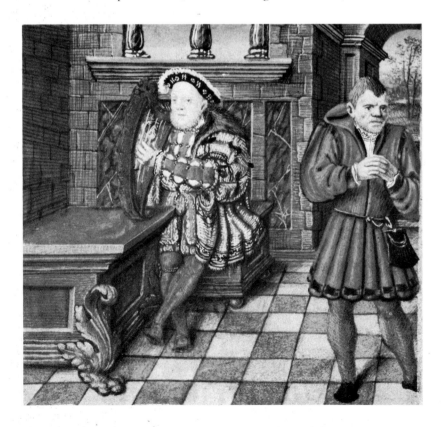

King Henry VIII and his jester, Will Somers, from a psalter decorated for the King himself about 1540. British Library, London

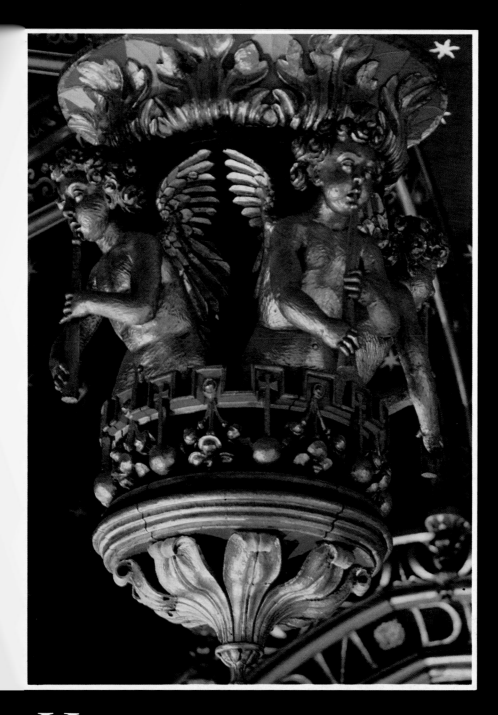

Hampton Court, built by Cardinal Wolsey, was presented by him to King Henry VIII in 1525 in a desperate and unsuccessful attempt to regain the King's favour. During his reign, Henry turned Hampton into one of the most luxurious of palaces

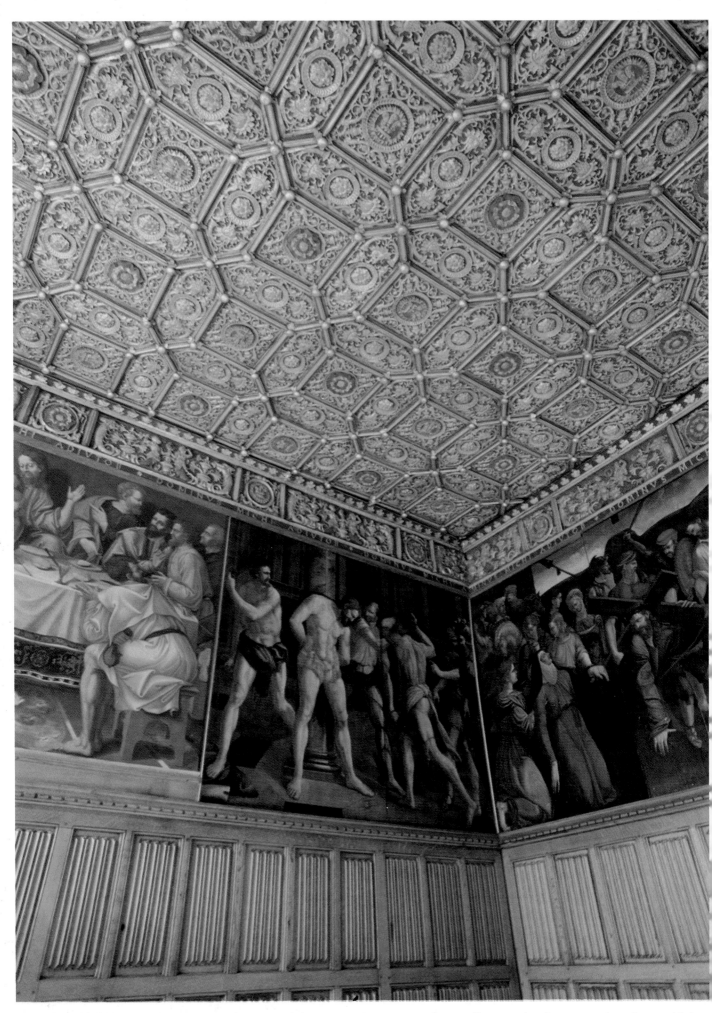

Above: Detail from Wolsey's Closet. The panels, by several different Northern European artists, illustrate Christ's Passion. The ceiling is gilded with Tudor roses and the feathers of the Prince of Wales. Below the frieze, Wolsey's motto, *Dominus michi adjutor*, is repeated. Opposite: the vaulted wooden ceiling of the Chapel Royal, Hampton Court. This ceiling was added to the chapel by King Henry VIII in 1535–6. The rest of the chapel interior was designed by Wren. Carvings between the windows are by Grinling Gibbons.

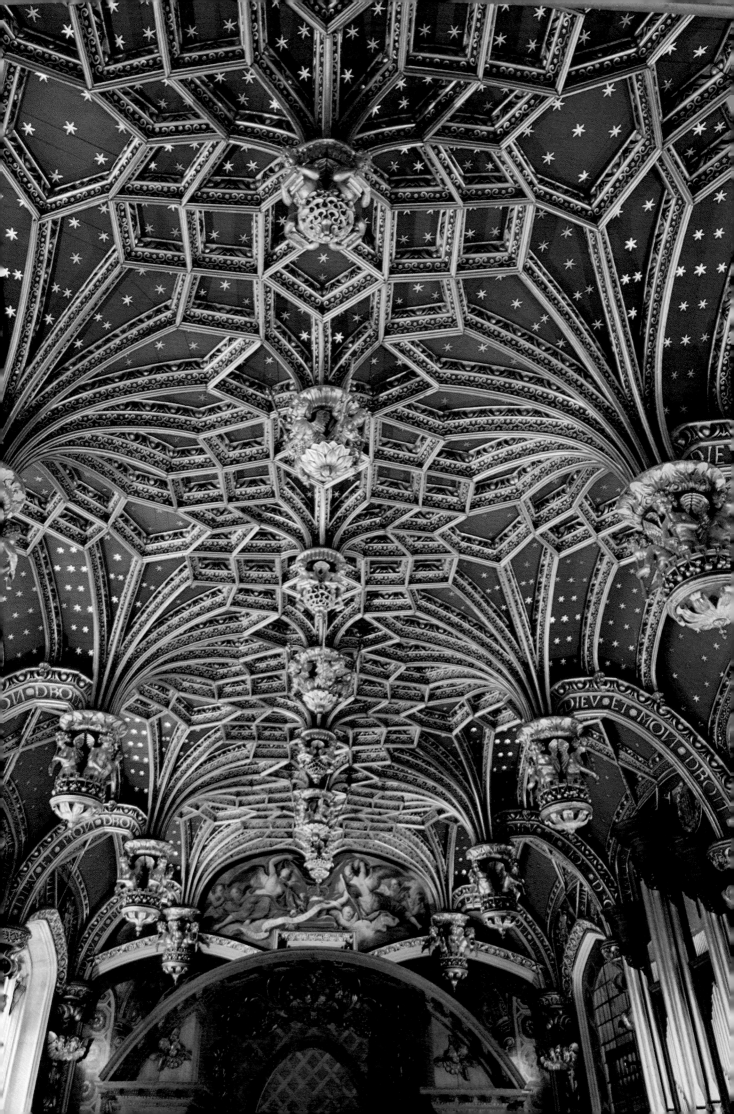

1 Studio of Hilliard, miniature of
  Queen Elizabeth I from the
  Armada Jewel, *c.* 1600. Victoria
  and Albert Museum, London.
2 The Mermaid Pendant, German,
  late sixteenth century.

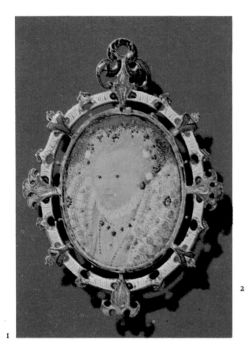

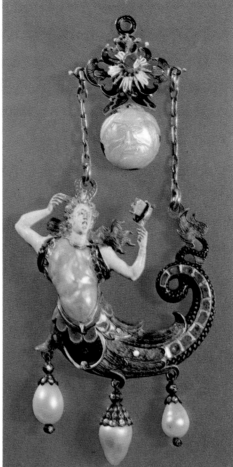

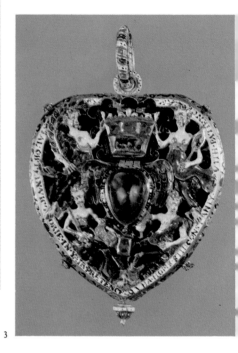

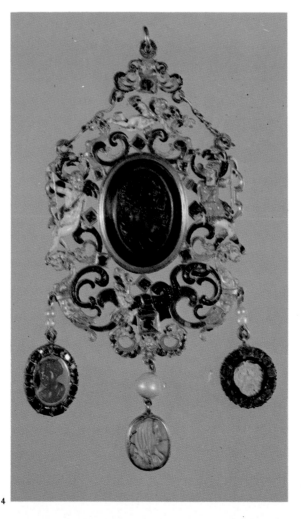

3 The Lennox or Darnley Jewel,
  made to the order of Margaret
  Douglas, Countess of Lennox, in
  memory of her husband, the
  Regent Lennox.
4 Enamelled Pendant, Italian, early
  sixteenth century

making a progress through the home counties. When deeply in love with Anne Boleyn he wrote what is possibly his best work, the motet *O Lord, Maker of all Kings*, which is still often played. In the same year he wrote *Quam Pulchra Est*, which has survived through the centuries and is still sung. Music, whether a mass or a bawdy drinking song, was a daily necessity for Henry, and a passion which lasted right through his life. The last portrait that we have of him is in the Psalter that he used. He is there, with his jester, Will Somers, looking old and battered, tired almost to death, yet playing still on his Welsh harp, finding solace in his music.

Music fulfilling so deep a personal need, the King became a great patron of musicians. His parsimonious father had kept very few: there were trumpeters to herald his approach on formal occasions, and one or two minstrels to provide a song or a tune at dinner, but few others on the royal payroll. By the standards of European courts, Henry VII's was a very meagre establishment. His son rapidly changed this. He preferred what English talent he could find and in the early years of his reign persuaded Robert Fayrefax, the organist of St Albans Cathedral, to join his court. Fayrefax composed both religious and secular music of the highest quality, was the first to use the counter-tenor extensively as a solo voice, and when he died, in 1521, the King paid for his burial at St Albans. However, Henry realised that the finest musicians were to be found in Europe, and he offered very large salaries indeed to entice Italian, Flemish and German musicians to join his court. Some, like the Bassano family, who provided royal musicians until the civil war, became firmly rooted in English court life. Others, like Memmo, only stayed for some years. Memmo, an organist of St Mark's, Venice, brought his own instrument with him and captivated Henry and his courtiers with his music. Indeed he was largely responsible for building up a superb band of musicians. As Dr Neville Williams has written, 'Under a sovereign who cared deeply about their work and was bent on providing the finest resources for music-making, they found the environment of the court stimulating. The royal musicians led the developments in instrumentation and composition and set standards of performance, certainly for the country as a whole, and probably for the courts of the West.'

All these musicians belonged to the Chapel Royal, but for most of Henry VIII's reign this was a name, not a place, the musicians following the King from palace to palace. In 1533, however, Henry provided a permanent home for them in his new palace at St James's, in the chapel that is still regularly used by the royal family. With a permanent home, the Chapel Royal could undertake both teaching and training.

Fine music played by outstanding musicians stimulated talent which, in Marbeck and Tallis, was able to meet the challenge of the English Reformation's demand for new settings for church services. Marbeck was the organist of St George's Chapel, Windsor, a somewhat too ardent supporter of the Reformation who very nearly got himself burnt as a heretic. The house where he lived, tucked away in a corner of Windsor Castle, is still occupied by the organist of St George's Chapel. Thomas Tallis, a greater composer than Marbeck, became the father of English cathedral music. He, too, was patronised by Henry, whose influence on the development of music in England is incalculable.

Understandably, the early 1530s were the high point of Henry VIII's creativity and patronage. The break with Rome, the divorce of Catherine and the marriage to Anne Boleyn had released the spirit of a man who was paralysed by the worry of taking decisions. Although in 1530, at the age of thirty-nine, he was, by the standards of his time, almost on the threshold of old age, he still jousted with skill, played tennis with his old vigour, found time to plan new palaces and extend old ones, patronise decorators and painters of outstanding skill, create one of the finest schools of music in the western countries, and compose his heart-felt songs and moving poetry of love.

But these great years of joy, pulsating with a sense of power, were soon darkened by old anxieties in new forms. Henry was once more haunted by guilt. Anne Boleyn's sister had been his mistress, so was this new marriage incestuous too? Was God's favour being withheld from him once more? At first irritated by his astrologers who had forecast a boy, he had taken the birth of his daughter, Elizabeth, as a mere prelude to a future heir. But when Anne failed to produce one, and her pregnancies proved false, Henry's own doubts were strengthened by his rapid tiring of her. In some ways Anne had only herself to blame. Her manner, which made her so provocative as a long-sought mistress, was disastrous when exploited by a queen. A miscarriage sealed her fate. Knowledge that she had had lovers before marriage and probably after (the rack made confession of crime certain, whatever the truth might be) brought her to trial in Westminster Hall and the block in the Tower.

As Catherine of Aragon had recently died, Henry VIII was now free to marry in the eyes of God and all mankind, whether catholic or protestant. Growing tasteless with age and power, Henry feasted with his new love, Jane Seymour, as Anne was buried. Jane Seymour, demure, virtuous, very gentle, produced the son, Edward, Prince of Wales, for whom the King longed, but died giving birth to him. Had she lived, the last ten years of Henry's reign might have been less terrible, less of a tragedy. In these years Henry aged quickly. His leg wound, which may have been a disease of the bone, osteomyelitis, gave him increasing pain. Extravagance, war, inflation, emptied his treasury and even the spoils of the monasteries failed to keep it full for long. And his personal life crashed from one disaster to another.

After Jane's death he was persuaded by his chief minister, the incomparably efficient Thomas Cromwell, to make a diplomatic marriage with a German protestant princess. Hans Holbein was sent scurrying back and forth to make sketches of promising brides – indeed he painted five out of nine possibles – and finally Henry decided on Anne of Cleves, not ravishing even in Holbein's portrait, but certainly as comely as Jane Seymour, again if Holbein is reliable. When Henry met her on Blackheath to escort her to Greenwich Palace, he was bitterly disappointed. She was awkward, and spoke little or no English. Nevertheless these qualities would not, I think, have deterred the King had she been far younger. Her age and maturity (she was thirty – very old for a sixteenth-century royal bride), combined, as they were, with naïvety in sexual matters, probably induced the impotence which seized the King. They slept in the same bed for a few nights, and then once again Henry was on the road to divorce, with Anne nothing loth to stop him.

A fiasco was followed by a disaster. His next bride, a beautiful, vivacious, tiny girl of twenty, Catherine Howard, proved to be a silly, wanton, sex-hungry girl who was willing to risk her head for pleasures

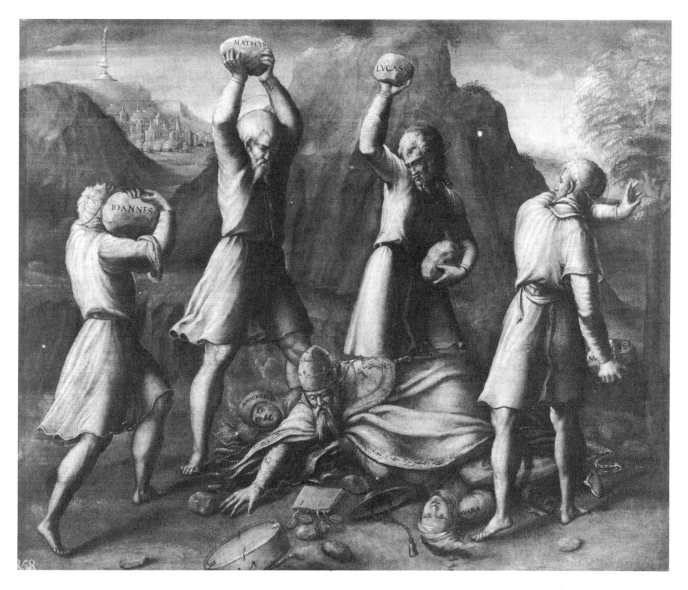

Girolamo da Treviso, *The Four Evangelists Stoning the Pope.* c. 1536

that her husband could not provide in the abundance she desired. Foolishly misled by the torrent of presents the King deluged her with, she behaved with complete indiscretion. This was even more foolish because she was a catholic and therefore the target of those sections of the court inclined to the reformed religion, who feared her influence with Henry VIII. Presented with the unsavoury facts about the Queen's behaviour by the Archbishop of Canterbury, the King's idolatry turned to raging hate. She, too, finished on the block in the Tower.

Then, at long last, Henry VIII married wisely – this time for talk. He chose a thirty-one-year-old blue-stocking, twice married to elderly men and twice widowed, who took delight in theology. Catherine Parr was a liberal catholic devoted to Erasmus, rather than a protestant, and so she could, and did, discuss divinity with the King without unduly raising suspicions about deep questions of faith. She also drew about her a circle of very able scholars and intellectuals, including Roger Ascham, who was to be Elizabeth I's schoolmaster, and John Cheke, to whom Henry entrusted the education of his son, Edward. As Catherine was also very fond of music, the last year or two of Henry VIII's reign echoed, if somewhat faintly, the years of his youth.

But they were untranquil years, for national problems weighed heavily on the King. Although he had broken with Rome, and could enjoy a

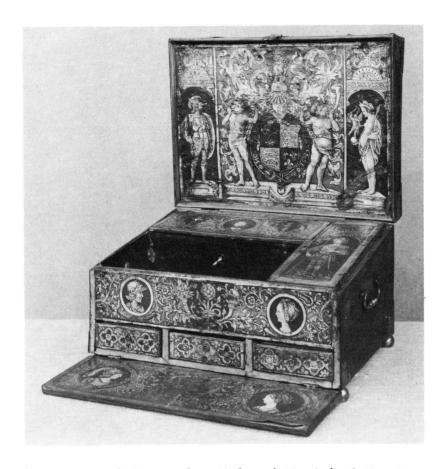

King Henry VIII's writing box. Victoria and Albert Museum, London

bitter, anti-papal picture such as Girolamo da Treviso's *The Four Evangelists Stoning the Pope*, he remained devoutly catholic, even as many of the leading men of power in the country, as well as wider classes of men, were being drawn towards the Reformation. In consequence a protestant might just as easily be thrown to the flames as a heretic as a loyal supporter of the Pope. Ill, often in pain, his flesh bloated, yet still exuding power, Henry VIII was a terrifying figure during his last two years. This is strongly conveyed in one of the last pictures of the King painted by Holbein for the Master Surgeons of London in 1543. There he sits, clothed in the robes and symbols of majesty, a towering, threatening figure as the surgeons kneel humbly about him. When at last he died, in 1547, England had lost its greatest, its most powerful, its most splendiferous of Kings, and certainly the most gifted. But he left his country like one of his own great ships – magnificent, richly equipped, but at the mercy of the tide.

Henry was buried by the side of Jane Seymour in St George's Chapel, Windsor. He should have had a tomb more splendid than his father's, fitting for a Renaissance prince. Long ago Torrigiano had designed one, but the King quarelled with him. Then he sent for the greatest of all craftsmen, Cellini, who refused the summons. At Windsor the King took over the enormous tomb designed by Wolsey for himself, but this, too, was never finished. The bronze was melted down by parliament in the civil war and, in 1805, Wolsey's sarcophagus intended for the King was shipped to London for the burial of Lord Nelson. And so, ironically, the greatest of the Tudors lacks the memorial he deserves.

The next eleven years were bitter, troubled times for England. Edward VI was painted several times – all kings need an official portrait, an image that can be repeated on seals and coins – and his father had been immensely proud of his son, so from babyhood had had his portrait painted. The most vivid portrait of all, by Guillim Scrotes in 1550, when the King was thirteen, shows a defiant, dignified little boy, but also very slight and vulnerable, standing in the pose that Holbein had created for his father, which gives the picture an exceptional poignancy.

Precociously intellectual, like most Tudors, rather precise and priggish, deeply religious, the young King became the plaything of rival factions. First the Duke of Somerset took control, then the Duke of Northumberland, who drove England fast into protestantism. But Edward VI, always sickly, died at sixteen. He had little time to build or collect. During his reign the chantries were abolished as popish. As well as saying masses for the dead, their priests often undertook schooling, and with the chantry funds some schools were founded in his name. Many survive; in one at Shrewsbury the old school house still stands. And when he was thirteen, a splendid collection of Holbein's drawings of his father's courtiers was bought for him.

His catholic half-sister, Mary I, who succeeded him, was soon burning protestants in Smithfield, as her predecessor had burnt catholics. There were more protestants, and some, like Archbishop Cranmer or Bishop Latimer, were men of very great distinction. The people hated the burnings, for a great number of ordinary folk suffered as well, but they hated Mary I's marriage with Philip II of Spain even more. They loathed Spaniards. Everywhere there was the scent of treason, and when Queen

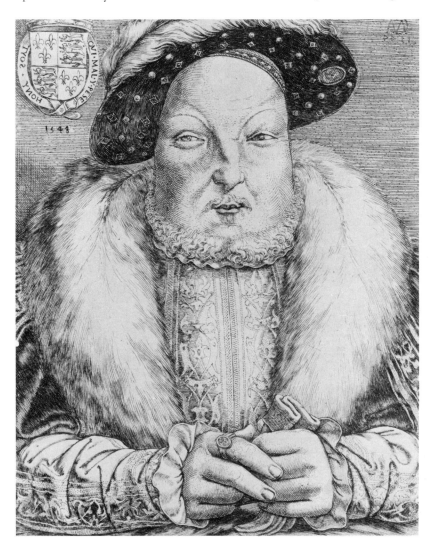

Cornelius Matsys. An engraving of King Henry VIII in old age. 1548

Mary died of dropsy in 1558, the nation felt an enormous sense of relief. This was God's crowning mercy, all protestants felt.

Queen Elizabeth I came to the throne at a perilous time. By 1603, when she died, she had given her name to the age, an age which succeeding generations, even to the present day, have come to regard as the most glorious in British history, matched only by the reign of Queen Victoria.

By 1558 Elizabeth had lived through heart-racking years of uncertainty. As a child of an executed queen, she had never been sure of her status, sometimes legitimate and cosseted at Court, sometimes regarded as a bastard and expelled from it. In Queen Mary's reign, she was in real danger, close to the block. She was sent to the Tower, but showed her spirit by sitting down at Traitors' Gate and refusing to budge! She spent many of her early years at the Old Palace at Hatfield, a royal hunting lodge. And at Hatfield can still be seen her stockings and gloves, and the hat she wore in the garden. There her character, and above all her taste were formed. Her tutor was Roger Ascham, a learned humanist with protestant inclinations, who wrote one famous book, *The Schoolmaster*. In the princess he discovered a very apt pupil. Like her father she was an intellectual who loved discussion and argument. She possessed an excellent memory; she learnt languages easily and well – she was fluent in Latin, French and Italian, and knew some Greek; she wrote superbly, not only fine flowery prose, but also in exquisite handwriting (she was a mistress of calligraphy, and many of her letters, had she not been Queen,

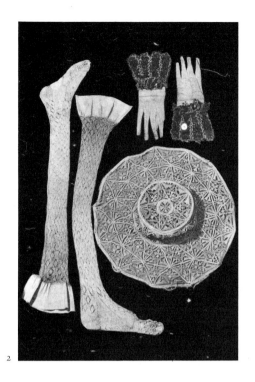

2

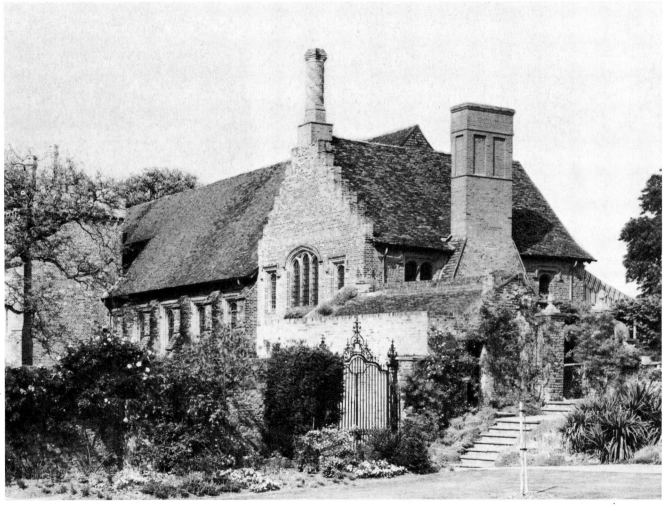

1

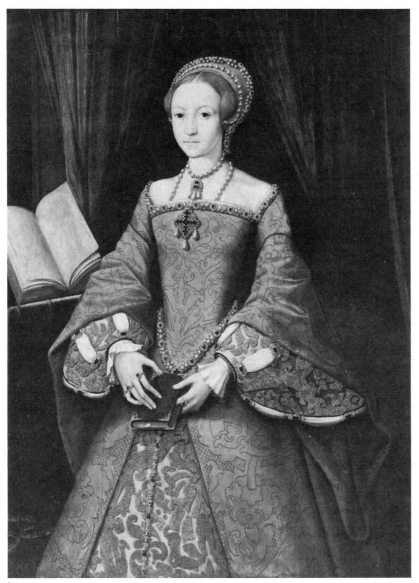

3

1 The Old Palace, Hatfield, the childhood
  home of Queen Elizabeth I. The original
  palace was built by Cardinal Morton, Bishop
  of Ely, and completed in 1497.
2 The garden hat, stockings and gloves worn
  by the young Elizabeth.
3 Artist unknown, *Elizabeth I when Princess*,
  aged about twelve. *c.* 1545.
4 Elizabeth's poem in her own handwriting as
  a child and a drawing of an astrolabe in
  the back of a French psalter

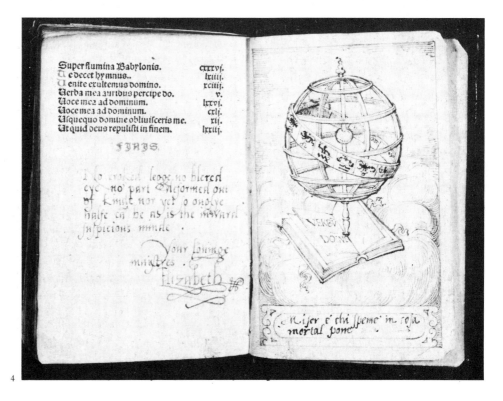

4

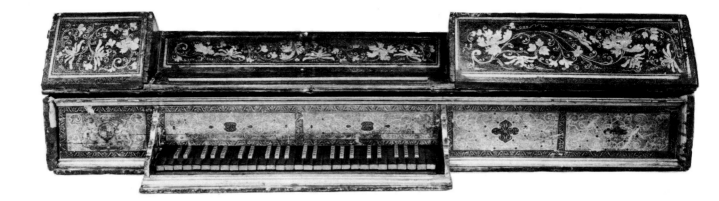

Elizabeth I's virginals. Victoria and Albert Museum, London

would have been cherished as works of art). It is not surprising that the best portrait of her as a young girl, painted by an unknown artist when she was thirteen, shows her with books. Like her father, she loved music. Her virginals can still be seen in the Victoria and Albert Museum. And she had throughout her life a passion for dancing.

At Hatfield not only was her intellect formed, but her character. When a young girl, she came very near to utter ruin. Thomas Seymour, the handsome brother of Protector Somerset, her brother's guardian, set about seducing her. He stalked into her bedroom, jumped on her bed, tickled her, aroused all her young sexual instincts, but never quite seduced her. He lost his head, she kept her virginity, but, as Wellington said of Waterloo, 'It was a damned close run thing!' But for her it was a traumatic shock; she learned what a prize she was; it strengthened the fears which her mother's fate had engendered. This and the terrible experience of her sister's reign made her relish *time*: to wait, to see, to put off action, and to relish even more her independence, her singularity. She realised that a virgin princess, a virgin queen, possessed power, authority, mystique, that no Lady Seymour could ever have had.

Perhaps it was fear of being confined, or the delight she took in the great park at Hatfield, which gave her a passion for being out of doors. She loved parks, loved long fast walks in all weathers. And she enjoyed hunting. All her life she tired her courtiers, striding with her long legs (for she was tall, like her father) through bracken at Greenwich, Richmond, Nonsuch, her favourite palaces. Although the palaces have vanished, the parks remain. Indeed, the royal passion for parks has enriched London immeasurably and helped to give it a far more balanced environment than most capital cities. As well as Richmond and Greenwich and the distant Nonsuch, there are Hampton, Bushey and Kew: deeper in the heart of the city are Kensington, St James's and Regent's – all crown lands that the public now enjoy.

The problems which Elizabeth I faced were immense. After the rejection of Roman catholicism there was the need to settle religion once again; but above all there was the need to avoid war, which the country could not afford, and, if possible, keep on amicable terms both with Spain, whose King Philip II, Mary's husband, had a tenuous claim to the throne, and with Scotland, where a violent conflict between catholics and presbyterians was raging. A catholic victory there could menace Elizabeth's position, for, unlike Elizabeth, there were no doubts about the legitimacy of the Queen of Scotland. She was descended from Henry VIII's sister. Worse, the crown of Scotland was also closely allied to

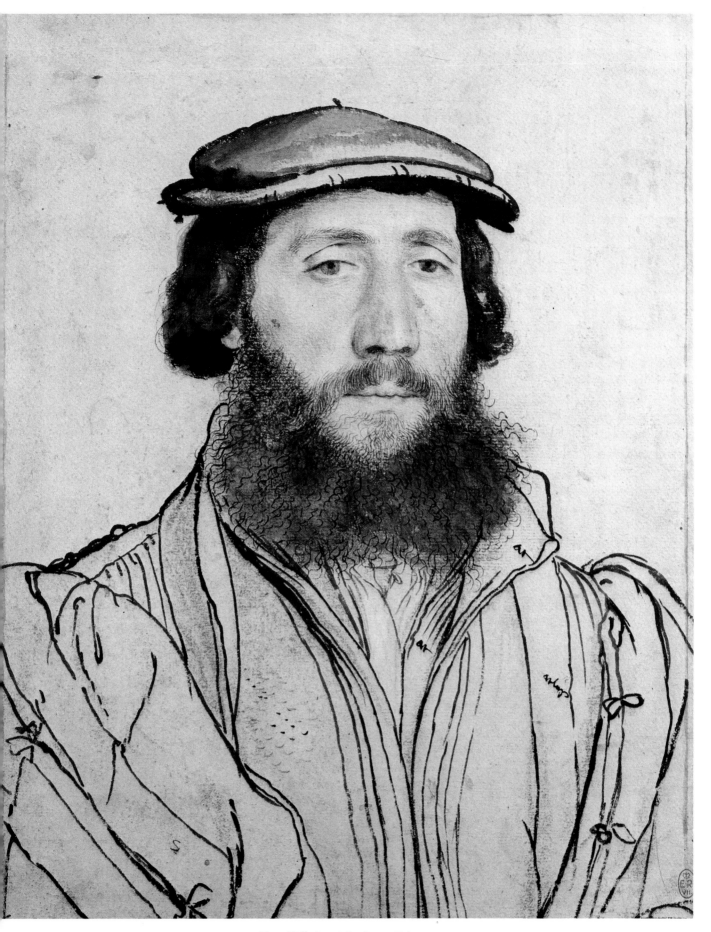

Hans Holbein, *A Gentleman: Unknown*

Hans Holbein settled in England in 1532, and by 1536 was in the service of King Henry VIII. A number of paintings (although none of his portraits of the King) are in the Royal Collection and the Royal Library at Windsor Castle has an unparalleled collection of his portrait drawings

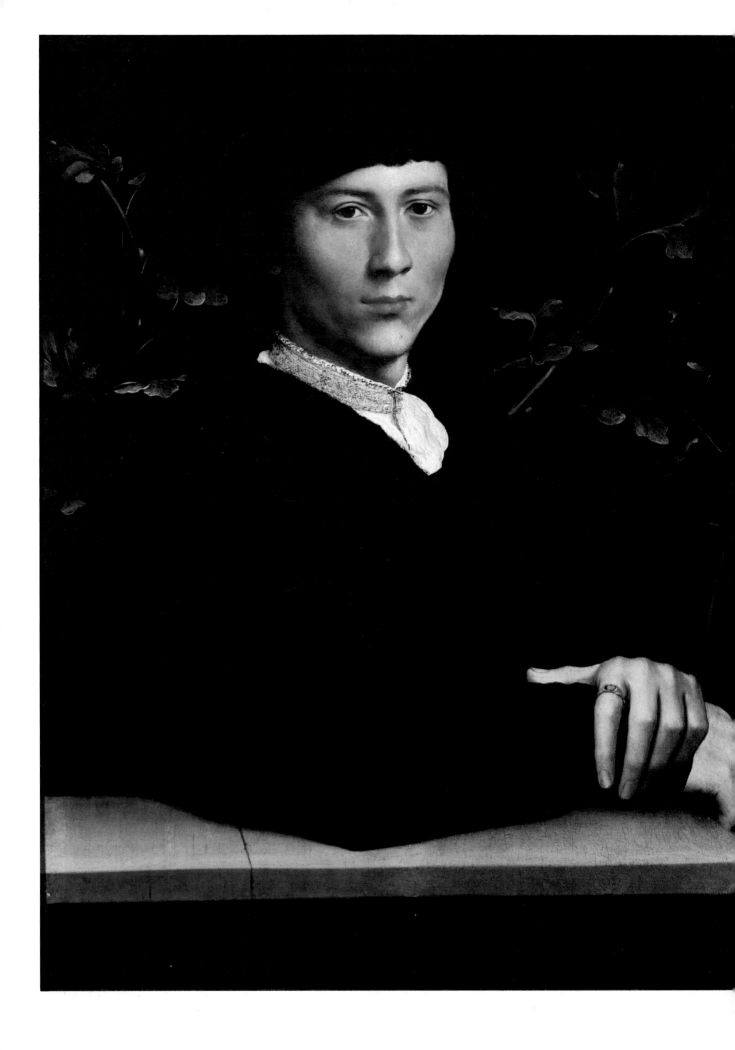

Hans Holbein, *Derich Born*, a merchant from Cologne. 1533

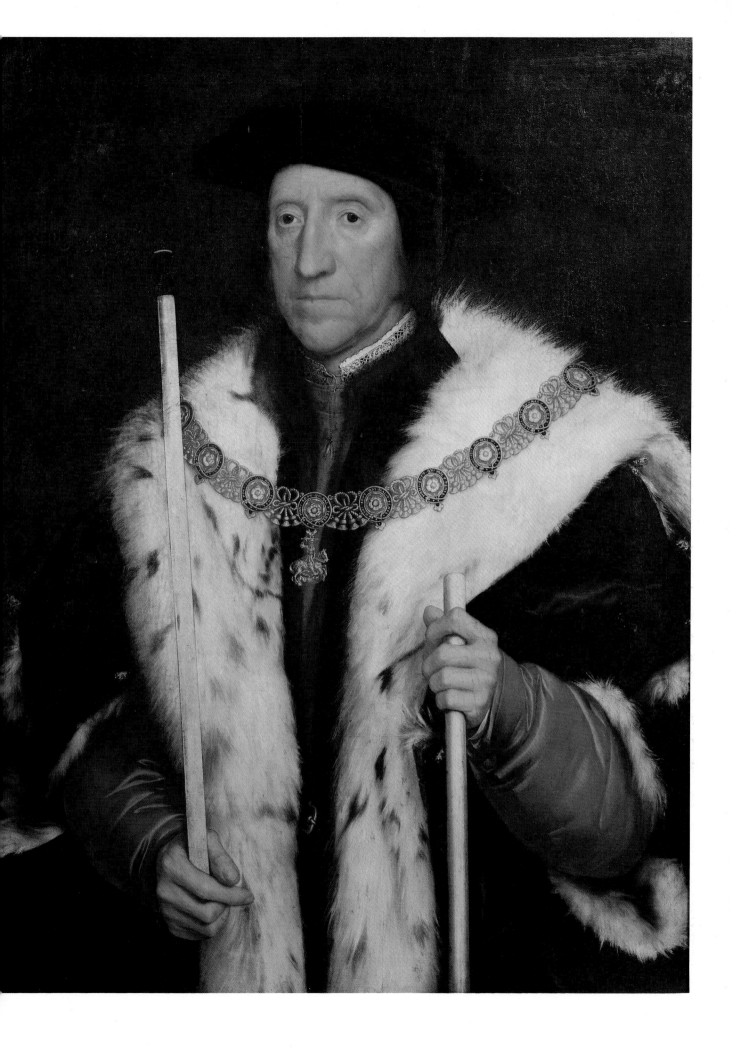

Hans Holbein, *Thomas Howard, Third Duke of Norfolk.* 1539/40

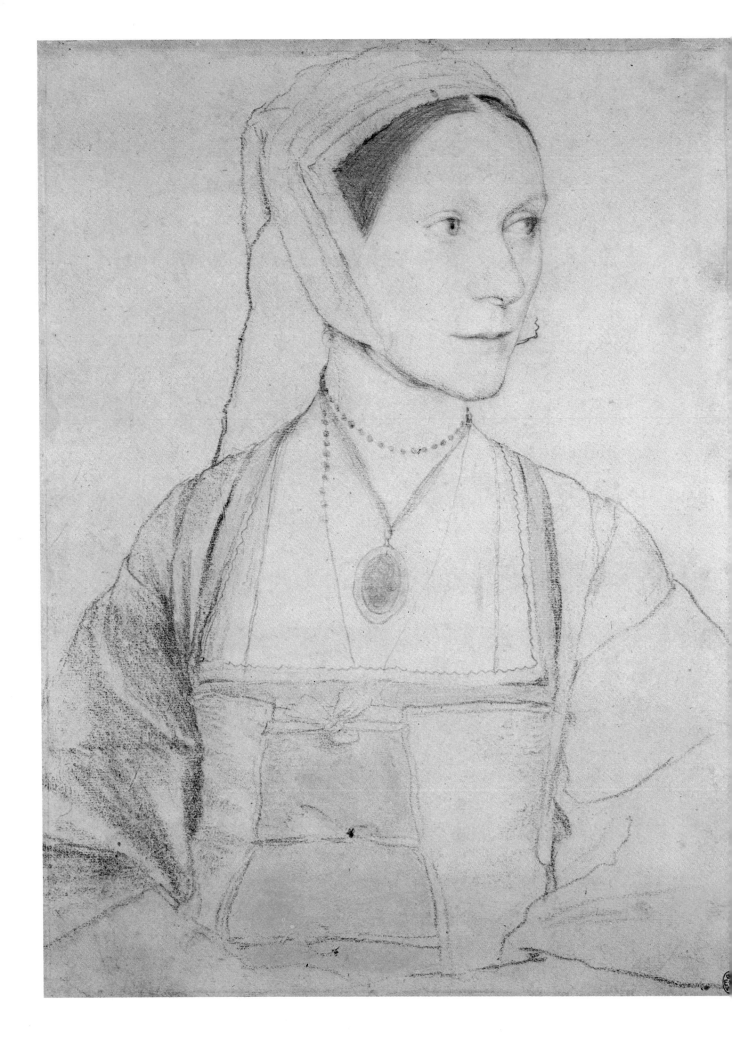

Hans Holbein, *Cecily Heron*, youngest daughter of Sir Thomas More

France through marriage. Menaces everywhere, and many of Elizabeth's counsellors thought she must marry for her country's sake. They saw that England could be plunged into civil war if she suddenly died, and death came easily in the sixteenth century.

For years, for diplomacy's sake, she might toy with the idea, encourage first this suitor, then that, give gracious and seemingly complying answers to her counsellors. She never married. Was it wisdom born of deep insight, or just that she could not? She loved handsome men – Dudley, Raleigh, the young Essex; painted for us in their outrageously expensive clothes, and posed with an air of fashionable melancholy in the brilliant miniatures of Nicholas Hilliard and Isaac Oliver. She flirted with them, but never yielded. Quite early in her reign, she began to play a role in which they, too, had their parts. She encouraged the cult of herself as a semi-divine virgin queen, surrounded by her worshippers, for which she dressed carefully and to which her courtiers took with Renaissance abandon. In her portraits – restricted to the official versions by privy council order, she presented the same image. Indeed, she became a living ikon. This is apparent in the work of both Nicholas Hilliard, the great miniaturist who may have been responsible for the first official portrait of Elizabeth I for the coinage, and Hans Eworth, the best portraitist of the early years of her reign. Eworth came from the Netherlands and we know very little about him. Although he painted with seeming realism – elaborate dresses in the most precise detail and portraits that realised the character of the sitter as clearly as Holbein – nevertheless even in the straightforward portrait of the Queen or the courtiers there is an allegorical quality, a sense that the subject has been set apart from common humanity, is of it but above it. There is a picture of Queen Elizabeth in the royal collection sometimes thought to be by Eworth that becomes pure allegory in which this concept of Elizabeth I as quasi-divine is clearly shown. She is robed and crowned in Majesty, carrying the orb and sceptre; before her, covered in alarm and confusion, are three goddesses, Juno (power), Pallas (wisdom), and Venus (beauty). This remarkable scene is taking place in Windsor Great Park.

Such adulation was not confined to royal painters. Just before this picture was painted, in 1569, the Queen had visited the University of Cambridge on one of her royal progresses, and the dons had greeted her with long Latin poems every bit as effusive as Eworth's painting. These royal progresses were pure theatre, as carefully stage-managed as a court masque. Elizabeth was carried in a litter like an idol, surrounded by her elaborately dressed courtiers who looked more like demigods than men. Wherever she went, her maids of honour had to dress in white, like vestal virgins. To sustain this role, the Queen dressed more sumptuously even than Henry VIII or his wives. She had a vast repertoire of dresses, and her 128 petticoats could be used in an infinite number of combinations. She preferred white or black, but richly embroidered in gold and colours – flowers, fruits, the themes were endless. And, of course, the decorations on her clothes were all emblematic, conveying messages to those educated in their symbolism; an ermine embroidered in silver on a sleeve, for example, indicated chastity. Other emblems acclaimed her wisdom, her power, her purity and her beauty, and her highly literary court read such symbols with ease. Her passion for jewels equalled her passion for clothes; her dresses, her wig, her fingers and neck were festooned with

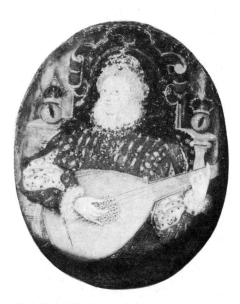

Nicholas Hilliard, *Elizabeth I with a Lute*. Trustees to the late Earl of Berkeley

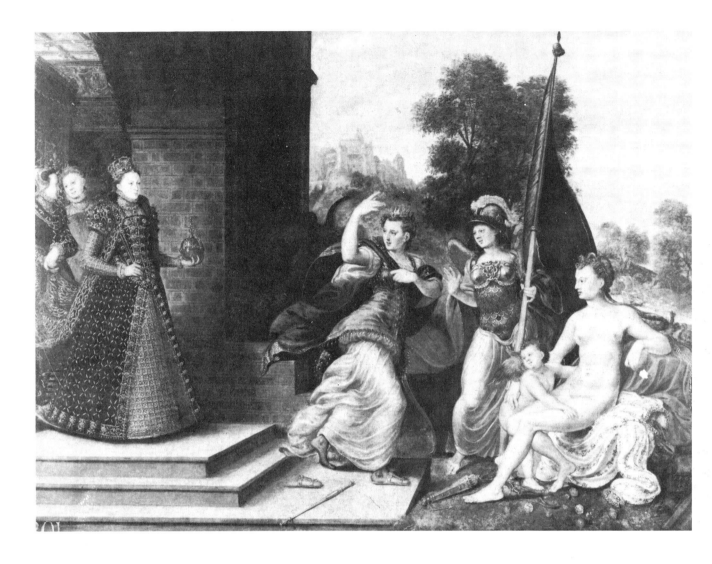

Attributed to Hans Eworth, *Elizabeth I and the Three Goddesses*. 1569. The Queen, attended by ladies-in-waiting, holds the Orb and Sceptre of State. Before her are Juno, Pallas Athene and Venus. In the distance is a view of Windsor Castle

them, and they, too, had their hidden meanings – pearls, for example, were another indication of chastity. All this extravagant clothing and jewellery proclaimed her to be Gloriana, Diana, the faery queen, the virgin, and so enhanced her power and helped Englishmen to feel that they were God's chosen people, blessed by Him with a queen who seemed more than mortal. Indeed, she became a living idol to her people, or rather a work of living art.

One can imagine what a fantastic sight it must have been for the Essex peasants and gentry, dropping to their knees to watch the great royal procession wending its slow way up the avenue to Ingatestone Hall, where Sir William Petre, one of her counsellors, with his family and retainers stood waiting to receive the Queen. The great retinue was led by the heralds, in their brilliant tabards. Then came her court and counsellors on horseback. Then the Queen in her great painted and gilded coach – no springs, and often bogged down in the mud – surrounded by her glittering courtiers on foot, flattering her, amusing her, making the slow time pass. They were like a cloud of gilded locusts. Sir William Petre had run up sheds behind the house for the hordes of retainers, only the closest courtiers and wisest counsellors being admitted into the house. The room, and probably the bed, used by the Queen still exist at Ingatestone. Such visits were an exercise in economy and propaganda, a mixture Elizabeth relished. The Queen and her court lived cheaply, and, above all, the ordinary people glimpsed god-like creatures and saw their triumphant virgin queen. It was pure theatre, but it worked. Petre was flattered, and his greatness in Essex society was underlined, but he never forgot the visit, not only for the honour, but also the cost: presents were expected by the Queen – jewelled swords, batons, daggers, golden darts of love were some of her favourites; but it was the food that ran away with the money. The bills which record everything they ate still exist: and locusts they were, three oxen, two calves, six sheep, sixty rabbits, along with fish and wild fowl galore, hundreds of chickens, herons from Kent, quail from London, and six dozen local peewits. 700 eggs seems a lot for a two-day visit, and there was enough wine to swim in.

Slowly Englishmen's self-confidence deepened; increasingly they felt that – as one bishop said – God was English and that He had destined them for greatness, and His holy work. But the fate of the nation, after twenty years of rule, even the fate of protestantism itself, still hung on the Queen's life. Spain, deeply involved in war with its rebellious Netherland provinces, strongly disliked the aid given to them, from time to time, by the English. From 1580 it became increasingly likely that the whole armed might of Spain might be turned against England. And there was the further problem of Mary Queen of Scots, Elizabeth's heir, but a catholic. Although she was in Elizabeth's custody, largely through her own folly, she presented a problem. Her catholicism allied her to Spain, her previous marriage and her French mother brought the support of France, and there were in Scotland, and perhaps in England, devout catholics prepared to put her on the throne of England by any means. So long as she lived she was a threat to Elizabeth I – as great a threat as Spain, but Scotland, England's hereditary enemy, was much closer at hand.

Scotland was a strange mixture: half catholic, half calvinist, the battleground of bitter feuding factions, where barbarism went cheek by jowl with wonderful Renaissance splendour. Linlithgow Castle, where Mary Queen of Scots was born of a French princess, Mary of Guise, was built by her father, and it illustrates this contrast perfectly. From across the loch the castle looks formidable, a great, brutal fortress; but within, what do we find? The High Renaissance: an exquisite fountain that would grace Rome, and a beautiful outside staircase that could come straight from the great Valois castle of Blois by the Loire.

The Stuart kings of Scotland were great builders. More often than not they used French masons, plasterers and decorators so that their castles were very distinctive, not at all English-looking. When Mary's son, James, was torn from his mother so that he might be brought up a calvinist, he was taken to another magnificent Stuart fortress, Stirling Castle, that stands, bleak and forbidding, above Bannockburn. Yet within, like Linlithgow, it was as sophisticated, as elegant, as replete with tapestries and pictures, as Hampton Court or Nonsuch. When James grew to manhood, another of his castles was Falkland Palace, which has been lovingly restored to evoke the splendour of the Scottish Stuarts. And certainly their jewels rivalled the Tudors'. When James was crowned in Stirling Church as James VI, he used the lovely Crown of Scotland, which is still a treasured part of the royal regalia, and indeed the oldest of all crowns.

Perhaps even Elizabeth would have failed to rule in Scotland. Mary

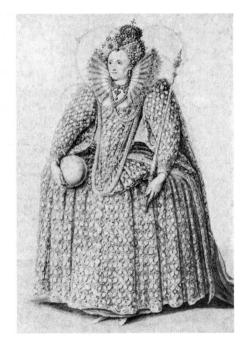

Isaac Oliver, Drawing of Queen Elizabeth I

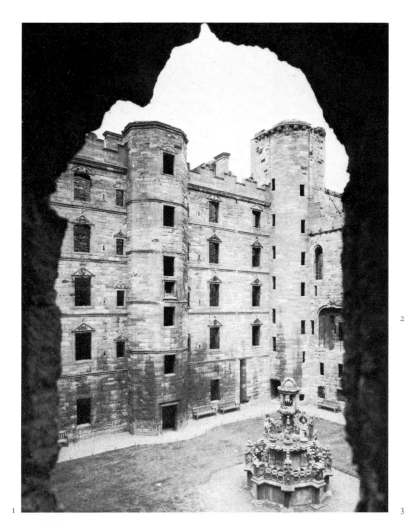

1

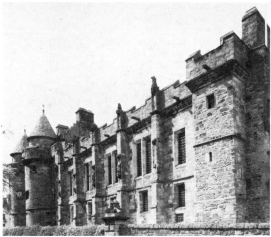

2

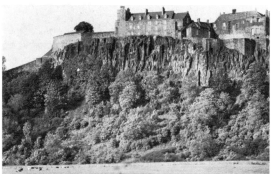

3

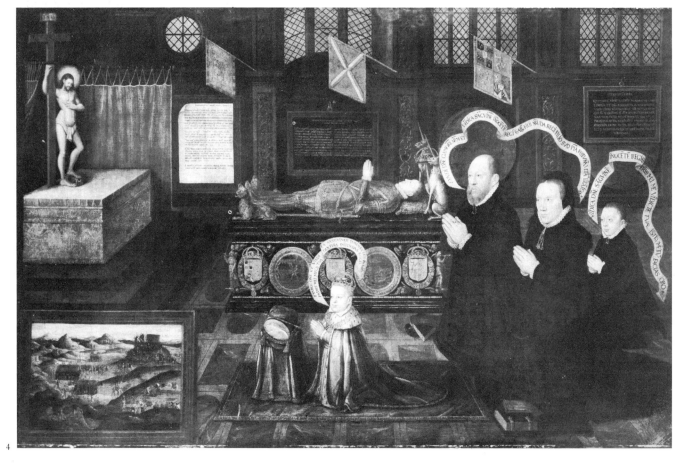

4

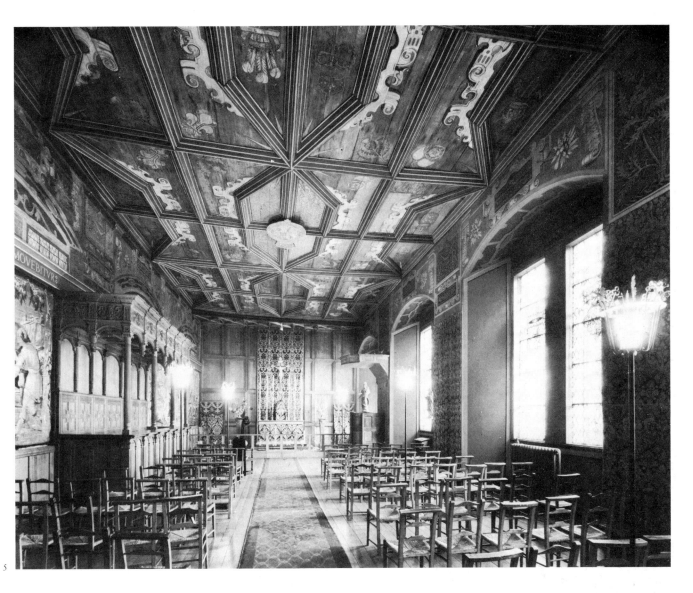

5

certainly did. Unlike Elizabeth, she married too often, and unwisely —
once to her cousin, Darnley. He was murdered by the man who became
her third husband, the Earl of Bothwell. At Holyroodhouse there is a
remarkable picture by Livinius de Vogelaare, *The Memorial of Lord
Darnley*, which tells with striking images the story of Darnley's murder,
and Mary's supposed implication in the plot. The inscriptions which
abound, and make crystal clear the picture's indictment, are now partly
obliterated, probably by her son who, after he came to the English throne
in 1603, did what he could to rehabilitate the memory of his tragic
mother, building for her a magnificent tomb in the chapel of Henry VII in
Westminster Abbey.

If Elizabeth wanted a warning against marriage, Mary's fate was
sufficient. Driven to disaster, Mary fled in 1568 to the protection of her
cousin, but only to exchange one prison for another, to become the tragic
heroine of the Stuarts, and of the Scottish people.

The end came in Fotheringay Castle. Elizabeth signed the death
warrant in 1587, regretted it, and wept and raged for days afterwards.
Yet it had to be. Mary had plotted with English catholics at the moment
of England's greatest danger, from the Spanish Armada, Philip II's 'great
enterprise,' which was to destroy protestant England. The tough-
minded men of Elizabeth's court felt that the presence of a catholic heir in

1 Linlithgow Castle. 2 Falkland Palace.
3 Stirling Castle. 4 Livinius de Vogelaare, *The
Memorial of Lord Darnley*. The inset picture
shows the battlefield at Carberry Hill.
5 Falkland Palace Chapel. 6 François Clouet,
Mary Queen of Scots — in widow's weeds

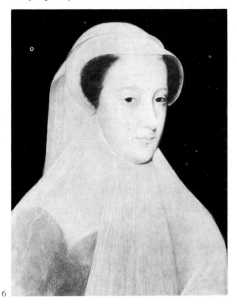

6

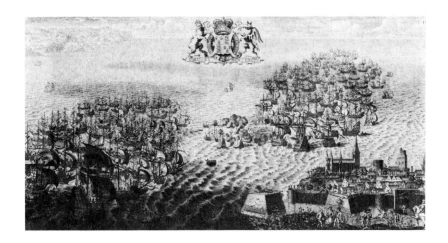

the country created too great a risk in case of invasion. When the Armada sailed up the Channel, Elizabeth I rose magnificently to the occasion. At the moment of greatest peril she rode down to Tilbury and spoke to her army. She used words as perfectly as she wore clothes, and her speech has resonated from generation to generation.

The defeat of the Armada was due to the fast English ships which outstripped the slow, heavy Spanish galleons, and the 'protestant gale' which did even more deadly work. This wind enabled the English to send in destructive fireships as the Spanish fleet took shelter on the French coast, and its furious force helped to wreck the Spanish galleons as they tried to round the Scottish and Irish coasts. Fair Isle, the Giant's Causeway, the wild coast of Clare, all claimed their victims. England's greatest triumph was, naturally enough, memorialised in pictures, tapestries and jewellery.

The defeat of the Armada put the seal on the belief that the English were truly God's people, and raised her navy and her sea-captains to the highest pitch of favour. Elizabeth I patronised the daring piratical tactics of Sir Francis Drake on the Spanish Main. She played her usual double game, denouncing him for Spanish benefit, and taking a cut of the profits for her own. Her sea-dogs had served her well.

The victory over Spain brought self-confidence and, often with royal encouragement, the true flowering of the Elizabethan Renaissance. Owing to inflation, a fall in the royal revenues and a natural parsimony, Elizabeth I built little. She loved exercise and so, in the fashion of her time, she built a long gallery at Windsor where she could stride up and down when the weather was too vile for the long walks that she loved. It now houses the Royal Family's books – a use which would have delighted Elizabeth I for she was an intellectual who loved to have witty, learned, word-skilled men about her. She adored the theatre in all its forms and was extremely fond of music and dancing. To the arts she loved she gave her patronage – or at least her blessing and encouragement for, unlike her father, she was not open-handed. Edmund Spenser's paean of praise, *The Faerie Queene*, and *The Shepheard's Calendar*, brought not a penny from the Queen, much as she delighted in the poetry and enjoyed the fulsome flattery of herself. Dramatists did better, for she loved pageantry, dressing up, repartee, symbolism both sonorous and elusive, and without her support William Shakespeare and Ben Jonson might have found fame far harder to achieve. She patronised both writers, and preserved the theatre which London's puritan councillors wished to

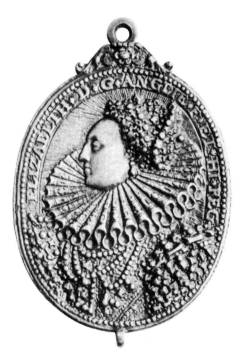

A silver medal commemorating the Spanish Armada, 1588. British Museum, London

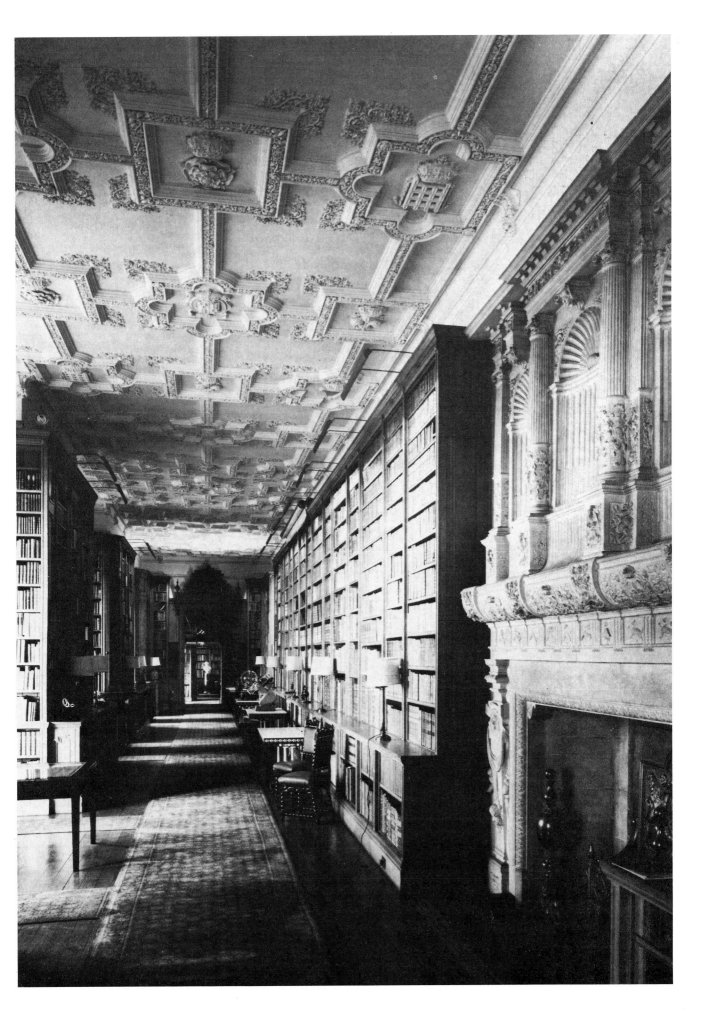

The Royal Library, Windsor, originally a long gallery built for Queen Elizabeth I. The fireplace is Tudor

close. She herself was at the first performance of *A Comedy of Errors*, and of *A Midsummer Night's Dream*.

As for masques and tournaments, these could never be too elaborate for Elizabeth, and each year on her Accession Day Sir Henry Lee, her Master of the Tilt, organised pageants and jousts of extraordinary complexity in which the emblems, symbols and allusions rioted with Elizabethan exuberance. And everywhere she went there was music. The Elizabethans took up with zest the madrigal, which had swept Italy half a century before, and produced masters of this art – Orlando Gibbons, William Byrd, Thomas Morley, and the greatest of all, John Wilbye. And although he never wrote madrigals, this, too, was the time of the sad nostalgic songs of John Dowland, as he himself said, 'Semper Dolens'.

Although Elizabeth patronised painting very little – apart, of course, from sitting for her carefully planned official portraits – there was one style that she loved – the miniature. Indeed, never has the art of miniature painting flourished so magnificently as in the last decades of Elizabeth's reign. This fashion was greatly stimulated by Nicholas Hilliard, the son of an Exeter goldsmith, and as we have seen, a keen admirer of Hans Holbein. He painted with great delicacy and his small pictures have a haunting nostalgia, for the poise and expression of his subjects expresses the melancholic mien which became fashionable amongst the elegant young men of Elizabeth's court, fitting, perhaps, for the autumn years of her reign. Miniatures were like jewels, they could be worn, they made delectable gifts. As well as Hilliard, Elizabeth and the court patronised Isaac Oliver, another great master of miniature painting.

Her last fifteen years were as difficult as any in politics and religion, and more difficult than all financially, yet they were culturally the greatest. For these were the years when the Elizabethan theatre was reaching new heights of greatness and the full genius of Shakespeare as a poet as well as a playwright began to be recognised. These were the years when Francis Bacon was distilling wisdom in brilliant essays, when John Donne was preaching sermons of impassioned and moving rhetoric. In music and in painting the achievement was remarkable and lasting. The wonderful success of her reign none could deny, and it was only fitting that England's Renaissance should revolve about her court – poets, playwrights, musicians and painters all sought her praise and hoped for her patronage. Wilful to the last, she refused to name her heir even as death seized her in her palace at Richmond in 1603. On that day England's greatest dynasty came to an end.

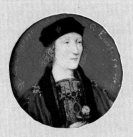

Nicholas Hilliard, *King Henry VII* (circular, 1⅜")

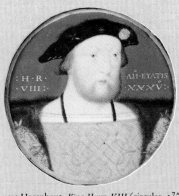

Lucas Horenbout, *King Henry VIII* (circular, 1⅞")

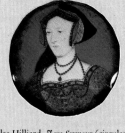

Nicholas Hilliard, *Jane Seymour* (circular, 1¾")

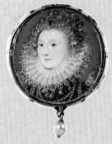

Nicholas Hilliard, *Queen Elizabeth I* (circular, 1")

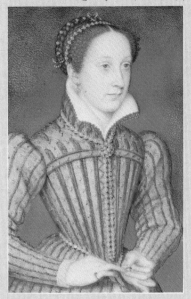

François Clouet, *Mary Queen of Scots* (3¼" × 2¼")

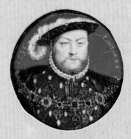

Nicholas Hilliard, *King Henry VIII* (circular, 1½")

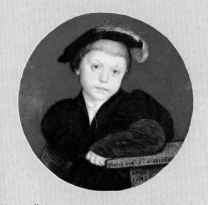

Hans Holbein, *Lady Audley* (circular, 2¼")

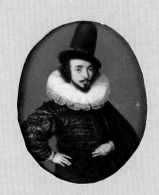

Isaac Oliver, *Self-portrait* (oval, 1¾" × 1½")

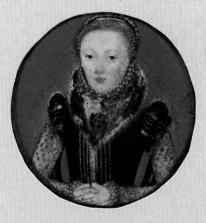

Queen Elizabeth I when young (circular, 1¾")

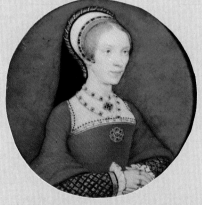

Hans Holbein, *Henry Brandon, Duke of Suffolk* (circular, 2¼")

T*he*
Royal Collection
*of miniatures is the largest and oldest in
existence. Those in this section are Tudor and
Stuart. Queen Elizabeth I kept in her
bedchamber 'divers little pictures wrapt within
paper, and their names written with her own
hand upon the papers'. King Charles I had
nearly eighty 'lim'd peeces' inventoried and
arranged in his Cabinet Room*

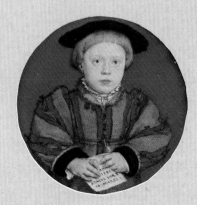

Hans Holbein, *Charles Brandon, Duke of Suffolk* (circular, 2¼")

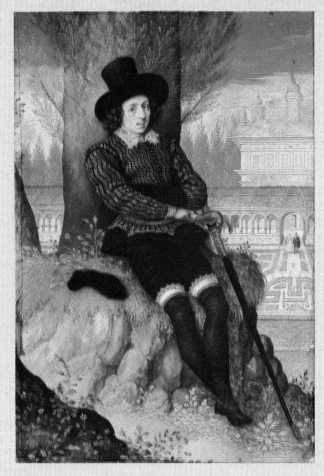

Isaac Oliver, *Portrait of a Young Man*, formerly called Sir Philip Sidney (5″ × 3½″)

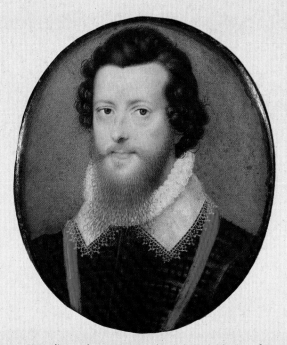

Isaac Oliver, *Robert Devereux, Second Earl of Essex* (oval, 2″ × 1⅝″)

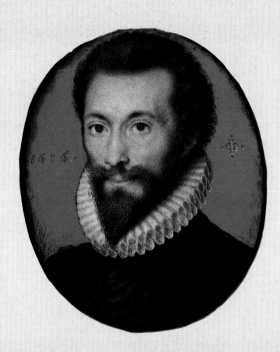

Isaac Oliver, *John Donne* (oval, 1¾″ × 1⅜″)

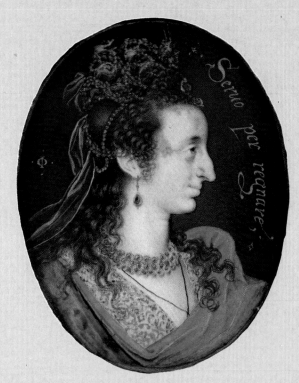

Isaac Oliver, *Anne of Denmark* (oval, 2″ × 1⅝″)

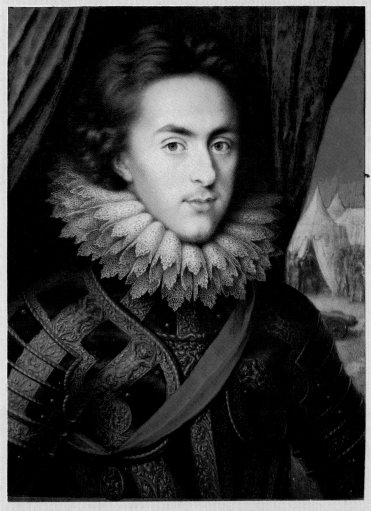

Isaac Oliver, *Henry, Prince of Wales* (5⅛″ × 4″)

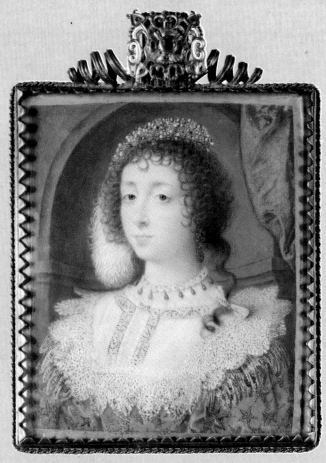

John Hoskins, *Henrietta Maria* ($3\frac{1}{2}'' \times 3''$)

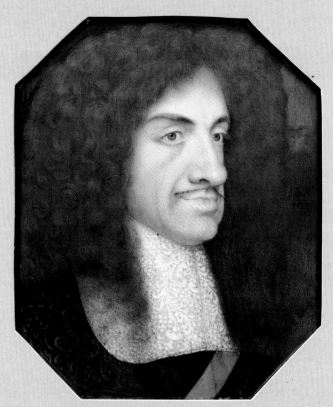

After Samuel Cooper, *King Charles II* (octagonal, $4'' \times 3\frac{3}{8}''$)

3

THE STUARTS

On a bitter winter's day, 30 January 1649, a small procession made its way across St James's Park. A King of England was going to his execution. Charles I entered his palace of Whitehall, where he was kept waiting almost interminably, but no anxiety touched the restrained dignity of his manner. He resolved to die like a king, and did. As he said on the scaffold, 'Death is not terrible to me. I bless God and am prepared'. This was true. And it was true because, he believed, 'I go from a corruptible to an incorruptible crown where no disturbances can be'. So, on that tragic day, England lost its king and the Church of England acquired a martyr. Already on that day the King's apology for his life, the *Eikon Basilike*, was on sale, with a frontispiece depicting Charles as a Christian martyr. Handkerchiefs reputedly dipped in his blood were on sale on the day after his execution. They worked wonders, the sacred touch still potent and divine. An Anglican churchman could describe him as 'a most lively image of Christ, so lively an image of him that amongst all the martyrs who followed Christ into heaven, bearing his cross, never was there any who expressed so great conformity with our Saviour in his sufferings as he did'.

It is hard for us to appreciate the traumatic impact of this act that sent a shudder of horror and fear through many puritan as well as royalist hearts. Kings had been done to death before, by assassins, in the deep and silent recesses of prisons, butchered by rivals or fanatics, killed in battle; but never before had a king been tried in public for misrule and executed in public like a traitor in the name of his people. This implied, even though it did not state, that men, not God, might choose princes; and rejected, therefore, that belief in the divine right of kings which Charles I shared with his father, James I. They believed in the very depths of their being that they were the chosen representatives of God's authority on earth – chosen by God by the very reason of their birth. This image had been rejected by Oliver Cromwell and his fellow puritans who had defeated Charles I in the civil war. They preferred the power of parliament to that of princes. The King dead, they abolished monarchy. And along with monarchy went its trappings – or rather the symbols and settings of monarchy. The regalia were broken up, the gold melted down and jewels sold, the silver and tapestries, even the chairs and carpets, all were put up for auction. And, most grievous of all, the great collection of pictures, drawings, bronzes and sculpture brought together by Charles I, one of the very finest made by any monarch at any time, was dispersed.

There is no space to list all of the great masterpieces that belonged to Charles I that were sold and now adorn the Louvre, the Prado, the museums of Vienna, Leningrad, Washington and elsewhere. And, alas, some have disappeared for ever. But one may sense the enormous loss to Britain by listing just those of his paintings which are now regarded as some of the finest treasures of the Louvre and the Prado. In the Louvre there are sixteen of Charles I's pictures: five Titians – his favourite painter – including three of his most famous pictures, *The Entombment of Christ*, *The Supper at Emmaus* and the haunting *Venus of Pardo*; a masterpiece of Leonardo's, *St John the Baptist*, returned home for it had belonged to Louis XIII; to these may be added two very fine Holbeins, the portraits of *Erasmus* and Henry VIII's astronomer *Nicolas Kratzer*; three outstanding Correggios; a brilliant Caravaggio, *The Death of the Virgin*, and Van Dyck's magnificent portrait of *Charles I à la Chasse*. The Prado was not quite

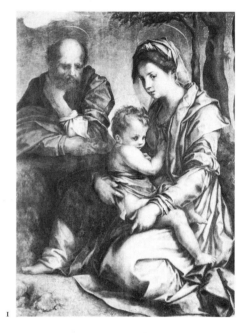

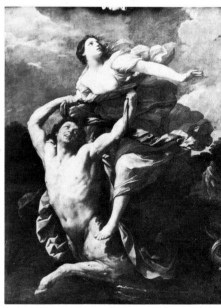

1 Andrea del Sarto, *Holy Family* – now in the Prado, Madrid.
2 Guido Reni, *Nessus the Centaur and Deianira* – now in the Louvre.
3 Sir Peter Paul Rubens, *The Apotheosis of James I*, the central panel of the ceiling of the Banqueting House, Whitehall

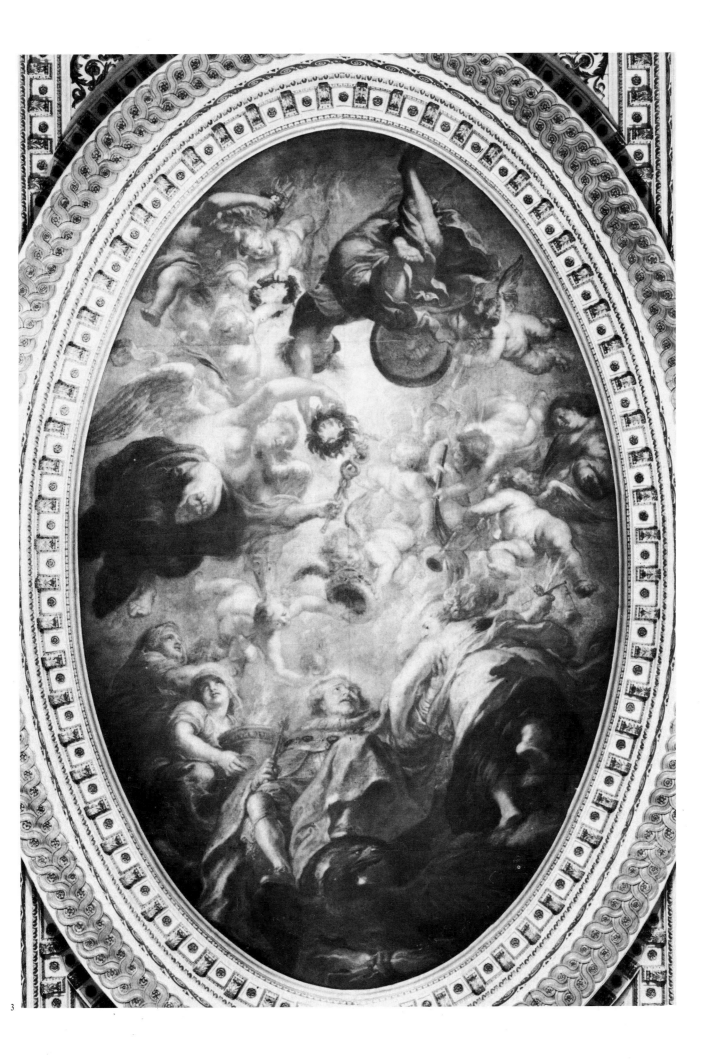

3

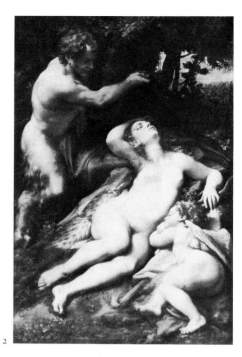

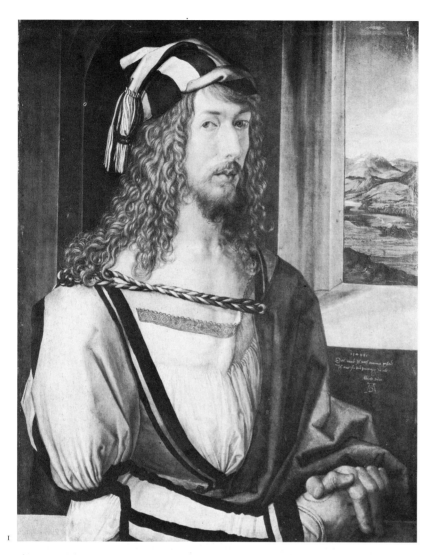

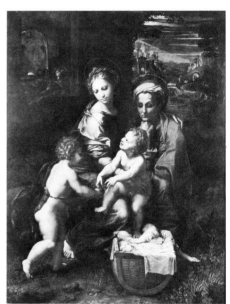

so fortunate, but fortunate enough – a Correggio, a Mantegna, a del Sarto, Dürer's greatest self-portrait and one of Raphael's finest paintings, *La Perla*.

Nor did Charles I's masterpieces fetch high prices: a Leonardo went for a mere £140 and a self-portrait by Rembrandt made only £5! Had those pictures, and others of exceptional distinction, remained with the crown, the royal collection would have been even more astonishing in its richness and variety than it is. To understand why this great heritage was dispersed, it is necessary to understand the image of monarchy that Charles I was quite deliberately projecting; an image which required an appropriate artistic setting. But although Charles collected and commissioned art, which enhanced and dignified his role, as we shall see, it also possessed deep personal meaning for him. He moved naturally in the world of painting and sculpture, possessing a marvellous eye and sensitive judgment, based on very great and detailed knowledge; indeed he was the greatest connoisseur to sit on the English throne. Nevertheless,

Six of the masterpieces from Charles I's collection that went to collectors abroad:
1 Albrecht Dürer, *Self-portrait*, the Prado, Madrid.
2 Correggio, *Jupiter and Antiope*, the Louvre, Paris.
3 Raphael, *La Perla*, the Prado.
4 Titian, *The Entombment of Christ*, the Louvre.
5 Titian, *Doge Andrea Gritti*, National Gallery of Art, Washington.
6 Caravaggio, *Death of the Virgin*, the Louvre

much of the art and architecture favoured by the King had a pejorative effect – sometimes directly, more frequently because of the lesson which it spelt out, in one splendid image after another – and nowhere so grandiosely as in the ceiling of the Banqueting Hall, painted by Rubens, under which, ironically, Charles moved to his death. It was a lesson Charles had been taught by his father.

James I of England and VI of Scotland was a slightly eccentric intellectual. As the great procession of coaches and wagons from Edinburgh made its way down the north-eastern coast in 1603, he understandably savoured the situation that he should be inheriting the crown of the kingdom which had executed his mother, Mary Queen of Scots. Taken from her when only a few months old, he had a difficult childhood. Scotland was riven by civil war, as noble catholic and noble calvinist battled for supremacy, with the infant James the prize of these bitter warring factions. That he survived, and in the end dominated the aristocracy, was because he was shrewd, clear-minded, intelligent and tough. True, he could be a pedant and a bore, but he could also write trenchantly. He did so extensively – on witchcraft, on tobacco-smoking, but most importantly on kingship, especially in *The Laws of Free Monarchies*. The only words one can use about this book are succinct, vivid, forceful and fatal. 'Kings are called Gods,' James announced, 'by the prophetical King David, because they sit upon God his throne in earth.' The king is absolute, bound only by God's laws, because he is God's appointed and anointed. And in Paul van Somer's portrait of James I the message was clear to all whose eyes could read the image. He is shown in the robes of majesty – orb and sceptre in hand, and crowned. Behind him the Banqueting House, built by the incomparable Inigo Jones, the most brilliant, most modern, building in London, where it was completed in 1622, totally different to any other. Why this odd juxtaposition? To those who knew, it was not in the least odd. The Banqueting House was a symbol. Its careful mathematical proportions spoke of the harmony of the universe, of peace, order and power – the virtues, in fact, of divine kingship. Hence it was an appropriate background for the king in majesty, fully crowned, holding his symbols of power and justice. That

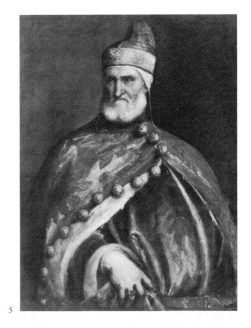

5

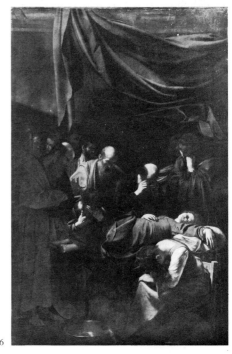

6

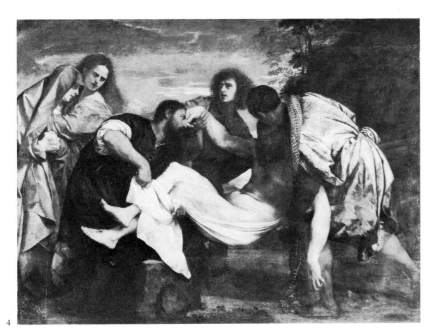

4

might have been a bit fanciful for James, who did not care overmuch for the visual arts – indeed, ugly fellow that he was, he hated being painted.

Nevertheless, for his son, bred in his doctrine and deeply versed in the iconography as well as the beauty of art, it would have symbolised eternal truth. Charles's artistic tastes were probably partly derived from his mother, Anne of Denmark, who possessed an alert eye, a delight in gardens, a quick appreciation of architecture, and a cultivated taste in the burgeoning art of the Netherlands. Both her sons – for Charles had had an elder brother, Henry, Prince of Wales, a young man of brilliant promise – possessed her eye; and they believed implicitly all that their father wrote about kingship. Hence theory and art were married in them. In his book, *Basilike Doron*, written for the Prince of Wales, James spelt out the absolute nature of kingship; justice and virtue, through his authority, must be imposed on his subjects. Their duty was to obey. This belief was buttressed by social institutions – 'No bishop, no king,' said James tersely. The Church of England was to reflect the divine nature of monarchy. So were poetry and the arts. The ceiling of the Banqueting House in Whitehall, painted by Rubens, is a great visual statement of the vision James gave his sons of the absolute right and God-given power of monarchs. It is also, incidentally, the only one of Rubens's major decorative schemes which still exists in its original setting. A part of the scheme emphasises the union of England and Scotland, but this, too, is seen as God's blessing – good fortune due to the king by reason of his birth. We are shown the attributes of kingship – the supremacy of wisdom, the divine authority, the king as the source of earthly justice, the king as defender of the faith and of the Church. The horrors of discord are banished. Peace reigns and the arts flourish. Not surprisingly, for one who has been so beneficial a father to his country, King James rises up through the empyrean to Heaven itself – having suppressed Ignorance, overcome Avarice, and quelled Rebellion.

The reality of James I's court, however – and this was obvious enough to his sons – did not reflect this God-like image of monarchy. Their father's adulation of young, handsome males was known and exploited; his courtiers were corrupt and immoral, politically as well as sexually vicious. It was an atmosphere against which Henry, Prince of Wales, had reacted strongly, and in his early youth he had begun to mould himself on the Renaissance concept of the ideal prince. He became a master of the martial arts – superb on horseback, devoted to the tournament, skilled with the sword and in love with the concepts of chivalry. Equally he patronised the arts. He was the first English prince to create a cabinet of works of art – Renaissance pictures, sixteenth-century bronzes and medals, classical statuary and coins, all brought together to create a sense of artistic splendour and regal taste. The Prince was known to 'valew none but extraordinary persons'; Thomas Howard, the Earl of Arundel, the greatest collector of antiquities in the kingdom, had become a member of his circle when the Prince was only thirteen. At sixteen the Prince made Inigo Jones, the most innovative British architect of the age, his surveyor. Like his mother, he adored masques, and Ben Jonson, the poet and dramatist, collaborated with Jones to produce some of the most spectacular and costly entertainments the court had ever seen. In 1610, they created *The Barriers* to celebrate Henry's investiture as Prince of Wales – an astonishing mixture of Arthurian romance and medieval

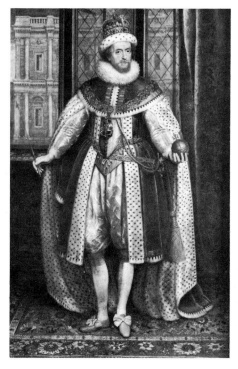

Paul van Somer, *James I*. The King wears the robes of State and holds the Orb and Sceptre. Through the casement window is seen the façade of the Banqueting House

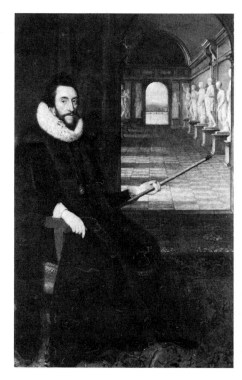

Daniel Mytens, *Thomas, Earl of Arundel*, the true 'father of vertu in England', whose example stimulated Henry, Prince of Wales's collecting. Mytens came to England in 1618, worked for the Earl of Arundel and King James I and subsequently was appointed by King Charles I 'one of our picture-drawers of our Chamber in ordinaire' for life. His self-portrait is reproduced on page 103. From the collection of the Duke of Norfolk

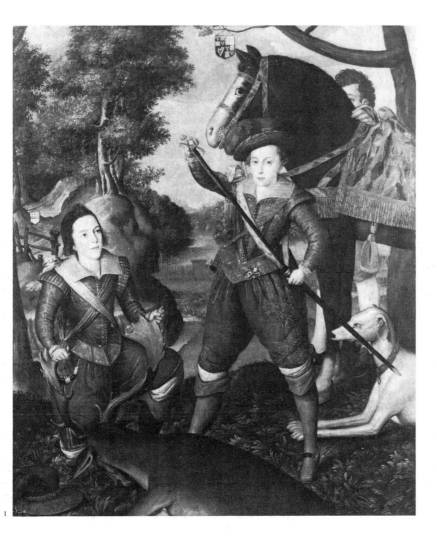

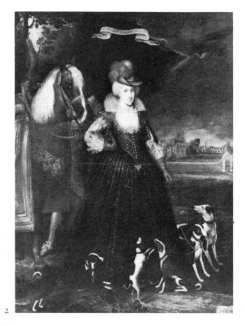

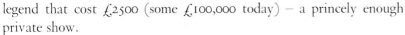

legend that cost £2500 (some £100,000 today) – a princely enough private show.

This was the world – vivid, beautiful, yet as private as it was regal – in which the young Charles's taste was formed. He was only twelve when, in November 1612, his brother suddenly died. Charles inherited not only Henry's collection of pictures, bronzes, coins, but also his attitude to kingship. He was to prove a greater connoisseur than his brother, to immerse himself more deeply in the private world of the masque, and become one of the greatest royal patrons of all time.

Charles I grew up from a shy, rather diffident boy with an embarrassing speech impediment into a complex young man. He craved for order and decorum. He strongly disapproved of the raffishness of his father's court, and, like his brother, reacted against it, even though he was powerfully attracted to his father's flamboyant favourite, George Villiers, Duke of Buckingham. Buckingham entered James's service as a page, yet at the King's death was the most powerful, as well as the richest, duke in the kingdom. He, too, was passionately fond of painting and sculpture, architecture and music, and spent lavishly. Somewhat frivolous, but a woman of discerning taste, the Queen, far more than her husband, moulded Charles's attitude to life. She and her husband had ceased to live together in 1606, and Inigo Jones was building the Queen's House at Greenwich for her when she died in 1619. Although money was too short to bury her for some days, he, appropriately enough, designed a magnificent hearse for her. The King wrote a few lines of poetry,

1 Robert Peake, *Henry, Prince of Wales, in the Hunting-Field*. The Prince has dismounted to deliver the *coup de grâce* to a stag whose antlers are held by the young Earl of Essex.
2 Paul van Somer, *Anne of Denmark*, in hunting costume in the park at Oatlands, which can be seen in the background.
3 Simon van der Passe, *Henry, Prince of Wales*, an engraving. 1612

concerned more with the divine attributes of princes than the death of his wife, which contained one line of superlative arrogance, 'Death serves but to refine their majesty'.

Charles I seems to have revered his brother more than his mother, for years later he ordered both Mytens and Van Dyck to paint large-scale portraits of Henry, based on the brilliant miniature by Isaac Oliver. As he grew to maturity, making friends with the cognoscenti of the court – Arundel, Buckingham, Somerset – his own taste began to form and grow. He developed, with Buckingham's encouragement, a deep attachment to the Venetians of the Renaissance, especially Titian; by 1623 he had already acquired, as well as four Titians, a Tintoretto. He was, however, not limited in his tastes, and he possessed a Van der Goes, as well as a Holbein. Nor is it suprising that he admired the greatest painter of his time, Paul Rubens. Rubens relished the sweet smell of patronage, and sent the Prince the picture of a hunt, but the Prince, realising it was studio work, sent it back. Charles was much more interested in obtaining

Two panels from the *Trinity Altarpiece* by Hugo van der Goes.
1 *King James III of Scotland*; behind him kneels his son, afterwards James IV.
2 *The Holy Trinity*. On loan to the National Gallery of Scotland, Edinburgh

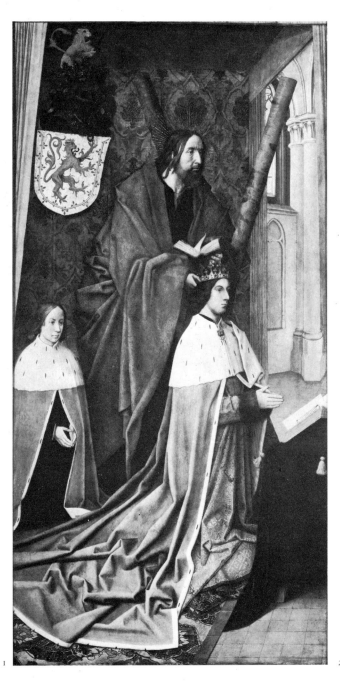

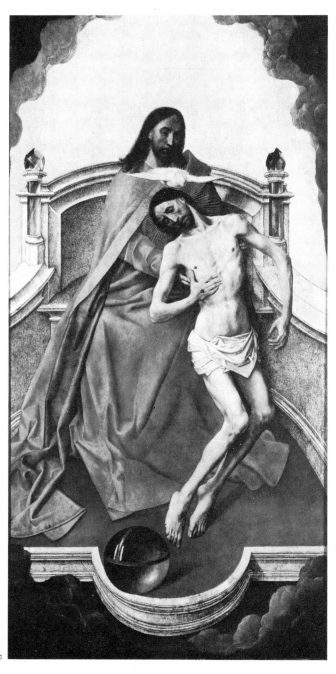

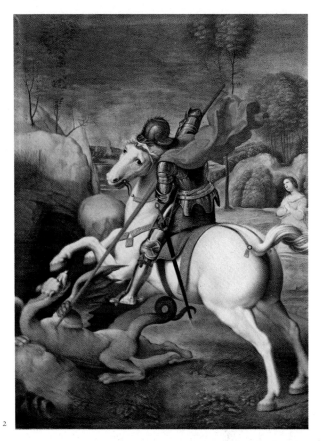

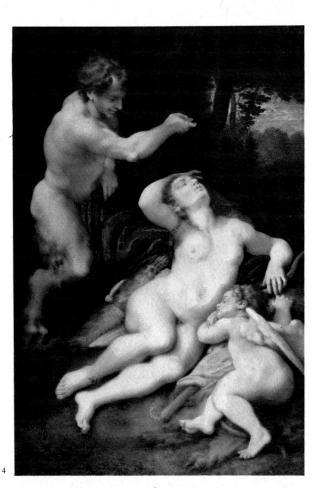

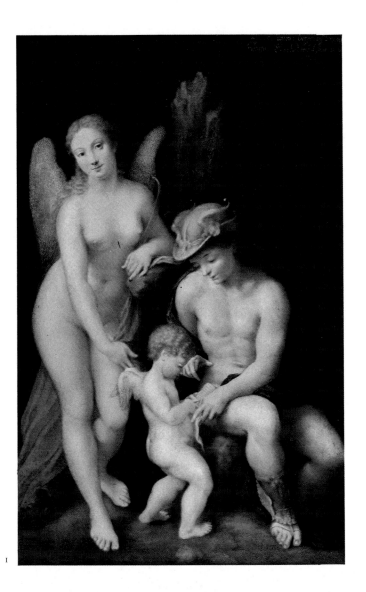

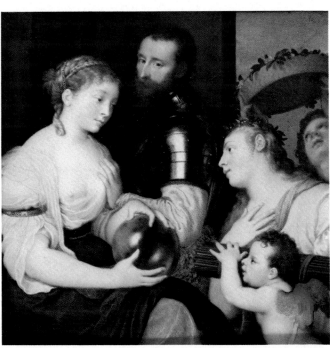

Peter Oliver, miniature copies of 1 Correggio's *Venus Mercury and Cupid*, 2 Raphael's *St George and the Dragon*,
3 Titian's *The D'Avalos Allegory*, 4 Correggio's *Jupiter and Antiope*

After King Charles I's execution, most of his superb collection was sold and much of it went abroad. The
miniatures above are copies of masterpieces lost to the Collection. The paintings on the following pages
are among those belonging to King Charles I which were either kept within or restored to the Royal Collection

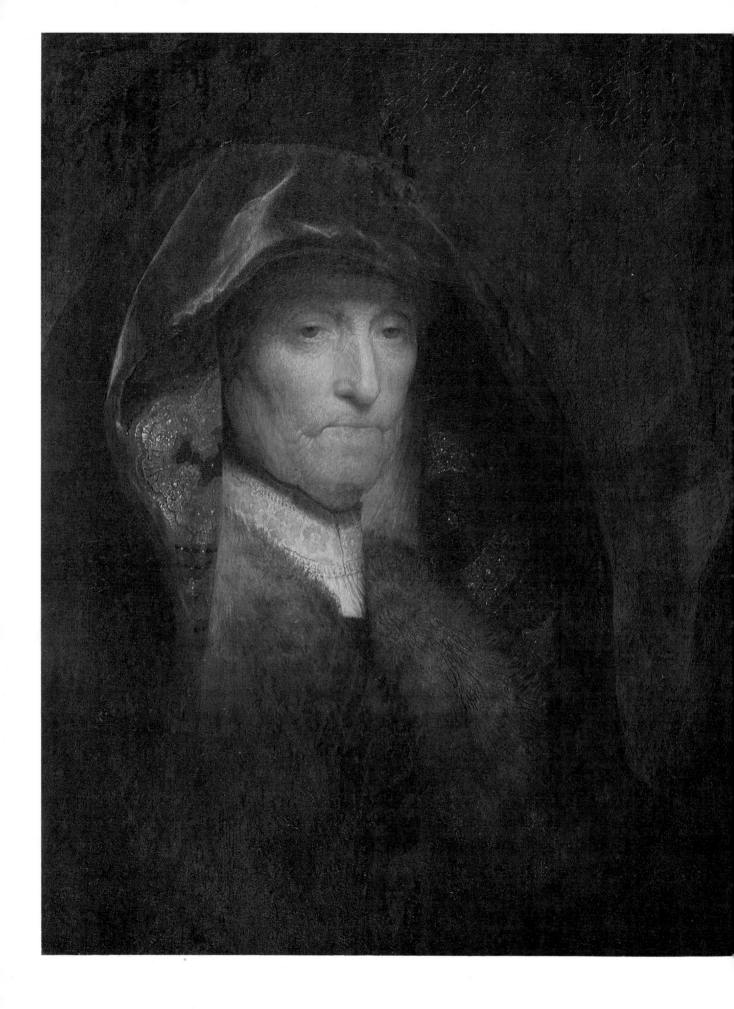

Rembrandt, *The Artist's Mother.* c. 1629

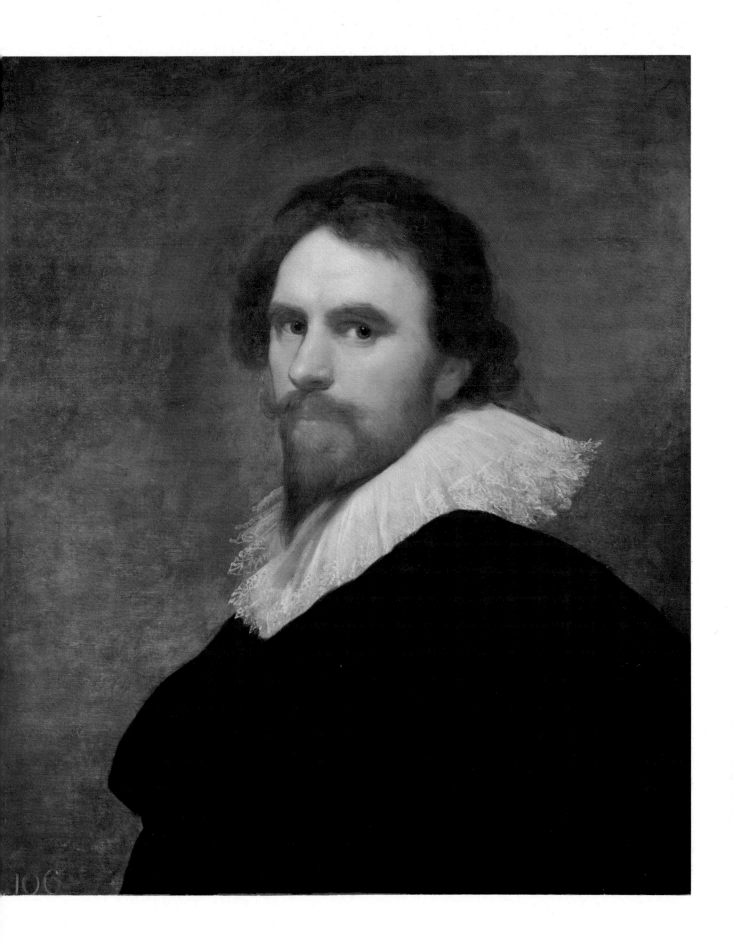

Daniel Mytens, *Portrait of the Artist*. c. 1630

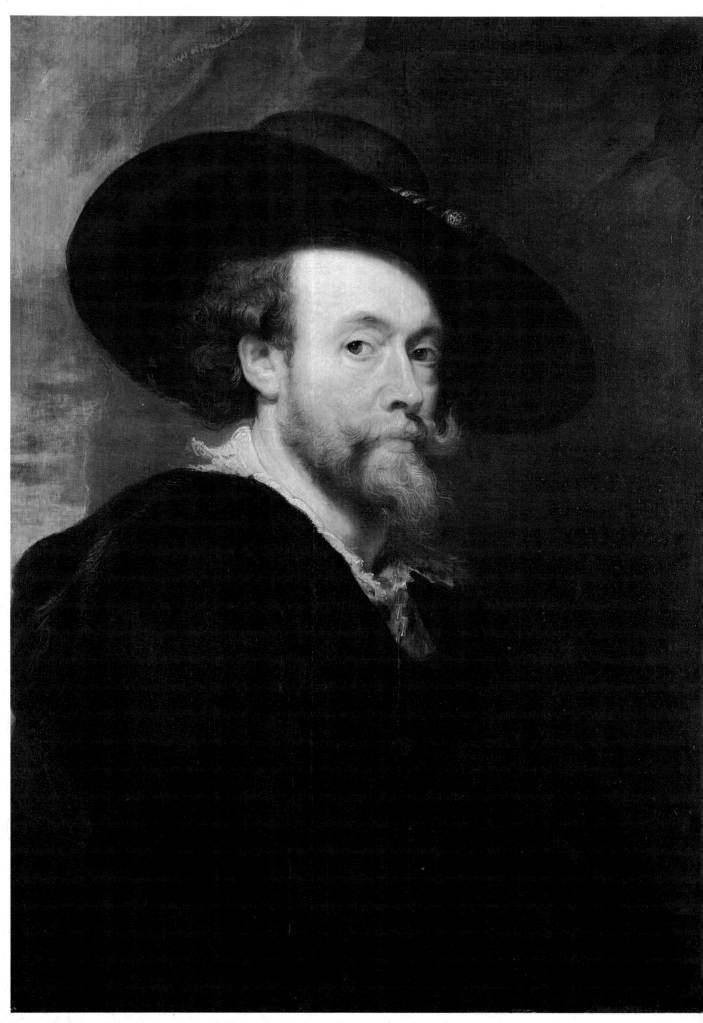

Sir Peter Paul Rubens: Above, *Portrait of the Artist*. 1623.
Opposite, Detail from *Landscape with St George and the Dragon*. 1629–30

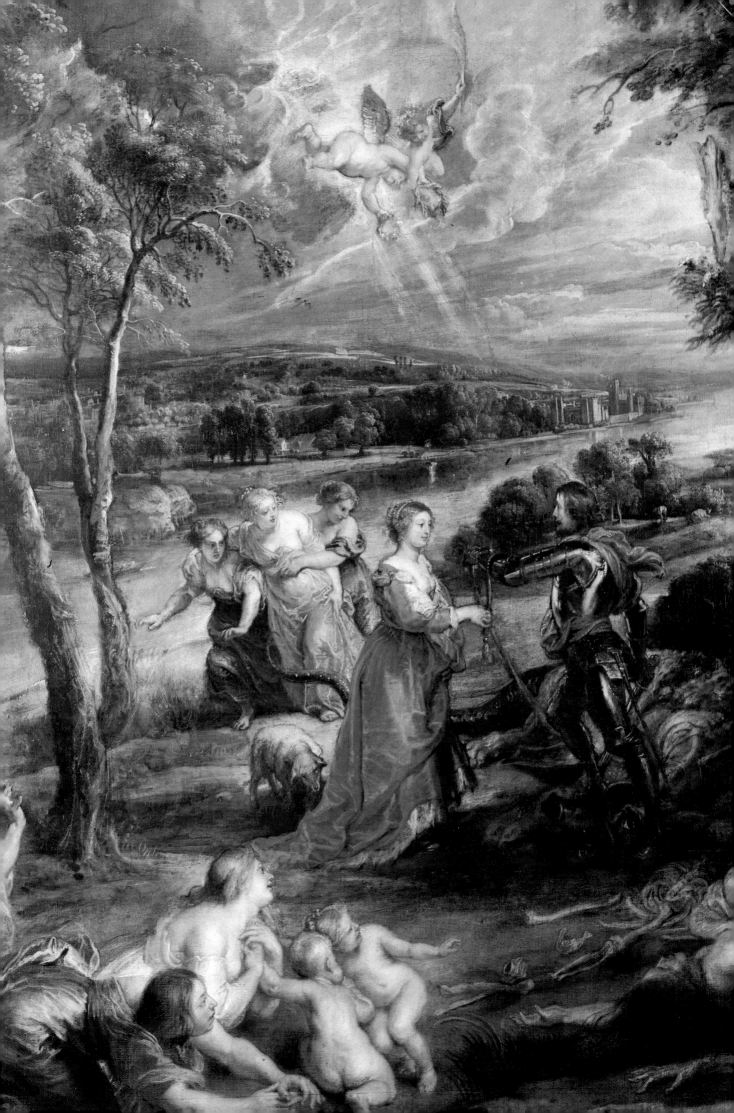

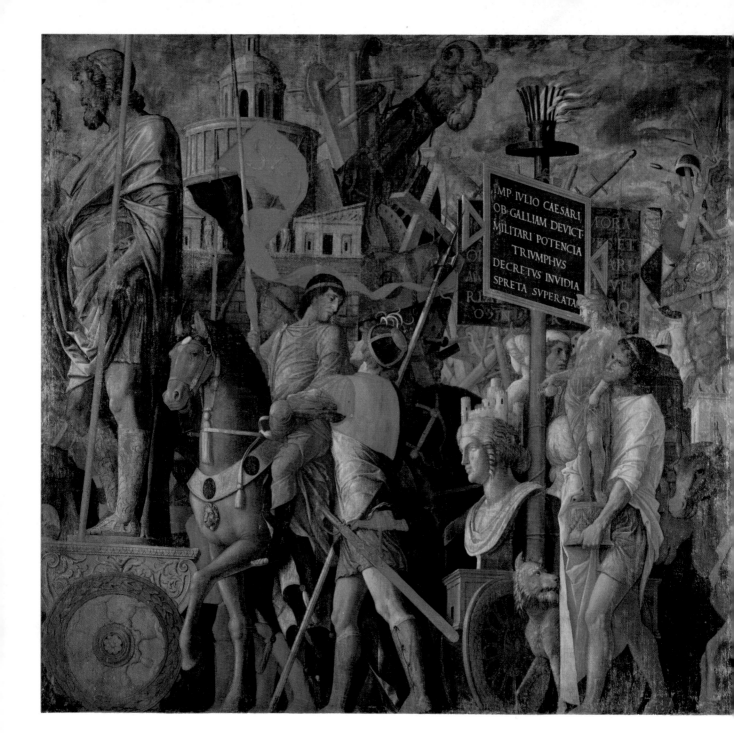

Andrea Mantegna, *The Triumph of Caesar*. 1485–94. *The Triumphal Car*

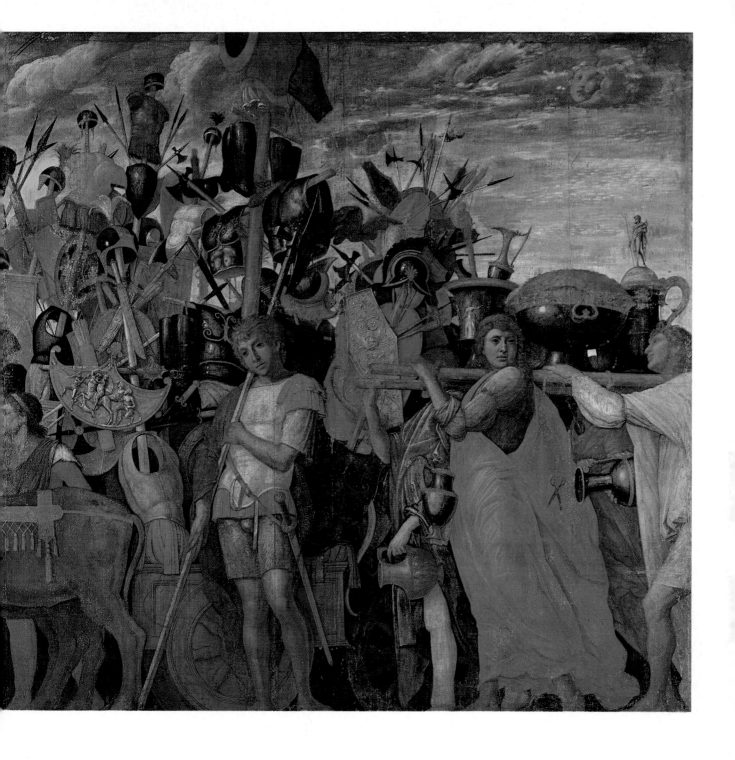

Andrea Mantegna, *The Triumph of Caesar.* 1485–94. *The Litter Bearers*

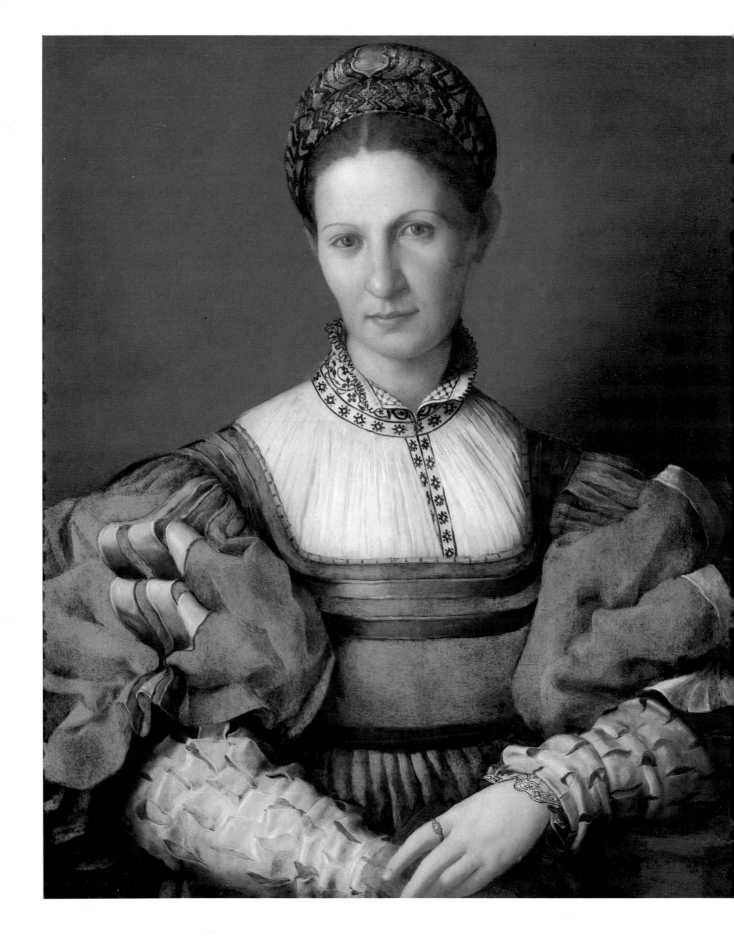

Agnolo Bronzino, *Lady in Green*

a self-portrait, and finally acquired the exceptionally fine picture which is one of the major works in the royal collection. Rubens, quick to discern the Prince's dedication to art (and to pay a compliment), called him 'the greatest amateur of painting amongst the princes of the world'.

By 1623 the time had come for Prince Charles to marry. As was usual with seventeenth-century princes, his plans for matrimony had been dictated by the needs of his father's foreign diplomacy. James I's search for a firm peace with Spain had first suggested a Spanish Infanta as a possible bride, and it was for that romantic reason that Charles visited Madrid in 1623. There, for the first time, he saw a great collection of European art. Fortunately, he was accompanied by two of England's greatest collectors – Buckingham and Endymion Porter – whose taste was close to his own, and, indeed, had helped to form it. Although Charles failed to win the Infanta, he received perhaps the most wonderful consolation prize in all history. Philip IV, the King of Spain, gave him *The Venus of Pardo* by Titian, now in the Louvre. Whilst in Spain, Charles was also quick to purchase the portrait of the Emperor Charles V by Titian, and it may have been the stimulus of seeing the Spanish collection that impelled him to send post-haste to Genoa, where the great Raphael cartoons were being offered for sale. These were needed for another royal enterprise – the foundation and encouragement of the Mortlake tapestry factory. No prince interested in the arts could fail to wish to have his own source of supply, and James I wished to wrest this monopoly from the

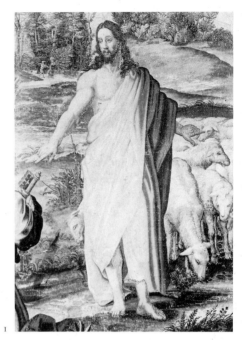

1

1 Detail of Christ from one of the tapestries woven at Mortlake from Raphael's designs. Mobilier National, Paris.
2 Raphael, *The Miraculous Draught of Fishes*, one of the original cartoons, now on loan to the Victoria and Albert Museum, London

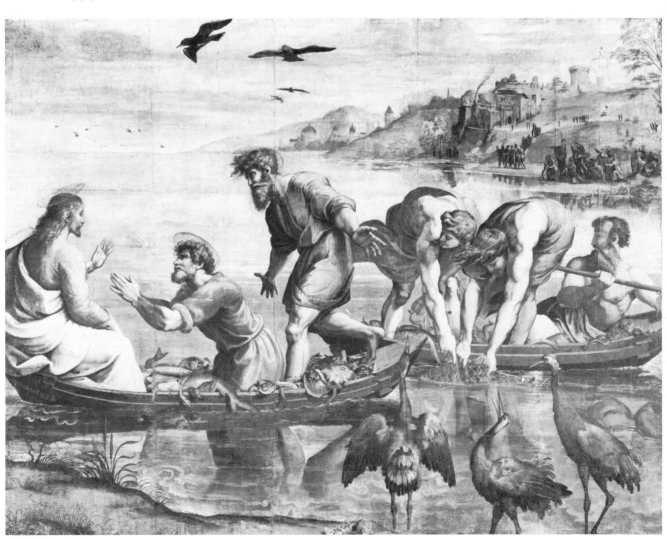

2

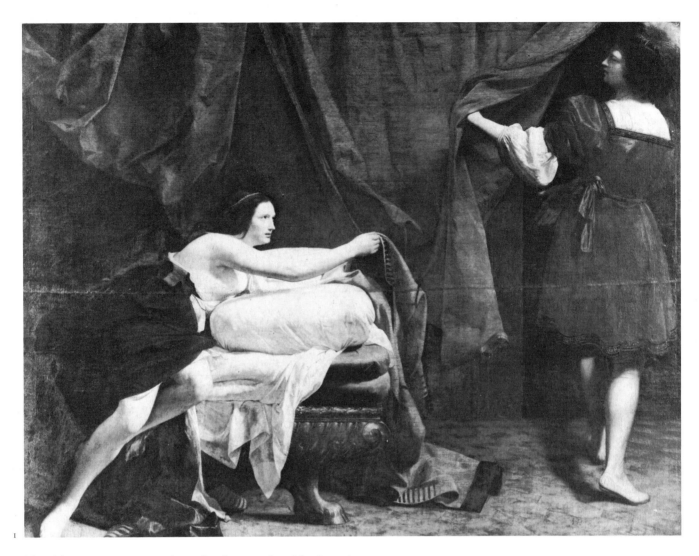

Flemish weavers. For a time the factory flourished, and many great tapestries were woven, including sets from the Raphael cartoons.

Charles returned from Spain by way of Paris, where he found his bride, Henrietta Maria, a catholic sister of the King of France, then only fourteen years old.

Although the marriage, two years later in 1625, began somewhat uneasily – perhaps due to the King's diffidence, it developed into a deep and abiding relationship. What was unusual in a seventeenth-century monarch, Charles I remained entirely faithful to his wife. Henrietta Maria was comely, rather than beautiful; cultivated, rather than intelligent; she, too, became deeply attached to her husband. They enjoyed domesticity. In 1630 Charles, Prince of Wales, was born and other children rapidly followed. Above all, they shared a common vision of life. A deeply sincere catholic, Henrietta Maria embedded the seeds of her religion in her children; most of them became catholic in later life, and in James II's case it ruined his reign.

Charles I lived and died in the Church of England, but was drawn to a ritualistic anglicanism whose ceremonies and vestments were so close to the practice of Rome that many of his calvinistically inclined subjects could see little difference. Indeed, these suspicions were strengthened when Henrietta Maria was given the use of the Queen's Chapel in St James's, newly designed by Inigo Jones – small, beautifully proportioned, noble rather than grand, where for the first time in England since

1 Orazio Gentileschi, *Joseph and Potiphar's Wife*.
2 The Queen's Chapel, St James's Palace. Built by Inigo Jones and given over by King Charles I to his Catholic wife, Henrietta Maria, for her use

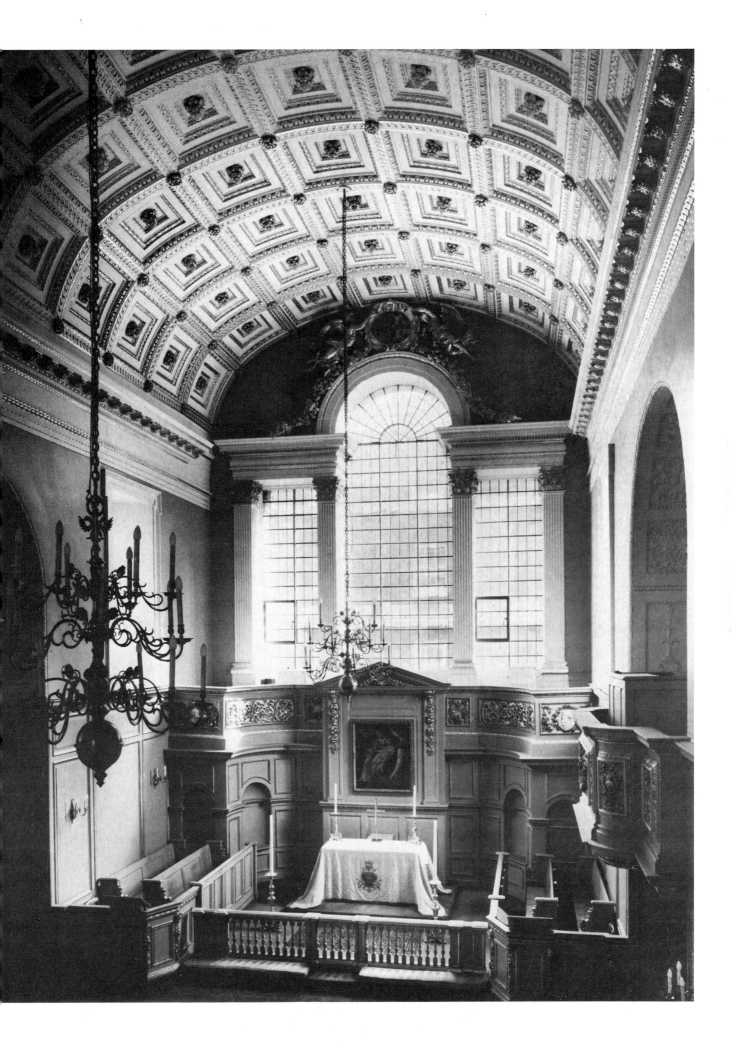

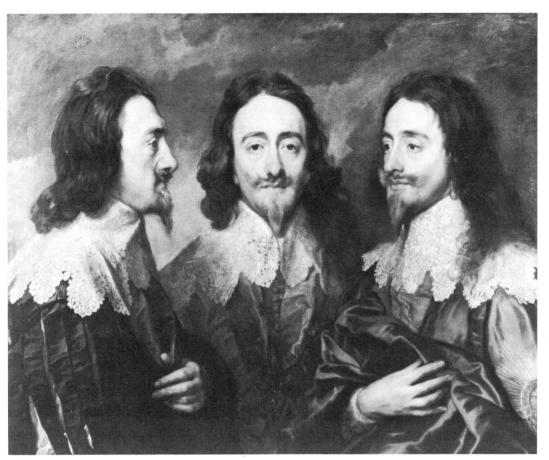

Sir Anthony van Dyck, *Charles I in Three Positions*. 1635. The King wears the ribbon and the star of the Garter – this was the likeness Bernini worked from when carving his portrait bust of the King

Mary's reign the catholic mass was said daily by priests. This heightened the suspicions of many men that the court was sliding towards Rome, suspicions that were strengthened when Rome itself saw an opportunity which it might exploit to its advantage. Even if they could not convert the King, they might at least try to ease the position of English catholics. Intriguers and flatterers soon found their way to court to exert pressures of every kind, and Rome did not forget the passionate interest which the King had in the arts. In 1635, for example, a group of pictures was sent over as a present to the King and Queen. From this relationship with Rome were born the great works of art that sprang from a collaboration between Van Dyck and Bernini. The Pope's nephew, Cardinal Barberini, commissioned Bernini to do a bust of Charles, alas lost in the great fire that destroyed Whitehall Palace in 1698, although fortunately a copy still exists at Windsor. In order that the artist could make this bust, Van Dyck painted Charles I's head in three positions – full face, half face, and profile. This magnificent triple portrait remained in the Barberini Palace until the early nineteenth century. George IV bought it in 1822. The bust delighted the Queen; for its exquisite artistry, for its likeness, and for the image it projected of Charles as King. These artistic links between Rome and London infuriated puritan pamphleteers, like the notorious William Prynne, who was to lose his ears for denouncing the Queen's passion for the theatre; he roundly denounced these attempts 'to seduce the King himself with pictures, antiquities, images and other vanities brought from Rome'. And this overt catholicism, this friendliness with Rome by the court in a deeply protestant country, offended men of power as much as the mob. Not that all seductions came from Rome. The Dutch, keenly protestant, were just as eager to pander to Charles's love

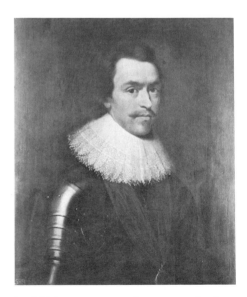

Daniel Mytens, *George Villiers, First Duke of Buckingham. c.* 1620–2. A favourite of James I and Charles I, and a lavish collector of works of art

of pictures. In 1636, to sweeten the King during discussions of improved Anglo-Dutch relations, they gave him five pictures including an *Adam and Eve* by Mabuse. However, the Dutch gift did not win Charles from his sympathy for his wife's religion. He had little use for calvinists, who were causing him enough trouble in his parliaments.

The King and Queen created for themselves a crystal world, an ideal arcadian court where peace and virtue reigned. But many members of parliament could only see luxury and extravagance. What irritated many close-fisted Puritans (and inflation and a sluggish economy gave them every right to close their fists) was the money spent on the Queen. She took over the Queen's House at Greenwich, which Inigo Jones had begun for Anne of Denmark; the result was the exquisite building we see today, in what was then the foreign (Italian Palladian) fashion. She patronised Orazio Gentileschi and his daughter, Artemesia, whose vigorous self-portrait is still in the royal collection. They had worked for the Queen of France, Marie de Medici, and had been drawn to London through the patronage of the Duke of Buckingham. The Duke's influence, at this time, was paramount in art as well as politics. Certainly he never discouraged spending, either by himself or by the King. In 1627, when his influence was at its height, Charles I began negotiations for his most spectacular purchase – the collection of the Duke of Mantua, which contained some of the greatest works of the Italian Renaissance – antique and renaissance sculpture as well as paintings, the results of a century's discerning patronage by the Gonzaga family. It included pictures by Titian, Raphael, Andrea del Sarto, Caravaggio, Correggio and the magnificent Mantegna cartoons of *The Triumph of Caesar*. These have recently been cleaned and are now, in spite of damage, much as they must have been when Charles I saw them unpacked. The greatest assembly of Italian art in the western countries bordering the Atlantic had been created at one stroke. Together with his Dutch and Flemish pictures, the

1 The Crouching Venus. A Roman copy of a Greek original. British Museum, London.

2 Page from the pictorial inventory of the statues in King Charles I's collection at Whitehall which were acquired from the Duke of Mantua in 1627. It includes the Crouching Venus

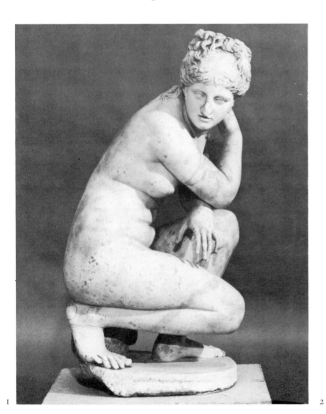

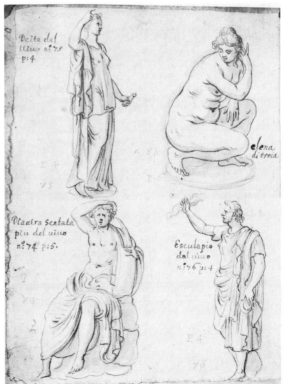

Dürers (which were to come to him as presents from Nuremberg) and the inheritance from his ancestors, Charles I, by 1635, owned the finest collection of art ever assembled by a British monarch. These great works adorned the royal palaces – Whitehall, Richmond, Hampton Court, Nonsuch, Oatlands, Greenwich, and the Queen's palace at Somerset House, which was pulled down in the eighteenth century.

These are the years which have been immortalised by Rubens's pupil, Anthony van Dyck, after him the greatest Flemish painter of his day. Arriving in London in 1632, he acquired a fine but jealous mistress, Margaret Lemon, whose lovely portrait by him is in the royal collection. Tempestuous and passionate, she threatened, according to Hollar, to bite his thumb off so that he could not paint. Had she done so, her exquisite body might not have been immortalised, for it has been suggested that she was the model for Psyche in his *Cupid and Psyche* – the most evidently Titianesque of Van Dyck's compositions for his patron. Perhaps because they were both tiny men, and more importantly because they shared a mutual admiration for Titian, the monarch and the painter quickly took to each other – and Van Dyck, knighted, was set up in a fine house by the King. Very much a courtier, he understood the inwardness of the King's vision of monarchy, and caught brilliantly 'the Majestie and Decorum of State'. His portraits of the King, his wife and his family have strong resonances of Rubens and of Titian; the poses, too, are often traditional, yet they are done with new and ravishing elegance of style. He painted three outstanding large portraits of the King, great works of art. Many critics prefer *Charles I à la Chasse*, where the King is in an unconventional pose, standing by his horse, held by a groom. The draughtsmanship is magnificent and texture brilliant; others, and I agree, prefer Charles on horseback, which hung at the end of the long gallery at Whitehall. It appeared as if the King himself were riding into the gallery. The picture reeks with a lofty regality, a mild arrogance combined with elegant serenity. The King's expression is touched with sadness – seeming to presage the dark and tragic future, and yet at the time these pictures were painted the future was bright with hope. In these portraits one sees a man who accepts calmly and with dignity the fact that, though still human, he is above all other mortal men. Again, the famous picture with his wife, although alive with affection, also possesses a sense of distance from common humanity. In these pictures of the King, Van Dyck projected the image of Charles I which has lasted until our own time. And it is essential to stress that, no matter how artificial or mannered Charles might seem to us, or to his critical subjects, there is an obvious sincerity in his face and in his carriage that expresses a truth about dedicated kingship that is most moving. In Van Dyck's subtle art Charles's courtiers are seen to be elegant, serene, with the mild and polished arrogance of men secure in their elevated states. How right the Banqueting House was for these creatures; how natural for them to dance and masque and behave as if they were men apart!

Long before he had reached middle age, Charles I had made his court a great centre of European art; indeed Rubens said of Whitehall Palace, 'When it comes to fine pictures I have never seen such a large number in one place as in the royal palace.' This was in 1630 when he was engaged in diplomatic negotiations with the English government, for Rubens was a diplomat as well as a painter, and was knighted by Charles on this

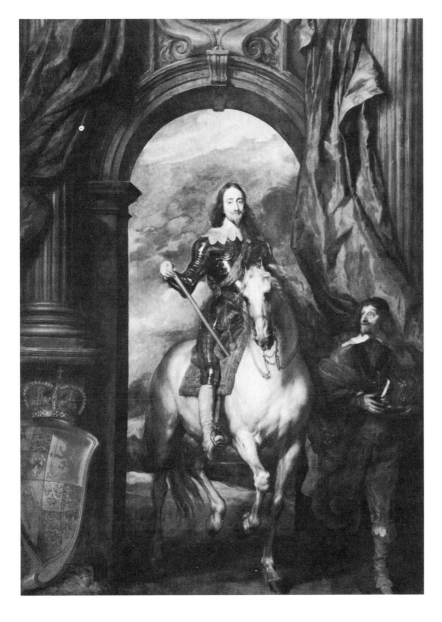

Sir Anthony van Dyck, *Charles I with M. de St Antoine*, the King's equerry. 1633

occasion as a tribute to his standing as an ambassador. He appreciated Rubens's art more than his diplomacy, and he was to acquire Rubens's outstanding painting, *St George and the Dragon*. St George, as the patron saint of England should, is fighting in the Thames Valley. All the haunting qualities of the English countryside, which Rubens thought to be of exceptional beauty, are impressionistically evoked by the artist.

During the first few years of his reign, Charles I was far more successful at collecting art than practising politics. His private world of divinely blessed monarchy was at variance, and sharply so, with what many men of influence felt they wanted of monarchy. Racked by inflation, terrified of popery, burdened with taxes, suspicious of luxury, detesting show and finery, they did not take kindly to Charles I's court. They were increasingly suspicious of his friendliness with the catholic powers of Europe. The King's ministers and friends, who took care of his business in the Lords and Commons, found parliament, during these years 1625–29, too intractable to manage; indeed, the opposition there became so menacing that in 1629 Charles dissolved parliament and decided to rule without it. He did not call another parliament until 1640.

During these eleven years of personal rule, the King withdrew more and more into a private world, isolated himself from bitter social and political reality, and became insensitive to the opinions of many of his subjects, including a great many men of power and influence. To support the splendour of his court, he was forced to exercise exceptional ingenuity in taxes, reviving the distraint of knighthood, by which men of very small estate either had to become knights or pay a fine, and old forest laws which had long fallen into disuse. Their revival caused increasing bitterness and as in the famous case of John Hampden, who refused to pay Ship Money, direct confrontation. The expensive masques of these years, their cost high enough but wildly exaggerated through gossip, rumour and malice, fanned the flames of discontent. And yet the opposition to the King was largely impotent. Without parliament there were few ways of attacking the court, and Charles acquired a false sense of security and of successful government.

In the decades before the Civil War and during it, many of the men and women of the Court were painted by some of the greatest miniaturists of all time – Nicholas Hilliard, Isaac and Peter Oliver, John Hoskins, and Samuel Cooper. And the miniaturists themselves show a developing psychological subtlety. Hilliard, true to his Elizabethan fame, is more ikon-like than his followers. The Olivers show a great concern with character. The most subtle of all, however, was Samuel Cooper, who lived through the turbulence of civil war and commonwealth, that testing time of men's characters, when tragedy struck many and unbelievable success, as with Cromwell, came to a few. Like their King, Charles's courtiers loved to give and receive tokens of friendship and love; miniatures were so easy to carry on journeys, or from house to house, from palace to palace.

Palace to palace. When bitter civil war broke out in 1641, and brought an end to masques, and the artificial life of the court, Charles still dreamed of a palace that would outshine the Louvre and the Escurial. Unbelievably, even after defeat in 1647, according to the architect John Webb, he was still discussing the rebuilding of Whitehall Palace, which would reflect his concept of monarchy, a concept shattered by the bloody civil war that had overwhelmed the country, often splitting families, dividing father and son, setting brother against brother. The civil war was the most desperate social upheaval this country has known in modern times; at the time probably the most traumatic experience since the Norman Conquest. Forced from London, Charles set up his court at Oxford. As defeat followed defeat, and the hopes of victory faded, harsh reality must have pressed in upon him. The brilliant life of the cavalier court over, the mood of nostalgia and defeat is beautifully evoked in these words by G. M. Trevelyan about St John's College, Oxford: 'They strolled through the garden, as the hopeless evenings fell, listening, at the end of all, while the siege guns broke the silence with ominous iteration. Behind the cannon on those low hills to northward were ranked the inexorable men who came to lay their hands on all this beauty, hoping to change it to strength and sterner virtue.' And in the portraits which William Dobson painted at this time the same elegiac note is struck.

Artificial, proud, exquisitely elegant and outrageously expensive Charles and his court had been; but the court was also very virtuous, very high-minded, deeply religious. It was the religion, no matter how

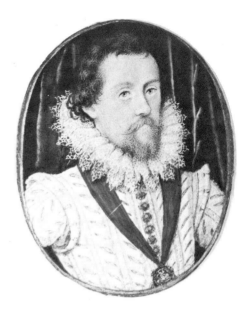

Nicholas Hilliard, *King James I*

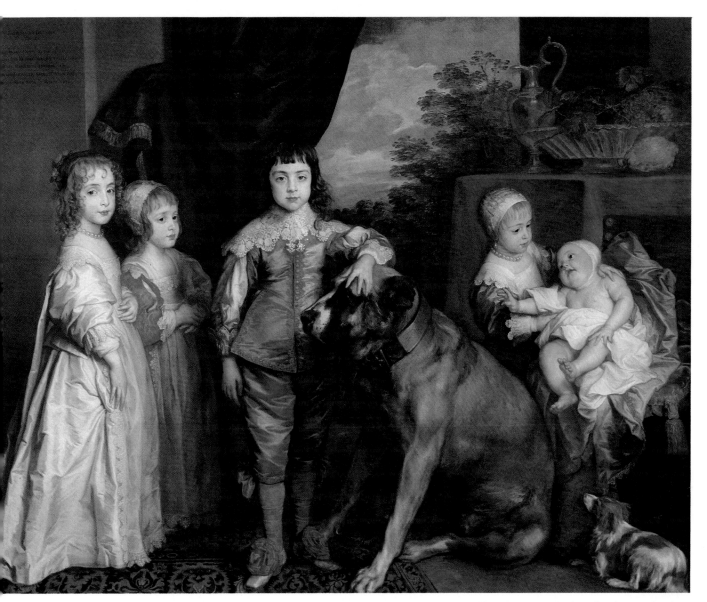

Sir Anthony van Dyck, *The Five Eldest Children of Charles I.* 1637. Princess Mary and Prince James stand beside Prince Charles who rests his hand on the head of a large dog. Princess Elizabeth is holding the infant Princess Anne

From 1632 until his death in 1641, Sir Anthony van Dyck worked above all for King Charles I and a great deal of his time was taken up with portraits of members of the royal family and of the court. The royal collection is still rich in Van Dycks (26 in all). Perhaps the finest, the portrait of Thomas Killigrew and (?) Lord Crofts reproduced on page 153, was acquired by Frederick, Prince of Wales, in the eighteenth century. The paintings reproduced here and on the following three pages were returned to the Royal Collection at the time of the Restoration

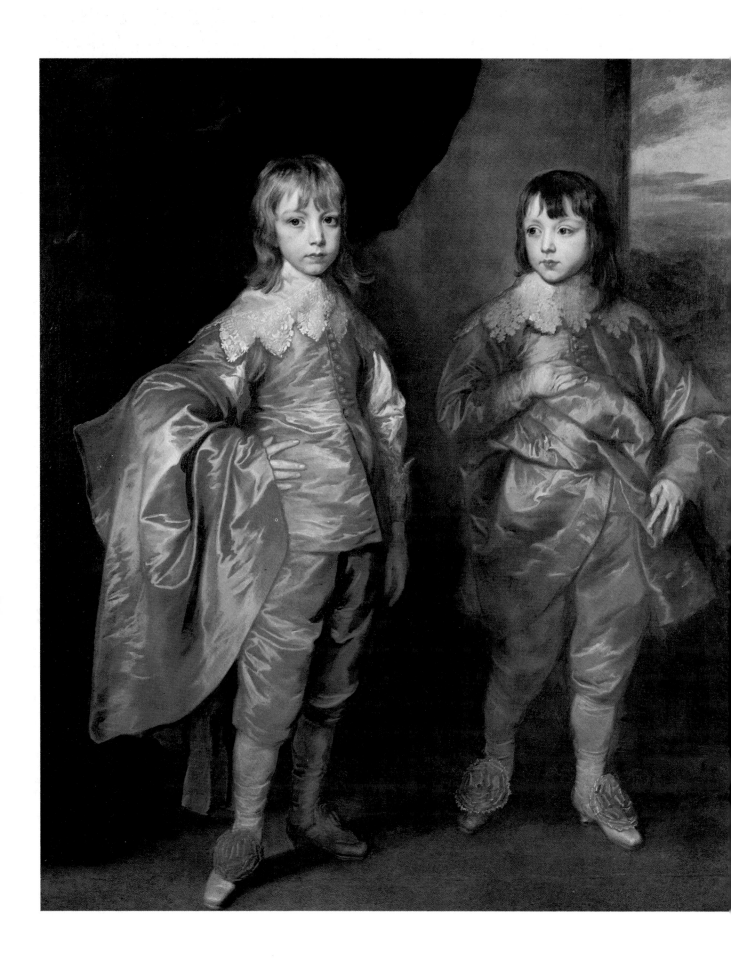

Sir Anthony van Dyck, *George Villiers, Second Duke of Buckingham, and Lord Francis Villiers.* 1635

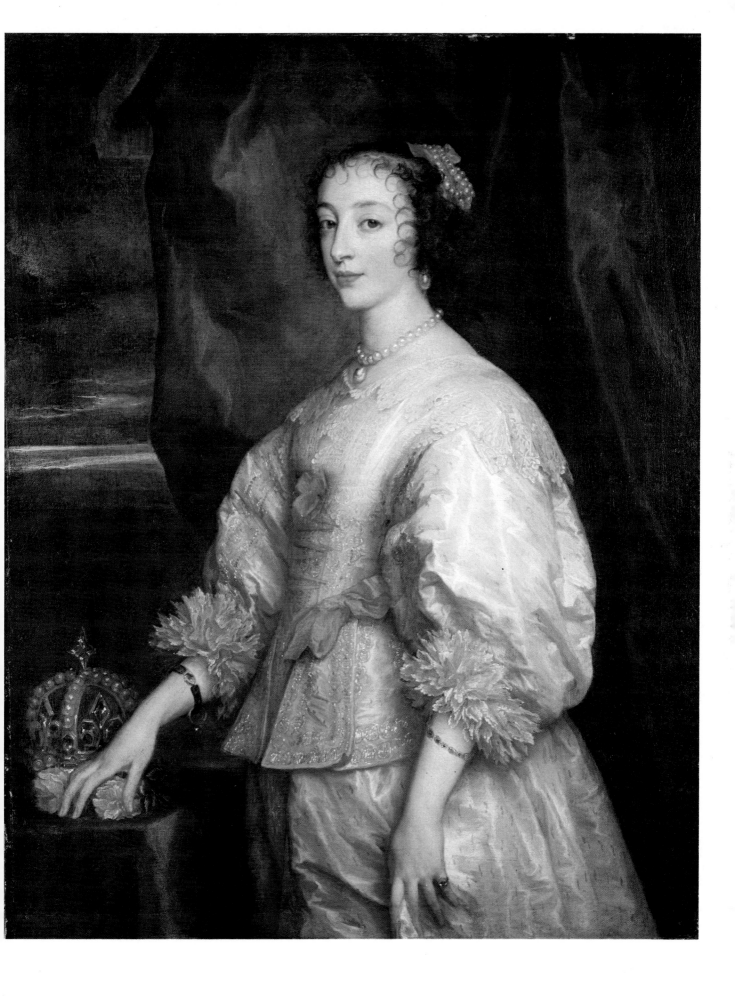

Sir Anthony van Dyck, *Henrietta Maria*

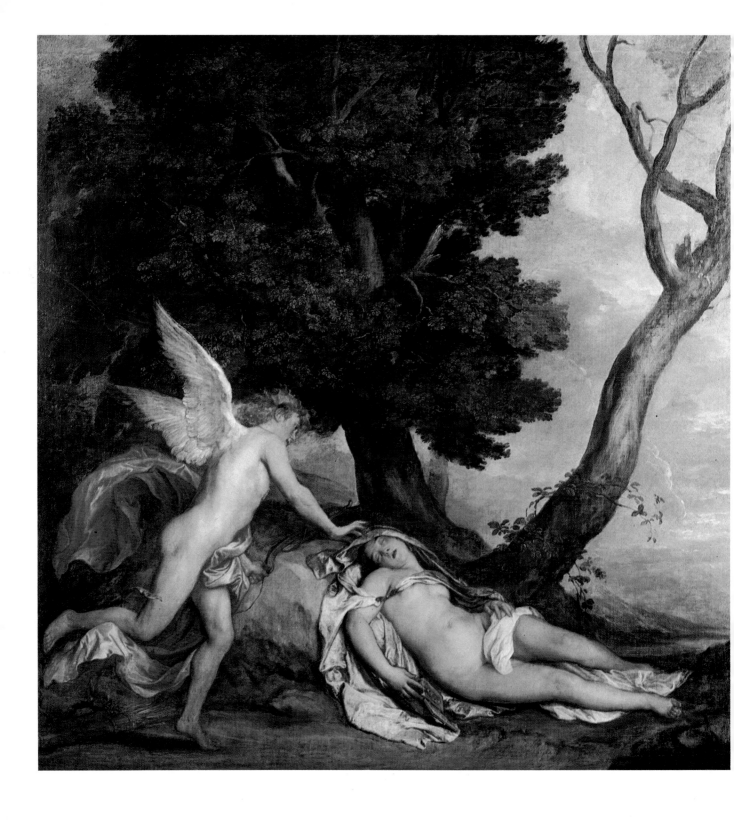

Sir Anthony van Dyck, *Cupid and Psyche*. c. 1639–40

deeply felt, of the aesthete – the beauty of holiness, in which ceremony and music, vestments discreet yet beautiful, movements of respect performed with grace, were a part of daily ritual. To the puritan the sin was in the beauty, in things outward, not inward and spiritual.

Forced to leave Oxford, and wandering almost aimlessly in search of friends and supporters, Charles came briefly to the church of Little Gidding, where the Ferrar family, under the leadership of Nicolas Ferrar, had created a religious community that embodied Archbishop Laud's concept of 'the beauty of holiness'. Archbishop Laud's church – the anathema of the puritans who regarded it as utterly popish – was the one true expression for them of the Anglican religion. And here, in the quiet Huntingdonshire countryside, Charles found solace. His religious sincerity was absolute. Captured by his enemy at last, and strictly confined to Carisbrooke Castle on the Isle of Wight, he read and annotated his Bible for his son. He believed that he was dying a martyr for his church; his belief stiffened his arrogance, as well as his spirit. On the day of his execution his great statement of regal faith, *Eikon Basilike*, was published. There he wrote: 'Well, God's will be Done. I doubt not, but my Innocency finds Him both my Protector and my Advocate who is my only Judge, whom I own as King of Kings.' In Charles's view, only God might judge kings, and to him his trial by parliament in the name of the people of England was a treasonable farce.

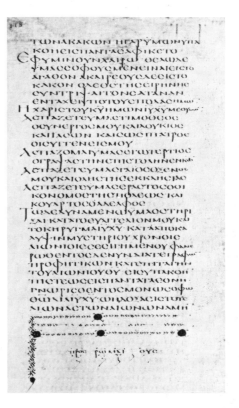

Detail from the *Codex Alexandrinus*. Early fifth century. One of the most magnificent of all manuscripts of the Bible, written in silver on purple vellum and presented to Charles I by Cyril Lucar, Patriarch of Constantinople. British Library, London

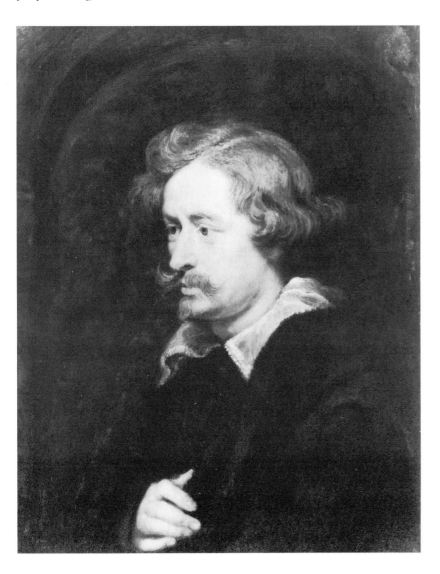

Sir Peter Paul Rubens, *Portrait of Van Dyck*. First recorded in the inventory of Charles II

Not so for Oliver Cromwell and his army, who fought, defeated, tried and executed the King. To them God had obviously shown His favour, spoken in a clear voice in battle. And their God did not like baubles. Indeed, one of the more ardent supporters of parliament, William Dowsing, went on a rampage, chopping off the carved angels from the roof trusses of the parish churches, and smashing with holy delight medieval stained-glass windows. To such men, the King's pictures, sculptures, tapestries and bronzes were 'vanities', unseemly in a godly commonwealth. Also, the commonwealth was uncommonly short of money, and gold, jewels, anything that could be turned quickly into money, were valuable and dispensable. The first £30,000 was desperately needed by the treasurer of the navy to pay the sailors. The royal regalia was dispatched to the mint, the gold of the crowns, sceptres and orbs melted down, the jewels sold off – to the great glee of the poet, George Withers, who stuck St Edward's crown on his head and cavorted around Westminster Abbey when the trustees for the sale were examining the crown jewels. He burst out into rhyme:

'We have seen the pride of Kings,
    with these much desired things,
Whence their vain ambition springs,
    Scorn'd, despis'd, and set at naught.
We their silk, their pearls, their gold
And their precious Jemms behold
    Scattred, pawned, bought and sold;
And to shame, their glory brought.'

However, the furnishings, the carpets, the armour, the books, let alone the vast collection of paintings, were a much more complex matter than the regalia, or the plate, which had also been melted down. It was decided to sell them off by auction, but the proceedings were lengthy and the emergence of Oliver Cromwell as Lord Protector made it necessary to retain some royal buildings and possessions in order to provide a proper stateliness for Britain's ruler. He favoured Hampton Court and Whitehall; Windsor was turned into an army barracks, and St James's Palace housed the royal library. The intention, never realised, was to set up a public library, with this great collection of books which had been begun by Edward IV. It contained over a thousand manuscripts, including the *Codex Alexandrinus*, one of the earliest manuscripts of the Bible, given to Charles I by the Patriarch of Constantinople. Many other rare manuscripts, some Saxon, had been rescued by John Leland for Henry VIII at the dissolution of the monasteries. The printed books, many of them from the earliest days of printing in England, were almost as precious as the manuscripts, and included Henry VIII's own copy of the tract against Luther, which, as we have seen, earned him the title of 'Defender of the Faith'. In the end this royal library did become public property when, in 1757, George II presented it to the recently founded British Museum, one of the many magnificent gifts from the English monarchy to that institution.

Unfortunately there was never any intention to set up a public art gallery or museum. That would have been quite contrary to strict puritan principles, for they disapproved of mythological paintings, pictures of saints or the Holy Family, and all female nakedness. And so the great dispersal of paintings began. The great European collectors

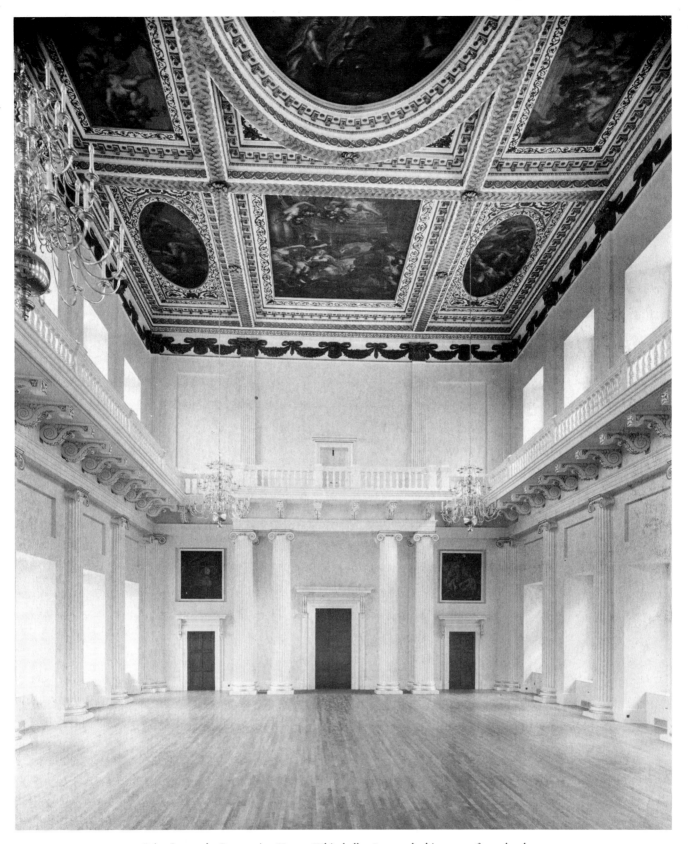

Inigo Jones, the Banqueting House, Whitehall, 1619–22, looking away from the throne

Inigo Jones (1573–1652), John Webb (1611–72) and Sir Christopher Wren (1632–1723) span the Stuart reigns. Jones established classical architecture in England: the Queen's House, Greenwich, the Queen's Chapel at St James's and the Banqueting House, Whitehall were all royal commissions. His nephew by marriage, John Webb, worked both with him and Wren. Wren worked for the crown at Hampton Court, Greenwich and Chelsea – where he designed the Royal Hospital

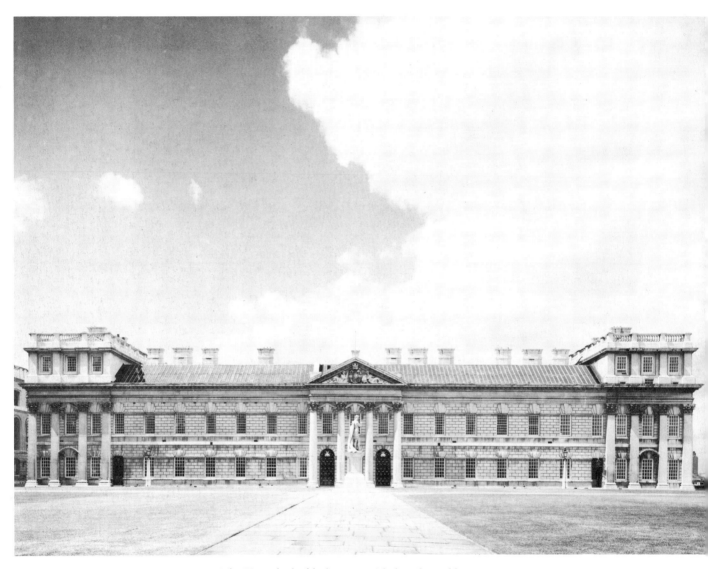

The King Charles block, Greenwich, by John Webb. 1662–9

The Fountain Court, Hampton Court, by Sir
Christopher Wren. Wren began alterations to
Hampton Court for King William III in 1689

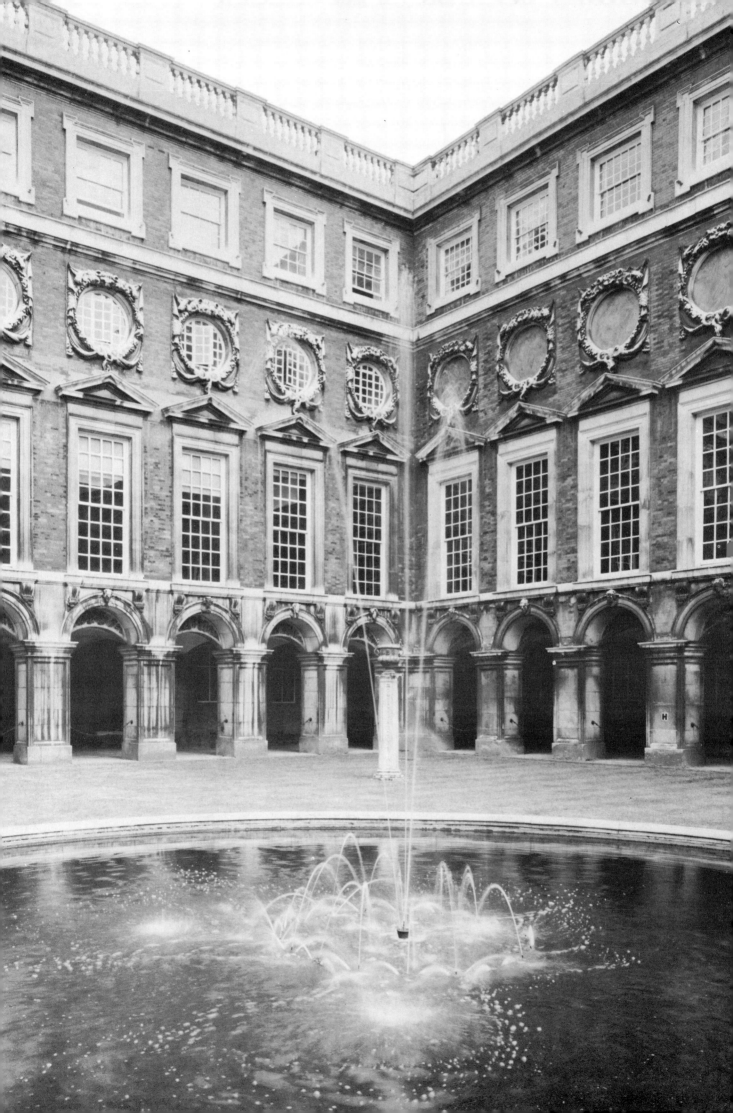

realised their splendid opportunity. Both the King of Spain and Cardinal Mazarin, the chief minister of France, sent their agents, who secured what are now some of the greatest treasures of the Prado and the Louvre. However, many London dealers and artists, such as Emanuel de Critz, snapped up what they could; de Critz, who formed a syndicate to buy a large number of the King's pictures, was said to have three rooms full of works of art, including the famous Bernini bust. Others went to citizens and noblemen who bought in the hope of further profit or of better times. A vast amount were sold – not only works of art and the furnishings of the palaces, but also the royal armour. We must be grateful to Edward Annesley, the keeper of the stores at the Tower, who purchased the splendid armour made at Greenwich for Charles I and his young son, Charles, Prince of Wales; they can be seen today in the armoury of the White Tower.

Grievous as the losses were, they might have been worse. Mantegna's *The Triumph of Caesar* was valued, offered for sale, and then, fortunately, withdrawn and kept at Hampton Court, maybe because no buyers for such huge canvases could be found, maybe because they were wanted for Cromwell, who can scarcely have been unmoved by the subject. They were sent to his Chamberlain at Whitehall in 1653, and their powerful representation of overwhelming military force can scarcely have failed to attract him. It may be, too, that Cromwell preserved the great tapestries, which told the story of the defeat of the Armada, for he was a passionate admirer of the power and vigour of Elizabethan England. Unfortunately these masterpieces were burnt in the great fire that destroyed the old Houses of Parliament in 1834. In all £20,000 worth of goods were reserved for official use – mainly for Whitehall Palace, which Cromwell used a great deal. In 1656 John Evelyn described it as 'very glorious and well furnished'. Even so, the loss to England was incalculable; one of the greatest collections of Renaissance art had been broken up forever.

From the moment that Charles I's head was struck from his shoulders in 1649, Britain drifted slowly but certainly back towards monarchical government. Cromwell, in the last years of his life, was as near to being a king as a man could be, short of coronation. And when Charles II finally returned as king, in 1660, the country went delirious with joy. The corporations of cities and the great companies of the city of London expressed their delight in the most practical way by sending him presents of silver plate of regal quality. Exeter Corporation sent a magnificent salt, Plymouth a splendid combined water fountain and perfume burner. Salts proved popular, for the King received eleven more. Nor was his need for plate for the Chapel Royal forgotten – some corporation or guild, we do not know which, sent a beautiful chalice and paten in gold. Because of the destruction that went before, this is the oldest plate of any magnitude in the royal collection.

Thirty years of age at his restoration, he was totally different from his father in temperament as well as physique. Six feet tall, with the long, saturnine, deeply-lined face of a man amused by the ironies of life, he had no intention of recreating his father's image of monarchy, no matter how much he longed for a strong and powerful government based upon himself and his brother, James, Duke of York. His boyhood and youth had been a series of defeats and humiliations. A child of twelve when the

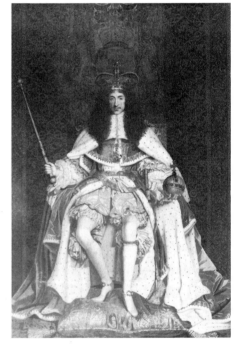

John Michael Wright, *King Charles II* (detail)

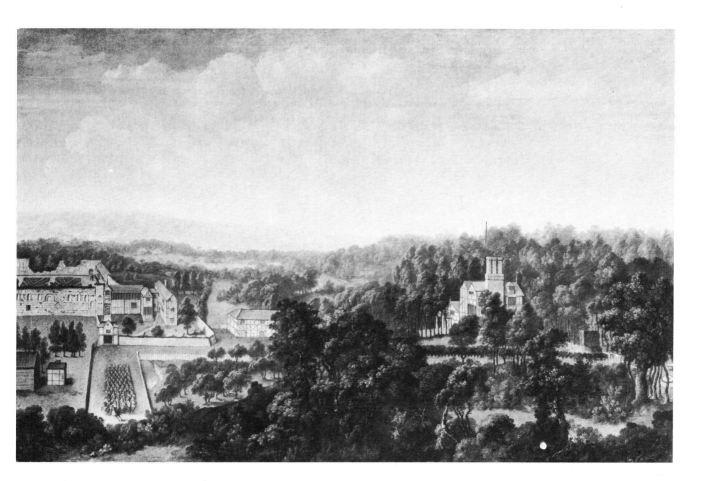

civil war broke out, he had nonetheless donned his armour and fought for the royalist cause. He had lived through the tragedy of his father's death. He had accepted the harsh terms of the Scottish covenantors, becoming a presbyterian before he was crowned their king at Scone. He had made a bold bid, in 1651, to win back England, only to suffer a most crushing and humiliating defeat at Worcester. He just escaped capture, hiding in the famous oak tree at Boscobel, living in priests' holes, travelling in the humblest disguises, until he got away to France. That traumatic escape haunted him, and he told the story of it over and over again, to the point of becoming a bore. After his restoration he commissioned Streeter to paint a curious picture, symbolic rather than topographical, of Boscobel and Whiteladies, his two major hiding places, in fact some miles apart but brought together in one picture. Engraved by Hollar it sold in hundreds. Pamphlets and ballads celebrated the story of the escape, and the royal oak became a favourite tavern sign. As one might expect, it became a symbol to which Charles II was firmly attached, and when he came to rebuild Windsor, he incorporated the motif in the plaster of the ceilings. In the long, shabby years of exile that followed the escape to France, Charles II was a royal pauper drifting from court to court, living in hope, cajoling with promises, sustained by his gusto for life and his strong, physical appetites.

Back on the throne, he wanted to enjoy what had been returned to him. He preferred to rebuild the authority of the crown slowly and subtly; to bind men of power to him in a hundred ways, from direct bribes to mere affability. No monarch has possessed a finer sense of the dimension of time in politics than Charles II. He was quite happy to mock and deride the tastes of the puritans, to stress the delights of life, to rule with unbuttoned ease, a public, not a private king. He preferred to go with a few cronies to Drury Lane, rather than sit through elaborate masques at court. He patronised actors, and fell in love with actresses. He discovered at Drury Lane the beautiful Nell Gwynn, the orange girl whose son he made a Duke. He had a passion for women, yet he remained on very good terms with his barren wife, Catherine of Braganza, and was unfailingly kind to her. He was kinder still to his succession of mistresses and their bastards, showering them with titles and, when he could lay his hands on it, money.

Charles II might cultivate an air of easy familiarity about his court, but he needed to keep up a proper state. His exile had given him a knowledge of the splendour of the courts of France, Spain and the Netherlands. He had also spent some time at the court of his aunt, Elizabeth of Bohemia, who, through her vivacity and charm, had drawn about her a highly sophisticated circle, many of them patrons of the arts. Although not a compulsive collector like his father, nor so great a connoisseur, Charles II loved pictures, and was keen to embellish the emptied palaces to which he had been restored. And naturally enough he was determined to recover whatever he could of his father's collection.

Three weeks before he landed in England, on 30 May 1660, parliament had set up a committee to search for Charles I's goods. Some very famous pictures and bronzes were quickly recovered. Francis Tryon, a merchant of London, had bought several pictures in the hope, one day, of presenting them to Charles II, including 'one raerre peese of the present King, the Princes Royall, the Duek of Yarcke, the Prinses Elizabett holding haer Suster the Prinsesse Anna upan haer lap, all in one peese, of Sir Antonio V'dike'. Unfortunately this picture did not remain for very long in the royal collection. James II probably gave it to his mistress, the Countess of Dorchester, and George III had to pay 500 guineas to get it back from her descendants. Other Van Dycks were among those in Emmanuel de Critz's three rooms of pictures. Peter Lely, whom Charles II, shortly after his accession, made the king's painter, possessed others. Many statues – difficult to identify, were recovered, and even some embroidery. Edmund Harrison, the late King's embroiderer, who lived in Grub Street, had got hold of a cloth of state, richly worked, and a fine carpet, that he claimed were worth £1000 – some £25,000 in modern money.

Important though the recoveries were, the gaps in the collection were enormous, and many of the finest old masters were irretrievably lost to the collection – sold abroad or untraceable. Indeed, Charles II had realised that this would be so even before he sailed for England, and he had purchased in the Netherlands from a dealer, William Frizell, seventy-two pictures, including one or two Dutch paintings. Charles II also enjoyed a stroke of good fortune. The Dutch government, which had been at war with Cromwell, hoped to maintain peaceful relations with the restored monarchy, and as a token of their goodwill they made Charles a magnificent present of twenty-seven old masters, including Titian's *Man in Black Holding a Book* and a splendid Lorenzo Lotto, as well as eight fine oriental lacquer cabinets.

However, pictures and furnishings were not the only concern of Charles II. He also required regalia for his coronation: crown, orb, sceptre, swords of state, all had to be made. They cost the government

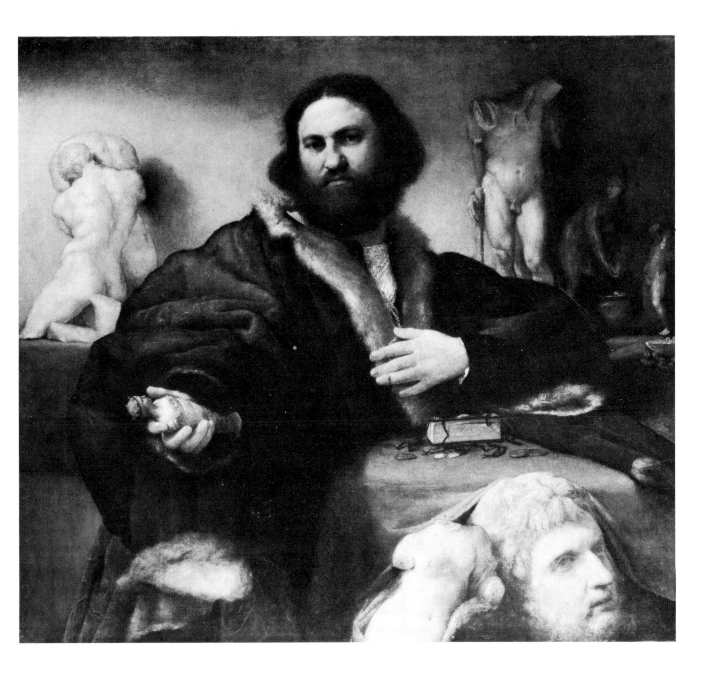

£31,978 9s 11d, and much is still used. The Queen's regalia were not made until 1685, when James II succeeded his brother, since at the time of the coronation Charles II was not married, and when he did Catherine of Braganza was never crowned.

Although remade, the regalia's form and symbolism stretched far back into the Dark Ages, as has been explained in Chapter I. Charles II's coronation caused almost as much hysterical delight as his first entry into London, but once securely on the throne the King became the target of much criticism, as the knowledge of his way of life spread through London. He flaunted his mistresses, especially Lady Castlemaine who made no secret of her relationship with the King; and he flaunted his bastard son, James Scott, whom he made Duke of Monmouth. He must have been delighted when his sister-in-law commissioned Sir Peter Lely to paint the leading beauties of the court. Pepys, who was greatly affected by Lady Castlemaine's charms, thought them 'good but not like'. Hazlitt later dismissed them as a 'set of kept mistresses, painted, tawdry', which was excessive. Certainly several of them had been targets for the amorous

Lorenzo Lotto, *Andrea Odoni*. Presented to King Charles II by the States General of Holland in 1660, together with works by Titian, Veronese, Tintoretto and others

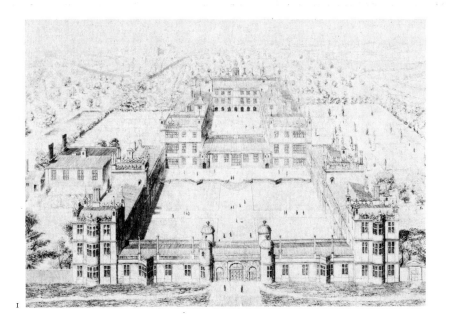

attentions of the King and his brother – not always with success – but some were entirely virtuous. What can be said is that all were beautiful, all skilfully painted, and that the pictures pleased James Duke of York. However, the most powerful and perhaps the most beautiful woman at Charles II's court is not amongst them – his French mistress, Louise de Kéroualle, Duchess of Portsmouth (her portrait in the Royal Collection is by the French artist Philippe Vignon), and she was the only one to exert real political influence over him. The others were for the bed, not the cabinet; Portsmouth graced both. His courtiers were as rakish as Charles II himself; some, like the notorious Earl of Rochester, who was banned from the court for writing an excessively obscene poem about the King, were even more licentious. Such wantonness upset not only the presbyterians, but also many anglicans, including Samuel Pepys who thought that the monarchy would fall into such disrepute that its very existence might be endangered. There was, however, conscious political art in Charles II's style of monarchy. He sensed that much of the country was sick of puritan prudery and repression. And he was right.

Charles I had withdrawn into a chaste, pious, highly aesthetic yet artificial Elysium. His son wanted to be close to his subjects. He would take walks in St James's Park – its privacy lost during the commonwealth to the citizens of London and never recovered – so that he could be seen, even approached. Many responded to his manner, secretly admiring his wenching, and the ballad singers did a good trade in the song 'In Good King Charles's Golden Days'. He was known familiarly to many as 'Old Rowley'.

Sauntering, theatre-going, the open relaxed life, all brought him closer to his people – and so did racing, which he patronised. He was to be seen frequently at Epsom. Like his grandfather, he preferred Newmarket, however, and built a small palace for himself there – all but the cellar has vanished long since; Nell Gwynn had a house close by, and the straight mile down the Devil's Dyke on Newmarket Heath is still called 'the Rowley Mile'. To stimulate racing he began the Royal Gold Plate races at Newmarket, a method also taken up by his niece, Queen Anne, who loved the turf and initiated Royal Ascot, with its splendid processions from Windsor to the course.

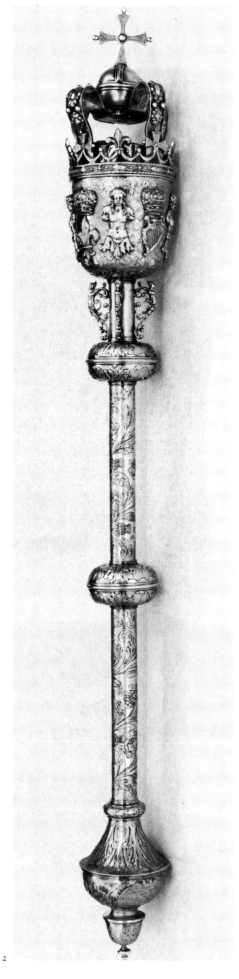

Apart from Whitehall, most of Charles II's palaces were badly dilapidated, and, with his love of racing, he decided in 1667 to buy Audley End – a vast house built by the Earls of Suffolk near Saffron Walden. He never really settled there, and although it remained a royal palace for the rest of the century, it was not greatly used. It was, unlike Windsor, just a little too remote from London, and not quite near enough to Newmarket. Until the railway and the telegraph made communication easy, it was very difficult for the monarchy to reside very far from London. Oddly enough, it had been far easier for the medieval kings who had taken their governments – including the treasury – around with them, moving in huge processions of cumbersome wagons. But government had become highly complex, stabilised in London, and daily decisions were frequently wanted from the King. For the same reason the project for a palace at Winchester, for which Sir Christopher Wren produced a design, never proceeded very far. Audley End, however, presages Sandringham and Osborne of later monarchs, a royal retreat, some distance from London.

Audley End proving unsuitable, not surprisingly Charles II set about making Windsor Castle truly habitable. He commissioned Hugh May to build a suite of apartments for himself and his Queen. This led to the old apartments of Edward III being gutted, but many of its walls were embedded in the new building. A century and a half later, George IV

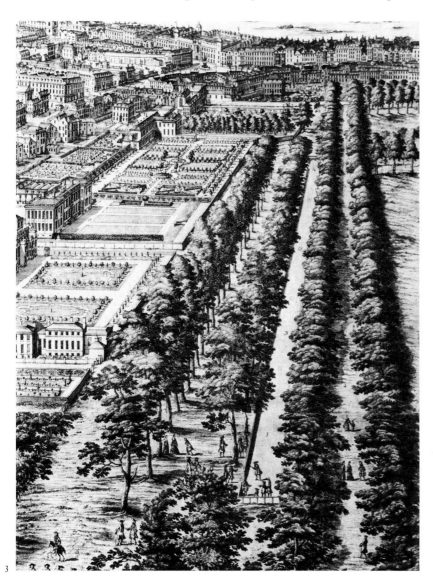

3

1 Engraving by Winstanley of Audley End, near Saffron Walden, which was built in 1667.

2 The Mace presented by Charles II to the Royal Society, and still in their possession.

3 *Vue et Prospective de la ville de Londre: Westminster et Parc St James*. Detail of an engraving by John Kip

remodelled these rooms again, but he left one or two of them intact so that it is possible to catch the flavour and style of Charles II's Windsor, particularly in the Queen's presence chamber, which possesses a splendid painted ceiling by the Italian artist, Verrio, and fine carvings by Grinling Gibbons. The Queen's audience chamber and the King's dining-room also retain their painted ceilings by Verrio. The theme of the paintings (a banquet of the Gods) and the carvings would betray the latter rooms' use, even if we did not know it. They abound with fruit, game, food in riotous variety. It was here that the King dined in public, and where anyone dressed as a gentleman and permitted by the guards could come and gape – a strange custom. This public eating by the monarch stretched back to the Dark Ages. But wherever the King and Queen went – Windsor, Whitehall, Hampton or Greenwich – they had to maintain this curious ceremony of eating their dinners by themselves, in public. Only in private could they sit and eat with other people.

Charles II possessed a keen visual sense and loved fine furniture, bronzes, medals, as well as paintings and drawings. Not much remains – a fine silver table, mirror and pair of candlestands, said to have been presented by the City of London in the early 1660s, a looking-glass, two distinguished cabinets in ebony, and little else. But fortunately his pictures, and above all his drawings, remain. Charles II may have made the greatest contribution of all to the royal collection – the collection

The Queen's Presence Chamber, Windsor. The ceiling was painted by Verrio, the carvings are by Grinling Gibbons

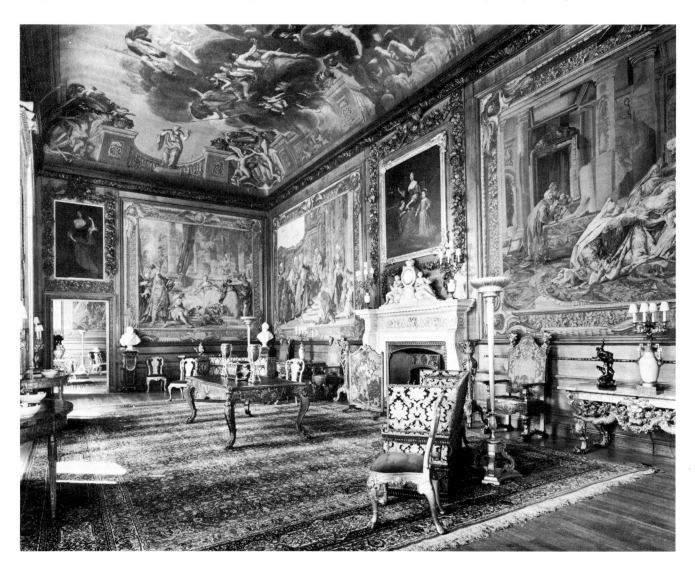

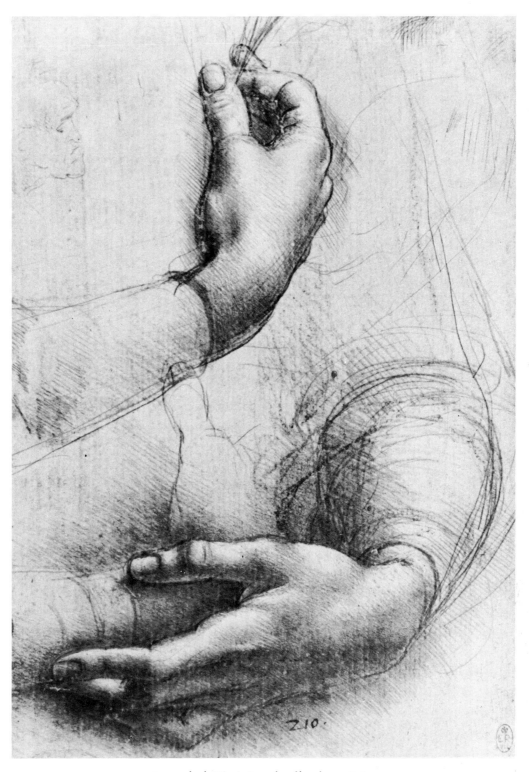

Leonardo da Vinci, A study of hands. 1478–80

The great collection of 779 drawings by Leonardo da Vinci, which is now in the Royal Library, Windsor, were
in the Royal Collection by 1690. It is thought they may have been acquired for King Charles II by Sir Peter Lely

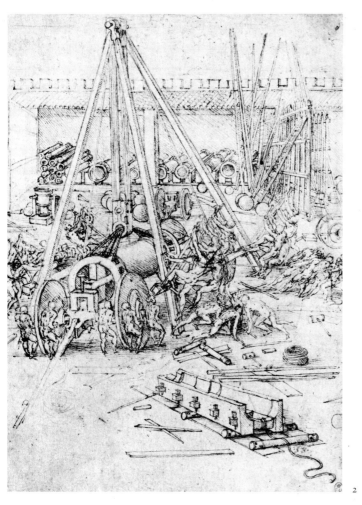

1

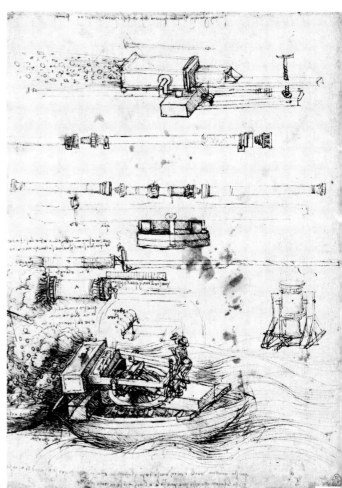

2

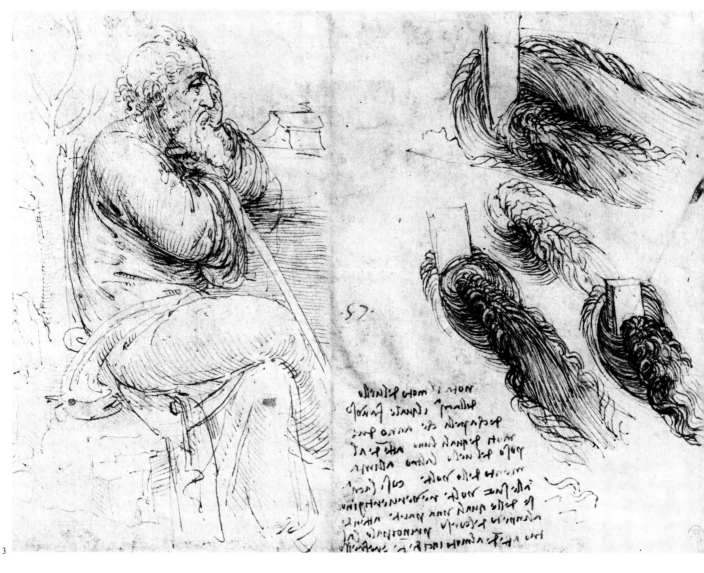

3

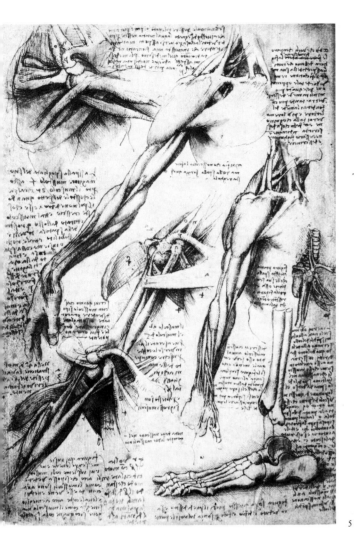

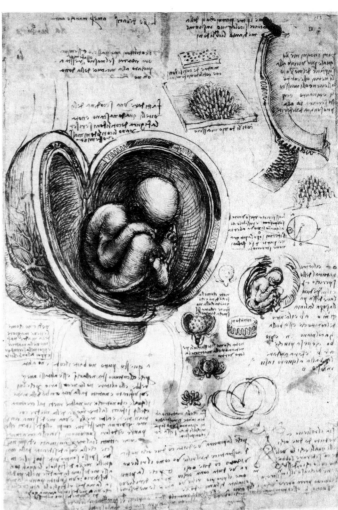

5

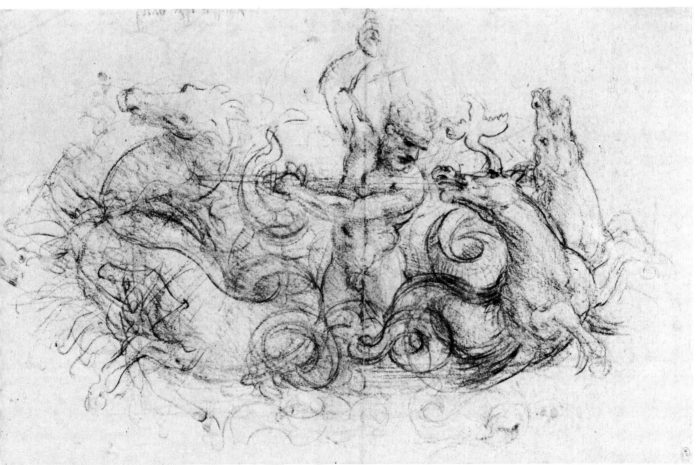

Drawings by Leonardo da Vinci: 1 A gun foundry. *c.* 1487. 2 Mortars and a gun cradle. *c.* 1485. 3 An old man meditating and studies of swirling water. *c.* 1510. 4 Dissection of a man's arm. *c.* 1510. 5 Cross-section of a womb. *c.* 1510. 6 Neptune and sea-horses. *c.* 1503/4

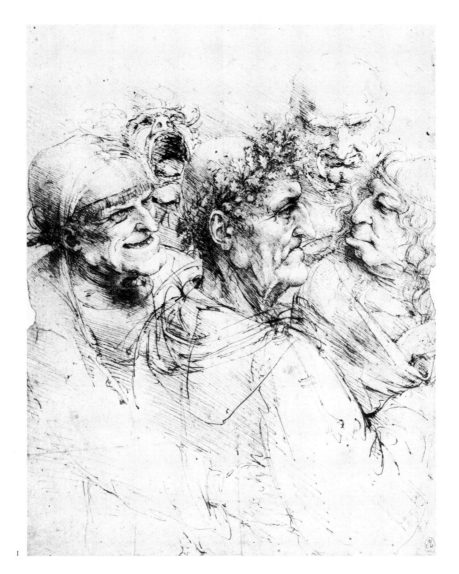

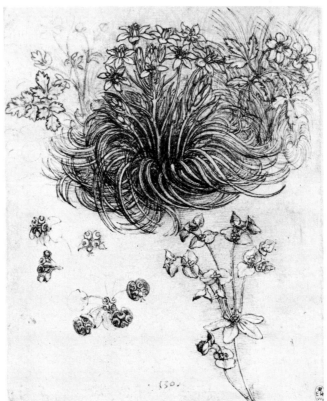

Leonardo da Vinci: 1 Caricature group. *c.* 1490. 2 Star of Bethlehem. *c.* 1506

now at Windsor of drawings of Leonardo da Vinci; 779 drawings on 234 folios – a collection of the greatest splendour covering his artistic life. They include two of his finest silver point drawings, the fully articulated study of a woman's hands and the profile portrait of a woman. How this collection came into the royal possession is not known. It was in the Netherlands in the later 1640s, belonging to the exiled royalist, the Earl of Arundel. In 1690 we know that it had joined the royal collection, for there is a reference to Queen Mary II showing it to a friend. It is just possible that William III and Mary brought it over, but unlikely. A purchase by, or a gift to, Charles II is more probable. And the drawings could easily, apart from their obvious beauty, have had a further interest for Charles II, as well as his brother James, and their cousin, Prince Rupert (the son of Charles I's sister, Elizabeth). Many drawings in the collection show evidence of Leonardo's passionate interest in nature and the way it functioned, from the flow of water to the anatomy of men and animals and in geometry and mechanical ingenuity such as the studies of the casting of cannon. These interests of Leonardo's very much chimed with the intellectual interests of the court in the 1660s and 1670s. Prince Rupert had his own laboratory and performed a number of distinguished

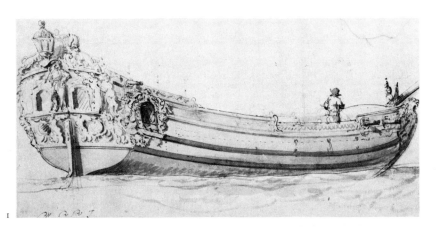

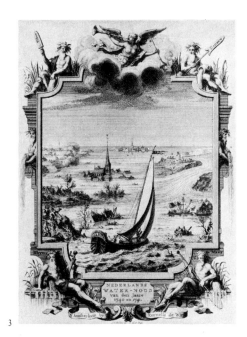

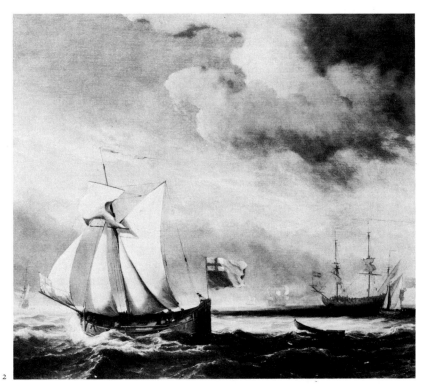

1 Willem van de Velde the Younger, *The English Yacht, Charles. c.* 1663. The yacht was built in 1662. National Maritime Museum, London.
2 Willem van de Velde the Younger, *The Royal Escape. c.* 1675.
3 Cornelius de Wit, engraving of a Dutch yacht

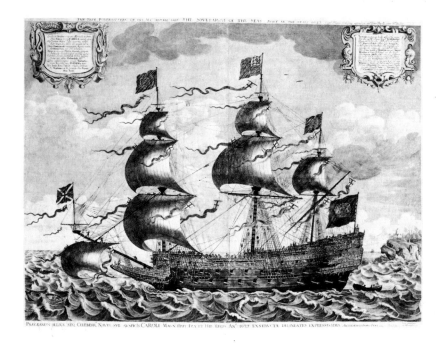

The Royal Yacht, *The Sovereign of the Seas*, built in 1637 and designed by Phineas Pett. National Maritime Museum, London

and important experiments in chemistry. Charles II patronised the new Royal Society, which was devoted to the exploration of nature through experiment and observation. He and his brother, James, were keenly interested in the experiments of Phineas Pett with double-bottomed boats. They were both very active yachtsmen, at a time when the yacht was being rapidly improved, and both preoccupied with improvements in sails and gear. Indeed, they became the founding fathers of yacht racing in order to test the efficiency of methods. Their yachts were the best in Europe, and Louis XIV of France was delighted to be presented with a pair. Charles also founded the Royal Observatory at Greenwich, in the hope of increasing the accuracy of navigation, as well as finding out about the stars with the aid of the recently invented and rapidly improving telescope.

In these interests Charles's brother, James, was as active as himself. He was a tough, efficient, obstinate man of principle, a natural bureaucrat with a splendid head for business. As Lord High Admiral he had helped to rebuild the British navy after the humiliations inflicted on it by the Dutch who, at one point, burnt British ships in the Medway. He was the ablest sailor ever to sit on the throne and fought, in 1672, one of the greatest naval battles of the seventeenth century at Sole Bay, just off Southwold in Suffolk. It was a remarkable fillip for British morale and naturally celebrated in a splendid series of tapestries, woven at Mortlake.

It was during Charles II's reign that a permanent British army came into being, partly made up of the regiments formed during the Commonwealth that had never been disbanded and others that were created by him. Many of Charles II's influential subjects detested this 'standing army' and feared for their freedom. But it was essential for the safety of the realm and for the protection of Britain's growing empire. And the wounded, sick and old soldiers of Britain's army were the object of a magnificent gesture of public patronage by Charles II. He commissioned Wren to design the great hospital at Chelsea where old soldiers still enjoy the fruits of his bounty and, not surprisingly, they celebrate 'Oak Apple Day' in memory of the King's escape after Worcester and his restoration in 1660.

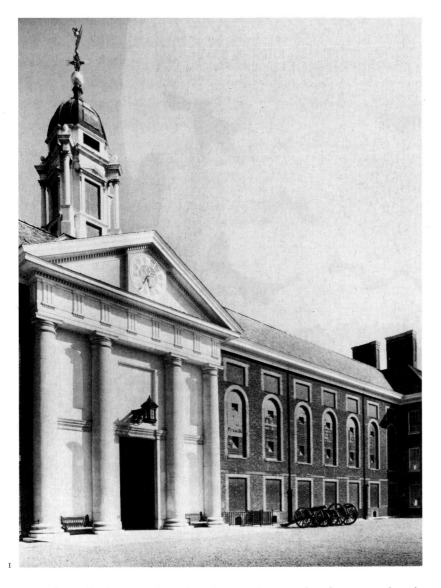

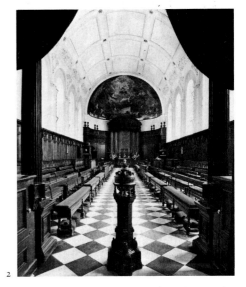

And so Charles II projected an image of monarchy that was relaxed, approachable, that took pride in its army and navy, yet loved common pleasures, horses, sailing, and women. It was a very masculine image, one that contrasted strongly with that of his father, and brought Charles considerable popularity. Privately he longed for greater power, and quietly, without unduly disturbing his purse-conscious subjects, he was rebuilding the great collections of art and creating a setting fit for monarchy.

His tough-minded, impulsive brother nearly wrecked it all. A convinced Roman catholic, who took a catholic bride, Mary of Modena, for a second wife, he went, as soon as he succeeded Charles II in 1685, bull-headed for complete religious toleration for roman catholics, who were severely repressed by law. His countrymen would not have it, and three years later he was in exile in France, succeeded by his protestant daughter, Mary II, and her husband, William III, the Stadholder of the Netherlands. Placed on the throne by parliament, it is the only time England has had two monarchs, for Mary was Queen in her own right. A special orb had to be made for her coronation, and has never been used since. Their succession put an end to any hope of absolute monarchy. No king could now rule alone, for his purse was controlled by parliament, which had therefore to meet every year.

1 The Royal Hospital, Chelsea, was founded by Charles II in 1682, as a home for army pensioners. It was designed by Sir Christopher Wren and completed in 1687.
2 The Chapel

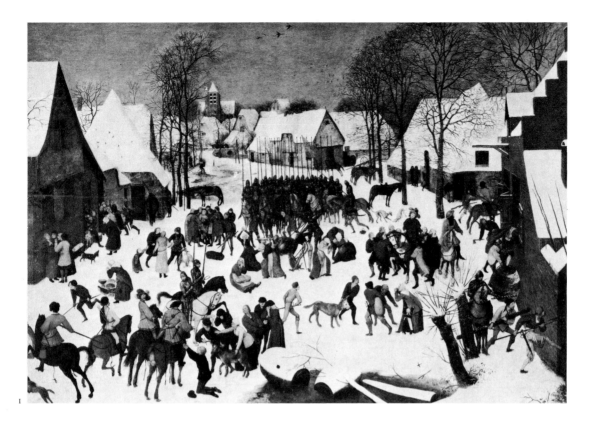

William III, a highly intelligent, but cold and reserved man, whose great ambition was to check the military ambitions of Louis XIV, was determined to mobilise England in his crusade against France. He accepted parliament's role, but, as he said, he did not intend to be 'A Doge of Venice'. Parliament might have become a permanent part of government, but so was monarchy. He certainly intended to maintain what he felt to be a proper state. He suffered, however, from asthma, and hated the coal smoke of London. He decided to create a new palace at Hampton Court – intending to pull down all of Wolsey's and Henry VIII's building, except the Great Hall. In Sir Christopher Wren he had at his command a brilliant architect, arguably the greatest ever produced by England. Wren built the Fountain Court at Hampton, together with the great staircase which leads to a majestic suite of state rooms – rooms far finer than those built at Windsor by Charles II. Queen Mary II was largely responsible for the decoration – and for the very positive Dutch style of furniture and china which her long residence in the Netherlands had taught her to love. Much, including the beds, has great splendour. She was also a great connoisseur and collector of the blue and white pottery made at Delft in imitation of the blue and white porcelain that was being imported in great quantities from China. This pottery makes a vivid contrast to the dark panelling, and the great tulip vases at Hampton Court are among the most important pieces of Delft ever made. Their size and complexity make the firing in the kiln difficult and hazardous, making failure far more common than success.

Mary II was a modest, retiring person who was greatly moved by the beauty of women, and she commissioned Sir Godfrey Kneller, who had succeeded Sir Peter Lely as chief court painter, to paint her ladies-in-waiting in imitation of Lely's great series of Windsor beauties. Alas, Charles II's girls certainly were not only more beautiful, but also far luckier with their painter. Mary II, however, was responsible for one

1 Pieter Bruegel, *The Massacre of the Innocents.* Acquired by Charles II.
2 Detail of the South Front, Hampton Court Palace, designed by Sir Christopher Wren and built for William and Mary as the Latin inscription records

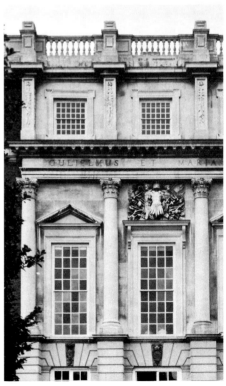

great act of patronage. Charles II had intended to build a great palace at Greenwich – so convenient for the yachting which he adored. Sir Christopher Wren had begun to build it but what is now known as 'King Charles block' was still unfinished in 1694 because the funds had run out (Charles was perpetually short of money). Mary II proposed to turn the buildings into a great hospital for seamen to match that at Chelsea for soldiers, and Wren's pupil, Nicholas Hawksmoor, undertook the work, which was not completed for many years. Today Greenwich Hospital is one of the most beautiful buildings in the country. It could scarcely have been created at a more appropriate time, for England's navy was rapidly expanding and was to be involved in battle for two decades.

Although work at Greenwich continued, the building and beautification of Hampton Court stopped abruptly in 1695 after Mary's sudden death the previous year. William III was far more deeply attached to his wife than his courtiers realised, and after her death, Hampton Court ceased to attract him. Nevertheless, the changes made by William III and Mary II extended Hampton Court's life as a royal palace for several more generations, and a great deal of money was spent by William and by Queen Anne, William III's sister-in-law and successor, in creating one of the finest gardens England had ever known. Indeed gardening was a major passion of William's, 'not only a Delighter but

Engraving by John Kip after Leonard Knyff of a bird's eye view of Hampton Court Palace at the time of William and Mary

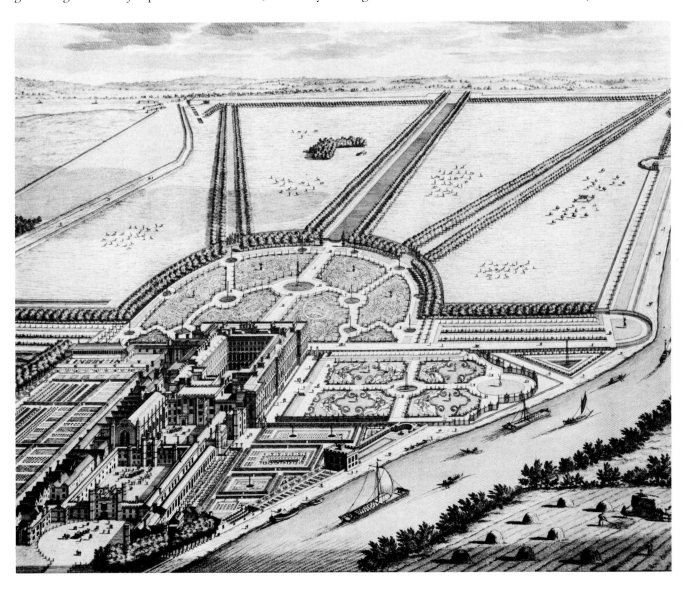

likewise a great Judge' as one contemporary called him. The garden was planned by Henry Wise, whose nurseries at the corner of Brompton Road and Knightsbridge provided innumerable rare shrubs and trees for aristocratic gardens. His design broke away, to some extent, from the highly formal gardens of the Dutch and the French; nevertheless, with their canals, strict avenues of trees, and controlled beds of flowers and scented shrubs they were far from the asymmetrical 'naturalness' that later became fashionable. Many features of Wise's garden are still discernible at Hampton Court, particularly in the planning of the avenues. The gates to the river walk, which still exist, are by the master of the late seventeenth-century ironwork – Tijou (see page 93).

To be nearer to London for the sake of official business, William III had bought Nottingham House, now Kensington Palace, just a short drive from Whitehall, but clear of the smoke and fog which was becoming intense in London and Westminster. It was a small house of no great natural beauty, and so needed remodelling as a royal residence. This was done by Wren, although both the alterations at Hampton Court and Kensington were not grandiose, and these palaces were hardly more splendid than the homes of the great ducal families who had brought William III to the throne. Indeed, Kensington had been the home of William III's Secretary of State, the Earl of Nottingham. Similarly, the furniture, the tapestries, the china echoed the taste of the whig aristocracy, whose sovereigns they were.

William III and Mary II had created a setting of monarchy that was dignified, regal, without being grandiose or overwhelmingly ambitious, and so it scarcely betrays the fact that England was becoming richer and more victorious than she had been for centuries. Only on Wren's great staircase at Hampton Court, painted by Verrio, does one get some sense of the drama of the continental wars in which England was involved from 1689 to 1715.

1 Anonymous early eighteenth-century engraving of a bird's eye view of Kensington Palace, showing the additions made by William and Mary, and the gardens as altered for Queen Anne.
2 The King's Staircase, Hampton Court, painted by Verrio. Finished and decorated 1700

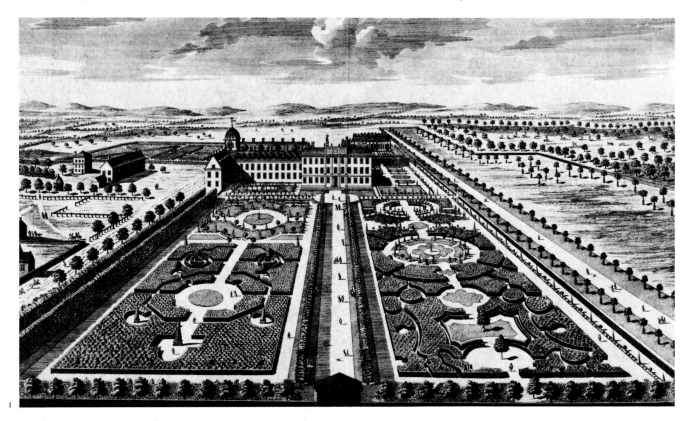

1

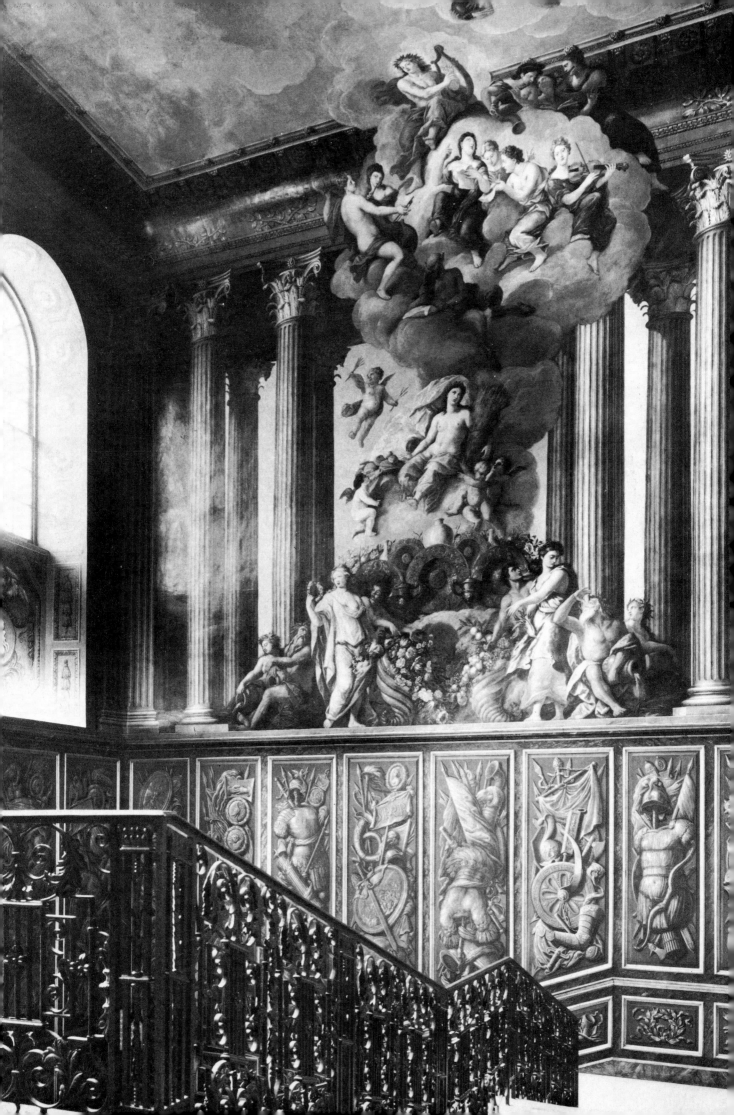

England's major victories in the war against France and Spain took place in the reign of Queen Anne. She had to be close to London, for she attended cabinet meetings almost every day, taking decisions about the great war in which England was engaged, which explains her preference for St James's to Kensington. She was a sad, ageing woman, overwhelmed by childbirth and the subsequent deaths of her children, very conscientious, and not at all unshrewd in politics and government. She was also very large, and disliked movement – apart from going to Windsor occasionally for the hunting and the racing at Ascot, she spent most of her time in St James's Palace. She refurnished St James's, building the ballroom, and a fine suite of state rooms. There she heard of Marlborough's victories, and of the triumphs of her navy. Her country had begun the long journey towards world supremacy. In her brief reign, from 1702 to 1714, crown and people had a common identity, a sense of unity and of national purpose. The tribulations of the seventeenth century, which had led to the execution of one king and the exile of another, were over. Absolutism had gone for ever; parliamentary monarchy and a stable throne had been established at last, or would be, if her successor could peacefully assume the crown.

THE HANOVERIANS

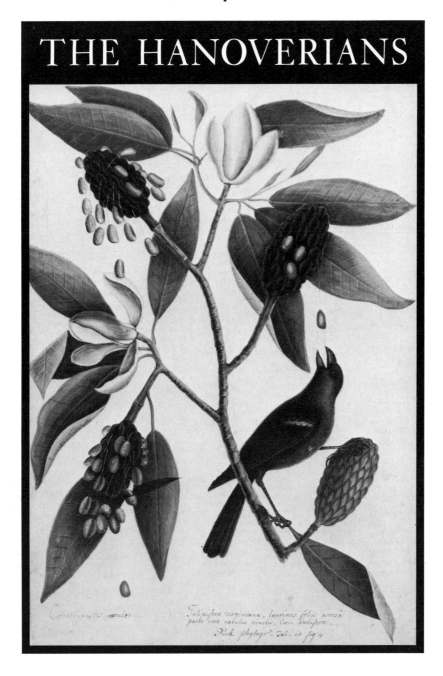

On 29 September 1714 most of the English aristocracy was at Greenwich, crowded in the Painted Hall, where Thornhill's decoration was finished in all but the ceiling. They were waiting, with considerable anxiety, for the arrival of their new king. In 1701, in the Act of Settlement, they and the House of Commons had decided the succession: in the first place it went to Queen Anne, who had given birth to seventeen children but they all died, so she was without a direct heir. Her Stuart relations were in exile, James II, her father, had died; his eldest son, known familiarly as 'the Old Pretender', claimed the English throne by strict hereditary descent, but he was a Roman Catholic. The majority of men of power preferred the protestant descendants of the daughter of James I, who were the Electors of Hanover. Queen Anne had, however, refused to allow even the Elector's son to reside in Britain, which inclined many to believe that she secretly favoured her Stuart nephew. She did not. Her dislike of the Hanoverians, however, meant that very few of the nobility had met their future king. And naturally enough they were a prey to anxiety. What they did know of George I was not encouraging. He was more or less ignorant of English, a middle-aged man set in his ways; his private life had been tragic and vengeful. He had discovered that his wife had a lover. The lover was killed and the wife imprisoned for life. He disliked social life and lived very privately with his two mistresses – both middle-aged like himself.

George I was coming to take charge of a country which had witnessed a century of unparalleled turbulence – two civil wars, a savagely suppressed rebellion, a bloody revolution, repeated plots, and endless instability. A war with France of global proportions had recently ended with what the whigs in parliament thought to be the thoroughly unsatisfactory peace at Utrecht (1713), and they were longing for revenge on the tories who had made it. English politics were full of rancour and the rage of party; they had been so since the civil war, and the political animosities between whigs and tories had deep roots in local and family feuds that stretched back for generations. The Whig Party embraced the great landed families and some of the richer merchants of London. They wanted to limit the powers of the crown in favour of parliament, and to promote toleration in religion (except for catholics). They were also commercially-minded, keen, whether merchant or aristocrat, to make money. The Tory Party, on the other hand, supported the powers of the crown, wanted no toleration in religion, and preferred an old-fashioned patriarchal attitude, instead of values based on money. In addition, thousands of Britons of all classes greatly preferred the Stuarts, and it is not surprising that many Europeans regarded Britain as ungovernable and rated the new dynasty's chance of remaining on the throne as small.

The problems of government were not merely political. Twenty-five years of warfare had greatly accelerated social change. England's expanding empire in the Caribbean, in India, in North America, could only be sustained by growing commerce, growing industry, growing public finance, and only maintained if protected by an efficient navy and professional army, both of which cost a great deal of money. Financial institutions had been devised to cope with this new, expensive, yet profitable world – the Bank of England, additional taxes with a growing army of bureaucrats to manage them, funded National Debt, and new-

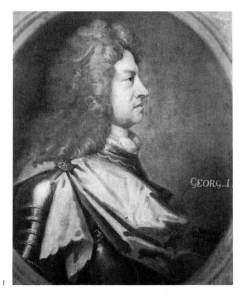

1 Studio of Kneller, *George I*.
2 Sir James Thornhill, Ceiling, Painted Hall, Greenwich Hospital. 1708–27

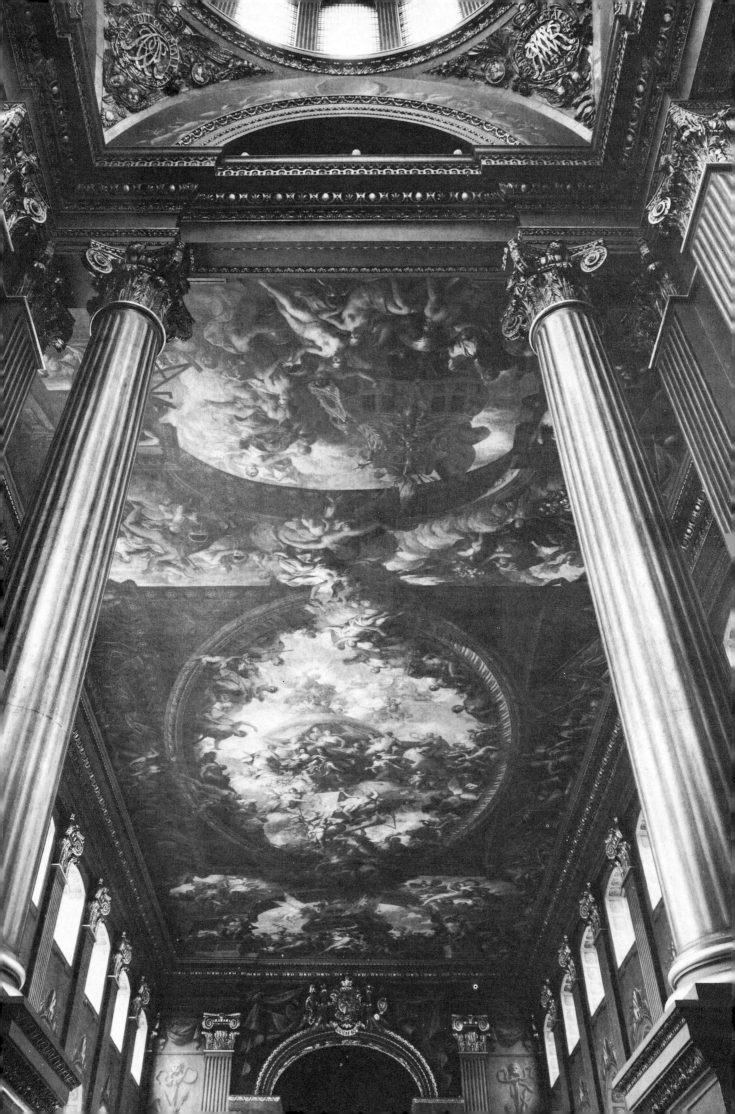

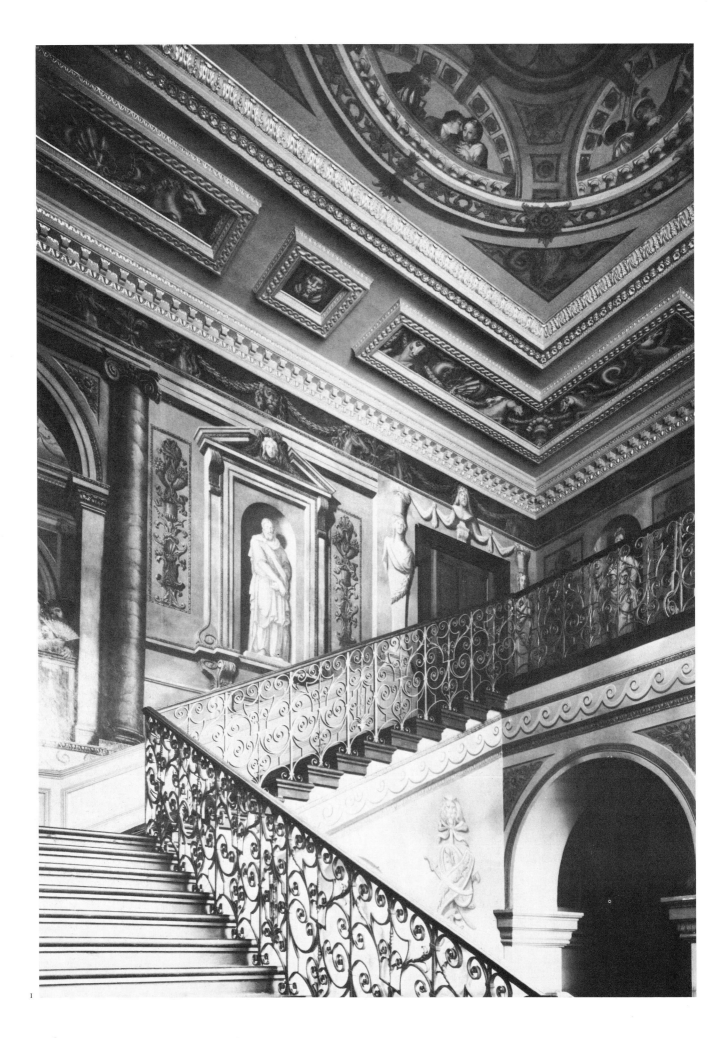

I

fangled insurance companies. These novelties bred anxiety as well as exuberance in the hope of riches. And rightly did they breed anxiety, for the control of these powerful new financial instruments was haphazard; their dangers far from being understood.

Thus George I inherited a divided country, which had been over-extended by war, and new institutions that were capable, if mishandled, of catastrophic effects. Two neighbouring countries, France and Spain, were bitter in defeat and ready for revenge, eager to exploit any troubles in which England might be involved. Both, not unnaturally, became warm supporters of the exiled Stuarts.

So George I arrived to govern a turbulent, explosive country, riven with dynastic strife and an almost certain target for invasion; a country in the midst of political revolution, financial revolution, commercial revolution. Could George I master the situation? Could he succeed with the help of his whig aristocrat allies and their supporters in the House of Commons, in the towns and countryside, in bringing his new nation the order, the stability, the peace for which they longed? In September 1714 the future was dark and violent storms followed, only to give way to years of glorious success.

In 1715 the Stuarts invaded. They were convincingly defeated, and 'the Old Pretender' scurried back to France. The financial system blew up in the South Sea Bubble, in which speculative mania in stocks and shares (a new development, this) ran riot. Government ministers had been bribed, bought by gifts of shares; the filthy waters of corruption lapped around the court. The new dynasty might easily have been submerged. Thanks to the political genius of Sir Robert Walpole, who withstood with great skill the attack on the court in the House of Commons and also restored confidence in government finance, it survived; and George I emerged from the crisis stronger than ever. When the whigs came to write their history, the majestic triumphs of the eighteenth century were theirs, for the disasters they blamed their kings. Indeed, the Hanoverians have always had a bad press – George I, dull; George II, a boor and a philistine; George III, stupid. Is this true? Emphatically not. They made, all of them, immense contributions to the greatness of Britain. Take George I. At times he worked a sixteen-hour day. Highly intelligent, versed and skilled in diplomacy, by indefatigable application he helped to create, through a complex web of foreign alliances, the peace that Europe and England needed. He brought an end to party strife in the country. Even during the South Sea Bubble he gave his loyalty firmly to the whigs. Afterwards he let them use royal power to obtain a grip on the political life of England. By 1721 the whig aristocracy was more powerful than it had ever been – more unified, more absolute in its control of power, and it ruled England for the rest of the century.

George I rapidly adopted in England the life-style which suited his temperament. He lived modestly, spending his evenings with one of his mistresses, usually the Duchess of Kendal. As a distraction from his work, he enjoyed cutting out beautiful and complex silhouettes – now all lost. Another pleasure was music, and when he appeared in public it was more often than not at the opera. His main act of patronage was to commission William Kent, the architect who was sponsored by the Earl of Burlington, the dictator of the taste of the whig aristocracy, to

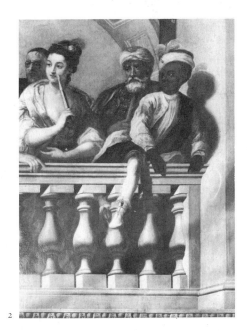

1 The King's Grand Staircase, Kensington Palace, built by Sir Christopher Wren in 1689.
2 A detail from the staircase

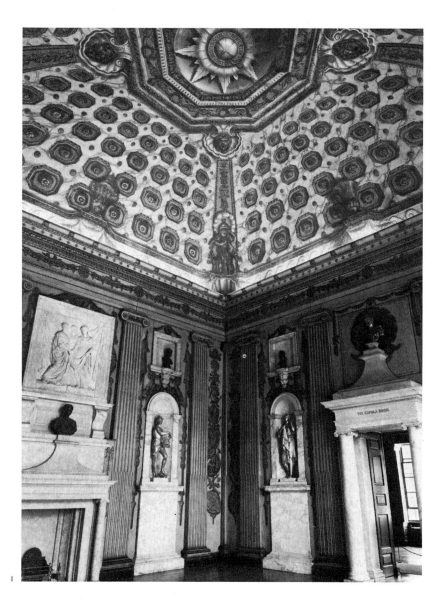

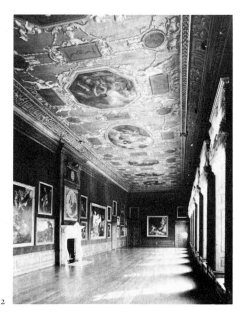

1 The Cupola Room, Kensington Palace, decorated for King George I by William Kent, who began work on it in 1722.
2 The King's gallery, designed by Nicholas Hawksmoor in 1695. The ceiling was painted by William Kent

remodel the state rooms at Kensington Palace. Kent also redecorated for the King a great staircase by Christopher Wren at Kensington, the palace George I liked most. Kent artfully worked in pictures of George I's courtiers, including his two very intelligent and able Turkish servants, Mustapha and Mahomet, whom the King had captured at the Siege of Vienna in 1683, and, inevitably, his own self-portrait.

The King was not very interested in grandeur, and the state rooms at Kensington were almost all the building that he undertook – which again was shrewd and wise. The whig dukes might live like kings, but their king should live like a duke. Even the Cupola Room, the finest of Kensington's state rooms, is not quite so splendid as the salon at Blenheim. Nor were the gardens at Kensington grander than those at Blenheim, fine as they are. Those which we see today were initially laid out by Henry Wise and Charles Bridgman, which replaced those created by Queen Anne. For their time they were very modern, making far greater use of grass lawns and natural landscape features than had been the fashion in the past. They were only completed in 1731 when a series of ponds were linked together to form the Serpentine.

Perhaps, too, it was only right that, as he and his ministers were triumphing over Jacobite invasion and financial disaster, Sir James

Thornhill should be completing the ceiling in the Painted Hall at Greenwich Hospital. It represents the victories of Britain over the French, offers a magnificent tribute to the great founder of whig monarchy, William III, and makes a splendid, emphatic statement of British self-confidence and ambition, based on triumphant sea-power and undefeated armies. An impressive theme, richly embroidered, indeed, a theatrical statement of Britain's imperial destiny that the ever-increasing wealth and riches, in spite of financial scandals, made more certain. The anxiety which George I's arrival at Greenwich had engendered had disappeared in ten years, to be replaced by an ever-increasing confidence, almost arrogance, which was the hallmark of the whigs. For them the future, not the past.

If George I was a good whig, who made certain of his dynasty's survival, George II was a better one, and his wife, Caroline, a better one still. Caroline was by far the ablest of our queens between the reigns of Elizabeth I and Victoria, and she has been greatly undervalued. Although rather plump, she was exceedingly comely, very regal in bearing, and possessed vivacity and charm. She had been very well educated and as a young girl she had displayed formidable intellectual powers. She possessed a strong inclination towards philosophy and corresponded regularly with the great German mathematician, Leibnitz; even greater

Engraving by Jean Rogue of Kensington Palace and gardens, as laid out by Henry Wise, 1736

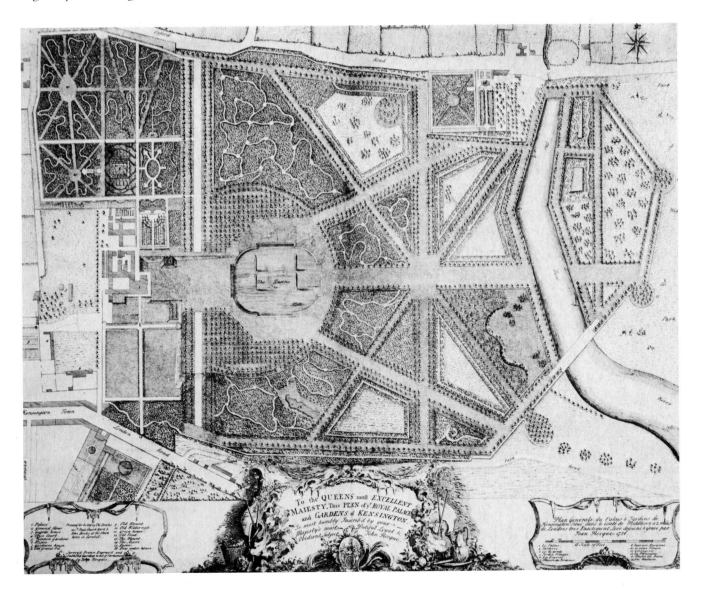

was her passion for theology, and she liked nothing better than to spend an hour or two arguing about the nature of the Trinity with Dr Samuel Clarke, one of the outstanding theologians of the day. Like Clarke, Queen Caroline inclined towards far greater toleration in religion than was customary at this time. But her greatest love was politics. She was fascinated by personalities in relation to power, to office, and to ideas. She spent a great deal of time with her husband's prime minister, Sir Robert Walpole, one of the most skilful managers parliament has ever known, and he came to regard her as one of his ablest allies. Walpole was also a very great patron of art. For his house in Norfolk, as well as for the cabinet room at Whitehall, he had commissioned the greatest architects, decorators, painters and sculptors in England. William Kent was responsible for the magnificent cabinet room. Walpole had made Sir James Thornhill the King's painter; he had given numerous commissions to Michael Rysbrack, the greatest English sculptor of the time; he supported scores of other able and distinguished painters; and he strongly encouraged Caroline's taste in the arts, as well as in politics.

The Queen commanded William Kent to build for her two extraordinary buildings at Richmond — one, called Merlin's Cave, was a thatched cottage, and the other, a Grotto, was a four-roomed Gothic cottage. This was to be a temple to the great geniuses of British learning and piety, and she began to have statues made for it by Guelfi, though he was rapidly succeeded by Michael Rysbrack. These made a splendid gallery of whig heroes — Sir Isaac Newton (who discovered the orderly reasonableness of the Universe); Henry Boyle (the father of modern chemistry); John Locke (the political philosopher of whiggery); Sir Francis Bacon (the great Elizabethan regarded as the father of science); Dr Samuel Clarke (the theologian, now long forgotten, but very popular at that time, strong on the immortality of the soul, but weak on the Trinity); and a Dr Wollaston (a great polemicist on behalf of the sweet reasonableness of religion, another theologian who helped to banish Hell from men's minds). The Queen was so delighted with Rysbrack's work that she visited his studio in 1735 to view his equestrian statue of William III, which the corporation of Bristol had commissioned. It still stands in Queen's Square, the finest equestrian statue of any of our monarchs, finer, even, than Le Sueur's of Charles I. Rysbrack was commissioned to sculpt busts of herself and her husband. Although she died before hers was finished, it was a magnificent likeness, as was the King's — certainly they are quite magnificent busts; the terracottas which survive are finer than the finished marble busts.

Queen Caroline also had a taste for history and she had Rysbrack make a series of terracotta busts of the kings and queens of England, beginning with Alfred the Great. Unfortunately most of these were accidentally destroyed in this century (only three survive), but her interest in the royal inheritance was very keen, and her collection of royal portraits which she bought from Lord Cornwallis still remains. Others she found in the royal collection — she discovered a collection of Holbein's drawings in a bureau at Kensington Palace. She also encouraged a far greater interest in, and systematic arrangement of, the body of royal drawings and portraits.

A delightful woman — intelligent, sensible, alive to the world of artists as well as scholars — she loved her husband, and, in spite of having a

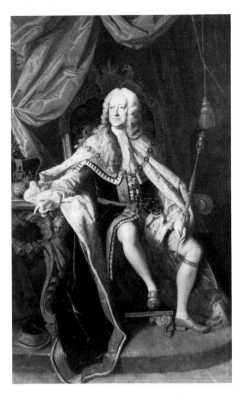

Thomas Hudson, *George II*. National Portrait Gallery, London

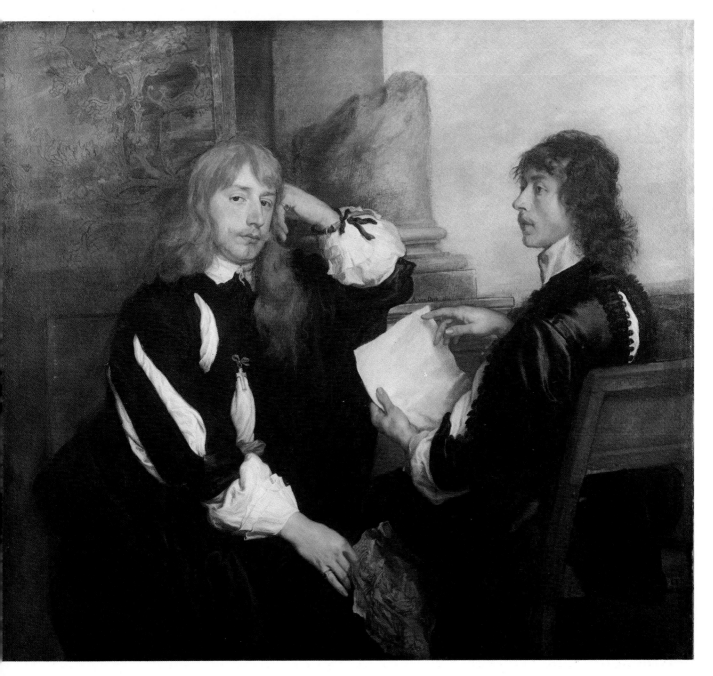

Sir Anthony van Dyck, *Thomas Killigrew and* (?)*William, Lord Crofts.* 1638

Frederick, Prince of Wales, King George II's eldest son, was the first of the Hanoverian dynasty to show a lively interest in the arts and formed an outstanding collection of Italian, Spanish, French and Flemish pictures. It is conceivable, too, that he acquired the splendid portrait by Frans Hals on Page 155. These four paintings reflect the range of his taste

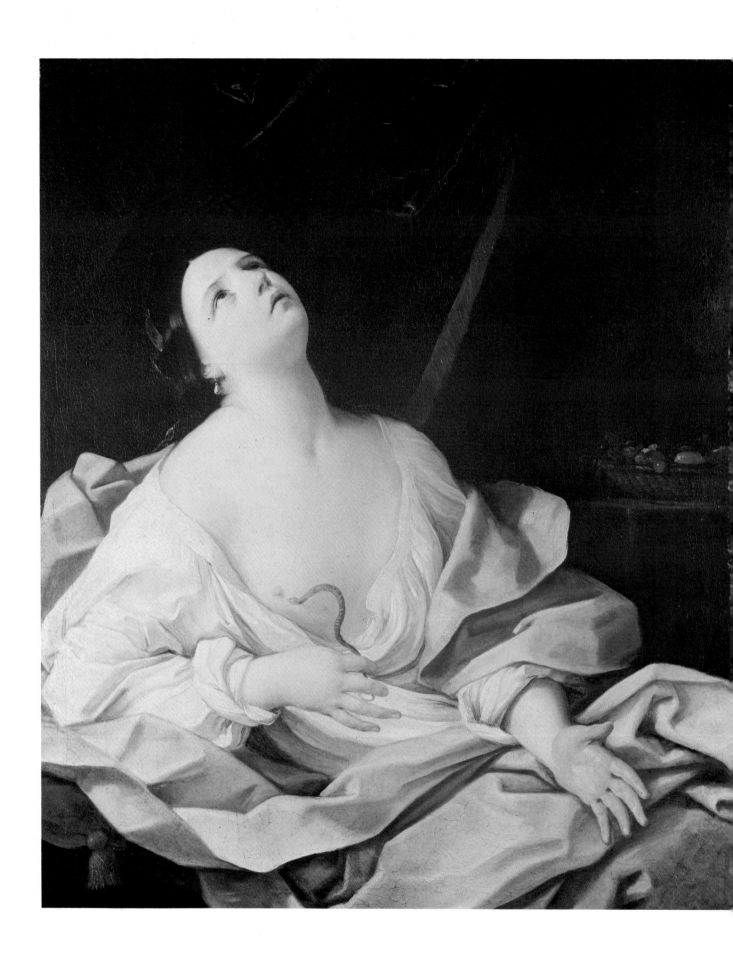

Guido Reni, *Cleopatra with the Asp*

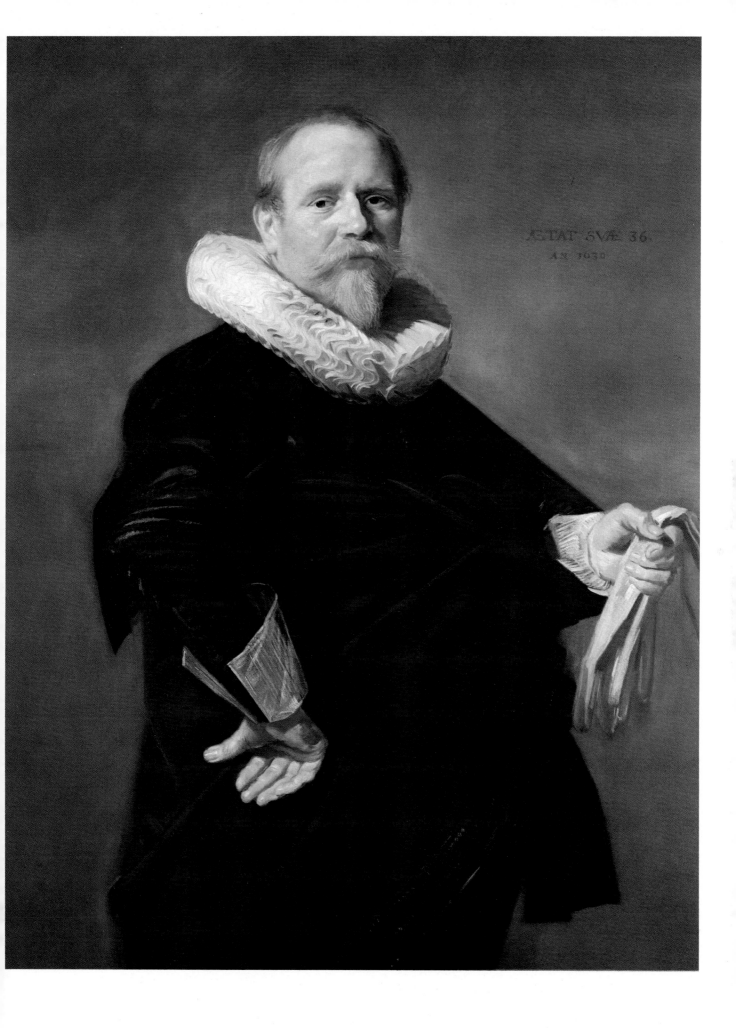

Frans Hals, *Portrait of a Man.* 1630

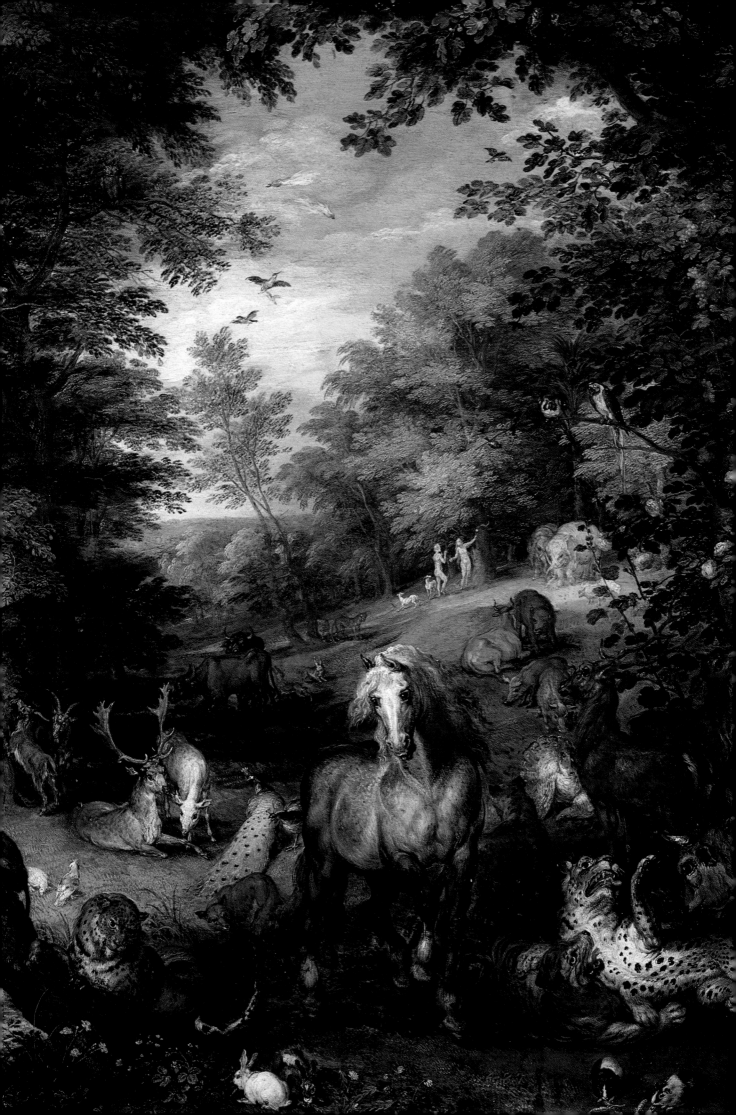

mistress (deaf, and largely for show), he loved her. On her deathbed she begged him to marry again; weeping, he said he could not, he would have mistresses instead. And he kept his word.

The King had little use for painting and poetry. A weakness, surely, but he had plenty of strengths, far more than historians have allowed. His sound political judgment always led him to yield in a crisis in the last resort for he knew the whigs were his masters but only in a crisis. In day-to-day business, however, he kept a firm hand, particularly on army appointments. He was extremely brave, and was the last king to fight in battle, at Dettingen in 1743, against the French and their allies. He loved the army, and gave strong support for William Kent's dramatic remodelling of Horse Guards' Parade, which became a fit setting for Trooping the Colour, first witnessed by George II, and so colourful because George and his soldier son, Cumberland, insisted that each regiment should dress alike (ie be uniform, hence 'uniforms'). The brilliant regimentals of the guards and other regiments were specified by the King to the smallest detail, and, to give an accurate representation of his army, George II ordered David Morier to paint with great exactitude the uniforms of the British army; dull pictures, maybe, but a very important record for the military historian.

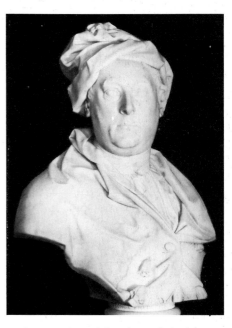

Louis François Roubiliac, bust of Handel

After the army, George II's other great passion, like his father, was music – music in all its forms, but most especially opera and the operas, oratorios and other music of George Frederick Handel. Handel had been George I's court musician in Hanover, but he had left in order to freelance in England. For a time he may have been in the Duke of Chandos's service, but when George I became King, he patronised Handel, giving him £1000 a year for the Royal Academy of Music, which was strongly supported by the whig aristocracy. Even the bitter feud which flared up in 1717 between the King and his son (nothing like so savage, however, as the quarrel between George II and *his* son, the royal family's passions were very volcanic!) could not keep them both from attending Handel's operas and oratorios, which became a paean of praise for Britain's triumphs in war and peace, a constant *Te Deum* to the success of Britain. This royal patronage of music, inherited, as we shall see, by generations of Hanoverians, helped to give England an incomparable musical life in the eighteenth century, and to make it a Mecca for continental musicians as well as its own considerable and often under-rated talents.

Frederick, Prince of Wales, George II's son, was an even greater lover of music than his father. He was a good performer – Philippe Mercier painted him playing his cello in the small banqueting house at Hampton Court, which became a miniature royal concert room. This picture was probably painted in 1733, when Frederick had just taken up the instrument. Although he is shown playing with his sisters, who had been taught by Handel, he was on very bad terms with them, as with the rest of his family.

Frederick has suffered a worse press even than his father or grandfather, or his son, George III. He is usually depicted as an ass, stupid enough to get killed by a cricket ball. He was not an ass, and he probably caught a chill and died of pneumonia. He has been underestimated for a variety of reasons, but mainly because it is difficult to believe that there was not something fundamentally wrong in a son whom his parents

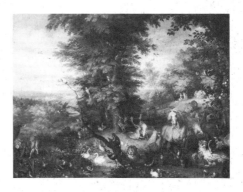

Jan Bruegel, *Adam and Eve in the Garden of Eden*. 1615.
Detail on facing page

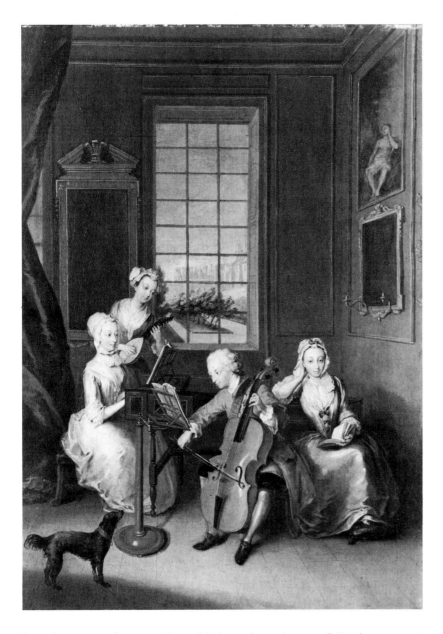

Philippe Mercier, *The Music Party.* c. 1733.
Frederick, Prince of Wales, with his three
eldest sisters, playing in the Banqueting
House, Hampton Court

hated so intensely. How deep this hatred was is very difficult to assess.
The most virulent examples – his mother Caroline, for example, wishing
him in hell – are derived from an extremely prejudiced source, the
malicious, bitter, brilliantly satirical Lord Hervey, a bisexual lap-dog of
the Queen's, the truth of whose magnificently amusing court memoirs is
very difficult to determine. Hervey and the Prince had shared the same
girl for a time, and they quarrelled, or certainly Hervey quarrelled. In
Hervey's memoirs Frederick appears as a foolish, ungrateful, treacherous
ass, rightly detested by his parents, and most historians have accepted
this version, even though they may have, on occasion, moderated the
violence and bitterness. There is, however, plenty of other evidence that
his parents and he got on badly together. That was in no way unusual
amongst the Hanoverians, or other European monarchs in the eighteenth
century for that matter. The King of Prussia considered executing his son
– afterwards Frederick the Great; and the Tsar of Russia did, in fact, kill
his. And there are uncontestable facts; Frederick's father stopped him
coming to England for as long as he could, would not allow him to marry,
and kept him in the schoolroom long after he was fully mature. The King
also ostentatiously favoured his brother, the Duke of Cumberland, a

tough soldier like his father. Frederick felt so threatened, for some reason or another, that he rushed his wife out of his father's palace just before her first labour – a foolish and dangerous act. Naturally his father was incensed. Not surprisingly Frederick took up, in 1737, with those politicians who were opposed to his father's minister, Sir Robert Walpole, which to the King was not far short of treason. And Frederick was able to use his influence with sufficient skill to be largely responsible for Walpole's fall from power in 1742, which blackened Frederick's reputation among orthodox whigs, who accused him of toryism. In the end, his politics failed. The massive citadels of the great whig families were too strong even for a King's son to storm. And so Frederick has been written off as a fool and all that most people remember of him is the doggerel written at his death:

'Here lies poor Fred who was alive and is dead.
We had rather it had been his father.
But as it's just poor Fred who was alive and is dead
There's no more to be said.'

In fact, there is a great deal to be said – and in his favour. Many of his interests and tastes may have sprung from the alienation from his parents. Against their devotion to Handel, Frederick patronised the Italian opera, and tried to establish it in London, not, however, with any resounding success. Maybe because his father disliked painting, Frederick took it up, but for whatever reason he became a true connoisseur. He bought wisely, patronised wisely, and greatly enriched the royal collection. His taste was deeply personal, and he frequently attended the

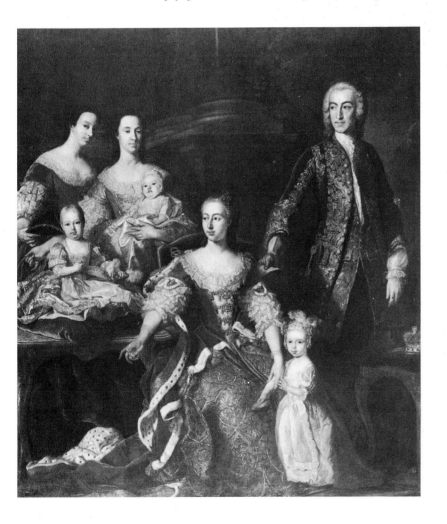

Jean-Baptiste Vanloo, *Augusta, Princess of Wales, with members of her Family and Household.*
173(9?)

auction rooms to make certain of purchasing what he wanted. He did not buy the great living Italian artists – the Ricci, Pellegrini, and the most popular of all with English collectors, Canaletto. His interest was that of Charles I, on whom he may have modelled his tastes. He had a passion for Van Dyck, buying five, including one of the greatest, the double portrait of Sir Thomas Killigrew and Lord Crofts, who are shown mourning Killigrew's wife. He also acquired two magnificent Rubens landscapes and, two of his best acquisitions, Jan 'Velvet' Breugel's *Kermesse* and *Adam and Eve*. He was also responsible for the purchase, at a high price, of an outstanding Holbein portrait of the Duke of Norfolk. He purchased for his own pleasure, hanging his favourites in his private room at Leicester House, his London home. Naturally so keen a connoisseur patronised British and foreign artists working in London, and here again his taste and discernment are obvious and personal. He preferred the easy relaxed style of Mercier, or Amigoni, who painted three portraits of him. He enjoyed the informality of conversation pieces and sporting pictures, and commissioned several pictures by John Wootton, the precursor of the great animal painter, George Stubbs. And when it came to state portraits, with unerring instinct he chose Vanloo, who, according to Sir Oliver Millar, painted 'what is perhaps the most original royal group since Van Dyck', the Prince's wife, her household and family. The Prince was very eager to support an academy for British painters and often discussed the project with George Vertue, the engraver and historian of art, but he died before he had the power to implement his idea.

For the decorative arts, like all good whigs – for Frederick claimed to be a better whig even than his father – he used William Kent, not only at his house at Kew, but also for a magnificent state barge, especially designed for him and the only royal barge of the eighteenth century that still exists. We forget how colourful the Thames must have been – the royal family and noblemen had their barges, alive with colour and heraldry, the city companies had theirs and, naturally, the Lord Mayor had a majestic one. Frederick did not use his barge solely for formal occasions, but also for musical concerts on the Thames – these were very popular – and also as a coach. The first time he went in the barge was in order to take his mother and five princesses from Chelsea to Somerset House to inspect the cleaning of some royal pictures. This barge, which would be at home in Venice, plied the Thames for over a hundred years; the last time it was used was in 1849 by Prince Albert, to open a coal wharf!

Prince Frederick was devoted to the Thames and sponsored rowing races: in 1749 he gave a silver cup, valued at seventy-five guineas, for a race between seven pairs of sculls between Whitehall and Putney. The Prince and his family turned out in style, using their new barge, and, adding a touch of fashionable chinoiserie, had their watermen dressed 'in Chinese habits'. When not at Leicester House or Kew, Frederick lived at Cliveden, further along the river, where he gave house parties that were famous for their concerts, amateur theatricals, and masquerades. He himself enjoyed country life, particularly shooting and fishing with his sons. He was the first member of the royal family to become a dedicated cricketer, which he also played with his children. Indeed, the Prince was a devoted family man, and when he had family groups painted, he liked

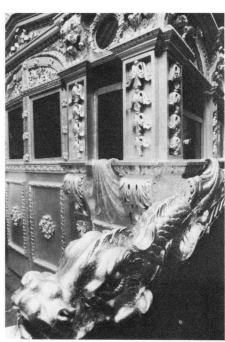

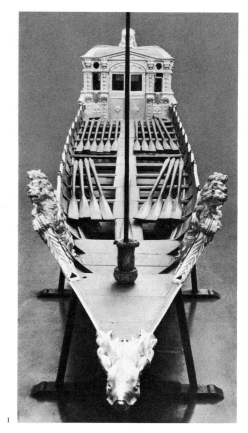

1 and 2 Prince Frederick's state barge, designed by William Kent and now in the National Maritime Museum, London

his sons and daughters to be doing childish things – playing with their toys or pets, not standing or sitting stiffly around him.

Fortunately for Frederick, his tastes were shared by his wife, Princess Augusta of Saxe-Gotha. Although the Prince seems to have been quite promiscuous as a young man, and once had a very unfortunate escapade when a girl of the town robbed him in St James's Park, marriage captured him completely. He loved his wife deeply and sincerely and enjoyed nothing more than her company, composing neat little poems to her, and making her the heroine of the masques which he enjoyed writing. Princess Augusta, too, has suffered from the usual bad Hanoverian press and is often denounced for miseducating her children in tory principles after her husband's death in 1751, and for becoming besotted with the handsome but pompous Lord Bute, to whom her eldest son, George III, also became disastrously and slavishly attached. Another myth manufactured out of a granule of truth. She shared most of her husband's tastes – music and pictures (she was responsible for the ravishing series of pastels by Liotard of her nine children) and their marriage was a great success.

The Prince's delight in family life is portrayed by George Knapton in a family group commissioned after his death as a tribute to him by his wife. There he looks down on his children engaged in pursuits and hobbies which he had encouraged; the future George III is with his brother, Edward, examining the plans and fortifications of Portsmouth (nearby are surveying and architectural drawing materials): the two younger princes are playing with a model yacht, one of the princesses plays on a lute, and their pet dog is with them. But the picture also spells out a lesson. The Act of Settlement, which brought the Hanoverians to the throne, is there, but so is Magna Carta. Nothing could be more whiggish; nor make a bolder claim that the Prince of Wales's family was the true guardian of whig principles. This picture demonstrates better than

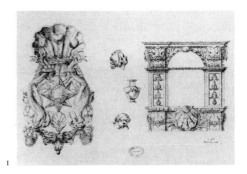

1

1 and 2 William Kent's designs for the state barge, 1732. Royal Institute of British Architects, London

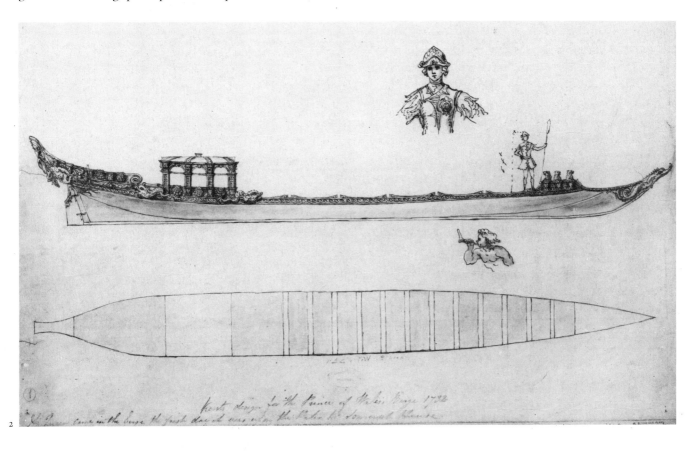

2

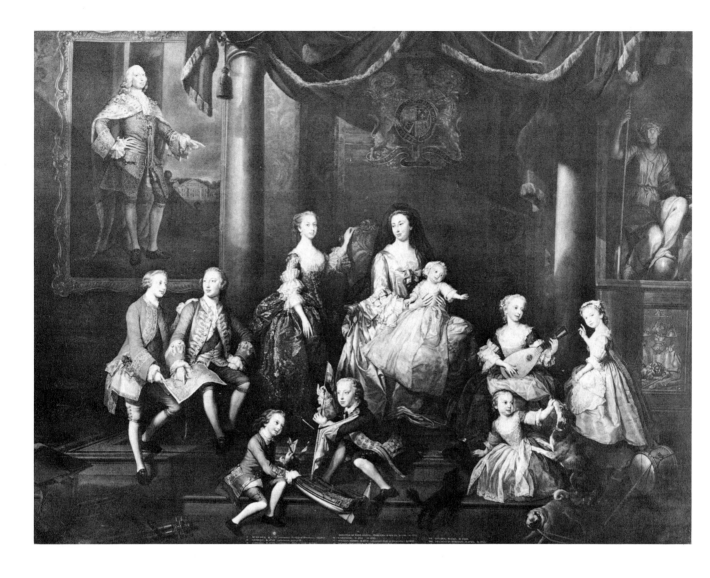

words could the principles, as well as the family background, of George III, who succeeded his grandfather in 1760. There was nothing tory at all about his upbringing, old-fashioned whig maybe, but not tory.

George III lost America; that is the one fact that most people know about him. After all, it says so in America's Declaration of Independence. 'The history of the present King of Great Britain is a history of repeated injuries and usurpations, all having in direct object the establishment of an absolute Tyranny over these states.' Then it goes on, page after page, listing the acts of tyranny, for which not George III but his parliament was responsible. Nevertheless, the accusation stuck. George III was accused of packing parliament with his friends, bribing and suborning the rest, and acting like a veritable Stuart, bent on destroying the freedom of parliament. Clap-trap that only a George Orwell could treat with the contempt it deserves! George III was no tory, no tyrant; his ministers, like his grandfather's, were all whigs. The nobility and gentry of his realm dominated parliament, and it was their policy that lost America. Naturally George III did not eye the American rebels any more favourably than his ministers. He regarded them as traitors, which is technically what they were. It is often forgotten that to eighteenth-century Englishmen America was as much a part of Britain as Wales or Scotland, or, for that matter, Devon or Yorkshire, and that the war with America was a civil war. George III certainly demanded firmness and

George Knapton, *The Family of Frederick, Prince of Wales*. 1751. Augusta, Princess of Wales, wears a black veil to mark her recent widowhood. A portrait of the Prince (who had died on 20 March 1751) is in the background. George, Prince of Wales, later King George III, is seated to the right of his mother

resolution from his ministers, and it was very difficult for him to envisage compromise with rebels. But then George III possessed a very principled, if very rigid, mind; to him rebellion was quite simply rebellion. In any case, neither King nor parliament could have placated America.

Recently George III has received a somewhat kinder and fairer treatment, but he is still misunderstood, still denied not only virtues, but accomplishments, too often depicted as a stupid, well-meaning man of very limited intelligence; a compulsive talker, with a passion for irrelevant detail; frugal to the point of miserliness, and interested only in farming. This, again, contains grains of truth savagely distorted. Few monarchs have been less wasteful, more careful of their finances, but he could – and did – spend large sums wisely, on the promotion not only of the arts, but also the sciences. To understand his tastes, one must go back to his father and mother and their children, to the White House at Kew, where George III grew up.

His father, Frederick, was as passionately interested in plants as he was in pictures and music. The distant worlds of Asia, Indonesia and North and South America, were providing botanists in England with thousands of new plants, often trees and shrubs, like the camelia, of exquisite beauty. Frederick's friend, Lord Bute, was a passionate botanist and encouraged him to plant and breed exotic new species at Kew – and so began the Royal Botanic Gardens. When Frederick died, Peter Collinson, the greatest importer of rare plants, lamented that 'gardening and planting here lost their best friend'. But the Princess of Wales continued to buy, to plant and to beautify what rapidly became a treasure house of trees and shrubs and flowers. In the eighteenth century a large garden needed buildings – follies, they were called – temples, false ruins, that sort of thing, as well as plants. They provided seats for rest, closed the long perspective of an avenue or came as a sudden surprise in a serpentine walk. Princess Augusta asked Sir William Chambers to build for her; he produced 'Roman' ruins, and several charming temples. When her son succeeded, money was a little easier, so she commissioned Chambers to build a magnificent Orangery, which, as well as providing her court with a plentiful supply of oranges, also acted as a shelter for other tender plants needing heat. It still adorns Kew. But the most remarkable of all of Chambers's works there was the octagonal Pagoda – a

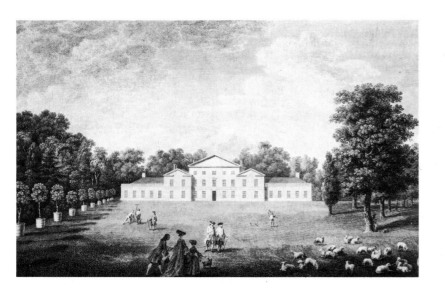

The White House, Kew, where King George III spent his boyhood. An engraving after W. Woollett. *c.* 1760

Chinese building ten stories high. It was not merely a whim, for it gave an incomparable view of the rapidly extending gardens, and so helped in designing the plantations and walks.

George III grew up at Kew, in a world of new and expanding knowledge of nature; and botany was one of the most rapidly developing sciences of the eighteenth century. Neither he nor his wife, Charlotte of Mecklenburg-Strelitz, whom he married in 1761, ever lost their passion for Kew or their interest in botany. He bought, for example, Mark Catesby's *Natural History of Carolina, Florida and the Bahamas*, with the artist's original drawings, for what was in 1768 a vast price for a book—£160. This interest also brought one of the rarest of all botanical books into the royal library. About 1785 Lord Bute gave Queen Charlotte a nine-volume work by himself entitled *Botanical Tables containing the different Familys of British Plants*. With total disdain for public acclaim, he had only twelve copies of this printed, at a cost of £12,000 (about £150,000 today), which must make it one of the most expensive books ever published.

Enough has been said to demonstrate that Frederick and his wife were

The Royal Botanical Gardens at Kew were begun by Frederick, Prince of Wales. His son, King George III, developed the gardens and bought, for the royal library at Windsor, some rare and beautiful botanical books.

1 *Sophora Japonica*, a remnant of Hanoverian planting still surviving in the Gardens at Kew.

2 The title page of Lord Bute's *Botanical Tables containing the different Familys of British Plants*. *c.* 1785

3 and 4 Two engravings after W. Woollett, *c.* 1760, of the Royal Gardens at Kew.

5 *The Red Curlew*, and 6 *The Four Eye'd Night Butterfly with branches of Philadelphus and Smilax* – two plates from Mark Catesby's *Natural History of Carolina, Florida and the Bahamas*, 1731–43.

7 *Caterpillars*, pupae and moths on Solanum-Indicum spinosum, a drawing on vellum for Maria Sibylla Merian's *Metamorphosis Insectorum Surinamensium*, published 1705

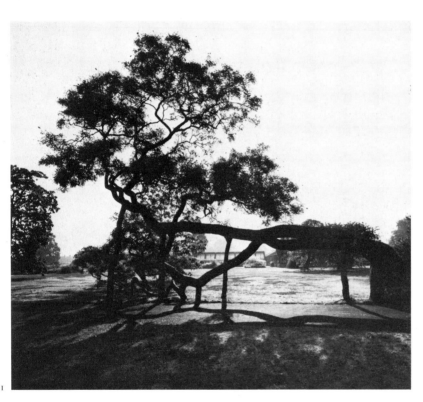

1

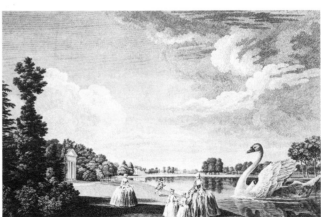

2

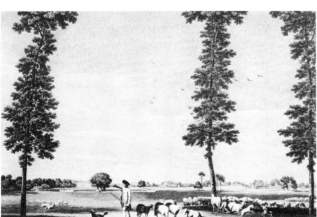

3

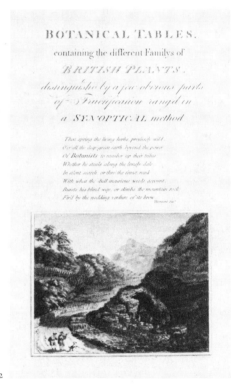

4

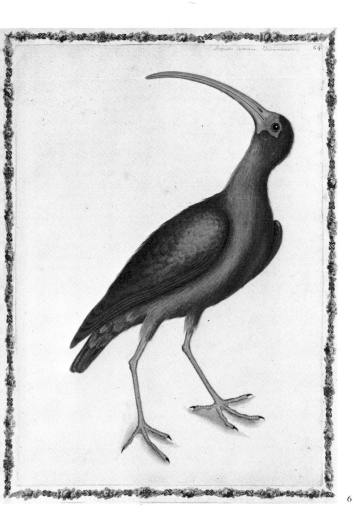

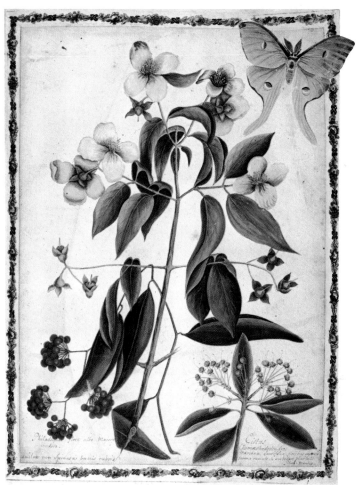

6

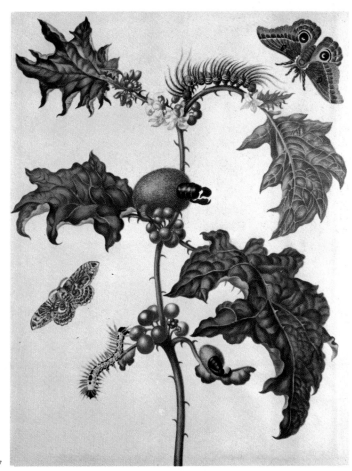

7

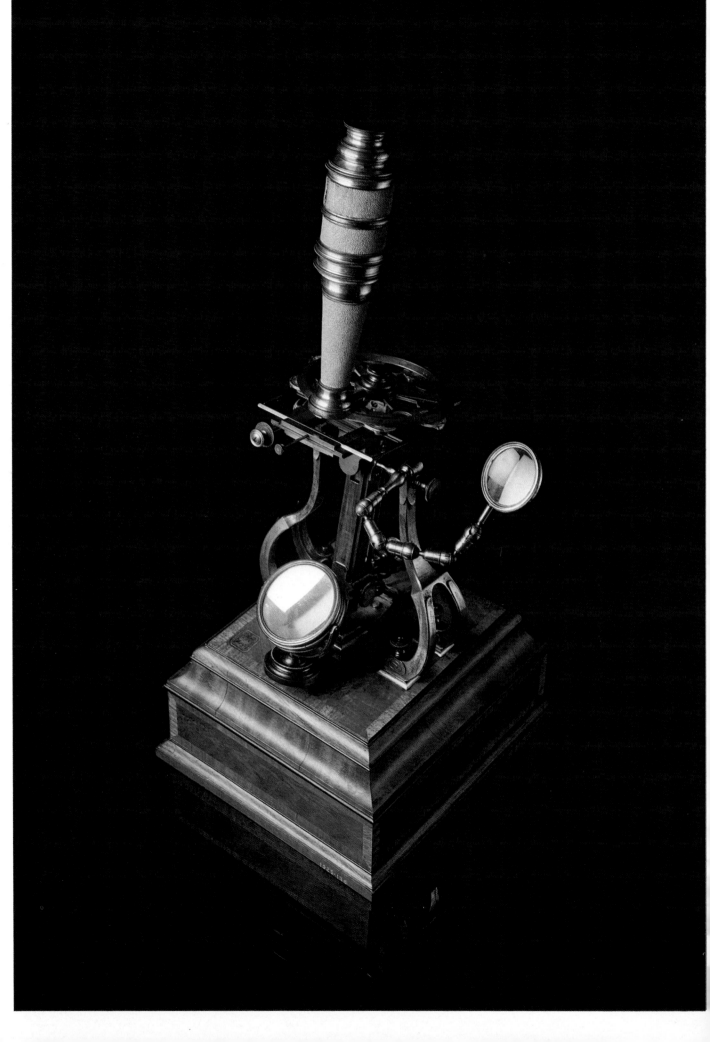

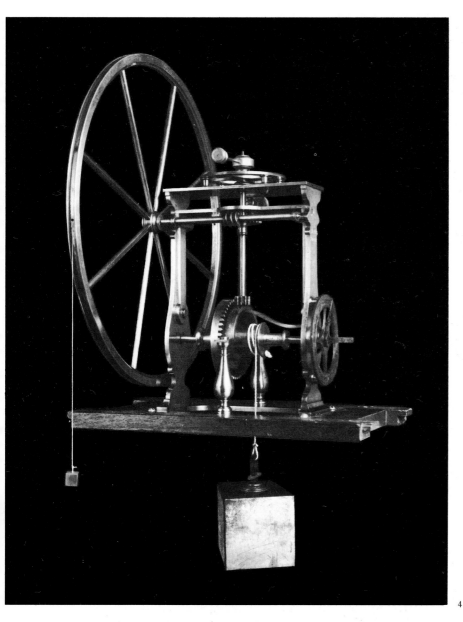

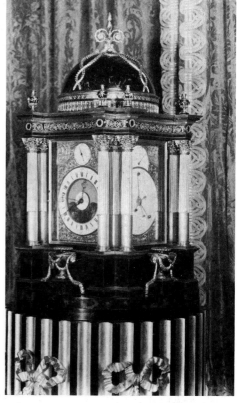

King George III's scientific interests were wide. His microscope (opposite) is now in the Science Museum, London, as is the compound engine (2), both made by George Adams.

3 Directions, in King George III's handwriting, for assembling a watch.

4 Four-sided astronomical clock by Christopher Pinchbeck, 1768. The four dials show: the time of day; a planetarium; the tides at forty-three points; and the signs of the zodiac and sidereal time

4

3

highly cultivated people. There was, it is true, in Frederick a streak of rashness, of impatience which made him at times irritated with the shyness and social awkwardness of his eldest son, and led him to prefer his younger brother, the Duke of York. Nevertheless, neither he nor, after his death, his wife were likely to neglect the education of their son, who would be king. They did not. He was taught to read and write French, German and Latin, grounded in mathematics by Scott, a Fellow of the Royal Society, and he was the first British monarch to study physics, chemistry, botany and astronomy. He grew to love books and, whatever subsequent historians have said, he was impeccably grounded by Bute in sound whig history, which is demonstrated by a large bundle of essays that he wrote for Bute, and which still remain in the royal archives. These sentiments about the revolution of 1688 would have done credit to the great whig historian, Macaulay: '... this Convention [ie the parliament of 1689] with all its blemishes saved the nation from the iron rod of arbitrary power ... let us remember that we stand in debt for our liberty and religion to the success of 1688'.

He was naturally taught the usual social accomplishments – to dance, to fence, to ride, to shoot – and he was always to enjoy a vigorous outdoor life, but he enjoyed the arts as well. He became a competent musician, playing the harpsichord with skill. Even at fourteen he was buying the scores of Handel's oratorios, and he was delighted to receive ninety-seven autograph volumes of Handel's works, which he had especially bound. This remarkable collection was given in 1957 by Queen Elizabeth II to the British Library. Music remained his life-long passion, and was shared by his wife who played the organ as well as the harpsichord.

George III was also taught drawing by Joseph Groupy and George Michael Moser, and architecture by Sir William Chambers. The precision of architectural drawing appealed to him very much and underlay his taste in painting. It was also during his childhood that he developed a passion for the theatre. His father adored amateur theatricals and

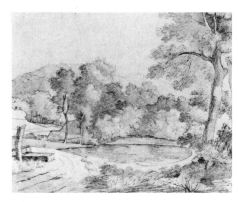

A landscape drawing by King George III when Prince of Wales

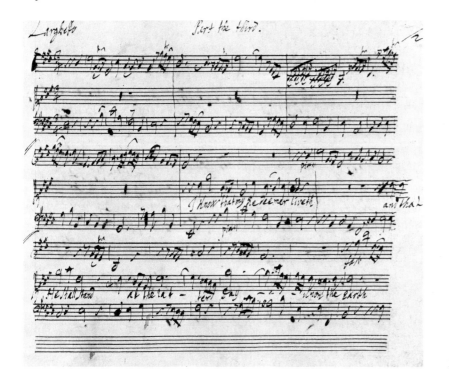

A page from Handel's *Messiah*. The composer's son, his amanuensis, gave ninety-seven autograph volumes of his father's works to King George III and these are now in the British Library, London

delighted in producing a play with his children in the major roles. George III himself, as a boy, was not a good actor (no one ever praises him), but he certainly acquired a taste for the theatre.

These were the tastes and accomplishments that were expected of a polished prince, but to them George III added an addiction all of his own – a passion for books. Indeed, he is the only true bibliophile in the long line of British monarchs. He bought over 67,000 books on every conceivable subject; they filled room after room at Buckingham House, which George III had bought for his wife shortly after their marriage in 1762, and formed the nucleus of the British Library at the British Museum. It contained over 200 Bibles, in every language from Finnish to Iroquois, massive quantities of Shakespeare, twenty-six books printed by Caxton, a first edition of *Paradise Lost*, and most eighteenth-century British authors – Fielding, for whom the King had a passion, Samuel Johnson of course, Boswell, Smollett, Sterne. He also purchased foreign authors, even Rousseau and Voltaire, whom he detested. Not surprisingly the King's bibliographical and musical interests fused, and he purchased rare Dutch, French and Italian song books, and bought massively at the sale of the library of William Boyce the composer, who had been the Master of his band. By 1785 the King had assembled the greatest collection of musical books in England.

The King allowed £1500 a year for purchases of books, and frequently exceeded it; in 1765, for example, he spent £10,000 on Joseph Smith's

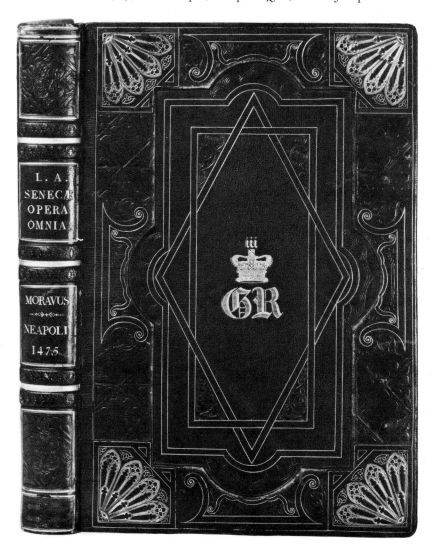

A binding from King George III's library. British Library, London

collection which contained remarkable early printed books. Even earlier he had bought the *Thomason Tracts*, 32,000 pamphlets, broadsheets, newspapers and books relating to the English civil war in the seventeenth century. Realising their importance to scholars, he gave them at once to the British Museum. Not that he kept scholars out of his own library – far from it, it was open to them all. Dr Johnson used it, and was honoured by a visit from the King whilst he was there. Even radicals like Dr Joseph Priestley, whose support of the cause of America and for the reform of parliament the King deplored, were made welcome. John Adams, the second President of the United States, visited the library in 1783, when he was the first American ambassador to the court of St James. He was no admirer of George III, naturally enough, but he was a scholar and a book lover. He wrote, 'The King's library struck me with admiration. I wished for a week's time, but had but a few hours. The books were in perfect order, elegant in their editions, paper, binding, etc, but gaudy and extravagant in nothing. They were chosen with perfect taste and judgment; every book that a King ought to have always at hand … In every apartment in the whole house, the same taste, the same judgment, the same elegance, the same simplicity, without the smallest affectation, ostentation, profusion or meanness.' To service so magnificent a library required its own bindery, and shortly after Adams's visit in 1786 George III established the first royal bindery, whose tools are still in use today.

The library filled a great deal of Buckingham House – or the Queen's House, as it was known. This was the first new palace to be acquired in London for two centuries. It had belonged to the illegitimate daughter of

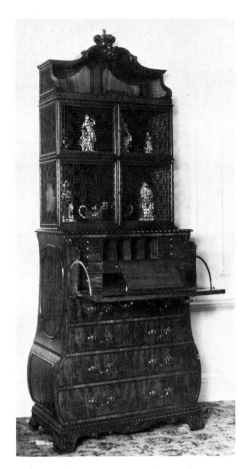

Bureau-cabinet by William Vile. Made in 1762 for Queen Charlotte's apartments in St James's Palace

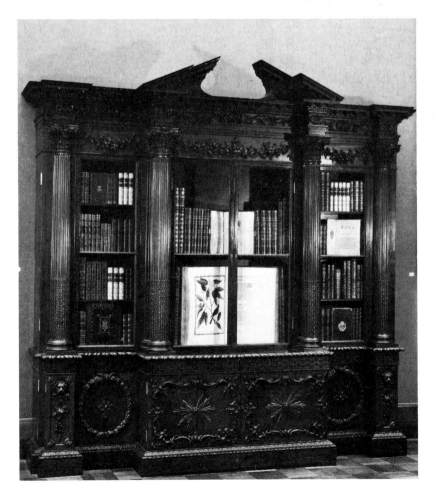

Bookcase by William Vile. Made in 1762 for the furnishing of Buckingham House

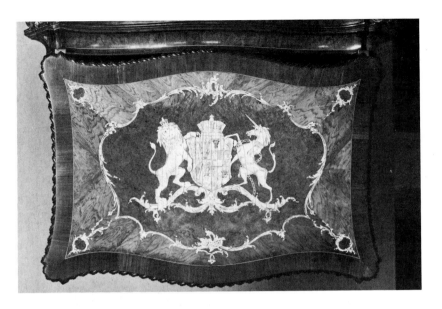

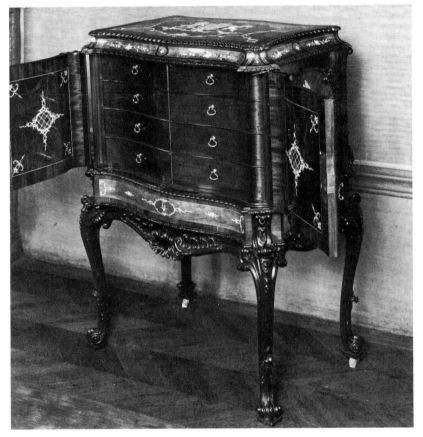

Jewel cabinet made by William Vile for Queen Charlotte in 1762. The top is inlaid with the Royal Arms

James II, the Duchess of Buckingham, and though a small house by royal standards, it had a large garden which gave it great privacy, unlike St James's Palace which had almost none. For generations, almost for centuries, the British monarchs had toyed with the idea of building a new great palace in London. For George II William Kent had designed a magnificent Palladian palace to be built in Hyde Park. It never was. And it was this modest house which ultimately was to become the major royal palace in London.

When purchased in 1762 it was far too small, and new rooms had to be built, including a splendid Octagon Room for the library. All rooms needed both furniture and pictures, and George III and Queen Charlotte shopped happily. Fortunately English cabinet-making had achieved an

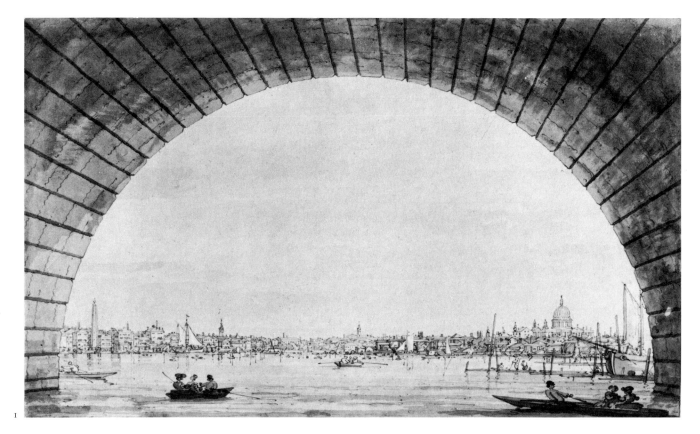

exceptional degree of elegance and splendour, with Thomas Chippendale and William Vile, and it was the latter whom the King and Queen particularly favoured. He built a noble bookcase for the King, surely worthy of the library, which is now in the royal collection again, after having been owned for many generations by a younger branch of George III's family. Vile also made a number of pieces of furniture for the Queen, including an elaborate jewel cabinet which ranks amongst the finest pieces of furniture made in eighteenth-century England. The King had lavished jewels on the Queen at their marriage, most of them now lost to the royal collection, as in the nineteenth century they were successfully claimed by the Hanoverian branch of the family, much to Queen Victoria's chagrin.

As well as furniture, the King and Queen also needed pictures. In 1762, through the help of Lord Bute's brother, George III made a spectacular purchase which immediately transformed the royal collection – the pictures and drawings, old masters and modern masters, which had been assembled at Venice by Consul Smith. Joseph Smith acted as a cicerone for many young aristocrats on the Grand Tour, advising them about purchases and often acting as an intermediary with Venetian painters. At the same time he had built up his own outstanding collection. George III purchased it for £20,000; although some years later Catherine the Great of Russia was only to pay £33,000 for the vast collection of old masters which Sir Robert Walpole had brought together earlier in the century, by any standards this was a bargain. Amongst the old masters was one of the world's great pictures, Vermeer's *A Lady at the Virginals*, and a fine portrait of a young man by Giovanni Bellini. The heart of the collection, however, was contemporary, or near contemporary, Italian pictures, mostly Venetian, and very much in accord with the taste of the English nobility, whose sons were now being sent to

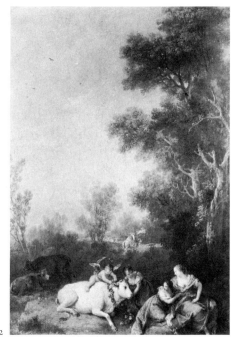

1 Canaletto, drawing of *London; St Paul's seen through an Arch of Westminster Bridge.* *c.*1746/7.

2 Francesco Zuccarelli, *Europa and the Bull.* Bought for King George III with the collection of Consul Smith and painted for the Consul, probably in the 1740s

Italy to finish their education and rarely came back without modern Italian paintings. Apart from two charming genre scenes by Longhi, *Blind Man's Buff* and *The Morning Levée*, the bulk of the collection consisted of topography and landscapes. There were fifty paintings by the Ricci, mainly landscapes with slight classical allusions. George III was attracted to Zuccarelli's style and later bought five more canvases from this artist, who came to England in pursuit of patronage. Finally there were the Canalettos – fifty paintings and 150 drawings, mainly of Venice. Indeed, one can make the journey, picture by picture, down the length of the Grand Canal. These paintings had been commissioned by Consul Smith, whose liking for systematic topographical representation and exact detail chimed with the King's own tastes. A view of the Thames, seen through an arch, looking towards Westminster, which Canaletto had painted during his visit to England, exactly recalls for us the bustling life of the Thames of George III's day.

During the early years of his reign, George III also acquired a collection of drawings from Cardinal Albani, which contained magnificent works by Domenichino, the Carracci, and Poussin. George III clearly liked drawings almost more than paintings, because he also purchased another collection, from Richard Mead, a successful physician who was also an ardent collector, which contained yet more drawings by Poussin. Some of the finest drawings in the royal collection may have entered it during the early years of George III's reign – may have, because little is known of the provenance of many of them; some of the fine Michelangelos and Raphaels may have been purchased by his father, or entered the collection even as early as Charles I's time, but they are first listed in George III's reign, and he could have bought them.

Marco Ricci, *The Courtyard of a Country House*. Also from the Consul Smith collection

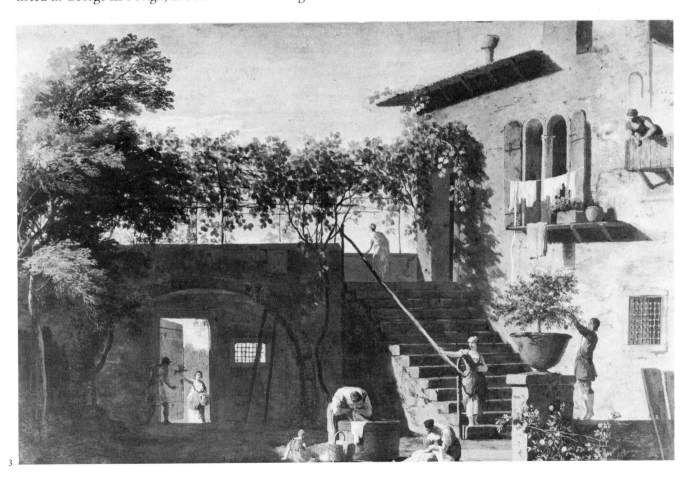

3

George III stopped collecting pictures as soon as his purpose – adorning Buckingham House – was achieved, but he never ceased to be a splendid, if erratic, patron of British art. He was responsible for the foundation of the Royal Academy, provided rooms at Somerset House for its annual exhibitions, and throughout his active life remained interested in its affairs. He drew up the diploma to be given to an academician on his election himself, provided £400 a year out of his own pocket, reserved the appointment of the treasurer to himself, and made certain that the aims of the academy, which was dedicated as much to education as to display, were carried out. He regularly attended the annual banquet and visited the exhibitions until 1806, when his eyesight began to fail.

As on so many matters, George III depended initially on Bute for advice on British painters. Bute rightly favoured a fellow Scotsman, Alan Ramsay, who produced a brilliant state portrait of the King and a flattering one of the Queen. His portrait of the King enjoyed an astronomical success; most of the great aristocratic families of England, and scores of corporations, bought copies, and yet more were sent as presents throughout the world, to the Great Mogul as well as to the Governor of the Bahamas. This portrait made Ramsay a fortune; never before had a coronation portrait of a monarch been so widely dispersed. Although Joshua Reynolds became the first President of the Royal Academy, and was knighted by the King, George III never liked his work. As he told Lord Eglington, who was pushing Reynolds, with some asperity, 'Mr Ramsay is my painter, my Lord'.

For a time he took a great deal of pleasure in the work of Thomas Gainsborough, who painted by far the most beautiful picture of Queen Charlotte. He also commissioned him to paint all of his children, to match the series by Liotard which his mother had ordered of her children. These were shown at the academy and Gainsborough was extremely anxious that they should be hung precisely as he wanted them. Later they became jumbled, until George VI had them rehung in the Long Corridor at Windsor, precisely as Gainsborough wished them to be arranged. George III often dropped a painter with remarkable alacrity and although Gainsborough had painted exceptional portraits of them – that of Queen Charlotte is quite brilliant – he abruptly ceased to patronise him. Other members of the royal family remained loyal to Gainsborough. One of the most beautiful of all Gainsborough's portraits was of the King's brother, the Duke of Cumberland, and his wife out for a walk that now hangs in the Queen's dressing-room at Windsor. The Prince of Wales, afterwards George IV, also patronised Gainsborough, not only for his own portraits, but also for those of the beautiful young actress, Perdita Robinson, who was his mistress, and of his boon racing companion, Colonel St Leger, who gave his name to the classic race. One of the more enduring favourites of the King was Benjamin West, an expatriate American, who became the second President of the Royal Academy. A man of soaring ambition, he painted vast historical pictures which projected the heroic virtues of courage, endurance, patriotism, virtues deeply admired by the King. Although a very skilled painter, these pictures now seem overstrained and bathetic, whereas his more informal portraits of the Queen and the royal children still delight. Throughout his life the King switched his patronage abruptly and

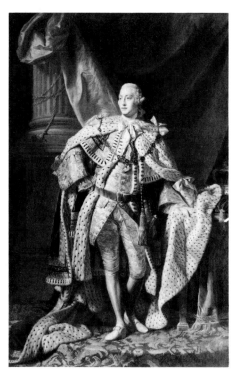

Alan Ramsay, state portrait of King George III. 1760

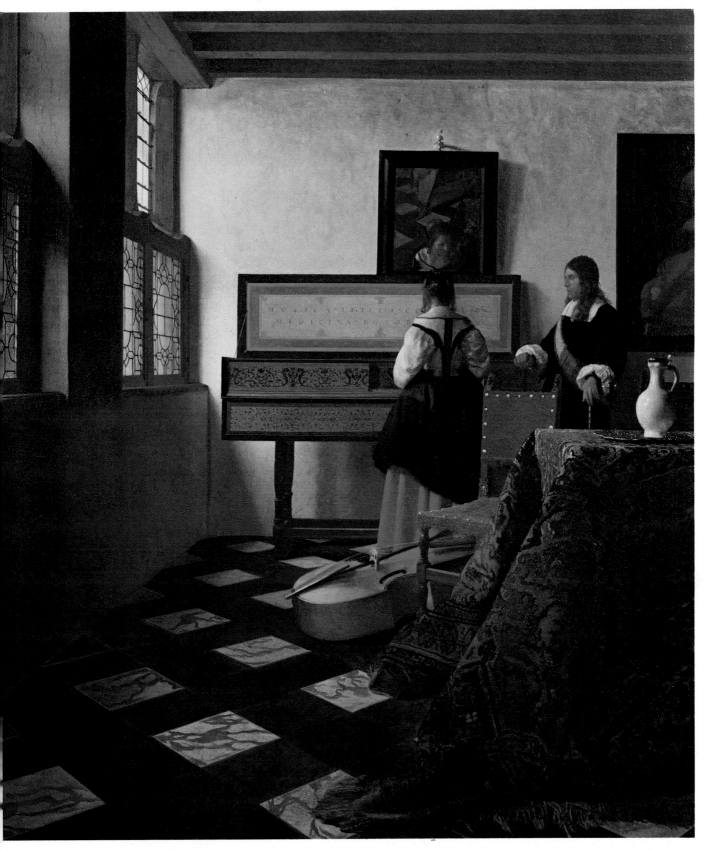

Johannes Vermeer, *The Music Lesson: a Lady at the Virginals with a Gentleman Listening. c.* 1665–70

In 1762 George III *bought practically the whole of the collection of Consul Smith of Venice: coins, medals, prints, books, cameos, drawings and paintings. Smith's superb collections were almost certainly intended for Buckingham House, which the King had bought that year for Queen Charlotte. Reproduced here are four of the paintings*

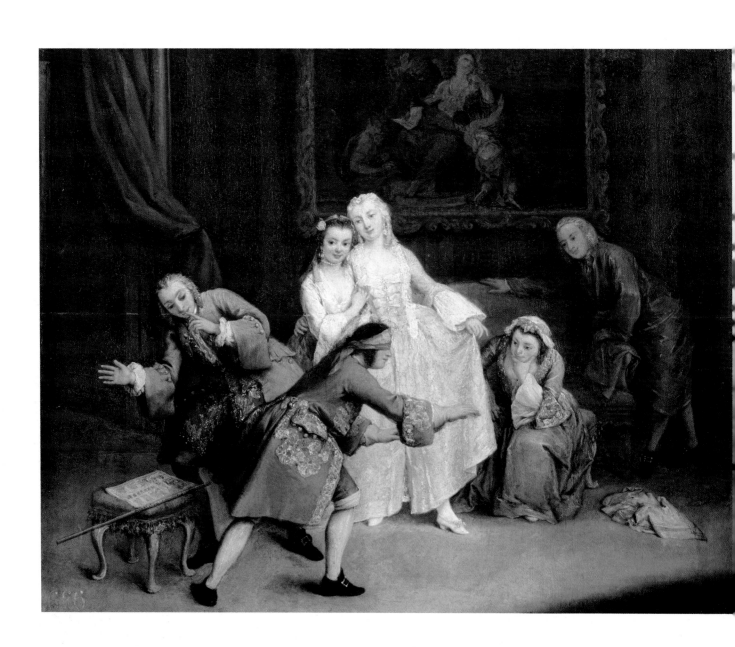

Pietro Longhi, *Blind Man's Buff*. 174(?)

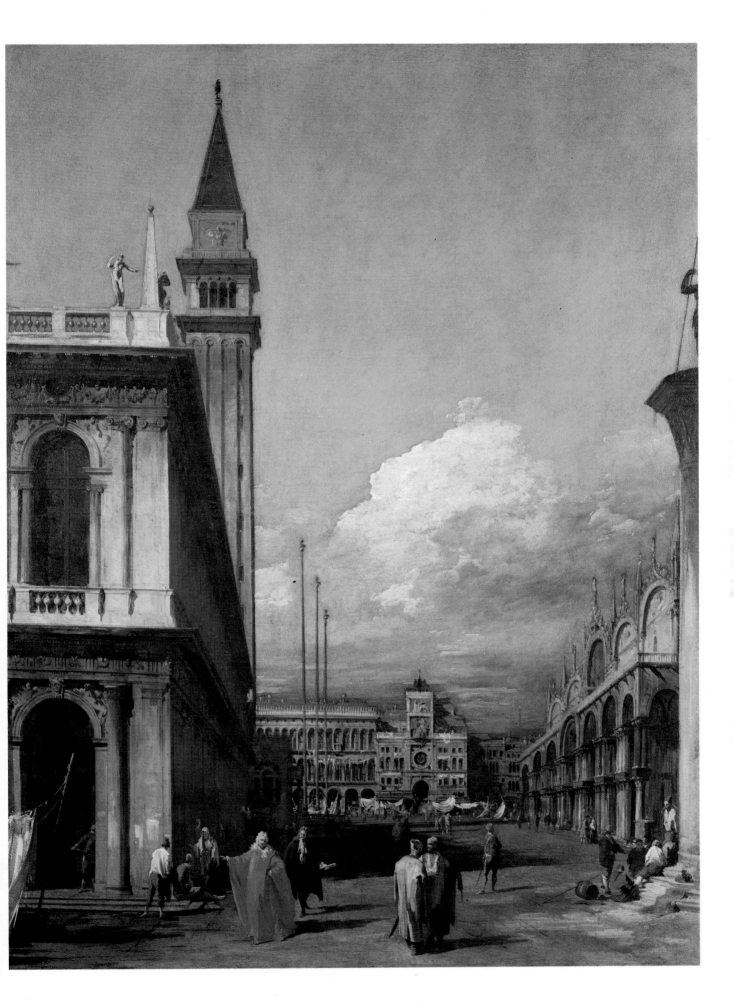

Canaletto, *The Piazzetta, Venice*

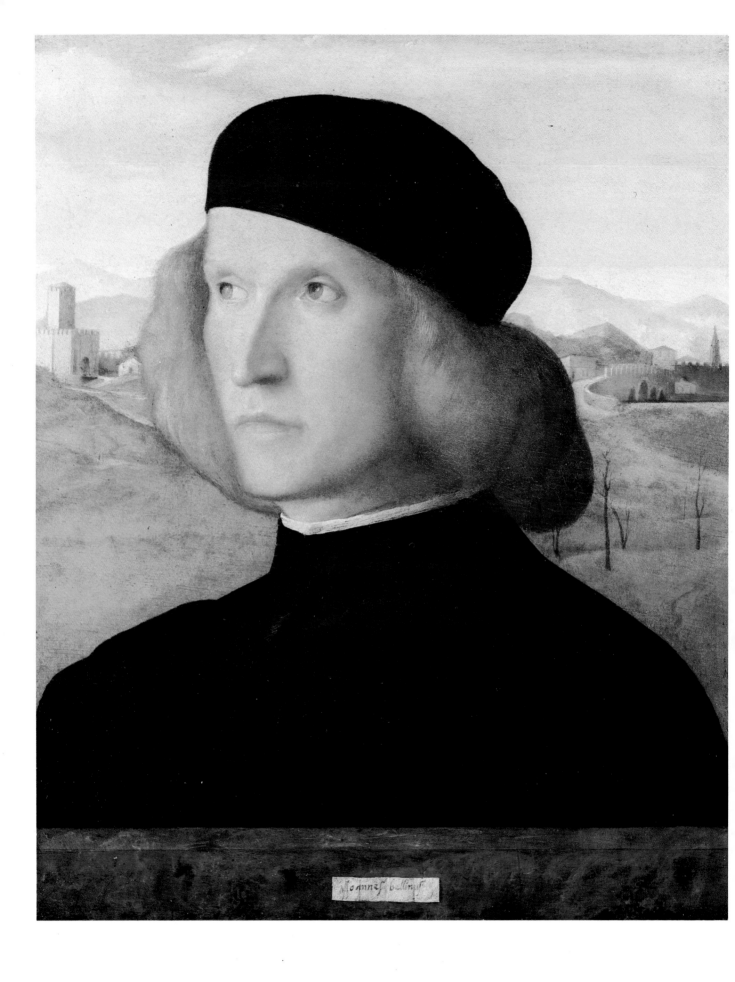

Giovanni Bellini, *Portrait of a Young Man*

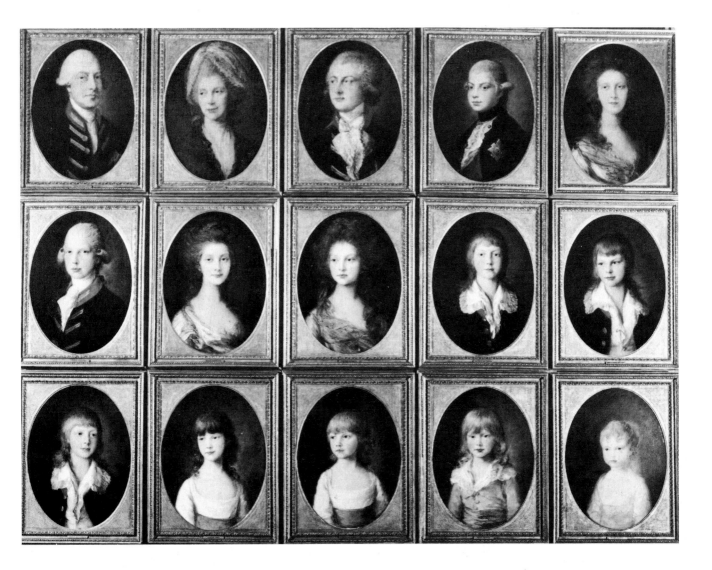

decisively, but Johann Zoffany remained in favour, the informal gaiety and accuracy (always a strong point with the King) of his pictures delighting him and the Queen. Zoffany painted the great group portrait of the first Royal Academicians 'most likenesses strong', as Horace Walpole wrote. (The two lady academicians are shown by portraits – as a nude male model was posing it would have been indelicate for them to be personally present!)

George III had come to the throne, fortunately, when Britain was full of creative exuberance, of a sense of power and purpose. Agriculture booming, commerce flourishing, industry growing, Britain seemed certain of a glorious future. Indeed, the year before George III's accession, 1759, had been the Year of Victories, that *annus mirabilis* when the church bells never stopped ringing – the French and their allies defeated in Germany, in Canada, in India, in the Caribbean; Britain triumphant everywhere. No wonder that George III told his first parliament that, 'born and educated in this country, I glory in the name of Britain', or that his new state coach should riot in the symbolism of victory. The design of this astonishing coach – the most famous of all royal coaches – was orchestrated by Sir William Chambers and the painting done by Cipriani. The King is symbolised as monarch of the sea, and the coach is festooned with tritons blowing on their conches, but perhaps the paintings speak louder still in their obvious symbolism: here Peace is

Thomas Gainsborough, George III, Queen Charlotte and thirteen of their children. The portraits were painted in September and October 1782

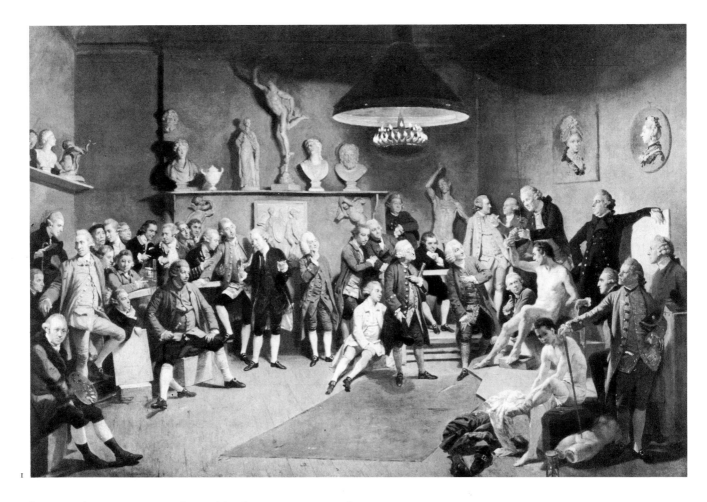

burning the instruments of War (timely, as France was about to accept the humiliating Treaty of Paris), History recording the reports of Fame, and, the most appropriate, 'Industry and Ingenuity offering a cornucopia to the Genius of Britain'.

A young King, a victorious nation, 'commerce', as Edmund Burke wrote, 'made to flourish through war'. Happy in his marriage, with Bute at his side, all seemed set fair. Yet within three years the political life of the nation was in turmoil and in turmoil it remained for most of George III's reign. The Treaty of Paris in 1763, which brought the long war with France to an end, was not humiliating enough for many London merchants, who wanted to grind France into oblivion. This bitterness was forcibly expressed by John Wilkes, whom the government handled with such ineptitude that he was able to raise one fundamental constitutional issue after another. For ten years, whenever they appeared on the London streets, George III and his ministers were almost deafened with cries of 'Wilkes and Liberty'. In bitter essays or savage cartoons a free press began to heap calumnies on the King which, softened and modified, were to slip into the textbooks of history – the most insidious that he sought to re-establish the arbitrary power of the Stuarts.

The King was involved in politics more than his grandfather had been, partly because he had to be, and partly because – ineptly – he wanted to promote Lord Bute. Bute was a most civilised man, but utterly incompetent, as he himself quickly realised, to manoeuvre with skill in the jungle of power politics. The whig oligarchs hated him, but whig oligarchy was no longer what it had been. The old, established figures were dead or ageing, their successors were quarrelsome, power-hungry,

Johann Zoffany: 1 *The Academicians of the Royal Academy. c.* 1768. 2 *The Tribuna of the Uffizi.* (See colour detail, page 196)

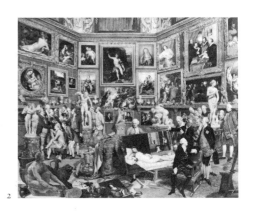

factious, so that, time and again, the young King was forced to reconstruct his ministries. True, the whigs made him get rid of Bute, but they were unable to provide a reliable and successful prime minister. With America, in addition, on the verge of revolution, one can realise how heavy were the burdens on the young King's shoulders, and marvel that he found so much time for his intellectual and artistic interests.

Like any world in which there are great extremes of riches and poverty and little social control, George III's London experienced considerable violence, robbery and mayhem, and highway robbery in Hyde Park was nothing untoward. Life had crudity and violence as well as glitter, and the peacock-like aestheticism in clothes and coaches contrasted with the grime and ugliness, the hatred and cruelty which was expressed so vividly in the caricatures and the satires of Hogarth. The age was so vivid, so full of colour and darkness, that we tend to be distracted from its most remarkable aspects – a spreading sense amongst all classes of vital growth, the feeling that the British were becoming richer, that life could be, and should be, materially more enjoyable. This pervaded every aspect of life, and never before had men and women been so active in seeking for wealth, in looking for markets, in applying their ingenuity to producing new goods. Agriculture, as well as commerce and industry, was infused with this spirit of optimism and experiment. Never had the majority of Englishmen been so well fed; though there could be, and was, ugly starvation amongst the rural as well as the urban poor, by previous standards England abounded in food and was abundant with meat in the eighteenth century. Not surprisingly this was the age which had invented the song 'The Roast Beef of Old England' back in the King's grandfather's day. This spirit of enterprise and experiment in agriculture deeply interested the King, indeed involved him as much as did the developments in art, or in music; perhaps more so.

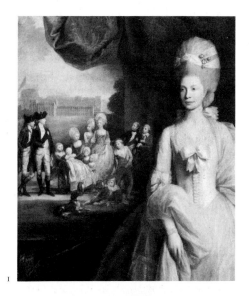

He farmed at Richmond, and later ran three large farms in the Great Park at Windsor, where he bred cattle and, particularly, sheep. He was responsible for introducing merino sheep and crossing them with English breeds in order to produce finer wool. A frugal man, who loved accuracy, he kept a sharp eye on his accounts and made a profit. His farming brought him very close to the economic heart of his age.

Accuracy, precision, regularity of habit, these were the very fundamentals of the King's character, and he was fascinated by mechanical and scientific instruments, particularly elaborate clocks. Every room in Buckingham Palace had clocks especially designed for him, and kept in perfect accuracy by his chief clockmaker, Benjamin Vulliamy. One of the most remarkable of these is the four-sided astronomical clock which shows mean and solar time, gives the time at various places of different longitude, and the tides at forty-three different places, mainly in the British Isles. If that were not enough, it tells the phases of the moon, the days of the week, the month, the position of the stars and the sun, and traces the movement of six planets! And the King himself, with Sir William Chambers, designed the magnificent case in which this quite remarkable clock is placed.

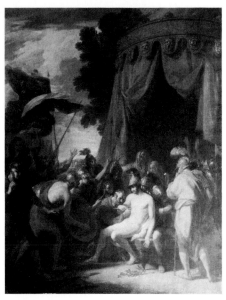

Another extraordinary clock which also records the weather, designed especially for George III by Alexander Cumming, is the barograph for which he paid in 1765 the very considerable price of £1178; the mechanism is ingenious and the case is of exceptional richness and

Benjamin West: 1 *Queen Charlotte.* 1779. A detail. Her thirteen children are grouped behind her. 2 *The Death of Epaminondas.* 1773

beauty. He owned what has been described as 'perhaps the most historically important watch in the world', made for him in 1769 by Thomas Mudge, the inventor of the lever-escapement which this watch incorporates; even more remarkably it is the first pocket watch which automatically adjusts itself to changes in temperature.

George III was also a practitioner of horology, able to take to pieces and reassemble the most complicated watches – he carefully drew up in his own hand a list of the complex and methodical processes that he had to follow. His love of accuracy, precision and a proper sense of order also led him to take delight in astronomy, and make a close friend of William Herschel, a talented musician turned astronomer of genius, who discovered the planet Uranus in 1781, and so expanded the bounds of the solar universe. Like most astronomers, Herschel wanted bigger and bigger telescopes, and the King financed a forty-foot instrument (through which he insisted on walking before it was fitted up) at a cost of £4000, and annual maintenance of £200 (all, of course, out of his private purse). In the earlier days of his reign the King had a small observatory at Richmond, but in order to watch the transit of Venus across the sun, decided to build a much larger one at Kew to take a bigger telescope. Captain Cook had been sent – with royal blessing – to observe the transit on the other side of the world, and consequently discovered New Zealand and made a thorough exploration of the Pacific; but the weather held fair in England, and the King watched the transit at Kew.

Clocks and the stars were not George III's only scientific interest. He made a collection of fine instruments, many of them novel and ingenious, such as the Compound Microscope and the Compound Engine, both made by George Adams, the leading inventor of such instruments. In many ways George III was a natural technologist, and would have made an excellent engineer or draughtsman. But, as Napoleon rightly remarked, he ruled a nation of shopkeepers. Commerce flourished as never before, and commerce stimulated industry; both needed markets, expanding markets, so the leaders of commerce and industry sought, and obtained, royal patronage. Josiah Wedgwood, the great potter, was early in the field. Having received an order for a creamware service, he obtained permission to call it 'Queen's ware', which immediately multiplied his sales. He cultivated the royal interest, and made a medallion to mark the recovery of the King from illness in 1789. This sold splendidly, as did other profiles of the royal family, but he was not the only potter patronised. Queen Charlotte purchased a superb Chelsea dinner service, perhaps the finest ever made by that factory, and combining the King's love of clocks with the Queen's delight in china, the same firm produced two remarkable porcelain clock cases. The King and Queen also visited Worcester to inspect the porcelain factory there in 1788. Matthew Boulton, who partnered James Watt, the inventor of the steam-engine, had a three-hour interview with the King and Queen in 1770, and was delighted to obtain an order for his splendid, and rightly famous, Derbyshire blue-john vases.

The King was happiest at Kew. He could drive over to his observatory, spend happy hours in the ever-growing botanical gardens, retire to the thatched *cottage orné* which Queen Charlotte had had built, and there take tea or listen to his daughters play on the harpsichord or mandolin, or help them with their sketching. Indeed, he loved Kew so

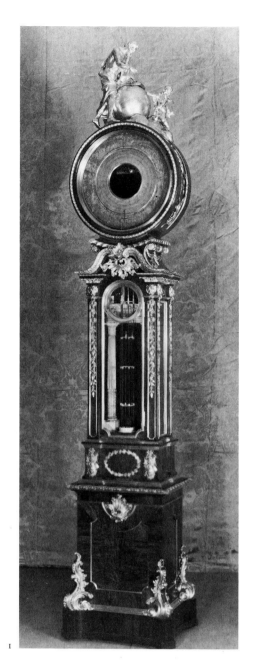

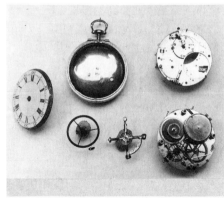

1 Barograph by Alexander Cumming. Commissioned by King George III, it was purchased by him in 1765.

2 Gold watch made by Thomas Mudge for the King in 1769 – the first watch to have lever-escapement

much that he pulled down his parents' house and began to build, at last, a large palace by the river. It was designed in the revival of the Gothic style, which was just beginning to be fashionable. The work was slow, indeed the palace remained a half-built dream and never became a lived-in reality. Unfinished, it was demolished in 1828, and no vestiges remain. Whilst it was being built, the King moved into a charming small house in Kew Gardens, built in the Dutch style in the seventeenth century by a prosperous London merchant, which had been used previously as a home for his elder sons with their tutors.

The domestic happiness which George III enjoyed unfortunately did not last long. The struggle with America and her European allies had ended in the disaster at Yorktown, where the British army was defeated and America secured her independence. In this defeat the King felt a personal sense of humiliation, made worse by the triumphs of the opposition politicians whom he detested. As turbulent as ever, large sections of the population demanded parliamentary reform, and a new, more aggressive radicalism developed. Great national problems were worry enough, but the King's anxieties were made deeper by the behaviour of his children. He had fifteen, and preferred daughters to sons. Indeed, he adored them so much that he hated them marrying. His sons he liked when they were small, but adolescence led to conflict with them all. It is true that they were a strange and difficult brood. They all got into scrapes, set up expensive mistresses, piled up debts, and often behaved with extraordinary eccentricity. Most of them were warm-hearted, impulsive and generous to a fault. Their blatant immorality, their injudicious marriages (which most of them came to with the utmost reluctance) and their mountainous debts darkened the King's days, and added immensely to the burdens which he carried.

To cap all, the King most probably suffered from a rare metabolic disorder, porphyria. It was not identified until the twentieth century, and as the symptoms were akin to madness – extreme irritability, compulsive talking, hallucinations – the family and the nation thought that he had become insane when he went down with a severe attack in 1789. The Prince of Wales, expecting immediately to become Regent, if not succeed to the throne, behaved with so total a lack of judgment that when the King recovered their relationship worsened even further. Naturally the King himself thought that he had been mad, and dreaded a further attack. The illness, followed almost immediately by the French Revolution and renewed war between Britain and France, together with the riotous behaviour of his sons, began to turn the tide of popularity towards the King.

During the second half of his long reign George III had come to live at Windsor, which he took under his wing like some benevolent squire. He refused to live either at Hampton Court, Kensington Palace or St James's because his grandfather had (he could be very obstinate in his dislikes). He continued to work at St James's when in London, giving audiences and the like, but he would not live there. Windsor attracted him because of its hunting, and occasional visits led, in the late seventies, to longer stays, for a time, in the house that Queen Anne had used. Sir William Chambers began to put some of the rooms of the Castle in order, and from the middle 1780s onwards George III used Windsor frequently. Queen Charlotte was quite unhappy to move back into the castle, and began to

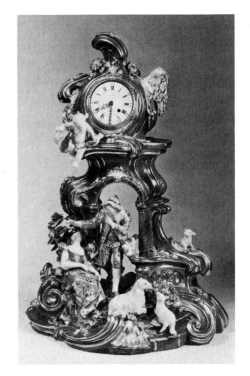

One of a pair of Chelsea porcelain clocks by William Strigel, that belonged to Queen Charlotte. *c.* 1760

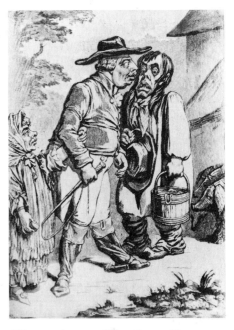

Gillray, caricature of King George III as 'Farmer George'. 1795. The caption reads 'Well, Friend, where a'you going, hay? – What's your Name, hay? – where d'ye Live, hay? – hay?'

use frequently her house at Frogmore, with the beautiful landscaped garden. Certainly the Castle and St George's Chapel, which the King also repaired, were saved from becoming totally ruinous. He enjoyed strolling with his family along the North Terrace, stopping to chat with the families from Windsor that were allowed to walk there. He loved visiting and being visited by the boys across the river at Eton, and they still celebrate his birthday with a parade of boats down the river Thames flowing by the Castle. He would frequently stroll in the town, browsing in the bookshop for items for his library. And he actively promoted the building of a theatre at Windsor which, once established, he visited once a week.

His generosity and his avid curiosity, which always led to a flood of questions, stimulated a warmth and loyalty that gradually spread further and further from Windsor, so that when he made his visit to Weymouth or Cheltenham to take the waters his journeys took on the air of a triumphal procession. Both Kew and Windsor were a great solace and one sorely needed, for the 1790s proved a bitter decade: defeats for Britain's allies on the continent, bad harvests and near starvation at home, even a naval mutiny, in 1797, at the Nore; and after a century's peace rebellion in Ireland. All immensely agitated the King, and made his precarious health worse. Only at the very end of the decade did the victories of Nelson in the Mediterranean and further victories in India bring some comfort. He had further attacks of his illness which steadily gained ground, but was well enough to appreciate the importance and significance of Trafalgar, when Nelson destroyed the combined fleets of France and Spain and so secured Britain from the threat of invasion. But his eyesight began to fail, further attacks of illness weakened the King, destroying the happiness that he had created for himself. His interest in agriculture, in art, in science died long before he did.

From time to time he was well enough to visit his small, much-loved palace at Kew, but in the end his mind gave way and they brought him to Windsor. He became totally blind, almost deaf, and wandered about his rooms in a purple dressing gown, Lear-like with his wild white hair and beard, lost to reality. Sometimes he played on his harpsichord and he never ceased talking, talking of men and women long since dead, of the days when he was a young prince of infinite promise.

By the time he died, in 1820, the Britain of 1760 had been transformed. Politics, society, culture had all changed, and the Hanoverian monarchy, which had seemed so stable, so permanent at his accession, was once more in seeming jeopardy through the excesses of his sons, particularly the Prince Regent, who succeeded him. Yet the jeopardy soon passed, and the excesses of the Prince brought Britain a remarkable inheritance.

An engraving by C. Turner of King George III in old age. 1820

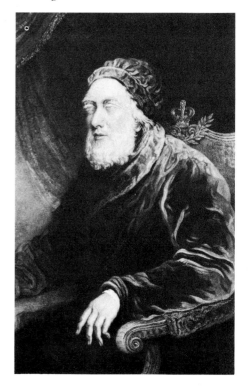

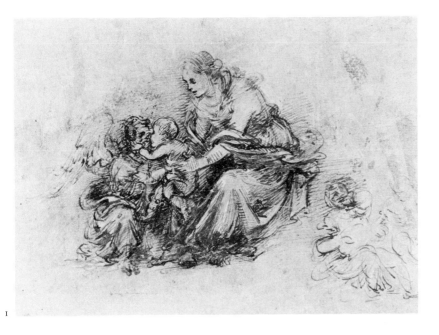

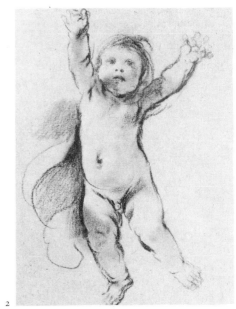

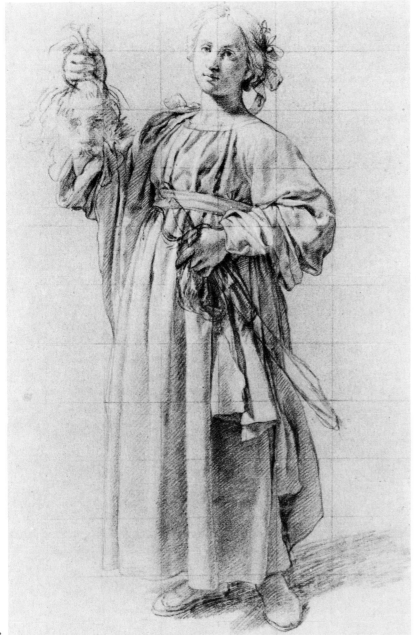

Splendid old master drawings entered the
royal collection in the Hanoverian period.
In 1762 King George III purchased two
remarkable collections, that of Consul
Smith, and the Albani collection bought for
him in Rome by James Adam. In this section
are some of the Italian drawings acquired by
the King.

1 Filippino Lippi, *An Angel Receiving the Child
  from the Virgin*
2 Guercino (Giovanni Francesco Barbieri),
  Study of a Flying Putto.
3 Sassoferato (Giovanni Salvi), *Judith with the
  Head of Holofernes*

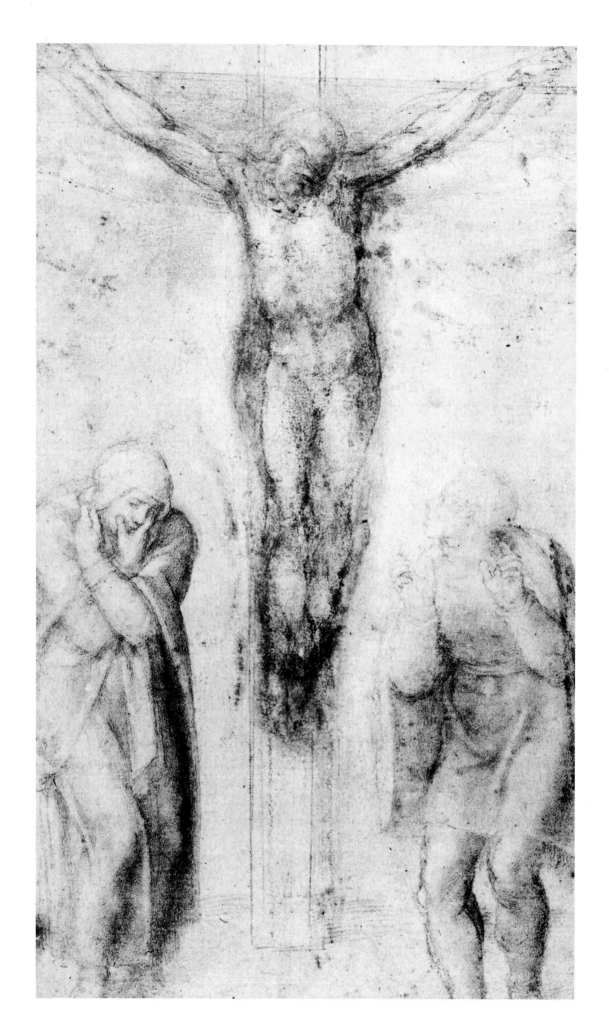

Michelangelo, *Christ on the Cross between the Virgin and St John. c.* 1540

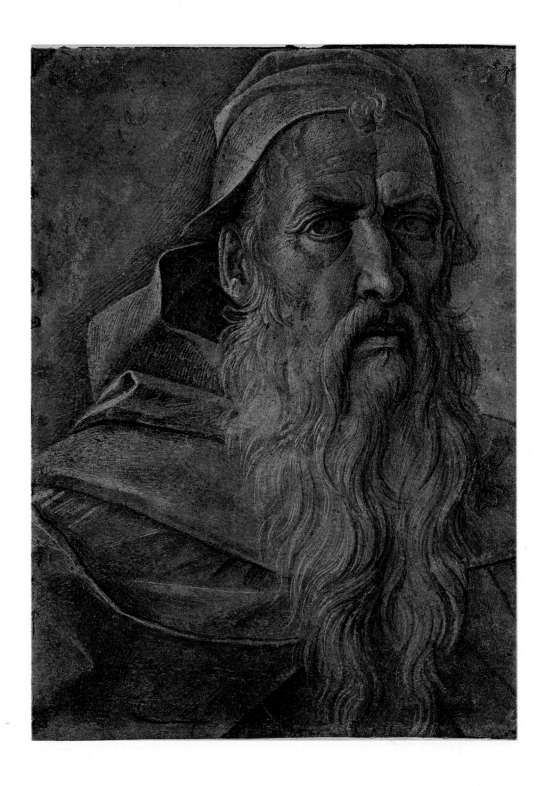

Giovanni Bellini, *Head of an Old Man. c.* 1460

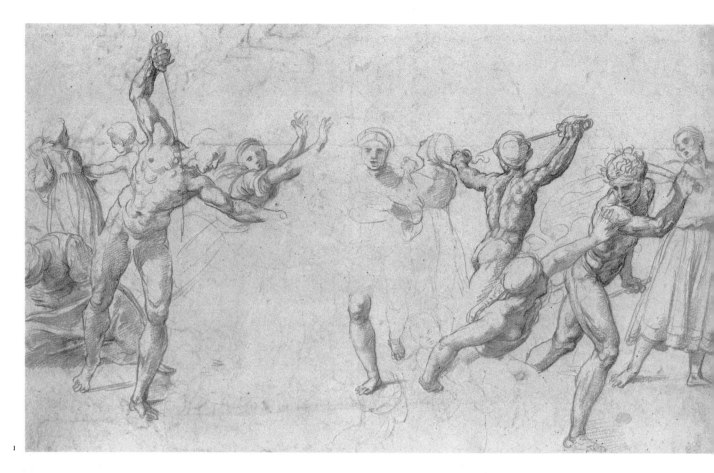

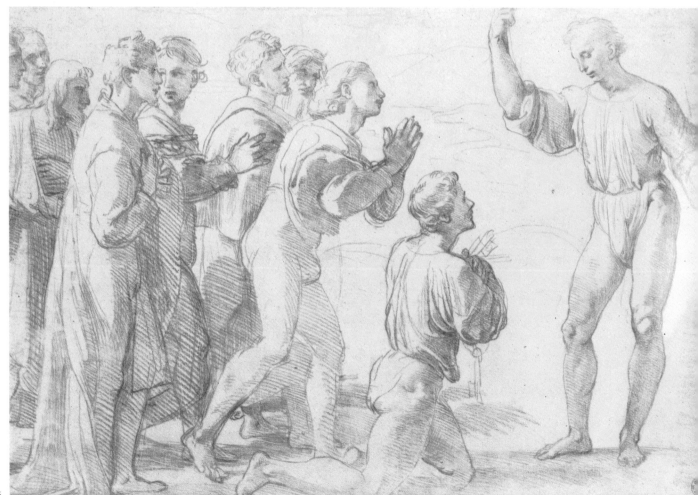

Raphael: 1 *The Massacre of the Innocents. c.* 1510. 2 *Christ's Charge to St Peter.* 1515

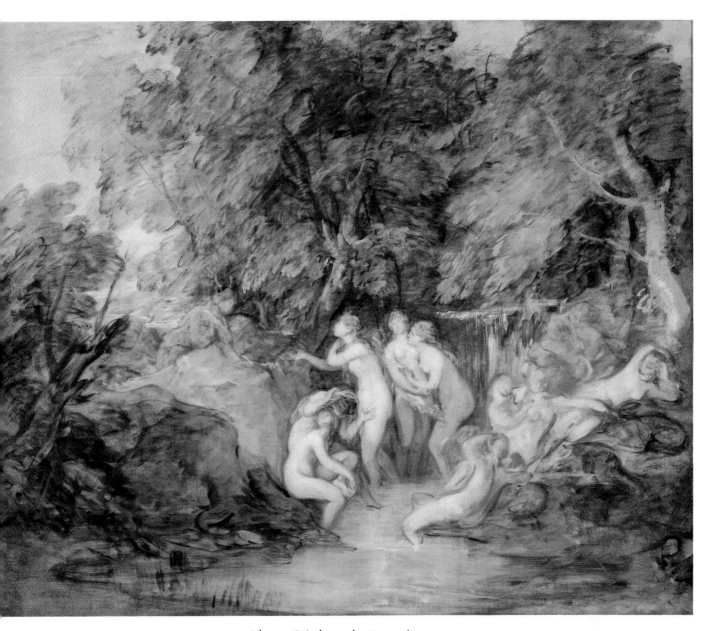

Thomas Gainsborough, *Diana and Actaeon*

Three painters, all of whom were patronised by the Hanoverian Court: Thomas Gainsborough, Jean-Etienne Liotard and Johann Zoffany

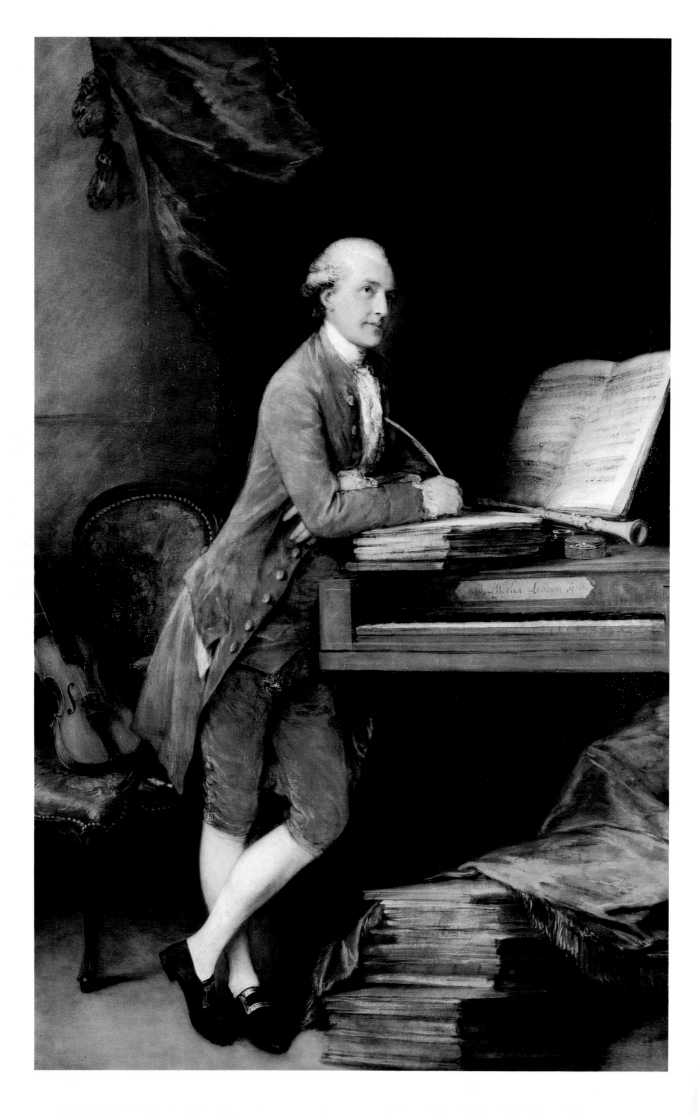

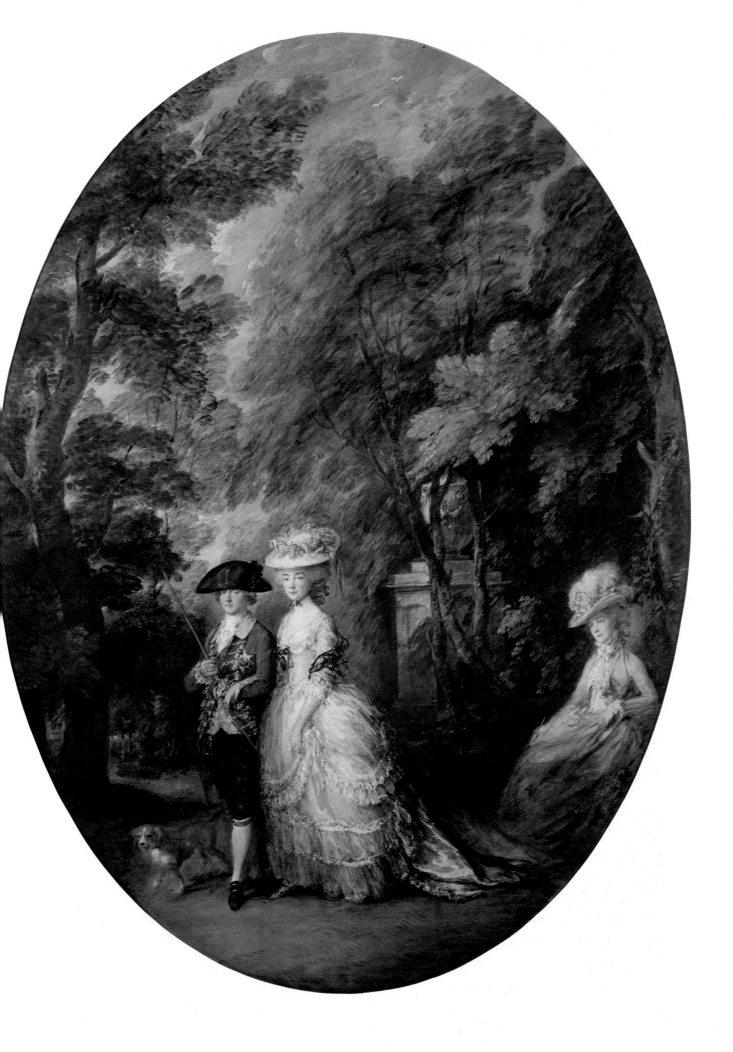

Thomas Gainsborough: *Johann Christian Fischer* (left) and *Henry, Duke of Cumberland, with the Duchess of Cumberland and Lady Elizabeth Luttrell*

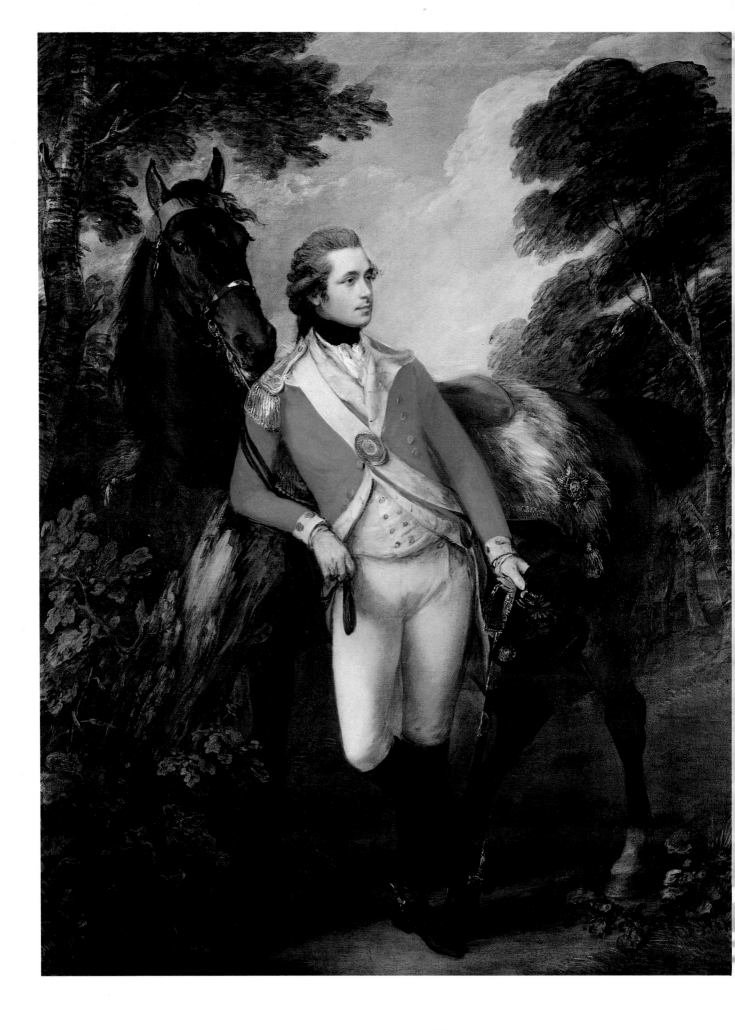

Thomas Gainsborough, Colonel John Hayes St Leger

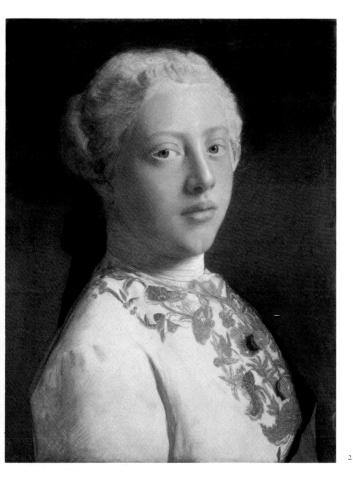

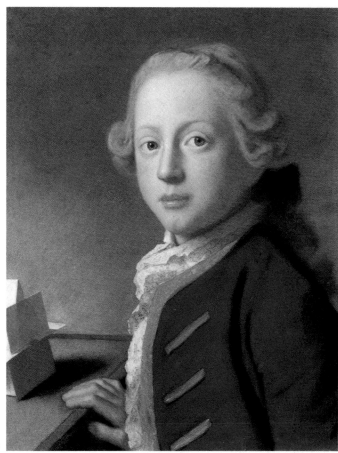

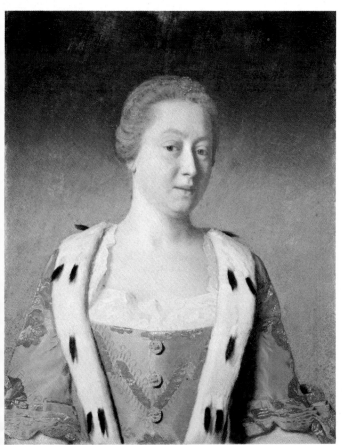

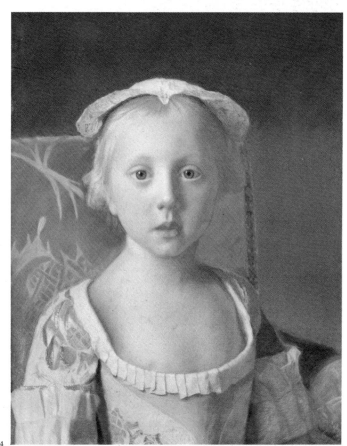

Jean-Etienne Liotard: 1 *George, Prince of Wales*. 2 *Henry Frederick, Duke of Cumberland*. 3 *Augusta, Princess of Wales*. 4 *Princess Louisa Ann*

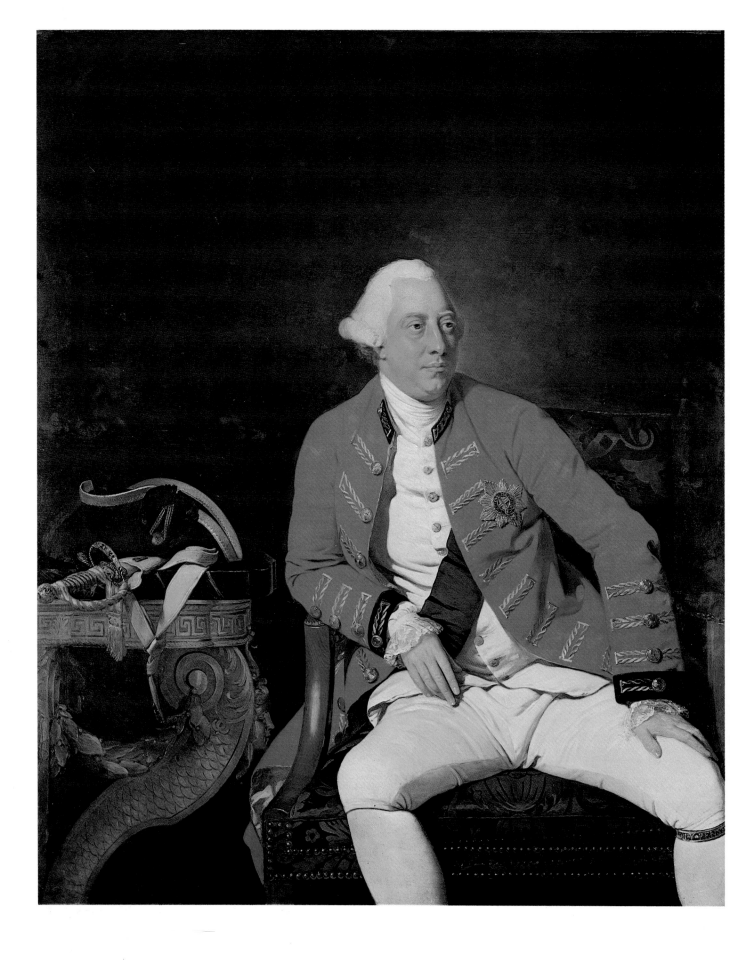

Johann Zoffany, *George III.* 1771

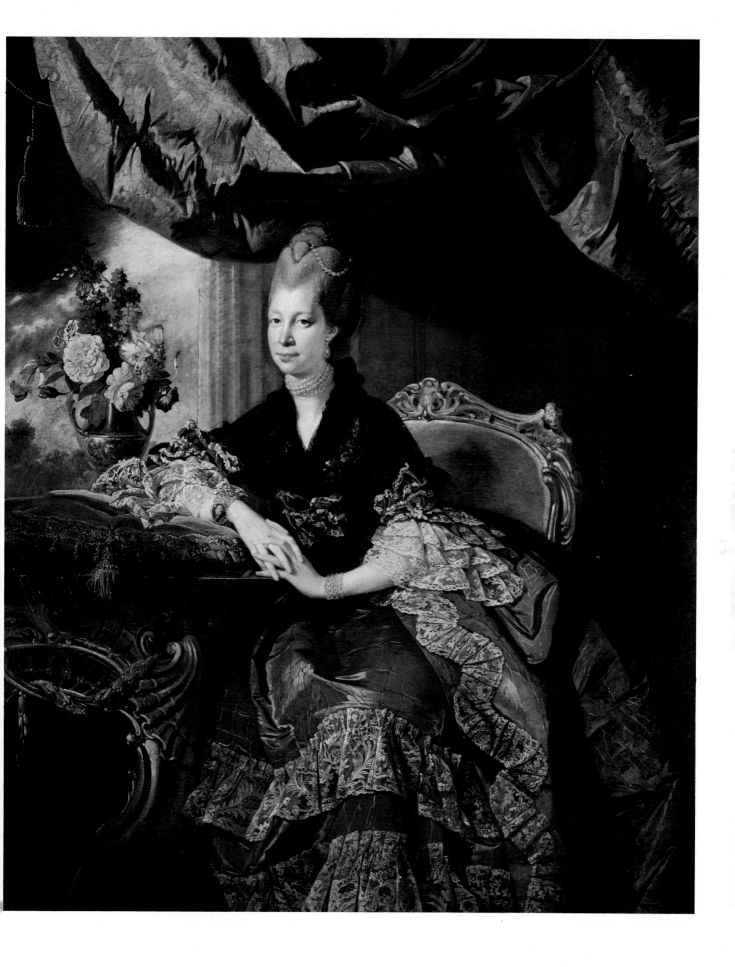

Johann Zoffany, *Queen Charlotte*. 1771

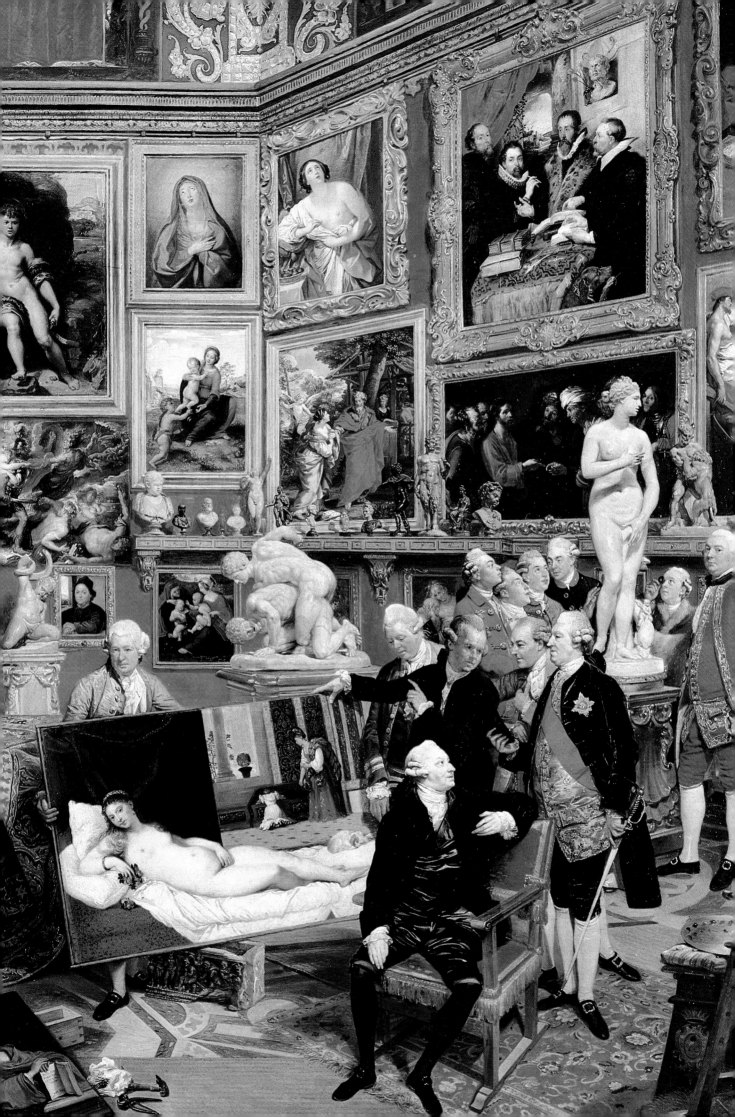

5

GEORGE IV

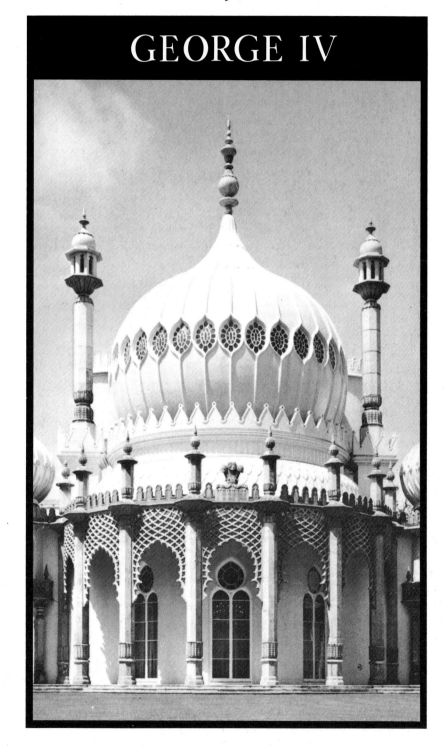

A Prince, the Prince of Princes at the time,
With fascination in his very bow . . .
Though royalty was written on his brow,
He had, then, the grace too, rare in every clime,
Of being, without alloy of fop or beau,
A finished Gentleman from top to toe.

Byron, Don Juan, Canto XII, lxxxiv

Who can look at Brighton Pavilion, George IV's marine villa, with indifference or boredom, or wonder what kind of man could ever wish to live in it? Outside, Indian and Moorish minarets mingle with eighteenth-century elegance of sash and bow windows to create a unique building that baffled the understanding as much as it provoked the emotions. William Cobbett, the home-spun radical, described it as 'a little Kremlin'; for William Hazlitt, the literary critic and essayist, it was a rare collection of stone pumpkins and pepper boxes; naturally an anonymous journalist was more vituperative, calling it 'a madhouse or a house run mad'. The best quip came from the greatest wit of the age, the Reverend Sidney Smith, who dismissed the pavilion in one sentence: 'The Dome of St Paul's went down to the sea and pupped'.

Thousands of visitors to Brighton's seaside, generation after generation of them, stare at the pavilion uncomprehendingly and make it the butt of their witticism. Aesthetes and connoisseurs gush over it, but few accept it for what it is – a fantasy in bricks and plaster of a sad, ageing, self-indulgent, very rich King, who possessed taste but little judgment, vivid imagination and no control. What control there was came from the standards of his age and the instinctive practice of his architects. The pavilion is a dream, belonging neither to Russia nor India nor China nor Mongolia nor to Moorish Spain, although it has affinities to the architecture of all of them, but simply to the Prince's longing for a chic originality that would astound his friends. The inside, like the outside, is a strange pastiche; at times, with its strong reds and yellows and blues, it is almost but not quite vulgar. On first viewing it is overpowering and slightly repellent: the huge lotus-like chandeliers, the dragons writhing down the walls, the imitation blue skies, palm trees in cast iron, banana trees in bronze, seats pretending to be dolphins, and everywhere bamboo chairs, bamboo beds, bamboo bookcases, bamboo seats – but, of course, imitation painted bamboo – even bamboo in iron. The pavilion shocks as few other buildings do; it creates immediately the atmosphere of a life; the true setting for the man who made it. It is easy to imagine these rooms grossly over-heated, to see again the vast kitchen, teeming with gargantuan piles of food and noisy with sweating cooks and scullions, orchestrated by Carême, one of the greatest of French chefs, to provide excitement for the palates of the twenty or so old roués with their wives or mistresses who sat with the Prince in his Banqueting Room. This room and the Music Room are the two most extravagant and extraordinary rooms, not only in the Pavilion, but in Great Britain.

The Banqueting Room is dominated by its central chandelier – a vast structure, in 1818 immensely modern because it was lit by gas, not candles.[1] It weighs a ton and consists of a bronze-leafed plantain tree

---

[1] The Prince incorporated all the technical achievements of his time; the pavilion is the first house to use cast-iron pillars both for structure and decoration.

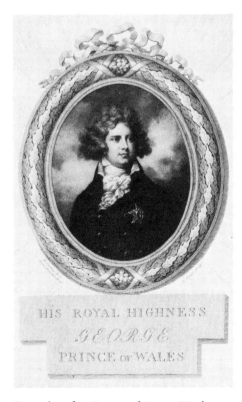

Engraving after Cosway of George IV when Prince of Wales. 1795

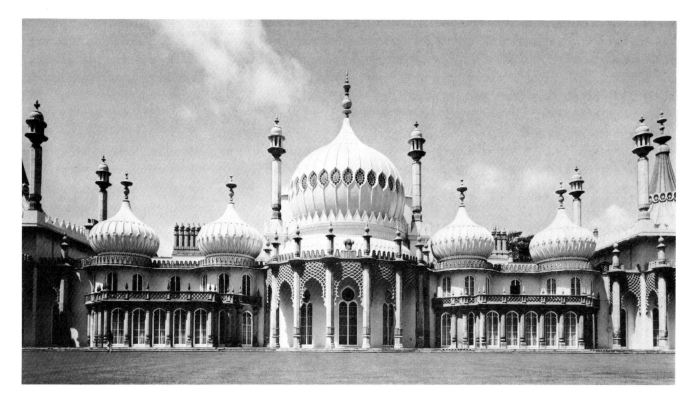

The Royal Pavilion, Brighton, by John Nash. 1815–22

from which hangs a large silver dragon holding in his claws an enormous glass bowl and around its rim are six smaller dragons with lotus flowers in their mouths. The cost was £5613 9s 0d (well over £50,000 today). There are four other enormous water-lilies and eight ten-foot-high standard lamps – a pedestal of gilt dolphins, a huge, deep blue Spode vase topped by a lotus flower of tinted glass (cost £5322 4s 0d). The room itself is painted with Chinese scenes; the decoration is crimson, gold and blue. The decorative work cost £8339 11s 0d and the furniture £9710 8s 0d. The total cost of the room was the equivalent of about £450,000.

The Music Room is in many ways more astonishing still. It was of this room that the Princess Lieven, one of the most sophisticated women of her time, wrote: 'I do not believe that since the days of Heliogabalus, there has been such magnificence and such luxury. There is something effeminate in it which is disgusting. One spends the evening half-lying on cushions: the lights are dazzling: there are perfumes, music, liqueurs' (as might be expected, the Prince loved perfumes and cases of quart bottles were constantly being sent to Brighton). The room seemed to recall Marco Polo's description of the great tent of Genghis Khan. As in that, serpents writhed head first down the columns which divided the great panels of red lacquer painted in gold with Chinese scenes. The recesses of the great convex ceilings have roofs of beribboned bamboos. The central ceiling is a vast dome, decorated with diminishing scales. Flying dragons abound, and the central chandelier is a Chinese water-lily. Again the cost was prodigious and the result fabulous.

As one walks through these rooms, the question becomes more insistent. What was he like, this man who turned a modest villa into a fantastic pleasure dome? As with the pavilion, opinion about George IV was deeply divided. For Leigh Hunt, the essayist, he was 'a libertine over head and ears in debt and disgrace'. Shelley, the poet, called him 'a crowned coward and villain'. Those who knew him liked him far more:

his doctor thought him 'the most perfect gentleman', Sir Walter Scott loved dining with him, and greatly admired his wide knowledge; and the Princess Lieven, who could and did judge by the highest standards of European sophistication, wrote that 'he adorned all the subjects that he touched'. Most loved or hated him; few were indifferent to him.

It is very easy to mock George IV, to criticise his self-indulgence and extravagance; his faults were glaring and too often masked his virtues and his deep humanity. Indeed, it is difficult to do justice to him. He was a very odd man, perhaps the strangest of all our monarchs. He ate too much, he drank too much, he fell in love too often. He was impulsive, open-hearted, compulsively extravagant. He was a man of romantic imagination with the impulses of an artist and some of the temperament of an actor. As a young man he was extremely handsome; even in old age, when he had run to excessive fat, he still possessed the magnificent ruins of good looks. And his courtesy, his style, which combined ease with a sense of royal dignity, gave him the well-deserved title of 'The First Gentleman of Europe'. Yet in spite of his style and polish, he could be quick to take offence; deep down he was an uneasy man, insecure, longing for some great creative success; it never came. Or is that fair? After all, he had the energy to make his dreams a reality at Windsor, as well as Brighton, and so gave Britain two of the most dramatic buildings in Western Europe. And that is not all. He was a splendid patron, personally persuading his reluctant Commissioners of Crown Lands to accept John Nash's vast scheme by which the royal palaces in London were linked by Regent Street to Regent's Park, which was to be surrounded by imposing terraces of great beauty. To do this required tearing down miles of poor streets and mean buildings. Regent's Park, rightly named, replaced a piece of open country called Marylebone Park; and the Zoo, again, is rightly where it is, because George IV helped to bring it into being. The whole concept has a sweep and a grandeur, a sense of scale worthy of a great capital, that appealed to the Prince Regent. He wanted London to be worthy of a triumphant and expanding nation not only visually but also culturally.

The Prince grew up in a rapidly changing world. Leadership in the industrial revolution, combined with an expanding empire in the east, was creating new sources of wealth for Britain, enabling the country to support not only large fleets, but also large armies, pour money into the treasuries of its continental allies, and bring about the defeat, in the end, of France and Napoleon. The battles of the Nile, Trafalgar, Waterloo symbolised more than victory in war: they meant, and the Prince knew it, that Britain had become the richest and most powerful country in the world. He wanted its symbols to be worthy of its role. Often, of course, he interpreted this in a very personal way, such as turning the rather small Buckingham House into a great palace – another of his architectural triumphs. He wanted a vast palace not simply because he himself liked vast palaces and great buildings, but also – and rightly – because he felt that St James's was not worthy of the nation. London needed an imposing palace, and in Buckingham Palace he created one.

He realised that he was living in very revolutionary times – not merely because of the vast upheaval in politics and the destruction of social privileges brought about by the French revolution – the changes went deeper, far deeper. More and more men and women were accepting

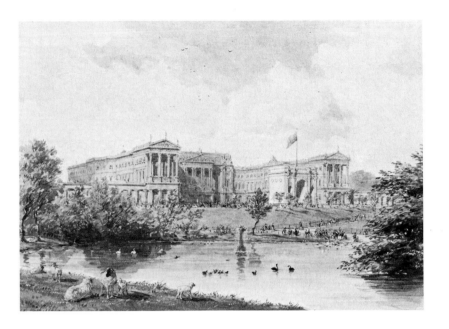

Buckingham Palace at the time of George IV, drawn by Joseph Nash

new attitudes to life, believing more absolutely than ever before in the inevitability of material progress, looking with eagerness towards the future, and showing increasing impatience with the past. There was a growing sense of the excellence of modernity, whether it was the music of the waltz compared with that of the minuet, or the simple, almost diaphanous clothes that women wore, compared with the complex and elaborate dresses of the immediate past. Indeed, the Prince himself had pioneered a revolution in men's everyday dress, giving his seal of approval to the simple, elegant lines and subdued colours favoured by his friend, Beau Brummel. Fine craftsmanship, whether new or old, certainly always caught his eye and emptied his pockets, but so did originality and novelty, and he was prepared to take risks. He first used cast iron in building the conservatory of his London home, Carlton House, but later used it in his kitchen at Brighton, where it had to support the full weight of the building, and not merely glass. He realised its importance and wanted both to exploit its possibilities and also to give it the seal of his approval. Not content with cast-iron pillars, he also introduced elaborate cast-iron staircases. Similarly he adopted gas-lighting for his palaces as soon, almost, as it was invented. His brother, William IV, had it torn out of all the palaces as too dangerous, but some of George IV's gas standards may still be seen outside Kensington Palace.

He was acutely aware that royal patronage helped to support new technology. He was interested in scientific as well as technological creations; he bought, maybe experimented with, electrical batteries. Most certainly he patronised the Royal Institution, whose president, Humphry Davy, the great chemist of the age, he impulsively knighted. This side of his complex nature needs stressing because it is so easily overlooked in the emotional riot of his life, or in the compulsive, almost manic collecting in which he indulged. The most awesome aspect, however, of the Prince's character was his gargantuan appetite for life, his fantastic gusto. His collections – pictures, statuary, watercolours, prints, furniture, porcelain, armour – are stupendous in size; he built or remodelled four great palaces; he purchased, personally and with attention, prodigious quantities of furs, perfumes, handkerchiefs, walking sticks, jewels, clothes in multicoloured variety; his social life was

packed, his love life involved and inordinately preoccupying. He ate and
drank to excess from youth to age, and yet managed somehow to be
deeply involved in politics and diplomacy. To many – relations, friends
and subjects – this compulsive, wanton self-indulgence, this rioting
creativity, was extravagant, hateful, thoughtless and selfish at a time
when the country was racked with unemployment and poverty, or in the
throes of a great war. More Englishmen hated him than loved him
throughout his life; fewer still understood him, either during his life or
after his death. He has rarely been given his due. He created the setting
of monarchy as we know it.

We possess many pictures of George IV as a boy, usually with his
brothers, especially Frederick, Duke of York, with whom he grew up and
to whom he remained devoted; in all of them there is great charm, a
warm, open countenance, a sense of dignity not merely the painter's
creation. And we know that he was a very eager, yet sometimes wilful
child. He received instruction in Latin and Greek with ease, learned to
sing and play the cello, and was taught to draw, to paint in watercolours,
and to appreciate art. He learned French as easily as Latin and had a good
knowledge of German and Italian. He took at once, oddly enough, to
military engineering, and the careful precision drawing that went with
it. He was exceptionally well grounded in literature and history – with
his good looks and exquisite manners, he was almost a paragon. But, as
his tutor said of him and his brother Frederick, 'They could never be
taught to understand the value of money'.

By seventeen the young Prince was a charming, witty, polished and
generous companion. He could be, and usually was, captivating to men
and women alike; he was full of animal spirits, full of appetite for life,
eager to give himself to love, to friendship, longing to be the Princely
Maecenas. At the same time, he was deeply attached to his family – his
sisters adored him, his brothers, at times maybe envious, could never
resist his attraction for long; they all exploited his affection, his absurd
generosity. He was devoted to his mother, who very genuinely cared for

Johann Zoffany: 1 *George, Prince of Wales, and
Frederick, later Duke of York. c.* 1765. The two
children are in a room at Buckingham House.
2 A detail from a later painting of the two
children, *c.* 1770, modelled on Van Dyck's
portrait of George and Francis Villiers (see
page 118), which hangs on the wall to the
left in the first painting

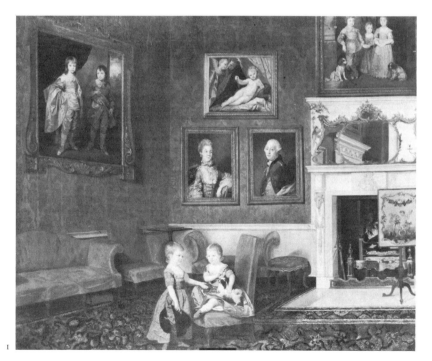

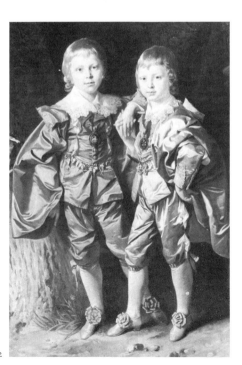

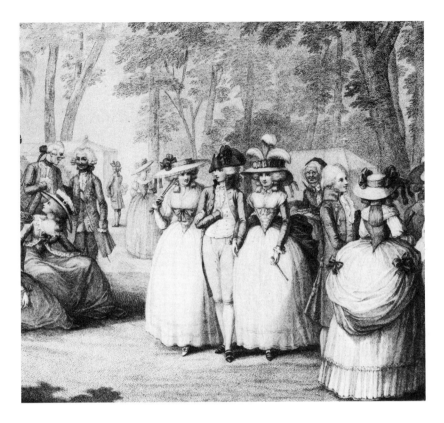

Detail of an engraving by W. Dickinson after H. Bunbury, 1784, showing the Prince of Wales at a party in the grounds of Carlton House

him, irritated and alarmed as she often was by his irresponsible actions and monstrous debts. He stood in awe of his father, the warmth of his emotions somehow frozen. Family trouble there was bound to be. George III liked a quiet, orderly, somewhat frugal domestic life, one that was highly moral and conscientiously dutiful. Even though he could never have regarded the natural excesses of his son with benignity, he was certainly not a puritanic ogre. Nevertheless, his parents' household became very oppressive to the young Prince.

The household of his rakish uncle and aunt, the Duke and Duchess of Cumberland, enticed him – balls, dinner parties, gambling, women and whig politics that mocked as well as criticised his father's political predilections. Nothing was done by these friends to discourage his extravagance. His debts mounted. At eighteen he set up a lovely actress, Perdita Robinson, as his mistress. He wrote her letters, and they proved costly; she had to be bought off with a handsome pension. As a leader of fashion, his bills for clothes, for jewels, for all the accoutrements of fashionable life, were spectacular, but his monumental debts were due to gambling, partly at cards, but mainly through horses. As might be expected, he adored horses. By the time he was a young man the racehorse had been bred not only to a remarkable degree of efficiency, but also to great beauty. Horses had also been carefully bred for carriage work, and more and more attention was given by carriage makers to lightness, to balance, to new steel leaf-springs, in order to enhance speed. On heavily used roads the gradients, too, were being lowered and the surfaces properly engineered. Amongst the *jeunesse dorée* this helped to engender a love of speed, and everyone who was rich enough lavished their money on horses and carriages. No one catches the excitement, the aesthetic pleasure in horses and phaeton better than George Stubbs. It is not surprising that, with the Prince's eye for excellence, he should have engaged Stubbs to paint himself driving a phaeton – one of the best of

Stubbs's pictures, and one of the best portraits of the Prince as a young man. And the Prince, never doing anything by halves, assembled one of the finest collections of Stubbs in existence, one of the glories of the royal collection.

The Prince – much to his father's delight – was a superb horseman. He rode to Brighton and back within ten hours, and even more impressively he drove his phaeton twenty-two miles in two hours. Of course the excitement of driving, as well as racing, was heightened by gambling. When his debts permitted, the Prince was a great patron of the turf; his horses won innumerable races for him at Newmarket, Ascot, Brighton and elsewhere; and, at least in racing, the Prince enjoyed quite phenomenal luck, although some of his racing friends attributed this to his superb judgment of a horse. Colonel St Leger, a member of a famous Yorkshire racing family whose father had founded the first 'classic', run in 1776, was one of the boon companions of his youth; their portraits were painted by Gainsborough and exchanged, and the Prince showered St Leger with lavish presents, including the superb saddle which appears in St Leger's picture. Two other favourite companions were Sir John Lade and his wife, Letty, whom he had picked up in a brothel. She rode as well as her husband and swore more formidably; they, too, gambled to excess and Sir John went broke. Nevertheless, he settled down quite happily for the rest of his long life as a coachman on the London-Brighton run. These raffish youngsters, who were friends of Cumberland and became friends of the Prince, enraged the King as much as the debts. George III did what he could to check the natural excesses, the ebullient uninhibited vitality and extravagance of the Prince, but to no avail.

At twenty-one, the Prince could not be denied his own establishment. His whig friends did their best to secure him huge financial provisions, but the King was adamant. In the end the crisis was resolved, and the Prince received £60,000 down to help settle his debts, and about £62,000 a year and a house of his own. To the Prince it was as if the gold mines of South Africa had been opened for his plundering. He erupted on the London scene like a dazzling firework display. With great energy and total indifference to the cost, he set about creating at Carlton House, which the King had granted him, a setting worthy of himself and of the heir to the British monarchy. He more or less gutted it, and added to it the great portico which is now the side entrance to the National Gallery in Trafalgar Square. He built ballrooms and conservatories where he held dinners, balls and breakfasts on an unrivalled scale; one breakfast for hundreds of guests lasted until six in the evening. He bought neighbouring houses and tore them down to make way for his garden with its Italian temples and observatory.

Colossal as his alterations were, and the great crimson Drawing-Room and Silver Dining-Room were certainly splendiferous and grandiose, they paled into financial insignificance when compared with what he spent on furniture and pictures. Like any aristocrat or royal person of his day, he bought mainly French furniture or English furniture in the French taste. The most splendid eighteenth-century pieces now in the royal collection were bought by him; many of the *bureaux plats*, side-tables, cabinets, armchairs and settees are by the finest *ébénistes* of eighteenth-century France. Whether he had money or not, the Prince bought bronzes, candelabra, clocks and porcelain to adorn his furniture. When the French

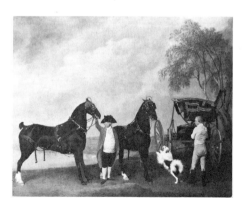

George Stubbs, *Prince of Wales's Phaeton*. 1793. (See colour detail page 207)

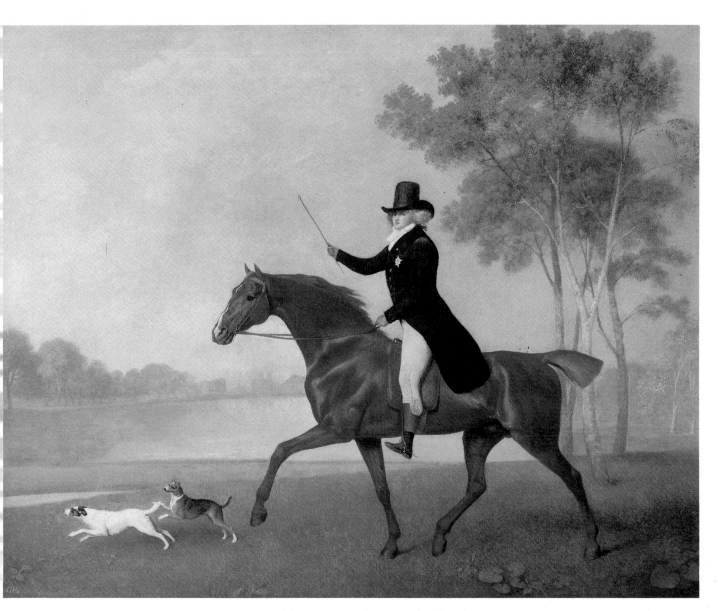

George Stubbs, *George IV when Prince of Wales.* 1791

George Stubbs raised the art of animal painting to a new level. The Royal Collection is richly
endowed with his works, many of which were painted for King George IV

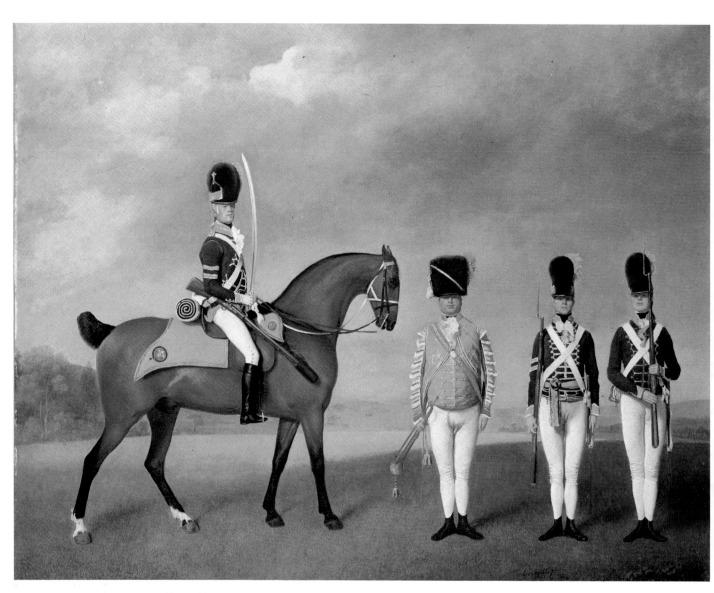

George Stubbs, *Soldiers of the Tenth Light Dragoons*. 1793. The Prince of Wales was Colonel of the Regiment

George Stubbs, Detail from the
Prince of Wales's Phaeton. 1793

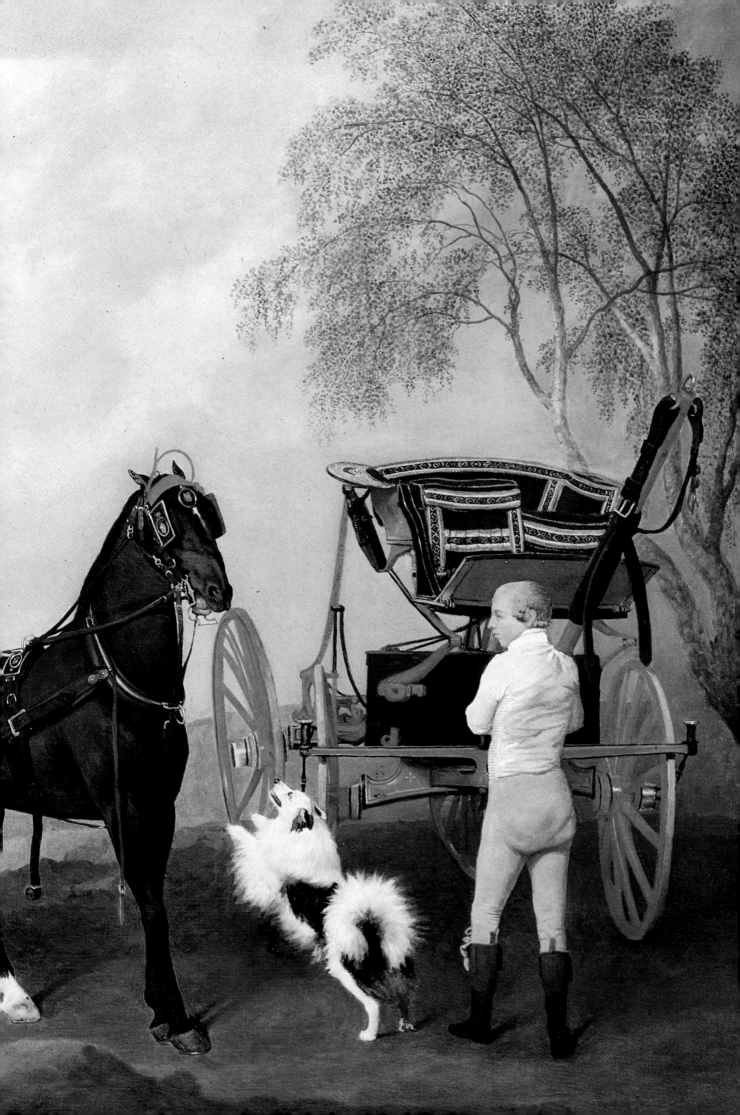

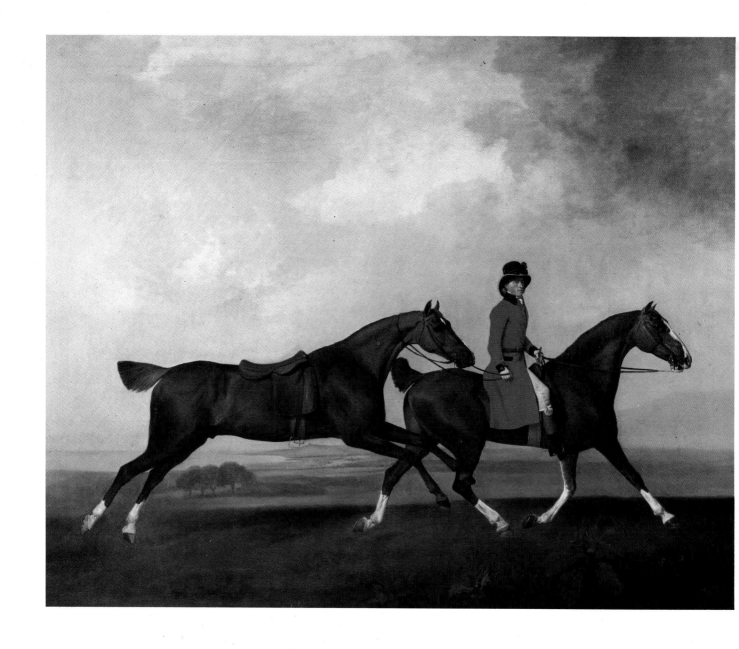

George Stubbs, *William Anderson with Two Saddlehorses.* 1793

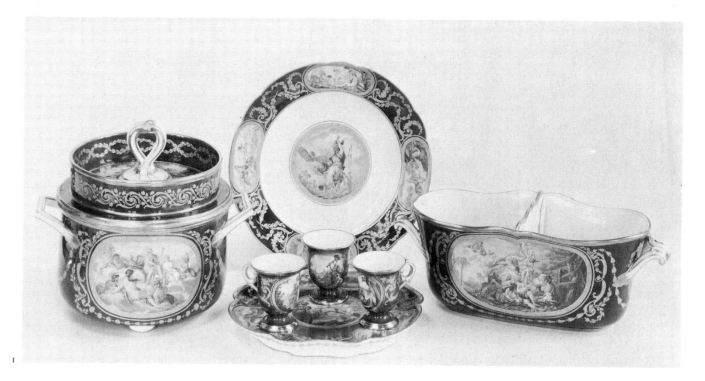

Revolution emptied the palaces of the French aristocracy, he naturally bought massively. It was at that time that he acquired the Sèvres dinner service which was being made especially for Louis XVI. It was so costly that only a few pieces could be made each year, but by the time of the French King's execution in 1793 it had built up to a vast service. The Prince seized his opportunity and bought it. He also possessed another magnificent Sèvres service which is regarded today as one of the finest produced by this great porcelain factory. Unlike most great services of that period, it is still used for state banquets at Buckingham Palace and Windsor.

Naturally the Prince also purchased fine Gobelins tapestries and superb Aubusson carpets. Carlton House, however, was not furnished entirely in the French style. The Prince's delight in creativity led him to buy some very original and splendid English furniture which adorned the Throne Room in Carlton House. Simplicity and functional quality, however, could attract him as much as ornate decoration; he particularly admired a neat, comparatively small writing table, which subsequently acquired the soubriquet of 'Carlton House Writing Table' and was frequently copied, became very fashionable, and still is the perfect table for writing a letter or a hurried note. But the dominant theme of Carlton House was of grandeur, echoing the French palaces of Versailles and the Trianon, rather than St James's and Buckingham House. But the Prince being the Prince, there was also a stronger note of fantasy than one finds either at the Trianon or at Versailles. From the very first he took delight in Europe's vision of Cathay and ordered the architect, Henry Holland, to use the Chinese motive in one of his drawing-rooms at Carlton House. The fantasy and whimsicality of chinoiserie grew in its appeal to the Prince, reaching its climax in the pavilion at Brighton, but his other strong personal note lies in the Gothic Drawing-Room and Gothic Conservatory. Neo-Gothic created for him not only a sense of nostalgia for the medieval past, but also a note of grandeur and regality which he felt appropriate to monarchy. The fascination with the Gothic he

1 Part of a Sèvres porcelain service made for Louis XVI, 1783–92, and bought by George IV.
2 Detail from one of the Gobelins tapestries bought by George IV in 1825

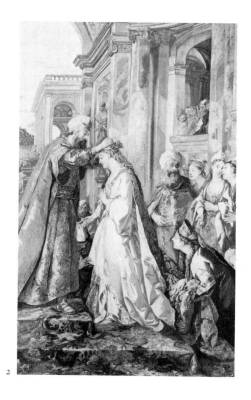

acquired at this time was never to desert him; it found its full expression when he came to re-model Windsor Castle in the evening of his life.

As important as the furniture and the decoration of Carlton House were the pictures. Throughout his life George IV spent a great deal of money on pictures, sometimes buying a block from an important collection, sometimes a single picture, and sometimes selling what he had previously bought in order to improve the quality of his collection. Very early he had patronised Stubbs, Gainsborough, Cosway and others. He loved portraits of himself to give to his friends and to receive theirs. Carlton House called for Dutch and Flemish pictures – such paintings had been the rage in France throughout the eighteenth century, and it was believed that they made a perfect marriage with French furniture, bronzes and porcelain. By 1816, 136 pictures adorned the great suite of state rooms at Carlton House, sixty-seven were in the attics or the Prince's bedroom, and 250 more in store. By then the Prince had acquired a number of masterpieces, more than any monarch since Charles I.

He bought outstanding Rembrandts: in 1811 he purchased *The Shipbuilder and his Wife*, painted by Rembrandt at the height of his powers and acknowledged to be one of the greatest of his portraits. He also bought *The Lady with a Fan*, another Rembrandt of exceptional quality. In 1819 he added *Christ and the Magdalene at the Tomb*. He and his advisers bought together many Dutch masterpieces: de Hooch, *The Card Players*, Steen, *The Morning Toilet*, Ter Borch, *The Letter* are of the highest quality. Landscapes delighted the Prince as much as portraits or genre scenes; there are two evening landscapes in the collection, both typical of the artists who created them and both representative of their best work: Cuyp and Ruisdael. Fine as these are, they are surpassed by Rubens's *The Farm at Laeken*, a lyrical landscape painted with all the self-confident assurance of genius.

Within twenty years, the Prince had assembled one of the finest collections of Dutch and Flemish paintings in existence. When he decided to pull down Carlton House, his vast collection went mostly into store and there it remained until early in the reign of Queen Victoria, when they were hung four deep in the new Picture Gallery in Buckingham Palace. Some are still there, some adorn other rooms there or at Windsor. Once again they can be seen in the setting of fine French furniture for which the Prince bought them.

But this is to run ahead. The early extravagances of the Prince at Carlton House needed no huge purchases of old masters to plunge him deeply into debt. At twenty-one he was spending £1000 a week on furnishings, and his bills for wine, food and candles were prodigious. He gave parties for all the bold young whigs whom the King hated: Charles James Fox, the most profligate of men, yet a splendid orator and a man of deep human compassion; the playright, Sheridan, as witty at a party as on the stage and a man to whom the Prince was strongly attracted, for he drank as deeply as the Prince and had an unfailing capacity to amuse. At the general election in 1784 the Prince came out vigorously in support of his whig friends whom the King was trying to defeat. It was the King, not the Prince, who had the resounding success. But there was worse than debt and political defeat in store.

The Prince was deeply in love with a twice-widowed Roman Catholic six years older than himself, Mrs Fitzherbert. Mrs Fitzherbert was a

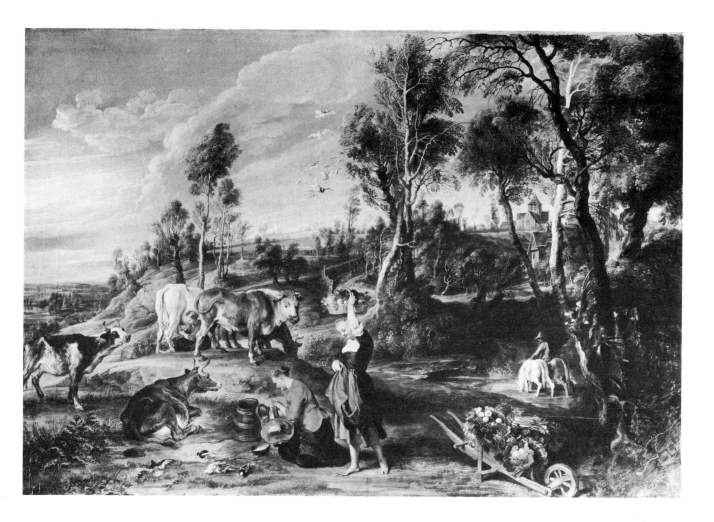

Sir Peter Paul Rubens, *The Farm at Laeken*.
c. 1618. Bought by George IV in 1821

rather plain woman of austere morals. The Prince pleaded, threatened suicide, offered to leave England, poured out presents of jewellery, all to no avail. Desperate, he went through a marriage ceremony with her, totally illegal in English law, but binding in the eyes of the Roman Catholic Church and Mrs Fitzherbert. Naturally, the secret lasted no more than a few days, and cartoons and caricatures poured from the press. The King was not amused, either by the marriage or by the debts which now amounted to £269,878 6s 7½d – equivalent to about £3 million today; very impressive indeed for a young Prince in his twenty-fourth year.

The Prince always possessed a strong sense of theatre. Knowing he was getting nowhere with his father he shut up Carlton House, dismissed his staff, and ostentatiously took an outside seat on the public coach to Brighton, where he had rented a small marine villa. Mrs Fitzherbert followed. The Prince, utterly in love, appeared to be as happy as he had ever been, living a life which, for him, was of unnatural simplicity. He should have been racked with anxiety. The rumours of the marriage became so intense that a denial or an affirmation had to be made for the Prince by his friends in parliament. Affirmation would mean the loss of the prospect of the throne and, probably, continued poverty combined with social ostracism. Denial meant labelling the woman he loved a whore. It is easy to condemn the Prince's choice, but for a man of his temperament anything but denial would have been suicide. His friends denied his marriage; Mrs Fitzherbert, mortified, left him; once again he threatened suicide, but became desperately and genuinely ill, sick with love and grief. Mrs Fitzherbert returned, and at the cost of her reputation he had secured his position as heir apparent who might still beget legitimate offspring. So arrangements were made to cope with his debts; he received an extra £10,000 a year from his father, £161,000 from a somewhat disgruntled parliament, and £60,000 to help complete the never-to-be-completed Carlton House.

In optimistic expectation that his debts would be settled, the Prince's fertile creative mind had already begun to dwell on rebuilding his villa at Brighton. There he had enjoyed perhaps the greatest happiness he was to know. Why not live there? And living there, why not a home fit for a Prince? Henry Holland had been sent for, the villa had vanished, and a small army of bricklayers, carpenters, plumbers, plasterers and decorators were rushing up a miniature but sumptuous palace – completed, at least sufficiently for the Prince to take up residence, in little more than three months. This was to remain the core of the Brighton Pavilion, its classical lines discernible even when enriched with the oriental fantasies of John Nash. Small versions and pastiches of it abound in seaside resorts and spas; its elegant bow windows and classical lines were rapidly copied at Brighton, in the South and North Parades that were built shortly afterwards.

Brighton Pavilion, like Carlton House, was constantly changing, always growing in size and splendour, taking on at the end that air of astonished fantasy that strikes every visitor to Brighton today. Inside it was vivid with colour, fashionable neo-classical in decoration, the furniture French, some pieces having been sent from Carlton House. It was, however, comparatively cheap, costing the Prince a mere £22,338.

Although the Prince's private life at Brighton was all harmony and bliss, his public life over the next few years was catastrophic. His debts, which should have been paid off, had not been; once he had his hands on the money he still lived with all his old extravagance – impulsively giving a tradesman £600, buying shirts by the score and suits by the dozen; and Mrs Fitzherbert must have the clothes and jewels of a princess. His friends were entertained with regal profusion and life was too dull without gambling at cards, billiards or the horses. He might be living modestly, but only by *his* standards.

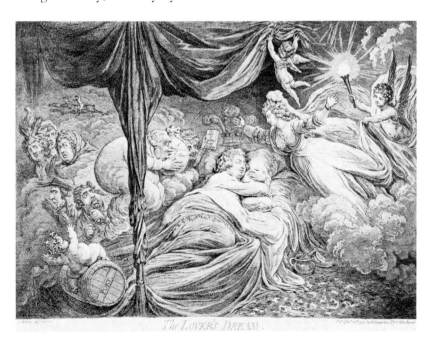

The LOVER'S DREAM.

A caricature of George IV's marriage by Gillray. 1795

But the Regency crisis caused by the King's illness did him most harm. The Prince wept with deep and genuine emotion when he saw his father's apparent madness, but his imagination, stimulated by his friends, glowed at the prospect of power. The Prime Minister, William Pitt, knowing that he must go if the Prince had full powers as Regent, stalled and proposed in parliament some limitations on the Prince's authority, which his friends, Fox and Sheridan, fought tooth and nail. Already in his imagination the Prince was dismissing ministers, dispensing honours, creating governments, but Pitt stalled long enough for George III to recover. The King regarded the Prince's behaviour as a disgrace, a sentiment shared by all but his closest friends, and the Prince went back to Brighton and Mrs Fitzherbert with a bruised reputation which he was never quite able to live down. Once again the heat of his imagination combined with his lack of judgment betrayed him.

With the years, his compulsive appetite to buy and spend grew. When the French revolution forced the aristocracy of France to sell their splendid furniture, tapestries, bronzes and china, the Prince – fortunately, in the end, for posterity – found the temptation irresistible, and in the early 1790s he began to buy very heavily. By 1796, his debts had soared to over £640,000 (about £12 million today). To pay off the debts the King insisted on conditions. They were that the Prince must marry and get an heir. According to the Prince, 'one damn'd *frau* is as good as another', and he let his father choose. When he saw the choice, Princess Caroline of Brunswick, he called for brandy and, according to Queen Victoria, Lord Melbourne told her that he only got through the marriage ceremony because he was drunk. The Princess was coarse in feature, foul in language, with strong body smells and devoid of all common sense. Worse, she was to develop a rampant sexuality. No woman could have offended the susceptibilities of the Prince more than she. However, a child was conceived and born – the Princess Charlotte, but this accomplished, the Prince refused to live any more with the Princess, and begged Mrs Fitzherbert to return which, after consulting Rome, she did with some reluctance; and in the process drove the Prince once more frantic and hysterical. Quaintly enough, it was not only Rome, but the royal family which helped to overcome Mrs Fitzherbert's hesitation – Princes and Princesses called on her, and even the King and Queen no longer regarded her with absolute disfavour.

The years that followed his broken marriage were sweetened by Mrs Fitzherbert's return, but in many other ways they were bitter enough for the Prince. He naturally longed to fight in the wars against France; to play a similar role in war to his great hero, Louis XIV, the Sun King. George III forbade it absolutely, a bitter decision for a Prince whose brothers, particularly the Dukes of York and Clarence, saw active service. York became Commander-in-Chief of the army, and Clarence, who steadily rose in rank in the navy, became Admiral of the Fleet in 1811.

So the Prince had to play out in private what he could not do in public. He became obsessed with the war and its battles, and a compulsive collector of trophies and mementoes of his country's victories. He was delighted when his father at last made him Colonel of the Dragoons. Not that he would be allowed to smell battle, but he could indulge the family passion for uniforms and regimentals. He had himself painted by Beechey in full dress and carefully preserved the uniform itself, which is still at

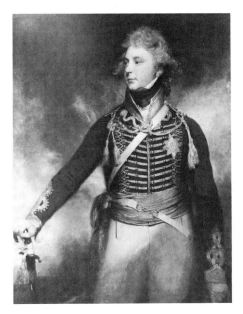

Sir William Beechey, *George IV when Prince of Wales*. 1803

Windsor. Like his ancestors, the Prince knew everything that was to be known about uniforms. He built up a collection of military prints, drawings and watercolours, running into thousands, many of exceptional quality. It now adorns the library at Windsor.

But the Prince was artist as much as collector. His military accoutrements – swords, powder horns, pistols – were beautifully made by the finest craftsmen – and nothing pleased him more than a present of fine arms, such as the splendid pair of double-barrelled flintlock pistols given to him by Louis XVIII of France. Arms and armour poured into Carlton House and later into Windsor, and its display intrigued the Prince as much as its acquisition. Finally he decided to use them to decorate the Grand Vestibule and the Queen's Guard Chamber at Windsor, which were to house his military relics and provide a dramatic entrance to the Waterloo Chamber. They now form one of the most magnificent displays of firearms, swords and armour in existence.

The Prince's passion for the army and navy went beyond mere collecting. He was deeply patriotic, loathed the French revolution as the work of a king-killing mob, and longed for Napoleon's defeat, even though he admired the genius of the man himself. If he could not take part in the war, at least he could collect relics of great battles or have his military painter depict the battles for him, as Dighton did at Waterloo. Like most of his countrymen, he worshipped Nelson and Wellington. He commissioned Hoppner to paint what is perhaps the most convincing likeness of Nelson. After Trafalgar, which finally established Britain's command of the seas, he commissioned Turner's great battle piece; it was the only Turner that the Prince ever bought: one would have expected him to be sympathetic to Turner – the painter's feeling for visual drama matched the Prince's liking for military drama.

A devoted Englishman, named Children, knowing George IV's passion for victory over the French, wanted to present him with a chair made from the elm that Wellington sat under at Waterloo, an odd, rather ugly memento. It was eventually presented to Queen Victoria in 1838. George IV was also extremely proud of the despatch Wellington

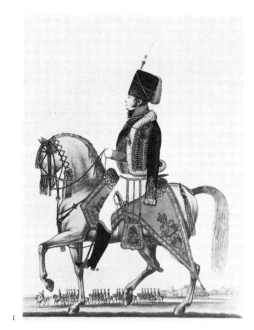

The Prince of Wales was actively interested in all military matters and extremely proud of the British victory at Waterloo.

1 An engraving by I. C. Stadler, after C. Rosenberg, of the Prince Regent on horseback. 1811.

2 Denis Dighton, *The Battle of Waterloo: The Charge of the Second Brigade of Cavalry*. Within minutes, 15,000 French were fleeing and two field batteries destroyed.

3 A chair made by Chippendale the Younger from the elm tree that Wellington stood under at Waterloo and presented to Queen Victoria.

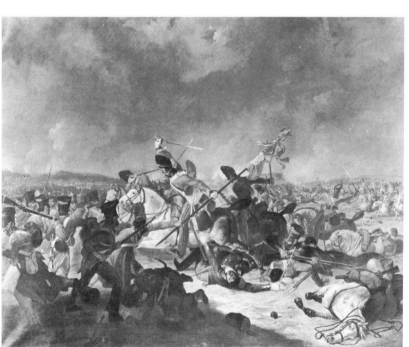

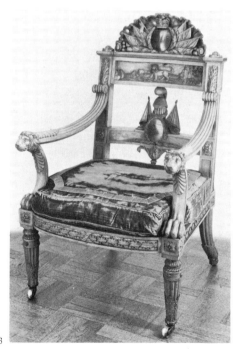

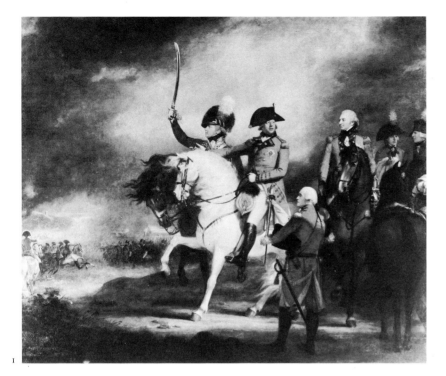

1 Sir William Beechey, *George III at a Review*. 1797–8. On horseback beside his father the Prince brandishes his sabre as Colonel of the 10th Light Dragoons.

2 One of a pair of double-barrelled flintlock pistols presented to the Prince by Louis XVIII on 20 December 1814. They are inlaid in gold with the arms of the Prince.

3 The burnished-steel hilt of an English smallsword, which dates from after 1798

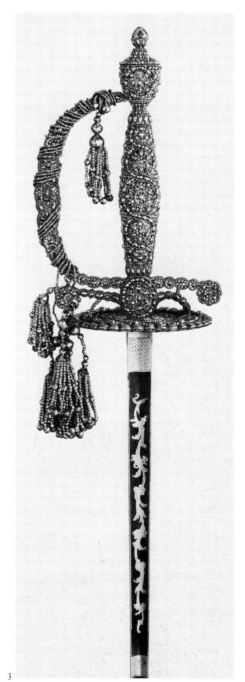

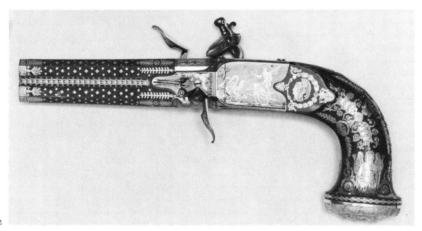

wrote after the battle to the government, a copy of which he kept as a most prized possession. For years afterwards he read it repeatedly to his guests. It arrived dramatically. Lord Liverpool, the Prime Minister, and the Regent were at a ball in St James's Square – Mrs Boehme's. Major Percy had ridden posthaste from Waterloo in under two days, and was still blood-stained and dusty when he arrived. The ladies withdrew; Lord Liverpool read the despatch announcing victory; the Prince, gracious as ever at a moment of high drama, turned and said, 'I congratulate you, *Colonel* Percy' – giving the major instant promotion. Then he wept – wept at the thought of friends dead or maimed. And for the rest of his life Waterloo haunted him – its glory, its drama, its toll of death. Like any artist, he identified deeply, so deeply indeed that his descriptions of battles he had never fought were as real as if he had been there. There was an occasion when he described, in the Duke of Wellington's presence, a charge down an almost perpendicular hill, and looked to the Duke for confirmation. 'Very steep, Sir, very steep,' said the Duke, never at a loss for a word.

Waterloo was the crowning victory, and George IV decided to create a room at Windsor worthy of Wellington and his victorious allies. The

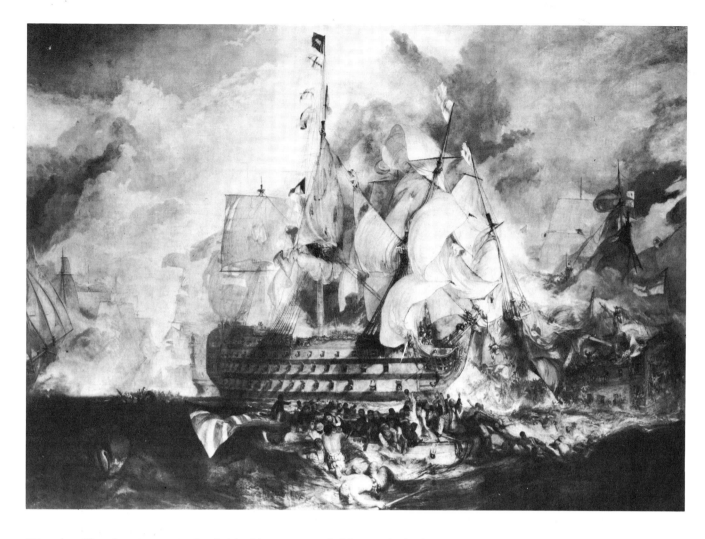

J. M. W. Turner, *The Battle of Trafalgar*.
The only Turner commissioned by George IV.
National Maritime Museum, London

Waterloo Chamber was not quite finished in George IV's lifetime; he had planned it towards the end of his reign. The portraits by Sir Thomas Lawrence, commissioned by the King, dominate the room; there are thirty by him, painted at the height of his powers. Wellington, of course, takes pride of place, but all around the room are the sovereigns, generals and leaders of Britain's allies – the Tsar of Russia, for example, whose visit to London so embarrassed the Regent when the Londoners received him rapturously whilst ignoring or hissing their own Prince Regent. And there is, naturally, General Blücher, a good soldier but appalling guest, who got so abysmally drunk at Oxford that the Regent, with charming good manners, made an elegant speech of thanks to the University from the few words of German grunted by the General. Better Blücher on the battlefield than at the banquet! Prince Metternich, who was neither a sovereign nor a general, hangs here, and rightly so; astute, yet deeply conservative, he was the main architect of the peace in 1815. He secured a formidable ally in George's boon companion, the Princess Lieven, who had been Metternich's mistress and who relished politics even more than love. George, from the time of his regency, rightly appreciated that Metternich's diplomacy had kept Europe at peace after Napoleon's defeat, and his admiration never flagged. The most surprising portrait, perhaps, to hang in this gallery is that of Pope Pius VII, who played no part in the wars, and only a minor part at the Congress of Vienna, which settled the destiny of Europe. The Prince had a fondness for the Pope and he had behaved with his usual generosity towards him.

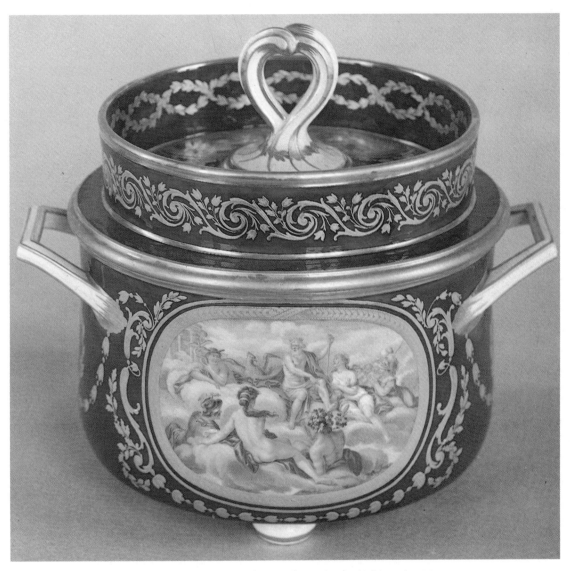

A Sèvres porcelain ice pail, part of a service made for Louis XVI

King George IV collected French works of art on an extensive scale and much of Carlton House was furnished in the French style. His acquisitions make one of the finest collections of French art ever assembled outside France

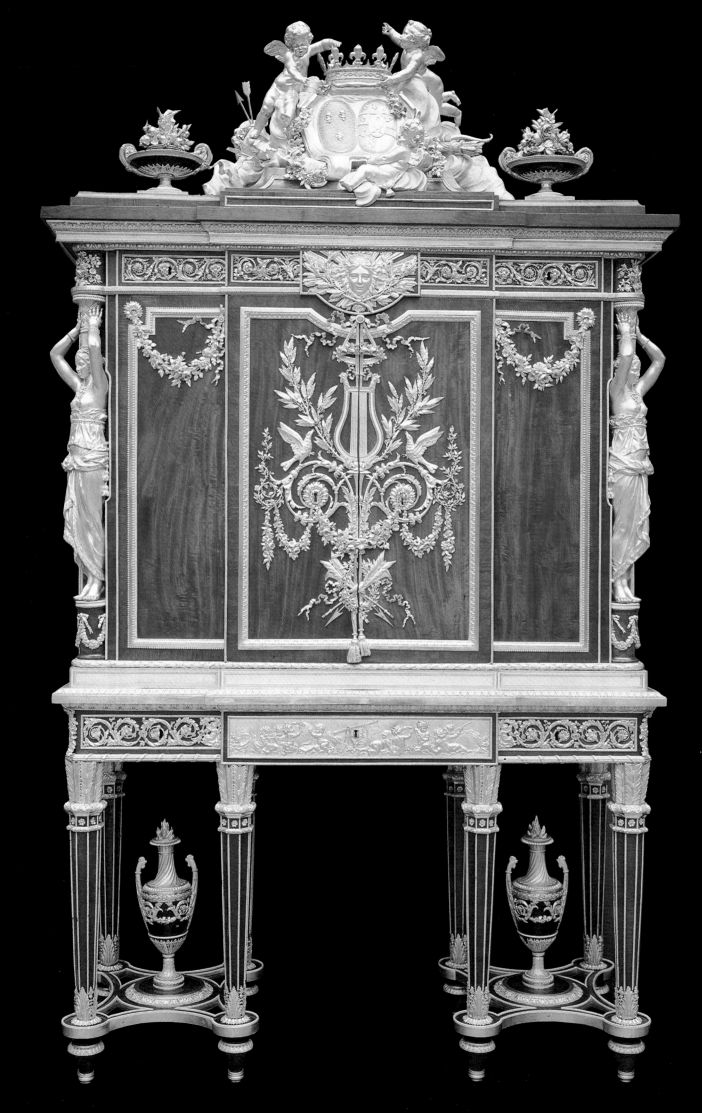

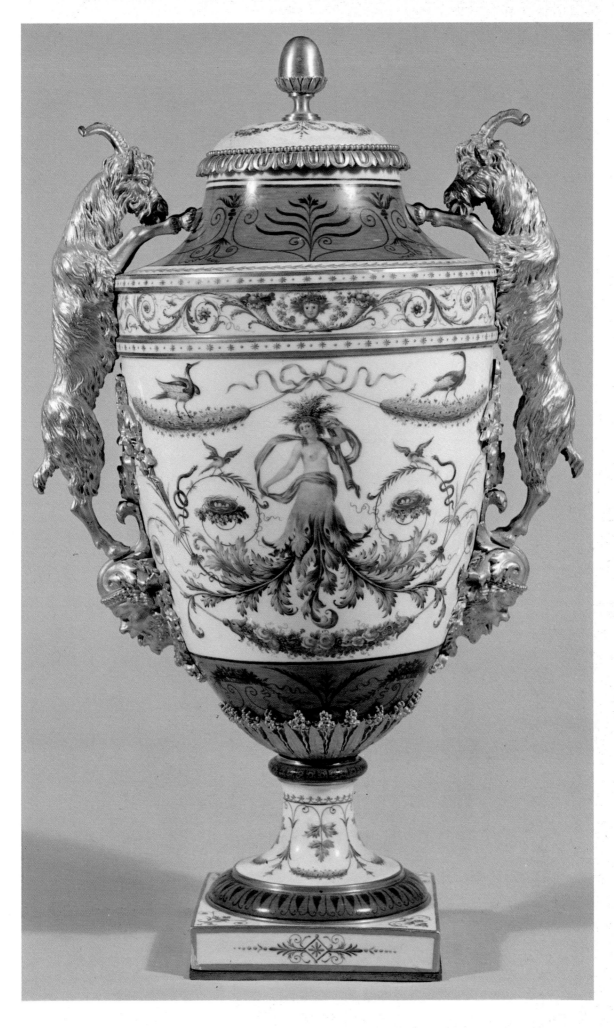

Opposite: Jewel cabinet by J. H. Riesener. *c.* 1785

Above: One of a pair of vases, in hard-paste Sèvres porcelain, dated 1782, made by P. P. Thomire for Louis XVI. George IV bought them in 1812

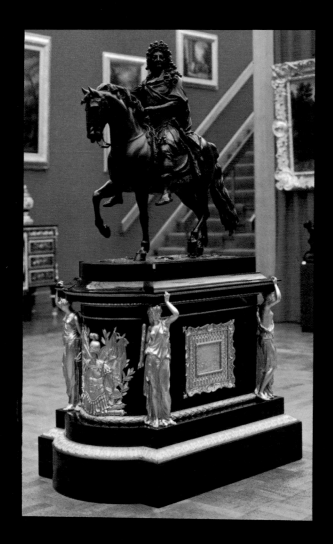

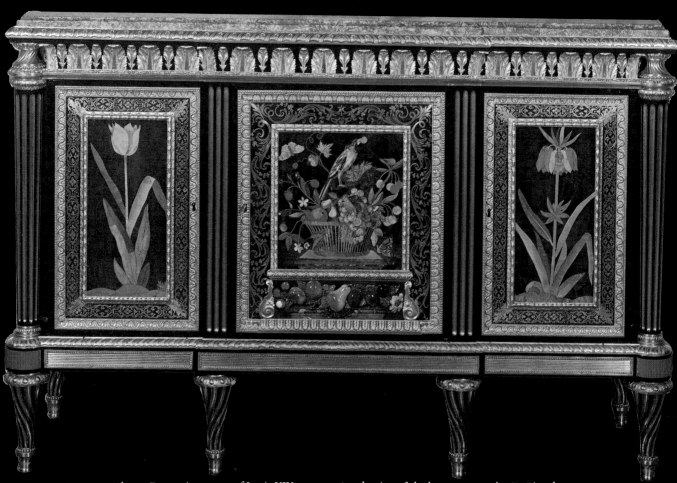

Above: Equestrian statue of Louis XIV. *c.* 1700. A reduction of the bronze statue by F. Girardon
Below: Cabinet by A. Weisweiler. Late eighteenth century

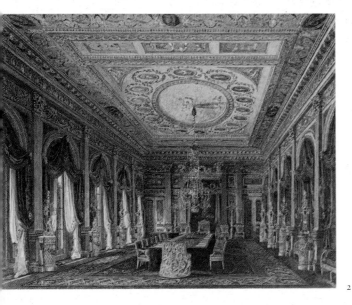

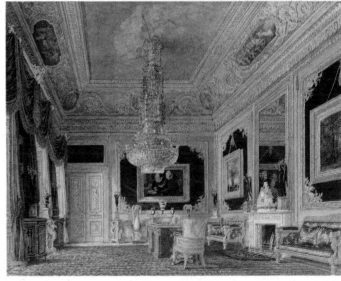

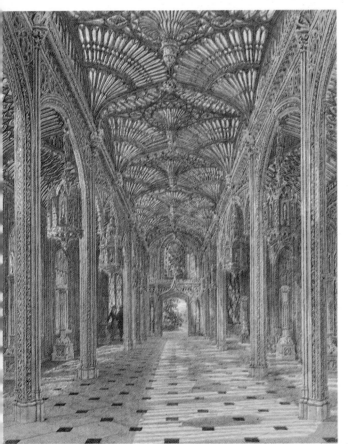

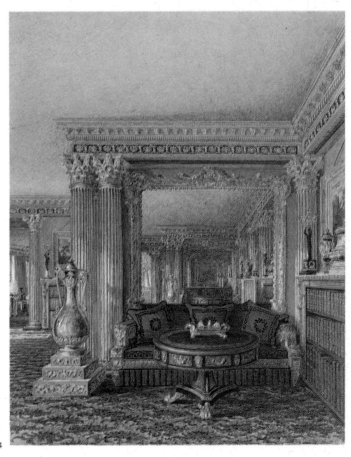

Watercolours of the interior of Carlton House published as engravings in W. H. Pyne's *The History of the Royal Residences*, London, vol. III, 1819.
1 The Throne Room. 2 The Blue Velvet Room, the Prince of Wales's Audience Room. 3 The Gothic Conservatory. 4 A corner of the Library

K*ing George IV built Carlton House as his London home. The architect was Henry Holland. The building was*
demolished in 1827

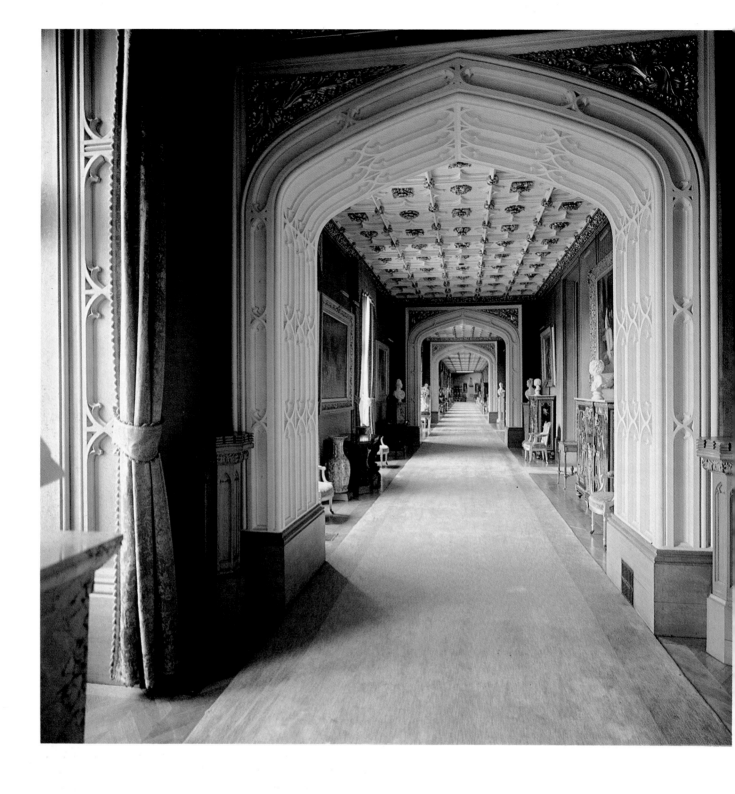

The Grand Corridor, Windsor Castle, by Sir Jeffrey Wyatville

Two great monuments to King George IV as patron of architecture: the additions made to Windsor Castle towards the end of his life, and the Royal Pavilion, Brighton, the flamboyant masterpiece of his earlier years

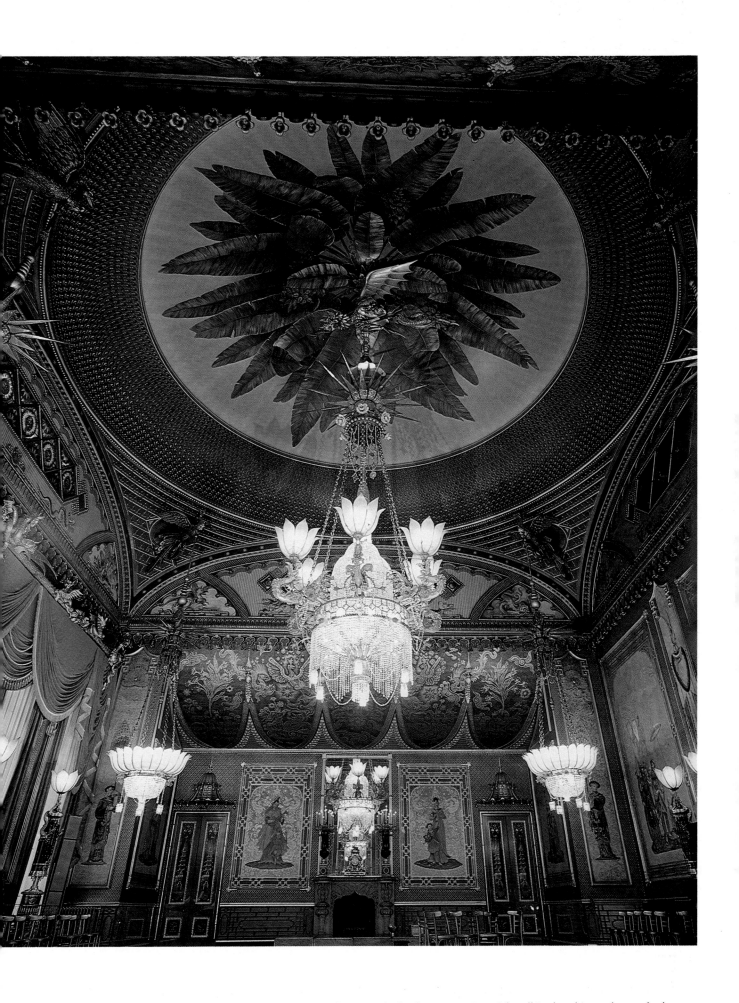

The central gasolier, in the Banqueting Room of the Royal Pavilion, thirty feet high, almost a ton in weight, all in the Chinese theme of a dragon, dolphins, waterlilies and lotuses and composed of links of pearls and rubies

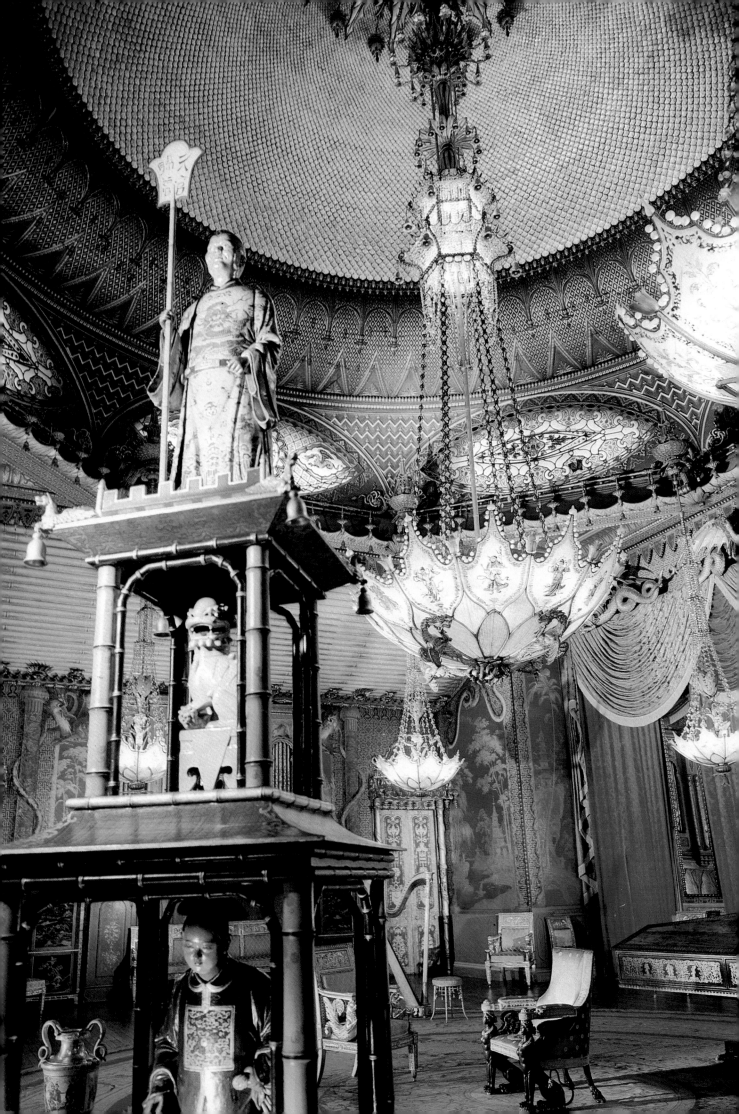

Pius VII said that he and the papacy were too poor to pay for the return of the works of art Napoleon had taken from the Vatican to adorn Paris, and offered to give them instead to the Regent. The Regent refused and paid for their return to Rome – a touch of theatre, as always with the Regent, but still a grand gesture.

More than his ministers, far more than his people, George IV had an intuitive sense of the greatness of events. He had witnessed the rise and fall of Napoleon, a dramatic career was bound to enthral him, and he was greedy for grandeur and romance, so he collected mementoes of

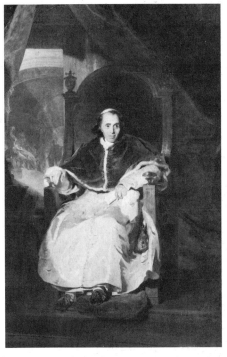

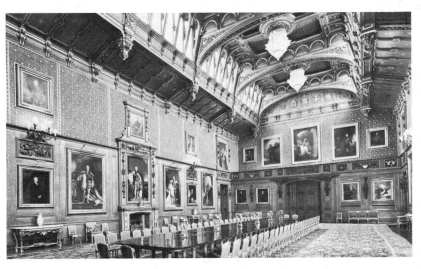

Sir Thomas Lawrence, knighted by George IV in 1815, gave help and advice to the King on the formation of his collection of paintings, and was his principal painter.
1 Sir Thomas Lawrence: *William Pitt.* 2 *Pope Pius VII.* 1819.
3 The Waterloo Chamber at Windsor, hung with portraits by Lawrence

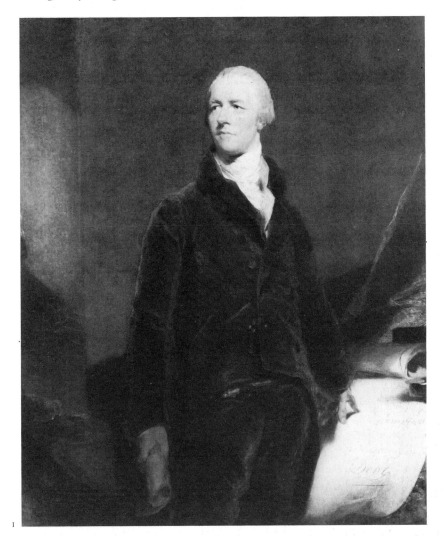

Opposite: The Music Room at the Royal Pavilion, Brighton

Napoleon with his usual ardour – swords, of course, and batons used in battle. He was also very keen to obtain possession of one of the acknowledged masterpieces of the Sèvres porcelain factory – the famous Table of the Great Generals – which Napoleon himself had ordered from Sèvres in 1806. It depicts Alexander the Great, surrounded by the great generals of antiquity. It took six years to make, and cost a small fortune. The Regent offered to buy it, but a grateful Louis XVIII made him a present of it. Perhaps his most famous purchase was the oversized nude statue of Napoleon by the most distinguished sculptor of the time, Canova. Napoleon hated it, the Regent admired it, bought it, and, generous as ever, presented it to the Duke of Wellington, who set it up in the vestibule of his London home, Apsley House, where it still remains. Canova, Napoleon's favourite sculptor, became the Regent's. He bought several remarkable statues from him and commissioned others. His fondness for Canova illustrates the exceptional range of the Prince's taste – his appreciation of the fashionable neo-classical style never inhibited his love of Gothic or Chinese fantasies, or even of the taste of the previous generation. Napoleon spurned a superb jewel cabinet by the greatest of all eighteenth-century cabinet makers, J. H. Riesener, as 'too old-fashioned'. Some years later George IV bought it up at a London sale; it became one of his most prized possessions, and is one of the most splendid pieces of furniture now in the royal collection (see page 218).

The Regent's fascination with Napoleon leads us, at last, to one of the deepest springs of his character. Although at times he appears to be a magpie collector (snapping up jewels, bronzes, furniture, china, pictures, drawings, prints, medals) there was, beneath it all, a very powerful ambition. A magnificent statue at Windsor of Louis XIV perhaps gives us the key to it. It is a reduction, but a very large version of the most famous equestrian statues of Louis, cast to celebrate his great victories. Britain

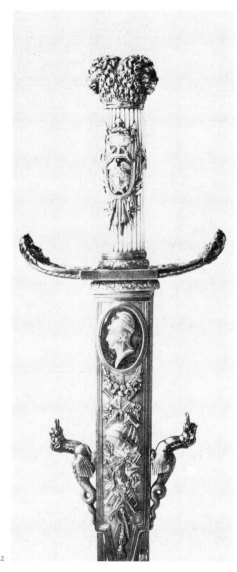

2

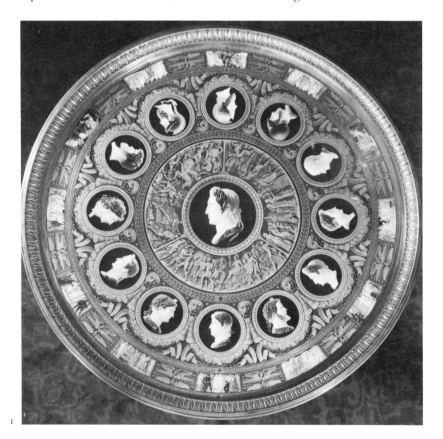

1

1 'Table of the Great Generals.' Commissioned by Napoleon in 1806 from the Sèvres manufactory and given to George IV by Louis XVIII in 1817. The porcelain top is painted with the head of Alexander the Great in the centre and twelve commanders from antiquity.
2 The hilt of Napoleon's sword when First Consul, also acquired by the King

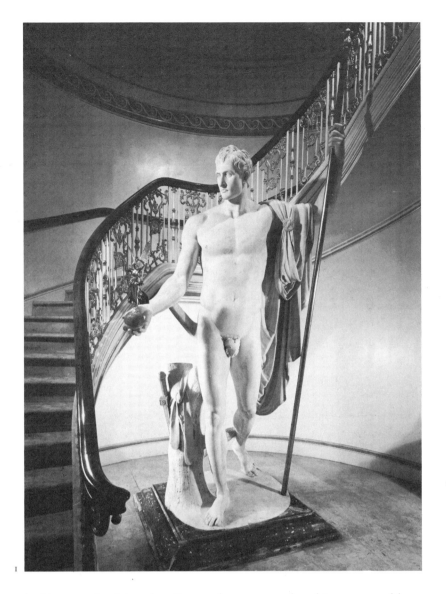

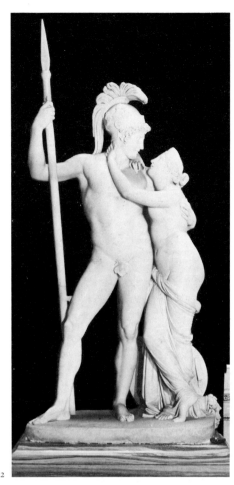

Antonio Canova: 1 His statue of Napoleon at
Apsley House, presented by George IV to
the Duke of Wellington. 2 *Mars and Venus*,
commissioned by the King following
Canova's visit to England in 1815 and placed
in the Conservatory at Carlton House

had become far richer than France, but possessed nothing comparable to
Versailles, Louis's huge palace built in the late seventeenth century. Nor
did Britain possess a museum comparable to the Louvre, with its
outstanding collection of European art. Throughout his life, George IV
wanted to correct this loss – to give England palaces worthy of the King
of the world's most powerful nation, and collections of art that would be
unsurpassed by any other country. He hoped, too, that British artists
and craftsmen would outshine the world's, but his model, his hero, was
Louis XIV. He collected bronzes of Louis, and acquired magnificent busts
of his marshalls, Vauban, the great military engineer, the Duc de Villars,
Marlborough's most formidable rival, and the handsome Condé – along
with Turenne, the greatest of Louis XIV's generals.

George IV might have made a hero of Louis XIV, but in spirit he was
closer to his great grandson, Louis XV, the great patron of French
craftsmen, the best cabinet-makers, tapestry-weavers, and bronze-
casters of the eighteenth century, whose work George IV never stopped
buying, so that his collection of eighteenth-century decorative art is one
of the greatest in the world.

Fantasy and reality had always been fused in the Prince's mind,
sometimes one, sometimes the other having the upper hand. Self-
indulgent he might be, and certainly extravagant, yet deep-feeling. And

life had buffeted him pretty hard. Often he felt useless to his country; his wife behaved abysmally – a loose-mouthed hoyden; his only child proved first difficult, then tragic: married happily and very young to Leopold of Saxe-Coburg, she died in childbirth in 1817; nor did the baby survive. The most profound relationship of his life, that with Mrs Fitzherbert, had collapsed in 1803. He subsequently fell in love with the large and matronly Lady Hertford, who kept the relationship entirely platonic but exploited its financial advantages ruthlessly, as did her vast successor, Lady Conyngham. Like many deeply sensuous and self-indulgent men, he became the target for exploitation with growing age. No wonder, then, that, like so many men with a fissured artistic temperament, he was compelled to withdraw into his own world, his own dreams; to create a deeply personal setting for his private life.

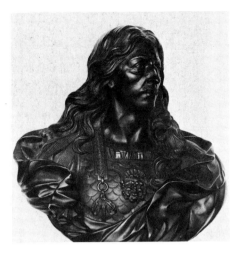

Bronze bust of Condé, after A. Coysevox

That had always meant Brighton, where his personal happiness had been greatest. He had never been totally happy with Holland's villa. He created additions in 1802 and began to adopt the Chinese theme, creating a corridor which was a fanciful interpretation of the inside of a Chinese lantern. For a time, however, his attention was distracted by the building of palatial stables and a gigantic riding school, designed by Humphrey Repton, one of his greatest architectural achievements. The central cupola was eighty feet in diameter and sixty-five feet high, lit by great leaf-shaped panels of glass; the base housed the royal horses in forty-five stables, and the harness rooms and grooms' rooms were on the first floor connected by a circular balcony; in the middle, for watering horses, a huge fountain played.

The stables astonished everyone who saw them and for once the Prince felt that he had achieved the grandeur which he sought. They were the key to the pavilion's future, for in many ways they were closer to a great mosque built by the Moguls than to the Halle des Blés, from which their original inspiration came. Also, they made the pavilion seem very small and mean. After toying with Repton's scheme for a more Indian treatment of the pavilion, the Prince finally decided to accept John Nash's scheme in 1815, and work was started on the building that we know today.

Contemporaries were astounded by the kitchen, as much as by the food. 'Such contrivances for roasting, boiling, baking, stewing, frying, steaming and heating,' wrote his friend, Croker, 'hot plates, hot chests, hot air and hot hearths, and with all manner of cocks for hot water and cold water, and warm water and steam, and twenty saucepans all ticketed and labelled, placed up to their necks in a vapour bath.' The Regent was immensely proud of his kitchen, and once had a carpet spread in it so that he could dine with his cooks. Food of the highest quality gave him great pleasure.

So it was here, in the great rooms which have already been described, that the Regent created an intensely private world for himself, a world of almost oriental luxury and extravagance, in which food, gossip, drink and music played the dominant roles, all, even including the gossip, on the grandest possible scale. The Regent could be totally indiscreet about his ministers, mimic them brilliantly to his friends, give away state secrets and express the strongest opinions on foreign affairs quite at variance with the cabinet's. There was nothing reserved or secretive about this Regent, certainly not to his friends.

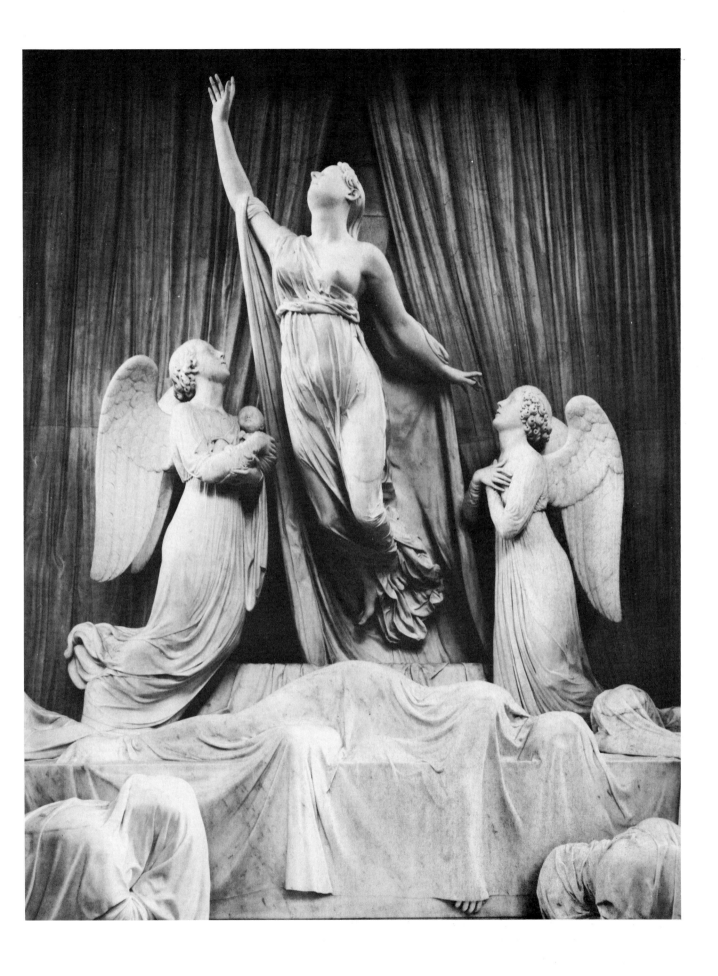

Monument to Princess Charlotte, by Matthew Wyatt, in St George's Chapel, Windsor, erected by King George IV after his daughter died in childbirth in 1817

But music was more important than gossip, as important as the gigantic quantities of food and wine, a profusion that was intended to delight the eye as much as the palate of his guests, for no small party of twenty could have consumed the 116 elaborate dishes placed before them. The Regent was equally extravagant with his musical entertainment. There were state trumpeters and the King's Band of Musicians in Ordinary, as well as the singers and musicians at the Chapel Royal, yet the Regent could not do without a private band to perform whenever he wanted. There were forty-two musicians in this band, all practitioners of wind instruments. In 1825, apart from clothes, they cost £5780, but said they were starving and demanded an £885 19s 6d pay increase for 1826. And to this must be added the star performers – the great singers, great pianists, such as Rossini whom the Regent loved to entertain at Brighton – who naturally charged a large fee. So the cost of the band was enormous but, as ever with the Regent, the result was splendid; most visitors to Brighton were as bewitched by the music as they were by their host.

In Brighton the Regent was secure, above all from the hatred of the mob and the bitter attacks of the radical press. The extravagance of Brighton, however, contrasted ill with the poverty and desperate social conditions that followed the Napoleonic wars, and led to violent outbursts and harsh repression. It was the middle class who hated the

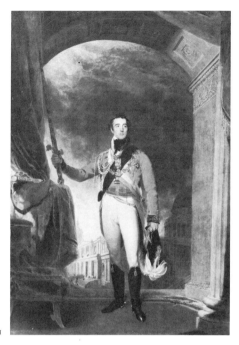

1 Sir Thomas Lawrence, *Arthur Wellesley, First Duke of Wellington.* 1814–15.

2 William Hogarth, *David Garrick with his wife Eva-Maria Veigel.* King George IV bought the picture in about 1826

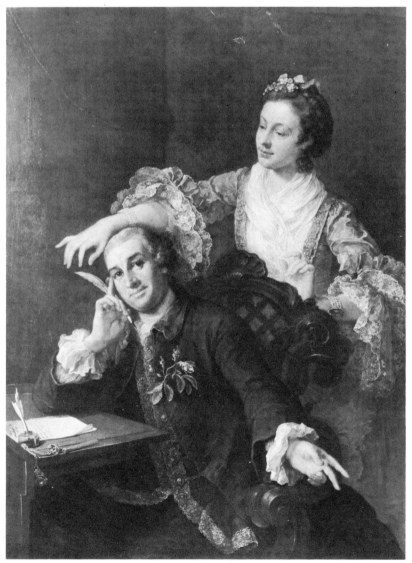

Regent most; after all they, not the poor, paid the taxes and so footed his extravagant bills. Many detested him so heartily that increasingly they took up the cause of his wife and encouraged her to claim her rights as Queen when the Regent at last succeeded his father in 1820. She was, by any standards, a coarse, flamboyant, almost certainly adulterous woman, but such was her support that the King's attempt to divorce her failed and increased his unpopularity, at least in London. Yet he could never quite believe in this unpopularity, and drove it from his mind. His love of pageantry, his sense of the dignity and grandeur of the monarchy, the theatrical side of his nature, all from time to time pulled him away from his private fantasy world into public performances as colourful, as grandiose, as the pavilion itself.

Theatre fascinated George IV. His hero was David Garrick, the great actor of his early youth; he purchased a splendid picture of him and his wife by Hogarth and collected 116 prints of Garrick alone. Like all George IV's collections, his collection of theatrical prints is enormous. At times he was buying fifty prints at once from Colnaghi. No one was a more ardent spectator of opera and ballet, so he brought a very professional interest to his own coronation. He himself designed the costumes, which are fanciful Tudor, a period in which aesthetic interest was beginning to revive. He commanded that the designs be printed with descriptions of them and of the coronation service in a huge double elephant folio printed in gold, which is now in the royal library at Windsor. No tittle of pageantry was cut from the coronation, and for the last time the King's Champion, resplendent in armour, charged into the banquet in Westminster Hall and threw down his gauntlet. For the last time the Herb Woman with her attendants strewed her sweet-smelling flowers.

As well as the costumes, George IV turned his hand to jewellery and produced an enchanting circlet of gold, diamonds and other precious stones which is now worn by Queen Elizabeth when she goes to open parliament. And, as might be expected, George IV acted splendidly in the title role – everyone praised his dignity and, in spite of his corpulence, the elegance of his movements. Fortunately the Queen made a fool of herself, demanding to be let into the coronation ceremony. For once her actions made him, and not her, popular in London.

Certainly George IV enjoyed his coronation, and he shrewdly saw the public value of this pageantry of monarchy. So he planned state visits to all his dominions. Ireland came first. No English king had ever visited Ireland except at the head of an army. The journey was, much to the King's delight, made memorable by the first royal use of a steamship, and although the visit was slightly muted by the sudden death of Queen Caroline, the King was rapturously received. Just as well, since he had a hideous and dangerous return voyage. Then he went to Hanover, his German Kingdom, which had last been visited by George II. On the way, he visited Waterloo with the Duke of Wellington, who was surprised by the obvious boredom of the King; but it was pelting with rain, and dripping fields are no great stimulus to the imagination. However, the King did show one sign of emotion, bursting into tears when he was shown the grave of his friend Paget's leg, which had been blown off in the battle. In Hanover he was received rapturously, much to his delight, but it was the visit to Scotland that had the most lasting results.

No monarch had visited Scotland since Charles II had taken refuge there. The country meant a great deal to George IV. He admired Sir Walter Scott, whose novels he read and praised. He enjoyed Scott's company and had his portrait painted by Lawrence. Also, he was full of compassion for the exiled Stuarts, on whose behalf the Scottish Highlands had flared into rebellion in the famous '45. He had taken care of James II's remains when they were moved in France, and when the last Stuart, Cardinal Henry of York, died, George IV had a vast memorial erected at his own expense in St Peter's, Rome – again by Canova – an action which irritated his whig friends immensely, but made him new allies in Scotland. And rather than let them be dispersed, he bought up all the Stuart papers, along with what remained of their jewels – including Charles I's coronation ring. His sense of identity with the Stuarts and with Scotland was very close. He intended to take Scotland by storm, and did.

Of course, George IV paid great attention to his costume. He sported the Stuart tartan and kilt and even though his flesh-coloured tights caused some hilarity, most Scotsmen were deeply impressed by the King. He opened up Holyroodhouse – no monarch had set foot there since James II made a visit when Duke of York – and held a glittering levée that made the Scots at last feel that they, too, had a King. With Sir Walter Scott's help he resuscitated the ancient traditions of the Scottish monarchy. Compared with this, the visits to Ireland and Hanover were mere rehearsals. His visit worked to perfection. The Stuarts were not obliterated, but were, in a sense, enfolded in the royal past; they became romantic family ghosts. The reality was the flashing splendour of George IV.

Aelbert Cuyp, *An Evening Landscape. c.* 1650

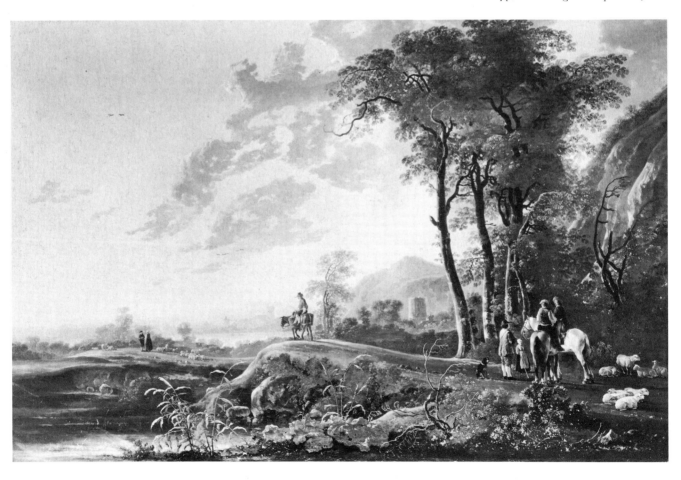

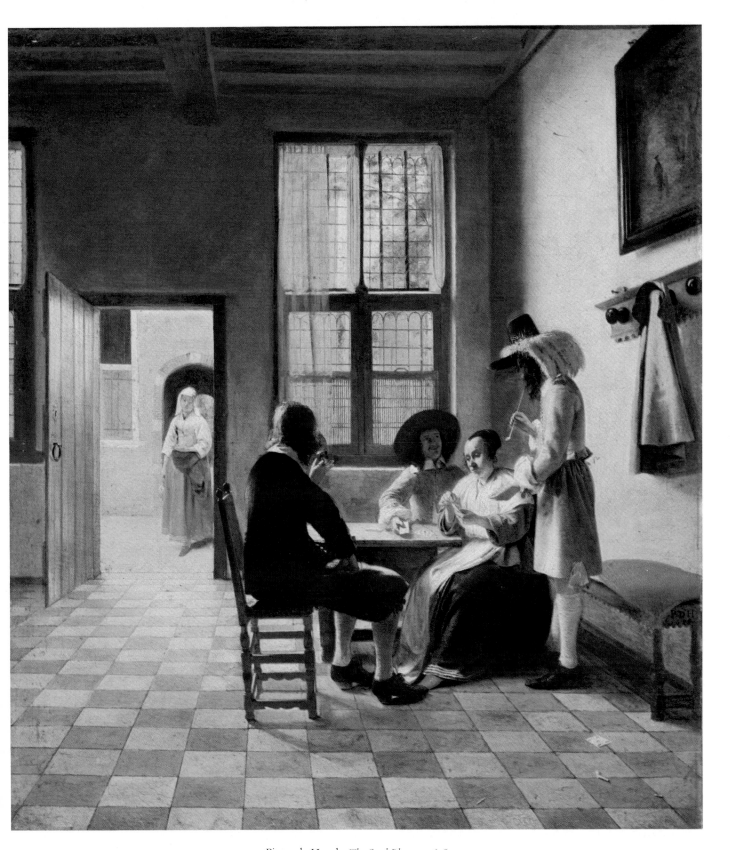

Pieter de Hooch, *The Card Players*. 1658

King George IV assembled a fine collection of Dutch old masters, most of which hung at
Carlton House and are now at Buckingham Palace

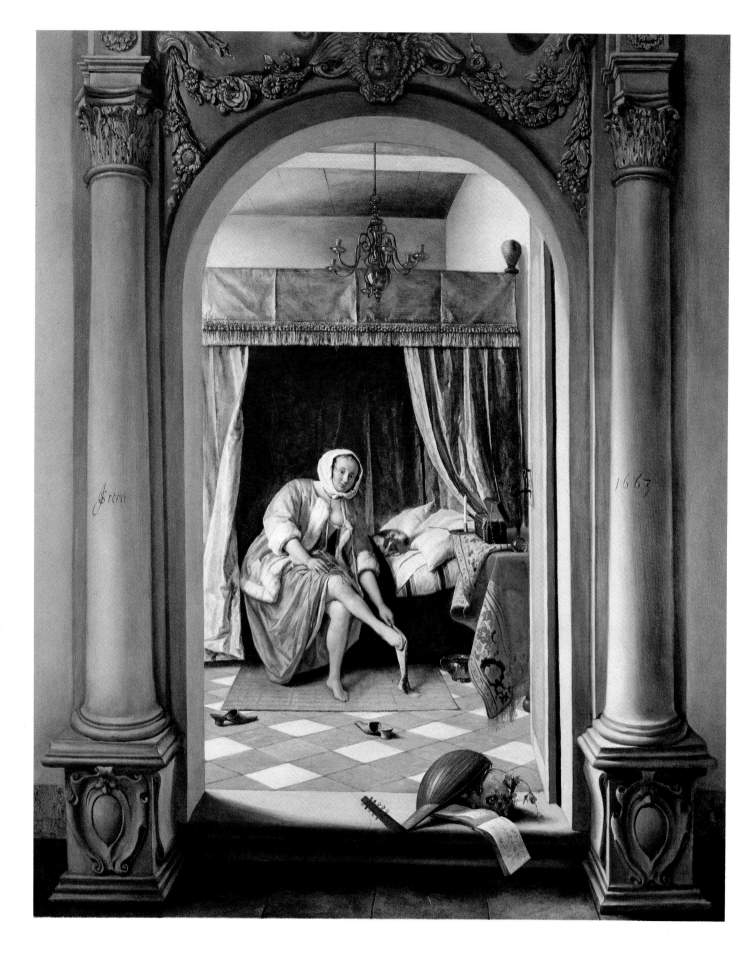

Jan Steen, *The Morning Toilet.* 1663

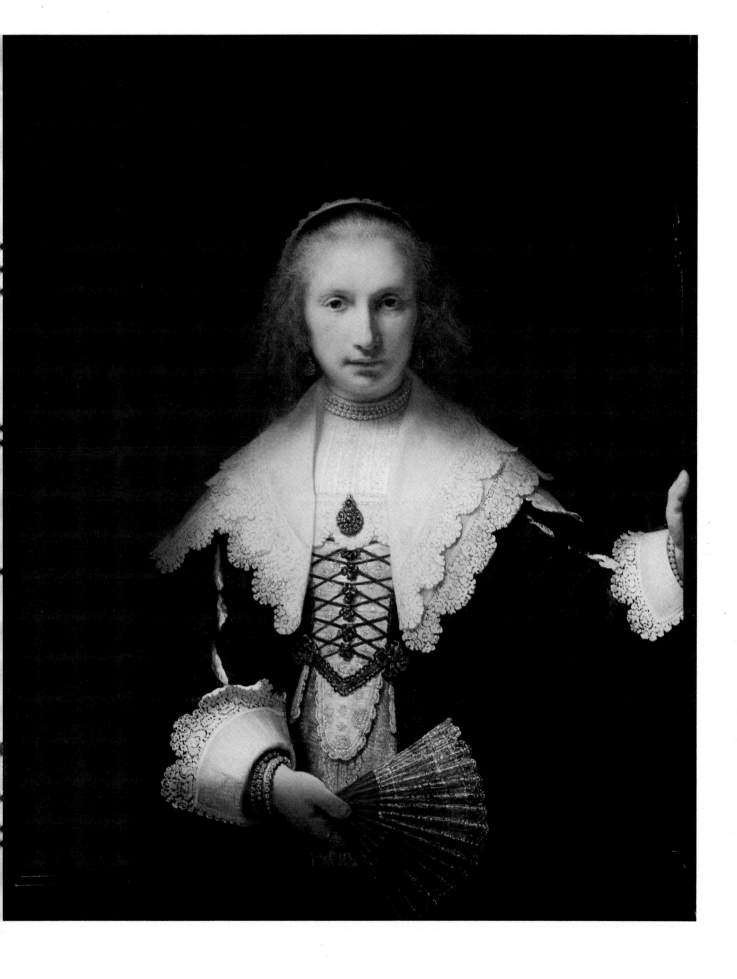

Rembrandt, *The Lady with a Fan.* 1641

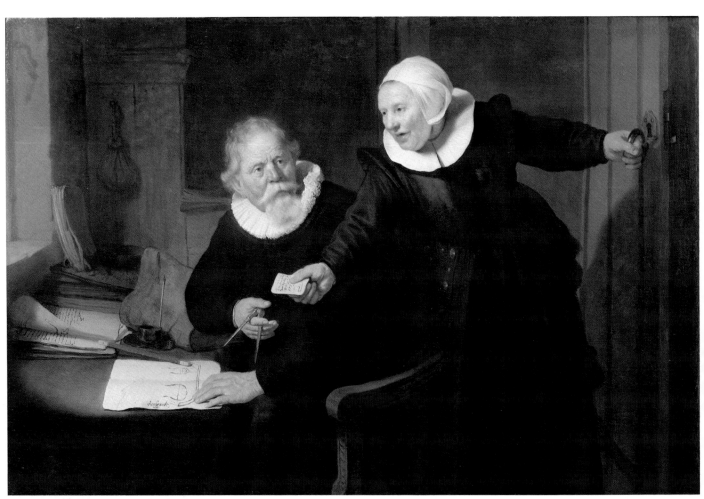

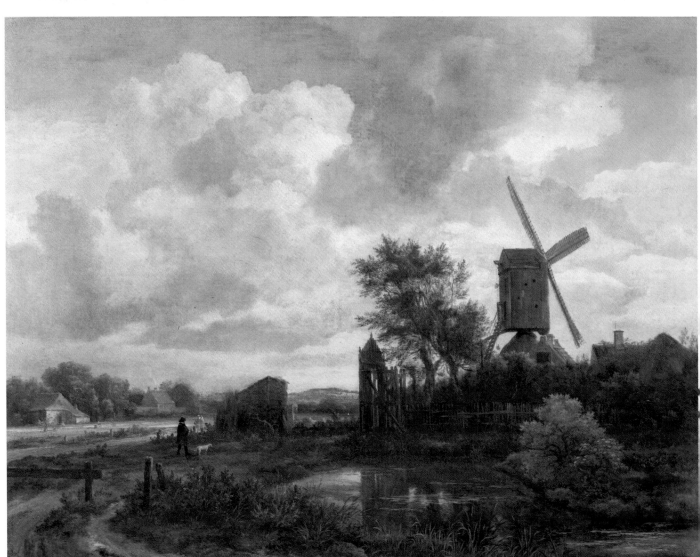

Since that day Scotland has had a special place in the lives of British kings and queens. With the coronation, and these visits, the pageantry of monarchy had been reborn. Nor, equally important, was it a private pageantry. Now, for those who could not be present, there were prints that sold by their thousands. By these great state visits George IV began to bring the monarchy towards that wider public exposure which was to give it such strength in the following century.

Although, in a sense, it was all too late – the King was over sixty, overweight, and far from healthy – his artistic energies were prodigious and his ambition to create a setting worthy of the British monarchy undimmed. His interest in art and literature and science were as lively as ever. Sir Walter Scott was not the only novelist the King admired. He had always been a devotee of Jane Austen, and had her novels in his library; under royal persuasion she dedicated *Emma* to him. Byron, whom he had met at Brighton, he read with avidity. George IV's patronage led to the foundation of the Royal Society of Literature, which still flourishes. Scientists he admired as much as writers. Yet his great passions remained art and architecture. He was partly responsible for getting the Elgin marbles for the British Museum; he pressed his government to buy the famous Angerstein collection of old masters, and start the National Gallery; and he continued to buy with discernment for his own collection, no longer extensively, but filling the gaps with works of the first quality. In the last year of his life he bought Claude's *The Rape of Europa*, which now hangs at Windsor. And, of course, he went on patronising British artists – buying narrative paintings by Wilkie and Haydon, not in the same class as the great old masters, but of great merit. Curiously he never bought a Constable.

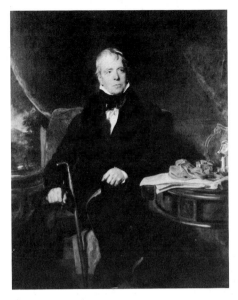

Sir Thomas Lawrence, *Sir Walter Scott*

Sir David Wilkie, *The Entrance of George IV at Holyroodhouse*, in August 1822. The King receives the keys to the palace. Begun the same year, but not finished until seven or eight years later

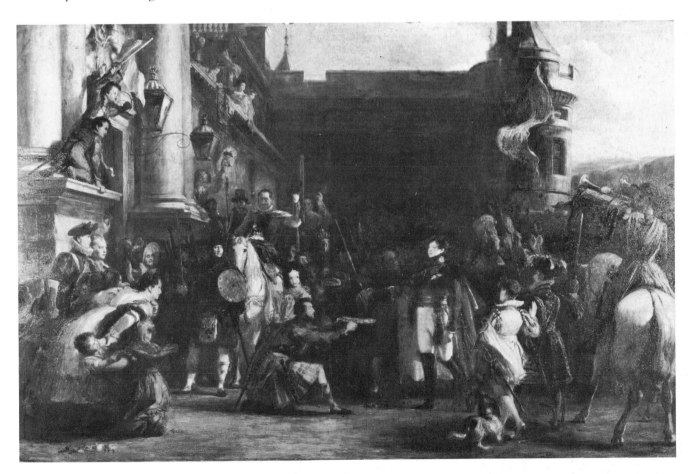

Opposite, top: Rembrandt, *The Shipbuilder and his Wife*. 1633. Bottom: Jacob van Ruisdael, *An Evening Landscape*. c. 1660

As he grew older, architecture obsessed him more and more. Deciding that Carlton House was too small, and Windsor too dilapidated, he tore down Carlton House and rebuilt Buckingham Palace, but it was Windsor that became his passion. This was to be his Versailles, a truly regal setting for the brilliant furniture and pictures from Carlton House. This, too, was his government's wish; in making a very large grant, his ministers said that they wanted the building to be 'to a degree of splendour that was becoming to the sovereign who ruled over the country, and also the country over which he ruled'. But Windsor was a great medieval fortress, and George IV decided that his additions must be in the Gothic taste. To make them he chose Jeffrey Wyatt – a creative artist who was even less interested in costing than the King himself. Wyatt was so besotted with the splendour of his position that he begged to be allowed to change his name to Wyatville; George IV replied that 'Veal or Mutton, he could call himself what he liked'. Soon the King was mimicking Wyatt's Derbyshire accent to perfection, but he never mocked his work. He admired him intensely, knighted him for it, and

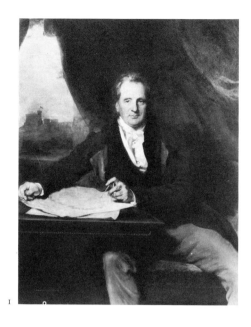

1

Sir Thomas Lawrence: 1 *Sir Jeffrey Wyatville*, the architect who reconstructed Windsor Castle for the King. 2 *George IV*. *c*. 1822. Wallace Collection, London

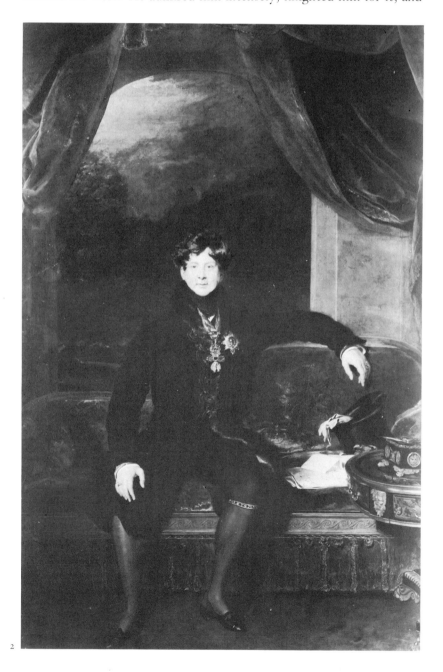

2

had his portrait painted by Lawrence. At a cost of £800,000, 500 workmen transformed Windsor. One of its most original features was the Grand Corridor, 550 feet in length, linking the private apartments and state rooms, but it was also perfect for the display of the King's china, bronzes, medals and pictures. It became a memorial of the past, for here he placed the busts of the dead friends of his gilded youth – Charles James Fox, Sheridan, and Thurlow, the hard-drinking, crotchety Lord Chancellor – and amongst them William Pitt, his old enemy, but now forgiven. At twilight these busts were as luminous as ghosts.

As one year passed into the next, George IV lived more and more at Windsor. He was rightly proud of his magnificent suite of drawing-rooms, the red, the green and the white, where he held his last parties, and entertained his ageing family and friends. Though they fall short of Versailles in regal splendour, they are, perhaps, the most beautiful royal rooms of all the Queen's palaces; the furniture he loved best at Carlton House is here – some of his finest pictures, china and bronzes.

And yet what irony these rooms contain! For as the King's setting

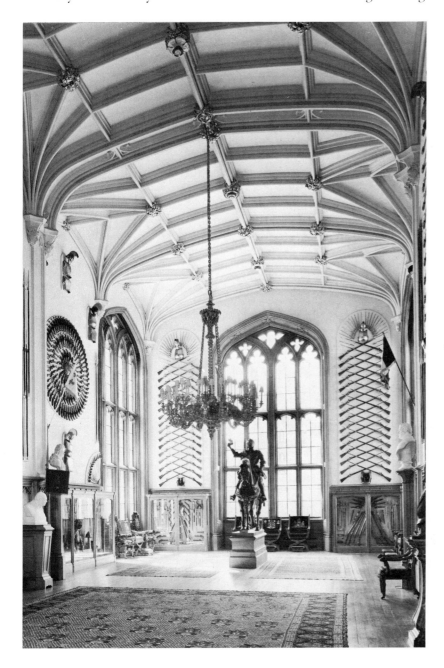

The Guard Chamber, Windsor Castle

became more regal, so his power diminished. He had long forgotten his whig principles, if not his whig friends. More and more he came to idolise the conservative dedication (some would call it obstinacy) of his father. As a young Prince, he had warmly supported the movement to give catholics, who were excluded from the franchise, the vote; now, as an old man, he did his utmost to prevent it. But rail as he might against the British Constitution, he had to obey it and catholics got the vote. It was one more dark reminder of a new world, a new generation that he liked less and less, driving him increasingly to privacy; to the creation and perfection of his private world at Windsor.

One of his most imaginative acts there was to create the great Eastern terrace, and to open up from the castle the vista of the Long Walk – a great avenue that Charles II had planted. He commanded Westmacott to make an equestrian statue of his father which he intended to place at the end of the avenue, an act of piety and contrition. He suffered as his father suffered – probably from the same disease. This brought him to a deeper understanding of his father's qualities. In life his father had often rejected him; in death he could not, and although George IV never saw the statue impressively placed in the great vista, once more it was his act of creative imagination that put it there.

Increasingly confined to Windsor, he found solace in driving in his phaeton round the park or down to Virginia Water, which his great uncle Cumberland had created. Sometimes he sent for his niece, the Princess Victoria, whose company he enjoyed. She later recollected how she 'met the King in his phaeton, and he said "Pop her in", and I was lifted and placed between him and Aunt Gloucester, who held me round the waist. I was greatly pleased, and remember that I looked with great respect on the scarlet liveries'. The King was on his way to Virginia Water, where he would fish with Lady Conyngham, using the tackle which still remains. A few musicians, usually on a barge, would play music for them. At times they would picnic with friends, sometimes in the tents which the King had erected for the summer, sometimes in the Roman ruins of Leptis Magna, which he had had transported from Libya. Or he would have his friends driven down to his menagerie. As always with the King's collections this grew very fast and included gnus, kangaroos, and a vast collection of rare birds; but his greatest prize was a young Nubian giraffe, whose beauty entranced him. 'Nothing could give an idea of the beauty of her eyes.' One of his last commissions was a picture of the giraffe by Agasse. It is on loan to the Zoological Gardens, for one of the last acts of George IV's patronage was to sanction the founding of the zoo, to which his own collection of animals and birds was promptly dispatched by William IV, who had no more use for rare animals than for gas lighting.

No matter how sick or old, the King still maintained an astonishing gusto for life. Sensation, both in its most refined and in its coarsest sense, still dominated his life. The beauty of Windsor haunted him as much as the fleeting beauty of the young giraffe. At the same time he could gorge and drink with an appetite that was suicidal. Already a dying man, in April 1830 he consumed for breakfast 'a pidgeon and beef steak pie of which he ate two pidgeons and three beef steaks, and drank three parts of a bottle of Mozelle, a glass of champagne, two glasses of port and a glass of brandy'. Since he combined such meals with massive doses of laudanum to kill the pain, it was a miracle that he lasted another two months.

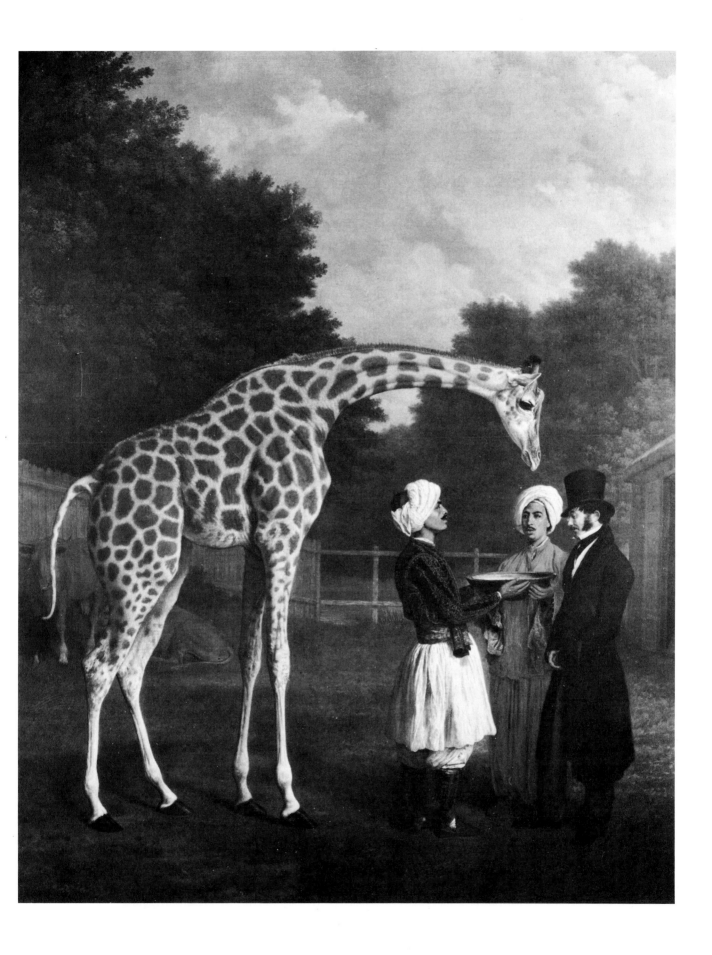

Jacques-Laurent Agasse, *The Nubian Giraffe*. 1827. With it are two Egyptian cows (probably used as wet nurses), two Arab keepers and Edward Cross, importer of, and dealer in, foreign birds and beasts at the Royal Menageries. The giraffe was given to George IV by Mehemet Ali, Pasha of Egypt, and the King constructed a spacious paddock for it at Windsor, but it only lived two years

He died in the castle which he had renewed and embellished, making it the finest of all the palaces of the British monarchy; there he brought together once more in one great building the royal medieval past, the long centuries between, and the living present.

At his death he was praised by two of the greatest men of his age. The Duke of Wellington said, 'He was, indeed, the most extraordinary compound of talent, wit, buffoonery, obstinacy and good feeling – in short a medley of opposite qualities with a great preponderance of good – that I ever saw in any character in my life'. As might be expected, Prince Talleyrand, the great French statesman, was pithier: 'King George IV was *un roi, grand seigneur*. There are no others left'.

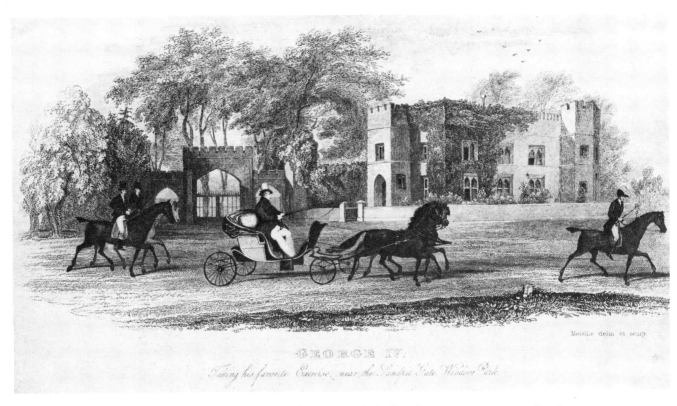

King George IV in old age, riding in a phaeton in Windsor Great Park. 'Taking his favourite exercise . . .' reads the caption to this engraving by Melville

6

VICTORIA AND ALBERT

William IV, George IV's younger brother and, like him, Queen Victoria's uncle, reigned briefly – a strange, eccentric man, very gruff, very down to earth. He had no pretensions to artistic taste whatsoever, and thought that all religious pictures were indecent and should be destroyed. He cut what he thought to be the antique flummery of the coronation – no herb strewer for him, no champion bursting into the feast; indeed, no great feast at Westminster Hall at all. Many of the peers whose coronation duties were cut became furious, but fortunately he permitted some expenditure. He and his wife, Queen Adelaide, had two very beautiful rings made for the coronation, so fine that they have become a part of the regalia and, apart from Queen Victoria, have been used by all sovereigns since at their coronations.

His reign also witnessed some splendid additions of porcelain to the royal collections. Either the King, or, far more probably, his gentle, warm-hearted, retiring Queen, bought a magnificent Rockingham dessert service which gave a great fillip to this factory, and two other magnificent services were ordered from Worcester and Davenport. And more importantly, he did not call a halt to the great architectural plans of his brother. During William IV's reign, the Waterloo Chamber was finished at Windsor, and several of George IV's plans for Buckingham Palace came to fruition, although for a brief moment they were put at risk. Often William IV spoke and acted impulsively and once he suggested that Buckingham Palace should be scrapped altogether.

Brief as his reign was, it was in remarkable contrast to his brother's, and in one way, at least, it was important for the developing image of the monarchy. William IV loved to mingle with his people; walk up and down the pier at Brighton, or stroll about St James's Street and even attend the wedding of a friend. Bluff, hearty, talkative, he enjoyed close contact – being seen on ordinary, as well as state, ceremonial, or organised occasions. At Brighton, London or Windsor he and Queen Adelaide were much more *visible* – a trend which was steadily to strengthen, and to influence the monarchy. The public responded by wanting to see more and more of them which, with a rapidly growing population at Brighton and Windsor, as well as London, made the privacy of remoter homes absolutely essential. This trend was to influence deeply the life style of Queen Victoria, who succeeded her uncle in 1837.

Queen Victoria had a difficult childhood. Her father, the Duke of Kent, died soon after she was born. Her mother was the sister of Prince Leopold of Saxe-Coburg, who had been the husband of George IV's daughter, Charlotte, and was heartily detested by the King. Since George IV hoped either that he would marry again, or that his brother, William, would have children, he tended to ignore the Duchess and her child. The Duke of Kent's debts were monumental, but George IV would do nothing about them and Leopold had to support the Duchess and her daughter. Both he and his sister believed passionately in the young Victoria's destiny, and time and again, as their hopes appeared dashed, death came to their aid and removed potential threats to Victoria's accession. But for seventeen years the Duchess fought George IV and William IV for a proper recognition both of Victoria and of herself, for she expected to be Regent.

By the middle 1830s all had come to look upon Victoria as the heir

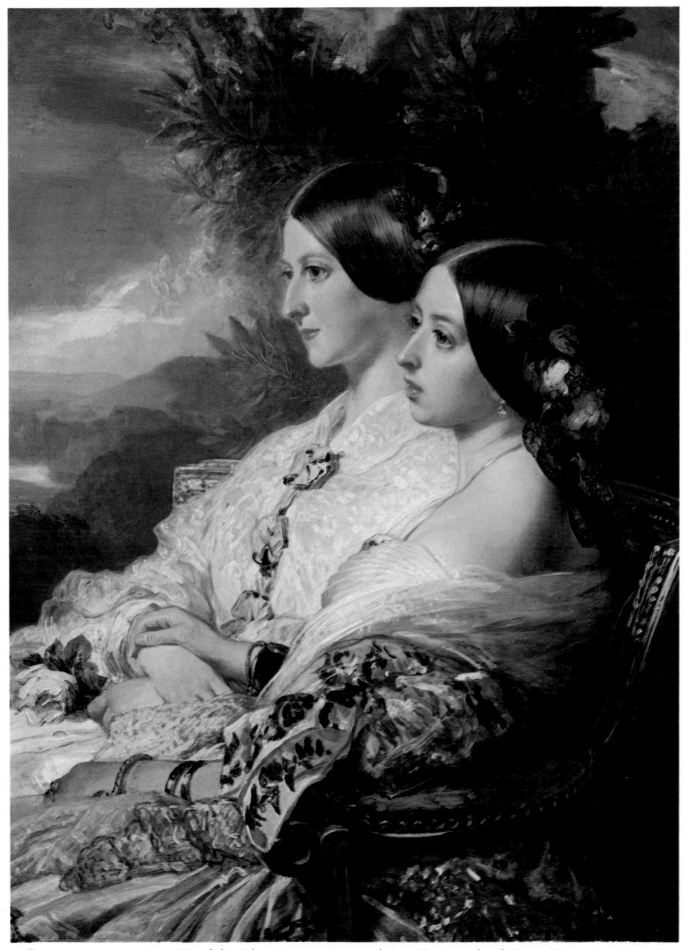

Frans Xaver Winterhalter, *The Cousins: Queen Victoria and Princess Victoire, Duchesse de Nemours*. 1852

Queen Victoria and Prince Albert added contemporary pictures to the Royal Collection. As well as portraits by Winterhalter, the last of the great court painters, there are technically brilliant pieces of popular painting, like the Frith and Landseer reproduced here

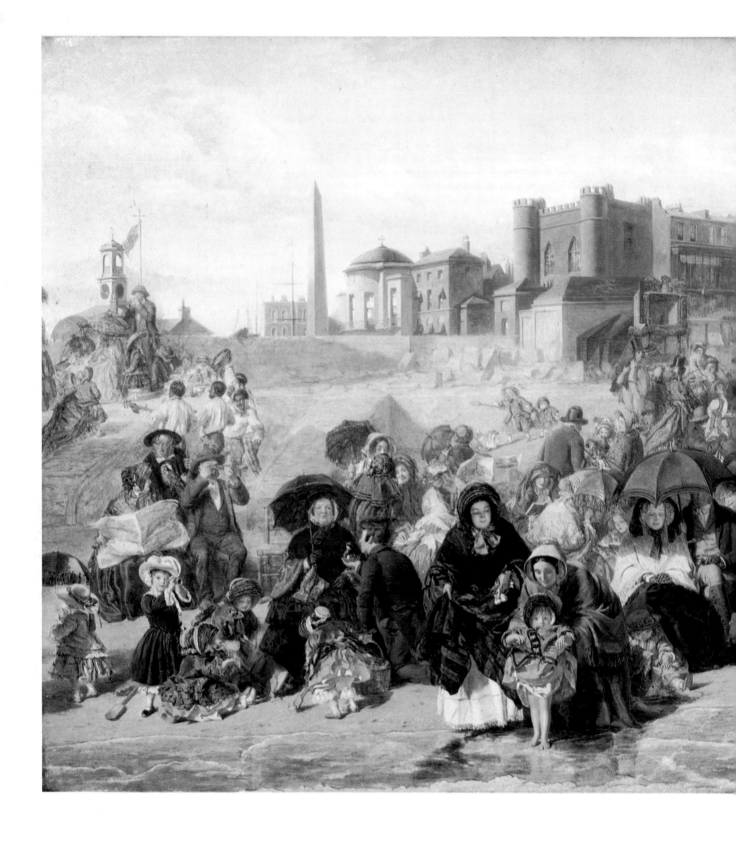

William Powell Frith, *Ramsgate Sands*. 1854

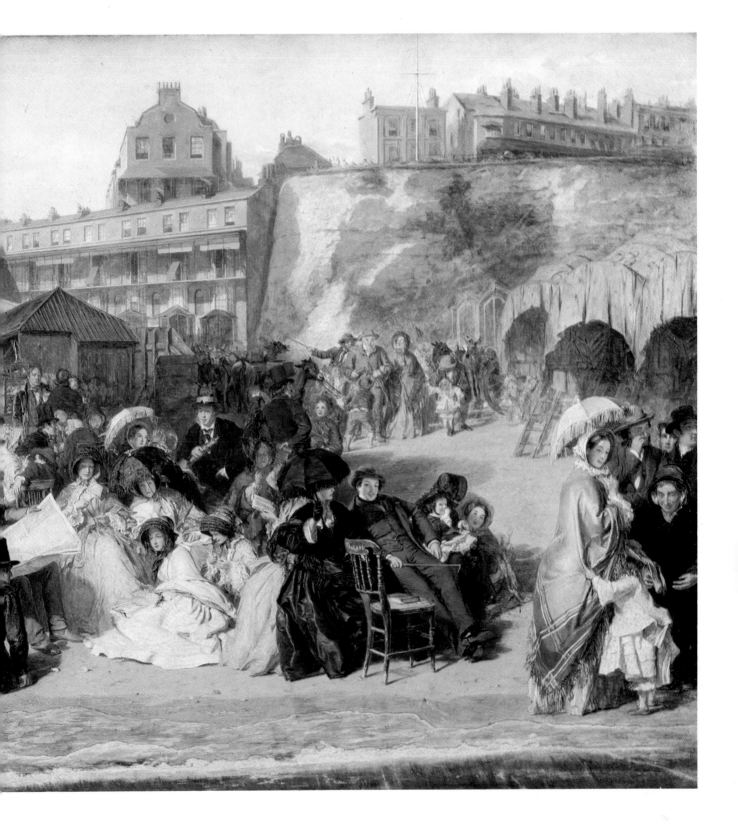

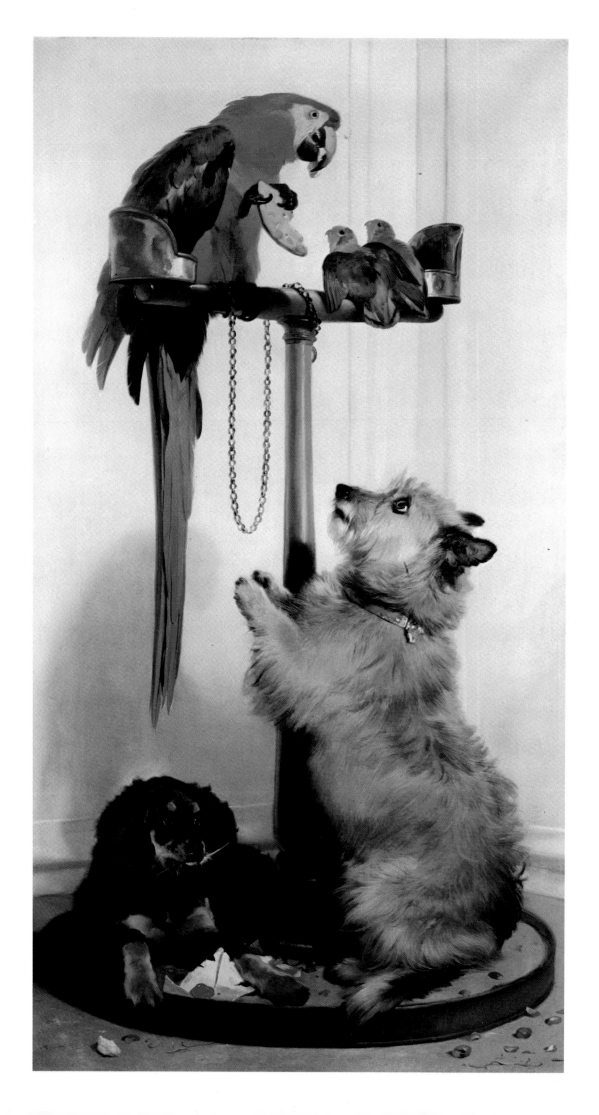

presumptive. By then the Duchess had secured, after a great deal of effort, a better suite of rooms at Kensington Palace, the one that we associate with the girlhood of Queen Victoria. Most of her childhood and youth, however, were spent in gloomier circumstances – in dark and cramped rooms on the ground floor. Her mother was terrified that she might fall under someone else's influence so, until she became Queen, Victoria slept in the same room as her mother. She was never allowed to speak to anyone without a third person being present. This oppressive atmosphere, which Queen Victoria recalled nearly fifty years later, caused great tensions. She clung to her governess, the admirable, if possessive, Baroness Lehzen, and adored her elder half-sister, Feodora, as lively as she was beautiful. She longed for the company of girls and boys of her own age, for gaiety, or 'mirth' as she called it: instead she spent hours with the dolls which still remain. With these, made by her and Lehzen after characters they had read about in stories or from operas they had seen, she invented conversations, games, stories. From time to time such deprivation caused passionate outbursts, particularly with those to whom she was deeply attached, for the rest of her life. Yet the strong emotional tensions – the need for security, for trust, never touched the surface of her life. Very early, Victoria was taken on semi-royal progresses by her mother, so that she could be seen by the people. Triumphal arches, mayors and aldermen in their scarlet liveries, fanfares of trumpets, the booming of guns, kaleidoscopic firework displays, became a natural part of her existence. She responded with exceptional grace and dignity. As Lady Wharncliffe said, 'She is born a Princess without the least appearance of any art or affectation'.

She was, of course, carefully educated. Her school books still exist at Frogmore, with her name proudly inscribed in them, from the first shaky 'V' to the clear and bold VICTORIA. She loved drawing, which she was taught by Westall and practised it all her life with considerable skill. She was very fond of music, and sang with a light, pure and very exact soprano voice. Above all, she was taught to behave like a Queen. But

1 A group of dolls, made by Queen Victoria when a child. Now in the Museum of London.
2 A page from one of her schoolbooks with her tutor's corrections

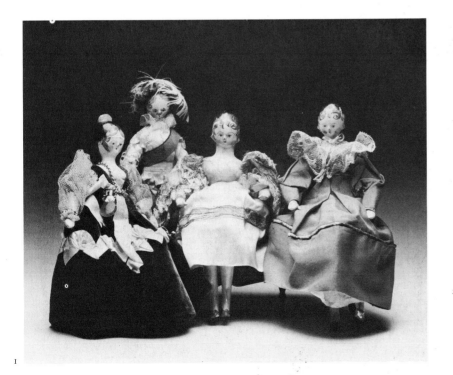
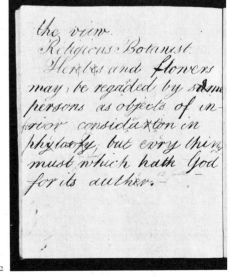

Opposite: Sir Edwin Landseer, *Islay and Tilco with a Red Macaw and two Lovebirds*. 1839. Five of Queen Victoria's pets

much as she enjoyed her role she also longed to escape from it into privacy, into loving security with another human being. As many do, her riven nature found consolation in writing. Her journal and her innumerable letters throughout her long life were her way of relieving tension. No matter how packed with events a day might be, she always found time for one or two thousand words.

How well she describes the most dramatic event of her life at Kensington Palace. 'I was awoke at six o'clock by Mama . . . I got out of bed and went into my sitting room (only in my dressing gown) and *alone* . . . Lord Conyngham (the Lord Chamberlain) then acquainted me that my poor Uncle, the King, was no more . . . and consequently that I am *Queen*.' Later in the day the Queen held her first council, and impressed all of her ministers and particularly the leader of the government, Lord Melbourne, by the firmness and dignity of her manner. This scene was painted by Sir David Wilkie. The Queen ultimately disapproved strongly of the picture. Wilkie painted her in white, but she should have been in black for mourning. With her literal mind, that was enough for the Queen to change her artistic loyalties. Afterwards she gave her preference to Sir George Hayter, who painted her coronation and, later, her marriage.

Young, impulsive, as yet naïve in the art of politics, the Queen was fortunate in having Lord Melbourne as her first minister. Old, wise, and rather lonely, yet he knew how to amuse, and how to persuade – even persuading her to take up riding again and they were often seen together in the park. On these occasions, Melbourne would find Victoria very interested in people and events, especially of her own royal family. Melbourne belonged to a franker age and the Queen herself was no prude; correct, yes, but not prudish, and she enjoyed the stories of her wicked uncles. At the same time Melbourne was teaching her about men and

Sir David Wilkie, *The First Council of Queen Victoria*. Before her stands Lord Melbourne with a State Paper. Wilkie altered her dress from black to white to emphasise her innocence – an inaccuracy which offended the Queen as she had actually been wearing mourning for her uncle, William IV

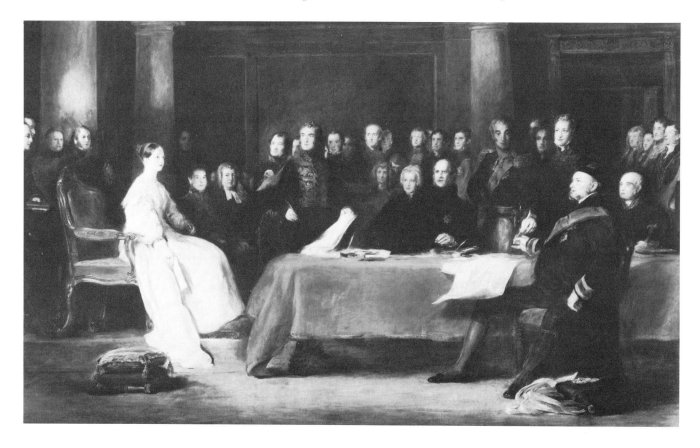

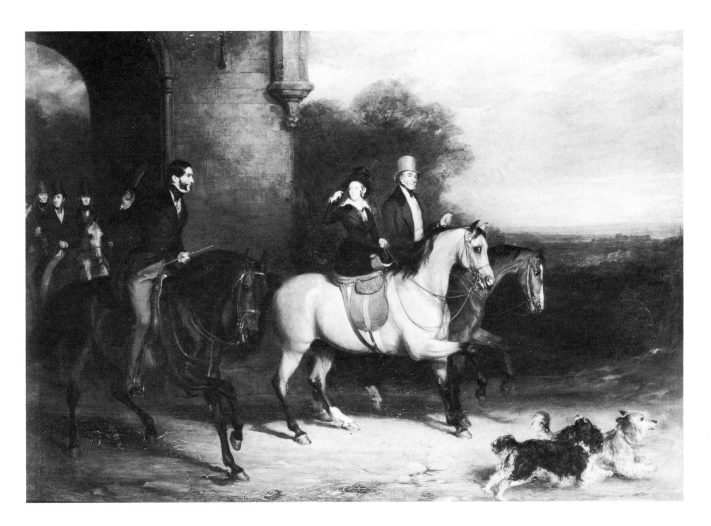

Sir Francis Grant, *Queen Victoria riding with Lord Melbourne at Windsor*

politics and, equally important, the limitations of her position. Victoria grew extremely attached to Melbourne, who was so much more amusing than Baron Stockmar whom her uncle Leopold, himself a pompous bore, had made her chief personal adviser. And Melbourne quickly learned not only to appreciate the Queen's qualities – the directness, the truthfulness of her response (for she was totally without guile or artifice) and her dedication to her role in life – but also her weaknesses, her underlying anxieties, the passionate and romantic aspects of her nature.

Melbourne realised quickly that she was very susceptible indeed to male charm – England was not likely to have a second Virgin Queen. Both Victoria and her advisers wanted an early marriage. Leopold, however, had already decided that her husband would be her cousin, Albert of Saxe-Coburg-Gotha, who for some years had been groomed for the part. On his first visit to London with his brother, he had made quite an impression on Victoria, but Leopold had felt that he was still insufficiently polished and had sent him off to Italy for a year. This year in Italy was to influence Albert's taste profoundly.

Outwardly Albert was a paragon of a prince. He rode beautifully, danced to perfection, possessed a fine figure and strong good looks. He was intelligent, well versed in music, knew a great deal about the mechanics of architecture as well as its aesthetic qualities. He could draw, paint watercolours, etch. He was fluent in four languages – German, English, French and Italian. He was methodical, hard-working and dedicated to the concept of constitutional monarchy. And yet, in spite of these obvious virtues and abilities, his new fellow countrymen did not, unlike their Queen, take him to their hearts. Perhaps it was the accompanying air of dutiful dedication which he brought to all that he did which dampened their response. Perhaps they sensed that, in spite of all his accomplishments, there was a lack of gusto for life. For some reason the deepest springs in his being were never released and so Victoria's love was greater, more demanding, than his. Young as he was, he very soon became the young Queen's mentor, almost as much father as husband.

They were married on 10 February 1840, a day of utter delight, if endless ceremony, for the Queen. She still found time, however, to write a few hundred words in her journal. 'The ceremony was very imposing, fine and simple . . . I felt so happy when the ring was put on, and by Albert.' He rapidly became the core of her life, the arbiter of her tastes and habits – or so she liked to believe. The truth was less idyllic. She had a passionate, not easily governed temper. She could be imperious and she rarely forgot that she was Queen. She took pregnancies badly. Albert usually met her outbursts with detachment and sent her kindly argued letters, which added to her frustration. The storms passed, and her love, if not his, was total. She was more than willing to let Albert mould her artistic tastes.

Children were expected; indeed, soon after their marriage Victoria and Albert bought a splendid seventeenth-century German cradle ready for their first-born, who proved to be a girl, named after her mother, and known as the Princess Royal. She subsequently became the Empress of Germany. The Prince of Wales was born shortly afterwards, and a steady stream of princes and princesses followed. So, almost immediately, they were faced with a problem of where to live. Albert disliked Windsor – he believed, rightly, that the drains were unhealthy and dangerous; both of them hated Brighton, where they were too exposed to a prying public; and Buckingham Palace, as conceived by George IV, did not allow for a

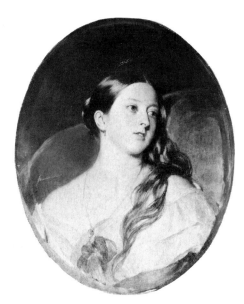

Frans Xaver Winterhalter, *Queen Victoria when Young*

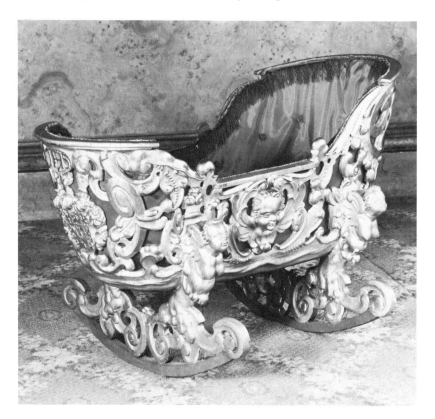

The seventeenth-century cradle bought by Queen Victoria for her first baby

large family of royal children: there were no convenient nurseries, and in any case it was totally unsuitable for the kind of family life that Albert envisaged. In addition, Albert was a believer of the virtues of pure air, and throughout her life, Victoria liked air not only pure but *cold*. So when, on Sir Robert Peel's advice, they inspected a property in the Isle of Wight, by the sea at Osborne, they were enchanted by it; bought it and started to build their own home. New technology made it just possible for them to move that far from London; the railway and the steam ferry meant that ministers could get to Osborne and back in twenty-four hours. Victoria, if needed, could be back in London in a few hours. It was possible, at last, to live remotely yet still reign effectively. And Osborne was fun, particularly for Albert; serious fun.

Throughout his life Prince Albert craved for isolation; for relief from the oppressive grandeur of royal palaces. Maybe this was the influence of his childhood and youth spent at Rosenau – a very small castle, embedded in the hills and woods some five or six miles from the huge, almost threatening Schloss Ehrenberg that dominated Coburg itself. But the isolation of Osborne delighted them both. 'Life is so quiet,' wrote Albert, 'when we are on the Isle of Wight and no Court surrounds us.' In order to intensify the privacy which he sought, Albert had been careful to separate the private royal apartments from the royal household by putting them in a separate building joined to the household's apartments by an open corridor. This arrangement was very congenial to Victoria, who liked nothing better than having Albert to herself. She wrote in her journal, 'It is impossible to imagine a prettier spot and we have a charming beach quite to ourselves – we can walk anywhere without being followed or mobbed.'

Keenly interested in architecture, and an ardent reader of *The Builder*, Albert had great faith in Thomas Cubitt's modern mass-production methods, and admired his monumental terraces in Belgravia. He asked Cubitt to join with him in designing Osborne. For its time it was a very modern house, as fireproof as it could be made, with up-to-date bathrooms. Although the Italian influence at Osborne is strong, for Albert was deeply moved by the early Renaissance, the villa never quite throws off the air of Kensington. The terraced and statued gardens, which were quickly followed both by the old aristocracy and the *nouveaux riches*, such as the Rothschilds, have, with their carefully pruned magnolias and gravelled walks amidst the laurel and the yew, the indelible stamp of the Victorian age. Indeed Osborne, both house and garden, soon began to pup vigorously and the Osborne skyline, suburban Italianate villa, with tower, could be discovered within a decade not only throughout Britain, but also in Germany, France, and frequently in the middle-west of America. If the building is not truly successful, the setting of terrace, wooded hillside and sea is triumphant.

Furniture, carpets, tiles, door fittings, were carefully designed by the Prince with the advice of Gruner, a German fresco painter and decorator of great skill and sound taste, who had accompanied Prince Albert during his visit to Italy before he was married. The colours are brilliant, very Italian, and perfect for the bright light of the island. The Copeland door furniture is exquisite, yet very modern and up-to-date, far easier to wipe than brass would be to clean. Nothing pleased Albert more than marrying art and science, which became his great theme, his great ambition.

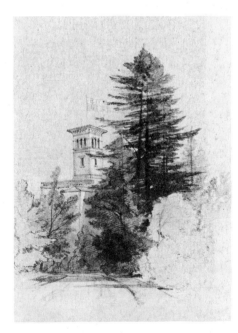

Edward Lear, watercolour of Osborne, July 1846. Lear was one of the Queen's tutors in drawing

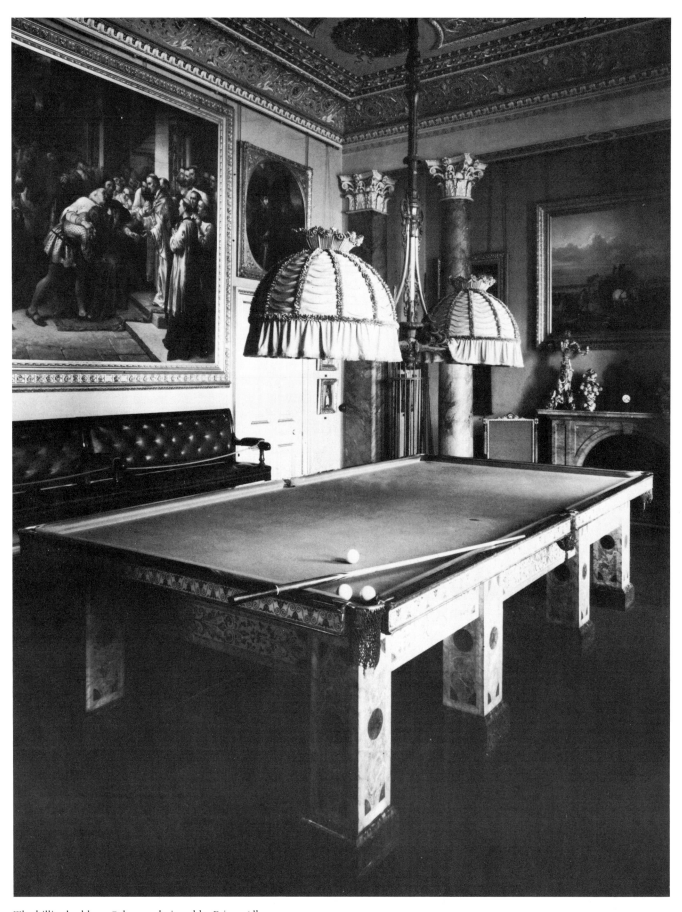

The billiard table at Osborne, designed by Prince Albert

His wish to make Osborne a smooth, easily worked, yet beautiful machine in which to live is best illustrated, perhaps, by the strange shape of the Queen's drawing-room. Her Gentlemen of the Household could not sit in her presence, but round the corner of this room they were not visible to her, so they could not only sit, but play billiards on the table, whose base with its Raphaelesque decoration was designed by Albert.

Osborne was also intended from the very first to display the pictures and statues in which Albert had a passionate interest. Probably under Gruner's influence, he had been captivated by the painters of the early Renaissance who, in 1840, were far from fashionable. He began to collect early Italian, German and Flemish pictures, and it was Gruner who secured some of the finest. He was responsible for the magnificent triptych by Duccio di Buoninsegna, one of the glories of the royal collection, and the earliest of its masterpieces, probably painted about 1300. The Queen, who rapidly acquired the Prince's taste, bought him two magnificent pictures for his birthday in 1846 – Daddi's *Marriage of the Virgin*, and the triptych, *The Coronation of the Virgin*, then thought to be by Gaddi (as indeed was the former picture) and now attributed to

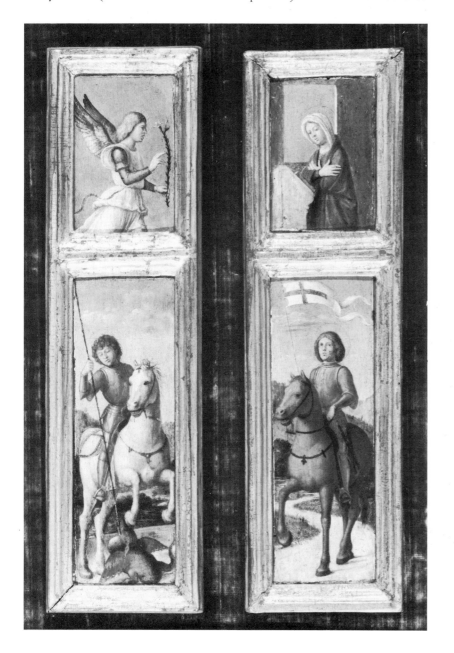

Cima da Conegliano, Detail of *Four Saints and the Annunciation*. Purchased in 1847 and given by the Queen to the Prince Consort on his birthday

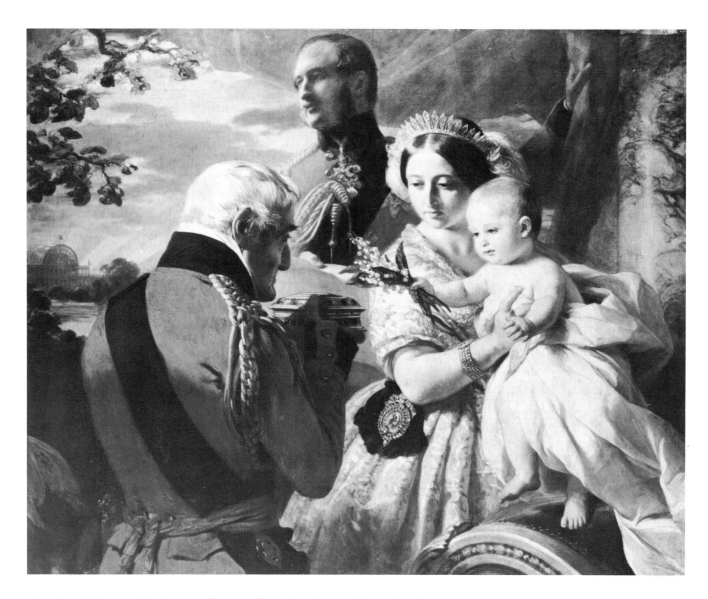

the school of Jacopo di Cione. For his next birthday she gave him Cima da Conegliano's *Four Saints*. These were, surely, some of the finest birthday presents ever received by a sovereign's consort and the Prince was steadily adding to his collection by his own purchases – a Gentile da Fabriano, a lovely Fra Angelico, a tiny Gozzoli. Nor did the Prince confine himself to Italian paintings; he snapped up an excellent Cranach. Some of the finest of these pictures hung on the walls of the Prince's dressing-room at Osborne.

Fortunately for the nation, the Prince was a natural proselytiser and encouraged Charles Eastlake, the Director of the National Gallery, to purchase early Italian paintings at a time when the trustees, still deeply attached to the High Renaissance, were very reluctant to allow Eastlake to buy fifteenth-century pictures. Albert was concerned for Eastlake because he believed profoundly in the educational and moral value of art. Art, he believed, helped to uplift society, to make it conscious of ideals of thought and feeling. A society without art would have been an unthinkable disaster, so from the earliest days of his marriage he naturally patronised modern painters and sculptors. He was very quick indeed to appreciate Winterhalter's panache as a portrait painter, and Landseer's skill as an animal painter, the greatest since Stubbs.

In the patronage of contemporary artists, the Queen's influence was

Frans Xaver Winterhalter, *The First of May 1851*. Painted 1852. The 82nd birthday of the Duke of Wellington and the first of his godson, Prince Arthur. The Great Exhibition had been opened that morning by the Queen. The Crystal Palace can be seen in the background

quite strong; indeed she had purchased and been given Landseers before her marriage. She loved the present and wanted it preserved; so every child was painted and sculpted at an early age – even their tiny feet and hands and ears carved in marble. The Queen's and Prince's dogs were painted by Landseer, or even, as with Albert's favourite greyhound, Eos, moulded in zinc. Modern portraits and pieces of marble sculpture adorned their birthday tables alongside, maybe, a glowing old master. Most of the best and earliest portraits are by Winterhalter, many of great charm and splendid *panache*, such as his fine portrait of Prince Arthur, or the moving picture of the old Duke of Wellington making his birthday presentation to his baby godson; or the brilliantly posed family group, with its sensitive treatment of the young Prince of Wales in Russian costume.

Osborne was full of children – born mainly in the 1840s and early 1850s, when life seemed so very insecure for many European monarchs. As Queen Victoria wrote to her uncle, Leopold, 'When one thinks of

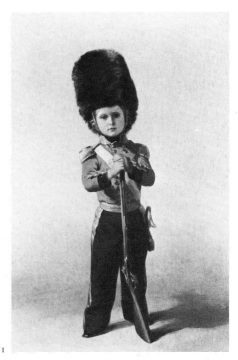

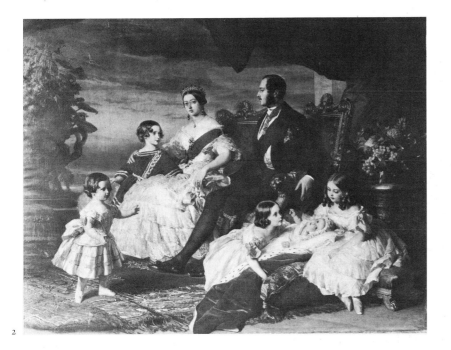

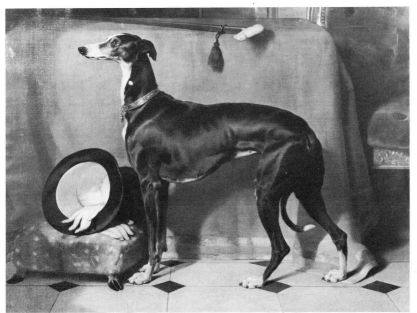

Frans Xaver Winterhalter: 1 *Prince Arthur*. 2 *The Royal Family in 1846*. Painted 1846. The children are, left to right, Prince Alfred, the Prince of Wales, Princess Alice, Princess Helena and Princess Victoria. 3 Sir Edwin Landseer, *Eos*, Prince Albert's favourite greyhound

one's children, their education, their future, I always think and say to myself "Let them grow up fit for *whatever stations* they may be placed in, high or low".' The sentiment was really Albert's, who set about putting it into practice. All the royal children had gardens – their tools still exist, marked with their initials. Their work was professionally criticised, and they were paid by the hour. They also made bricks. In 1854, Prince Albert put up the Swiss Cottage at Osborne, the first prefabricated house to be put together in England. There the princesses were given the most up-to-date kitchen equipment, and they cooked; one of the girls' scones, buns or cakes always graced the royal tea-table. Nor were science and the arts of war forgotten; they had their museum for fossils and geological specimens and an excellent model fort to play at soldiers. Both boys and girls were taught – goodness knows why – to erect tents!

Osborne was a haven of domestic bliss. Tense at times, particularly for the Prince of Wales whose relationship with his parents was never easy, it nevertheless gave that sense of privacy and security for which Queen Victoria always felt a need. It also gave her a novel experience, impossible for her anywhere else: on 30 July 1847 for the first time she bathed in the sea, with her maids, in a commodious and discreet machine. She was utterly delighted until she put her head under water, and then she was not amused.

Much as they loved Osborne, the Queen and the Prince could not avoid either Buckingham Palace or Windsor, which were the proper settings for the great occasions of the court – the Levées, the drawing-rooms, the fancy-dress balls, usually for a charity in which the Queen took an interest. They were so pleased with their dresses for a medieval ball, to which they went as Edward III and Queen Philippa, that they had themselves painted by Landseer in their costumes. But Buckingham Palace was regarded as too small, too unimposing for the greatest state affairs, and certainly lacking in the amenities needed for the Queen's growing family, so Marble Arch was moved to its present position and Blore, with the Prince looking over his shoulder, designed an imposing but rather dull new front block. The balcony, where they could show

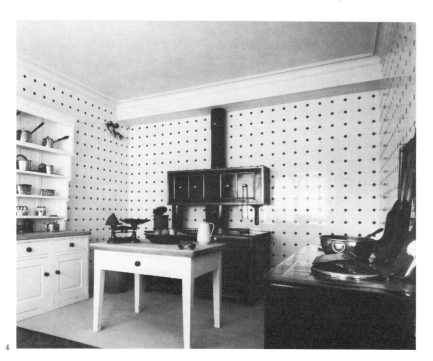

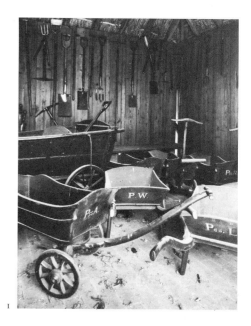

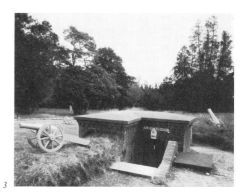

Osborne: 1 The Royal children's gardening tools, marked with their initials. 2 Their shop – 'Spratt, Grocer to her Majesty'. 3 Their fort. 4 Their kitchen

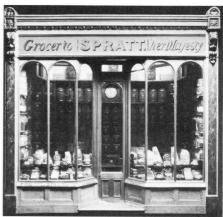

themselves, all of them, to their loyal subjects, was Albert's idea and has since become a dramatic focus of great occasions in the royal family's and the nation's life.

Prince Albert's other great triumph at Buckingham Palace, this time with a different architect, Pennethorne, was the ballroom, which still remains much as he intended it. With George IV's grand staircase and now the ballroom, the British monarchy had a setting in London worthy of the wealth and power of their country – one grand enough, at last, for the greatest of royal occasions, the state visits of other European monarchs. These visits were a nineteenth-century development. No monarch had visited England in state during the seventeenth or eighteenth centuries. The first occasion had been after the defeat of Napoleon, when the sovereigns of our most powerful allies visited London. However, Queen Victoria's ministers encouraged her to invite both Louis Philippe and his wife, and then Napoleon III and Eugénie, in order to give a spectacular public demonstration of the entente cordiale with France. And it was at Windsor or at Buckingham Palace where many of the visits of other European monarchs took place. Louis Philippe presented the Queen with a *char à banc* – a remarkable vehicle, and invented by a Frenchman. The Queen always viewed these visits with expectant apprehension, but just as often she recollected them as occasions of pure delight. The visit of Louis Philippe led to an agitated exchange of letters with his daughter, the Queen of the Belgians, about the King's habits – his food, how hard he liked his bed, whom he should meet. She awaited his arrival with tremulous excitement, rose to the occasion, and regretted his departure as intensely as she had feared his arrival.

What she did so thoroughly enjoy was to be with someone she could treat, and who could treat her, as an equal. If, like the French King, they accepted her husband as equal too, she was swept away with joy. Although she loved Louis Philippe and his Queen, she succumbed even more completely to Napoleon III and to Eugénie's beauty and style. Their state visits to Buckingham Palace and Windsor, and their private one to Osborne were spectacular events that lived in the Queen's memory. She dedicated a memorial album to their visit and had the most lavish festivities painted – including the State Ball at Buckingham Palace.

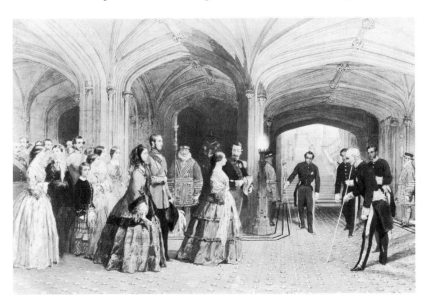

Watercolour by G. H. Thomas, of the reception of Napoleon III and the Empress Eugénie at Windsor, 16 April 1855. From Queen Victoria's Souvenir Albums

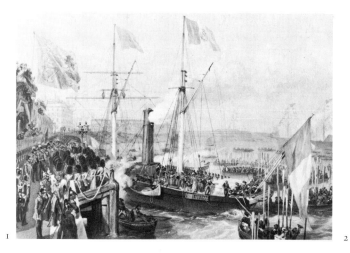

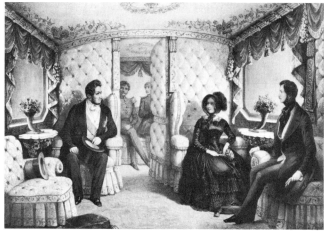

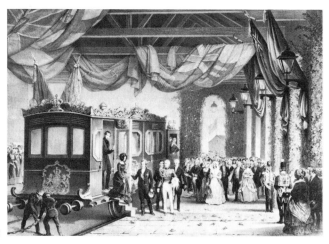

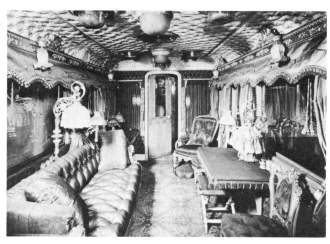

Preparations for this visit had agitated her more than usual (years later the Empress Eugénie was still muttering about the frightful bed curtains in the bedroom at Windsor especially furnished for her), but what had alarmed the Queen more was the irony of entertaining a Napoleon – a *parvenu* and a member of the family of England's greatest enemy. In the event, the Emperor made so vivid an impression on her that she had to get all down in words.

'That he *is* a very extraordinary man, with great qualities there can be *no* doubt – I might almost say a mysterious man. He is evidently possessed of *indomitable courage, unflinching firmness of purpose, self-reliance, perseverance*, and *great secrecy*; to this should be added a reliance on what he calls his *Star*, and a belief in omens and incidents as connected with his future destiny, which is almost romantic – and at the same time he is endowed with wonderful *self-control*, great *calmness*, even *gentleness*, and with a power of *fascination*, the effect of which upon all those who become more intimately acquainted with him is *most sensibly* felt.'

His charm for her strengthened, rather than weakened. She enjoyed a return visit to Paris later in August 1855, when the beautiful and elegant Eugénie became a life-long friend. Naturally this visit, too, was recorded – not only in the inevitable water-colour album, but also by photography, which might have been invented for Queen Victoria, with her passion for fixing a moment of time for eternity.

Queen Victoria loved travel. She always hated leaving, but thoroughly enjoyed arriving. She was the first British monarch of modern times to travel extensively in Europe, both on state occasions and privately,

Ceremonial travel: 1 Watercolour by G. H. Thomas of the arrival by royal yacht of Napoleon III at Dover, 16 April 1855.

2 Engraving by J. David, after E. Pingret, of King Louis-Philippe of France, Queen Victoria and Prince Albert in the royal train during the French King's State Visit to England in 1844.

3 Engraving by Bayot and Cuvillier, after E. Pingret, of the arrival of the royal party at Portsmouth Station, during that visit.

4 Photograph of the interior of the saloon carriage used by Queen Victoria from 1869 to the end of her life, from the train made for her by the London and North Western Railway Company

and from her girlhood she made constant visits in her own realm. All this was possible because steam, and later the telegraph, enabled her to be easily reached. Railway and steamship brought the essential papers to be dealt with. There was never any need for a Regency, whether she was in Biarritz or Balmoral. But steam not only eased communication, it also brought an ease and comfort to travel that no other monarch had known. Whereas Queen Elizabeth I had had to ride pillion behind her steward on the way to visit Burghley, Queen Victoria sped there by royal train with comfortable sitting-rooms and bedrooms. She preferred, however, to stop at stations for her meals; Perth and elsewhere maintained a special room for her with her own silver, linen, china and furniture.

The first royal yacht, the *Royal George*, was borrowed from the navy. It was an uncomfortable ship, and both the Queen and the Prince were delighted when it was replaced by the *Victoria and Albert*, a steam ship which belonged to them. The vessel showed such power that it outdistanced the fleet on its first royal voyage in 1843, carrying them to visit Louis Philippe at the Château d'Eu, the first visit of a reigning English monarch to France since Henry VIII had met François I at the Field of the Cloth of Gold. The Queen and the Prince both loved the *Victoria and Albert*, dressed their sons up as little sailors (thereby starting a fashion) and used the yacht whenever they could.

To travel in comfort and very royally was bliss – not only for the Queen and her husband, but also for millions of their subjects. Railways had synchronised time throughout England, but also made arrival at a given hour more or less certain. Huge crowds could gather knowing that they would see the Queen and her husband. Furthermore, it was now

William Wyld, watercolour of Manchester, 1852. Commissioned by Queen Victoria

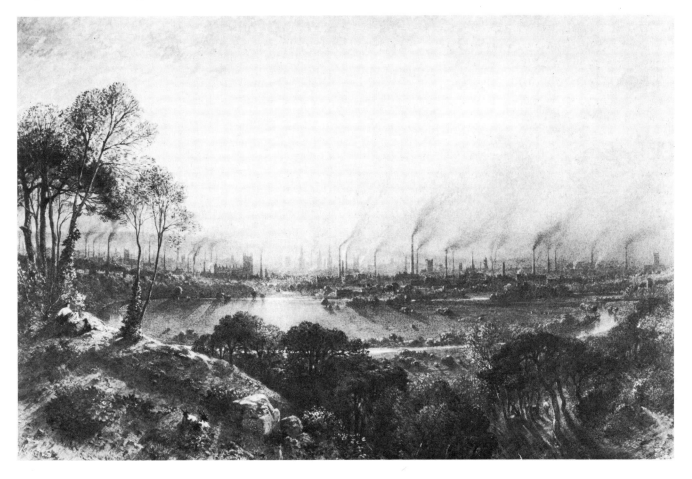

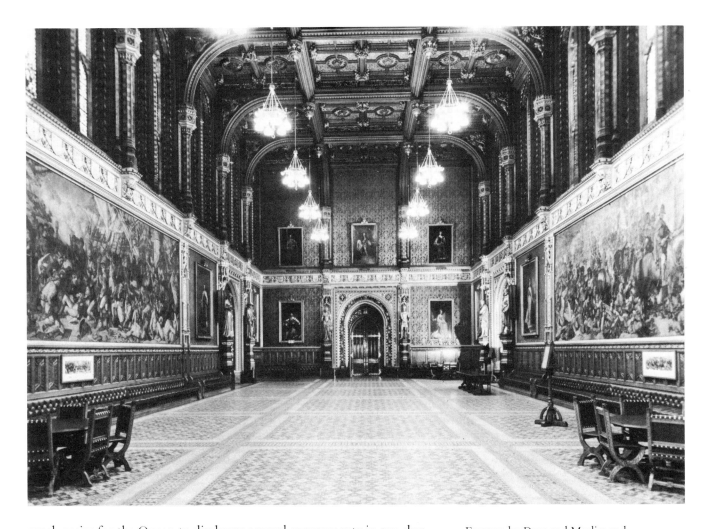

Frescoes by Dyce and Maclise and decorations by Barry and Pugin in the Royal Gallery, Houses of Parliament, Westminster

much easier for the Queen to discharge several engagements in one day. There was no town of any consequence which she did not visit and so she was seen, in the flesh, by millions of her subjects and with exuberant loyalty the growing provincial towns of the midlands and the north would burst out into floral bowers, triumphal arches and brilliant fireworks. As ever, Queen Victoria loved mementoes of the scene, and cherished the prints, water-colours and, increasingly, the photographs of her visits. However, she was quick to notice the glaring poverty behind the flowers and, even as a small girl of thirteen, was appalled by what she saw in the Black Country. She wrote in her diary: 'The country is very desolate everywhere; there are coals about, and the grass is quite blasted and black. I just now see an extraordinary building flaming with fire. The country continues black, engines flaming, coals in abundance, everywhere, smoking and burning coal heaps, intermingled with wretched huts and carts and little ragged children.' These royal visits gave Victoria and Albert a deeper knowledge of their country than any previous monarch possessed. Their progresses were widely portrayed in the press; and millions followed their tours in the newspapers.

Sir Robert Peel, who had as sharp an eye for a painting as a personality, realised that Prince Albert was a man whose taste, discernment and decision must be employed. The Palace of Westminster was a royal palace – the wrecked remains of the medieval palace made worse by the burning of the Houses of Parliament in 1834. Its rebuilding had begun and its decoration had become imperative. The Prince proved an astute, hard-working and innovative Chairman of the Royal Commission set up by Peel to undertake this task. He took great delight in Barry's design and Pugin's splendid neo-Gothic furnishings, but was himself almost entirely responsible for the great frescoes by Dyce, Maclise and other English painters which decorated its rooms and corridors. The art of fresco had been almost lost, and its revival was due to the famous Nazarene school in which Gruner was deeply interested. The total effect was grand, a far grander setting than parliament had ever had before. It gave added majesty to the state openings of parliament, which in the old house had been very subfusc, but could now glow with pageantry, expressing England's new wealth and expanding Empire. Indeed, it glowed so strongly in the House of Lords that the Queen thought the effect 'brassy'. Time has mellowed it.

The Prince's belief in the need for science, for improving technology, together with his love of art in all its forms, convinced him that art must be a living public reality, linked with science, with industry, with government at all levels, for the sake, as he saw it, of its deep moral quality. His vision – and it was a grandiose one – is contained in South Kensington and its complex of museums. Here he wished to bring together a great museum of design and of ornamental art, which would also include science and technology. The Prince and his advisers hoped to entice the Royal Academy, the Society of Antiquaries and the Royal Society to the site, so that lectures and conversazzione might embellish the exhibitions. There was the further hope that the British Museum and its huge library might also be housed there. Of course, these hopes were never fully realised, otherwise England would enjoy one of the greatest centres of art, science and learning in the world; as it is, the South Kensington site is impressive, and a fitting memorial to Prince Albert's unremitting efforts to educate the British public in design.

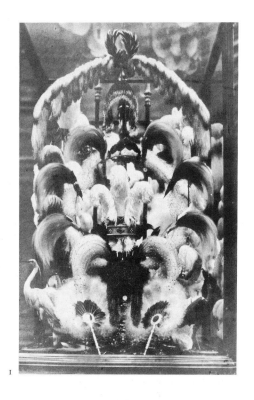

Calotypes from the 1851 Great Exhibition Jury Reports. 1 A stand of egrets' feathers. 2 The upper galleries of the Exhibition

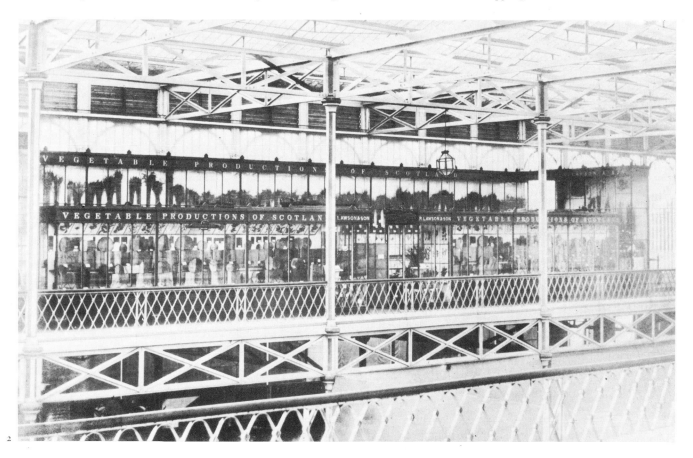

The concept and its partial fulfilment came out of the Prince's greatest achievement – the Great Exhibition of 1851. Although the Prince enjoyed visiting the aristocracy, his visits were rarely merely social. At Chatsworth, for example, he was particularly impressed by the Duke of Devonshire's model village of Edensor, where each house had running water – which he copied at Osborne and at Balmoral. The Duke's ingenious conservatory, planned and constructed by his gardener, Paxton, intrigued the Prince even more. Albert and his advisers, particularly Henry Cole, had begun to plan a huge international exhibition of the art and industries of all nations, with, of course, a very special emphasis on Britain. The concept had aroused bitter opposition, but the Prince's dogged determination and unremitting energy carried the day. Paxton was his man.

The advanced cast-iron and glass Crystal Palace, designed by Paxton, came in for major criticism. As the Prince somewhat tartly wrote to Frederick William IV of Prussia, 'The mathematicians worked out that the Crystal Palace must collapse after the first strong wind; the engineers claimed that the galleries would break up and crush the visitors; the economists predicted that prices would rise drastically as a result of the vast influx of people, while doctors warned of a reappearance of the black

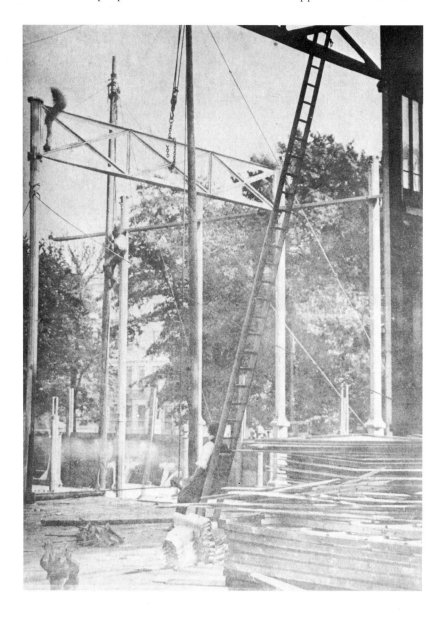

Photograph of the dismantling of the Crystal Palace in 1852. It was reopened at Sydenham Hill in 1854

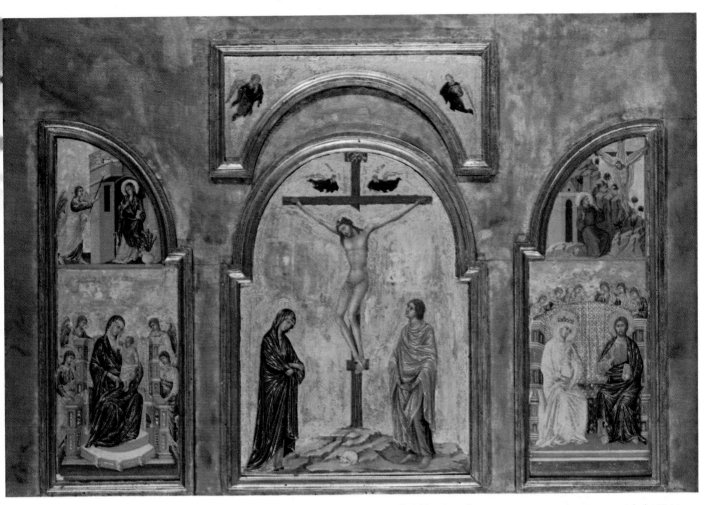

Duccio di Buoninsegna, *Triptych: The Crucifixion; the Annunciation with the Virgin and Child enthroned; St Francis receiving the Stigmata with the Virgin and Child enthroned*

P*rince Albert had, from youth, been interested in Italian art and, mainly during the 1840s, made an impressive collection of Italian primitives*

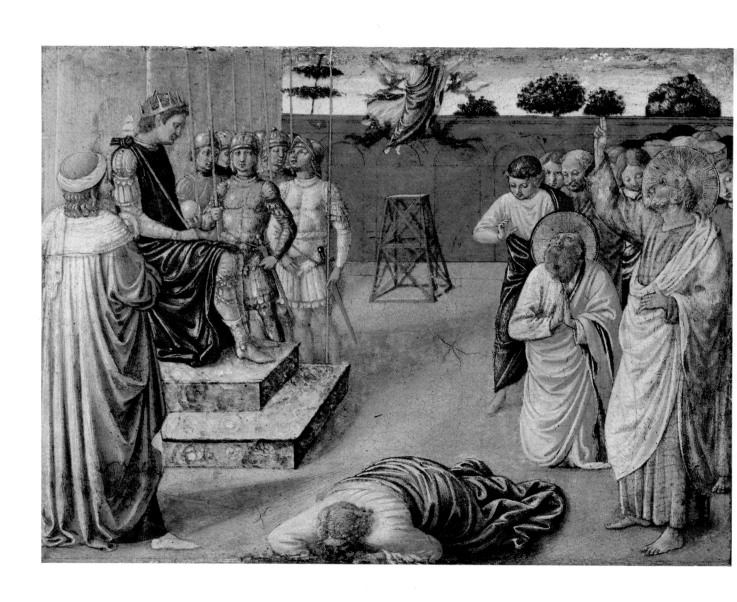

Benozzo Gozzoli, *The Death of Simon Magus*

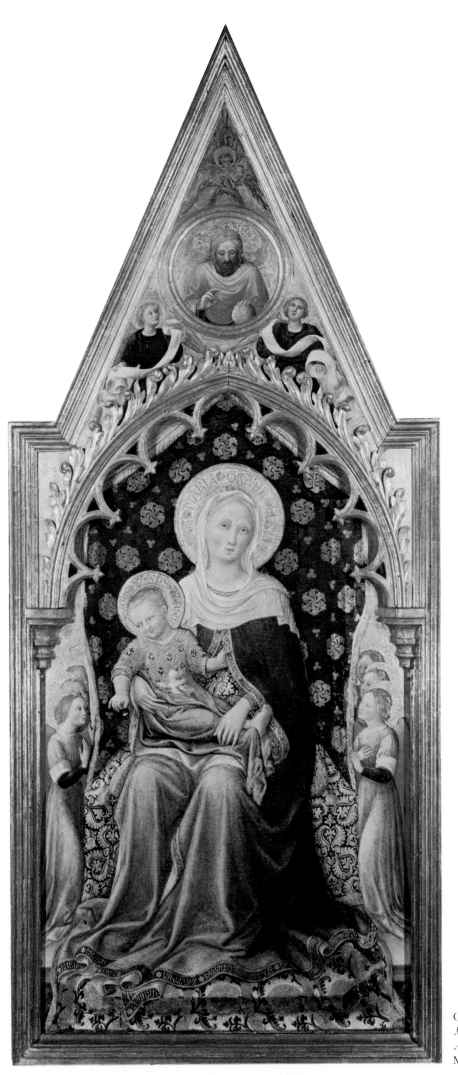

Gentile da Fabriano,
*Madonna and Child with
Angels.* Completed by
May 1425

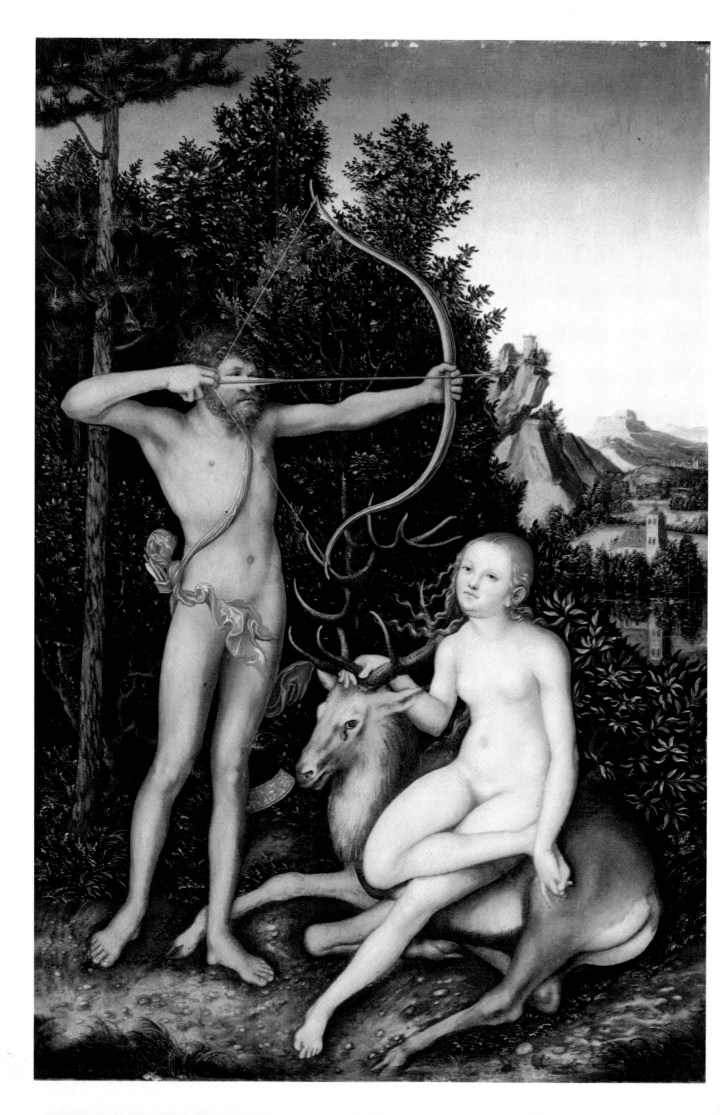

death of the Middle Ages as a result of these crowds, which reminded them of the crusades. The moralists predicted that England would become impregnated with all the evils of the civilised and uncivilised worlds, while the theologians argued that this second Tower of Babel would also incur the vengeance of an insulted God.' In fact it was a triumphant success. Few would have disagreed with what the Queen wrote in her diary after formally opening it: 'The *greatest* day in our history, the *most beautiful* and *imposing* and *touching* spectacle ever seen . . . Albert's dearest name is immortalised by this *great* conception, *his* own.'

The Queen went thirty-four times. The proudest occasion, the opening ceremonies apart, was after the exhibition had been moved to Sydenham, where she took Napoleon III and Eugénie on 20 April 1855. They received a huge welcome from tens of thousands – a scene which moved the Queen deeply, for not only was this Albert's great work, but also the proud display of the conquering wealth and industry of her kingdom, and a statement of quality and design.

As well as the fabulous Koh-i-noor diamond, whose cutting Albert had supervised, the Queen lent the beautiful yet restrained Axminster carpets, designed by Gruner for the Green Drawing-Room at Windsor, and which still adorn it today. From Osborne came the huge glass candelabrum, eight feet tall, made by Oslers of Birmingham. Each of her exhibits was intended to display the artistic quality of British craftsmanship, and naturally both the Queen and the Prince from time to time made a well-publicised purchase.

Six million people visited the exhibition, often travelling on the railway for the first time and dumbfounded by the grandeur of London, let alone the exhibition. In the end a profit of £186,000 was made, and the 1851 Commissioners still provide large scholarships for scientific research.

Much to the Queen's delight, the reputation of Prince Albert soared. He became the established authority on the commercial public display of art and science. Considering that he also kept up with the details of diplomacy and politics, more often than not drafting letters and memoranda for the Queen, he was incredibly active in these spheres.

Albert was partly responsible for Trafalgar Square as we know it. The National Gallery was extended to accommodate the great acquisitions which the Prince had encouraged them to buy. At the same time, the lay-out of Trafalgar Square was completed by the addition of four magnificent lions on the plinths. Nor did Prince Albert confine his patronage to London and its museums. He was a passionate crusader in the cause of art for public display. When laying the foundation stone of the Midland Institute at Birmingham, he took the opportunity to make a powerful speech on the application of art and science to industry. He visited with pleasure the new St George's Hall at Liverpool, supported the National Gallery of Scotland, and in 1857 helped to make a success of the first great loan exhibition of art and sculpture at Manchester (he and the Queen lent some of their finest pictures). Indeed, he wanted the public to share the royal treasures, and from 1854 deliberately used the *Art Journal* for publishing articles, with engravings, of the treasures of the royal collection. About two dozen a year were contributed for seven years, and did much to strengthen the sale of the *Journal*.

In spite of royal commissions, the Queen's dispatch boxes, pre-

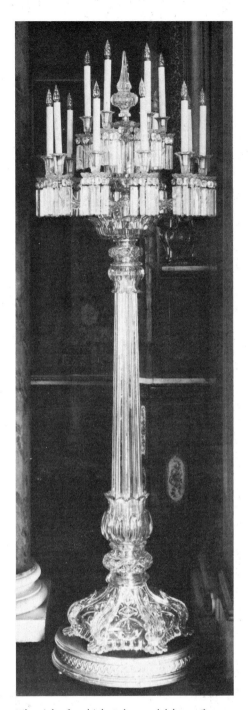

The eight-foot-high Osler candelabrum from the Drawing-Room at Osborne

Opposite: Lucas Cranach the Elder, *Apollo and Diana*

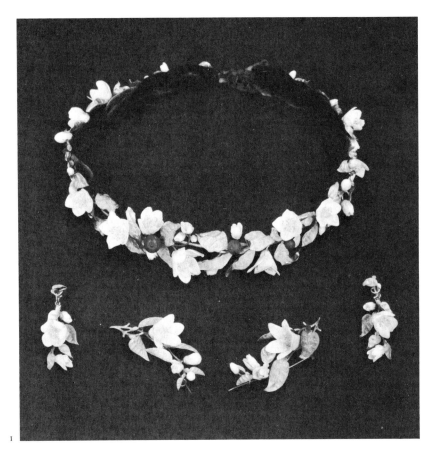

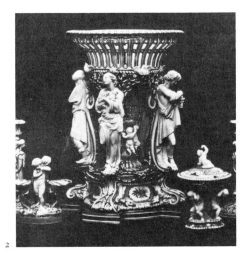

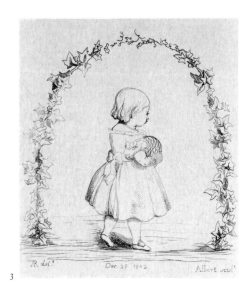

1 Prince Albert's present to Queen Victoria, Christmas 1845 and 10 February 1846. Orange blossom circlet, earrings and brooches designed by the Prince and made in enamel, porcelain and gold. Five small green oranges represent their children.
2 One of the Minton exhibits, commissioned by Prince Albert and shown at the Great Exhibition.
3 The Princess Victoria, drawn by Queen Victoria and etched by Prince Albert, 27 December 1842

occupation with his children, and especially the Prince of Wales (their relationship was a mutual torment), the restless nature of the royal life (Windsor, Osborne, London, Scotland, and repeated provincial and European tours), this astonishing man still found time for creative work, which he executed with great competence. For example, he designed the dairy at Windsor – a temple of hygiene, decorated with Minton tiles and brought to life by fountains (see page 279). He loved jewellery and insignia, designing the Star of India, advising on the Victoria Cross, and creating a great deal of jewellery for his wife. His present to her in 1845 was a circlet of orange leaves of frosted gold, with small enamelled green oranges and white porcelain blossoms, with matching brooch and earrings. His grander designs in silver were less successful. He painted watercolours well, if not so well as his wife; he taught her to engrave and they dabbled in lithography together. They both loved music, but his taste was far better; he taught her to love Handel almost as much as her Hanoverian ancestors; he patronised Mendelssohn (they listened to his music most days); and it is likely that he introduced the Queen to Bach and Gluck, whom she found 'old-fashioned'. He wrote a *Te Deum* that was performed in St Paul's, and other organ music which is worthy, if not of great distinction. He was a far better practitioner than composer, and he played the organ with considerable skill.

He and the Queen spent evenings together sorting, cataloguing, and studying the huge collection of drawings in the library at Windsor. Albert attended to their mounts, and the boxes they now repose in were ordered by him. With his librarian, Ruland, he compiled a great photographic record of Raphael's work – one of the first of its kind in the history of art. Prince Albert had an immense influence not only on the development of constitutional monarchy, for which he is justly admired, but also on the formation of the more admirable aspects of Victorian taste, for which he is rarely praised.

This strange man, over-industrious, overburdened with a restless moral sense, worked himself into premature old age. A tense man, he kept his emotions towards his wife on a very tight rein, but they became uncontrollable over the Prince of Wales. When he discovered that the Prince had had an affair with a young actress, he lost all sense of proportion. Shortly afterwards Albert caught typhoid from the putrid drains of Windsor and, as Queen Victoria sadly realised, he seemed to lack all will to live. He was forty-two when he died in 1861, plunging his widow into a paroxysm of grief. She had already suffered to an alarming degree at the death of her mother earlier in the year.

It was the Queen's nature to harp on anniversaries, to establish memorials of every kind. From babyhood her children were painted, sculpted, drawn and photographed year in year out. The rooms in all her palaces and castles were crowded with pictures of her relations and friends, her horses and dogs. It is not surprising, therefore, that for a husband who had been so much of her life, she should let her grief run riot in memorials. Osborne was immediately frozen – nothing was allowed to be changed, even his watch-case was left hanging on the bedhead above where he would have slept. And she built, in the gardens of Frogmore, a huge mausoleum (see pages 277–8). Albert had already planned one for her mother, the Duchess of Kent; so Frogmore was a natural choice. The Duchess's mausoleum had echoes of the one that Albert and

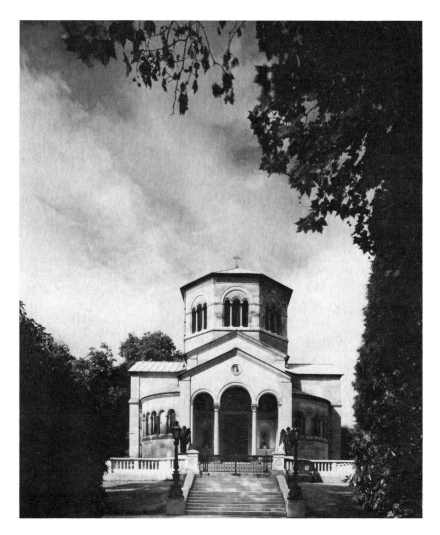

The Royal Mausoleum, Frogmore.
Consecrated in 1862 and completed in 1871

his brother had designed for their father at Coburg, which Queen Victoria so greatly admired that she wanted to be buried in it. The Mausoleum for Albert was built in thirteenth-century Italian style, but in vast blocks of granite culled from all over the British Isles. The sarcophagus is the largest block of flawless granite in the world. The brooding heaviness of the building and its huge tomb is relieved by the decoration, which the Queen commanded should be in the style of Raphael, the Prince's favourite artist. The effigy was by Marochetti; he made hers at the same time, but it was forty years before she joined her husband and by then it had been misplaced and took some time to find. After the Chapel of Henry VII at Westminster Abbey, this is by far the grandest funeral monument to any of the British monarchs.

Each year, when the anniversary of the Prince's death came round, the bitterness of loss was renewed, and she mourned again. 'Day turned into Night', as she phrased it. Statues of Albert quickly multiplied. In 1865 she travelled to Coburg, where his statue had been raised in the market place – a scene which, naturally enough, she had immortalised by a painting and by photographs. In 1866 she unveiled the first to be raised in Britain, at Wolverhampton. More importantly, and overriding Albert's express wish, she placed a statue on the memorial to the 1851 Exhibition, plans for which had been sanctioned by Albert; Britannia was to have stood where he now stands. Much more impressive was the huge memorial that was raised to him in Kensington Gardens. The public, like the family, were never to be allowed to forget her beloved Albert, any more than she could. She withdrew to Osborne, and for years avoided state occasions, and visited London as little as possible. Fortunately she had one other more remote home where the memory of Albert was as alive as at Osborne – Balmoral.

Although Victoria and Albert designed Osborne, it was not enough. Albert longed for the mountains and the pine forests of his youth; for the valleys, lakes and swift-moving streams of Thuringia. He found them on Deeside. They discovered Balmoral in 1848 and the Queen found 'the wilderness, the solitariness of everything is so delightful'. Albert's interest in Scotland was quickly fired; he built cottages, started arts and crafts centres, established, as at Osborne, huge plantations, and was soon tearing down old Balmoral and building and designing the castle we see today. Remote as it was, railway and then the telegraph made it possible for the Queen to be there for months. The prime ministers as well as other ministers had to make the journey, and a small suite was kept for them – it still is. Albert's taste was far more successful at Balmoral than at Osborne. The castle sits four square and strong in a magnificent setting of wood and mountain; but the famous tartan carpets, often mocked, give a lightness and colour to the inside of the house that seems to draw in the green and blue light of the landscape. And this lightness is increased by the furniture in pine and maple designed by Albert; even the silver hinges of their entwined initials add to the sense of light (see page 243). No detail was too small for Albert's attention, whether it was the bas-reliefs of St Hubert, St George and St Andrew by John Thomas, which adorn the outside, or the beautiful, if odd, candelabra of Highland chieftains in Parian marble which grace the main drawing-room. The scale remains small and domestic – even today the heir to the throne has to make do with a study-bedroom – and yet most of the royalty of

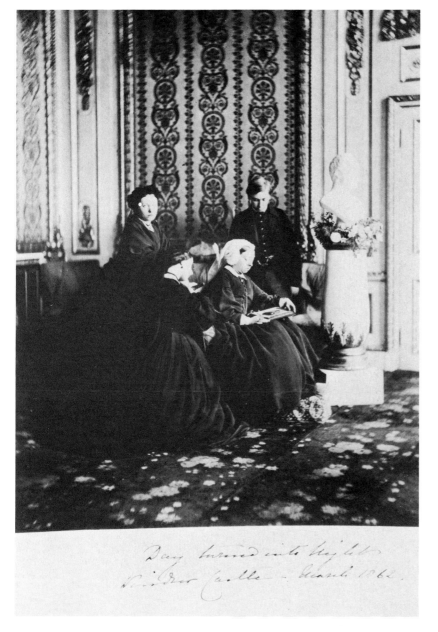

Queen Victoria and her daughters mourning Prince Albert's death, Windsor Castle, March 1862. 'Day turned into Night' is her own caption to this photograph

Europe came to visit Queen Victoria here; when Tsar Nicholas of Russia arrived, the whole of Deeside was commandeered for beds.

Much as the Queen enjoyed these visits and the visits of her children, she preferred Balmoral to herself and her memories. She and Albert had always believed strongly in memorial albums, covering not only the public, but the private events and scenes of their lives. In Leitch and Carl Haag they found excellent painters and so the Queen could turn to her albums of Balmoral and relive the years with Albert and some of the remarkable journeys across the Highlands, when they crept off *incognito* and stayed at simple inns at Fettercairn and Dalwhinnie. Their stamina was quite remarkable; they loved cold air and seemed impervious to rain – a good Scottish mist made Queen Victoria quite happy; what she hated was heat – and forty or fifty miles driving and riding across rugged Highland tracks were taken in their stride. If anyone showed wear and tear, it was the Household. At other times they made wider sweeps – often on their journey to Balmoral – staying with the Roxburghs, the Buccleuchs, the Atholls, reviewing Highland regiments, patronising Highland games, which they also supported on Deeside at Braemar.

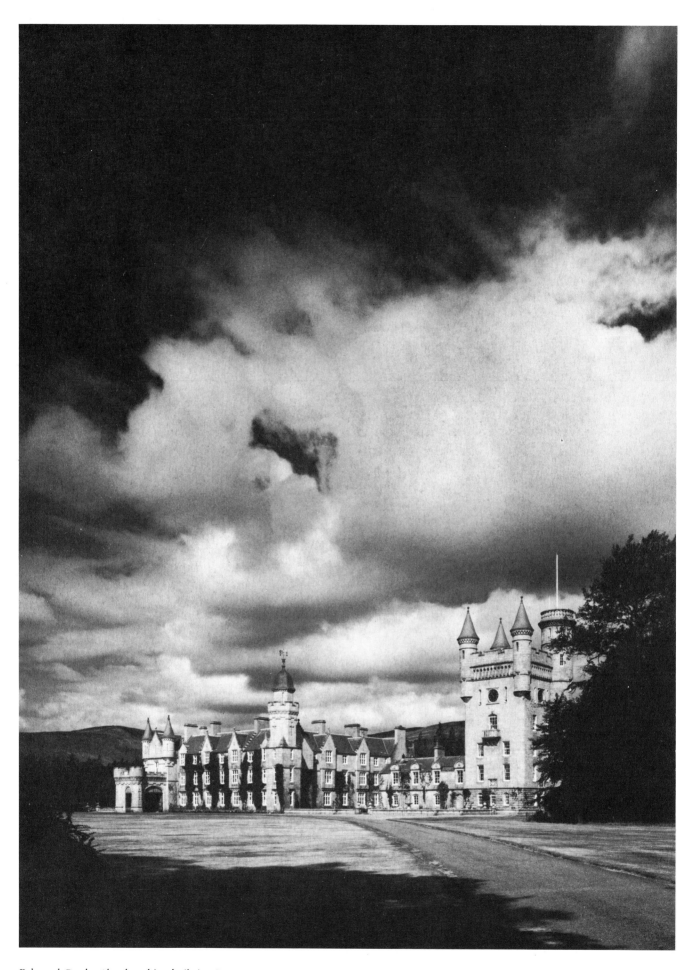

Balmoral Castle, Aberdeenshire, built in 1853

They both loved the Scottish scenery, and their obvious joy in Scotland, their delight in Balmoral, also helped to set a vogue. Wealthy businessmen from Glasgow began to build their miniature Balmorals in the Trossachs; increasingly the English aristocracy bought deer forests and set up their own hunting lodges. The Highlands of Scotland ceased to be a wild, dangerous, lawless world – in a sense they began to be the Switzerland of Britain.

It was a semi-private world, so distant from their English homes, that the Queen deeply loved. Her photographs and pictures recalled other private family moments – the building of a cairn to mark the Castle's purchase, or the famous evening when Prince Albert brought home by torchlight the great stag which he had shot; the climb of Loch-na-Gar, fording the Tarff, or one of the last of the family occasions – the luncheon at Cairn Lochan some two months before the Prince died. She and Albert had often withdrawn further into the Highlands to live at the Shiel of Althnaguisach, which was little larger than a suburban villa perched on a mountainside, and indeed looked rather like one. There they could sketch and paint, or he could work at his innumerable memoranda or plan his buildings and farms. Now she longed for something remoter and in wilder country and she built an equally suburban-looking house, The Glassalt, in the deep, narrow glen at the head of Loch Muick, very secluded. There, with the smallest of staffs, she could spend a few days remembering the past. It remains as she left it, her sitting-room and bedroom intact. On the bedhead of the four-poster where she lay and grieved a watch case of Albert's still lies; on the dressing-table is a beautiful Minton service, painted with leaping salmon. Yet, Glassalt is not all sadness, but often rings with laughter and the music of children, for the royal family loves its privacy as much as Queen Victoria did, but for different reasons. There they can have their barbecues, their family suppers in freedom.

The Queen and the Prince loved their Highland servants as much as the Highlands, adopted their dress, their music and their dances, and did all that they could to sustain the arts and crafts still practised on Deeside. The great event which nothing could stop – scarcely, even, a royal death – was the Gillies' Ball. It was held in the ballroom, the Queen herself dancing reels with her favourite attendant, John Brown.

This withdrawal into the Isle of Wight and the Highlands and the very special privileges she showered on her devoted servant, John Brown, which led to her being slanderously called Mrs Brown, made Queen Victoria very unpopular for about ten years. Brown was a handsome, rough-spoken, hard-drinking Highlander, who irritated the court as much as he pleased the Queen. (He could be devastatingly rude to the royal children, including the Prince of Wales who loathed him; indeed, the first thing that the Prince did when he succeeded his mother was to move the huge statue of Brown from the front of Balmoral, and dump it in the forest a considerable distance from the castle.) Nothing, however, could shake the Queen's admiration and affection for Brown and he acquired a singular distinction: he has a memorial in the Mausoleum of Frogmore – discreetly placed at the base of a column, made discreeter by Edward VII removing the gilt from the lettering, but nevertheless there he is, in the most sacred of all royal Victorian places, a measure of Queen Victoria's regard.

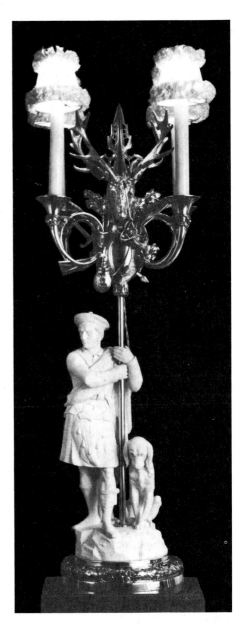

One of a pair of Minton candelabra of Highlanders in Parian marble. From the main Drawing-Room at Balmoral

Although she avoided the public, the Queen's isolation never led her to evade her public duties – coping with dispatches even as she went for a ride. In the end she was teased back into public life and to a popularity that bordered on idolatry, by three things. Her family, which had spread by marriage throughout the courts of Europe, drew her into diplomacy. There was scarcely a throne from Spain to Russia whose ruler or heir apparent was not related to her. An indefatigable correspondent, writing millions of words every year, she knew the interaction of family life, politics and diplomacy could not be avoided, and she became very skilled at exerting subtle personal pressure on governments far more autocratic than her own. She also felt it encumbent to maintain family affection in spite of governmental differences; so her role remained an active one, which required her not only to write letters, but also to entertain. And no one responded more regally than she to the visits of foreign sovereigns.

This emergence, without Albert's help, into the world of European diplomacy was skilfully exploited by Benjamin Disraeli, whom she found in her middle age as fascinating as Lord Melbourne in her youth. Like Melbourne, he was deliciously indiscreet, but unlike Melbourne a master of gross flattery. He gave approval to the publication of her *Some Leaves from a Journal to the Highlands*, the first book published by a reigning monarch for over 200 years. It had a remarkable success – its artful artlessness and its powerful evocation of the royal style of living deserved it. Disraeli's greatest stroke was to make her Empress of India, which quickened her interest, always strong, in that country. But more important than Disraeli, or even her vast family, was her own innate delight in life. Unlike Albert, she had always possessed gusto. She enjoyed being alive, she had insatiable curiosity about people and about things, and she enjoyed her food as much, probably more, than her grief. And she was often amused, and burst out in genuine laughter. Certainly she blossomed more and more as her reign began to take on the air of a saga. For most of her subjects, by the 1870s, she had been Queen throughout their adult lives, through a time in which Britain's Empire and wealth grew to unprecedented heights.

This great Empire the Queen longed to visit, but she was never able to; fortunately, however, she could visualise it exactly – through the roving eye of the camera. From the earliest days of daguerreotype, Queen Victoria had been fascinated by so magical a method of preserving the past. She pored over the photographs of the Crimean War, of which she formed a magnificent collection; sent off Bedford, one of the finest photographers of the time, to make a photographic album of Coburg; followed the Prince of Wales's visit to India in 1875/6: gave an audience to Charles Dickens because he possessed some superb photographs of the American Civil War. And from their earliest days, of course, the royal children, their wives and husbands, their children and *their* wives and grandchildren had been photographed over and over again, so that the royal photographic collection is, perhaps, one of the greatest in the world – both of people and of events.

At Balmoral, in Prince Philip's dressing-room, there is a frieze of family photographs of the 1860s that runs round the wall of a turret. At that time these photographs, called *cartes de visite* (because they were the size of visiting cards), were all the rage, and sold in tens of thousands to

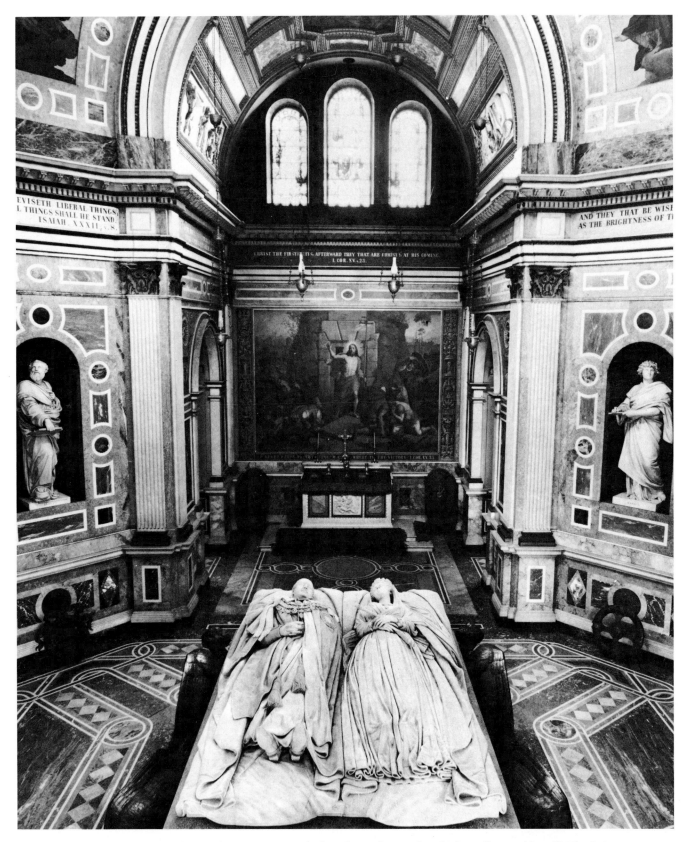

Queen Victoria had the Royal Mausoleum at Frogmore built to house the remains of Prince Albert and herself. The designer was Professor Ludwig Gruner, the Prince's artistic adviser, and the architect was A. J. Humbert. The tomb was designed by Carlo Marochetti

Buildings which, in different ways, owe much to Prince Albert. The Raphaelesque decorations of the Royal Mausoleum were a tribute to him in the style of his favourite painter. The Dairy at Windsor shows the Prince's interest in modern manufactures and practical improvements which also found expression in his support for the Great Exhibition of 1851

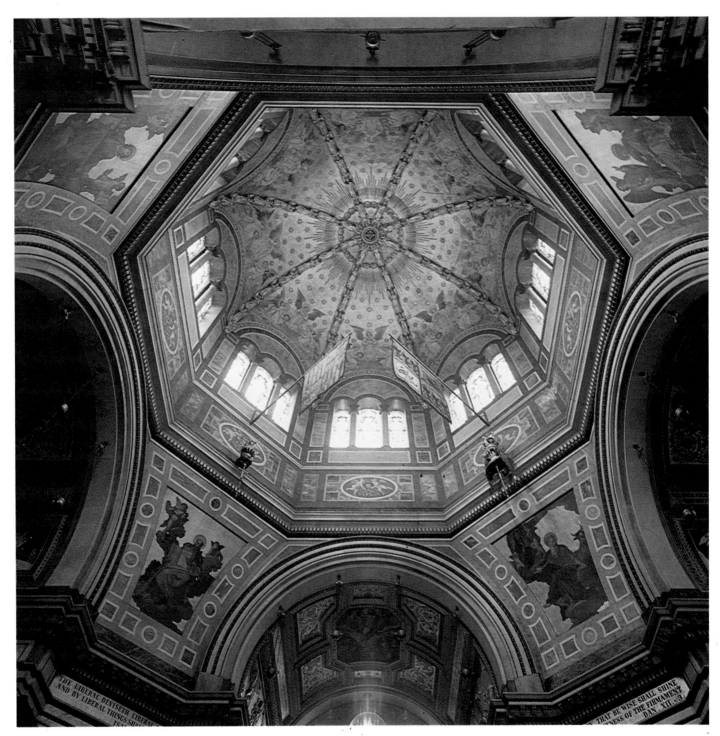

The Dome of the Royal Mausoleum, Frogmore

Opposite: 1 The Royal Dairy, Windsor. 2 Detail of one of the Minton tiles which decorate the Dairy

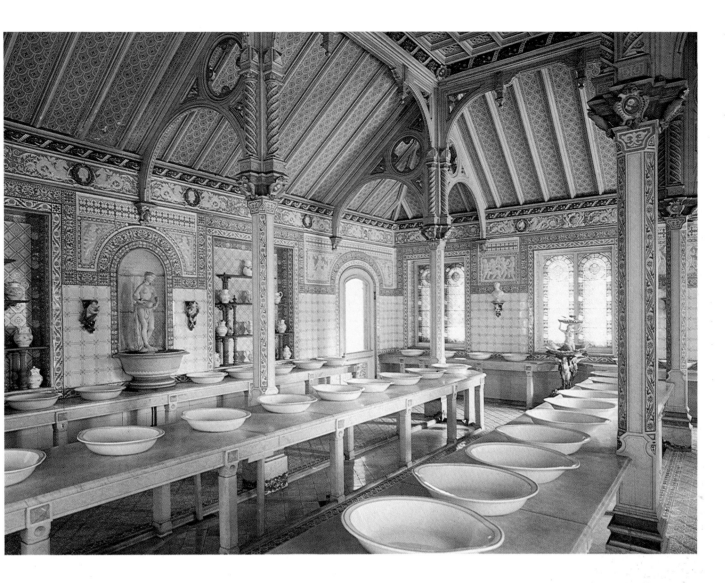

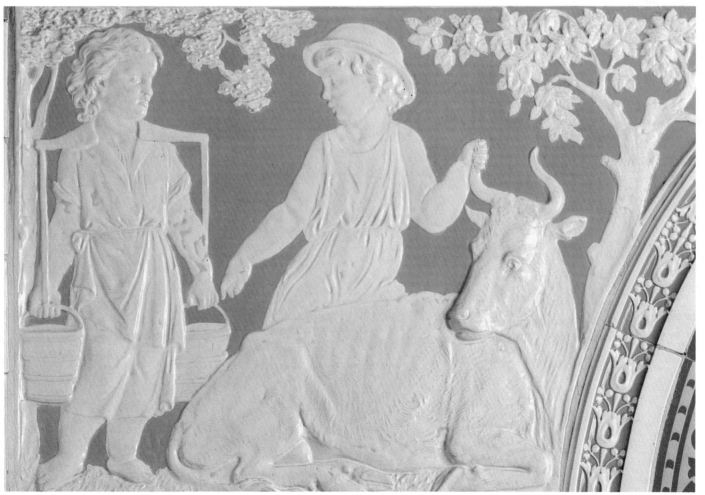

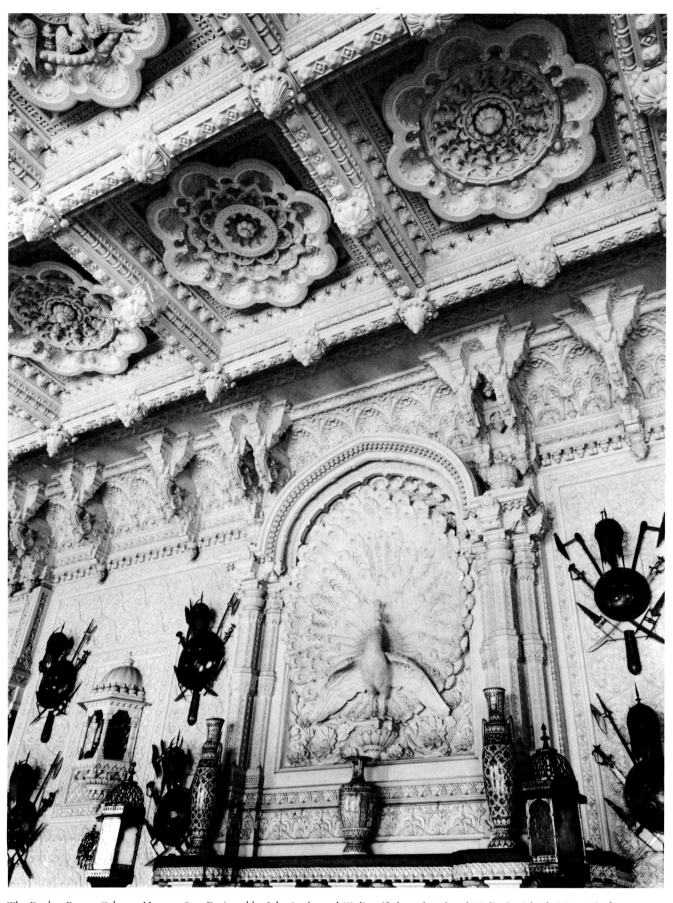

The Durbar Room, Osborne House, 1890. Designed by John Lockwood Kipling (father of Rudyard Kipling) with Bhai Ram Singh, an expert in Indian decorative techniques

the public. Mayall, a popular American photographer, made, even in the 1860s, £35,000 a year in royalties from his photographs of the royal family. The most popular was that of the Princess of Wales, the beautiful Alexandra, with the young Duke of Clarence riding piggy-back; a pose which thousands of mothers copied. The importance of photography in bringing not only the likeness of royalty into the humblest cottages, but also in permitting her subjects to visualise the great state events of her reign, cannot be overestimated. Certainly Queen Victoria had no doubts; she had everything photographed – rooms and dogs, as well as state visits and royal weddings – and so her life is pictorially recorded with an exactitude that no previous monarch could match. In the evening of her life she was quick to see the vast possibilities of the cinema, and films were being shown at Windsor in the 1890s. The use of photography by the newspapers whetted the public's appetite for royal events and also helped to satisfy it. Even so, it was only a beginning. By present-day standards royalty appeared seldom in the public press; but then they also appeared only rarely in public. This was the beginning.

In old age the Queen projected a very powerful yet consistent image – an image, as it were, of the world's grandmother – timeless, serene, yet exuding power. Europe had found its matriarch, and she began to see herself, consciously or unconsciously, in this dual role of Queen and mother. Nothing demonstrates this more clearly than her attitude to India and her great jubilee celebrations. Her interest in India had always been intense and she was far more sympathetic to the Indians than many of her ministers. The Durbar Room at Osborne is the physical expression of that love and interest, containing, as it does, echoes of Indian culture and art and the presents – good, bad or indifferent, but all preserved – which flowed to her from its princes and peoples. She was totally free from colour prejudice, indeed loathed it, and in the evening of her life Hafiz Abdul Karim, an Indian known as 'Munshi', who taught her some Hindustani, played much the same role as John Brown – much to the horror of her Household. He was a strikingly good-looking man, not so high caste as he would have the Queen believe, but clever, subtle and very sensitive to slights, which came often. He saw more confidential papers than he should have and probably influenced the Queen's attitude to India and its problems. Certainly he made her more sensitive to prejudice. These words of hers, written on 29 May 1898, have a stinging relevance. 'The future Viceroy [of India] must really shake himself more

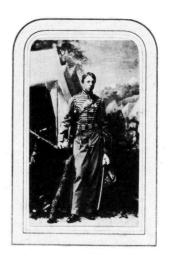

2

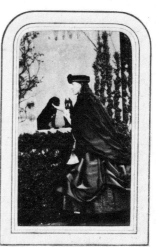

1

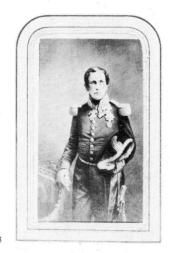

3

Carte de visite photographs of European royalty were immensely popular – the public bought them in huge numbers and the Royal family collected them. These are from the Royal Library, Windsor. 1 Louis, Comte d'Eu. 2 Grand Duchess Constantine. 3 King Leopold I of the Belgians. 4 The Prince Imperial. 5 Grand Dukes Vladimir and Alexis Alexandrovich, sons of the Emperor of Russia

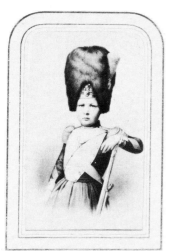

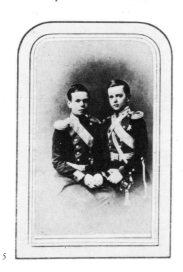

4

5

and more free of this red-tapist, narrow-minded Council and entourage. He must be more independent and *hear* for *himself* what the *feelings* of the Natives really are and not be guided by the *snobbish* and vulgar and overbearing and offensive behaviour of many of our Civil and Political Agents, if we are to go on peacefully and happily in India, and to be liked and beloved by high and low, as well as respected as we ought to be, and not trying to trample on the people and continually reminding them and make them feel that they are a conquered people.' In this there is a deep and true concern for human values.

This message, this concern, the assumption of the role of universal mother, was clear in her great jubilee celebrations of 1887 and 1897. Her family wanted her, in 1887, to dress up in robes of state. She refused. She knew her people's image of her and, spurning the State carriage, she

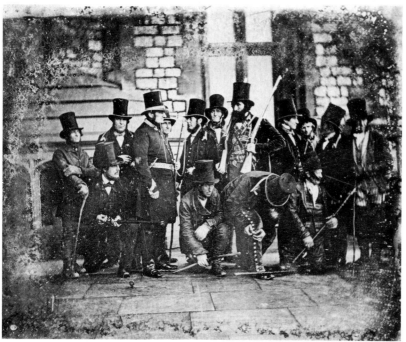

1

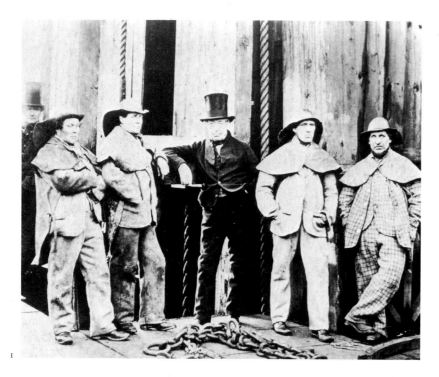

3

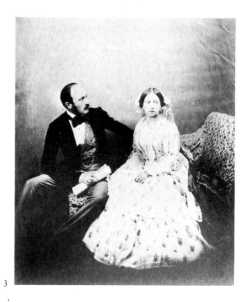

2

The photographs in the Royal Archives, Windsor, reflect Queen Victoria's and Prince Albert's interest in domestic and current affairs. Many are also splendid examples of early photography.

1 A team of rescue workers at a mine disaster in the north-east of England, by W. Downey, 1862.
2 Game-keepers at Windsor Castle, daguerreotype, *c.* 1847.
3 Queen Victoria and Prince Albert. A hand-tinted photograph by R. Fenton, 1854.
4 The Chartist meeting at Kennington Common, South London, in 1848. A daguerreotype by W. Kilburn.
5 Staff at the Royal Mews, Buckingham Palace, in 1847. The Queen was present when this was taken

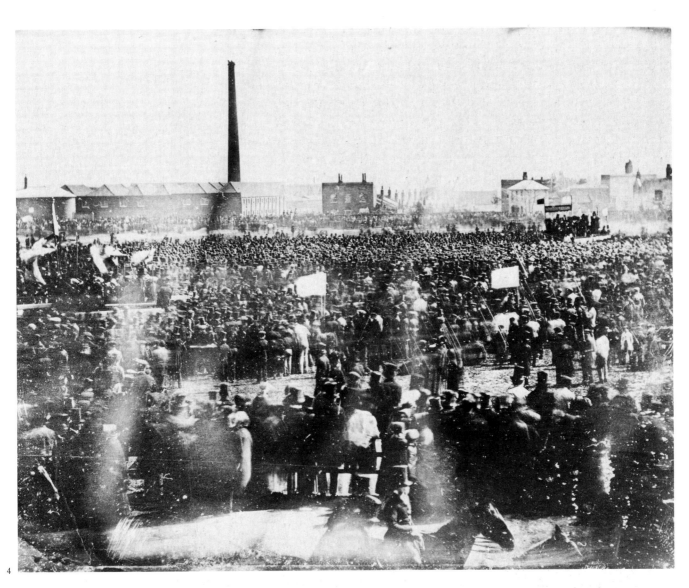

4

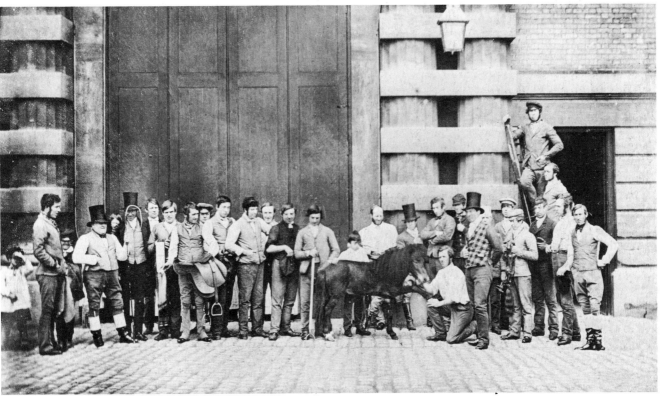

5

drove in an open landau, dressed in simple black with an ordinary black bonnet trimmed with white lace. The contrast with the glitter of emperors, kings and princes, preening in peacock uniforms, ablaze with jewels and orders, was vivid, and her instinct surely right. Similarly in the Abbey, sitting in the chair of state to receive the homage of her extensive royal family, she thrust aside protocol and warmly embraced them all. A few old people with long memories would recall how, as a girl at her coronation, she had left her throne to help the aged Lord Rolfe who had stumbled as he knelt to do homage. Time and time again in triumphal arch, in painted slogan or bad verse, this theme echoed, 'Not Queen alone, but Mother, Queen and Friend'. Not merely sentimental and lachrymose, this contained a deep tribal truth for the British,

The photographic record at Windsor also covers events abroad.

1 A Mission Wedding, South Africa, from the album of 1879.

2 Huts of the guards at Balaclava, in the Crimean War, by James Robertson.

3 Kimberley diamond mine: the Big Hole. 1879 Album

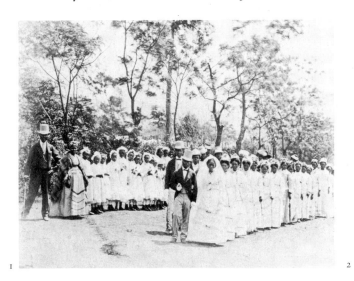

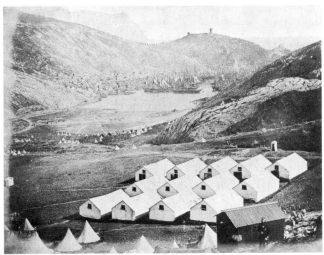

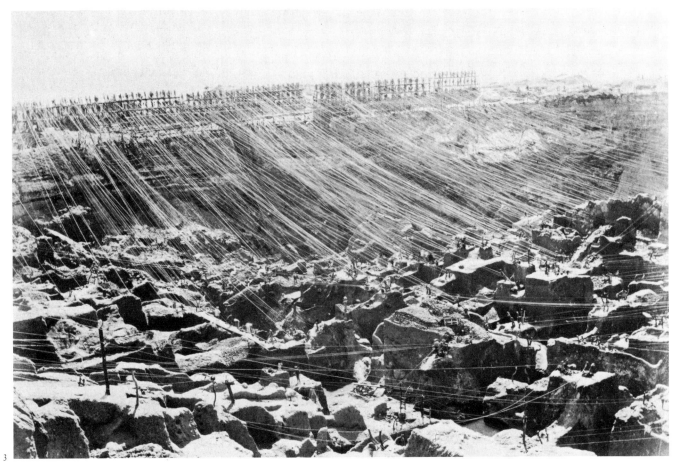

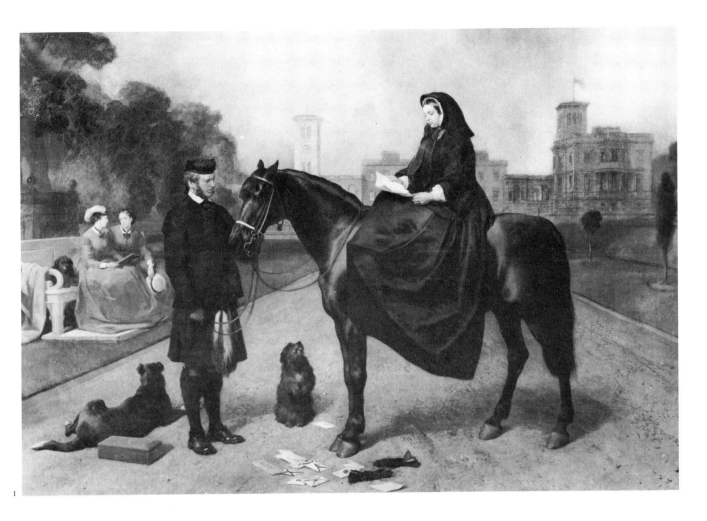

wherever they might be. The Queen, with simplicity and dignity, sailed through the packed days of celebration in which, on both occasions, her nation and her empire rioted – a small, black figure that dimmed the colourful splendour of half the royalty of Europe and the East.

Still the compulsive writer, she was never too weary to set down her thoughts: 'Amply repaid for my great exertion and fatigue, by the unbounded enthusiastic loyalty and devotion conveyed from all parts of my vast Empire by high and low, rich and poor, far and near, which has sunk deep in my heart'. So she sailed on, seemingly immortal, as indefatigable as ever; taking off in her royal train or yacht with sixty servants to Nice, to Berlin, to Ireland; never stopping the work of dispatches, memoranda, minutes, appointments; never ceasing to write letters to her innumerable family or to add another thousand words to her journal; finding time to sketch and paint (she painted an exceptionally good portrait of one of her Indian servants when she was seventy-three); taking regular exercise and indulging her insatiable curiosity. But death never ceased to inflict its dark pain. In 1900 her son Alfred, Duke of Edinburgh, died of cancer, and she knew her daughter, Victoria, was dying of it too. A grandson died in South Africa. Lady Churchill, the friend of fifty years, died on Christmas Day 1900, and she hated, as she had always hated, the pain and suffering of her soldiers, fighting, as they now were, in South Africa. Even her deep, almost visceral attachment to life at last gave way and she died at Osborne on 22 January 1901, ironically enough in the arms of her grandson, Kaiser Wilhelm, Emperor of Germany.

1 Sir Edwin Landseer, *Queen Victoria on Horseback*, reading letters in the grounds of Osborne, 1866. John Brown holds the reins.
2 The Queen's memorial to Brown, her 'faithful and devoted Personal Attendant and friend', in the Mausoleum at Frogmore

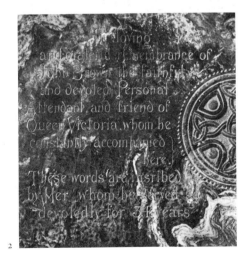

Not only Britain, but the whole of Europe and much of the East, was convulsed in a paroxysm of grief. With full military honours, she moved solemnly through the silent, sorrowing crowds to lie by the side of the husband she had mourned so long.

Queen Victoria in the grounds at Frogmore, with one of her Indian servants

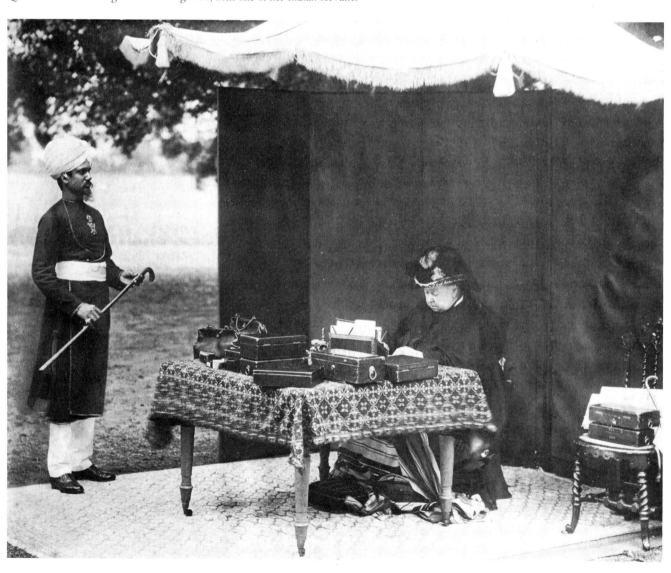

7

THE TWENTIETH CENTURY

When the grief at the death of Queen Victoria passed, the people and the press turned to Edward VII and his wife with eager expectation. In spite of the devotion which the old Queen inspired as her long reign proceeded, she had not been frequently seen. Except when entertaining visiting sovereigns, she did not go to race meetings, to regattas, or to the opera and theatre. She might visit friends in the Highlands, or stay with them on an official visit, but never once did she dine in a subject's house in London. She had very strict ideas on what a queen should or should not be seen doing.

Fortunately for the monarchy, her son, Edward VII, loved company, hated to be alone for an hour, delighted in shooting, racing and regattas, adored the theatre and was fascinated by the new invention of the motor-car. He was gregarious, outward-going, a man who loved to see and be seen. On the average he undertook every year thirty public occasions – opening universities, bridges or hostels, attending banquets to promote humanitarian causes and always full of grace and good humour, adept at making short public speeches. Indeed, he was probably the most accomplished impromptu speaker the royal family has so far produced. At his accession in 1901, he spoke to his assembled council for eight minutes, explaining why he was taking the name of Edward VII and expressing how deeply he felt the obligations of monarchy, without any notes but with an eloquence and dignity that deeply impressed everyone present.

Edward VII was far more visible to his subjects than any monarch had ever been before. Surely Queen Victoria was photographed and the Court Circular reported her movements and her guests, but Edward VII and his beautiful Queen, Alexandra, the sister of the King of Denmark, were the objects of such intense interest that their lives were almost lived in public. They were photographed at Ascot, at Newmarket, at Cowes, at the theatre and opera. The balls they gave, the dinners – private as well as public – were extensively reported in the press; the Queen's and King's clothes, their jewels, their dogs, their food – the press and its photographers could never have enough. Never before had the private, as well as the public life of monarchy been so exposed to public view. And not only in the press, but also on the screen, at the new 'picture houses' or cinemas that were springing up in the first decade of the twentieth century. Edward VII responded to life on a public stage with an accomplished dignity and affability that the most professional of actors would have found hard to equal. Many of the puritan middle class deplored his gambling, worried about his extravagance and fretted their souls about his peccadilloes, but the majority of his subjects, particularly the working class, adored him. They loved his gusto for life. They made a cult of Mrs Lillie Langtry, the Jersey Lily, to whom he was attached and whom he had helped launch on an acting career after financial disaster. They betted heavily on his horses and were as delighted as he was when Persimmon, whose statue is a dramatic feature in the grounds at Sandringham, won the Derby in 1896, and doubly so when Diamond Jubilee won the race in 1901.

Edward VII belonged to Europe almost as much as he belonged to Britain. He was uncle, first or second cousin of nearly all the royalty of Europe and half the sovereign princes of Germany. The Emperor of Germany and the Tsar of Russia were his nephews, the Queen of Spain his niece, the King of Denmark his brother-in-law, and so one might go

1 King Edward VII, April 1902.
2 Albert Edward, Prince of Wales, with the jockey Watts mounted on Persimmon, and the horse's trainer, Richard Marsh, Newmarket, September 1897.
3 'The Prince's First Tiger.' The Prince of Wales with his shooting party, India, 1875–6.
4 King Edward VII shooting, early 1900s.
5 On board the *Britannia* for the start of the Queen's Cup, August 1896. The Prince of Wales is in the centre

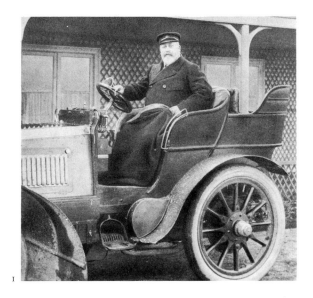

1

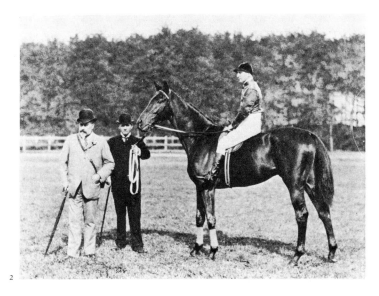

2

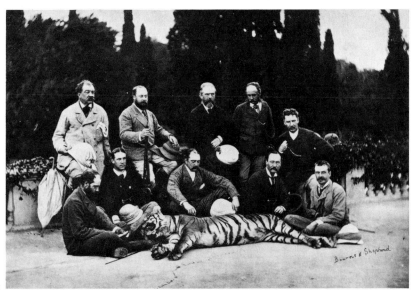

3

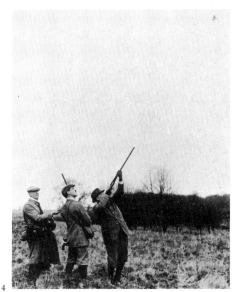

4

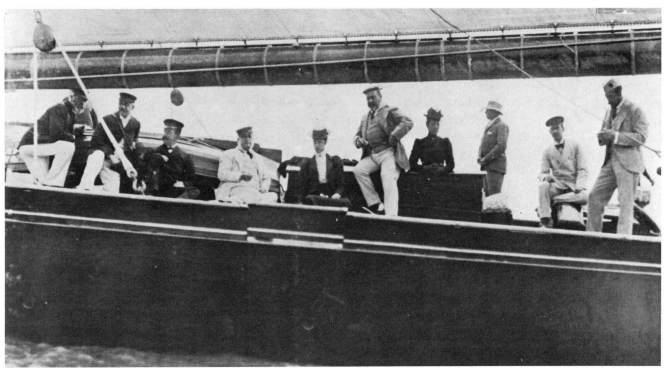

5

from court to court. They all visited each other for family reasons, for state reasons, for diplomatic reasons, attempting to ease tensions and abate the dangerous rivalries of the European power game, but always, at least in Edward VII's case, under the control of the ministers. His popularity in Europe was almost as great as it was in England. He adored France and took a yearly holiday at Biarritz; he dieted and gambled at the German spas of Baden-Baden and Homburg.

Beyond Europe lay his empire, the largest the world had ever known. He had paid an extensive visit to India in 1875/6, which he had enjoyed immensely. The diversity of the land, both its magnificence and its poverty, caught his imagination, though the attitude of many political agents to the Hindus and Moslems infuriated him by its obvious racial prejudice. His mother, unfortunately, was very ambivalent towards the royal reception which he received and so he visited his empire far less than he desired. His son, George V, like the royal family today, travelled far more widely.

Gregarious as he was, Edward VII always returned to Sandringham with special delight. It was his home. It had never belonged to any of his ancestors. He and his wife built it, furnished it, created the landscape about it – the lakes, the woods, the brilliant shrubberies of rhododendron and azalea, and the rare trees that make the gardens of Sandringham some of the loveliest in England. Sandringham had been bought, on the

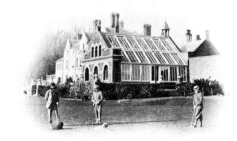

Croquet at Sandringham, 1864. The Prince of Wales is on the right

Sandringham: the west front with the rockery on the right

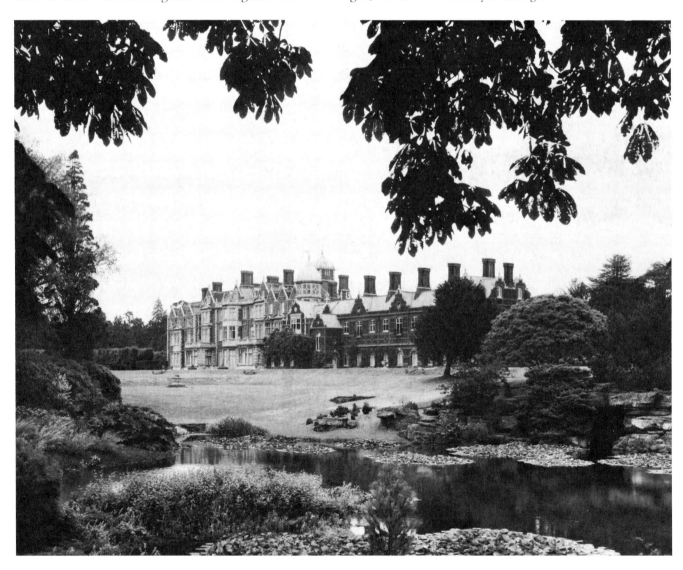

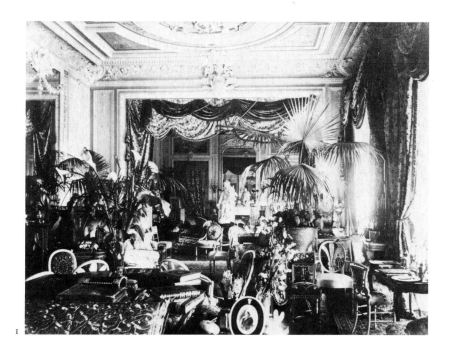

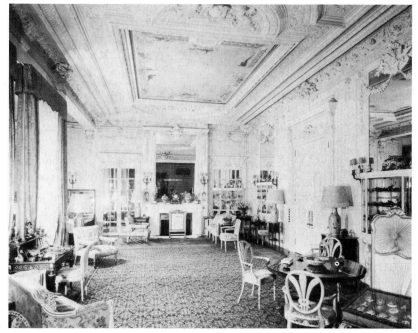

1 The drawing room at Sandringham in 1899.
2 The same room, seventy-five years later

advice of his earnest father, who hoped the Prince might put down his roots as a country gentleman, manage his estate, grow attached to it, as he and Queen Victoria had to Osborne and Balmoral. The result was both more and less than his father expected. Nothing could turn the Prince into a country squire, yet he certainly put down roots. Sandringham was his home as no other palace was. He loved Christmases there, with his children and grandchildren about him; indeed, both George V and George VI felt, as Edward VII did, that Sandringham was a special place for their family. When his grandson, Prince Charles, was born, George VI wrote to his mother, Queen Mary, full of excitement that now there was the prospect of five generations at Sandringham!

The house was the King's creation. He pulled down the Georgian house, which itself had replaced, scarcely a hundred years previously, the old Tudor one of the Hostes, a family allied both to Sir Robert Walpole and to Lord Nelson. Only the old bowling alley of the former house remains, converted into a long, narrow library. The new house was built in warm brick. It is long and rambling, full of nostalgia for Tudor architecture, yet in no way a copy in design or in detail. Autumn light suits it best, when the glowing brick and stone harmonise with the dying leaves of red, gold and brown of the trees and woods that surround it.

The interior is a great surprise. A typical Victorian *porte cochère* leads one to expect a vast entrance hall and an imposing staircase down which royalty could sweep. Actually, the door leads straight into the drawing-room the King used after dinner – a room furnished and decorated for comfort. There is no grandeur, no splendour. The Tsar of Russia, the Emperor of Germany and other crowned heads of Europe who came to Sandringham for the magnificent shooting which it provided (bags of up to 30,000 a season were nothing untoward) must have been astounded by the domesticity and absence of rooms of state. Of course, it was a big house – and needed to be. A large retinue of court officials and servants necessarily followed the King and Queen wherever they went, and naturally enough their royal guests brought their suites with them and of course their servants. So there were warrens of small rooms, but the state rooms were neither numerous nor very grand. Like the after-dinner sitting-room, the dining-room was not large. The furniture, a vast mahogany dining-table with stout fluted legs, and a large suite of chairs – heavy, almost ponderous furniture, but made with fine craftsmanship – was by Holland and Sons, nineteenth-century cabinet-makers of con-

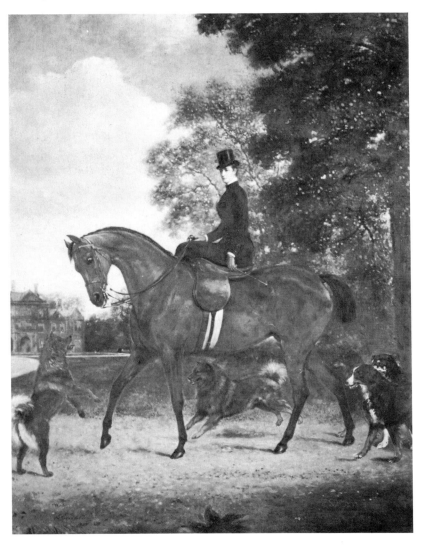

Jean-Edouard Lacretelle, *Queen Alexandra when Princess of Wales*, 1885

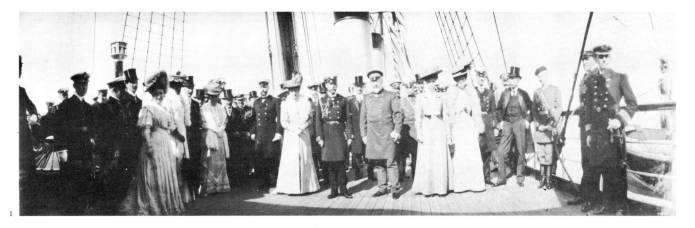

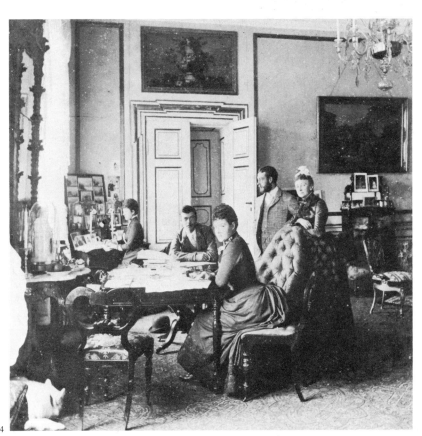

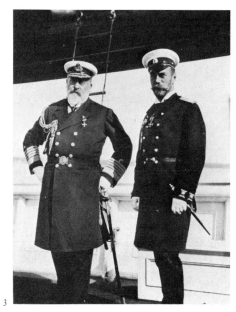

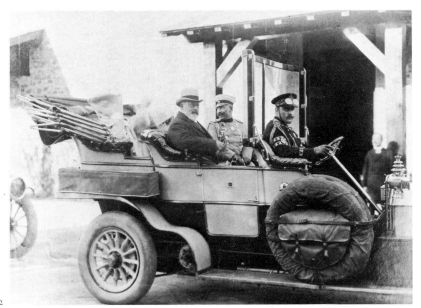

The social gatherings and official visits of the Royal Families of Europe are also recorded in photographs in the Royal Archives.

1 Group on board yacht. Reval, 1908. To the right of the King are Queen Alexandra and Tsar Nicholas II; to his left, Grand Duchess Olga Alexandrovna, Princess Victoria and Grand Duke Michael Alexandrovich of Russia.

2 King Edward VII and Kaiser Wilhelm II in a motor car. Friedrichshof, 1906.

3 King Edward VII and the Tsar on board the Royal Yacht. Reval, 1908.

4 A royal group at leisure: from left to right, Alexandra, Princess of Wales, Tsarevich Nicholas Alexandrovich of Russia, Empress Marie Feodorovna of Russia, Prince George of Wales and Queen Louise of Denmark. Fredensborg, 1889

siderable distinction who were responsible for much of the furniture at Sandringham. The most impressive feature of the dining-room is a series of tapestries. These were given to the King in 1876 by Alfonso XII of Spain. They are replicas of Spanish tapestries and two of them were based on paintings by Goya.

One of the most charming rooms in Sandringham is the Queen's sitting-room, with its delightful embossed wallpaper, which looks out towards the west where the garden catches the light of the dying sun. This room is pervaded by the nostalgia of an Edwardian afternoon. The brilliant main drawing-room, in gold and white and blue, is even more nostalgic, recalling beautiful women, handsome men, rich, elegant, sophisticated and serene people, who had no knowledge, no vision of the war that within a few years was to ravage Europe, destroying so many of its royal dynasties. Although the drawing-room is almost a wedding cake of a room, it is not trivial, not over-decorated or over-gilded. It belongs as completely to its own age as the music room at Brighton or the tower at Osborne do to theirs. And it contained what is so appropriate for its time – a quite remarkable collection of objects made by Carl Fabergé and his master craftsmen.

The core of the collection was formed by Queen Alexandra. Her sister was the Dowager Tsarina of Russia, her nephew, Tsar Nicholas II, had married a granddaughter of Queen Victoria, so the Russian and English royal families were exceptionally close. Queen Alexandra was, like her sister, a woman of great beauty, who created for herself a personal style of elegance, particularly in clothes. Even the French aristocracy rushed to imitate her hats and dresses and parasols. She was a woman of generous personality, who cared deeply for her husband and enjoyed the same pleasures and hobbies. She tolerated with grace the beautiful and lively women with whom he liked to surround himself in later years – and was sympathetic to his need for the company of a Mrs Keppel or a Lady Randolph Churchill – when her extreme deafness made prolonged conversation difficult. She always retained her husband's deepest affection and regard throughout their long marriage.

Their friends were diverse – not necessarily aristocratic, mostly, but not all, rich, for Edward asked at least one well-known radical to Sandringham because the King enjoyed his conversation. He refused to wear evening dress, so his meals were served on a tray in his bedroom. Many European sovereigns, particularly the Germans and Russians, twitched their anti-semitic noses at the fact that some of Edward VII's closest friends were Jews – Rothschilds, Kassels, Sassoons – and he was the first British monarch to attend a synagogue. His very rich friends were eager to give him and Queen Alexandra presents at Christmas, at birthdays, indeed on every possible occasion. But Queen Alexandra insisted on modest gifts and refused, for the most part, to receive any personal jewellery except from her immediate family. However, she adored Fabergé, so her friends and her husband knew how to please her and this led to one of the most remarkable collections of Fabergé ornaments in the world.

Carl Fabergé was a goldsmith and jeweller of St Petersburg (his shop still exists in Leningrad). He developed a style reminiscent of the great French goldsmiths of the eighteenth century, yet intensely personal. He could be both austere and whimsical and combine surprise with elegance.

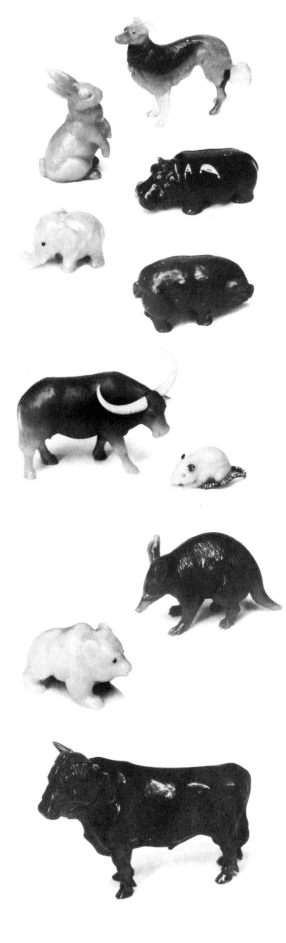

Carl Fabergé, animals carved in semi-precious stones

Even his most elaborate pieces have a clarity and restraint that are almost mathematical in their impact. He worked in gold and silver and very precious stones, but he was also drawn to the variety of colour and texture of semi-precious stones – malachite, agate, jade, rose quartz and many others.

Queen Alexandra took great delight in the whimsical side of Fabergé's invention and, as their prices were then relatively modest – £30 or £100 – never discouraged her friends from adding to her extensive Fabergé menagerie of animals, birds and fish. At Sandringham there are about 300 animals carved in semi-precious stones. There is a charming dormouse with diamond eyes and golden whiskers; elephants in rock crystal and jade, standing, sitting, trumpeting – some scarcely half an inch, others monsters of five inches. There are tiny frogs, and birds of every variety – parrots, toucans, cockatoos, flamingoes, and a grave grey pelican. And, of course, dogs – dachshunds, poodles, collies and bulldogs. In 1907 Edward VII sent for Fabergé's modellers from St Petersburg; they worked hard and fast making clay models of all the animals at Sandringham – the pigs, the hens, the turkeys, the huge shire horses that pulled the wagons, the prize shorthorn bull, the King's dog, Caesar (who had his own footman), and the Queen's favourite Pekinese. The most famous animal of all at Sandringham, Persimmon, Edward VII's great Derby winner, was cast in silver; the rest in semi-precious stones. As might be expected, Queen Alexandra was overjoyed when she saw them all set out in the dairy.

As well as animals she collected what are perhaps the most beautiful of all the productions of Fabergé's workshops: rock crystal vasès containing a stem of flowers or fruit. One contains a single spray of gold-spun catkins, another of bleeding heart in rhodonite and chalcedony, another a stem of rowan, the berries in purperine. Everything by Fabergé was welcome – paper knives, boxes (some with exquisite views of Sandringham in sepia), cigarette boxes (plain, in gold and enamel, or disguised as a travelling trunk), photograph frames, even bell pushes and parasol handles!

The passion for Fabergé lasted for three generations. Queen Mary added some of the most splendid pieces to her mother-in-law's collection, including two of the Imperial easter eggs – elaborate surprises which Fabergé made for the Tsar to give to his mother and his wife on Easter Sunday. They were not made for anyone else. The more lovely of the two in the royal collection is the one given by Tsar Nicholas to his wife at Easter 1914. This opens to disclose a cameo upon which are carved portraits of the five Imperial children, all to be slaughtered four years later with their parents during the Russian Revolution. Queen Mary's love of Fabergé was passed on to her son, King George VI, who made a small but very fine collection of cigarette boxes, still crisp and sharp although he used them constantly.

Marlborough House, Edward VII's London home when he was Prince of Wales, has now been emptied of its treasures, so the Fabergé and the white and blue drawing-room at Sandringham now recall one aspect of the Edwardian age as nowhere else does. It was a world for the rich and aristocratic: a secure, elegant, whimsical world in which everything was taken lightly. Yet in Edward VII himself there was a sense of serious commitment. He might delight in the frivolity of Fabergé, but he could devote long hours to working-men's housing conditions, write bitter

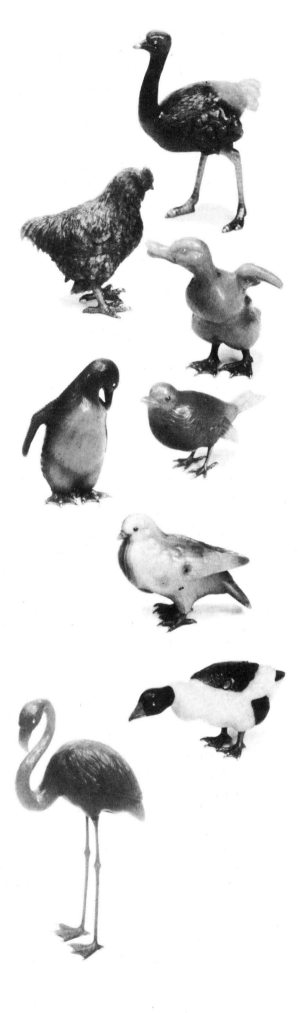

letters to his mother about the treatment of Indians by English political agents, go from one busy public function to another with dignity, warmth and wit. The newly formed and rapidly growing Labour Party adored him. And everywhere he went, the red dispatch boxes followed, reminding him, if he needed to be, that he was far more than the King of Great Britain.

There is a room – the antechamber to the library – at Sandringham which symbolises one of the most important roles that Edward VII had to discharge. It is redolent of empire, with its Mogul lamps, a strange room deep in the heart of so much domesticity and there, to one side, is a red pillar box for posting letters – the link, as it were, between Sandringham and the far-flung empire over which Edward VII ruled and on which the sun never set. We almost forget over how much of the earth's surface the British monarchy reigned, even in the reign of Edward VII.

Throughout the nineteenth century many territories had been added to the old established empire: in the East, in the Pacific, in Africa, even in the Southern Atlantic – huge land masses such as Burma, or Egypt and the Sudan, or tiny and remote islands from Tristan da Cunha to Pitcairn Island in the Pacific. As the century progressed these were tied even more closely to the mother country by cable along which telegrams could pass, and above all by the postal service which England did so much to develop. Sir Rowland Hill introduced the adhesive postage stamp: it was to become both a new art form and a vast new territory for the compulsive collector. The first members of the royal family to become interested in stamps were King Edward when Prince of Wales, and his brother Alfred, Duke of Edinburgh, afterwards Duke of Saxe-Coburg and Gotha. They visited De La Rue's printing works on 8 April 1856, when a block of forty imperforate 6d stamps was specially printed for them. This was preserved and became the first documented item in what was to become the greatest stamp collection in the world. Prince Alfred later became the Honorary President of the Royal Philatelic Society London, but it was his nephew, afterwards George V, who was responsible for the organisation, definition and extent of the collection. George V com-

The following four pages show postage stamps, and material related to their design and production, in the Royal Collection.

PAGE 297 *Rare stamps from the era of the Classics and the Primitives.*
Britain's first postage stamps, the 1d Black and the 2d Blue, were issued on 6 May 1840. 1 1840 1d Black from the first printing (indicated by the 'Page 1' in the margin). 2 1840 2d Blue from the first printing. 3 1840 1d Black from Plate 4, showing the Maltese Cross cancellation applied by the Post Office to prevent stamps being reused. 4 1847 Trinidad, the first colonial stamp, privately issued for local use by the master of the steamship *Lady McLeod*. 5, 6 1847 Mauritius 1d, 2d, the first stamps officially issued by a Colonial Post Office. They were printed one at a time from a copper plate engraved by J. Barnard, a local watchmaker and jeweller. Only fourteen 1d and twelve 2d stamps are known. 7, 8 1850 New South Wales 1d, 2d showing a primitively engraved view of Sydney. 9 1851 Canada – the famous Twelve Pence black. 10 1854 Bermuda 1d printed and signed by the local Post-master, W. Perot. 11 1856 British Guiana 4d printed locally from type and initialled by a postal official. 12 1854 India 4d printed with the head inverted in error. 13 1854 Western Australia 4d showing the error caused when the lithographer placed the transfer of the frame inverted relative to the swan. 14 1855 New Zealand 1/-. One of the many early stamps based on the Chalon portrait of Queen Victoria. 15 1855 Tasmania (Van Diemen's Land) 2d, engraved from the watercolour by Corbould shown on the next page. 16 1861 Cape of Good Hope triangular penny printed blue instead of red, and joined to a normal 4d blue. The error was caused by one of the 1d stereos being accidentally included when the plate for the 4d was made up. 17 1857 Newfoundland 1/-, one of the rarest of the early heraldic designs. 18 1859 Ceylon 4d, another of the famous early rarities.

1 Letter sheet designed by William Mulready, addressed to the Duke of Cambridge, uncle of King George V.
2 Caricature by John Leech of the Mulready envelope – letters hang even from the lion's tail.

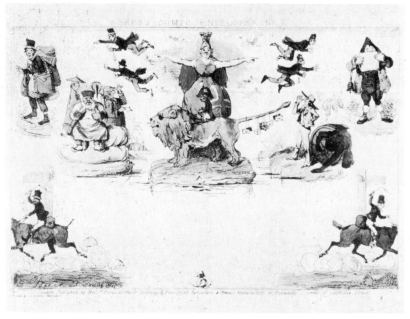

2

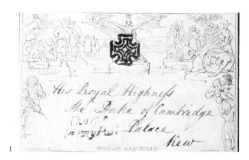

1

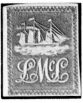

1

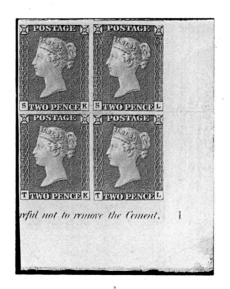

2

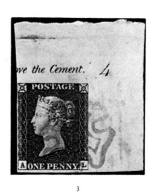

3

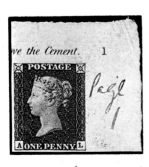

4

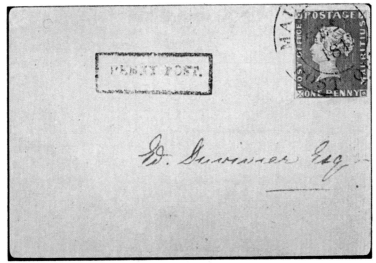

5

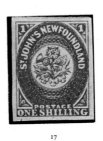

6

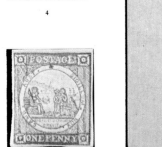

7

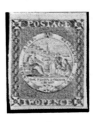

8

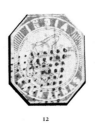

9

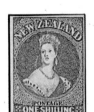

10

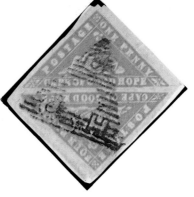

11

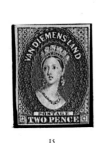

12

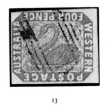

13

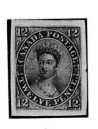

14

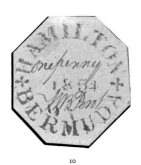

15

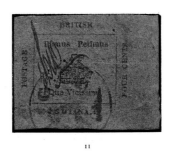

16

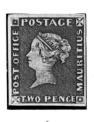

17

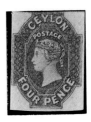

18

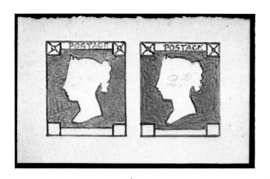

1

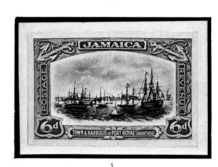

2

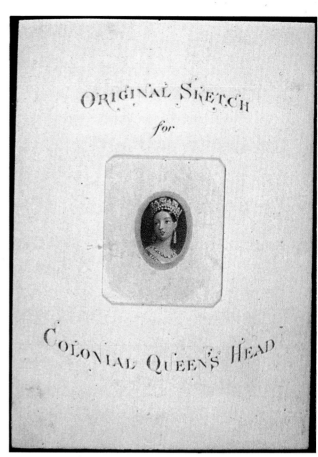

3

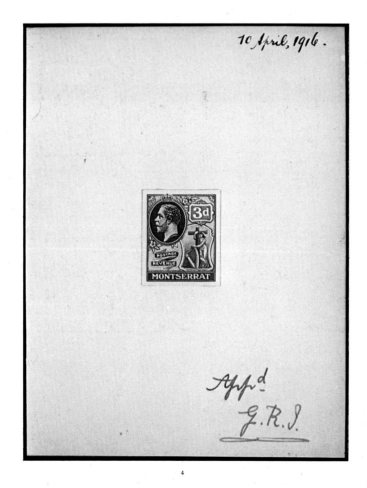

10 April, 1916.

4

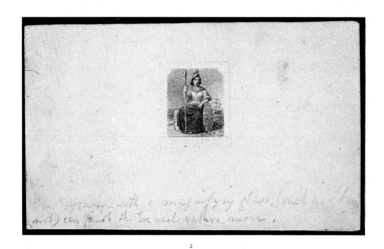

5

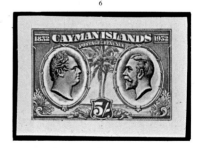

6

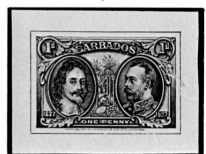

7

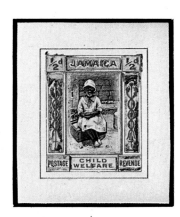

1

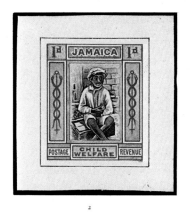

2

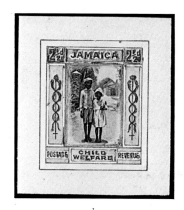

3

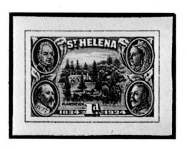

4

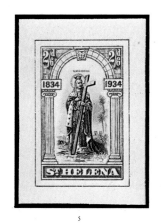

5

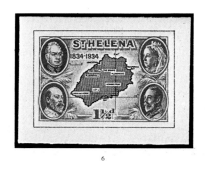

6

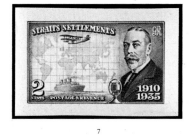

7

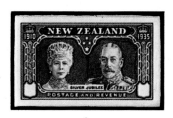

8

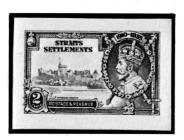

9

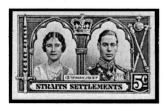

10

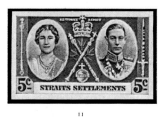

11

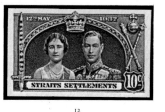

12

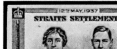

13

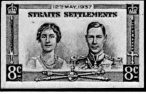

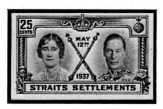

14

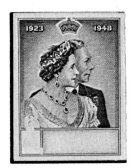
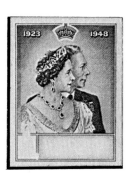
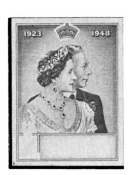
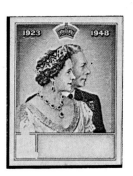

1

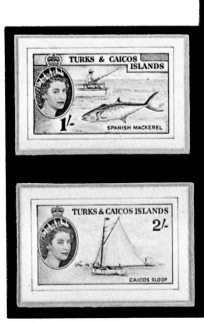
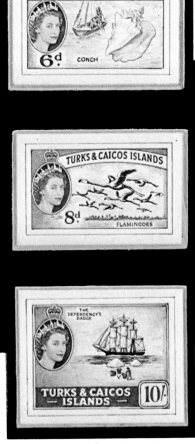
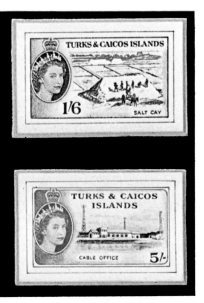

2

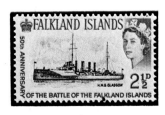
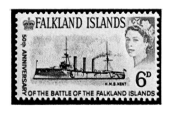
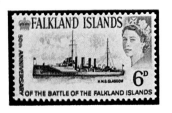

3   4   5

municated his enthusiasm to his son Albert, Duke of York, afterwards George VI, who sought to deepen the collection by bringing together all aspects of the stamp's production, from the artist's first drawing, through all stages of engraving and printing. It has been continued in this way up to the present day.

George V first became fascinated by stamps about 1890, probably through the influence of his uncle who envisaged that the young sailor prince's visit to the West Indies could provide a source for many additions to his own collection. By 1893, the prince had become Honorary Vice-President of the Royal Philatelic Society, succeeding the Earl of Kingston in the more executive position as President in 1896, and so giving great prestige to what was regarded as a rather crankish pastime. He began as a general collector. One of his wedding presents in 1893 was a collection of 1500 carefully selected stamps, given to him by his fellow enthusiasts. He astounded the world in 1904 by bidding £1450 for an unused 2d 'Post Office Mauritius', one of the rarest stamps in the world, and now almost priceless. By 1906 he had decided to concentrate on British and British Empire issues only, and arrangements were made for him to be presented with examples of every stamp produced by the Post Office and also those supplied by the Crown Agents for the Colonies. From 1910, following a suggestion from the Postmaster General, he received examples of all stamps registered with the Universal Postal Union at Berne, which meant, in effect, a copy of every new issue throughout the world. He generously gave all the foreign issues to the Royal Philatelic Society. For the rest of his life, George V, when in London, devoted three afternoons a week to his stamps. When he died, his collection contained at least one example of almost every stamp of Great Britain and the British Empire, housed in 325 albums – a collection, like the Leonardo or Holbein drawings, so substantial and so important of its kind that its philatelic value is incalculable.

The range is astonishing, starting with the earliest of all stamps, the famous penny black, a number of which probably came to him when his father bought the Duke of Edinburgh's collection and made him a present of it. This stamp, and others of the 1840s such as the twopenny blue, are masterpieces of careful, simple engraving. Printing these stamps, and developments like accurate perforation, required craftsmanship of the highest order; and here Britain led the world, and doubtless his sense of British achievement strengthened George V's interest. His appreciation of the superlative craftsmanship and the creative ingenuity which went into postage stamps gave him a special interest in many of the early experiments, such as the illustrated Mulready, a stamped postal envelope which was developed along with the first adhesive stamps. In fact, this envelope proved to be a disaster; it was exceptionally ornate, and one of the angels in the engraving had a leg missing, which led to an outburst of caricatures, some of which are in the royal collection. Mulready's envelope was withdrawn, but the idea flourished and spawned a host of privately produced illustrated envelopes, attacking slavery, supporting temperance and Sabbath Day Observance, or being used merely as trade advertisements. Indeed, the illustrated envelopes in the royal collection provide a vivid commentary on the social life and attitudes of Victorian England.

Although the adhesive postage stamp was surprisingly slow to spread

PAGE 298 *Artists' sketches for early stamp designs.* These stamp-sized miniature works of art, of which there are many in the Royal Collection, were used for approved designs, and as references for the engravers.
1 1840 watercolour sketch for the first stamps.
2 1848 Edward Henry Corbould watercolour sketch of Britannia. He has written, in pencil, 'The engraver with a magnifying glass (such as I have not) can finish the toenails rather more'. This sketch was used for the design of stamps for Barbados, Mauritius and Trinidad. 3 1854 Corbould watercolour sketch, used for Tasmania (Van Diemen's Land), see previous page. 4 1916 Montserrat, De La Rue artist's design for the new issue of stamps personally initialled as approved by King George V. 5 1922 Jamaica, De La Rue artist's design showing Port Royal. 6 1927 Barbados, Bradbury Wilkinson artist's watercolour drawing for the issue to commemorate the Tercentenary of British Settlement, showing King Charles I and King George V. 7 1932 Cayman Islands, Waterlow artist's watercolour drawing for the issue to commemorate the Centenary of the Legislative Assembly, showing King William IV and King George V.

PAGE 299 *The Pictorial Era: King George V Silver Jubilee and King George VI Coronation*
1, 2 and 3 Artist's watercolour drawings for a series of Jamaican stamps to be sold at a premium of ½d each for the Child Welfare League. 4, 5 and 6 1933 watercolour drawings for St Helena, for stamps to commemorate the Centenary of British Settlement, showing the heads of successive sovereigns, an island scene, a map and a representation of St Helena. 7, 8 and 9 1935 King George V, Silver Jubilee stamps. An unused design showing means of communication round the world, the design adopted for New Zealand and that adopted for the Crown Colonies, showing Windsor Castle. 10–14 1937 King George VI Coronation Stamps, a series of trial drawings – the issued design was based on the last shown.

PAGE 300 *King George VI Silver Wedding to Queen Elizabeth II*
1 1948 King George VI Silver Wedding colour trials. 2 1957 Turks and Caicos Islands, designs of local interest: a conch, flamingoes, a Spanish mackerel, Salt Cay, a Caicos sloop, the Cable Station, the Dependency's Badge depicting salt raking. 3, 4 and 5 1964 Falkland Islands. The first two stamps are the normal 2½d and 6d designs, the second 6d has a printing error and shows the wrong combination of frame and central design. The centre shows H.M.S. *Glasgow* (the design for the 2½d) and not, as it should, H.M.S. *Kent*

to the world at large, within the British Empire it flourished. Tiny islands such as Trinidad, Mauritius and Bermuda were quicker to realise its value than France or Russia, and by the time George V began to assemble his vast collection it had spread to the farthest corners of the empire. Pictorial stamps, which were developed during his reign, are a vivid memorial to its extent. There are seals sprawling on the coast of Newfoundland, the strange Booby birds gracing one of the stamps of the Cayman Islands, a view of Sydney in its infancy, the black swans of Western Australia, harbour scenes of colonies in the Caribbean, in the Pacific, in the Indian Ocean. These brilliantly etched little pieces of gummed paper encapsulate the imperial role of the British monarchy; on all the stamps, above the dhows passing some remote promontary, or the lonely freighter ploughing through empty seas, is the regal yet benign profile of George V.

The encouragement of this hobby by his uncle and his father was a brilliant intuitive act. Edward VII was deeply attached to his sons, particularly George V – their relationship was a vivid contrast to the troubled and difficult childhood he had experienced with his own parents – and yet the contrast in their two personalities was remarkable. Edward VII brought back colour and pageantry to the monarchy. He loved state occasions, the brilliance of the uniforms, the massed bands, the grandeur that surrounded the visits of his brother monarchs. Beneath the surface of these glittering occasions were political and diplomatic tensions, particularly between Germany and Britain, that Edward VII worked with all his diplomatic skill and personal charm to ease. That he failed was no fault of his. The conflict was too deep for any monarch to bridge.

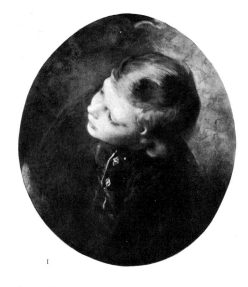

1

1 James Sant, *King George V when a Boy.*
2 The Game Museum, Sandringham

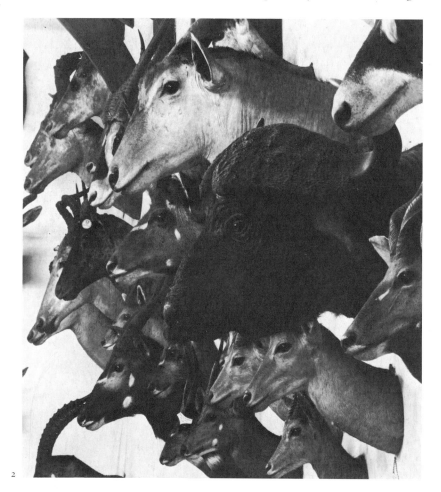

2

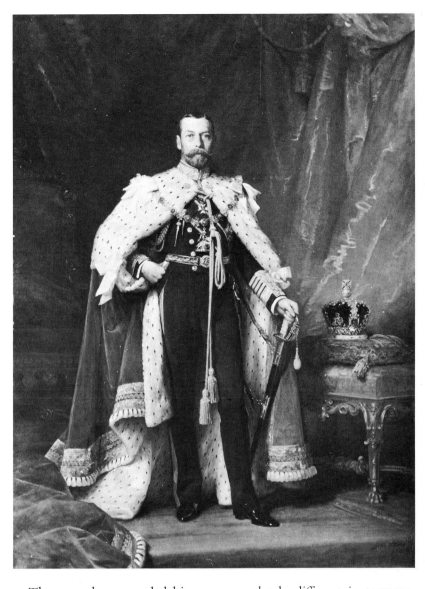

Sir Luke Fildes, *King George V*. 1912

The son who succeeded him was completely different in temperament. As King he went on living, until his mother died in 1925, in a modest villa, York Cottage, at Sandringham. The King's sitting-room and study there are no bigger than one would find in a double-bayed house in Wimbledon or Clapham. The bedroom in which Queen Mary gave birth to all of her children, save one, is modest in size. Both naturally retiring people, they loved the house for its domesticity. The King enjoyed country pursuits. He was a splendid shot – many of his trophies are in the Game Museum at Sandringham – and he sailed with great skill; sailing was one of the great passions of his life (as it had been his father's), and he raced regularly at Cowes, often in friendly combat with Sir Thomas Lipton, the tea merchant. Unlike his father, whose horses won the Derby twice, and who undoubtedly increased his vast popularity by his patronage of the turf, racing was for George V a pleasant formal duty rather than a passionate enthusiasm. Again, unlike his father, he did not enjoy large weekend parties, endless dinners, cards and gossip. In the evening he preferred either to work in his study, or better still, sit with Queen Mary and read aloud to her. In this he seems, like his father, to have found instinctively a style which accorded with what their subjects thought right for their monarchs, one which matched the age in which they lived. The Edwardians expected a profuse ostentation. George V and Queen Mary, however, were to live through not only the terrible disasters of the first world war, but the grim years of the 1920s that culminated in the General Strike of 1926, the bitter conflicts in Ireland, the terrible depression of the 1930s and the renewed menace of fascism in Germany and Italy. In a desperate world of shifting and changing values, of revolution and disaster, they reflected an image of quiet dignity and family probity, a monarchy that was dignified, dedicated, and given in no way to excess.

But before catastrophe came, in 1914, there was one occasion of imperial splendour which Edward VII would have fully enjoyed and to which George V looked forward with considerable trepidation: the great Durbar which he held as King-Emperor at Delhi in December 1911. His father, as Prince of Wales, had visited India and enjoyed every moment of it – its colour, its beauty, its antiquity, the splendour of its princes and the richness of its game. But he had gone as the Queen's representative; 1911 was the first time a reigning monarch had visited India. Already there was a strong and vigorous movement towards independence, a growing criticism of the archaism of princely India; the King was well aware of all this and his forebodings seemed to be confirmed when he rode into Delhi through a crowd of 50,000, mainly silent, Indians. In fact they were confused – they expected their Emperor to ride in on an elephant and he had passed them on his horse before they quite realised who he was. The great Durbar that followed, with the Princes of India making their homage, was planned with impressive grandeur. The King and Queen sat crowned and in their robes of state and so not outmatched by the dazzling jewel-bedecked costumes of the princes, some of whom were richer than some European sovereigns.

As his grandmother had done on her tours, the King had taken along with him an official artist, Jacomb Hood, to record the highlights of the Durbar, but photographers and film makers went, too. The steady development and improvement of still and movie cameras were making unposed, outdoor action shots of royal occasions both easier and more dramatic. No monarch had been photographed so extensively as Edward VII and he was the first to be frequently filmed, but the exposure to the

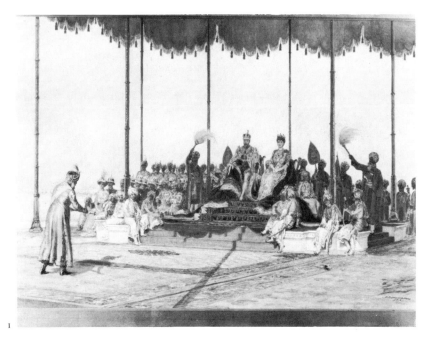

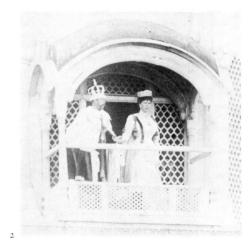

1 Jacomb Hood, watercolour of *The Delhi Durbar*.
2 King George V and Queen Mary at the Durbar, 12 December 1911

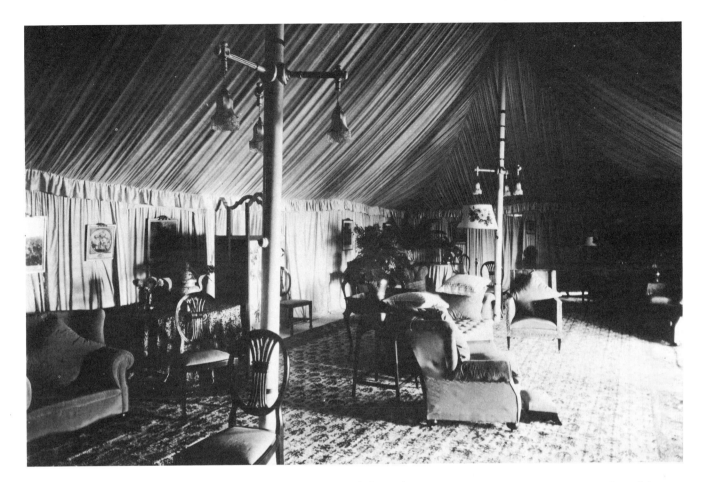

Queen Mary's sitting-room at the Delhi
Camp, December 1911

camera and, therefore, to the world's press steadily increased throughout
the twentieth century. Gradually more intimate scenes of royal family
life were published in newspapers and magazines, to the delight not only
of millions of Britons, but also of Europeans and Americans. This
development was carefully fostered by George V's descendants, who
acceded to the ever-increasing demands of their subjects, while retaining
both the dignity of monarchy and a core of personal privacy; this delicate
balance has been maintained with an exceptional skill that has met the
challenge of television as easily as that of action photography and film.
Although film of the 1911 Durbar now appears quite primitive in
technique, it was startling at the time. It brought royal events enacted in
India into tiny picture palaces scattered throughout Britain. After the
Durbar more and more royal activities were eagerly followed on the
screen and in consequence ordinary people became much more aware of
the burden of the monarchy – the relentless nature of its yearly rituals.

Not only did improvements in cameras and filming please the public,
it also greatly pleased the royal family itself. By the accession of George V
the royal photographic collection was immense, but it grew even more.
His mother, herself an excellent photographer, had added a very large
number of prints. Queen Mary, a natural collector, possessed a most
sympathetic eye for photography, and was quick to seize on human and
moving situations for her own collection. One of the finest photographs
in her albums is of the shy, reserved, yet easily moved King bending
down to talk to a tiny, ragged young steel worker in Sunderland; a
twinkle in the King's eye and a broad toothy grin across the boy's face.
This picture was taken in the desperate conditions brought about in the
twenties by the social and economic upheavals caused by the first world

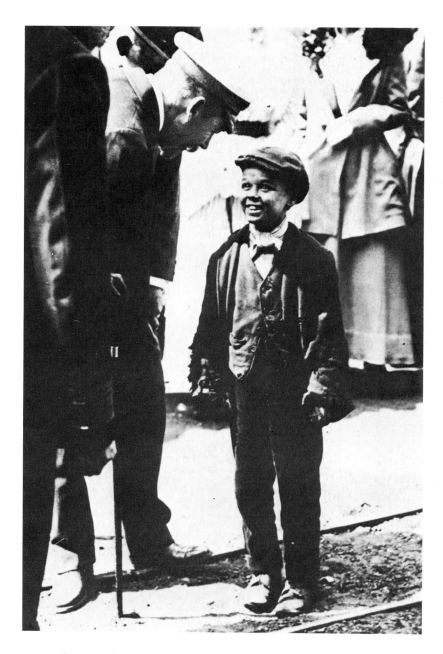

King George V and a boy. Sunderland, June 1917

war. The British monarchy survived these crises, which brought the world in which George V and Queen Mary had grown up to ruins, as strong as before. During the war the King visited his troops in France as often as his ministers would let him. His son, Edward Prince of Wales, was eager to serve in the trenches. The future George VI was a midshipman at the Battle of Jutland. Queen Mary, the Princess Royal and other members of the family helped the King on his endless visits to factories, ports, troop camps, and hospitals. They went out to the people as Edward VII had done when he interested himself in slum housing — shirking none of the horrors, and never closing their eyes to the shortcomings of their society or the tribulations which ordinary men and women were experiencing. All of these activities were recorded and the films and the photographs are a priceless part of the royal inheritance, giving vivid life to one of the most critical phases of Britain's destiny.

It was also a bitter experience for the royal family itself. The King and Kaiser Wilhelm of Germany were cousins and although frequently infuriated by the Kaiser's arrogance, they had been moved both by his charm and his devotion to his grandmother, Queen Victoria. It was a

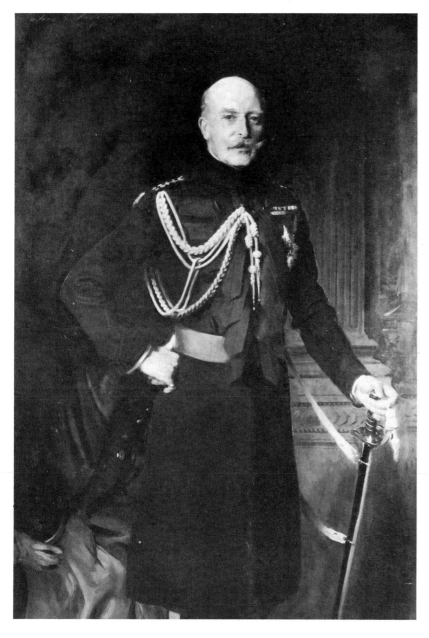

John Singer Sargent, *Arthur, Duke of Connaught*

hideous experience to be locked in battle with his country; even more hideous was the slaughter of the entire family of their Russian relatives to whom they were closely attached.

Every British family had its tragedies, and the royal family was no exception. The King also suffered severe injury during these war years. Whilst visiting troops his horse took fright, reared, threw him and then rolled on him, breaking his pelvis. He returned to England in immense pain, unfortunately having experienced at first hand the suffering and physical torment of so many of his wounded soldiers. Yet these years that were so disastrous for many of the thrones of Europe forged deeper bonds between the King and Queen of Britain and their people. Their total dedication, without a hint of flamboyance, increased their popularity. At the same time both maintained an air of regality. Queen Mary particularly, by the cultivation of an intensely personal, somewhat idiosyncratic style of dress, seemed beyond fashion, yet everyone's idea of a Queen. Less striking, perhaps, than the Queen's, the King's style too was very personal and recalled the stability, the order, the traditions of an earlier age in a world adrift and over-excited by the new and the fashionable. Although they were constantly seen, photographed and filmed, they maintained some of the ancient mystique of monarchy in an age where class barriers were crumbling and the demand for a wider social democracy grew ever more loud. Wherever they went they drew enormous crowds.

George V and his wife were well matched. But both were very shy, somewhat inarticulate when it came to expressing their emotions and, therefore, awkward and reserved towards their children. They felt deep anxiety over their eldest son, afterwards Edward VIII. He seemed too eager to participate in the fast, sophisticated life of the 1920s. Yet his charm was so immense that he captivated the people as much, if not more, than his parents, and the illustrated papers and the news films were rarely without his picture, whether he was hunting in the shires, dancing in a night club, or visiting a working men's institute. In the twentieth century the royal family have acquired a daily audience of hundreds of millions, for Americans and Europeans follow their lives with avid interest. Nevertheless, when Edward VIII's liaison with Mrs Simpson began, the British press was all discretion, judging more wisely than he the mood of his people. This dialogue between monarchy and the press has been of exceptional importance to the monarchy in the twentieth century and one which required great skill in its handling. When used with brilliance, it has been of immense service to the popularity of the monarchy.

There is no doubt that the shy, retiring Queen Mary was as instinctively skilful as any King or Queen of this century in strengthening the affection in which monarchy was held. She possessed curiosity about people as well as things and a warmth towards people. In the second world war hitch-hiking members of the armed forces in Gloucestershire, where Queen Mary lived at Badminton House, would be astonished to see the royal Daimler draw up. He or she would be bidden to get in. Gentle, kindly questions about family followed and sincere best wishes as they were put down on their way to home or camp. An abiding curiosity that was energetic, perceptive and tireless was an important feature of Queen Mary's character – and one which responded deeply to her husband's great inheritance. She acquired a great knowledge of every aspect of the royal buildings and collections. She herself compulsively collected everything from bibelots and mementoes to important works of art, but was more concerned with the decorative arts than with old master paintings and drawings. A superb embroiderer herself (she often worked the tapestries used to re-cover eighteenth-century chairs), she had a keen eye for furniture and decorative objects – particularly those which reached a high degree of craftsmanship. She did appreciate portraits, particularly if they had a connection with her ancestors, and nothing gave her more delight than a bibelot with a portrait of a former sovereign, such as the exceptionally fine tea caddy of cedarwood, decorated in ivory and ebony, with portrait medallions of George III and Queen Charlotte, or the magnificent tortoiseshell snuff box with a gold lid bearing a fine profile medallion of George IV as Prince Regent. Over a very long life, she acquired scores of Chinese snuff bottles, Battersea enamels, *Vernis Martin* boxes, and fine jades. Magnificent examples of eighteenth-century English and European porcelain filled the rooms of Marlborough House, where she spent so many years of her widowhood. She was a regular

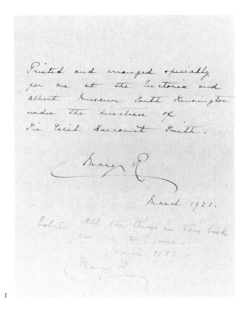

1

Pages from the illustrated catalogue to Queen Mary's collection.
1 Her autographed notes on the contents.
2 A page from the catalogue

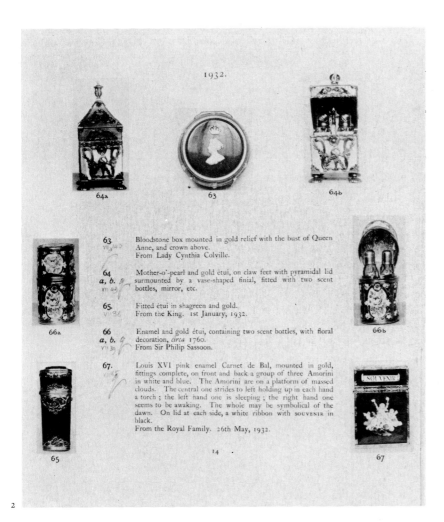

1932.

64a	63	64b

63. Bloodstone box mounted in gold relief with the bust of Queen Anne, and crown above.
From Lady Cynthia Colville.

64 a, b. Mother-o'-pearl and gold étui, on claw feet with pyramidal lid surmounted by a vase-shaped finial, fitted with two scent bottles, mirror, etc.

65. Fitted étui in shagreen and gold.
From the King. 1st January, 1932.

66 a, b. Enamel and gold étui, containing two scent bottles, with floral decoration, *circa* 1760.
From Sir Philip Sassoon.

67. Louis XVI pink enamel Carnet de Bal, mounted in gold, fittings complete, on front and back a group of three Amorini in white and blue. The Amorini are on a platform of massed clouds. The central one strides to left holding up in each hand a torch ; the left hand one is sleeping ; the right hand one seems to be awaking. The whole may be symbolical of the dawn. On lid at each side, a white ribbon with SOUVENIR in black.
From the Royal Family. 26th May, 1932.

66a   66b

65   67

14

visitor to small antique shops in Cambridge or King's Lynn, as well as to the famous dealers in Bond Street. In 1937 the catalogues of her acquisitions ran to three stout volumes, and she herself wrote in her own hand what was the origin and the purpose of her collecting: 'The nucleus of the collection ... was formed in 1893, from the personal gifts to the Queen on the occasion of Her Majesty's marriage. The collection has been added to by gifts and purchases, and, in extending it, Her Majesty has aimed principally at the acquisition of objects of historical and personal interest relating to the Royal Family.'

The gifts recall nostalgically the empire that is no longer ours; indeed Queen Mary lived long enough to witness its passing. There is a pair of diamond-studded bracelets given by the Maharajah of Bikaner in 1907, a star-shaped box of beaten gold set with rubies given by the ladies of Singapore in 1901, an Indian necklace with gold coins and diamonds given by the Sultan of Lahej at Aden in 1901, and a carved ivory box with gold mounts given by the tea planters of Ceylon. Not great works of art, surely, but mementoes of imperial voyages, of an age that passed quickly and is now touched with pathos and nostalgia. On these voyages, particularly that to India in 1911, the Queen's discerning eye was captivated by the beauty of seventeenth-century Mogul art, and she was able to slip away from the exhausting formalities for a sufficient time to make one or two outstanding purchases, including two fine crystal cups of the early seventeenth century. She never lost this passion for the Mogul decorative arts, and for the next twenty-five years and more she steadily added pieces of great quality, so that the Mogul section is one of

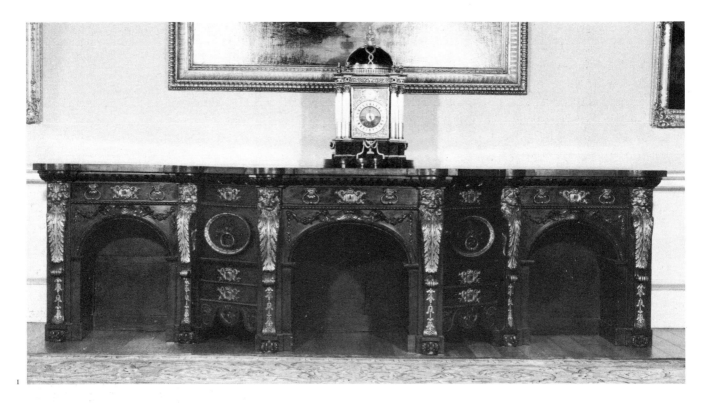

the most distinctive strands of the collection as a whole. But the finest contribution Queen Mary made was probably furniture. William Vile, as distinguished, many would say, as Thomas Chippendale, made many pieces for George III for Buckingham Palace, and Queen Mary greatly admired his work. She was able to buy a richly carved mahogany sideboard and a gilt and mahogany commode which may date from the early years of William Vile's career when the influence of William Kent, the great decorative artist of the early eighteenth century, was still very strong. Once they were confidently attributed to him but it is so difficult to make definite attributions without evidence of bills or other documents that there is now considerable doubt as to their authorship. Whether by Vile or not, they are superb pieces of furniture worthy of a royal palace.

As much as collecting Queen Mary enjoyed restoring to their original homes long parted objects – furniture moved from Brighton Pavilion or Windsor or Buckingham Palace. When the Corporation of Brighton decided to restore Brighton Pavilion to what it had been in the days of the Prince Regent, the curators found a tireless patron in Queen Mary. She ransacked the bedrooms and attics of Buckingham Palace and Windsor, ferreted through storerooms in search of furniture and objects bearing the Pavilion mark, and when she discovered them, persuaded first her husband and then her son, George VI, to loan them to Brighton, where they belonged. H.M. the Queen has continued to embellish the pavilion with furniture that is known to have belonged there. Often, too, Queen Mary's knowledge and quick eye would discover a pavilion piece in an antique dealer's; immediately it was on its way to Brighton. Her enthusiasm and her dedication were invaluable in the restoration of one of the most exotic of all royal palaces in Europe. Brighton's debt to her was immense.

As with Brighton, so with Holyroodhouse, the royal palace in the heart of Edinburgh, the ancient home of King George V's Stuart fore-

1 Mahogany sideboard attributed to William Vile, 1740.
2 A case of Queen Mary's collection of jades. These were in her Dining Room at Marlborough House, but are now at Buckingham Palace – still in their original showcase

bears. The old palace had been swept away, except for King James IV's Tower which contained the historic rooms associated with Mary Queen of Scots. Although her bedroom has suffered many alterations, two panels of needlework embroidered by her hang over the fireplace. The rest of the palace was replaced by a classical Palladian building, the first in Scotland, designed by Sir William Bruce and begun in 1671 by Charles II. It was still unfinished in 1680 when the money ran out, and it was still unfinished when King George and Queen Mary came to the throne. They decided to complete the building and to use it regularly. The restoration was undertaken with scholarly care so that the new panelling and stucco-work harmonised exactly with the old. And naturally Queen Mary took an eager interest in securing appropriate furniture for the newly completed rooms. They used their new palace at Edinburgh frequently for state visits and enjoyed residing there; so have their children and grandchildren so that, once again, Scotland possesses a formal palace as well as a royal home. The palace has continued to be embellished, and Queen Elizabeth II and Prince Philip have added a distinguished collection of pictures by modern Scottish painters.

The restoration of Brighton Pavilion and the completion of Holyroodhouse showed Queen Mary and George V's passionate interest in the royal inheritance and their dedication to its preservation. At both Brighton and Holyroodhouse the highest standards both of scholarship and preservation were maintained; both King George and Queen Mary regarded themselves (as, indeed, had many of their ancestors, particularly George IV and Prince Albert) as guardians rather than owners of national treasures. During Queen Mary's lifetime, there was scarcely a

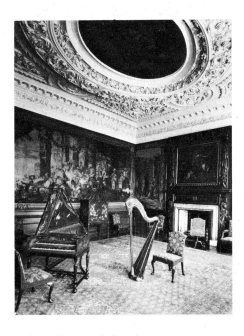

Holyroodhouse, Edinburgh

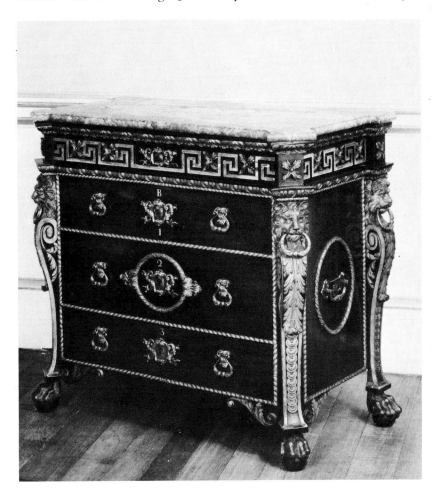

Mahogany and gilt commode attributed to William Vile – about 1740

major exhibition, at the Royal Academy or elsewhere, to which the royal collection did not make an important contribution; and no exhibition of any magnitude went without a visit from the Queen. She was a pillar of strength to the directors of London's museums and particularly the Victoria and Albert Museum, in which she took a special interest. She learned a great deal about conservation, about the need for careful cataloguing, and for proper scholarly research into so vast a collection as she and her husband possessed. During this reign, the royal collections were placed in the hands of distinguished scholars in the world of art – a process which has continued and expanded until the present day.

Queen Mary's devotion to the decorative arts and the time and care she spent on the royal houses and palaces led, in 1920, to a group of people choosing a gift that would serve as a gesture of good will to the Queen and, at the same time, help raise money for her favourite charities. This was the origin of the Queen's Dolls' House. It was first exhibited at the Great Empire Exhibition at Wembley in 1926 and has continued to draw tens of thousands of visitors a year to Windsor Castle. It is a brilliant, almost unbelievable *tour de force*, the most elegant and the most successful.

Queen Mary had always delighted in miniature objects. She had added many tiny Fabergé pieces to Queen Alexandra's collection and she rarely failed to purchase a small object of high craftsmanship; so the idea of a dolls' house was appropriate and, as the promoters well knew, miniaturism has always had an immense popular appeal. The dolls' house is really a Palladian country house of regal splendour. It was designed by Sir Edwin Lutyens, an ebullient man who combined tradition with orig-

Queen Mary's Dolls' House. The ceremonial entrance hall and staircase

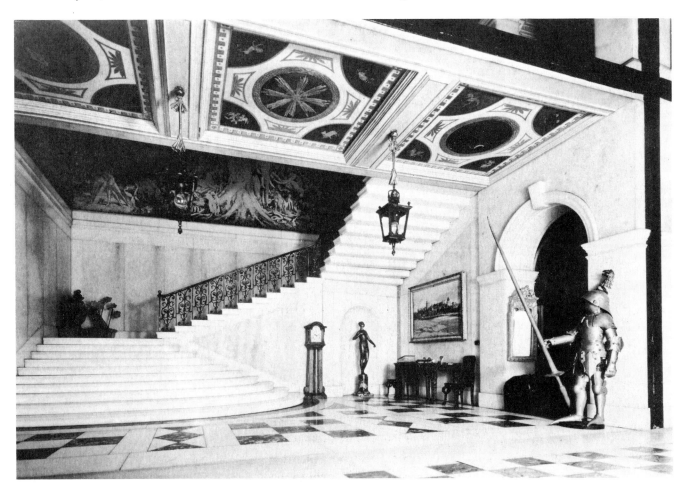

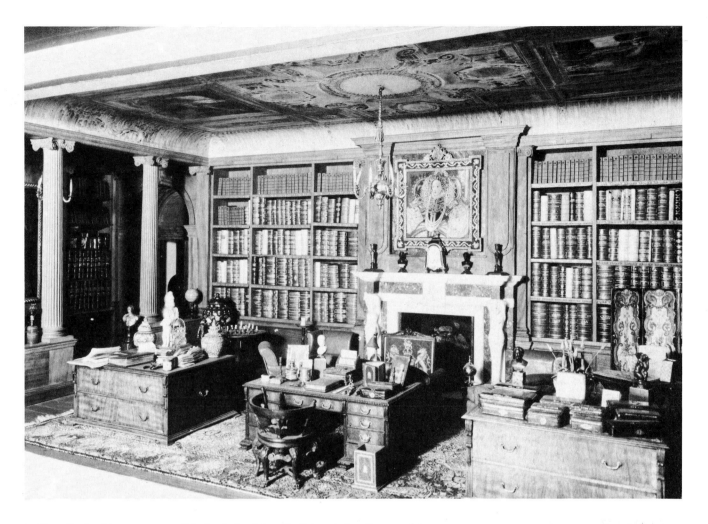

inality (he had been responsible both for New Delhi and the Cenotaph).
Everything in the house was to be to the scale of one-twelfth: if a book
was twelve inches high, for the dolls' house library it had to be one inch.
From the nursery to the garage, everything is there and perfect. There
were difficult technical problems: wire made to the scale required would
not lie flat on a pulley, so fine fishing line was used for the lift ropes, and
the lifts work perfectly! Similar problems were overcome for the leather
and paper of books, and for the linen; only the taps in the scullery slightly
jar because of their size – odd because the silver taps in the King's
bathroom not only seem correct, but work perfectly to fill the marble
bath or washbasins. Indeed, everything works, no matter how small –
the electric lighting, the almost paper-thin door locks and keys, the
knife-grinding machine in the kitchen, the minute clocks on the man-
telpieces. And all rooms show a remarkable perfection of craftsmanship:
the silver candelabra in the drawing-room; the sofas and settees in the
salon, the King's canopied bed, the roll-topped desk in the Queen's
bedroom, with its garniture of miniature porcelain; and the minute
uniforms and swords in the King's wardrobe. When enlarged by photography these appear as perfect as they would have been had they been
made for a royal palace.

What was most remarkable was the enthusiasm with which so many
distinguished men and women entered into the project. The writers and
artists of the day responded magnificently and the library contains two
very remarkable collections. There are over 700 tiny prints, drawings
and watercolours. Adrian Stokes, Edmund Dulac, Sir William Nicholson,

The Dolls' House library. Most of the books
were specially written for it; the authors
include Hardy, Conrad and Kipling. Above
the marble fireplace hangs Sir William
Nicholson's portrait of Queen Elizabeth I. The
two cabinets contain a collection of miniature
drawings

Mark Gertler, Paul and John Nash, and many other artists contributed, including a number of cartoonists – H. M. Bateman, Heath Robinson and 'Fougasse', amongst others. Other painters provided the pictures for the walls; two splendid state portraits of King George and Queen Mary by Sir William Orpen flank the chimney-piece in the drawing-room; A. M. McEvoy presented an astonishing pastiche of Winterhalter's famous painting of Queen Victoria, the Prince Consort and their family, and Sir Alfred Munnings painted Edward Prince of Wales on horseback. Even in so tiny a picture Munnings manages to create a sense of movement and of the wide-open midland shires. Authors, as well as painters, were invited to contribute to the dolls' house and the library is full of tiny, beautiful leather-bound volumes. Not surprisingly Sir James Barrie, a self-involved little man, presented his own autobiography; Max Beerbohm wrote *The Meditations of a Refugee*, and M. R. James, naturally enough, *The Haunted Dolls' House*. Conan Doyle found a miniature story for Sherlock Holmes, *How Watson Learned the Trick*. Arnold Bennett produced a small story about Xmas, but Joseph Conrad contented himself with a small quotation from a published book. Poetry, light-hearted for the main part, abounded – Thomas Hardy, Robert Bridges, Edmund Blunden, Aldous Huxley, Robert Graves, and many others. Even A. E. Housman. The only note of gravity was struck by Viscount Haldane, who produced *An Essay on Humanism*, and by C. F. Voysey, who offered *Ideas in Things*, scarcely a miniature subject; and Sir James Frazer copied three conventional extracts from *The Golden Bough*. Never before and never again will so distinguished a clutch of authors write for a dolls' library!

The most distinguished practitioners in every field were eager to help. Not surprisingly the wine-cellar was handed over to George Saintsbury, the greatest wine-bibber of his age, who was also a literary critic of great distinction. The bottles are one inch high, and are filled with some of the most precious vintages that Saintsbury had enjoyed in a very long life of daily drinking – a Château Margaux 1899, Château Yquem 1874, a Cockburn port of 1874, and Madeira (an especial favourite of Saintsbury's) of 1820. As a Professor at Edinburgh, Saintsbury learned to love single malts and there are quarter casks of fine whisky, along with bottled Bass, and Bass in cask. Nor did Saintsbury forget the tools of the butler's trade – there are miniature corkscrews, bottle-baskets, wine-funnels, and the rest.

As with the wine cellar, so with the garden, for so regal a dolls' house necessitated a garden, and there was only one choice for the designer – Gertrude Jekyll, the greatest designer of her day, who had for years given her advice to the royal family. Perhaps this is the most ingenious of all parts of the dolls' house, for the garden had to be stowed away in one of the drawers in the base. So each tree had to be designed to lie down horizontally when the drawer was closed, which meant that it had to avoid the flower beds and the shrubberies. There are four flower beds, filled with summer flowers – irises, carnations, sweet peas, tiger-lilies, tiny tubs of azalea and rhododendron. There are butterflies on the flowers, a snail or two, birds, and a thrush's nest with eggs. Like everything else in the house, the ingenuity and craftsmanship are quite remarkable. It is whimsical, almost frivolous at first sight, but astonishing in its completeness: the tiny lavatory pans actually flush, the lift lifts, and one can play the gramophone or the grand piano.

The public loved it when they first saw it at Wembley, and it still raises great sums for those charities in which Queen Elizabeth the Queen Mother, to whom the dolls' house now belongs, is specially interested.

Both the King's stamp album and the Queen's Dolls' House are, in a sense, symbolic of the route that the monarchy was taking. In the homes of millions of their subjects there were humble collections of stamps for the boys, small dolls' houses for the girls; as the aristocracy and gentry of Regency England could identify with the Prince Regent's interest in important pictures and fine furniture, so could millions of ordinary men and women identify with the King's hobby and the Queen's delight. And in more profound ways, too, the monarchy began to reach out to the poorest, the most deprived and hard-pressed of their people. No matter how bitter the industrial strife, or how wretched the conditions, the King and the Queen never hesitated to visit and to comfort, blunting by their presence the razor-edge of social bitterness, and helping to promulgate the sense of one family, one people. At the time the great economic crisis, which plunged England into the deep depression of the 1930s, the King and his advisers decided that words of comfort, hope and endeavour spoken by him on Christmas Day would be deeply appreciated by the nation, and so, in 1932, he made his first Christmas Day broadcast from Sandringham. Millions of families throughout England, the Empire and the world sat in silence around their wireless sets and listened to his words of hope. Twenty-five years later, millions more were able to watch Queen Elizabeth II give her Christmas message on television, from the same study that her grandfather had used.

George V's Christmas messages to Britain and the Empire were few. His health, from the time of his injury in France, was never strong, and in the twenties he suffered severe illnesses that forced him against his will to give up, for a time, his public duties. In the end his frail constitution gave way, and England lost a King who showed instinctive skill in adapting the monarchy to the modern world – making it constantly visible without losing its dignity and mystique. Far more than any of his ministers he realised and readily recognised the strict limitations of constitutional monarchy, as well as its duties and its right to warn and advise. Even when denied a knighthood for a man of outstanding accomplishment by Lloyd George, he accepted with wry good humour, whereas his grandmother or his father would have exploded with indignation. The depth of his country's feeling for him was apparent when the BBC announced the fatal words, 'The King's life is drawing peacefully to a close'. The nation itself mourned and kept vigil.

Edward VIII who, within months, plunged the country into its first serious constitutional crisis since the seventeenth century, had little time to add either to the buildings or the collections. Before his accession he had restored the derelict Fort Belvedere in Windsor Great Park, where he created a beautiful garden. He was an ardent gardener, as indeed was his brother, George VI, who succeeded him.

Both George VI, by his simplicity and dignity, and Queen Elizabeth, by her charm and grace, and by their constant devotion to their royal duties, quickly re-established the popularity and the traditional role of monarchy. Yet they had hardly begun to rule before their country was plunged into the crises that resulted in the cataclysm of the second world war. Never had Britain been in greater peril than in 1940, never before had her people suffered the terrible ravages of war at home. The monarchy, like the people, responded nobly. The King visited Coventry the morning after its bombing; both the King and the Queen picked their way through the rubble of the East End of London, giving encouragement and bringing hope. They shared with their fellow countrymen the experience of being bombed – Buckingham Palace was hit twice, the chapel devastated, the King's study windows blown in. They kept a record in photographs and film, which illustrated the heroism of ordinary men and women as well as their own deep concern for the sufferings of their people. And never were the Christmas messages from Sandringham more welcome than during those bitter years.

They spent the nights and some weekends at Windsor with their young daughters, who themselves played as active a part as their age allowed in the war effort. On one remarkable occasion the young Princess Elizabeth spoke words of comfort and of hope to the children of England. At Windsor the King and Queen took solace in gardening. When victory came, the people thronged to Buckingham Palace in their thousands for the traditional moment – the appearance of the royal family on the balcony; from Queen Mary to the young princesses, the royal family had to return again and again to their cheering people.

The King's health, never strong, had been weakened by the strain of war and the years of economic and social crisis that followed took their toll. When he could escape from the constant round of public duties he spent time encouraging the construction of the splendid Savill Gardens, named by the King's command after Sir Edward Savill, who also designed the even more beautiful Valley Gardens. The King was also actively concerned with the garden at the Royal Lodge. This was not a time for excessive expenditure on old masters, whose prices soared astonishingly, but both the King and the Queen gave their patronage during their reign to British artists and John Piper did a notable series of paintings of Windsor Castle that evoke the storm-ridden years of the second world war and its aftermath. After the war the King, realising perhaps how fundamentally Europe had changed, assembled for the Long Gallery at Windsor a collection of medals and orders that recalled the days of his father and grandfather when Europe glittered with them.

Meanwhile the King's health grew worse. Visits to Australia and New Zealand had to be postponed and he underwent drastic surgery. He seemed to recover, but died suddenly at Sandringham, the house he loved best of all, on 6 February 1952.

So England had a young and radiant Queen, whose coronation was the most spectacular royal event television had ever recorded. Queen Elizabeth the Queen Mother moved to Clarence House, to whose furnishing and adornment she brought her discerning eye. She had added several pictures of exceptional quality, two lovely impressionists – a Monet and a Sisley – excellent sporting pictures by the Herrings and James Seymour. And she patronised many outstanding British painters. She also formed a splendid collection of Chelsea porcelain, amongst which are many plates from the famous Hans Sloane service, perhaps the finest ever made by eighteenth-century English manufacturers of porcelain. She could also be brave, as well as wise, in her patronage, sitting for her portrait by Graham Sutherland, the finest yet the most candid of English portrait painters today. The result is a miraculously human portrait –

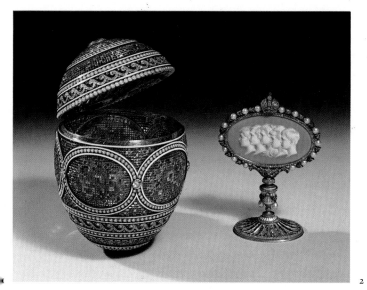

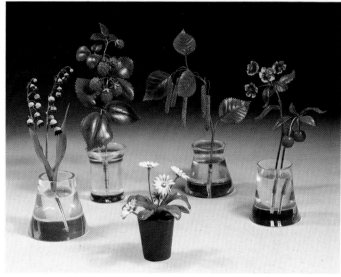

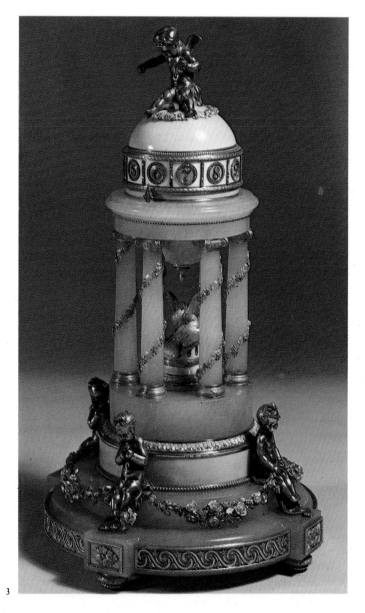

Carl Fabergé: 1 Easter egg in platinum and gold, containing a stand showing portraits of the children of Tsar Nicholas II. Originally presented by the Tsar to the Tsarina. Dated 1914. 2 Flowers and fruit in rock crystal pots. 3 The Colonnade Egg, presented to the Tsarina by Tsar Nicholas II. *c.* 1905

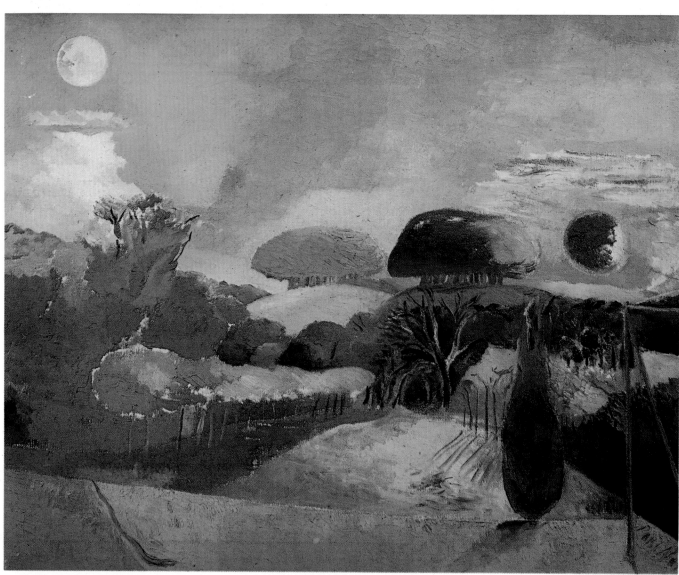

1

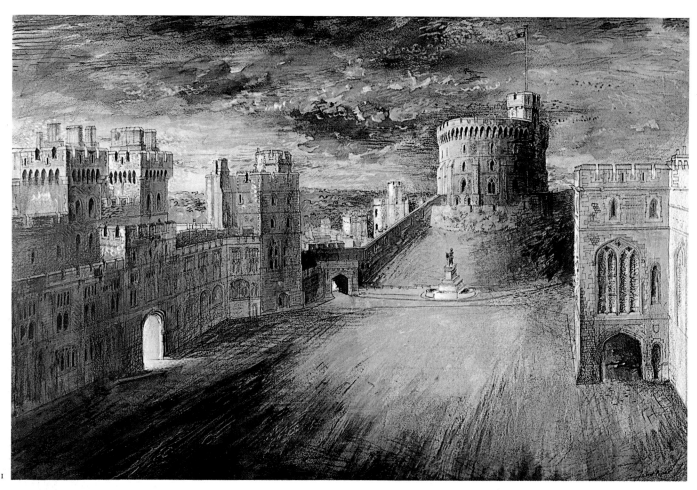

2

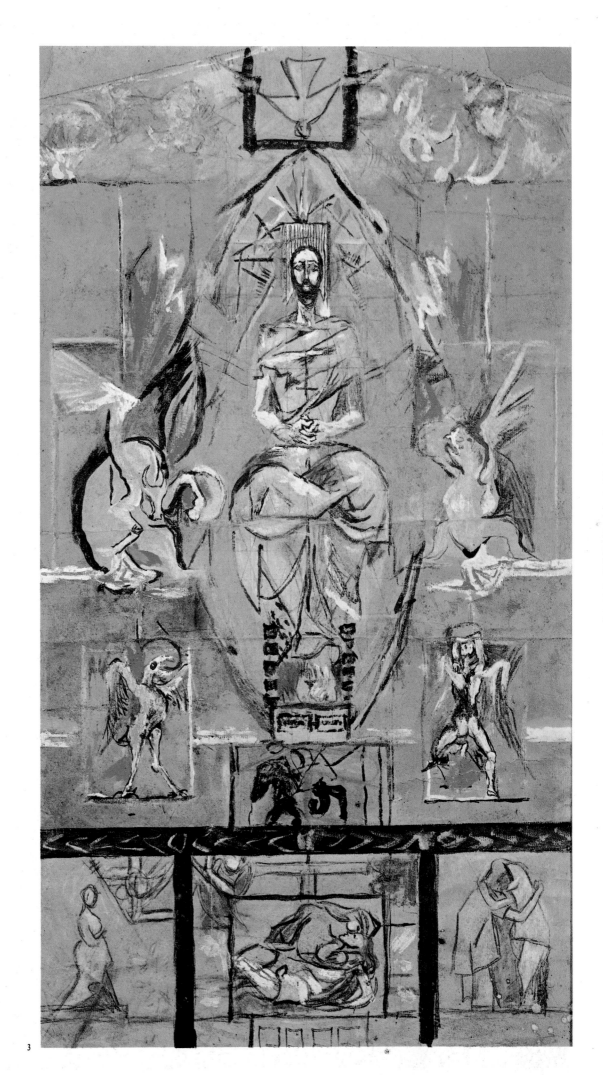

John Piper, *Windsor Castle*: the Quadrangle looking towards the Round Tower. 1942. Paul Nash, *Landscape of the Vernal Equinox*. Painted in 1934. Bought by Queen Elizabeth the Queen Mother. Graham Sutherland, *Study for Christ in Glory*. A study for the tapestry at Coventry Cathedral. In the lower section is a triptych with a Pietà in the centre, Annunciation on the left and Visitation on the right. Purchased by the Queen in 1962

3

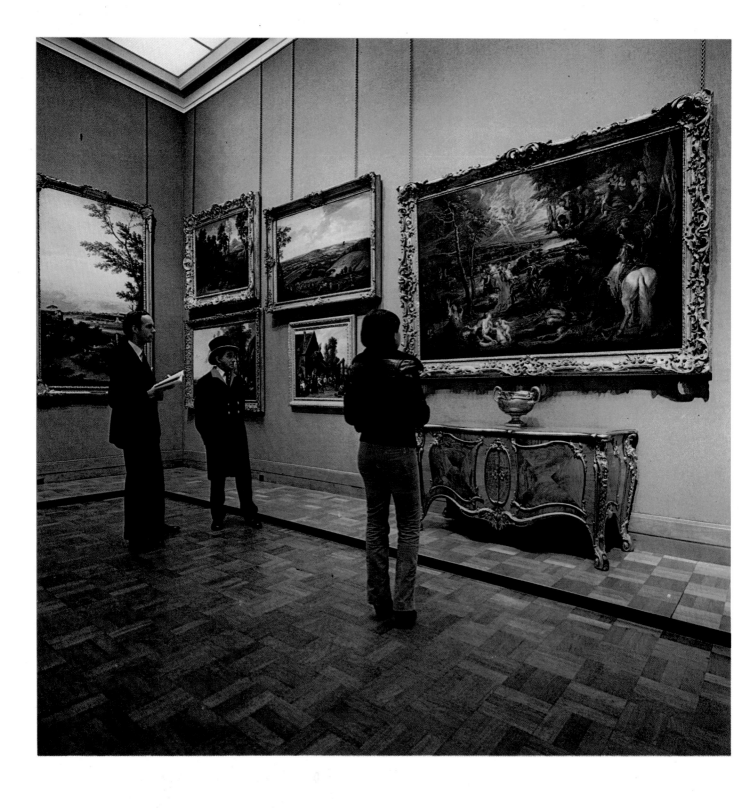

The Queen's Gallery, Buckingham Palace, was opened to the public in 1962. Exhibitions of works from the Royal Collections are regularly held there

light-years away from some of the stuffy state portraits that all monarchs have to endure. Her delight in the arts has also made her a willing and generous patron not only of music and the opera, but also of those societies bent on presenting the artistic heritage of Britain, to which she herself has made a notable contribution.

On the wild north coast of Scotland, there was a very small but perfect sixteenth-century castle at Mey, rapidly falling into decay. Another decade of neglect and the castle would have been so ruinous that repair would have been impossible. The Queen Mother bought the castle from her own funds and restored it with the utmost care for the authenticity of detail and so created what perhaps will be the last royal castle – small, remote, a gem preserved. And even on these wild shores the Queen Mother conjured a tiny traditional garden appropriate to that furthermost part of Scotland. There her sitting-room looks out to the most storm-ridden shores of Britain.

There is a tiny harbour just below the castle, and when the Queen Mother first took up residence the royal yacht, *Britannia*, steamed into the bay with her family, coming to greet her in her new home. *Britannia* is the last of a long line of royal yachts going back down the centuries. Three previous yachts had been named *Victoria and Albert*; the last had been built in 1899. After the war it was too out of date for further use. Royal yachts are expensive, yet essential. There are still foreign

The Castle of Mey, Caithness, Scotland

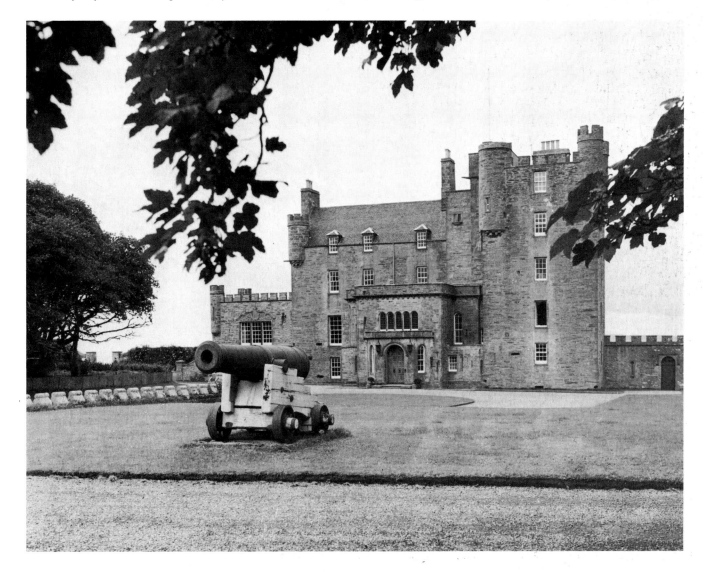

countries, as well as the great dominions and tiny islands of the commonwealth, demanding the royal presence. On state visits to foreign countries the Queen has to entertain on a scale that is often not possible in her smaller embassies; also the yacht gives greater security in a dangerous world. And yet to Queen Elizabeth II and her husband a yacht for themselves seemed too vast an expense. So the yacht *Britannia* was designed for a dual purpose – for a hospital ship in case of need and as a royal yacht.

Prince Philip's deep knowledge of ships and his long experience of the sea played a great part in creating the finest royal yacht ever built. Since it was commissioned, in 1959, it has travelled over 50,000 miles, encircling the globe several times. Comfort and efficiency are never in conflict. The royal apartments (these can be transformed into wards) were decorated by Sir Hugh Casson, and they contain, as does the ship as a whole, mementoes of the past as well as presents made to the royal family on recent voyages. The ornate binnacle on the verandah deck comes from the *Royal George*, the yacht used by George IV on his visit to Ireland – the first to use steam, although at that date merely as a supplement to sail. Relics of Queen Victoria's yachts are more frequent and the ever-inventive Prince Albert was responsible for the gimbal table in the drawing-room. This room, also, contains an impressive amount of furniture that came from the *Victoria and Albert II*.

The dining-room is at its most impressive when the table is laid for a state occasion. Then the beautiful silver nefs are set out. These are models in silver of the carracks which sailed across the oceans of the world on voyages of discovery in the late sixteenth and early seventeenth centuries – ships which hark back to the great seafarers of Elizabethan England – Drake, Frobisher, Gilbert and the rest. The detailed craftsmanship of these small silver ships is exceptionally fine, but it is their historic symbolism which, perhaps, is their most remarkable

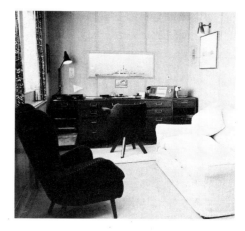

H.M.Y. *Britannia*: Prince Philip's sitting-room

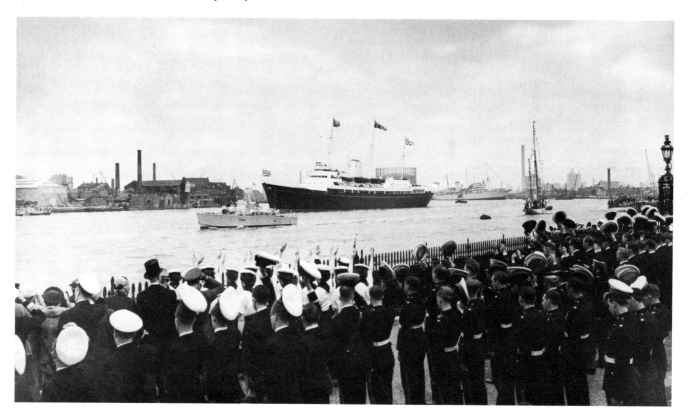

The royal yacht *Britannia*, sailing up the Thames past the Royal Naval College, Greenwich

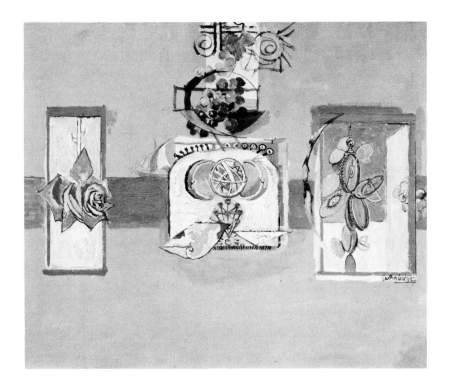

Graham Sutherland, *The Armillary Sphere*. 1957. An abstract painting on the theme of exploration: the armillary sphere in its case; Drake's Dial; the English rose; grapes to symbolise the wine trade; and a background of the sea and a ship

feature. As well as the nefs, there are two imposing silver-gilt urns, masterpieces of the neo-classical style, that were subscribed for by the nation to mark Nelson's triumph at Trafalgar – one in his honour, the other in honour of Admiral Collingwood, who assumed command after Nelson's death and completed the victory. These are inscribed with eulogies in the sonorous rhetoric of the day. The one to Nelson reads as follows:

As a lasting memorial of
The Transcendant and Heroic Achievements
of the ever to be lamented Warrior
Horatio Viscount Nelson
Baron of the Nile
Who while the British Fleet under his command
conquered or destroyed
The United Fleets of France and Spain
off Cape Trafalgar
on the 21st of October 1805
Gloriously fell in the moment of Victory
This Vase is Presented
To his Relict
Viscountess Nelson
By the committee of the Patriotic Fund

The Queen can entertain fifty-six people to dinner at this table; here kings and presidents have sat by her side in Asia, in Africa, and most recently in America when the Queen and President Ford celebrated the Bicentennial of England's defeat in America. Time heals, and no monarch could have had a more tumultuous welcome than Her Majesty as she sailed across the Hudson River to New York in the *Britannia* on 9 July 1976.

Strolling through the rooms and along the deck of this elegant ship, one is amazed by its compact efficiency. Not an inch of space wasted, it is

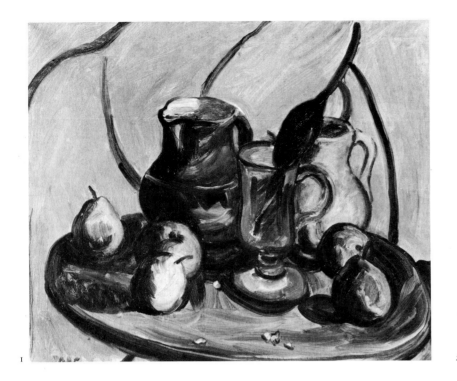

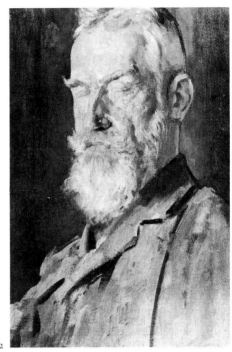

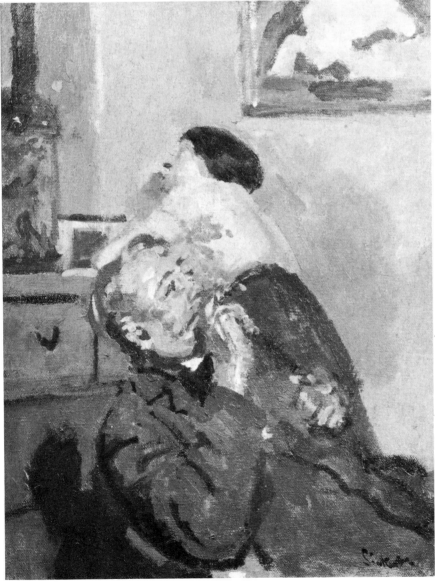

King George VI and Queen Elizabeth the Queen Mother were enthusiastic collectors of English paintings:

1 Sir Matthew Smith, *Still Life: Jugs and Apples*. 1939.
2 Augustus John, *George Bernard Shaw: 'The Philosopher in Contemplation' or 'When Homer Nods'*. 1915.
3 Walter Richard Sickert, *Ennui. c.* 1913

like a beautiful, perfectly made engine. As well as being stirred by mementoes from the great royal yachts of the past, one is constantly reminded, as one moves from room to room, of the extraordinarily extensive journeys the royal family has made in the last twenty-five years – pictures by Sir Edward Seago of Prince Philip's visit to Antarctica in 1956, a cricket bat and ball from Samoa, slate daggers from New Guinea, steel drums, as well as more humble presents from loyal and distant subjects. The most moving of all, perhaps, is a wooden carving of a shark signed by every adult of Pitcairn Island, the remotest island of the Commonwealth, given when the yacht visited the Southern Pacific in 1971. Like film and television, the royal yacht has contributed to the ubiquity of monarchy. In the nineteenth century few in distant places expected to see their Queen, now almost everyone's hopes are fulfilled.

Not only is the royal presence more visible, but so, too, are the royal homes and royal possessions. Queen Elizabeth, Prince Philip, Prince Charles and Queen Elizabeth the Queen Mother are deeply concerned

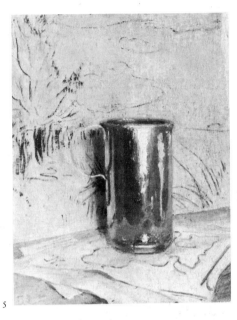

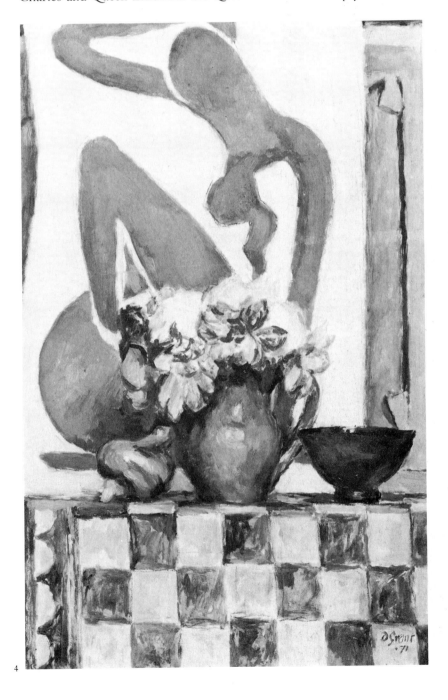

4 Duncan Grant, *Still Life*. 1971
5 Sir William Nicholson, *The Gold Jug*. 1937

not only with their inheritance, but also that it should be made available to a wide and ever wider public. To further this end the bomb-blasted royal chapel at Buckingham Palace was rebuilt as a gallery in which the royal treasures could be displayed. A modern, admirably lit gallery was constructed, and since 1962, when it opened with an exhibition of the major treasures of the royal collection, more than a dozen exhibitions of superlative quality have been held, from Leonardo's drawings to the finest stamps in the collection. During the last fifty years the scholarship of the fine arts has grown both in extent and depth and the Queen has been advised by scholars of great distinction. Lord Clark, Sir Antony Blunt, Sir Oliver Millar and others have encouraged the compilation of a series of outstanding catalogues of the Queen's drawings and pictures. Attributions now are more exact, the delicate work of restoration is carried out systematically and with the highest skills. As with the drawings and pictures, so with the armour, the silver, the porcelain, the furniture, sculpture and bronzes and the castles and palaces themselves where the work of preservation is never ceasing. The royal buildings and collections are in a finer state of repair than they have ever been.

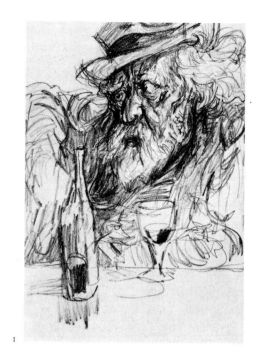

1

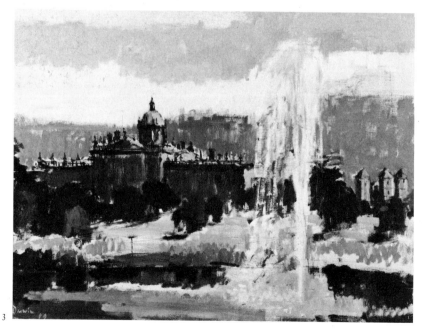

2

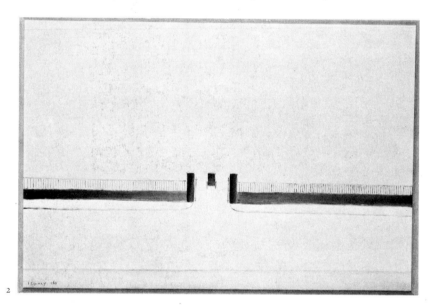

3

The Queen and the Duke of Edinburgh have collected modern British and Commonwealth pictures:

1 Feliks Topolski, *Augustus John*. Black chalk drawing from a set acquired by The Duke of Edinburgh.
2 L. S. Lowry, *The Carriage*.
3 Sir Robin Darwin, *Castle Howard*. 1950

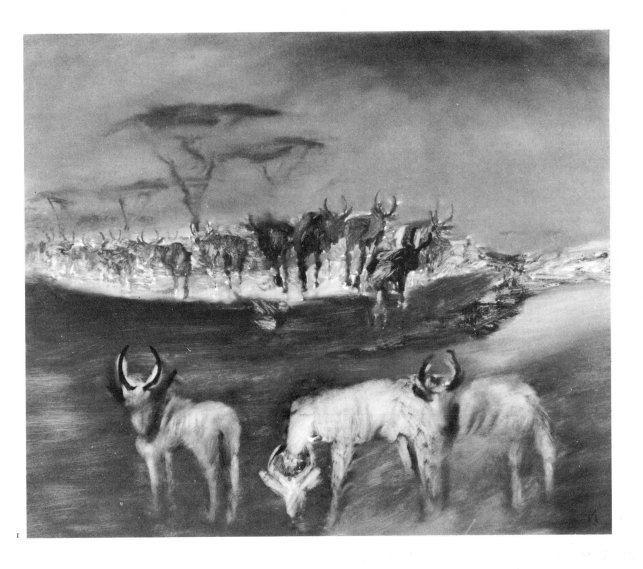

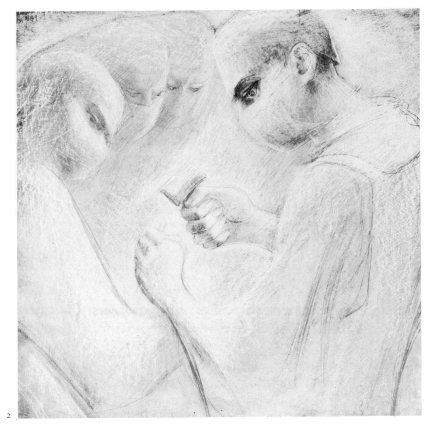

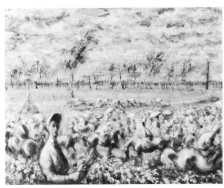

1 Sidney Nolan, *Herd at the Waterhole*. 1963.
2 Dame Barbara Hepworth, *Arthrodesis of the Hip*. 1949. Painted after the artist had watched an operation undergone by her daughter.
3 William Dobell, *A Country Race Meeting*

More widely known, far better catalogued, more extensively reproduced, the royal collection has naturally been in great demand in an age which is addicted to exhibitions. And so the royal treasures are constantly on the move, for unless the frailty of a painting or object, dangers in movement to a different climate, or the problems of transport put it at risk, it is rare for a request for a loan to an exhibition of importance to be refused. The possession of so many riches has stimulated both the Queen's and her husband's interest in art; they have bought modern pictures, fine examples of Graham Sutherland, L. S. Lowry and Sidney Nolan amongst others. Maybe it was living amidst so much beauty that led both Prince Philip and Prince Charles to take up painting themselves. The Queen herself has purchased pictures of outstanding importance to the collection – Samuel Cooper's brilliant miniature of Hugh May, who was responsible for Charles II's alterations at Windsor, the fine Kneller of George I's Turkish servant, Mahomet, two outstanding Blanchets of the last two Stuarts – Prince Charles Edward and Cardinal York, and many others; indeed Her Majesty's additions to the collection are the finest since the death of the Prince Consort.

But the purchases are never for themselves alone; indeed, they have never been. George IV insisted, nearly two centuries ago, that his

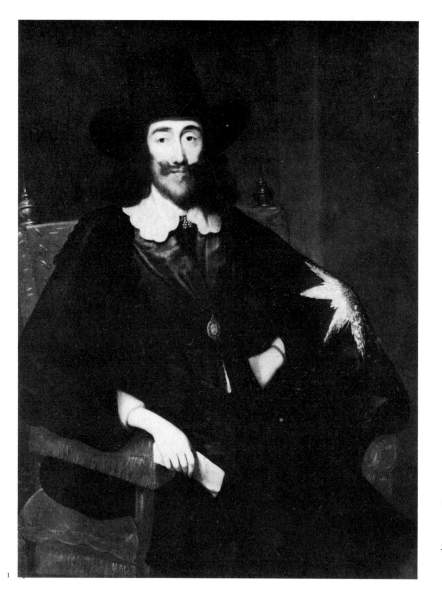

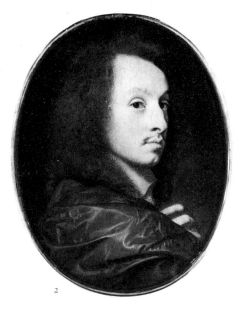

Two pictures, of royal significance, that have been brought into the collection in modern times:
1 Edward Bower, *Charles I at his Trial*. Bought by Queen Elizabeth the Queen Mother in 1951.
2 Samuel Cooper, miniature of Hugh May, who remodelled the interior of Windsor for Charles II. Acquired by Queen Elizabeth II

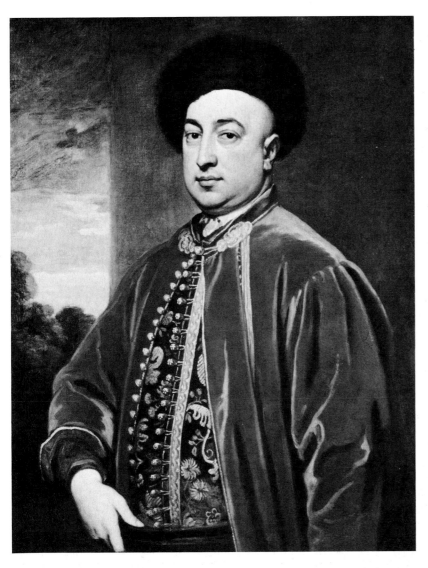

Sir Godfrey Kneller, George I's Turkish servant, Mahomet. Also acquired by Queen Elizabeth II

collection was for the nation. But never could he have expected the way in which the royal treasures have been brought to so many millions of people. Hundreds of thousands visit Windsor, throng to Osborne, walk in the policy of Balmoral and swarm at Sandringham, now both house and gardens are open to the public. All is available. Not, of course, all the time on every occasion; that would be impossible. But sooner or later, whether it be the Leonardo drawings, the great Holbeins, the huge array of old masters, the stamps, or the splendid collection of vintage motor cars and carriages, all are put on display. Now even the family photographs and the family letters, invaluable source material for social history, are available for scholars. Almost every day a scholar of great distinction, English, American, European, or maybe Asian, will be seen toiling up the great medieval staircase of the Round Tower to the archives, or making his way to the Elizabethan library at Windsor with its incomparable collection of prints and drawings.

By such methods – exhibitions, loans, the opening of houses and palaces – only hundreds of thousands could be reached; with the generosity and deep sense of public responsibility which is so marked a feature of the royal family, the Queen and her husband wished that their inheritance, of which they are such dedicated guardians, should be seen by millions. And with the new perfection of colour television there was no more splendid a vehicle for carrying out their wishes.

THE FILM CREW

Executive Producer:	Richard Cawston
Producer:	Michael Gill
Associate Producer:	Ann Turner
Director:	David Heycock
Film Cameramen:	Kenneth MacMillan
	Henry Farrar
Sound Recordists:	Malcolm Webberley
	Stan Nightingale
	Alan Dykes
	John Hale
	John Ramsey
Film Editors:	David Thomas
	Howard Billingham
	Pam Bosworth
	Alan Bradley
	Jonathan Crane
	Christopher Rowlands
Research:	Robert McNab
	Jenni Pozzi
Royal Household Liaison:	Thomas Barnham
Producers' Assistants:	Diane Sullivan
	Dorothy Stainforth
	Julia Hancock
Rostrum Camera:	Ivor Richardson
Stills:	Roynon Raikes
	Mike Sanders
Electricians:	Dickie Woods
	Arthur MacMullen
	Bob Julian
	Bert Wright

This account of two years' work by the BBC production team was written by the producer, Michael Gill

Thirteen of us were waiting in the Throne Room, chilly in the grey November morning. The camera tripod looked incongruous on the edge of the Persian carpet, facing the length of the large red and gold room originally designed by Nash for George IV. At the far end stood the battery of thrones: the heavy square one with the carved crown which had been Victoria's; the smaller throne of George V and George VI and their consorts, flanking the dais on which under a tall purple canopy stood the thrones with the monograms of Queen Elizabeth II and Prince Philip. All were unoccupied. The Queen was at Westminster opening Parliament and we were waiting for her return.

Ken MacMillan, the cameraman, Malcolm Webberley, the sound recordist, and I had been together through the making of *Civilisation* and *America*. Now we were about to film the opening sequence of this series which had already been under way two years.

Films are rarely shot in the order in which you see them, and we had to wait so long because there was only one day in the year when the Imperial State Crown left The Tower and was at Buckingham Palace. It was coming now. Through the windows we saw the cavalcade of glittering coaches and carriages pass under the arch into the central quadrangle. The guards crashed to attention, the band played the anthem. The plumed Life Guards clattered in to ride past The Queen; three officers, seated impressive in their grey cloaks and tricorns, might have ridden from the field of Waterloo.

Two officials in morning dress hurry into the Throne Room carrying a large black box with a brass handle. A door on the side of it opens and there is the Crown cushioned in white satin. William Summers the Royal Jeweller lifts it out carefully. Beside it he lays his tools: a magnifying glass, a small brush and two pairs of pliers.

'They won't be needed, I hope,' he says, giving a quick dust to the jewelled arches. The Crown is not large, but wherever you move the glitter of over 3000 precious stones catches your eye.

It sits alone on its cushion in front of the camera. The lights are switched on. The Queen comes in. She is wearing the diamond circlet which George IV had designed for himself, but which ever since has been worn by female members of the Royal Family. Her long dress and fur-edged coat of lace are also a-shimmer with diamonds. She has just returned from what must be one of the most taxing of her duties yet seems bubbling with energy.

'Did you see that horse?' she says to a colonel in scarlet and spurs. 'He came to a full stop a dozen yards before he should. Gave the coach a frightful jerk. The coachman was trying to make him go, but he wouldn't budge. The other horses had to drag him with them. He just slid along, all four feet down.'

She demonstrates with a graphic push forward of her wrists, and then walks over to the Crown. Her face, so expressive and animated in private conversation, takes on its familiar thoughtful expression.

'What do you think of this?' She picks up a rough lump of glass, larger than a cricket ball. It is a model of the original Cullinan Diamond, one part of which is now in the Crown. She had remembered it and had thought, rightly, that we would like to include it in the sequence.

The filming begins. Turning the Crown on its cushion, the Queen says:

> 'The Crown as you see it now was made for Queen Victoria in 1838 but many of the individual stones have a much longer history.
>
> 'The story goes that this strangely shaped ruby was given to the Black Prince after a battle in Spain in 1367. I always like to think of it being worn by Henry V in his helmet during the battle of Agincourt.
>
> 'This great diamond is a more recent addition. The first Star of Africa is even bigger and is in the sceptre. Both of them are parts of an immense diamond which was found quite by chance by the manager of a mine in South Africa in 1905. Apparently he just dug it out of the rock face with his walking stick.
>
> 'The whole Cullinan Diamond, as it came to be known, was given to my great-grandfather, King Edward VII, on his birthday.
>
> 'The Dutch jeweller who had to split it before it could be polished was so overcome by the responsibility that he fainted as he struck the blow, but he did it perfectly. There are two smaller pieces which my Grandmother always referred to as the "chips".'

After the sound filming there are the cutaways – the close-ups that will illustrate the different jewels referred to by the Queen. There are not many to take; we have already filmed the Crown in detail in the claustrophobic confines of the Jewel House at the Tower months before.

Then there are the still photographs for the *Radio Times*. The Queen places her hand on the cushion beside the Crown, takes it away, looks down, looks up, remains good-humoured. It is nearly two o'clock when we bow our farewells and are led away by Tommy Barnham, an ex-official at the Palace, who is our guide on all such occasions.

We head for the nearest pub, but there is no lunch break yet for The Queen. As we leave she is donning State Robes. Another photographer, Peter Grugeon, is already setting up his lights and curious white umbrellas. He is going to take the official photographs for the Silver Jubilee. There are other engagements later in the day, which has gone non-stop since the arduous Opening of Parliament.

Discussions between the Palace and the BBC on the televising of the Royal Collection had begun more than two years before. In 1974 a committee chaired by the Duke of Edinburgh was set up. One of the BBC members, Richard Cawston, the Head of Documentary Department and producer of the *Royal Family* film, asked me to produce the projected series. At first I could not see how to do the programmes appropriately. A week later I had a dream in which the whole opening sequence of the Queen, the Crown, the Throne Room appeared. When I woke up I wrote it down and went on to write the sketch of the whole series. Visual ideas

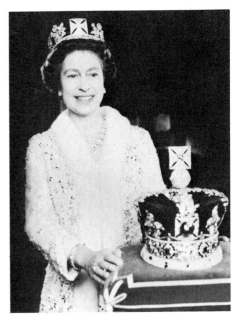

The Queen in the Throne Room at Buckingham Palace with the Imperial State Crown

often come in a sort of daydream, but rarely, in my experience, in such a complete and vivid form.

First entry to Buckingham Palace for me was through the front gate on the right as you look from the Victoria Memorial. A policeman checks your name on a list; over the gravel; past a hover of uniformed men at the door; up in the lift; very long corridors, too wide to be private, too discreet to be public; lots of paintings, some look familiar. It is a bit institutional? Perhaps this is just the subjective effect of nerves? No time to decide. Into a large square room with splendid Chinese wallpaper, carved dragons beside the fireplace. Brought up from Brighton by the Prince Consort, another arrival explains. He is Geoffrey de Bellaigue, Surveyor of The Queen's Works of Art.

The other members of the Committee are assembling: Lord Maclean, the Lord Chamberlain; Colonel Johnston, the Assistant Comptroller; Sir Oliver Millar, Surveyor of The Queen's Pictures; John Charlton, a Principal Inspector, Ancient Monuments, Department of the Environment; Lord Brabourne, the independent film producer. From the BBC, Alasdair Milne, Director of Television Programmes, and Richard Cawston. The chat is well-bred and dependable, like the atmosphere of a London club. It is on the co-operation and goodwill of these Palace officials that the programmes will rely through the years of their making.

Out of the tall windows is an unfamiliar angle on a well-known view: over the railings to the long perspective of the Mall. Could you identify this window later from out there? A rustle of expectancy draws you back into the room. In palaces there is always a footman to signal the arrival of Royalty. The Duke of Edinburgh enters. As you bow you refocus. He is not as tall as expected, but broader and sharper. Business begins briskly: it usually does when the Duke is in charge.

'Where's the sequence in furniture? Chairs and desks and Riesener cabinets – how do we make a flaming sequence out of them?'

Huw Wheldon shoves nose and jaw forward accusingly and then collapses back into his chair with a melodramatic groan of disbelief.

Across the table Jack Plumb, small and round and determined, sets his mouth in an obstinate *moue*.

'Well we can't avoid it because it's difficult, Huw. George IV is by far the greatest collector of furniture in the British monarchy. There are just dozens of important pieces.'

We pause. We are in the middle of a script conference at the BBC Television Centre. We are discussing the pilot film, which will ultimately be transmitted late in the series. Programme One will not be made until we have assessed the strengths and weaknesses which will emerge from the making of the pilot.

We are moving into uncharted seas. Plenty of biographies of kings and queens exist, and there are scholarly works on individual aspects of the Royal Collection, but nothing that combines and condenses all aspects together.

The size and variety of objects that have accrued around the monarchy is daunting: the collecting of George IV, the subject of our discussion, has produced two fat volumes of notes and clippings from our Courtauld-trained researcher, Robert McNab.

'That's all very well, Jack, but it doesn't make a sequence. We can't run a catalogue of furniture.'

We all know Huw is right. A sequence is the muscle that moves a film forward. At its simplest it involves a recognisable coherence in time and space, going through a door, surveying a room, going in close to individual objects; but for a purpose, to carry the story forward. No groups of film shots of different pieces of furniture will do that.

Ann Turner, the associate producer, suggests we could combine film of the furniture today with water colours that show the same pieces in Regency times.

'We'd have to make one example of each sort stand for all the rest,' says Huw thoughtfully. 'That's all there would be time for.'

We try it. Ultimately the sequence goes into the film.

Long before that, as a result of our round table discussions, the director has drawn up a short running order of the film: places, and paintings and objects on one side of the page, progression of ideas on the other. Then Jack Plumb writes an essay, embodying all this and much more. Using it as the backbone, Huw Wheldon writes the script he will speak on locations at many different times and places. The director puts beside it his camera shots, making such amendments as this entails. Many other modifications will follow as the script turns into the film. A television programme is a plant that is pruned and tended by many hands.

The Duke of Edinburgh is in the Royal Chart Room of the Royal Yacht *Britannia*, anchored at Gourock in the Forth of Clyde. He is surrounded by maps and ship designs and beautifully carved and gilded models of 17th-century ships that have been brought up specially from the Maritime Museum at Greenwich.

How to introduce these models has been discussed with the director, David Heycock, and the cameraman, Ken MacMillan. The Duke turns from them to the camera. The cueing device, which normally displays the script on a roller beside the camera lens, has broken down, but he is word perfect within minutes.

'It was Charles II and his brother, James, the Duke of York, who were largely responsible for the introduction of yachting and yacht-racing into England. Charles and James had learnt to sail during their exile in Holland. The word "yacht" is in fact derived from the Dutch and the description covers private pleasure sailing craft as well as the more heavily decorated boats of the officials such as the Burgomaster.

'The fore and aft rig of yachts allowed them to sail closer to the wind and made them much more manoeuvreable than the square-rigged ocean-going ships. It was this manoeuvreability, of course, that made yachting such a pleasure.

'This 17th-century scale model would have been very similar to the *Catherine* in which Charles once raced his brother from Greenwich to Gravesend and back. This is how the diarist, John Evelyn, described the race: "The King lost it going – the wind being contrary, but saved stakes in returning. There were divers noble persons and lords on board, His Majesty sometimes steering himself."'

We were more than six months into the filming. The pilot programme

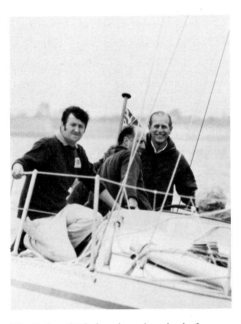

The Duke of Edinburgh at the wheel of *Yeoman XIX*

had been completed and we were shooting the rest piecemeal. This was for the story of the Stuart kings. We had already taken the sequence that would follow it in the film.

Two months before, the Duke had flown down to Portsmouth, landing on a jetty near the smaller helicopter equipped with a special camera mount which we had hired. Our pilot, Lyall Thomson, with over 25 years of flying was experienced in the difficult art of aerial photography. One cameraman would fly with him. David Heycock and another unit were in a power launch; Ken and Malcolm and I were on *Yeoman XIX*, the yacht which the Duke was to sail. The idea was to demonstrate practically the points the Duke had made about the manoeuvreability of yachts and the speed with which they could change course.

As we sailed out into the Solent past the grey warships the wind blew stronger and rain, at first threatening, came down in flurries and then continuously. The Duke borrowed an old windcheater but the crew of six, all volunteers, had to stay in their soaking jerseys. Filming had begun and continuity demanded that they kept to the distinctive green colours of the Yeoman yachts. They took it cheerfully, rushing about the slippery decks to change the tackle and winding furiously on the small aluminium wheels that had replaced the rope hauling I had naïvely expected.

Yeoman XIX was 40 feet long with a mast that rose 50 feet from the sleek lines of her aluminium alloy hull. I had never sailed in such a large yacht and was amazed at the speed at which we flashed over the waves when the spinnaker was out and how quickly, with a great crashing of water and creaking and groaning of stays and spars, we could go about.

We had walkie-talkies to communicate with each other, but they broke down from time to time and co-ordination was not easy. The launch kept shipping water and spray would fog the lens during a crucial manoeuvre. Meanwhile Ken lay back braced in the bows of *Yeoman*, photographing along the length of the boat under the whipping boom; and the helicopter buzzed overhead.

At last we reached the final shot: the Duke slid the yacht alongside the stationary launch within a foot or so of the camera, and we were heading back past Spit Sand Fort for Portsmouth. Perversely the rain abated and watery patches of sunlight flecked the sea.

'Pity about the rain,' I said.

The Duke leant back from the wheel.

'Oh, I don't know. Could have been flat calm. Force Four is the right wind for this sort of thing.'

He looked across the gusty waves. We were nearing the harbour and sea-gulls came up squalling. He took a trickle of spray from his chin.

'I expect it's the only sail I'll get this year.'

The great medieval doors of Chinon Castle were closed. I had to pull the ancient iron bell rope several times before the guardian appeared, grumbling, through a wicket gate. We were too early; the château did not open till nine-thirty. He looked distastefully at the laden film crew struggling over the bridge across the empty moat.

Diane Sullivan, my assistant, produced the letter of permission from the Service Départemental du Tourisme in Tours.

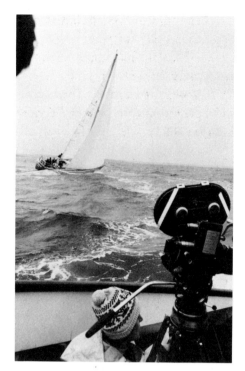

Filming *Yeoman XIX* from the launch in the Solent

It only makes him angry. Salauds. He had not been informed. Nothing had been prepared. We would have to come back at the official time.

I pointed out we had permission to film now, eight o'clock, because we needed the castle to ourselves. He shrugged his shoulders, turning away. That was our concern; if he had been told. . . .

There was only one thing to do: make a scene.

'Monsieur, je vous demande de téléphoner à votre supérieur.'

He was taken aback, but then gave a quick flash of cunning.

'Où est l'autorisation pour un coup de téléphone? Il est très tôt.'

Why did my French never get any better? Over the years I had been involved in many variations of this small drama. Why had I not picked up more forceful and picturesque phrases? Still, shouting helped; after a few minutes we were within the walls and streaming along the battlements.

It was a marvellous morning. The overnight rain had left the air clear and brilliant and the sun was coming up strongly. Below us the old town lay in a crumple of sharp roofs along the broad sweep of the Vienne. Opposite, the green woods faded up into small hills with slopes of vines.

We had chosen a bastion that took advantage of the outlook. Huw leant against a crenellation and we began.

'Henry II was a singularly vivid and energetic man and the central position of this fortress allowed him to make the frequent and unexpected journeys through and by which he governed. He was here, there and everywhere throughout the realm, always on the move. He was famous indeed for refusing, more often than not, to sit down either before or after his evening meal, even if he'd been travelling hard on horseback all day. He kept on walking about, powerful and barrel-chested, full of energy. His poor entourage had no alternative but to stand up as well until they were finally released and could totter off to their couches, absolutely worn out. It was while stomping about in this way, no doubt, that he uttered his most famous sentence – "Who will rid me of this turbulent priest?" It was only impatience, but it led to the murder and martyrdom of Becket.'

It was an excellent performance but the sound recordist was not satisfied.

'We're picking up a lot of background from the town, and the trouble is we can't see it.'

We all listened. It was true: distant dogs barked, doors and windows banged, chickens cackled, children trooping to school called out; all the delicious sounds of a small French town coming to life drifted up to us. But the camera view behind Huw was a curve of the empty Vienne.

'It'd be better if we moved; then the walls would mask the noise.'

I wanted the view, however, so we tried another take and another. As the morning progressed heavy *camions* on their way to Tours came roaring up the hill, changing gear on the corners below us. Altogether we tried thirteen takes in two different locations.

As we packed up to go on to Fontevrault, where Henry II was buried with his son, Richard Coeur de Lion. Huw turned to me:

'From my point of view only two of these are right, you know.'

'Yes, takes 1 and 4.'

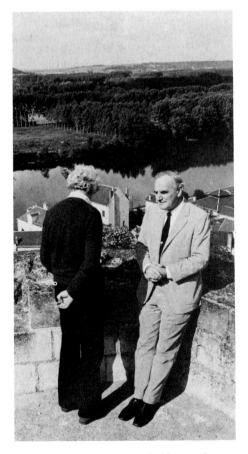

Michael Gill and Sir Huw Wheldon on the battlements of Chinon Castle

Only in those performances had he achieved a peculiarly sardonic note on the words 'absolutely worn out' that was entirely appropriate.

Months later, when editing, I found I was able to use Take 1. The background noise was acceptable, though the sound recordist had been right to draw my attention to it.

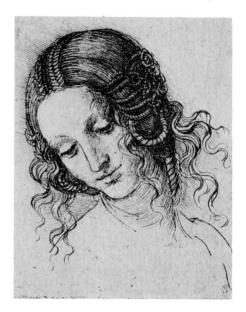

The drawing of Leda by Leonardo da Vinci which was filmed while having the Victorian backing removed

The razor was poised inches above one of the most famous Leonardo drawings: a study for Leda of a woman with downcast head and coiling hair. At a cue from the director the blade descended, slashing through the cardboard surround to the drawing millimetres from the edge of the paper. It was as breathtaking as watching an operation. The surroundings were similarly clinical: the white walls, gleaming instruments, bottles of chemicals, the overalled wielder of the knife, his glasses glinting under the harsh lights. Only the arrow-slit window set deep in the stone seemed to belong to a different world. The real one, for this was Windsor and the Leonardo under attack was not a fake, nor was the pile of Holbeins and other Old Master drawings along the bench.

We were filming one of the more bizarre acts of conservation. In the late 19th century the Leonardo drawings in the Royal Collection had been painstakingly mounted on numbered sheets of cardboard. The drawings had been glued directly onto the backing and over the years this had tended to warp. Moreover, though it had not yet happened to the Leonardos, glue could turn to acid and produce the brown stains on the paper surface known as foxing. Because of these dangers it was decided to remove the mounts and fix the drawings between individual sheets of perspex.

The card surrounding Leda had been cut away. The picture restorer, Michael Warnes, turned the drawing over and began to peel off the layers of the backing with deft strokes of the scalpel. As he approached the surface of Leonardo's paper he abandoned the scalpel and began to scrabble it off with his fingers. The drawing twirled rapidly, surrounded by growing divots of cardboard.

'How much would you say it was worth?' Our electrician was watching fascinated.

'Probably about £200,000,' said Jane Roberts, the Curator of the Print Room, who was keeping an eye on us.

'You've got quite a few of them, haven't you?'

'A few? Over 700.'

Michael Warnes smiled at his amazement and laid down the drawing.

'I'll show you something else surprising. I can't do any more with this one at the moment. I shall have to soak off the rest of the cardboard with a solvent. Look at this.'

He pulled open a shelf and took out another drawing. (I've never known a man who kept so many Leonardos in his bottom drawer.) This was of two horses' heads at the top of a dirty half-empty folio.

He turned on an ultra-violet lamp and switched out the main lighting. Under the purplish glow two further drawings appeared as if by magic on the folio – a cavorting horse with flowing mane and a dog scratching himself. Done in metal point they had faded from human vision, but their lines had been etched on the paper.

Next time we returned we would see the back of the Leda which no one had viewed for over 80 years. We were brought back from the feeling of privilege by Jane's voice, warning us to submit our script before editing the film.

As the Land Rover bumped over the rising ground the film crew came into sight waiting by the track higher up the hillside. Prince Charles, who was driving, studied them.

'That's the cameraman, isn't it? And that's your assistant. I've met them before, haven't I? Just remind me of their names.'

He had met them once during a couple of hours filming a year earlier.

This Sunday morning in October on the slopes of Tom Bad a Mhonaid, near Balmoral, the filming took only took an hour. Prince Charles found time to talk to every member of the unit, including the most retiring.

After church service at Crathie and lunch, we were filming at Glassalt Shiel, the plain small house Queen Victoria had rebuilt for herself after the death of Prince Albert. Much of Royal Deeside is surprisingly lush and gentle for those whose experience of Scotland relates to the Western Highlands. The appeal of Deeside to Prince Albert is understandable – the rolling wooded slopes of its valleys and meandering streams are reminiscent of Germany. But Glassalt is built in scenery as harsh as any on Mull or Skye.

A black wall of mountain, Creag Bhiorach, falls sheer into the dark waters of Loch Muick. It is over 250 feet deep. On the opposite shore of the loch, in a grove of trees beside a burn which tumbles restlessly into it, is the square stone house. It is not a comforting place for a widow to have chosen.

Clouds were massing when we reached there after the six-mile climb from Balmoral, but the rain held off. Prince Charles was to be recorded rowing on the loch, apparently alone. In reality Ken MacMillan, the cameraman, the sound recordist and an electrician with a small battery-light were with him. All three squeezed together in the stern of the small rowing boat. The prow rose three feet in the air and the stern sank within inches of the icy loch. Prince Charles pulled valiantly and the boat

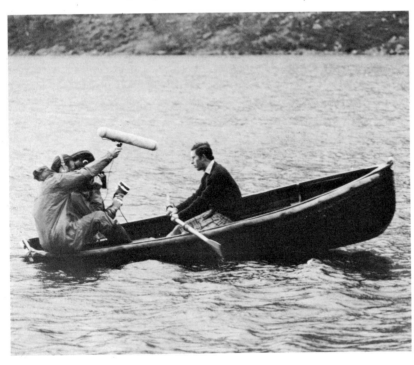

Filming Prince Charles rowing on Loch Muick

with its bizarre cargo of crouching men, pointing camera, microphone, tape recorder and upheld lamp, slid away over the dark water.

'It's the first time I've rowed uphill.'

Resting on the oars he told of his appreciation of Queen Victoria's Highland Journal.

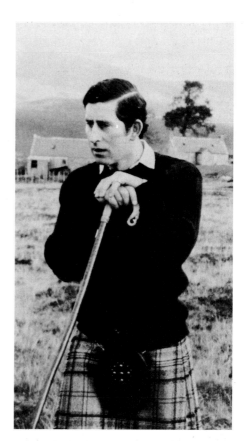

Prince Charles during filming on the hills near Balmoral

'I remembered when I first read the journals myself several years ago, and they immediately struck a chord. For instance, her first impression of Balmoral when she wrote, "All seemed to breathe freedom and peace, and to make one forget the world and its sad turmoils". Exactly what I feel. If you know and love Balmoral and its neighbourhood as much as I do, you can instantly recognise the places she describes.

'The most entertaining descriptions in the journals are those of the expeditions organised by Prince Albert when, with Queen Victoria usually mounted on a pony, and ghillies to lead the way, the whole family, sensibly wrapped in plaids and with good stout boots, trekked to all corners of the estate and beyond – to the beautiful Garballt Falls . . . or to climb the mountain Lochnagar (wrapped in mist, more often than not) – and so beautifully described by Lord Tennyson in his poem: Dark Lochnagar.

'On other expeditions Queen Victoria and Prince Albert would ride miles over the hill tracks to put up incognito at some small inn. If they were lucky the food was reasonable, but in one particular place all they got was a scrawny old chicken, with, as Queen Victoria put it, "no pudding and no fun". What the journals show more than anything else is her essential humanity – whether she was amused – and she was *constantly* amused – or moved by people's kindness. In all her letters and journals, the most complimentary thing Queen Victoria could say about anybody was that they were "straightforward", and the direct – almost blunt – speech of the Highlanders appealed to her most.

'She hated leaving, much as I hate leaving this marvellous place.'

After the Highlands Caithness is surprisingly flat. Windswept fields roll down to broad sandy bays. White crofts hug the bent grass of Dunnet Head, the most northerly point of Britain, but, surprisingly, in a shallow depression near the cliffs is a grove of trees and looming above them, crenellated turrets.

This is the Castle of Mey, the Scottish home of Queen Elizabeth The Queen Mother. In August the gardens, sheltered by tall stone walls, are full of flowers. The castle was built in the 16th century. It is small and stony but not at all grim.

The Queen Mother explains how she came to live there.

'I was driving along from a high road over there, we looked down and saw this old castle. We went and had a look at it and then I discovered that it was going to be pulled down. I thought I must try and save it, because it is one of the few 16th-century houses left in this part of Scotland.

'So I took it on. It wasn't in a very good state – the roof was really off – it took about 12 years to build it up, little by little. Roof on first, bathrooms, water, electric light, which was a great thrill. It's been rather a lovely thing to build up something that might have gone forever, and I think everyone feels it's a happy house which also is a very nice thing to feel, isn't it?

'I think there are too many ruins about nowadays; if only one could save more. Anyway this is saved for the moment.'

The next day we filmed along the coast. Oyster catchers rose from the grass with their sharp whistling cries. In the bay below the castle a seal floated lazily, drifting, nose-up, among the kelp. Across the Pentland Firth, looming and receding in the transient light, were the Orkneys: the tall spire of the Old Man of Hoy clearly recognisable towering above intervening cliffs like a giant shin bone.

In the evening the Royal Yacht, *Britannia*, sailed past with her naval escort, the frigate HMS *Penelope*. The last of the sunlight, reflected off the water, glittered on the sides of the ships. Their crews lined the decks in orderly rows. Rockets flashed up from the castle and were answered by star-shells. A sheet waved from the battlements. Across the water came the faint sound of cheering. The ships swept on majestically, rounding St John's point, heading south.

A hawk veered and plunged across the clifftop fields raising flocks of small birds in fluttering protest.

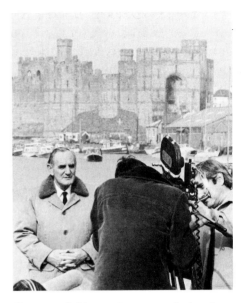

Sir Huw Wheldon at Caernarvon during the filming of the sequence on the first Prince of Wales

'I'd like you to look at the opening titles; I think they're beginning to come right.'

David Thomas, the film editor, was sitting in front of the metal table across which ran the celluloid tracery of film and sound tracks. He pressed a button and images appeared on the small screen at the back. The accompanying music, tinny and distorted by the weight of the spools, was undoubtedly impressive.

'I say, that music is . . .'

'Zadok the Priest. Now we've dropped the sequence on the Coronation we don't need it later and it seems to fit this parade of kings.'

It did. My original intention had been to use aerial views of the principal palaces as the background to the titles. The music I had chosen was a brass fanfare. When we had put it together, it had seemed very insipid. About a week before I had begun thinking of alternatives, using a series of portraits of the better known British monarchs as a starting point.

'I wonder if we can clear that recording; it's absolutely terrific.'

The more you looked the righter it seemed; but it had to be clearable on copyright for world distribution before we could use it.

'Another thing, David: we must get Edward IV reshot; his eye-line's definitely too high.'

Each close-up Royal portrait faded into the next, the process known as 'mixing'. In such a sequence of static images of faces, it was essential that all their eyes were at the same level. It was on the eyes that the viewers' attention would unconsciously be fixed and if they did not come through in precisely the same place it would create an uncomfortable effect, a sort of visual jolt or hiccup.

After more viewings we agreed that there were only one or two images to change and then the opening titles would be all right.

'Let's see what they do to the next sequence.'

We watched in silence for a few minutes, our pleasure evaporating.

The title sequence and the accompanying music of 'Zadok the Priest' were so powerful that they made the following images much too low-key. Editing a film is a bit like kneading dough; bang it into place in one area and it will puff out at another.

'I've had a note from Jack Plumb about your final script on the first programme, Huw. It's all OK except for one thing.'

'What's that?'

'He says we can't say that Edward I made his son Prince of Wales immediately he was born. The title wasn't conferred for several years.'

'Oh, Lord. That's in synch., old boy.'

The final commentary had yet to be recorded and any changes were therefore easy to make. But the synch. passages, those parts which Huw Wheldon spoke directly to camera, had been filmed in various locations months before.

'We shall have to cut it out.'

Jack Plumb was our arbiter on historical accuracy; we would have to accept his ruling.

'But we can't cut it, Huw. It leads directly into the sequence on Prince Charles's Investiture.'

We looked at the text gloomily. '. . . a child was born at Easter, he was a son and Edward immediately declared him Prince of Wales. . . .' When someone is speaking in vision there is no way you can cut out a few words without an inacceptable physical jump in the film.

It seemed an insoluble problem. Then I remembered a similar one on *Civilisation*, and how we had solved it.

'Can you think of a single word, about the same length as "immediately", that would put it right?'

Huw was rarely at a loss for a word.

'Yes. Subsequently. "Edward subsequently declared him Prince of Wales."'

'Right, we'll record that in the dubbing theatre, cut out "immediately" from the sound track and substitute "subsequently". You'll still be mouthing "immediately", but what the audience will hear is "subsequently".'

As the months rolled into years experience modified our reactions. Palace corridors lost their terrors and became familiar landmarks. The film cans mounted in piles in the vaults; the schedules, the detailed listing of technical requirements, of times on locations, of security clearance of vehicles and personnel, of accommodation booked, of special effects needed, of individual props ordered, and sets required, and officials informed, grew into volumes.

Initially the pressure fell most severely on Jack Plumb. He kept an awesome writing rate; his immense historical grasp was valuable throughout; he never failed to respond immediately and thoughtfully to every inquiry. Later the tension shifted to the efforts of the production team and Huw Wheldon. Like Henry II, a singularly vivid and energetic man, he was here, there and everywhere, stomping from location to location, one day with the Tudors, the next with Victoria, and taking the journey between to polish up the Plantagenets. Yet a few months before transmission it was impossible to say whether the programmes would be successful, even whether they would be ready on time.

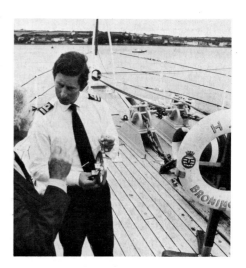

Prince Charles during the filming on board his command HMS *Bronington*

Such hazards are the commonplace of creative effort. Afterwards it would be unique events that people would recall with pleasure. For Ann Turner it was filming Prince Charles in the cramped but hospitable bridge and wardroom of his command, the mine-hunter HMS *Bronington*, and afterwards being winched off by helicopter at the beginning of a Force Five gale. For Ken MacMillan it was the sight of Queen Victoria's Mausoleum at Frogmore. She had built it for Prince Albert.

'It brought home forcibly in stone and marble how much he had meant to her. It has echoes of San Vitale in Ravenna while at the same time embodying in a very visual way many of the good things the Victorians stood for.'

For David Heycock it was arranging for the Gold State Coach, designed and built for the young King George III, to be refurbished and brought out of the Royal Mews. It was drawn down the Mall with appropriate ceremony as it had last been at the 1953 Coronation. 'It was strange to see the grooms eating sandwiches in shirt sleeves in the Mews, and then, once they were out on the Mall, transformed by their uniforms and the magic of the coach almost into figures from a fairy tale.'

The excitement of being able to study at close hand the meticulous line of a Holbein drawing or the brush strokes of a Gainsborough; the unexpected felicities like the early Stuart miniatures, the exquisite painting on 18th-century Sèvres china; the poignancy of the flakes of gold braid still adhering to the bullet that killed Nelson – the Collection rarely failed to reward. A microcosm of so much human achievement on so many diverse levels, it impressed also for the amount of care and effort devoted to its preservation. A preservation given added meaning by its still being in use, not stored away in museums.

We came to realise what a hard-worked structure the Royal Household was and to appreciate the good humour and help that we got from the servants of the Queen. Especially this was true of those at Windsor. Windsor was our favourite palace. It seems to express the genius of the British and their peculiar conception of monarchy in the way that Versailles formulates the rational intellect of the French. Rambling, old, enduring, full of surprising beauty and some ugliness, added to and modified through a thousand years, Windsor is built into the landscape, so as to seem an essential and enhancing part of it. It speaks for a noble past yet is quite well adapted for modern living. It stirs you more than you expected.

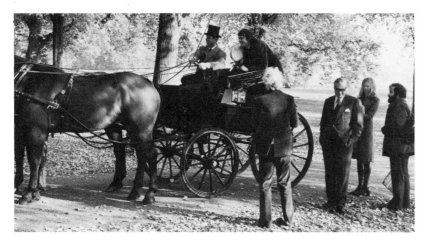

Filming the Duke of Edinburgh driving a four in hand in Windsor Royal Park. Left to right: The Duke, Kenneth MacMillan, Michael Gill, Richard Cawston, Diane Sullivan, Roger Twynan (assistant cameraman)

ACKNOWLEDGEMENTS
ILLUSTRATIONS
AND INDEX

ACKNOWLEDGEMENTS

We have had the assistance of many people in assembling material for this book and we should like to make acknowledgement here of our sincere thanks.

In the Royal Library and Archives at Windsor Castle, we are grateful first of all to the Curator of the Print Room, The Hon. Mrs Roberts, for her scholarship and ungrudging assistance in finding prints and drawings; in addition we would like to thank the Registrar of the Archives, Miss Jane Langton for information and Miss Frances Dimond of the Photographic Collection. At the Lord Chamberlain's Office, Mrs Margaret Cousland and Miss Sarah Wilson, Assistants to the Surveyor of the Queen's Pictures, have given invaluable help. We are also grateful to the following for making arrangements for Mr Michael Freeman to take photographs specially for this book: Capt. Alastair Aird, Comptroller to Her Majesty Queen Elizabeth The Queen Mother; Mr Julian Loyd, Land Agent, Sandringham; Col. William McHardy, Resident Factor, Balmoral Castle; Major William Nash, Superintendent, Windsor Castle; Mr Godfrey Bass, Chapter Clerk, St George's Chapel, Windsor Castle, and all other people who made special facilities available to us. Mr Freeman's photographs are credited in the following list.

J. H. PLUMB
HUW WHELDON

THE ILLUSTRATIONS

Unless otherwise stated, the illustrations in this book are from works in the Royal Collection and are reproduced by gracious permission of Her Majesty The Queen. The plates on pages 318, 324 and 325 are reproduced by gracious permission of Her Majesty Queen Elizabeth The Queen Mother. As paintings and works of art in the Collection are often moved from place to place, locations have not been given, except in the case of items in the Royal Library and Royal Archives at Windsor, which are marked accordingly.

Page numbers of colour illustrations are given in *italic* figures.

Half title and title, details of the gates to King Henry VII's Chapel, Westminster Abbey. Courtesy of the Dean and Chapter, Westminster Abbey. Photos Michael Freeman

Contents, the cover of a prayer book, belonging to Queen Elizabeth I. British Library, London

Page 11 The arms of John of Gaunt in stained glass. Victoria and Albert Museum, London

12 1 The Coronation of Queen Elizabeth II. Fox Photos. 2 St Edward's Crown. 3 The Imperial State Crown. Both Crown Copyright. Reproduced with permission of the Controller of Her Majesty's Stationery Office, London

13 4 Hilt and scabbard of the Jewelled Sword, made for the coronation of King George IV. 5 The Ampulla and Spoon. 2–5 Crown Copyright. Reproduced with permission of the Controller of Her Majesty's Stationery Office, London

14 1 The King's Orb and the Sceptre with the Cross. Crown Copyright. Reproduced with permission of the Controller of Her Majesty's Stationery Office. 2 King Edward I's Coronation Chair, Westminster Abbey. Courtesy of the Dean and Chapter, Westminster Abbey. Photo Michael Freeman

15 3 The south face of the White Tower. Department of the Environment. 4 Detail from the Bayeux Tapestry of Harold crowned King. Phaidon Press

17 St John's chapel, Tower of London. Department of the Environment. Photo Michael Freeman

18 Tomb of King Henry II, Fontevrault Abbey. Photo Viollet

19 King John's Cup. The Charter Trustees, King's Lynn. Photo P. M. Goodchild. Tombs of Richard I and Eleanor of Aquitaine, Fontevrault Abbey. Photo Viollet

20 1 Nicholas Broker and Godfrey Prest, Effigy of Anne of Bohemia, Westminster Abbey. Photo Edwin Smith. 2 Nicholas Broker and Godfrey Prest, Effigy of King Richard II, Westminster Abbey. Photo Edwin Smith. 3 Effigy of King Edward III, Westminster Abbey. Courtesy of the Dean and Chapter, Westminster Abbey. Photo Michael Freeman

21 Pietro Torrigiano, Effigy of Margaret Beaufort, Westminster Abbey. Courtesy of the Dean and Chapter, Westminster Abbey

22 and 23 Details of tiles from the floor of the Chapter House, Westminster Abbey. Courtesy of the Dean and Chapter, Westminster Abbey. Photo Michael Freeman

24 King Henry V. Cotton MS Julius EIV, Art I, fo. 8v. The British Library, London

25 King Edward IV receiving Wavrin's Chronicle. Royal MS 15 E IV vol. 1 fol. 14r. The British Library, London

26 1 Warriors encamped at the wall of a town. MS Royal 20 C. VII 27v. 2 The King delivers a speech from a scaffolding rostrum. MS Royal 20 B. XX 29v. 3 Two knights jousting. MS Royal 20B. XX 53r. 4 The coronation of King Richard II. Royal MS 14 E. IV vol. III f. 10r. 5 The King enthroned. Royal MS 14 C. VII f. 8v. All from the British Library, London

27 The building of the Tower of Babel. Add. MS 18850. British Library, London

28 Fifteenth-century view of London. Royal MS 16 F, II, fo. 73. British Library, London

29 1 Harold II, penny. 2 Edward I, silver penny. 3 Edward III, gold noble. 4 Edward III gold half-florin. 5 Henry III, gold penny. All from the British Museum, London

30 Caernarvon Castle. Aerofilms

31 1 Conway Castle, Aerofilms. 2 Beaumaris Castle. Airview, Manchester Ltd

32 1 A charter of King Edward I, 1280–1, granting land to Waltham Holy Cross Abbey. Public Record Office, London. 2 and 3 The Great Seal of King Edward I. The British Library, London. 4 The Privy Seal of John of Gaunt. B. M. Harleian Charter, 43 E. 14. British Library, London

33 The Eleanor Cross, Hardingstone. Courtauld Institute of Art, London. 2 The Great Seal of King Edward III. Public Record Office, London

34 The Treaty of Calais Chest, $9'' \times 37'' \times 9\frac{1}{2}''$. Public Record Office, London

35 Top, Wenceslas Hollar, engraving of the Tower of London. Royal Library, Windsor. Bottom, A joust, from *The Life and Acts of Richard Beauchamp, Earl of Warwick* by John Rous. B. M. Cotton MS. Julius E. IV, Art. VI, fol. 15v. British Library, London

36 and 37 *The Wilton Diptych*. National Gallery, London

38 A prisoner dragged along by horses. *Les Chroniques de Saint-Denis* (B. M. MSS. Roy. 20. C. vii). British Library, London

39 The Royal Gold Cup of the Kings. British Museum, London

41 St George's Chapel, Windsor. By permission of the Dean and Canons, St George's Chapel, Windsor. Photo Michael Freeman

42 1 The hammer-beam roof, Eltham Palace, Kent. Photo Michael Freeman. 2 Detail of the Royal Arms from the south porch of King's College Cambridge. Photo Edwin Smith. 3 The nave, King's College Chapel, Cambridge. Photo Edwin Smith

43 Detail of decoration from Queen Elizabeth I's virginals. Victoria and Albert Museum, London

44 Frontispiece to Raphael Holinshed's *Chronicles of England, Scotlande and Irelande*, 1577. British Library, London

45 1 Pietro Torrigiano, bust of King Henry VII. Victoria and Albert Museum, London. 2 The first column from the chapter on King Henry VIII, from Holinshed's *Chronicles*. British Library, London

46 King Henry VII's Chapel, Westminster Abbey. Courtesy of the Dean and Chapter, Westminster Abbey. Photo Michael Freeman

47 The tomb and effigies of King Henry VII and Elizabeth of York, designed by Pietro Torrigiano. Photo Michael Freeman

48 1 Hans Holbein, *King Henry VIII*. Thyssen Gallery, Lugano. 2 *Henry VII and Henry VIII*, from Holbein's cartoon for the fresco at Whitehall. National Portrait Gallery, London

49 Pietro Torrigiano, bust of King Henry VIII. Metropolitan Museum of Art, New York, Fletcher Fund, 1944

50 *Cardinal Wolsey*. National Portrait Gallery, London

51 Albrecht Dürer, woodcut portrait of Emperor Maximilian I. Royal Library, Windsor

52 The Royal Tudor Clock Salt. Worshipful Company of Goldsmiths, London

53 Silvered armour, made in Flanders for King Henry VIII. Master of the Armouries, Tower of London

54 and 55 Top, *The Embarkation of Henry VIII*. Bottom, *The Field of the Cloth of Gold*

56 King Henry VIII's foot armour and the Maximilian helmet. Master of the Armouries, Tower of London

57 1 Artist Unknown, *The Family of Henry VII with St George and the Dragon*. 2 Panelling from Nonsuch. Photo, Courtauld Institute of Art, London

58 St James's Palace. The Clock Tower, built by King Henry VIII in 1533. Photo Michael Freeman

59 Georg Hoefnagel, engraving of Nonsuch Palace. Royal Library, Windsor

60 Hans Holbein, design for a dagger handle. British Museum, London

61 After Quentin Matsys, *Erasmus*

62 Remigius van Leemput, *Henry VII, Elizabeth of York, Henry VIII and Jane Seymour*

63 Hans Holbein, design for a fireplace at Bridewell Palace. British Museum, London

64 King Henry VIII and his jester Will Somers. From a psalter decorated for the King himself. British Library, London

65 Detail from the ceiling of the Chapel Royal, Hampton Court. Department of the Environment, London. Crown Copyright. Photo Michael Freeman

66 Detail from Wolsey's Closet, Hampton Court. Department of the Environment, London. Crown Copyright. Photo Michael Freeman

67 The ceiling of the Chapel Royal, Hampton Court. Department of the Environment, London. Crown Copyright. Photo Michael Freeman

68 1 Studio of Hilliard, miniature of Queen Elizabeth I from the Armada Jewel. Victoria and Albert Museum, London. 2 The Mermaid Pendant. 3 The Lennox or Darnley Jewel. 4 Enamelled Pendant

71 Girolamo da Treviso, *The Four Evangelists Stoning the Pope*

72 King Henry VIII's writing box. Victoria and Albert Museum, London

73 Cornelius Matsys, engraving of King Henry VIII in old age. Royal Library, Windsor

74 1 The Old Palace, Hatfield. Photo Michael Freeman. 2 Queen Elizabeth I's hat, stockings and gloves. The Marquess of Salisbury

75 3 Artist unknown, *Elizabeth I when Princess*. 4 Elizabeth's handwriting as a child and a drawing of an astrolabe from a French psalter. Royal Library, Windsor

76 Elizabeth I's virginals. Victoria and Albert Museum, London

77 Hans Holbein, *A Gentleman: Unknown*. Royal Library, Windsor

78 Hans Holbein, *Derich Born*

79 Hans Holbein, *Thomas Howard, Third Duke of Norfolk*

80 Hans Holbein, *Cecily Heron*. Royal Library, Windsor

81 Nicholas Hilliard. *Elizabeth I with a Lute*. Trustees to the late Earl of Berkeley. Photo Courtauld Institute of Art, London

82 Attributed Hans Eworth, *Elizabeth I and the Three Goddesses*

83 Isaac Oliver, drawing of Queen Elizabeth I. Royal Library, Windsor

84 1 Linlithgow Castle. 2 Falkland Palace. 3 Stirling Castle. All photographed by Keith Gibson. 4 Livinius de Vogelaare, *The Memorial of Lord Darnley*

85 5 Falkland Palace Chapel. Photo Keith Gibson. 6 François Clouet, *Mary Queen of Scots*

86 1 Armada Tapestry. Engraving by J. Pine. Royal Library, Windsor. 2 Silver medal commemorating the Armada. British Museum, London

87 The Royal Library, Windsor. Photo Michael Freeman

89 1 Nicholas Hilliard, *King Henry VII*. 2 Lucas Horenbout, *King Henry VIII*. 3 Nicholas Hilliard, *Jane Seymour*. 4 Nicholas Hilliard, *Queen Elizabeth I*. 5 François Clouet, *Mary Queen of Scots*. 6 Nicholas Hilliard, *King Henry VIII*. 7 Hans Holbein, *Lady Audley*. 8 Isaac Oliver, *Self-portrait*. 9 *Queen Elizabeth I when Young*. 10 Hans Holbein, *Henry Brandon, Duke of Suffolk*. 11 Hans Holbein, *Charles Brandon, Duke of Suffolk*

90 1 Isaac Oliver, *Portrait of a Young Man* (formerly called Sir Philip Sidney). 2 Isaac Oliver, *Robert Devereux, 2nd Earl of Essex*. 3 Isaac Oliver, *John Donne*

91 1 Isaac Oliver, *Anne of Denmark*. 2 Isaac Oliver, *Henry, Prince of Wales*

92 1 John Hoskins, *Henrietta Maria*. 2 After Samuel Cooper, *King Charles II*

93 Detail from the Tijou gates at Hampton Court. Photo Michael Freeman

94 1 Andrea del Sarto, *Holy Family*. Prado, Madrid. 2 Guido Reni, *Nessus the Centaur and Deianira*. Louvre, Paris

95 Sir Peter Paul Rubens, *The Apotheosis of James I*. The centre panel of the ceiling painting at the Banqueting House, Whitehall. Department of the Environment. Crown Copyright

96 1 Albrecht Dürer, *Self-portrait*. Prado, Madrid. 2 Correggio, *Jupiter and Antiope*. Louvre, Paris. 3 Raphael, *La Perla*. Prado, Madrid

97 4 Titian, *The Entombment of Christ*. Louvre, Paris. 5 Titian, *Doge Andrea Gritti*. National Gallery of Art, Washington. Samuel H. Kress Collection. 6 Caravaggio, *Death of the Virgin*. Louvre, Paris

98 1 Paul van Somer, *James I*. 2 Daniel Mytens, *Thomas, Earl of Arundel*. By permission of the Duke of Norfolk. Photo Courtauld Institute of Art, London

99 1 Robert Peake, *Henry, Prince of Wales, in the Hunting-Field*. 2 Paul van Somer, *Anne of Denmark*. 3 Simon van der Passe, *Henry, Prince of Wales*. Royal Library, Windsor

100 Hugo van der Goes, two panels from the *Trinity Altarpiece*. Left, *King James III of Scotland* and his son, afterwards James IV. Right, *The Holy Trinity*. National Gallery of Scotland, Edinburgh. On loan from the Royal Collection

101 Peter Oliver, miniature copies of 1 Correggio, *Venus, Mercury and Cupid*, 2 Raphael, *St George and the Dragon*, 3 Titian, *The D'Avalos Allegory*, 4 Correggio, *Jupiter and Antiope*

102 Rembrandt, *The Artist's Mother*

103 Daniel Mytens, *Portrait of the Artist*

104 Sir Peter Paul Rubens, *Portrait of the Artist*

105 Sir Peter Paul Rubens, Detail of *Landscape with St George and the Dragon*

106 Andrea Mantegna, *The Triumph of Caesar – The Triumphal Car*

107 Andrea Mantegna, *The Triumph of Caesar – The Litter Bearers*

108 Agnolo Bronzino, *Lady in Green*

109 1 Detail of Christ from the Mortlake tapestry. Mobilier National, Paris. 2 Raphael, *The Miraculous Draught of Fishes*. Victoria and Albert Museum, London. On permanent loan from the Royal Collection

110 Orazio Gentileschi, *Joseph and Potiphar's Wife*

111 The Queen's Chapel, St James's Palace. Photo Michael Freeman

112 1 Sir Anthony van Dyck, *Charles I in Three Positions*. 2 Daniel Mytens, *George Villiers, First Duke of Buckingham*

113 1 The Crouching Venus. British Museum, London. 2 Page from the pictorial inventory of the statues in King Charles I's collection at Whitehall. Royal Library, Windsor

115 Sir Anthony van Dyck, *Charles I with M. de St Antoine*

116 Nicholas Hilliard, *King James I*

117 Sir Anthony van Dyck, *The Five Eldest Children of Charles I*

118 Sir Anthony van Dyck, *George Villiers, Second Duke of Buckingham, and Lord Francis Villiers*

119 Sir Anthony van Dyck, *Henrietta Maria*

120 Sir Anthony van Dyck, *Cupid and Psyche*

121 1 Detail from the *Codex Alexandrinus*. British Library, London. 2 Sir Peter Paul Rubens, *Portrait of Van Dyck*

123 Inigo Jones, The Banqueting House, Whitehall. Photo A. F. Kersting

124 John Webb, The King Charles block, Greenwich. Photo Michael Freeman

125 Sir Christopher Wren, The Fountain Court, Hampton Court. Department of the Environment. Crown Copyright. Photo Michael Freeman

126 John Michael Wright, *King Charles II* (detail)

127 Robert Streeter, *Boscobel House and Whiteladies*

129 Lorenzo Lotto, *Andrea Odoni*

130 1 Winstanley, engraving of Audley End. Royal Library, Windsor. 2 The mace presented by Charles II to the Royal Society, London, and still in their possession

131 *Vue et Prospective de la ville de Londre: Westminster et Parc St James*. Detail of an engraving by John Kip. Royal Library, Windsor

132 The Queen's Presence Chamber, Windsor

133 Leonardo da Vinci, A study of hands. Royal Library, Windsor

134 and 135 Drawings by Leonardo da Vinci: 1 A gun foundry. 2 Mortars and a gun cradle. 3 An old man meditating and studies of swirling water. 4 Dissection of a man's arm. 5 Cross-section of a womb. 6 Neptune and sea-horses. All from the Royal Library, Windsor

136 Leonardo da Vinci: 1 Caricature group. 2 Plant drawing, 'Star of Bethlehem'. Both from the Royal Library, Windsor

137 1 Willem van de Velde the Younger, *The English Yacht, Charles*. National Maritime Museum, London. 2 Willem van de Velde the Younger, *The Royal Escape*. 3 Cornelius de Wit, engraving of a Dutch yacht. Royal Library, Windsor

138 The Royal Yacht, *The Sovereign of the Seas*. National Maritime Museum, London

139 1 The Royal Hospital, Chelsea. Photo Michael Freeman. 2 The Chapel of the Royal Hospital, Chelsea. Photo Michael Freeman

140 1 Pieter Bruegel, *The Massacre of the Innocents*. 2 The South front, Hampton Court Palace. Department of the Environment. Crown Copyright. Photo Michael Freeman

141 Engraving by John Kip after Leonard Knyff, bird's eye view of Hampton Court Palace. Royal Library, Windsor

142 Anonymous early eighteenth-century engraving of a bird's eye view of Kensington Palace. Royal Library, Windsor

143 The King's Staircase, Hampton Court. Photo Michael Freeman

145 *The Blue Gross-beak on a branch of sweet flowring bay*. A plate from Mark Catesby, *Natural History of Carolina, Florida and the Bahamas*

146 Studio of Kneller, *George I*

147 Sir James Thornhill, Ceiling, Painted Hall, Greenwich. Royal Naval College, Greenwich. Photo Michael Freeman

148 The King's Grand Staircase, Kensington Palace. Photo Michael Freeman

149 A detail from the Staircase. Photo Michael Freeman

150 1 The Cupola Room, Kensington Palace. Photo Michael Freeman. 2 The King's Gallery, Kensington Palace. Photo Michael Freeman

151 Engraving by Jean Rogue of Kensington Palace and gardens. Royal Library, Windsor

152 Thomas Hudson, *George II*. National Portrait Gallery, London

153 Sir Anthony van Dyck, *Thomas Killigrew and (?) William, Lord Crofts*

154 Guido Reni, *Cleopatra with the Asp*

155 Frans Hals, *Portrait of a Man*

156 and 157 Jan Bruegel, *Adam and Eve in the Garden of Eden*

157 Louis François Roubiliac, bust of Handel. Photo Courtauld Institute

158 Philippe Mercier, *The Music Party*

159 Jean-Baptiste Vanloo, *Augusta, Princess of Wales, with Members of her Family and Household*

160 1 and 2 Prince Frederick's state barge. Photo Michael Freeman. National Maritime Museum, Greenwich

161 1 and 2 William Kent's designs for the state barge. Royal Institute of British Architects, London

162 George Knapton, *The Family of Frederick, Prince of Wales*

163 The White House, Kew. An engraving after W. Woollett. Royal Library, Windsor

164 1 *Sophora Japonica*, Kew Gardens. Photo Michael Freeman. 2 Title page of Bute's *Botanical Tables containing the different Familys of British Plants*. Royal Library, Windsor. 3 and 4 Two engravings after W. Woollett of the Royal Gardens at Kew

165 5 and 6 Plates from Mark Catesby's *Natural History of Carolina, Florida and the Bahamas*. Royal Library, Windsor. 7 Drawing on vellum for Maria Sibylla Merian's *Metamorphosis Insectorum Surinamensium*. Royal Library, Windsor

166 George III's compound microscope. Photo Michael Freeman. Science Museum, London. On loan from the Royal Collection

167 2 George Adams, Compound Engine. Photo Michael Freeman. Science Museum, London. On loan from the Wheatstone Collection, King's College, London. 3 George III's directions for assembling a watch. Royal Library, Windsor. 4 Christopher Pinchbeck's four-sided astronomical clock

168 1 A landscape drawing by King George III. Royal Library, Windsor. 2 Autograph page from Handel's *Messiah*. British Library, London

169 A binding from King George III's library. British Library, London

170 1 Bureau-cabinet by William Vile. 2 Bookcase by William Vile

171 Jewel Cabinet by William Vile

172 1 Canaletto, drawing of *London; St Paul's seen through an Arch of Westminster Bridge*. Royal Library, Windsor. 2 Francesco Zuccarelli, *Europa and the Bull*

173 Marco Ricci, *The Courtyard of a Country House*

174 Alan Ramsay, *King George III*

175 Jan Vermeer, *The Music Lesson: A Lady at the Virginals with a Gentleman Listening*

176 Pietro Longhi, *Blind Man's Buff*

177 Canaletto, *The Piazzetta, Venice*

178 Giovanni Bellini, *Portrait of a Young Man*

179 Thomas Gainsborough, George III, Queen Charlotte and thirteen of their Children

180 1 Johann Zoffany: *The Academicians of the Royal Academy*. 2 *The Tribuna of the Uffizzi*

181 Benjamin West: 1 *Queen Charlotte*, a detail. 2 *The Death of Epaminondas*

182 1 Barograph by Alexander Cumming. 2 Gold watch made by Thomas Mudge

183 1 Eighteenth-century Chelsea porcelain clock by William Strigel. 2 Gillray, cartoon of King George III as 'Farmer George'. Royal Library, Windsor

184 C. Turner, engraving of George III in old age. Royal Library, Windsor

185 1 Filippino Lippi, *An Angel Receiving the Child from the Virgin*. 2 Guercino (Giovanni Francesco Barbieri), *Study of a Flying Putto*. 3 Sassoferato (Giovanni Salvi), *Judith with the Head of Holofernes*. All from the Royal Library, Windsor

186 Michelangelo, *Christ on the Cross between the Virgin and St John*. Royal Library, Windsor

187 Giovanni Bellini, *Head of an Old Man*. Royal Library, Windsor

188 Raphael: 1 *The Massacre of the Innocents*. 2 *Christ's Charge to St Peter*. Both from the Royal Library, Windsor

189 Thomas Gainsborough, *Diana and Actaeon*

190 Thomas Gainsborough, *Johann Christian Fischer*

191 Thomas Gainsborough, *Henry, Duke of Cumberland, with the Duchess of Cumberland and Lady Elizabeth Luttrell*

192 Thomas Gainsborough, *Colonel John Hayes St Leger*

193 Jean-Etienne Liotard: 1 *George, Prince of Wales*. 2 *Henry Frederick, Duke of Cumberland*. 3 *Augusta, Princess of Wales*. 4 *Princess Louisa Ann*

194 Johann Zoffany, *George III*

195 Johann Zoffany, *Queen Charlotte*

196 Johann Zoffany, *The Tribuna of the Uffizi*. A detail

197 The Royal Pavilion, Brighton. Brighton Corporation

198 Engraving after Cosway of George IV when Prince of Wales. The Royal Library, Windsor

199 The Royal Pavilion, Brighton. Brighton Corporation

201 Buckingham Palace at the time of George IV, drawn by Joseph Nash. Royal Library, Windsor

202 Johann Zoffany: 1 *George, Prince of Wales, and Frederick, later Duke of York*. 2 Detail from a later painting of the two children

203 Detail of an engraving by W. Dickinson after H. Bunbury, showing the Prince of Wales at a party in the grounds of Carlton House. Royal Library, Windsor

204 George Stubbs, *Prince of Wales's Phaeton*

205 George Stubbs, *George IV when Prince of Wales*

206 George Stubbs, *Soldiers of the Tenth Light Dragoons*

207 George Stubbs, *The Prince of Wales's Phaeton*. A detail

208 George Stubbs, *William Anderson with Two Saddle-horses*

209 1 Part of a Sèvres porcelain service made for Louis XVI. 2 Detail from one of the Gobelins Tapestries

211 Sir Peter Paul Rubens, *The Farm at Laeken*

212 Gillray, caricature of George IV's marriage. Royal Library, Windsor

213 Sir William Beechey, *George IV when Prince of Wales*

214 1 Engraving by I. C. Stadler, after C. Rosenberg, of the Prince Regent on horseback. 2 Denis Dighton, *The Battle of Waterloo: The Charge of the Second Brigade of Cavalry*. 3 Chair, made by Chippendale the Younger from the elm that Wellington stood under at Waterloo

215 1 Sir William Beechey, *George III at a Review*. 2 One of a pair of double-barrelled flintlock pistols presented to George IV by Louis XVIII. 3 The burnished-steel hilt of an English small-sword

216 J. M. W. Turner, *The Battle of Trafalgar*. National Maritime Museum, London

217 Sèvres porcelain ice pail. Part of a service made for Louis XVI

218 J. H. Riesener, Jewel cabinet

219 Thomire vase in Sèvres porcelain, made for Louis XVI

220 1 Equestrian statue of Louis XIV. 2 A. Weisweiler, cabinet

221 Four water-colours of Carlton House, published as engravings in W. H. Pyne, *The History of the Royal Residences*, London, vol. III, 1819. 1 The Throne Room. 2 The Blue Velvet Room, the Prince of Wales's Audience Room. 3 The Gothic Conservatory. 4 A corner of the Library. All from the Royal Library, Windsor

222 The Grand Corridor, Windsor Castle. Photo Michael Freeman

223 The central gasolier in the Banqueting Room of the Royal Pavilion, Brighton. Brighton Corporation

224 The Music Room at the Royal Pavilion, Brighton. Brighton Corporation

225 Sir Thomas Lawrence: 1 *William Pitt*. 2 *Pope Pius VII*. 3 The Waterloo Chamber, Windsor Castle

226 1 Table of the Great Generals. 2 The hilt of Napoleon's sword

227 Antonio Canova: 1 Statue of Napoleon at Apsley House. Photo Victoria and Albert Museum, London. 2 *Mars and Venus*. Photo Courtauld Institute, London

228 A. Coysevox, bust of Condé. Photo Courtauld Institute, London

229 Monument to Princess Charlotte, by Matthew Wyatt, in St George's Chapel, Windsor. Photo Michael Freeman

230 1 Sir Thomas Lawrence, *Arthur Wellesley, First Duke of Wellington*. 2 William Hogarth, *David Garrick with his wife Eva-Maria Veigel*

232 Aelbert Cuyp, *An Evening Landscape*

233 Pieter de Hooch, *The Card-Players*

234 Jan Steen, *The Morning Toilet*

235 Rembrandt, *The Lady with a Fan*

236 1 Rembrandt, *The Shipbuilder and his Wife*. 2 Jacob van Ruisdael, *An Evening Landscape*

237 1 Sir Thomas Lawrence, *Sir Walter Scott*. 2 Sir David Wilkie, *The Entrance of George IV at Holyroodhouse*

238 Sir Thomas Lawrence: 1 *Sir Jeffrey Wyatville*. 2 *George IV*. Permission of the Trustees of the Wallace Collection

239 The Guard Chamber, Windsor Castle

241 Jacques-Laurent Agasse, *The Nubian Giraffe*

242 King George IV in Windsor Great Park. An engraving by Melville. Royal Library, Windsor

243 A silver door hinge at Balmoral with Victoria and Albert's initials entwined. Photo Michael Freeman

245 Frans Xaver Winterhalter, *The Cousins: Queen Victoria and Princess Victoire, Duchesse de Nemours*

246 and 247 William Powell Frith, *Ramsgate Sands*

248 Sir Edwin Landseer, *Islay and Tilco with a Red Macaw and two Love-birds*

249 1 Queen Victoria's dolls. Photo Michael Freeman. Museum of London. 2 A page from one of the Queen's schoolbooks. Royal Archives, Windsor

250 Sir David Wilkie, *The First Council of Queen Victoria*

251 Sir Francis Grant, *Queen Victoria riding with Lord Melbourne at Windsor*

252 1 Frans Xaver Winterhalter, *Queen Victoria when Young*. 2 The seventeenth-century cradle bought by Queen Victoria for her first baby

253 Edward Lear, watercolour of Osborne, July 1846. Royal Library, Windsor

254 The billiard table at Osborne, designed by Prince Albert. Photo Michael Freeman

255 Cima da Conegliano, Detail of *Four Saints and the Annunciation*

256 Frans Xaver Winterhalter, *The First of May, 1851*

257 Frans Xaver Winterhalter: 1 *Prince Arthur*. 2 *The Royal Family in 1846*. 3 Sir Edwin Landseer, *Eos*

258 Osborne: 1 The Royal children's gardening tools. 2 Their grocer's shop. 3 Their fort. 4 Their kitchen. Photos Michael Freeman

259 Watercolour by G. H. Thomas of the reception of Napoleon III and the Empress Eugénie at Windsor, 16 April 1855. From Queen Victoria's Souvenir Albums. Royal Library, Windsor

260 1 Watercolour by G. H. Thomas of the arrival by royal yacht of Napoleon III at Dover, 16 April 1855. 2 Engraving by J. David, after E. Pingret, of King Louis-Philippe of France, Queen Victoria and Prince Albert in the

royal train during the French King's State Visit to England in 1844. 3 Engraving by Bayot and Cuvillier, after E. Pingret, of the arrival of the royal party at Portsmouth Station, during that visit. All from the Royal Library, Windsor. 4 Photograph of the interior of the saloon carriage used by Queen Victoria from 1869 to the end of her life, from the train made for her by the London and North Western Railway Company. National Railway Museum, York. Crown Copyright

261 William Wyld, watercolour of Manchester. Royal Library, Windsor

262 Frescoes by Dyce and Maclise and decorations by Barry and Pugin in the Royal Gallery, Houses of Parliament, Westminster

263 Calotypes from the 1851 Great Exhibition Jury Reports. 1 A stand of egrets' feathers. 2 The upper galleries of the Exhibition. Royal Archives, Windsor

264 Photograph of the dismantling of the Crystal Palace in 1852. Royal Archives, Windsor

265 Duccio di Buoninsegna, *Triptych: The Crucifixion; the Annunciation with the Virgin and Child enthroned; St Francis receiving the Stigmata with the Virgin and Child enthroned*

266 Benozzo Gozzoli, *The Death of Simon Magus*

267 Gentile da Fabriano, *Madonna and Child with Angels*

268 Lucas Cranach the Elder, *Apollo and Diana*

269 Osler candelabrum, Osborne. Photo Michael Freeman

270 1 Circlet, earrings and brooches designed by Prince Albert for Queen Victoria. 2 One of the Minton exhibits shown at the Great Exhibition. 3 Princess Victoria, drawn by Queen Victoria and etched by Prince Albert. Royal Library, Windsor

271 The Royal Mausoleum, Frogmore. Photo Michael Freeman

273 Photograph of Queen Victoria and her daughters mourning Prince Albert's death, Windsor Castle, March 1862. Royal Archives, Windsor

274 Balmoral Castle. Photo Michael Freeman

275 One of a pair of Minton candelabra of Highlanders in Parian Marble. Photo Michael Freeman

277 Queen Victoria and Prince Albert's tomb, Royal Mausoleum, Frogmore. Photo Michael Freeman

278 Dome of the Royal Mausoleum, Frogmore. Photo Michael Freeman

279 1 The Royal Dairy, Windsor and 2 Detail of one of the Minton tiles which decorate the dairy. Photos Michael Freeman

280 The Durbar Room, Osborne. Photo Michael Freeman

281 *Carte de visite* photographs of 1 Louis, Comte d'Eu. 2 Grand Duchess Constantine. 3 King Leopold I of the Belgians. 4 The Prince Imperial. 5 Grand Duke Vladimir and Alexis Alexandrovich. All from the Royal Archives, Windsor

282 1 A team of rescue workers at a mine disaster in the north-east of England, by W. Downey, 1862. 2 Game-keepers at Windsor Castle, daguerreotype, *c*. 1847. 3 Queen Victoria and Prince Albert. A hand-tinted photograph by R. Fenton, 1854

283 4 The Chartist meeting at Kennington Common, South London, in 1848. A daguerreotype by W. Kilburn. 5 Staff at the Royal Mews, Buckingham Palace, in 1847. All from the Royal Archives, Windsor

284 1 Mission Wedding, South Africa, 1870. 2 Huts of the guards at Balaclava, in the Crimean War, by James Robertson. 3 Kimberley diamond mine: the Big Hole. All from the Royal Archives, Windsor

285 1 Sir Edwin Landseer, *Queen Victoria on Horseback*. 2 The Queen's memorial to John Brown at Frogmore. Photo Michael Freeman

286 Queen Victoria in the grounds at Frogmore with one of her Indian servants. Royal Archives, Windsor

287 King Edward VII and Queen Alexandra on board Royal Yacht, Cowes, 1903. Royal Archives, Windsor

289 1 King Edward VII, April 1902. 2 Albert Edward, Prince of Wales, with the jockey Watts, mounted on Persimmon, and the horse's trainer, Richard Marsh. Newmarket, September 1897. 3 'The Prince's First Tiger', India, 1875–6. 4 King Edward VII shooting, early 1900s. 5 On board the *Britannia* for the start of the Queen's Cup, August 1896. All from the Royal Archives, Windsor

290 1 Croquet at Sandringham, 1846. Royal Archives, Windsor. 2 Sandringham. Photo Michael Freeman

291 1 Drawing-room at Sandringham, 1899. Royal Archives, Windsor. 2 The same room, seventy-five years later. Sandringham Estate

292 Jean-Edouard Lacretelle, *Queen Alexandra when Princess of Wales*

293 1 Royal group on board yacht, Reval, 1908. 2 King Edward VII and Kaiser Wilhelm II in a motor car in Friedrichshof, 1906. 3 King Edward VII and Tsar Nicholas II on board the Royal Yacht, Reval, 1908. 4 Royal group at leisure, Fredensborg, 1889. All from the Royal Archives, Windsor

294 and 295 Carl Fabergé, animals carved in semi-precious stones

296 1 William Mulready, letter sheet. 2 John Leech, caricature of the Mulready envelope

297 1 1840 1d Black from the first printing. 2 1840 2d Blue from the first printing. 3 1840 1d Black from Plate 4, showing the Maltese Cross cancellation. 4 1847 Trinidad. 5 and 6 1847 Mauritius 1d, 2d. 7 and 8 1850 New South Wales 1d, 2d. 9 1851 Canada 12d Black. 10 1854 Bermuda 1d. 11 1856 British Guiana 4d. 12 1854 India 4d with the head inverted. 13 1854 Western Australia 4d with error. 14 1855 New Zealand 1/-. 15 1855 Tasmania (Van Diemen's Land) 2d. 16 1861 Cape of Good Hope triangular penny printed blue instead of red. 17 1857 Newfoundland 1/-. 18 1859 Ceylon 4d.

298 1 1840 watercolour sketch for the first stamps. 2 Edward Henry Corbould, watercolour sketch of Britannia. 3 1854 Corbould watercolour sketch of Queen Victoria. 4 1916 Montserrat, De La Rue artist's design, initialled by King George V. 5 1922 Jamaica, De La Rue artist's design showing Port Royal. 6 1927 Barbados, Bradbury Wilkinson watercolour. 7 1932 Cayman Islands, Waterlow watercolour drawing

299 1, 2 and 3 Artist's watercolour drawings for ½d stamps for Child Welfare League. 4, 5 and 6 1933 watercolour drawings for stamps to commemorate the Centenary of British Settlement. 7, 8 and 9 1935 designs for King George V Jubilee stamps. 10–14 Trial drawings for 1937 King George VI Coronation

300 1 1948 King George VI Silver Wedding stamps. 2 1957 Turks and Caicos Islands, designs of local interest. 3, 4 and 5 1964 Falkland Islands 2½d, 6d, and 6d with a printing error

302 James Sant, *King George V when a Boy*. 2 The Game Museum, Sandringham. Photo Michael Freeman

303 Sir Luke Fildes, *King George V*

304 1 Jacomb Hood, *The Delhi Durbar*. Royal Library, Windsor. 2 King George V and Queen Mary at the Durbar. Royal Archives, Windsor

305 Queen Mary's sitting-room at the Delhi camp. Royal Archives, Windsor

306 King George V and a boy. Sunderland, June 1917. Royal Archives, Windsor

307 John Singer Sargent, *Arthur, Duke of Connaught*

308 and 309 Pages from Queen Mary's illustrated catalogue to her Collection

310 1 Mahogany sideboard attributed to William Vile, 1740. 2 A case of Queen Mary's collection of jades

311 1 Holyroodhouse, Edinburgh. Department of the Environment. Crown Copyright. 2 Mahogany and gilt commode attributed to William Vile

312 Queen Mary's Dolls' House. Entrance hall and staircase

313 The Dolls' House library

317 Carl Fabergé: 1 Easter Egg containing portraits of the children of Tsar Nicholas II. 2 Flowers and fruit in rock crystal pots. 3 The Colonnade Egg

318 1 John Piper, *Windsor Castle: the Quadrangle looking towards the Round Tower*. 2 Paul Nash, *Landscape of the Vernal Equinox*. Both reproduced by gracious permission of Her Majesty Queen Elizabeth The Queen Mother

319 Graham Sutherland, *Study for Christ in Glory*

320 The Queen's Gallery, Buckingham Palace

321 The Castle of Mey, Caithness, Scotland. British Tourist Authority

322 1 H.M.Y. *Britannia*: Prince Philip's sitting-room. Royal Naval Official photograph. Crown Copyright. 2 H.M.Y. *Britannia*. Radio Times Hulton Picture Library

323 Graham Sutherland, *The Armillary Sphere*

324 1 Sir Matthew Smith, *Still Life: Jugs and Apples*. 2 Augustus John, *George Bernard Shaw*. 3 Walter Richard Sickert, *Ennui*. All reproduced by gracious permission of Her Majesty Queen Elizabeth The Queen Mother

325 4 Duncan Grant, *Still Life*. 5 Sir William Nicholson, *The Gold Jug*. Both reproduced by gracious permission of Her Majesty Queen Elizabeth The Queen Mother

326 1 Feliks Topolski, *Augustus John*. 2 L. S. Lowry, *The Carriage*. 3 Sir Robin Darwin, *Castle Howard*

327 1 Sidney Nolan, *Herd at the Waterhole*. 2 Dame Barbara Hepworth, *Arthrodesis of the Hip*. 3 William Dobell, *A Country Race Meeting*

328 1 Edward Bower, *Charles I at his Trial*. 2 Samuel Cooper, miniature of Hugh May

329 Sir Godfrey Kneller, George I's Turkish servant, Mahomet

332 The Queen in the Throne Room at Buckingham Palace. BBC photo

334 The Duke of Edinburgh at the wheel of *Yeoman XIX*. BBC photo

335 Filming *Yeoman XIX*. BBC photo

336 Michael Gill and Sir Huw Wheldon. BBC photo

337 Leonardo da Vinci, drawing of Leda. Royal Library, Windsor

338 Prince Charles rowing on Loch Muick. BBC photo

339 Prince Charles during filming near Balmoral. BBC photo

340 Sir Huw Wheldon at Caernarvon. BBC photo

341 Prince Charles on board HMS *Bronington*. BBC photo

342 The Duke of Edinburgh driving a four in hand in Windsor Royal Park. BBC photo

INDEX

Italic references are to illustrations

abbeys, *see* Fontevrault, Waltham Holy Cross, Westminster
Adam, James, 185
Adams, George, 167, 182
Adams, John, US President, 170
Adelaide, Queen of William IV (1792–1849), 244
advertising, 301
Africa, South, 284, 285
Agasse, Jacques-Laurent, *The Nubian Giraffe*, 240, 241
Agincourt, battle of, 35, 42
Albani, Cardinal Alessandro, 173, 185
Albert, Prince Consort of Victoria (1819–61), 160, 243–86, 291, 311, 322; collection of paintings, 255–6; death, Royal Mausoleum, 271–2; education, 251; Great Exhibition, 264–9; jewellery design, music, collecting, 270; Marble Arch and Buckingham Palace, 258–9; marriage, 252; Memorial, 272; Osborne and architecture, 253; Palace of Westminster, 262; South Kensington museums, 263
Alexander I, Tsar of Russia, 216
Alexander the Great, 226
Alexandra Feodorovna, Empress of Russia, 320
Alexandra of Denmark, Queen of Edward VII (1844–1925), 281, 287, 288, 292, 293, 312; character, 294–5; Fabergé, 294–5
Alexis Alexandrovich, Grand Duke, 281
Alfonso XI, King of Spain, 294
Alfred, Duke of Edinburgh, son of Queen Victoria, 257, 285, 296, 301
Alfred the Great, 13, 152
Alice, Princess, 257
Althnaguisach, Shiel of, 275
America, North, 146, 162–3, 181, 183, 276, 323
Amigoni, 160
Anchiennes et Nouvelles Chroniques d'Angleterre, 25, 26
Andrea del Sarto (1486–1531), 96, 113; *Holy Family*, 94
Angelico, Fra, 256
Angerstein collection, 237
Anne, Princess, daughter of Charles I, 117
Anne, Queen (1665–1714), 13, 130, 141, 142, 144, 146, 183
Anne Boleyn, 2nd Queen of Henry VIII (1507–36), 63–4, 69, 70
Anne of Bohemia, 1st Queen of Richard II (1366–94), 24, 38–9; effigy, 20
Anne of Cleves, 4th Queen of Henry VIII (1515–57), 70
Anne of Denmark, Queen of James I (1574–1619), 91, 98, 99, 100, 113
Annesley, Edward, 126
Apsley House, 226
Aquinas, Thomas, 60
Armada, Spanish, 85–6, 86; Armada Jewel, 68
arms and armour, 50–1, 53, 56, 126, 214, 215, 226
army, 22, 138, 146, 157, 183, 200, 214
Arthur, King of Britain, 36–7, 44
Arthur, Prince of Wales, son of Henry VII, 44, 45

Arundel, Thomas Howard, Earl of, 98, 100, 137
Ascham, Roger, 71, 74; *The Schoolmaster*, 74
Aubusson carpets, 209
Audley, Lady, 89
Audley End, 130, 131
Augusta, Princess of Wales (d. 1772), 159, 161, 162, 163, 164–8, 193
Austen, Jane, *Emma*, 237

Bach, J. S., 270
Bacon, Sir Francis, 46, 88, 152
Badminton House, 308
Baker, Sir Richard, *Chronicle*, 45
Balmoral, 243, 261, 264, 276, 291, 329; candelabra, 272, 275
Barberini, Cardinal Francesco, 112
Barry, Sir Charles, 262, 263
Bassano family, 69
Bassett, Lord, 40
Battle Abbey, 15
Bayeux tapestry, 15, 15
Bayot, 260
Beaufort, Margaret, mother of Henry VII (1443–1509), 46, 48–9; effigy, 20
Beaumaris Castle, 29, 31, 31
Bedford, John, Duke of (1389–1435), son of Henry IV, 39, 39
Bedford, photographer, 276
Beecher, Sir William (1753–1839), *George III at a Review*, 215; *George IV when Prince of Wales*, 213
Bellini, Giovanni (1430–1516): *Head of an Old Man*, 187; *Portrait of a Young Man*, 172, 178
Beowulf, 36
Berkeley Castle, 33
Berkley, William, 40
Bernini, Giovanni (1598–1680), 112, 126
Berny, Duc de, *Les très Riches Heures*, 39
Blanchet, 328
Blore, Edward, 258
Blücher, Prince von, 216
Blunt, Sir Anthony, 326
Boleyn, Anne, *see* Anne Boleyn
Boleyn, Sir Thomas, 63
books, 37–40, 122, 164, 169–70; bibles, 121, 122, 169
Books of Hours, 27, 38–41
Boscobel, 127, 127
Bosworth, battle of, 44
Bothwell, Earl of, 85
Boulton, Matthew, 182
Bower, Edward, *Charles I at his Trial*, 328
Boyce, William, 169
Boyle, Sir Henry, 152
Brandon, Charles, Duke of Suffolk, 89
Brandon, Henry, Duke of Suffolk, 89
Bridewell Palace, 57, 61, 63
Bridgman, Charles, 150
Brighton, 204, 211, 212, 244, 310
Brighton, Royal Pavilion, 197, 198–9, 199, 200, 201, 209, 211, 222, 230, 252, 310, 311; Banqueting Room, 198–9, 223; Music Room, 199, 224; Stables, 228
British Empire, 146, 200, 276, 281–2, 290, 296, 302, 309
Broker, Nicholas, 20
Bronzino, Agnolo (1503–72), *The Lady in Green*, 108
Brown, John, 275, 281, 285
Bruce, Sir William, 311
Bruegel, Jan 'Velvet' (1568–1625): *Adam and Eve*, 156, 157, 160; *Kermesse*, 160

Bruegel, Pieter (1525–69), *The Massacre of the Innocents*, 140
Brummel, Beau, 201
Buckingham, Duchess of, 170–1
Buckingham, George Villiers, Duke of (1627–87), 99, 100, 109, 113, 202; portraits, 112, 118
Buckingham House, 169, 170–2, 181, 200; furnishing, 171–4; Octagon Room, 171
Buckingham Palace, 57, 200, 201, 209, 238, 244, 252–3, 258, 310, 316; ballroom, 259; picture gallery, 210; Queen's Gallery, 320, 326; staff of Royal Mews, 283
Burghley, 261
Burke, Edmund, 180
Burlington, Earl of, 149
Bushey Park, 76
Bute, John Stuart, Earl of (1713–92), 161, 163, 168, 174, 180, 181, 239; *Botanical Tables*, 164, 164
Byrd, William, 88
Byron, Lord, 198, 237
Byzantium, 13, 29, 30

Caernarvon Castle, 16, 29–31, 30
Calais, 52; Treaty of, Chest, 34
Cambridge, Duke of, uncle of George V, 296
Cambridge University, 42, 48–9, 64, 81; King's College Chapel, 40, 42, 44, 64
Canaletto, Antonio (1697–1768), 160; *London*, 172, 173; *The Piazzetta, Venice*, 177
Canova, Antonio (1757–1822), 226, 232; statue of Napoleon, 227; *Mars and Venus*, 227
Canterbury Cathedral, 18, 24
Caravaggio, M. A. da (1569–1609), *The Death of the Virgin*, 94, 97
caricatures, 183, 211, 212, 296
Carisbrooke Castle, 121
Carlton House, 201, 203, 204–12, 209, 217, 221, 223, 227, 238, 239
Caroline of Anspach, Queen of George II (1683–1737), 151–3, 158
Caroline of Brunswick, Queen of George IV (1768–1821), 213, 231
carpets, 209, 269
Carracci, the, 173
Casson, Sir Hugh, 322
Castiglione, Baldassare, *The Courtier*, 52
Castlemaine, Lady, 129
castles, *see* Beaumaris, Berkeley, Caernarvon, Carisbrooke, Chester, Chinon, Conway, Corfe, Criccieth, Dover, Flint, Fotheringay, Gaillard, Harlech, Linlithgow, Mey, Newark, Norwich, Richmond, Stirling, Tintagel, Windsor
Catesby, Mark, *Natural History of Carolina, Florida and the Bahamas*, 145, 164, 165
cathedrals, *see* Canterbury, Coventry, North Elmham, St Albans, St Paul's, Worcester
Catherine Howard, 5th Queen of Henry VIII (d. 1542), 70–1, 79
Catherine of Aragon, 1st Queen of Henry VIII (1485–1536), 50, 54–5, 60, 62–3, 69–70
Catherine of Braganza, Queen of Charles II (1638–1705), 128, 129
Catherine Parr, 6th Queen of Henry VIII (1512–48), 71
Catherine the Great, of Russia, 172
Caxton, William (1422–91), 29, 44, 48, 169

Cellini, Benvenuto, 51, 72
Cerdic, King of Wessex, 13
Chambers, Sir William, 163, 168, 179, 181, 183
chapels, *see* Cambridge, King's College; Hampton Court, Chapel Royal; St James's Palace, Queen's Chapel; Tower of London, St John's Chapel; Westminster Abbey, Henry VII's Chapel; Windsor, St George's Chapel
Charles I, King (1600–49), 14, 94–7, 98, 99–121, 126, 128, 210, 232; bust by Le Sueur, 152; civil war, 116–22; collection of paintings, 100–9, 113–15; *Eikon Basilike*, 94, 121; execution, 94, 121; parliament, 115; portraits, 112, 115, 328; religion, 110–13, 116–21
Charles II, King (1630–85), 14, 45, 57, 61, 62, 110, 117, 121, 126–39, 140, 141, 311, 328; Leonardo drawings, 132–7; mace, 130; paintings, 128; palaces, 131–2; portraits, 92, 126; racing, 130; regalia, 128–9; yachts, 138
Charles V, King of France, 39
Charles Edward, Prince, the Young Pretender, 326–8
Charles, Prince of Wales (1948–), 30, 291, 325, 328
Charlotte of Mecklenburg-Strelitz, Queen of George III (1744–1818), 164, 170, 171, 179, 183, 202–3, 213; portraits, 180, 195
Charlotte, Princess, daughter of George IV (1796–1817), 213, 228; monument, 229
charters, 13, 32, 32
Chatsworth, 264
Chaucer, Geoffrey (1340–1400), 34, 37; *Canterbury Tales*, 37
Cheke, John, 71
Chelsea porcelain, 182, 183, 316
Chelsea Royal Hospital, 138, 139
Chester Castle, 16
chinoiserie, 160, 163–4, 199
Chinon, 16, 18
Chippendale, Thomas, 172
Chippendale, Thomas, the Younger, 214
chivalry, 35–7, 40, 52, 57, 98
Chronicles, 25, 37–40, 38, 44–5
Chroniques de Saint-Denis, 26, 38
Church, the, 16, 22, 33, 69–70, 71–2, 76, 98, 110–13, 121
Churchill, Lady Randolph, 294
Cima da Conegliano, Giovanni Battista (c. 1460–1508), *Four Saints and the Annunciation*, 255, 256
cinema, 288, 304–5
Cipriani, Giambattista, 179
civil service, 31–3
Clarence, Albert, Duke of, 281
Clarence House, 316
Clark, Lord, 326
Clarke, Dr Samuel, 152
Claude, *The Rape of Europa*, 237
Cliveden, 160
clocks, 59–60, 167, 181–2, 182, 183
clothes, 19, 37, 74, 81, 157, 181, 201, 203, 232, 294, 307
Clouet, François (c. 1516–72), *Mary Queen of Scots*, 85, 89
Cobbett, William, 198
Codex Alexandrinus, 121, 122
coins, 13, 29, 72
Cole, Henry, 264
Collinson, Peter, 163
Colnaghi, 231
Commonwealth, 122–6

Condé, Prince de, 227; bust after Coysevox, *228*

Connaught, Arthur, Duke of, son of Queen Victoria, 256, 257, *257*, *307*

Constable, John, 237

Constantine, Emperor, 30

Constantine, Grand Duchess, 218

Conway Castle, 29, 31, *31*

Conyngham, Lady, 228, 240

Cook, Captain James, 182

Cooper, Samuel (1609–72), 92, 116; miniature of Hugh May, 328, *328*

Corbould, Edward Henry, 297, 298

Corfe Castle, 19

Cornwall, Richard, Duke of, (son of King John), 36

Cornwallis, Lord, 152

Coronation: ceremony, 13–15, 316; chair, *14*, 15; regalia *12*, *13*, 14, 29, 83, 122, 128–9, 244; of Charles II, 128–9; of Elizabeth II, *12*, *13*; of George IV, 231; of Richard II, *26*, 38; of William IV, 244

Correggio, Antonio (1494–1534), 94, 96, 113; *Jupiter and Antiope*, *96*, *101*; *Venus, Mercury and Cupid*, *101*

Cosway, Richard, 198, 210

Coventry Cathedral, 319

Coysevox, Antoine, 228

Cranach, Lucas, the Elder (1515–86); 256, *Adam and Eve*, *268*

Cranmer, Thomas, 73

Crécy, battle of, 24

Crewe, Chief Justice, 42

Criccieth Castle, 31

Crimean War, 276, *284*

Critz, Emanuel de, 126

Crofts, Lord William, 117, *153*, 160

Cromwell, Oliver (1599–1658), 14, 94, 122, 126

crown, 14–15; Imperial State, *12*, 14; St Edward's, *12*, 14

crown jewels, *13*, 13–14, 29, 122, 232, 244

crusades, 18, 38

Crystal Palace, 264, *264*

Cubitt, Thomas, 253

Cumberland, Henry, Duke of, brother of George III, 174, *191*, *193*, 203, 204

Cumberland, William, Duke of, son of George II, 157, 158–9, 240

Cumming, Alexander, 181; barograph, *182*

Cuvillier, engraving of Portsmouth station, *260*

Cuyp, Aelbert (1620–91), 210; *An Evening Landscape*, *232*

Daddi, Bernardo, *Marriage of the Virgin*, *255*

Darnley, Lord, *84*, 85

Darwin, Sir Robin, *Castle Howard*, *326*

Davenport porcelain, 244

David, J., *260*

Davy, Sir Humphry, 201

Delft pottery, 244

Dettingen, battle of, 157

Devonshire, Duke of, 264

Dickens, Charles, 276

Dickinson, W., 203

Dighton, Denis, 214; *Battle of Waterloo*, *214*

Disraeli, Benjamin, 276

Dobell, William, *A Country Race Meeting*, *327*

Dobson, William, 116

Dolls' House, Queen Mary's, 312–15, *312*, *313*

Domenichino, 173

Domesday Book, 15

Donne, John, 88, *90*

Dorchester, Countess of, 128

Dover Castle, 16, 51, *54–5*

Dowland, John, 88

Dowsing, William, 122

Drake, Sir Francis, 86

Drury Lane, 128

Duccio di Buoninsegna (*c.* 1260–*c.* 1318), *Triptych*, *255*, *265*

Durbar, the, 304, *304*, *305*

Dürer, Albrecht (1471–1528), 114; *Emperor Maximilian I*, *51*; *Self-portrait*, *96*

Dyce, William, frescoes, 262, *263*

Dyck, Sir Anthony van (1599–1641), 100, 112, 117, *121*, 160; *Charles I à la Chasse*, *94*, 114; *Charles I in Three Positions*, *112*; *Charles I with M. de St Antoine*, 114, *115*; *Cupid and Psyche*, 114, *120*; *Five Eldest Children of Charles I*, *117*; *George Villiers, Duke of Buckingham, and Lord Francis Villiers*, *118*, 202; *Henrietta Maria*, *119*; *Thomas Killigrew and (?)William, Lord Crofts*, *153*

Eastlake, Charles, 256

Edgar, King of the English, 13, 15

Edinburgh, Philip, Duke of (1921–), 276, 311, 322–9; knowledge of ships, 322; painting, 326

Edward I, King (1239–1307), *14*, 23, 24, 29, *29*, 32, 34; lawgiver, 32–3; Welsh campaign, 29–31

Edward II, King (1284–1327), 30, 33

Edward III, King (1312–77), *14*, 24, *29*, 32, 33–4; effigy, *20*; garter, 40, 46, 131

Edward IV, King (1442–83), 25, 37, 40–2, 44, 46, 122

Edward VI, King (1537–53), 52, 70, 71, 72–3

Edward VII, King (1841–1910), *257*, 258, 270, 271, 275, 276, *287*, 288–96, *289*, *293*, 304; and the public, 288; Edwardian age, 295–6; Empire, 290; Europe, 288–90; monarchy, 302; Sandringham, 290–4; stamp collecting, 296, 302

Edward VIII, King (1894–1972), 30, 308, 314, 315

Edward, the Black Prince (1330–76), *14*, 40; tomb, 24

Edward the Confessor, King (*c.* 1003–66), 13, 14, *14*, 23, 34, 36, *36*, 37, 45

Edward, Duke of Albany, brother of George III, 161

effigies, *18–21*, 24, 33, 46–8, 272, *277*

Eglinton, Lord, 174

Ehrenburg, Schloss, 253

Eleanor of Aquitaine, Queen of Henry II (*c.* 1122–1204), 18; tomb, *19*

Eleanor of Castile, Queen of Edward I (d. 1290), 30, 33; Eleanor Cross, *33*

Elgin marbles, 237

Elizabeth I, Queen (1533–1603), *14*, 45, 52–7, 70, 71, 74–88; and Mary, 83–5; Armada, 86; clothing, *74*; cult of Virgin Queen, 81–3; handwriting, *75*; learning, 74; patronage of arts, 86–8; portraits, *68*, *75*, *81*, *82*, *83*, *86*, *89*; Spain, Scotland, 83; virginals, *43*, *76*

Elizabeth II, Queen (1926–), *12*, *13*, 23, 168, 231, 310, 311, 315, 316, 322–9; additions to Royal Collection, 326–8; preservation of royal homes and possessions, 325–6; royal tours, 322–5; sharing inheritance with public, 328–9

Elizabeth of Bohemia, daughter of James I, 128

Elizabeth, Princess, daughter of Charles I, *117*

Elizabeth the Queen Mother (1900–), 315–16, 321, 324, 325

Elizabeth of York, Queen of Henry VII (1465–1503), 46, 47, 57, *62*

Eltham Palace, 40–2, *42*

Erasmus, Desiderius (1466–1536), 48, 60, *61*, 71

Essex, Robert Devereux, second Earl of, 81, *90*, 99

Eton School, 184; chapel, 40

Eu, Comte d', 281

Eugénie, Empress, wife of Napoleon III, 259, *259*–60, 269

Evelyn, John, 126

Eworth, Hans, *Elizabeth I and the Three Goddesses*, 81, *82*

Exeter Corporation, 126

Fabergé, Carl (1846–1920), 294–5, *294*, *295*, 296, 312, *317*

Falkland Palace, 83, *84*, 85

Fayrefax, Robert, 69

Fenton, R., 282

Ferrar, Nicolas, 121

feudalism, 16, 33, 42, 44

Field of the Cloth of Gold, 51–2, *54–5*, 261

Fielding, Henry, 169

Fildes, Sir Luke, *King George V*, *303*

Fischer, Johann Christian, 190

Fisher, Cardinal John, 48

Fitzherbert, Mrs Maria (1756–1837), 210–12, 213, 228

Flint Castle, 29

Flower, Barnard, 46, 64

Fontainebleau, 51–2

Fontevrault Abbey, 18, 24

food, 83, 132, 198, 228, 230, 240, 258

Ford, Gerald, US President, 323

Fotheringay Castle, 85

Fox, Charles James, 210, 213, 239

France, 16–18, 24, 149; wars against, 140, 142–4, 146, 157, 179, 180, 183, 200, 213, 216

François I, King of France, 51–2, *54–5*, 261

Frederick, Prince of Wales, son of George II (1717–51), 117, *153*, 157–62, 164–8; botany, 163; music, 157; music and painting, 159–60; portraits, *158*, *162*; relationship with parents, 158–9; sport, 160; state barge, 160, *161*; wife and family, 161–2

Frederick the Great, 158

Frederick William IV of Prussia, 264

French Revolution, 183, 200, 208–9, 213, 214

Frith, William Powell (1819–1909), 245; *Ramsgate Sands*, *246–7*

Frizell, William, 128

Frobisher, Sir Martin, 323

Frogmore, 184, 249, *286*; mausoleum, 271–2, *271*, 275, *278*

Froissart, Jean, 38

furniture, 132, 170–2, *170*, *171*, 204, 209, *218*, *220*, 226, 252, 272, 292–4, 310, *310*, 311

Gaddi, Taddeo, 255

Gaillard Castle, 18

Gainsborough, Thomas (1727–88), 174, 204, 210; *Colonel St Leger*, *192*; *Diana and Actaeon*, *189*; *Henry, Duke of Cumberland, with the Duchess of Cumberland and Lady Elizabeth Lut-trell*, *191*; *Johann Christian Fischer*, *190*; *King George III, Queen Charlotte and thirteen of their children*, *179*

gardens, 150, *151*, 163–4, 253, 290, *290*, 316

Garrick, David, 230, 231

Garter, 40, 52

Gentile da Fabriano (1370–1427), 256; *Madonna and Child with Angels*, *267*

Gentileschi, Orazio (1563–1647), *Joseph and Potiphar's Wife*, 110

George I, King (1660–1727), 146–51, 157; character, 149; *Mustapha and Mahomet*, 150, 328, *329*; political and financial problems, 146–9; portrait, *146*

George II, King (1683–1760), 25, 34, 38, 122, 151–7, 171; army, music, 157; portrait, *152*

George III, King (1738–1820), 157, 161–84, *185*, 203, 204, 210, 211, 213, 231, 240, 308, 310; America, 162; background and education, 163–9; books, 169–70; caricature, 183; character, 163; clocks, microscope, *166*, *167*, 181–2; coach, *179*; farm, 181; furniture, 171–2; illness, 183; Kew, 164; landscape drawing by, *168*; pictures, 172–9; politics, 180–1; portraits, *162*, *174*, *179*, *184*, *193*, *194*; Windsor, 183–4

George IV, King (1762–1830), 13, 14, 112, 131–2, 174, 184, 198–242, 244, 259, 308, 311, 322, 329; Brighton, 228–30; Brighton Pavilion, 198–9; caricature, *212*; Carlton House, 204–10; character, 199–200, 226–8; collections, 201–2; coronation, 231; family, 202–3; horseman, 204; Mrs Fitzherbert, 210–12; music, 230; obsession with war, 213–26; patronage, 237; pictures, 210; portraits, *198*, *202*, *205*, 213, *214*, *238*; Princess Caroline, 213; royal tours, 231–7; Windsor, 238–42, *242*

George V, King (1865–1936), 290, 291, *293*, 298, *306*, 311; character, 303; first world war, 306; India, 304; monarchy, 307–8, 315; photography 304–6; portraits, *302*, *303*; stamp collection, 297–300, 301–2

George VI, King (1895–1952), 291, 295; monarchy, second world war, 315–16, 324; stamp collection, *299*, *300*, 301

George, St, 39, 44, 51, 52–7, 57, 115

Gibbons, Grinling (1648–1720), 67, 132, *132*

Gibbons, Orlando, 88

Gillray, James (1757–1815), caricatures: of George III; *183*; of George IV, *212*

Girardon, F., 220

Girolamo da Treviso, *The Four Evangelists*, 71, 72

Giulio Romano, tapestries, 52

glass, stained, 11, 46, 64

Glassalt, the, 275

Glendower, Owen, 31

Gloucester, Duchess of, 240

Gloucester, Humphrey, Duke of, son of Henry IV, 49

Gluck, 270

Gobelins tapestries, 209, *209*

Goes, Hugo van der (*c.* 1440–82), *Trinity Altarpiece*, 100, *100*

Gonzaga family, 113

Gozzoli, Benozzo, 256; *Death of Simon Magus*, 266

Grace de Dieu, 51, 54–5

Grant, Duncan, *Still Life*, 325

Grant, Sir Francis, *Queen Victoria riding with Lord Melbourne*, 251

Great Exhibition, 256, 263, 264–9, 270

Greenwich Palace, 45, 51, 70, 76, 114, 123, 141; Hospital, 141; King Charles block, *124*, 141; Painted Hall, 146, *147*, 150–1; Queen's House, 99, 113, 123; Royal Observatory, 138

Greenwich Park, 76

Groupy, Joseph, 168

Gruner, Ludwig, 253, 255, 269

Guelfi, 152

Guercino (1599–1666), *Study of Flying Putto*, 185

Guilford, Sir Henry, 61

Gwynn, Nell, 128, 130

Haag, Carl, 273

Hals, Frans (c. 1580–1666), *Portrait of a Man*, 155

Hampden, John, 116

Hampton Court Palace, 50, *54*, 59–60, 83, 114, 122, 123, 126, *140*, *141*, 183; Banqueting House, 157, *158*; Chapel Royal, 59, 65, 67; Fountain Court, *125*, 140; gardens, 141–2; Great Hall, 59, 64; King's Staircase, *143*; tennis court, 60; Tijou gate, *93*, 142; Wolsey's Closet, 66

Handel, George Frederick (1685–1759), 157, 159, 168, 270; bust, *157*; *The Messiah*, 168

Hanover, 231

Hanoverians, 145–86

Hardingstone, Eleanor Cross at, 33 or Cross at, 33

Harlech Castle, 29, 31

Harold II, King (c. 1022–66), 15, 29

Harrison, Edmund, 128

Hastings, battle of, 15

Hatfield Palace, 74, *74*, 75, 76

Hawksmoor, Nicholas (1661–1736), 141, *150*

Hayter, Sir George, 250

Hazlitt, William, 129, 198

Helena, Princess, 257

Henrietta Maria, Queen of Charles I (1609–69), 110, 112, 113; portraits, *92*, *119*

Henry II, King (1068–1135), 18, 22, 23; tomb, *18*

Henry III, King (1207–72), 22, 23–4, 29, 33, 34, 36, 40

Henry V, King (1387–1422), 24, 39, 42; portrait, *24*

Henry VI, King (1421–61), 24, 39, *39*, 40

Henry VII, King (1457–1509), 44–8, 62, 69; as administrator, 44–5; bust, 45–8; effigy, 47; portraits, *48*, 57, 62, 89

Henry VIII, King (1491–1547), 38, 45, 49–72; armour, 50–1, *53*, 56; bust, *49*; *Defence of the Seven Sacraments*, 60–1; divorce from Catherine of Aragon, 63–4; Field of the Cloth of Gold, 51, 261; music, 64–9; portraits, *48*, 62, *64*, *73*; Renaissance prince, 50; sport, 60; wives, 69–71; writing box, *72*

Henry, Prince of Wales, eldest son of James I (1594–1612), 98–9, 100; portraits, *91*, *99*

Henry of York, Cardinal, grandson of James II, 232, 326–8

Hepworth, Dame Barbara, *Arthrodesis of the Hip*, 327

heraldry, *11*, 35, 37, 40, 44, 46

Herring, John, 316

Herschel, Sir William, 182

Hertford, Lady, 228

Hervey, Lord, 158

Hill, Sir Roland, 296

Hilliard, Nicholas (1547–1619), 61, 68, 81, 88, 116; miniatures: *Elizabeth I*, *81*, 89; *Henry VII*, 89; *Henry VIII*, 89; *James I*, *116*; *Jane Seymour*, 89

Histoire d'Alexandre le Grand, 26

history, 23, 44–5, 152, 180

Hoefnagel, Georg, engraving of Nonsuch, 59

Hogarth, William (1697–1764), 181; *David Garrick*, 230, 231

Holbein, Hans, the Younger (1497–1543), 49, 57, 60, 61–2, 70, 72, 73, 77, 88, 152, 329; *A Gentleman: Unknown*, 77; *Cecily Heron*, 80; Chatsworth cartoon, 48; *Derich Born*, 78; design for fireplace, 63; *Erasmus*, 94; *Henry VIII*, 48; miniatures: *Lady Audley*, 89, *Charles Brandon, Duke of Suffolk*, 89, *Henry Brandon, Duke of Suffolk*, 89; *Nicolas Kratzer*, 94; *Thomas Howard, Duke of Norfolk*, 79, 160

Holinshed, Raphael (d. c. 1580), *Chronicles of England, Scotlande and Irelande*, 44, 45

Holland, Henry, 209, 212, 228

Hollar, Wenceslas, 35, 114, 127

Holyroodhouse, 83, 232, 237, *311*

Hone, Galyon, 64

Hooch, Pieter de (1629–c. 1684), *The Card Players*, 210, *233*

Hood, Jacomb, *The Delhi Durbar*, 304

Hoppner, John, 214

Horenbout, Lucas, *Henry VIII*, 89

Horse Guards' Parade, 157

Hoskins, John, *Henrietta Maria*, 92, 116

Howard, *see* Arundel, Catherine Howard

Hudson, Thomas, *George II*, 152

Hunt, Leigh, 199

Hyde Park, 171, 181

India, 146, 179, 184, 276, 281–2, *289*, 290, 304, 309

industrial revolution, 200, 261, 262, 282, *283*

industry, 179, 181

Ingatestone Hall, 82

Ireland, 184, 231, 232, 285

iron, cast, 198, 201, *222*, 264

Jacopo di Cione, 255–6

James I, King (1566–1625), 83, 94, 95, 97–9, 109, 146; *Basilike Doron*, 98; *Laws of Free Monarchies*, 97; portraits, 97, *116*; tapestry, 109–10

James II, King (1633–1701), 110, *117*, 126, 129, 130, 137–8, 139, 146, 232

James III, King of Scotland (1451–81), *100*

James IV, King of Scotland (1473–1513), *100*, *311*

James, the Old Pretender, 146, 149

Jane Seymour, 3rd Queen of Henry VIII (c. 1509–37), 62, 70, 72, 89

jewels, 68, 81–2, 231, 270, 294–5, 309; *see also* crown jewels

John, Augustus (1871–1961), 326; *George Bernard Shaw*, *324*

John, King (1167–1216), 13, 18, 19, 22; King John's cup, *19*

John of Gaunt, son of Edward III (1340–99), *11*, 32

Johnson, Samuel, 169, 170

Jones, Inigo (1573–1652), 97, 98, 99, 110, *111*, 113, 123

Jonson, Ben, 86, 98; *The Barrier*, 98

Jutland, battle of, 306

Karim, Hafiz Abdul, 281

Katherine, Queen of Henry V, 24

Kendall, Duchess of, 149

Kent, Duchess of, mother of Queen Victoria, 244, 249, 250, 271

Kent, Edward, Duke of, son of George III, 244

Kent, William (1685–1748), 149–50, 152, 157, 160, 171; Prince Frederick's state barge, 160, *161*

Kensington Gardens, 76, 150, 151, 272; Serpentine, 150

Kensington Palace, 142, *142*, 149–50, 152, 183, 201, 249, 253; Cupola Room, *150*; King's Gallery, *150*; King's Grand Staircase, *148*, 149

Keppel, Mrs, 294

Kew: George III's palace, 182–3, *184*; Observatory, 182; Orangery, 163; Pagoda, 163–4; park, 76, *164*; Royal Botanical Gardens, 163–4; White House, 160, *163*

Kilburn, W., *283*

Killigrew, Sir Thomas, 117, *153*, 160

Kimberley diamond mine, *284*

King's College Chapel, see Cambridge

Kingston, Earl of, 301

Kip, John: *Vue et Prospective de la ville de Londre*, *131*; *Hampton Court Palace*, 141

Kipling, John Lockwood, Durbar Room, Osborne House, *280*

Knapton, George, *The Family of Frederick, Prince of Wales*, 161, *162*

Kneller, Sir Godfrey (1646–1723), 140, *146*; George I's servant Mahomet, 328, *329*

Knyff, Leonard, 141

Kratzer, Nicolas, 59, 94

Lacretelle, Jean-Edouard, *Queen Alexandra when Princess of Wales*, *292*

Lade, Sir John, 204

Landseer, Sir Edwin (1802–73), 245, 257, 258; *Eos*, 257; *Islay and Tilco*, 248; *Queen Victoria on Horseback*, 285

Langtry, Lillie, 288

Latimer, Hugh, 73

Laud, Archbishop William, 121

Lawrence, Sir Thomas (1769–1830), 216; *Duke of Wellington*, 230; *George IV*, 238; *Pope Pius VII*, 225; *Sir Jeffrey Wyatville*, 238; *Sir Walter Scott*, 232, 237; *William Pitt*, 225

Lear, Edward, watercolour of Osborne, 253

Lee, Sir Henry, 57, 88

Leech, John, caricature of Mulready envelope, 296

Leemput, Remigius van, *Henry VII, Elizabeth of York, Henry VIII and Jane Seymour*, 62

Lehzen, Baroness, 249

Leibnitz, Gottfried, 151

Leicester, Robert Dudley, Earl of, 81

Leicester House, 160

Leitch, 273

Leland, John, 38, 122

Lely, Sir Peter (1618–80), 128, 129, 132, 140

Lemon, Margaret, 114

Lennox, Margaret Douglas, Countess of, 68

Leonardo da Vinci (1452–1519), 51, 52, 96, 133–7, 326, 329; drawings, *133–6*; *St John the Baptist*, 94

Leopold I, King of the Belgians, 218

Leopold of Saxe-Coburg, son-in-law of George IV, 228, 244, 251, 257

Leptis Magna, 240

Le Sueur, Hubert, 152

Lieven, Princess, 199, 200, 216

Linlithgow Castle, 83, *84*

Liotard, Jean-Etienne (1702–89), 164, 177, 189; *Augusta, Princess of Wales*, 193; *George, Prince of Wales*, 193; *Henry, Duke of Cumberland*, 193; *Princess Louisa Ann*, 193

Lippi, Filippino (c. 1406–69), *Angel Receiving the Child from the Virgin*, 185

literature, 37, 86–8, 169, 237

Little Gidding, 121

Liverpool, Earl of, 215

Lloyd George, Earl, 29, 315

Locke, John, 152

London, 28, 34, 35, 40, 140, 142, *172*, 181, 200, 269

Longhi, Pietro (1702–85): *Blind Man's Buff*, 173, *176*; *The Morning Levée*, 173

Loseley Park, 57

Lotto, Lorenzo (c. 1480–1556), 128; *Andrea Odoni*, 129

Louis XI, King of France, 40

Louis XIII, King of France, 94

Louis XIV, King of France (1638–1715), 140, 213, 220, 226–7

Louis XV, King of France, 227

Louis XVI, King of France, 209, 219

Louis XVIII, King of France, 214, *215*, 226

Louis-Philippe, King of France, 259, 261

Louisa Ann, Princess, daughter of Frederick, Prince of Wales, *193*

Louise, Queen of Denmark, *293*

Lowry, L. S., 328; *The Carriage*, 326

Lucar, Cyril, patriarch of Constantinople, 121

Luther, Martin, 61, 122

Luttrell, Lady Elizabeth, *191*

Lutyens, Sir Edwin, 312–13

Mabuse, Jan, *Adam and Eve*, 113

Macaulay, Lord, 168

Maclise, Daniel, frescoes, 262, 263

Magna Carta, 19, 161

Maiano, Benedetto, 50

Mallory, Sir Thomas, 44

Manchester, 269

Mantegna, Andrea (1431–1506), 96; *The Triumph of Caesar*, 106, 107, 113, 126

Mantua, Duke of, 113

manuscripts, illuminated, 13, 25–8, 34–5, 37–40, *38*

Marbeck, John, 69

Marble Arch, 258

Marchetti, Carlo, 272

Marie Feodorovna, Empress of Russia, *293*

Marlborough, Duke of, 144

Marlborough House, 295, 308

Marochetti, Carlo, 272

Marsh, Richard, trainer, *289*

Mary of Guise, 83

Mary of Modena, Queen of James II, 139

Mary, Princess, daughter of Charles I, *117*

Mary I, Queen (1516–58), 62, 73–4

Mary II, Queen (1662–94), 137, 139–42

Mary, Queen of George V (1867–1953), 291, 295, 303–15; as collector, 305, 308–15; character, 307–8

Mary, Queen of Scots (1542–87), 76, 83–6, 97, 311; portraits, 85, 89

masques, 88, 98–9, 116, 161

Matsys, Cornelius, engraving of Henry VIII in old age, 73

Matsys, Quentin, 61

Maximilian I, Emperor (1459–1519), 51, 51, 56

May, Hugh, 131, 328

Mayall, 281

Mazarin, Cardinal Jules, 126

medals, 86, 316

Medici, Marie de, 113

Melbourne, Lord (1779–1848), 213, 250–1, 250, 251, 276

Melville, engraving of George IV, 242

Memmo, Dionisio, 69

Mendelssohn, 270

Mercier, Philippe, 160; The Music Party, 157, 158

Merian, Maria Sibylla, Metamorphosis, 165

Metternich, Prince, 216

Mey, Castle of, 321, 321

Michelangelo Buonarroti (1475–1564), 46, 173; Christ on the Cross, 186

Millar, Sir Oliver, 160, 326

miniatures, 61, 88, 89–92, 101, 116, 326, 328

Minton porcelain, 275

monarchy: symbols and ceremony, 13–15; divine right of kings, 94, 97, 121; in 16th century, 57; medieval duties, 13, 16, 23; relationship to church, 16, 23, 38, 98; relationship to parliament, 22–3, 94, 121, 140, 144, 146, 149, 276; under Charles I, 121; under Charles II, 139; under Edward I, Edward II and Edward III, 33; under Elizabeth I, 81–2; under George IV, 237; under George V, 302, 308, 315; under Henry VIII, 51–2, 62; under James I, 97–8; under Victoria, 281; under William III and Mary II, 142

Monet, Claude, 316

Monmouth, James, Duke of, 129

Montfort, Simon de, 23

More, Sir Thomas (1478–1535), 45, 50, 59, 60, 61, 80; Utopia, 60

Morier, David, military paintings, 157

Morley, Thomas, 88

Morton, Cardinal John, 85

Moser, George Michael, 168

Mudge, Thomas, 182; pocket watch, 182

Mulready, William, envelopes, 296, 301

museums: British Library, 34, 169; British Museum, 38, 122, 169, 170, 263, 273; National Gallery, 237, 256, 269; South Kensington museums, 263; Victoria and Albert Museum, 312

music, 18, 64–9, 76, 76, 88, 149, 157, 159, 168, 201, 230, 270, 321

Mytens, Daniel (c. 1590–1648), 100; George Villiers, Duke of Buckingham, 112; Portrait of the Artist, 103; Thomas, Earl of Arundel, 98

Napoleon I (1769–1821), 182, 200, 214, 225–6, 259

Napoleon III (1808–73), 259–60, 259, 269

Napoleon, Eugène, Prince Imperial, 281

Nash, John (1752–1835), 197, 199, 200, 212, 228

Nash, Joseph, Buckingham Palace, 201

Nash, Paul (1889–1946), Landscape of the Vernal Equinox, 318

navy, 86, 138, 141, 144, 146, 184, 200, 214

Nelson, Lord, 72, 184, 214, 291, 323

Newark Castle, 19

Newmarket, 130, 204, 288, 289

Newton, Sir Isaac, 152

Nicholas II, Tsar of Russia (1868–1918), 288, 292, 293, 294, 295, 320

Nicholson, Sir William (1872–1949), 313; The Gold Jug, 325

Jug, 325

Nile, Battle of the, 200

Nolan, Sidney, 328; Herd at the Waterhole, 327

Nonsuch Palace, 57, 57, 59, 59, 76, 83, 114; park, 76

Norman conquest, 15–16, 116

North Elmham, 13

Northumberland, Duke of, 73

Norwich Castle, 16

Nottingham, Earl of, 142

Nottingham House, see Kensington Palace

Nottingham, mint, 31

Oatlands, 99, 114

Oliver, Isaac (c. 1560–1617), 81, 88, 100, 116; drawing of Elizabeth I, 83; miniatures: Anne of Denmark, 91; Henry, Prince of Wales, 91; John Donne, 90; Portrait of a Young Man, 90; Robert Devereux, 90; Self-portrait, 89

Oliver, Peter (1594–1648), 116; miniatures: Correggio's Jupiter and Antiope, 101; Correggio's Venus, Mercury and Cupid, 101; Raphael's St George and the Dragon, 101; Titian's D'Avalos Allegory, 101

Orléans, Charles, Duke of, Poems, 28, 34

Orwell, George, 162

Osborne House, 131, 253–6, 253, 257–8, 259, 264, 265, 271, 272, 285, 291, 329; billiard table, 254; candelabra, 269, 269; Durbar Room, 280, 281; Queen's drawing-room, 255

Osler candelabrum, 269

Oursian, Nicolas, 60

Oxford University, 42, 48–9, 64, 116

Paget, Archbishop, 231

palaces, see Audley end, Balmoral, Buckingham, Bridewell, Eltham, Falkland, Fontainebleau, Greenwich, Hampton Court, Hatfield, Holyroodhouse, Kensington, Kew, Newmarket, Oatlands, Richmond, St James's, Sandringham, Sheen, Somerset House, Whitehall

Paris, Treaty of, 180

Paris, Matthew, Chronica Majora, 26

parks, royal, see Bushey, Greenwich, Hampton Court, Kensington, Kew, Nonsuch, Regent's, Richmond, St James's, Windsor Great Park

parliament, 22–3, 32–3, 44, 94, 113, 115, 121, 122, 139, 146, 149, 180–1, 250–1, 276

Parr, Catherine, see Catherine Parr

Passe, Simon van der, Henry, Prince of Wales, 99

Paxton, Sir Joseph, 264

Peake, Robert, Henry, Prince of Wales, in the Hunting Field, 99

Peel, Sir Robert, 253, 262–3

Pennethorne, 259

Pepys, Samuel, 129, 130

Percy, Major, 215

Peter of Blois, 23

Petre, Sir William, 82–3

Pett, Phineas, 138; The Sovereign of the Seas, 138

Philip II, King of Spain, 73, 76, 85

Philip IV, King of Spain, 109

Philip, Prince, see Edinburgh

photography, 276–81, 304–5, 306

Pinchbeck, Christopher, 167

Pine, J., engraving of Armada, 86

Piper, Sir John, 316; Windsor Castle, 318

Pitt, William, 213, 225, 239

Pius VII, Pope, 216–17, 225

plate, 19, 39, 49, 122, 126, 160, 322–3

Poitiers, battle of, 24, 40

porcelain, 182, 183, 209, 209, 217, 219, 226, 244, 270, 275, 316

Porter, Endymion, 109

Portsmouth, Duchess of, 130

post, 296; see also stamps

Poussin, Nicolas, 173

press, the, 44, 157, 180, 211, 230, 262, 281, 288, 305, 308

Prest, Godfrey, 20

Priestley, Joseph, 170

printing, 29, 48, 122

Prynne, William, 112

Pugin, Augustus Welby, 262, 263

Pyne, W. H., The History of the Royal Residences, 221

Raleigh, Sir Walter, 81

Ramsay, Alan, George III, 174

Raphael (1483–1520), 52, 101, 173, 270, 272; cartoons, 109–10; Christ's Charge to Peter, 188; La Perla, 96; Massacre of the Innocents, 188; Miraculous Draught of Fishes, 109

Reformation, 23, 52, 62–3, 71–2

Regent's Park, 76, 200; Zoo, 200

Regent's Street, 200

Rembrandt (1606–69): Artist's Mother, 102; Christ and the Magdalene at the Tomb, 210; Lady with a Fan, 210, 235; Self-portrait, 96; The Shipbuilder and his Wife, 210, 236

Renaissance, 50, 60, 83, 86–8

Reni, Guido (1575–1642): Cleopatra with the Asp, 154; Nessus the Centaur and Deianeira, 94

Repton, Humphrey, 228

Reynolds, Sir Joshua, 174

Ricci, Marco (1676–1730), The Court-yard of a Country House, 173

Ricci, the, 160, 173

Richard, I, King (1157–99), 14, 18–19, 35; King Richard's Chanson, 18; tomb, 19

Richard II, King (1367–1400), 22, 34, 37, 38–9; coronation, 26; effigy, 20, 24; portrait, 36

Richard III, King (1452–85), 44, 45

Richmond Castle, 16

Richmond Palace, 45, 50, 76, 88, 114; Merlin's cave, Grotto, 152; observatory, 182

Richmond Park, 45, 76, 181

Riesener, J. H., jewel cabinet, 218, 226

Robertson, James, 284

Robinson, Perdita, 174, 203

Rochester, Earl of, 130

Rockingham porcelain, 244

Rogue, Jean, engraving of Kensington Palace, 151

Rossini, 230

Roubiliac, Louis François, bust of Handel, 157

Rous, John, Life and Acts of Richard Beauchamp, 35

Rousseau, J.-J., 169

Royal Academy, 174, 180, 196, 263

Royal Academy of Music, 157

Royal Collection, 60, 81, 109, 130, 132, 185, 204, 245, 312, 326, 397, 398

Royal Institution, 201

Royal Pavilion, see Brighton

Royal Philatelic Society, 301

royal residences, see Althnaguisach; Badminton House; Carlton House; Clarence House; Frogmore; Glassalt; Marlborough House; Mey, Castle of; Osborne; Tower of London; Windsor; and under palaces

Royal Society, 138, 263

Royal Society of Literature, 237

royal yacht, see under ships

Rubens, Sir Peter Paul (1577–1640), 100, 109, 114–15, 160; Apotheosis of James I, 95, 97, 98; Farm at Laeken, 210, 211; Landscape with St George and the Dragon, 105; Portrait of the Artist, 104; Portrait of Van Dyck, 121

Ruisdael, Jacob van (1628–82), An Evening Landscape, 210, 236

Rupert, Prince, nephew of Charles I, 137–8

Russian revolution, 295, 307

Rysbrack, Michael, 152; equestrian statue of William III, 152

St Albans Cathedral, 69

St Antoine, M. de, 115

St James's Palace, 57, 122, 144, 170, 171, 183, 200; Chapel Royal, 69, 126; Clock Tower, 58, 64; Queen's Chapel, 110, 111, 123; Tudor Friary Court, 64

St James's Park, 76, 94, 130, 131

St Leger, Colonel John, 174, 192, 204

St Paul's, 29, 172

St Peter's, Rome, 232

Sandringham, 131, 290, 290, 291, 316, 329; Game Museum, 302; York Cottage, 303

Sant, James, King George V when a Boy, 302

Sargent, John Singer, Arthur, Duke of Connaught, 307

Sassoferrato (1605–85), Judith with the Head of Holofernes, 185

Savill, Sir Edward, 316

sciences, 59–60, 137–8, 163–8, 182, 201, 240, 258, 263–9

Scone, 127

Scotland, 33, 76–7, 83–5, 231–7, 275, 321

Scott, Sir Walter (1771–1832), 200, 232, 237; portrait, 237

Scotus, Duns, 60

Scrotes, Guillim, 73

sculpture, 18–21, 45, 46–8, 47, 49, 50, 112, 113, 152, 157, 226–7, 227, 228, 229, 272

Seago, Sir Edward, 325

seals, 32, 32, 33, 72

Sensenhofer, Conrad, armour, 51, 56

Settlement, Act of, 146, 161

Sèvres porcelain, 209, *209*, 217, 219, *226*

Seymour, James, 316

Seymour, Jane, *see* Jane Seymour

Seymour, Thomas, 76

Shakespeare, William, 44, 52, 86, 169

Shaw, George Bernard, *324*

Sheen Palace, 45

Sheridan, R. B., 210, 213

ships: *Britannia*, 288, *298*, 321–5, *322*; *Grace de Dieu*, 51; *Royal George*, 261, 322; royal yacht of Napoleon III, *260*; state barges, 160, *160*, 161; *The Sovereign of the Seas*, 138; *Victoria and Albert*, 261, 321; *Victoria and Albert II*, 322

Sickert, Walter Richard (1860–1942), *Ennui*, *324*

Simpson, Mrs W., 308

Singh, Bhai Ram, *280*

Sisley, Alfred, 316

Smith, Consul Joseph, 169–70, 172, 175, 185

Smith, Matthew, *Still Life*, *324*

Smith, Rev. Sidney, 198

Smollett, Tobias, 169

Sobieski, *Book of Hours*, 39–40

Sole Bay, battle of, 138

Somer, Paul van (c. 1577–1622): *Anne of Denmark*, *99*; *James I*, 97, *98*

Somers, Will, *64*, 69

Somerset, Duke of, 73, 76

Somerset House, 114, 160, 174

Song of Roland, 37

Spain, 76, 85–6, 144, 149

Spenser, Edmund, *The Faery Queene*, *The Shepheard's Calendar*, 86

sport: billiards, 212, 254–5; cricket, 157, 160; croquet, *290*; fishing, 160; highland games, 273; horse racing, 130, 144, 204, 288, 303; horsemanship, 98, 168, 203, 228, 251; hunting, 16, 45, 144; jousting, 35–6, 51, 57, 60, 88; rowing, 160; shooting, 160, 288, *289*, 303; tennis, 60; yachting, 138, 141, 288, *289*, 303

Stadler, I. C., engraving of Prince Regent, *214*

stamps, 296–302, *297–300*

Steen, Jan (1626–79), *The Morning Toilet*, 210, *234*

Sterne, Laurence, 169

Stirling Castle, 83, *84*

Stockmar, Baron, 251

Streeter, Robert, *Boscobel House and Whiteladies*, *127*

Strigel, William, *183*

Stuarts, 83–5, 93–144, 146, 149, 180, 232, 327–8

Stubbs, George (1724–1806), 160, 203–4, 205; *George IV when Prince of Wales*, *205*; *Prince of Wales's Phaeton*, *204*, 207; *Soldiers of the 10th Light Dragoons*, *206*; *William Anderson with Two Saddle-horses*, *208*

Sutherland, Graham (1903–), 316, 321, 328; *Armillary Sphere*, *323*; *Study for Christ in Glory*, *319*

Sutton Hoo, 13

Talleyrand, Prince, 242

Tallis, Thomas, 69

tapestries, 15, *15*, 19, 37, 52, 86, *86*, 109–10, *109*, 126, 138, 209, *209*, 294, *319*

television, 315, 316, 325, 329

Ter Borch, Gerard, *The Letter*, 210

Thames, river, 160, *172*, 173

theatre, 86–8, 128, 168–9, 184, 231, 288

Thomas à Becket, 18

Thomas, G. H.: *Reception of Napoleon III and Empress Eugénie*, *259*; *Royal yacht of Napoleon III*, *260*

Thomas, John, 272

Thomason Tracts, 170

Thomire, P. P., 219

Thornhill, Sir James (1676–1734), Painted Hall, Greenwich, 146, *147*, 150–1, 152

Thurlow, Lord, 239

Tijou gate, at Hampton Court, *93*, 142

Tintagel Castle, 36

Tintoretto, Jacopo (1518–94), 100, 129

Titian (c. 1490–1576), 100, 113, 114, 129; *D'Avalos Allegory*, *101*; *Doge Andrea Gritti*, *97*; *Emperor Charles V*, 109; *Entombment of Christ*, 94, *97*; *Man in Black holding a Book*, 128; *Supper at Emmaus*, 94; *Venus of Pardo*, 94, 109

tombs, royal, 18, *18–21*, 23, 24–9, 45–8, 72, 272, 277

Topolski, Feliks, *Augustus John*, *326*

Torel, William, 24, 33

Torrigiano, Pietro (1472–1528): bust of Henry VII, *45*; bust of Henry VIII, *49*; effigy of Margaret Beaufort, *21*, 48; tomb and effigies of Henry VII and Elizabeth of York, 46–8, *47*

Tory party, 146, 161, 162

Tower of London, 15, 16, 34, *35*, 57, 70, 74; armoury, 50, 51, *53*, 126; St John's Chapel, 16, *17*; Tower, 34; White Tower, 15, *15*, *28*, 126

Trafalgar, battle of, 184, 200, 269, 323

Trafalgar Square, 204

transport, 131; barge, 160–1, *160*, *161*; coach, 179–80; landau, 282–4; phaeton, 203–4, *207*, 211, 240, 242; railways, 260–2, *260*; steamship, 231; vintage cars and carriages, 328; yacht, 138, *260*, 261, 288, *298*, 321–5, *322*

Trianon, 209

Trooping of the Colour, 157

Tryon, Francis, 128

Tudors, 44–88

Turner, C., engraving of King George III, *184*

Turner, J. M. W. (1775–1851), 214, 216

Urban VIII, Pope, 112

Urbino, Duke of, 52

Utrecht, Treaty of, 146

Vanloo, Jean-Baptiste, *Augusta, Princess of Wales*, 159, 160

Vauban, Marshal, 227

Velde, William van de, the Younger (1633–1707): *The English Yacht Charles*, *137*; *The Royal Escape*, *137*

Vergil, Polydore, 44–5

Vermeer, Jan (1632–75), *A Lady at the Virginals*, 172, *175*

Veronese, Paolo, 129

Verrio, Antonio (c. 1640–1707): King's Staircase, Hampton Court, 142, *143*; Queen's Presence Chamber, Windsor, 132, *132*

Versailles, 209, 227, 238, 239

Vertue, George, 160

Vertue, Robert, Henry VII's Chapel, *46*

Victoire, Princess, *245*

Victoria, Queen (1819–1901), 243–86, 288, 304, 306, 314, 322;

Albert, 251–2; Albert's collection of paintings, 255–7; Balmoral and Scotland, 272–5; childhood and education, 244–50; death of Albert, 271–2; Europe and the Empire, 276–82; Great Exhibition, 264–9; Jubilee, 282–4; King Louis-Philippe, 259; last years, 285–8; Melbourne, 250–1; music, 270; Napoleon III, 259–60; Osborne, 253–8; portraits, 245, 250, *251*, *252*, 256, *257*, 273, 282, 285, *286*; *Some Leaves from a Journal to the Highlands*, 276; travel, 260–2

Victoria, Princess Royal, daughter of Queen Victoria, 252, *257*, 270, 285

Vienna, 150; Congress of, 216

Vignon, Philippe, 130

Vile, William (c. 1700–67), 172, 310; furniture, 170, *171*, *310*, *311*

Villars, Duc de, 227

Villehardouin, Geoffroi de, 38

Villiers, Lord Francis, *118*

Vladimir Alexandrovich, Grand Duke, 218

Vogelaare, Livinius de, *The Memorial of Lord Darnley*, 84, *85*

Vuillamy, Benjamin, 181

Wales, 16, 29–31, 33

Walpole, Horace, 179

Walpole, Sir Robert (1676–1745), 149, 152, 159, 172, 291

Waltham Holy Cross Abbey, 32

Warham, William, Archbishop of Canterbury, 61

wars: American civil, 276; civil, 72, 94, 116–22; first world, 304, 305–7; Hundred Years, 34, 40; of the Roses, 40, 44; second world, 308, 315–16

Warham, William, Archbishop of Canterbury, 61

Waterloo, battle of, 200, 214–15, 231

Watt, James, 182

Watts, jockey, *289*

Wavrin, Jean de, 25, 37

Webb, John (1611–72), 116, 123; King Charles Block, Greenwich, *124*

Wedgwood, Josiah, 182

Weisweiler, A., cabinet, *220*

Wellington, Duke of (1769–1852), 76, 214, 215, 216, 227, 231, 242, 256, 257

West, Benjamin (1738–1820), 174; *Death of Epaminondas*, *181*; *Queen Charlotte*, *181*

Westmacott, Sir Richard, 240

Westminster Abbey, 13, 14, 16, 20, *21*, 32, 37, 57, 126, 262–3, *262*, 284; rebuilding of, 23, 24–9; Chamber of the Pyx, 29; Chapter House, 22, 23, *23*; Henry VII's Chapel, *1*, *3*, 45–8, *46*, *47*, 85, 272

Westminster Hall, 16, 22, 57, 70

Westminster, Palace of, 18, 22, 23, 31

Wharncliffe, Lady, 249

Whigs, 142, 146, 149, 150, 152, 159, 160, 161, 180–1, 210, 240

White Tower, *see* Tower of London

Whitehall Palace, 48, 61, 62, 94, 112, 114, 116, 122, 126, 131, 152; Banqueting House, 95, 97–8, 123

Whiteladies, 127, *127*

Wilbye, John, 88

Wilhelm II, Kaiser of Germany (1859–1941), 285, 288, 292, *293*, 306–7

Wilkes, John, 180

Wilkes, Sir David (1785–1841), 237; *First Council of Queen Victoria*, *250*;

George IV at Holyroodhouse, 237

William I, King (1027–87), 15–16, 19, *26*, 34

William II, King (d. 1100), 22

William III, King (1650–1702), 124, 137, 139–42, 151, 152

William IV, King (1765–1837), 201, 213, 244, 250, *298*

Williams, Neville, 69

Wilton Diptych, 36–7, *37*

Winchester, 18, 23, 131

Windsor, 16

Windsor Castle, 34, 69, 122, 127, 131–2, 133–4, 209–10, 237, 251, 252, 258, 259, 269, 271, *282*, 299, 316, *318*, *320*, 328, 329; George IV's Gothic additions, 238–42; Grand Corridor, *222*; Guard Chamber, *239*; Long Gallery, 86, 174, 316, 329; Queen Mary's Dolls' House, 312–15, *312*, *313*; Queen's Presence Chamber, 132, *132*; Royal Dairy, 270, *279*; Royal Library, 87; St George's Chapel, 40, *41*, 72, 229; Waterloo Chamber, 214, *215*–26, *225*, 244

Windsor Great Park, 81, *82*, 181, 240, *242*, 315; Savill Gardens, 316

Winstanley, Henry, engraving of Audley End, *130*

Winterhalter, Frans Xaver (1806–73), 256, *257*, 314; *First of May, 1851*, *256*; *Prince Arthur*, *257*; *Queen Victoria when Young*, 252; *The Cousins: Queen Victoria and Princess Victoire*, *245*; *The Royal Family in 1846*, *257*

Wise, Henry, 142, 150, *151*

Wit, Cornelius de, engraving of a Dutch yacht, *137*

Withers, George, 122

Wollaston, William, 152

Wolsey, Cardinal Thomas (c. 1475–1530), 50, 52, 54–5, 60, 61, 64, 72; and Hampton Court, 50, 59, 65; portrait, *50*

Woollett, William, *163*, *164*

Wootton, John, 160

Worcester, 127; Cathedral, 18; porcelain, 182, 244

Worde, Wynkyn de, 48

Wren, Sir Christopher (1632–1723), 67, 123, 131; Greenwich, 141; Hampton Court, 125, *140*, 142, *143*; Kensington Palace, 148, 149, 150; Royal Hospital, Chelsea, 138, *139*

Wright, John Michael, *King Charles II*, *126*

Wyatt, Matthew, monument to Princess Charlotte, *229*

Wyatville, Sir Jeffrey, 222, *238*, 238–9

Wyld, William, watercolour of Manchester, *261*

York, Edward, Duke of, son of Frederick, Prince of Wales, 168

York, Frederick, Duke of, son of George III, 202, *202*, 213

Yorktown, defeat at, 183

Zoffany, Johann (1734–1810), 189; *Academicians of the Royal Academy*, 179, *180*; *George, Prince of Wales, and Frederick, Duke of York*, 202; *King George III*, *194*; *Queen Charlotte*, *195*; *The Tribuna of the Uffizi*, *180*, *196*

Zuccarelli, Francesco (1702–88), *Europa and the Bull*, 172, *173*, 189